THOMAS COOK

On 5 July 1841 Thomas Cook, a 32-year-old printer from Market Harborough, in Leicestershire, England, led a party of some 500 temperance enthusiasts on a railway outing from Leicester to Loughborough which he had arranged down to the last detail. This proved to be the birth of the modern tourist industry. In the course of expanding his business, Thomas Cook and his son, John, invented many of the features of organised travel which we now take for granted. Over the next 150 years the name Thomas Cook became synonymous with world travel.

Today the Thomas Cook Group employs over 13,000 people across the globe and its Worldwide Network provides services to customers at more than 3000 locations in over 100 countries. Its activities include travel retailing, tour operating and financial services – Thomas Cook is a world leader in traveller's cheques and foreign money services.

Thomas Cook believed in the value of the printed word as an accompaniment to travel. His publication *The Excursionist* was the equivalent of both a holiday brochure and a travel magazine. Today Thomas Cook Publishing continues to issue one of the world's oldest travel books, the *Thomas Cook European Timetable,* which has been in existence since 1873. Updated every month, it remains the only definitive compendium of European railway schedules.

The *Thomas Cook Touring Handbook* series, to which this volume belongs, is a range of comprehensive guides for travellers touring regions of the world by train, car and ship. Other titles include:

Touring by train

On the Rails around France (Published 1995)
On the Rails around Britain and Ireland (Published 1995)
On the Rails around Europe (Second Edition Published 1996)
On the Rails around the Alps (Published 1996)
On the Rails around Eastern Europe (Published 1996)

Touring by car

On the Road around California (Second Edition Published 1996)
On the Road around Florida (Published 1995)
On the Road around Normandy, Brittany and the Loire Valley (Published 1996)
On the Road around the Capital Region USA (Published 1997)
On the Road around the South of France (Published 1997)
On the Road around the Pacific Northwest (Published 1997)

Touring by car, train and bus

Touring Australia (Published 1997)

Touring by ship

Greek Island Hopping (Published annually in March)

For more details of these and other Thomas Cook publications, write to Passport Books, at the address on the back of the title page.

TOURING

Southern
Africa

Independent holidays in
South Africa, Botswana,
Namibia, Lesotho, Swaziland,
Mozambique and Zimbabwe

Edited by
Melissa Shales

PASSPORT BOOKS
NTC/Contemporary Publishing Company

A THOMAS COOK TOURING HANDBOOK

Published by Passport Books, a division of
NTC/Contemporary Publishing Company
4255 West Touhy Avenue,
Lincolnwood (Chicago),
Illinois 60646-1975 USA.

Text: © 1997 The Thomas Cook Group Ltd
Maps and diagrams:
© 1997 The Thomas Cook Group Ltd

ISBN 0-8442-4759-6
Library of Congress Catalog Card
    Number: 97-66484
Published by Passport Books in conjunction
with The Thomas Cook Group Ltd.

Managing Editor: Stephen York
Project Editor: Deborah Parker
Editorial Assistant: Leyla Davies
Map Editor: Bernard Horton
Colour map: RJS Associates
City maps: RJS Associates
Route diagrams: Caroline Horton
Rail and bus information: Peter Bass

Cover illustration by Michael Benallack-Hart
Picture research: Image Select International
Text design by Darwell Holland
Text typeset in Bembo and Gill Sans using
    QuarkXPress for Windows
Maps and diagrams created using Macromedia
    Freehand and GSP Designworks
Text imagesetting: Riverhead Typesetters,
    Grimsby
Printed in Great Britain by Fisherprint Ltd,
    Peterborough

Written and researched by
Eric and Ruth Bailey
Paul Duncan
Melissa Shales

Book Editor
Melissa Shales

ABOUT THE AUTHORS

Melissa Shales is the Series Editor of the *Thomas Cook Touring Handbooks*, as well as editing and contributing to this volume. After a childhood in Zimbabwe, she returned to England to study History and Archaeology before embarking on a career as a freelance travel writer and editor. Formerly editor of *Traveller* magazine, *The Traveller's Handbook* and Series Adviser to the *AA/Thomas Cook Travellers Guides*, she has written 10 guidebooks, including several on France and India. Other Africa titles include Kenya and previous works on Zimbabwe and South Africa.

Eric and Ruth Bailey, a husband-and-wife team, are experienced journalists who turned to freelance travel writing some 17 years ago. Members of the British Guild of Travel Writers and The Society of Authors, both have travelled widely in Canada, Greece, Ireland, Mexico, the Philippines, South Africa and the US. The Baileys have written nine travel guides on their own account and have contributed to others, including *On the Rails around Britain & Ireland*, and *On the Road around the Capital Region USA*. They have a particular interest in inland waterways boating and are devoted dog-lovers.

Paul Duncan grew up in Cape Town before returning to the UK to study. He worked for some time at the Royal Fine Art Commission, and as a ghost writer and speech writer, and has also written several other travel guides, specialising in Italy and South Africa. He is currently back in Cape Town where he is continuing a flourishing career writing travel guides, travel articles for a broad range of international newspapers and magazines, and editing fashion journals. His proudest moment recently was when he was chosen to prepare the abridged version of Nelson Mandela's autobiography, *Long Walk to Freedom*.

PHOTOGRAPHS

The photographs in this book were supplied by Spectrum Picture Library, with the exception of the following: South African Tourism Board: back cover; section pp. 32–3, giraffe, lion; Cape Town; pp. 160–1, Durban; East London; Johannesburg; pp. 256–7, Kruger National Park. Melissa Shales: section pp. 32–3, car on road; baboon; game-viewing; pp. 256–7, Drakensberg Mountains; pp. 352–3, Victoria Falls. Trip: section pp. 32–3, baboon; protea; pp. 352–3, Sun City; Kalahari; Kalahari bushpeople. Eric Bailey: section pp. 32–3, Cape Town cable car; pp. 160–1, Lesedi; Soweto; pp. 256–7, elephant; pp. 352–3, Basotho people.

G. Weinberg; section pp. 160–1, De Hoop Nature Reserve; pp. 352–3, Khubus; Sossusvlei. Chris Fairclough Colour Library: section pp. 256–7, Bourke's Luck Potholes.

ACKNOWLEDGEMENTS

The authors and Thomas Cook Publishing have received an enormous amount of help during the production of this book from people who have generously given of their time, expertise and hospitality.

In Britain, special thanks go to Steve Dunn and Emma Cunningham of South African Airways, Alliance Air; Marion Deason of UTC; Alison Whitfield and Liz Wright of African Ethos; Dominic Shales, Kirsty Gaston and Judy Sykes for help with research; Naomi Graham, Naomi Graham International; Robert Schaerer, Three Cities Hotels Ltd; and Alison Whitfield, African Ethos. In Botswana, Air Botswana; the management and staff of Camp Okavango, Camp Moremi, Savuti South, Chobe Game Lodge and Mowana Lodge. In Lesotho, the Lesotho Tourist Board; Mick and Di Jones, Malealea Lodge; Christabel Jackson, Helang Basali Crafts. In South Africa, special thanks to Wilderness Safaris and the Eastern Cape Tourist Board for their hospitality and impeccable touring arrangements; Rovos Rail, Southern Sun, Karos Hotels, Simunye and the Conservation Corporation for their hospitality; Sue Partridge, Henry Bird and Evan Jones for fascinating tours; Sun International; Phillip Lategan, Afro Ventures; the management of Karos Safari Hotel, Rustenburg; Johan and Megan Richards, Pietermaritzburg; Bill and Mary Harrap, Original Balloon Safaris; Chris Olivier, tourist officer, Louis Trichardt; Essie and Daisy Esterhazan, Mayor and Mayoress of Ellisras; Johan Erasmus, Elliras Town Clerk; Dr Goosen, Ellisras; Johan Stemmet, Rhino Bushveld Eco-Park; Daan and Zena, Phalaborwa; Rita Miljo, Phalaborwa; Paul Bailey, Casa do Sol Hotel; Bobby Duffus, Lesedi Cultural Village; and the Park Hyatt Johannesburg. In Mozambique, thanks go to David Ankers of the Polana Hotel, for making the whole trip possible; Jays Camp and Arthur Delamere of Free Spirit for their hospitality; and Arlando Langa, one of Africa's most amiable guides. In Swaziland, HM King Msawati III; the Swaziland Ministry of Tourism; and Ruth Buck, Forester's Arms. In Zimbabwe, thanks go to Zimbabwe Sun, UTC, Hertz, Frontiers Adventures and Bushveld Safaris for their hospitality; and Laurie and Maureen Bond for the braais and picnics in the rain.

5

CONTENTS

ROUTES AND CITIES

In alphabetical order. For indexing purposes, routes are listed in both directions – the reverse direction to which it appears in the book is shown in italics.
See also the Route Map, p. 8, for a diagrammatic presentation of all the routes in the book.
To look up towns and other places not listed here, see the Index, p. 410.

7

REFERENCE SECTION

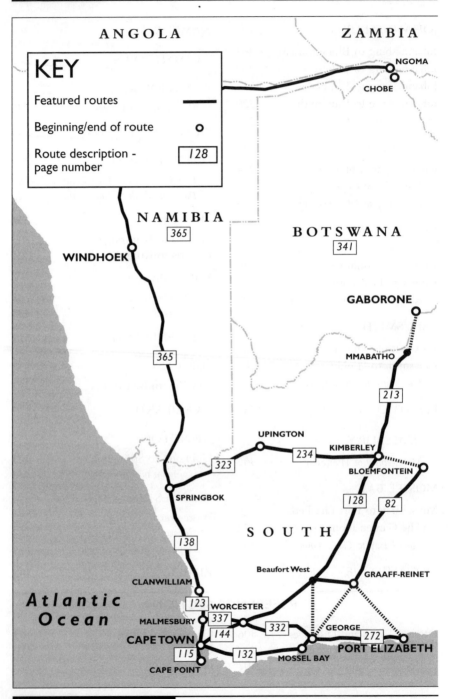

KEY

Featured routes ————

Beginning/end of route ○

Route description - page number 128

ANGOLA

ZAMBIA

NGOMA

CHOBE

NAMIBIA
365

WINDHOEK

BOTSWANA
341

GABORONE

MMABATHO

213

365

UPINGTON
234 KIMBERLEY

323 BLOEMFONTEIN

SPRINGBOK 128 82

SOUTH

138

Beaufort West GRAAFF-REINET

CLANWILLIAM

Atlantic
Ocean

123 WORCESTER

MALMESBURY 337

CAPE TOWN 144 332 GEORGE 272

115 132 PORT ELIZABETH

CAPE POINT MOSSEL BAY

8

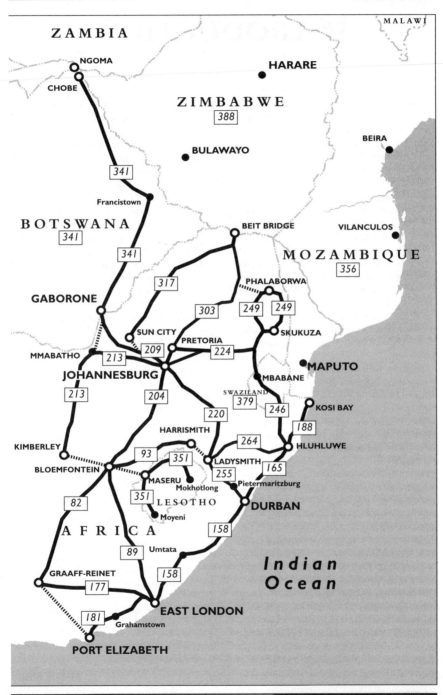

ZAMBIA

NGOMA

CHOBE

HARARE

ZIMBABWE

388

BULAWAYO

BEIRA

341

Francistown

BOTSWANA

341

341

BEIT BRIDGE

MOZAMBIQUE

VILANCULOS

356

317

PHALABORWA

GABORONE

303

249   249

SUN CITY

PRETORIA

SKUKUZA

MMABATHO

213   209

224

JOHANNESBURG

MAPUTO

MBABANE

213

204

SWAZILAND

379

246

KOSI BAY

220

188

HARRISMITH

264

HLUHLUWE

KIMBERLEY

93   351

BLOEMFONTEIN

LADYSMITH

165

255

MASERU   Mokhotlong

Pietermaritzburg

82

351   LESOTHO

DURBAN

Moyeni

AFRICA

158

89   Umtata

GRAAFF-REINET

158

177

Indian
Ocean

181   EAST LONDON

Grahamstown

PORT ELIZABETH

MALAWI

9

INTRODUCTION

Now that it has established itself as a democracy, the new South Africa has become the flavour of the decade. Tourism figures have soared, new hotels are appearing and more are scheduled, and charter flights are going into the major gateways. The local tourist trade is gearing up to offer an increasingly varied range of products, from a night in a beehive hut to game-viewing by elephant. South Africa has the beauty, the climate, the wildlife, the culture and the entertainment to offer year-round appeal. At the time of writing, it also has a favourable exchange rate against many other currencies. The surge of interest is also helping boost tourism in all the surrounding countries, as visitors branch out to the Victoria Falls, Okavango Delta, or Fish River Canyon, the beautiful mountains of Lesotho and Swaziland, or Mozambique's magnificent tropical beaches. Each of South Africa's neighbouring states has a special magic.

Southern Africa was made for touring. One of its greatest delights is the astonishing scenery. Whether it is the panoramic bushveldt stretching to purple horizons, the vast desert fields of brilliant flowers, the velvet rustle of the mountain grasslands, the dramatic escarpments, the rocky shores and smoking white sand dunes, or the thundering rivers and waterfalls, the usual clichés – spectacular, stunning, breathtaking, magnificent – are simply inadequate. Ten per cent of all the flowering plant species in the world grow here, and this is one of the last great wilderness habitats of the great African wildlife, home to many thousands of elephants, hundreds of species of bird, from ostrich to starling, great migrating herds of wildebeest and inquisitive burrows of meercats.

If that's not enough, you can try canoeing, white-water rafting, pony trekking, climbing, abseiling, hot air ballooning, skydiving, paragliding, bungee jumping, microlighting, off-road motorcycling, quad bike trails or hiking to remote rock paintings. On the coast, those fed up with sunbathing can try diving,

snorkelling, whale-watching, sports fishing, sailing, or surfing on world-class waves.

Finally, throw in generally excellent roads, comfortable accommodation, a genuinely hospitable welcome, fascinating history, and some of the nicest, friendliest and most entertaining people in the world.

Of course, things aren't perfect. The wind of change has blown away many old problems, but new ones have appeared that cannot be solved overnight. Crime is undeniably a major problem, and South Africa and Mozambique, in particular, do have no-go areas. However, with common sense and a willingness to follow local advice, the number of tourists who experience anything but a friendly welcome is minute. The possibility of catching malaria is sadly on the increase, but again sensible precautions, or simply travelling in winter, can alleviate most of the risk. You do have to be more careful about where you put your feet, or whether you feed the monkeys. But after all, this is Africa. Most people want just a tiny hint of danger to help sharpen the senses, heighten the impressions, and flavour their after-dinner stories.

The economies and currencies of this area are particularly volatile and the tourist trade is exploding into action. Together they mean that however hard we have tried to provide detailed, accurate information, some of it will inevitably be out-of-date by the time you read this. Nevertheless, we decided to put in prices so that you have a good idea of the costs involved, but these should be regarded as guidelines, not gospel.

There is so much beauty here, so much warmth from the people, as well as the sun, that any journey in southern Africa becomes an emotional, magical, experience. Go once and it will be in your blood. You will want to go again.

Melissa Shales

HOW TO USE THIS BOOK

ROUTES AND CITIES

Touring Southern Africa provides you with an expert selection of 30 recommended routes between key cities and attractions of South Africa, Botswana, Lesotho, Mozambique, Namibia, Swaziland and Zimbabwe, each in its own chapter. Smaller cities, towns, attractions and points of interest along each route are described in the order in which you will encounter them. Additional chapters are devoted to the major places of interest which begin and end these routes, and descriptions of each country. These chapters form the core of the book, from p. 78 to p. 405.

Where applicable, an alternative route which is more direct is also provided at the beginning of each route chapter. This will enable you to drive more quickly between the cities at the beginning and end of the route, if you do not intend to stop at any of the intermediate places. To save space, each route is described in only one direction, but you can follow it in the reverse direction, too.

The text is arranged in alphabetical order, led by a key destination in South Africa followed by chapters devoted to routes leading from that city to other major destinations. The first destination to be covered is Bloemfontein (pp.78–81), followed by routes from Bloemfontein: Bloemfontein to Cape Town (pp.82–88), Bloemfontein to East London (pp.89–92) and Bloemfontein to Harrismith (pp.93–99). Cape Town is described in the next chapter, followed by routes from that city, and so on. In some cases, the route may involve crossing the border between two countries, for example Kruger to Hluhluwe (pp.246–248). Information on border crossing times is given in the Travel Essentials chapter (p.18). The final pages of the book are devoted to briefer descriptions of the other six countries in the region. Each country is described in a separate chapter. The countries are arranged in alphabetical order and destinations within the country are in route order.

To find the page number of any route or city chapter quickly, use either the alphabetical list on the **Contents** pages, pp. 6–7, or the master **Route Map** on pp. 8–9. The routes are designed to be used as a kind of menu from which you can plan an itinerary, combining a number of routes which take you to the places you most want to visit.

WITHIN EACH ROUTE

Each route chapter begins with a short introduction to the route, followed by driving directions from the beginning of the route to the end, and a sketch map of the route and all the places along it which are described in the chapter. This map, intended to be used in conjunction with the driving directions, summarises the route and shows the main intermediate distances and road numbers; for a key to the symbols used, see p.13.

DIRECT ROUTE

This will be the fastest, most direct, and sometimes, predictably, least interesting drive between the beginning and end of the route, usually along major roads.

SCENIC ROUTE

This is the itinerary which takes in the most places of interest, often straying on to minor roads, a few of which may be gravel (all marked as such in the text). A very few routes are only suitable for 4x4, and these are also highlighted. Road directions are specific; always be prepared for detours due to road construction, etc. The driving directions are followed by sub-sections describing the main attractions and places of interest along the way. You can stop at them all or miss out the ones which do not appeal to you. Always ask at the local tourist information centre for more information on sights, lodgings and places at which to eat.

TRAINS AND BUSES

In some chapters, there are details of rail and bus routes, as an alternative to driving long distances. Information is taken from the *Thomas Cook Overseas Timetable* and relevant table numbers are given. Details of how to obtain a copy of the *Overseas Timetable* can be found on p.26 or p.223.

 SIDE TRACK

This heading is occasionally used to indicate departures from the main route, or out-of-town trips from a city, which detour to worthwhile sights, described in full or highlighted in a paragraph or two.

CITY DESCRIPTIONS

Whether a place is given a half-page description within a route chapter or merits an entire chapter to itself, we have concentrated on practical details: local sources of tourist information; getting around in city centres (by car, by public transport or on foot as appropriate); accommodation and dining; communications; entertainment and shopping opportunities; and sightseeing. The largest cities have all this detail; in smaller places some categories of information are less relevant and have been omitted or summarised. Where there is a story to tell or some fascinating background history to explain, we have placed **feature boxes** on subjects as diverse as 'Nelson Mandela', 'The Owl House' and 'Jock of the Bushveld'.

Although we mention good independently owned lodgings in many places, we always also list the hotel chains which have a property in the area, indicated by code letters after the hotel name. Many travellers prefer to stick to one or two chains with which they are familiar and which give a consistent standard of accommodation. A number of Southern African chains have been used in this book, which may be unfamiliar to readers. A brief description of each chain is given in **Hotel Codes** on p.407. The codes used for each chain are also explained there and central booking numbers are given.

MAPS

In addition to the sketch map which accompanies each route, we provide maps of major cities (usually the downtown area), smaller towns, regions, national parks, and so on. At the end of the book is a section of **colour road maps** covering Southern Africa, which is detailed enough to be used for trip planning.

THE REST OF THE BOOK

The **Contents** and **Route Map** pages have already been mentioned above. **Travel Essentials** is an alphabetically arranged chapter of general advice for the tourist new to Southern Africa, covering a wide range subjects such as accommodation and safety or how much to tip. We have also included a glossary in this chapter (p. 24), explaining unfamiliar Southern African words or phrases. **Country by Country** gives a brief and basic run-down on each of the seven countries in this book, covering subjects such as electricity, public holidays and telephones. **Driving in Southern Africa** concentrates on advice for drivers on the law, rules of the road, and so on. **Great Trains** describes the many wonderful railway journeys in this area and provides booking information. **Background Southern**

Africa gives a briefing on the history, geography, flora and fauna of this fascinating region. **Touring Itineraries** provides ideas and suggestions for putting together an itinerary of your own using the selection of routes in this book. At the back of the book, **Driving Distances** is a tabulation of times and distances between main cities, to help in trip planning. The **Conversion Tables** decode Southern African sizes and measures. Finally, the **Index** is the quick way to look up any place or general subject. And please help us by completing and returning the **Reader Survey** at the very end of the text; we are grateful for both your views on the book and new information from your travels in Southern Africa.

KEY TO MAP SYMBOLS

Route diagrams

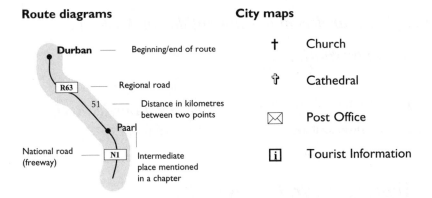

City maps

✝ Church

✢ Cathedral

✉ Post Office

[i] Tourist Information

KEY TO PRICE DESCRIPTIONS

It is impossible to keep up to date with specific tariffs for lodging and accommodation or restaurants, although we have given some general advice within the Country by Country chapter (pp.28–44). Instead, we have rated establishments in broad price categories throughout the book, as follows:

Accommodation (per person per night)

Cheap	Under R300
Moderate	R300–R500
Expensive	Over R500

Meal (three courses per person)

Inexpensive	Up to R40
Medium	R40–R70
Expensive	Above R70

ABBREVIATIONS USED IN THE BOOK
(For hotel chains, see p. 407)

Ave	Avenue (in addresses)	Mon, Tues	Monday, Tuesday, etc.
Blvd	Boulevard	N	National Road, e.g. N1
Dr.	Drive (in addresses)	Pl.	Place (in addresses)
hr(s)	hour(s)	R	Regional Road (in route
Jan, Feb	January, February, etc.		directions e.g. R311)
km	kilometre(s)	R5	Rand (in prices, e.g. 5 Rand)
kph	kilometres per hour	Rd	Road (in addresses)
M	Motorway, e.g. M3	St	Street (in addresses)
min(s)	minute(s)	4x4	four-wheel drive vehicle

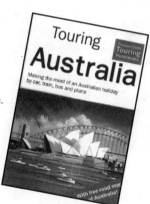

TRAVEL ESSENTIALS

Travelling in Africa is not always straight-forward, although Southern Africa certainly makes life easier than most of the continent. Your holiday will be one of the finest of your life, as long as you obey certain common sense rules. Read these guidelines and the country specific information in the Country by Country section (see pp. 28–44).

ACCOMMODATION

Southern Africa is blessed with a good selection of luxurious, historic country house hotels and game lodges, a growing number of excellent small bed and breakfasts and guesthouses, and plenty of cheap hotels, ranging from scruffy to seedy. South Africa also has a huge array of self-catering options, while most countries (with the exception of Mozambique, and that is being corrected) have excellent campsites, many of which also offer basic chalets. What is generally lacking, with the exception of the ubiquitous Holiday Inns and Protea Hotels, is a broad range of good, moderately priced hotels.

Outside South Africa, the options are far more limited (see also Country by Country, pp. 28–44), and full listings are virtually non-existent. Where possible, a broad range of suitable accommodation is listed within the text.

Whichever type of accommodation you are seeking, it is worth shopping around for atmosphere, location and price. Even some familiar hotel chains have properties of different grades, with their top-grade hotels costing three times as much as the more basic ones in the same city, while the bed and breakfast of your dreams may be 10 km out of the city centre – which is not much use if you don't have transport.

It is always worth enquiring about any special deals or weekend discounts at hotels. Most tourist offices in Southern African countries have lists of local accommodations available,

but few have information about rates, and counter staff are not allowed to make recommendations.

For the sake of this book, prices have been categorised into three sections, based on South African rates; these are shown in How to Use (p. 13). Those in other countries are roughly parallel, although Zimbabwe is noticeably cheaper and Mozambique, at present, is more expensive.

Bed and breakfast rates are usually R80–120, while a dormitory bed in a backpackers' hostel is around R25–40. Note that some of the most luxurious hotels and lodges are upwards of R1200, so check before booking.

Hotels

Since the ending of apartheid, a number of big new hotels have augmented South Africa's stock of guest rooms. However, most of these large hotels and resorts are in or close to the major cities. Hotels in smaller towns or in the country tend to have fewer than 30 bedrooms (some of the most exclusive have as few as 6), towns can be long distances apart and hotels fill up with business clients during the week and conferences at the weekend. With numbers of overseas visitors also rocketing in recent years, occupancy levels are generally high; it is wise to book ahead, especially in the peak summer season (Dec–Jan), and during school holidays.

Game Lodges and Camps

There is a magic about life out in the bush, sitting round a camp-fire, listening to the cackle of the hyenas and the snuffle of a grazing hippo. The game lodges are the reason most of us go to Africa. There is self-catering accommodation and camping in every national park, and you will be almost certain to see a good selection of animals. But to increase your chances of sighting the 'big five' and the more elusive species, you need expert assistance. It's well worth paying the extra to stay in an established bush camp or lodge where experienced guides know the

15

animals' most likely haunts and take visitors out in high, open vehicles for maximum visibility. You need two nights at any game park, even if you can only afford it once.

Southern Africa has become such a Mecca for tourists that some of the grander game lodges have pushed their rates through the roof. Locals complain that they have been priced out of the market, and that these properties are only interested in the wealthy overseas visitor. This is true, but do remember when wincing over the cost that you are usually paying an inclusive 24-hr rate to cover the room, all meals, game drives, the upkeep of the park, the expertise of the rangers and a variety of other recreational and leisure pursuits. Shop around carefully and you will usually find a lodge you can afford.

Although there are a couple in South Africa, Botswana has made a speciality of tented bush camps, which offer as many comforts and facilities as the brick or stone version. Large tents may be furnished with sturdy twin beds, bedside tables, clothes cupboard and chest of drawers. You will probably have your own shower and toilet within a few metres, or at least a folding stand and plastic bowl to wash in and a shared flush toilet. Some of these camps are in very remote places, and while the camps themselves are good value, you need to charter a light aircraft to hop between them (each camp offers a different environment with different wildlife) – and that is expensive. More easily accessible camps can keep expenses down.

Cultural Villages

There are relatively few of these so far, but cultural tourism is the new buzz word and everyone is rushing to get on the bandwagon. There are two types. The first is the cultural village, specially constructed with all mod cons and a programme of entertainments. The worst are unbearably tacky; the best, a fascinating and largely genuine experience, with local people living and working in the village. The second is the one that really benefits local people. Programmes of 'homestays' offer tourists the opportunity to experience life in the townships or a real bush village, sleeping, cooking and eating with the family in their circular, thatched mud huts. Africans are traditionally extremely hospitable, love having guests and are proud and happy to show off their traditional crafts, food, singing and dancing.

Bed and Breakfast

The bed and breakfast/guesthouse business is booming. Many of these are on farms, but they can also be found in towns and cities. Standards vary from basic to luxurious – quite a few are in delightful historic buildings, filled with antiques and set in beautiful grounds. Almost all have en suite bathrooms and are run by hospitable people, who offer a genuinely warm welcome. Many will provide an evening meal, as long as you request it in advance.

Prices vary, with little apparent relationship between facilities provided and the cost. Some of the best are surprisingly modestly priced, or you may be unlucky and arrive at a sparsely furnished room with a high price tag. It is cheaper to book direct, as booking through an agency can add 30% and a reservation fee to the price. However, when making arrangements from abroad, it is much easier to book through the agencies. Your choice. Always book ahead; many have only 2 or 3 rooms, and these are easily filled.

Self-catering

Self-catering accommodation is an excellent option, particularly in South Africa, although it is really only feasible if you have your own car, or are spending a few nights in one area. It is ideal for those who like to explore local markets and buy local foods. Most locals prefer to self-cater, so standards are excellent and the cost of the accommodation is considerably cheaper than other options. You can survive on the basics of tea, coffee and bread, as many largely self-catering places, such as national park camps, also have restaurants. However, for successful self-catering, you need to do plenty of pre-planning and have an efficient cool box. You may end up many miles from a store, and forgetting some important ingredient for a meal means going without. Check whether cutlery, crockery and bedding is provided; this varies. Some game camps will even provide a cook. All you have to do is hand over the ingredients and select a time for your meal!

South African Airways

Operating with a fleet of more than 50 aircraft, South African Airways, the national carrier, flies to 36 destinations in the UK and Europe, the USA, Far East, Australia, South America, the Middle East and other parts of Africa. On its international routes, SAA offers three classes of travel: Economy, with various discounted fares for the family or leisure travellers; Business, with wide armchair seats, individual CD music modules and personal seat-back TV screens; and First, with special sleeper seats with a 62-in seat pitch, superior in-flight entertainment, gourmet meals and Cape wines.

Both business and first class passengers are entitled to complimentary chauffeur-driven transport within a radius of 50 miles of London Heathrow or Manchester airports and fast-track check-in facilities. Through check-in is available for all classes of passengers from any British Midland point in the UK. In South Africa, the airline provides some 575 flights a week to major and secondary centres. A network of tertiary centres throughout the country is serviced by SA Express, an independent domestic airline affiliated to SAA, which also provides connecting flights to SAA's scheduled domestic and international flights. SAA's Voyager frequent flyer miles are available on SAA's domestic and international routes, and on flights operated by Lufthansa, American Airlines, Ansett, British Midland, Thai, SA Express and Alliance Air.

SAA UK Offices: *St George's House, 61 Conduit St, London W1R 0NE; tel: 0171-312 5000, fax: 0171-312 5009; and 4th Floor, 1 St Ann St, Manchester M2 7LG; tel: 0161-834 4436; fax: 0161-839 0639.*

Along the coast, there are numerous time-share blocks that also offer apartments for normal self-catering. These are listed with the tourist offices. There are also a great many privately owned cottages for rent, but these can be harder to find as there are no villa companies: check with local estate agents.

Camping

Camping and caravanning are both very popular here, although in a form that few Europeans would recognise. Firstly, the weather is ideally suited to the outdoor life, with plenty of sunshine and warm evenings – no huddling into your sleeping bags, dripping wet and frozen solid. Then there are the campsites, which are plentiful, beautiful and well furnished. Almost every town has a municipal site, while others are strewn liberally through game parks or near any sight of great natural beauty. Most have grassy pitches for tents and caravans, with their own cold water standpipes and bins, plenty of shady trees and well placed ablution and kitchen blocks. You are less likely to find electric and water hook-ups for caravans. Only infrequently will there be a restaurant, pool or other facilities, but you will almost certainly be provided with a copious supply of firewood for your *braai*, and there may well be wandering servants to do your washing-up, laundry and even cooking. Prices are very cheap.

Backpackers' Hostels

These are a new phenomenon in the region and are spreading like wildfire, particularly in South Africa and Zimbabwe, as Africa finally joins the backpacker's trail. There are several hostels in each of the big cities, with more and more of them getting Hostelling International affiliation. In Johannesburg, at least one of them provides free transport from Jan Smuts International Airport. Outside the cities, they are fewer, although they are springing up along the route of the 'Baz Bus' (see Country by Country, p.39), and at certain 'hippy' hangouts like Port St Johns on the Wild Coast (p.163). Most are clean, very spartan, reasonably secure and appear to have no rules of any kind.

BORDERS

Many visitors to Southern Africa arrange itineraries that include two, three or more countries. Crossing borders is not usually time consuming, though delays can occur when traffic builds up

Major Border Crossing Times

Namibia–Botswana
Buitepos 0700–1700
Mohembo 0600–1800
Ngoma Bridge 0600–1800

Narochas (Nakop) 24 hrs
Noordoewer 24 hrs
Oranjemund 0600–2200
Velloorsdrif 0600–2200

South Africa–Botswana
Bokspits 0800–1600
Martin's Drift 0800–1600
Parr's Halt 0800–1600
Ramatlhabama 0700–2000
Ramotswa 0800–1600
Tlokweng 0700–2200

South Africa–Swaziland
Bulembu/Josefsdal 0800–1600
Jeppes Reef/Matsamo 0700–1800
Lavumisa/Golela 0700–2200
Mahamba 0700–2200
Ngwenya/Oshoek 0700–2200

South Africa–Zimbabwe
Beit Bridge 0530–2230

South Africa–Lesotho
Calendonspoort open 24 hrs
Ficksburg Bridge open 24 hrs
Maseru Bridge 0600–2200
Tele Bridge 0800–2200
The other 5 crossings are on minor roads, some only accessible with a 4x4.

Swaziland–Mozambique
Lomahasha 0700–2200

Zimbabwe–Botswana
Kasane/Victoria Falls 0600–1800
Kazungula 0600–1800
Plumtree 0600–2000

South Africa–Mozambique
Komatipoort (Mpumalanga) 0600–1800

Zimbabwe–Mozambique
Forbes, Mutare 0600–1800
Nyamapanda 0600–1800

South Africa–Namibia
Klein Menasse 0600–2200

at the only border post between South Africa and Zimbabwe, or at busy times like Christmas. There are regular reports of difficulties and obstructionist delays on the land borders with Mozambique. For major border crossing times, see feature box, above. Details of other border posts' opening times between South Africa and neighbouring countries are obtainable from the **South African Department of Home Affairs**; tel: 011-314 8130. Please remember that if you need a visa for access to any country, it will be invalidated as soon as you leave, so even taking a short cut through Swaziland from the Kruger, or a day trip to Zimbabwe from Botswana means that you will need a multiple entry visa.

CHILDREN

Many people are frightened to take their children to Africa, scared of the diseases, the 'foreigness', and all the supposed nasties lurking round every corner. Forget it, this is childrens' paradise. As an area where the shops are well-stocked with baby food and nappies, the food and water hygienic, the quality of private health care excellent and the nannies plentiful and easily accessible, it· can also be a parent's paradise.

The weather is warm to hot, and almost always sunny. Children can play outdoors in clean, unpolluted fresh air all day. They must wear hats and sunblock and, if possible, shoes or sandals (against the various nasty creepy-crawlies). The towns have cinemas aplenty and Coke, hamburgers and ice-cream on tap, while the seaside resorts such as Durban are filled with entertainments, from funfairs to video arcades.

Swimming pools are common, although children should not to go near them unattended. Swimming in natural water should be avoided because of the risk of bilharzia (see Health Hazards, p.20). Sea swimming for children is only recommended on beaches with lifeguards or under careful supervision; many stretches of the coast have strong breakers and tides, while there are various nasty sea creatures, from jellyfish to sharks. Supervised beaches are known to be relatively trouble-free.

Game-viewing is not recommended with the under-5s, who have trouble sitting still and keeping quiet for long enough, and may get upset if you see a kill. As soon as they are old enough for explanations and instructions, they will be enthralled. Bush walking is fine as long as there is an adult to break the path and scare off snakes, and the children wear proper shoes.

Long car journeys are a nightmare with any children, so load up with tapes, games and other entertainments, or plan out a less ambitious itinerary. Starting a travel diary or some sort of collection can keep their minds focused and add to the learning experience. Several South African companies run parent-free adventure holidays for children of 7 and above. For a list, contact the **Dept of Environmental Affairs and Tourism**; tel: 012-310 3707.

CLIMATE

With a wide range of latitudes, altitudes, vegetation and even three oceans (Atlantic, Indian and Southern) affecting the weather, the climate varies quite dramatically, not only from country to country, but also from one part of a country to another. Southern Africa is known for its sunshine and warmth. Much of the region is sub tropical and, in the northern parts, tropical. Basically, summer is from Oct–Mar; winter from Apr–Sept. The rainy season is in summer. There is relatively little variation in the number of daylight hours, from about 0500–1900 in summer, 0700–1700 in winter.

Summer is often very hot, with daytime temperatures ranging from 24°C to nearly 50°C in the desert. Expect to meet temperatures in the mid 30°sC almost anywhere. Rain generally arrives as sudden storms, with crashing thunder and lightning, usually in late afternoon or at night. While the desert is obviously very dry, northern Natal and the Mozambique coast are heavily humid, clipped in Apr–May by the south-west monsoon. Winter is generally cooler (usually about 15–22°C), with crisp, dry, blue skies. Southern parts of South Africa, and anywhere over about 1000m, are prone to light frosts and a dusting of snow in winter; Lesotho and the Natal Drakensberg have enough for skiing. The southern Cape has a Mediterranean climate, with rain year-round. Summers are

Average Temperatures					
	Cape Town	Durban	Harare	Maputo	Windhoek
JANUARY					
Highest	78°F/26°C	81°F/27°C	78°F/26°C	86°F/30°C	85°F/29°C
Lowest	60°F/16°C	69°F/21°C	60°F/16°C	71°F/22°C	63°F/17°C
APRIL					
Highest	72°F/22°C	78°F/26°C	78°F/26°C	83°F/28°C	77°F/25°C
Lowest	53°F/12°C	64°F/18°C	55°F/13°C	66°F/19°C	55°F/13°C
JULY					
Highest	63°F/17°C	72°F/22°C	70°F/21°C	76°F/24°C	68°F/20°C
Lowest	45°F/7°C	52°F/11°C	44°F/7°C	55°F/13°C	43°F/6°C
OCTOBER					
Highest	70°F/21°C	75°F/24°C	83°F/28°C	82°F/28°C	84°F/29°C
Lowest	52°F/11°C	62°F/17°C	58°F/14°C	64°F/18°C	59°F/15°C

warm but rarely hot, while winters are sullen, cool and grey.

The best time to visit is probably in Sept, when the grass is short, the game-viewing good and the Namaqualand flowers bloom. Apr–May is also an ideal temperature.

CLOTHING

Coolness and informality are the keynotes for daytime wear. Cotton shorts and shirts are favoured by both sexes. In malaria zones, it is advisable to wear long trousers and long-sleeved shirts in the early morning and evening, when biting insects are most active. Smart casual clothing is ideal for evenings at restaurants or the theatre. Open-neck shirts are usually acceptable for men, but some of the more upmarket establishments may require jacket and tie, so check first or go prepared.

Wear drab colours (khaki, green, brown) for game-viewing. Even if the animals are colour-blind, the colour temperature can startle them. Walking boots are only necessary if you are planning a serious hike, but you will need reasonably solid boots with a good tread and ankle support for bush walking. A hat and sunglasses are also strongly advised.

Most golf courses welcome visitors, but when requesting a confirmed starting time from the club secretary, check the dress code. Jeans are usually against club rules.

Topless bathing is not advised.

CUSTOMS

See Country by Country, pp.28–44.

DISABLED TRAVELLERS

In South Africa, many city hotels have facilities for disabled people and others are generally very willing to try and help. Most rest camps in Kruger National Park offer access to the disabled visitor. Wheelchairs can be hired in most cities, and the larger car rental companies have a limited number of vehicles with hand controls. Early booking of these cars is advised.

Outside South Africa, facilities fade to almost nil, but with forethought and precision planning, it is almost always possible to get enough human muscle to literally carry you where you need to go.

Anyone with limited mobility, a heart condition or other physical problems should check facilities carefully, as most country hotels involve wooden boardwalks, bush paths and, often, many very steep steps. Game-viewing also involves clambering in and out of high-sided vehicles. It can be arranged, but the hotel should be notified well in advance to provide a more suitable room or assistance. **Wilderness Wheels Africa**; *tel: 011-648 5737*, is a tour operator specialising in game-viewing and bush adventures for disabled travellers. For other information, contact the **Satour National Accessibility Scheme**; *tel: 012-347 0600*.

EATING AND DRINKING

See Background, pp.72–73 and individual countries in Country by Country, pp.28–44.

EMBASSIES AND CONSULATES

See Country by Country, pp.28–44.

HEALTH

Check with your doctor which **inoculations** are necessary (or recommended) for the countries that you plan to visit. Defence against the risk of polio, tetanus, typhoid and hepatitis A may be advised; for Mozambique it is also advisable to have meningitis A&C and yellow fever (if going to the far north, near the Zambian border). Otherwise, a yellow fever vaccination is unnecessary, unless you are entering the area from a yellow fever zone. A rabies vaccination should only be required if you are planning to handle animals.

People on medication should take adequate supplies and a letter with full prescription details. This not only convinces the Customs authorities that you are not smuggling, but means you can get a quick and easy repeat prescription if necessary. A second pair of glasses or your vision prescription is also a good idea.

Health Hazards

Bilharzia is a disease which can damage the intestines, liver and urinary tract. It can be treated, but there is no vaccine available. It is caused by a parasite in slow-moving waterways or at the edge of dams. In South Africa, the freshwater snail which carries the parasite is,

Game-Viewing

You will need drab-coloured clothes, a jacket or blanket for early mornings and late evenings, binoculars, field guides to animals, birds and trees (see pp.26–27, and Background, pp. 59–61) and, of course, your camera, preferably with plenty of fast film. A 200mm lens is the shortest possible for half-way decent wildlife photography. If walking or riding, you should also take a hat, sunglasses, sunblock, water, and wear long trousers and shoes with a good tread and ankle support.

It is not necessary to go out in an open vehicle with a ranger, but it is strongly recommended, at least for your first couple of drives. The high vehicles give a far better view than a saloon car, and an experienced guide will see far more than you and help you 'tune in' your eye. You will also get instant identification and fascinating background material. In the private reserves, radio contact helps track more important sightings and you have the option of driving off the road. Many places also offer walking or horse safaris with a game guard, while in Zimbabwe and Botswana, it is now possible to travel by elephant.

The best viewing times are dawn–1000 and 1600–dusk. Most animals turn invisible as they wait out the midday heat in the shade. Game park animals are used to vehicles and should not be spooked, but talk quietly, don't stand up and never, never get out.

theoretically, found only in Kwazulu-Natal and in provinces north of the Vaal River. However, if infected humans have been nearby, they may have passed it on. It is widely spread in all the more northerly countries. Swimming in any natural fresh water is not recommended, unless you are assured that you are in a non-bilharzia area.

AIDS is rampant, so celibacy, or at least safe sex, is strongly advised. In South Africa, blood for medical purposes is carefully screened and treated; the situation is not always so clear elsewhere. Don't have a transfusion in Mozambique.

The **climate**, while generally benign, can turn on you if not respected. The sun here has a high ultraviolet rating. Sunscreen of factor 15 or more is recommended. Wear a sun hat and try to avoid long periods of exposure to the sun. All day sunbathing is unhealthy and may lead to skin cancer. If you begin to feel giddy or sick, go inside, have a cool bath and drink large quantities of cool liquid. If this doesn't help, you may have heatstroke (when the body's thermostat can't cope), and you will need a doctor.

Be particularly careful when hiking or in the desert; you need far more water to avoid dehydration. In the mountains, there is also the possibility, if the weather closes in, of hypothermia. At the least, always carry a space blanket, iron

rations of high energy food and some warmer clothes.

There are all sorts of unfamiliar, and possibly dangerous, **bugs** and **beasties**, including spiders, snakes, scorpions and ticks. Most will get out of your way, but always watch where you put your hands and feet, don't scramble up sunny rocks without being careful, shake out shoes and sleeping bags before you get into them and check yourself for ticks after walks through long grass. If you are bitten, try and stay calm – panic only raises your heartbeat and pumps the poison round the body faster. Get medical help as fast as possible.

Rabies shouldn't be a problem, as long as you don't handle animals or feed stray dogs and cats. If you are bitten, get help immediately. The treatment is totally effective, as long as the disease is caught in time.

Food and water are hygienic, and it is safe to drink the tap water almost everywhere in South Africa, Swaziland, Namibia, Botswana and Zimbabwe, although it is worth double-checking with the locals in poorer districts or remote rural areas. There is some doubt about the water quality in Lesotho, and it is certainly not recommended in Mozambique. Bottled water is available in the cities here; elsewhere, you will have to carry your own supply or use purifiers and filters.

Malaria

The single greatest health hazard in Southern Africa is malaria, which must be taken seriously. Malaria is a killer and the incidence is on the increase. Don't let it put you off going, but be very careful. Much of South Africa is malaria free – the only malarial areas are around the borders, particularly in northern Kwazulu-Natal, in the Kruger and parts of Northern Province. It is present in all the other countries and is particularly dangerous in the Zambezi Valley and Hwange areas of Zimbabwe, where the more virulent strain of cerebral malaria is present.

Alarmingly, some strains are developing resistance to the prophylactics. Get up-to-date advice from your doctor (or a specialist organisation like the School of Hygiene and Tropical Medicine in London) about exactly which type of anti-malaria protection is required for your particular destination (or destinations). It is necessary to start a course of anti-malaria drugs a week or more before you enter a malarial area, and for four weeks after your return. The most effective current drug, **mefloquine** (Larium), may produce a raft of unpleasant side-effects, from vivid dreams and hallucinations to fainting and outright psychosis. If you have doubts about taking it, speak to a local pharmacist. The other usual option is a powerful cocktail of chloroquine and paludrine, both of which may be bought from chemists without a prescription. One antibiotic, **Doxycycline**, also has some success as a prophylactic.

More importantly, try to avoid being bitten. The disease is spread by the female anopheles mosquito, which only flies between dusk and dawn. If you are bitten in daylight, although irritating, it is not serious. Use insecticidal creams, sprays, wipes or impregnated wrist and ankle bands, such as Autan or Jungle Formula. The crucial ingredient is a chemical known commonly as **Deet** – it is possible to buy 100% Deet preparations from specialist travel suppliers that you can soak your clothes in.

Those whose skin is sensitive to these preparations may suffer skin allergies, which can be as burningly irritating as vicious insect bites. Pharmacists the world over are always willing to help and advise, and in Africa many of them stock a product called **CER-8**, which deters insects without touching the skin. It is in the form of inch-square emanating pads, which adhere to the inside of your cuffs, under your collar, at your waistband, on your socks or sandals – at any vulnerable place. You press them to release the Citronella they contain, and although you may smell like a lemon grove, they do keep insects at bay. Wear long sleeves and trousers after dark and avoid perfume, which is said to attract insects. They apparently hate the smell of Vitamin B, so take supplements or eat Marmite. At night, use a mosquito net and coils, or a plug-in electrical device giving off insecticidal vapours.

Malaria symptoms may not manifest themselves for some weeks. Seek medical advice immediately if you develop flu-like symptoms at any time up to 6 months after your return, explaining which areas you have visited. If it's just a cold, you've wasted nothing but time, but early treatment is essential. Any type of malaria is dangerous; cerebral malaria, mercifully a rarer form, can be severe and even fatal within hours of being bitten.

Treatment

It is important to have good medical insurance as you have to pay for treatment in state hospitals as well as in private clinics, and for all doctors' consultations and prescriptions.

The best private health care in South Africa is up to the best in the world (this is the country that invented the heart transplant). Good, if less sophisticated, facilities can also be found in most of the surrounding countries, as long as you can pay. Most state hospitals are overstretched to bursting and standards of both care and cleanliness vary enormously. A flying doctor service, **MARS** (Medical Air Rescue Service) connects remoter areas of all these countries with good hospitals, often in South Africa.

HITCH-HIKING

Hitch-hiking is widespread, and many people hitch-hike without coming to any apparent harm. However, it is not recommended, and you should never hitch after dark. If you accept a lift from a black driver, you may be expected to contribute towards petrol costs.

Many Africans walk long distances, often with heavy loads. Although they would probably be good company, you have to harden your heart. The safety rule for visitors is to drive with doors locked and windows up, and never to pick up strangers.

To arrange or offer lifts safely ahead of time, contact **Backpackers** in Cape Town; *tel: 021-234 530*, or **Dial-a-Lift** in Johannesburg; *tel: 011-648 8136/8602*, or consult the noticeboards in some tourist information offices or backpackers' hostels.

INSURANCE

Full travel insurance is strongly advised. Theft or loss of possessions, damage to expensive items such as cameras, personal injury or illness – such things can ruin your holiday, and without sufficient insurance coverage they can ruin your bank balance too. Whether you buy insurance coverage from a travel agent, such as Thomas Cook, or whether you shop around among companies specialising in travel insurance, be sure to read the small print so that you know how well protected you are. Many 'adventure' activities, such as riding or canoeing, might be excluded and you may have to pay an additional premium on some policies.

LANGUAGE

See Country by Country, pp. 28–44.

OPENING HOURS

See Country by Country, pp. 28–44.

POLITICAL ETIQUETTE

While the New South Africa has become one of the most liberal countries in the world, it is still circumspect to gauge who you are talking to before opening your mouth. In the surrounding countries, particularly Zimbabwe and Mozambique, open and vocal criticism of the government can be unhealthy.

The presidents and other important politicians in many of these countries travel by fast-moving cavalcade, complete with motorcycle outriders. Other traffic must stop and clear aside to let them through. Do not point a camera at

Glossary

bakkie – small pick-up truck

biltong – salted sun-dried meat (see p.72)

boma – large sheltered enclosure for braais

braaivleis (braai) – barbecue

breyani – Cape Malay rice dish (see p.73)

burgher – Cape Dutch townspeople (not commonly used after British take-over in the early 19th century)

Cape British – earliest British settlers in Cape region of South Africa; Georgian and Victorian-style South African architecture

Cape Dutch – architecture (see p.114) and cooking (see p.72–73) of the early Dutch settlers in the Cape

Drosdty – combined government offices and magistrate's court in Cape Dutch South Africa

fynbos – Cape mountain flora (see p.59)

Karoo – large strip of semi-desert stretching across Western and Eastern Capes (literally 'land of thirst' in Khoikhoi)

kloof – hill, neck of high land in Afrikaans

kombi – minibus

koppie/kopje – small, rocky hill standing alone in flat surroundings

kraal – enclosure; used both for stockpen and enclosed village (not politically correct)

lekker – great, good, nice (Afrikaans)

mealies – corn on the cob

Randlord – the 19th-century diamond and gold millionaires (e.g. Rhodes), see p.201

rondavel – small, round, thatched cottage, based on African hut design

stoep – verandah

veldt – open savannah/scrub landscape, as in strandveldt (coastal), bushveldt

witblits – literally 'white lightning'; ferocious spirits home-distilled by Afrikaners

any official without permission. Nor may you photograph any strategic or military building, including, officially, bridges, railway stations and police stations.

SECURITY

Sadly, personal safety has become a real issue, particularly in the larger cities in South Africa. Sensible guidelines for visitors, which can equally be applied to the other countries in the region, are issued in a leaflet entitled *Explore South Africa*, available at major airports, distributed by the Safety and Security Task Group. Most of the recommendations are obvious but frequently ignored:

1. Never leave luggage unattended. It is difficult if travelling alone, but keep them with you at all times, unless locked in your hotel room or a luggage store. Insist the porter places your bags where you can see them as you check in.

2. Keep valuables in the safety deposit box, keep your room door locked whether you are in or out, and hand in your keys at the desk every time you leave the hotel.

3. Always carry a set of photocopies of all important documents, including passport, visa, traveller's cheque numbers and insurance. Keep them away from the originals. If anything is stolen, this will speed up the replacements.

4. If someone knocks unexpectedly on your hotel room door, ask who it is. If you have not made any request, phone room service, housekeeping, reception or whatever is applicable to find out if they have sent somebody.

5. Always take a cab after dark, however short your journey. Taxis do not cruise as a rule. If you need one, ask your hotel or the tourist office for the name of a reliable company and telephone. Most shops, restaurants and sights are happy to call one for you.

6. Do not carry large sums in cash and avoid displaying valuables, such as cameras and jewellery. Don't walk in dark, isolated areas at night. If possible, walk in groups in busy, well-lit streets, plan your route in advance and look purposeful.

7. Keep a firm grip on anything you are carrying. Pass your shoulder bag strap over your head and wear the bag with the fastening towards your hip. If it has a clip fastening or zip at the top, keep your hand over it. Use a hidden money belt for carrying valuables.

8. On the whole, foreigners (and not just

whites) should avoid the former townships, unless accompanied by a local or official tour guide who can vouch for you. If you are worried about a particular area, phone a police station or ask the locals for advice.

9. If you are faced by muggers, don't quibble. Hand over what they ask for and wait until they are out of sight before contacting the police. Muggers can be very violent, usually carrying knives or guns; the idea is to come out with your life intact.

For security in the car, see Driving in Southern Africa, p. 48.

Street Enterprise

Obvious tourists are usually targets for locals, who probably want to do nothing more sinister than cadge a bit of cash or sell you yet another wooden hippo. Park at the kerb to study a map and you may quickly find someone at the car window with a broad grin and outstretched hand. Or you may park, lock your car and be confronted with someone offering to wash the vehicle, or guard it during your absence for a tip. These people can be very persistent. Many add a sorry story about having to pay for a family funeral or their school books.

Such incidents are irritating, but are rarely menacing, and how you deal with them is up to you. Most people in Southern Africa are very nice and extremely poor, and your assistance is crucial. If they can perform a service instead of just begging, so much the better, and self-appointed car-watchers are often a good, cheap way of ensuring your car and your possessions are intact when you get back. Saying no may have the opposite effect! Beware of distributing largesse too openly, or you could soon find yourself among a forest of 'waving palms'.

Taxis

Communal minibus taxis have set routes, cover long distances, and sometimes even cross international boundaries. They are efficient and very cheap; they are also frequently unroadworthy, heavily overloaded and drive far too fast. The accident rate is appalling. Lone travellers, particularly young women, may also be at risk from fellow passengers. Imagine travelling several hundred kilometres in a minibus with miners who have just been paid after weeks away from home, and who have been celebrating with drink. It is safer to travel by scheduled coach, or to pool funds with trusted fellow hostel residents or campsite neighbours and hire your own vehicle.

Anyone roaming around southern Africa should telephone home at regular intervals, even if it means transferring the charges, to make sure that someone always has at least a vague idea of where you are. That way, someone might notice if you go missing, and have a rough idea of where to start looking.

Most importantly of all, don't allow fear to stop you travelling or to colour your perceptions of some of the kindest and most entertaining people in the world.

SMOKING

You are in a tobacco-growing region, cigarette prices are at rock-bottom and people still smoke far more than in Europe or North America. Restaurants with no-smoking areas are not thick on the ground, but if you want to eat in a smoke-free area, it is always worth asking. It may be suggested that you have a table on the balcony, but some of your fellow diners are sure to light up. Most bed and breakfast homes prefer guests not to smoke indoors. Some hotels may have non-smoking rooms.

TIME

Standard time in all countries in Southern Africa is two hours ahead of Greenwich Mean Time, one hour ahead of Central European Winter Time and seven hours ahead of Eastern Standard Winter Time. This applies year-round in all countries except Namibia, where time moves back 1 hr in winter (Apr–Sept), when it is one hour ahead of Greenwich Mean Time.

TIPPING

It is customary to tip waiters 10% of the restaurant bill if everything has been satisfactory – a service charge is rarely imposed. Porters should be given R1, or the equivalent, for each item of luggage. Taxi drivers usually receive tips of 10% of the fare. Petrol station attendants often deserve a tip. They not only fill the tank but also clean the windscreen thoroughly and offer to check tyres, oil and water, if required.

TOILETS

All petrol stations have clean and efficient public toilets; if locked, ask for the key. You will also find them in restaurants, cafés, department stores and at most museums or other visitor attractions. Out in the bush, they may be of the hole-in-the-ground variety; check under the seat for insects before sitting down. If using the bushes, try and cover your tracks.

TOURIST INFORMATION

The spread of tourist information is surprisingly good (except in Mozambique). Look for the almost universal lower-case 'i'. You may have to look hard in some towns. Tourist information offices are not necessarily centrally situated, and it sometimes seems that 'i' signs are rationed to one per town. Tourist information may be inside the town hall or public library. Addresses and opening times are listed, wherever possible, throughout this book.

The standard of service varies, but staff levels are low. You may encounter a young, inexperienced staff member valiantly coping alone, or you may get faultless expertise from a conscientious live wire of a tourist officer, with a thorough knowledge of the region and a flair for anticipating your needs. A tourist office may be drab, with only a few leaflets displayed, or it may be decorated with posters and photographs and have a range of local crafts on sale. Lists of local accommodation and restaurants are usually available, but you usually have to guess the price. It is worth asking if a reservation service is available. Frustratingly, most offices close over the weekend, but some hoteliers and proprietors of bed and breakfasts display up-to-date details of the tourist attractions in their area.

USEFUL READING

Most international guidebook series have a volume on South Africa. The Thomas Cook Travellers range of compact colour guides has a *South Africa* title (published by the AA/Thomas Cook Publishing in the UK and Passport Books in the USA). The AA *Explorer* series also has a South Africa title, by Melissa Shales (published

by the AA). Both available from any bookstore. If you intend to use **trains** or **buses** to any extent, you will find it useful, both for pre-planning and for use on holiday, to have the latest edition of the *Thomas Cook Overseas Timetable* (referred to throughout this book as the **OTT**). This gives up-to-date schedules for rail services and some long-distance bus services in South Africa. Published every two months, it is available at branches of Thomas Cook in the UK, or can be purchased by credit card from **Thomas Cook Publishing**, *PO Box 227, Thorpe Wood, Peterborough PE3 6PU, UK; tel: 01733 503560; fax: 01733 503596 (from outside the UK, the code is 44 1733).* Current prices inclusive of postage are £9.80 (UK 2nd class post), £11.90 (Europe airmail) and £13.30 (rest of the world airmail). US readers can order the OTT from **Forsyth Travel Library**, *1750 East 131st St, PO Box 480800, Kansas City, MO 64148*, for US$27.95 plus $4.50 shipping.

History and Politics

The Boer War, Thomas Pakenham (Wiedenfeld & Nicolson); *The Cape of Good Hope – A Maritime History,* Robin Knox-Johnston (Hodder & Stoughton); *The Scramble for Africa,* Thomas Pakenham (Wiedenfeld & Nicolson); *The Randlords*, Geoffrey Wheatcroft (Wiedenfeld & Nicolson); *The First Dance of Freedom*, Martin Meredith (Abacus); *The Founder – Cecil Rhodes and the Pursuit of Power*, Robert Rotberg (Oxford University Press); *To the Banks of the Zambezi*, TV Bulpin (Thomas Nelson & Sons); *The Washing of the Spears*, Donald Morris (Jonathan Cape); *Shaka's Children*, Stephen Taylor (Harper Collins); *People and Power*, Andrew Proctor (Academic Books); *History of Botswana*, T. Tlou and A. Campbell (Macmillan). *The A-Z of South African Politics,* ed. Anton Harber and Barbara Ludman (Penguin); *The Long Walk to Freedom*, by Nelson Mandela (Little, Brown & Co./Abacus); *The Rainbow People of God*, by Desmond Tutu (Doubleday/ Transworld); *Tomorrow is Another Country*, Allister Sparks (Struik); *Mugabe*, David Smith & Colin Simpson (Sphere).

Specialist Guides

Culture Shock! South Africa, Dee Rissik

(Kuperard); *Discovering Southern Africa*, TV Bulpin (Discovering Southern Africa Productions); *Hiking Trails of Southern Africa*, Willie and Sandra Olivier (Southern Book Publishers); *New South African Wine Guide*, John Platter (John & Erica Platter); *Myths and Legends of Southern Africa*, Penny Miller (TV Bulpin Publications); *Major Rock Paintings of Southern Africa*, ed. Tim Maggs (Indiana University Press); *Historical Buildings in South Africa*, Desiree Picton-Seymour (Struik); *Zimbabwean Stone Sculpture*, M. Arnold (Books of Zimbabwe); *Africa All-Stars — the Pop Music of a Continent*, Chris Stapleton and Chris May (Paladin). *Roberts Birds of Southern Africa*, Gordon Maclean (CTP); *Newman's Birds of Southern Africa*, KB Newman (Macmillan); *A Field Guide to the Larger Mammals of Africa*, Jean Dorst and Pierre Dandelot (Collins); *Southern Africa's Mammals*, Robin Frandsen (Frandsen); *Two Oceans, A Guide to the Marine Life of Southern Africa*, GM Branch, CL Griffiths, ML Branch and LE Beckley (David Philip); *Field Guide to the Trees of Southern Africa*, Eve Palmer (Collins).

Literature and Travelogue

The authors listed below have published other works; these are simply the best known.

My Traitor's Heart, Rian Malan; *The Grass is Singing* and *African Laughter*, Doris Lessing; *Nervous Conditions*, Tsitsi Dangarembga; *House of Hunger*, Dambudzo Marechera; *White Man Black War*, Bruce Moore-King; *Waiting for the Rain* and *Coming of the Dry Season*, Charles Mungoshi; *Bones*, Chenjerai Hove; *The Heart of the Hunter* and *The Lost World of the Kalahari*, Laurens van der Post; *Maru* and *When the Rain Clouds Gather*, Bessie Head; *Cry of the Kalahari*, Mark and Delia Owens; *A Dry White Season*, André Brink; *The Lying Days*, Nadime Gordimer; *Cry the Beloved Country*, Alan Paton; *Jock of the Bushveld*, Sir Percy Fitzpatrick; *A Hunter's Wanderings in Africa*, Frederick Selous; *The Story of an African Farm*, Olive Schreiner; *Mafeking Road*, Herman Charles Bosman; *A Walk in the Night*, Alex La Guma; *I Write What I Like*, Steve Biko; *Travels in South Africa*, Anthony Trollope.

COUNTRY BY COUNTRY

BOTSWANA

Capital: Gaborone. **Language**: Setswana is the main national language and English the official language of government. **Currency**: the pula (P). Botswana is not part of the monetary system of South Africa, Lesotho, Namibia and Swaziland, but rands are accepted at border posts for payment of vehicle levies, customs duties, and so on. US dollars, UK pounds and SA Rand are all easily exchanged. Access/MasterCard, American Express, Diners Club and Visa credit cards are accepted on a limited basis.

Passports and Visas
All visitors need a passport valid for at least 6 months from the date of entry, proof of onward travel and/or visible means of support (a credit card will usually do). Citizens of all EU countries, Scandinavia, South Africa and the USA do not need visas. Ghana, India, Mauritius, Nigeria and Sri Lanka are the only Commonwealth countries whose citizens require a visa. Visitors requiring visas must obtain them before entering the country. In general, a one-month entry permit is issued at the border. This must be renewed at the nearest immigration office if a longer stay is required.

Customs
Botswana is a member of the Southern Africa Customs Union. Visitors from other countries may import duty-free 400 cigarettes, 50 cigars or 250 grams of tobacco; one litre of spirits, two litres of wine, 250 ml of toilet water, six cans of beer plus new and used goods worth not more than R500. There are no restrictions on foreign currency imports, but no more than P50 may be exported. **Airport/Departure Tax**: P80.

Tourist Information
Dept of Tourism, *P/Bag 00047, The Mall, Gaborone; tel: 353 024, fax: 308 675; PO Box 439, Sir Seretse Khama Rd, Maun; tel: 660 492;* and *PO Box 66, River Rd, Kasane; tel: 650 357, fax: 650 851.* Offices open daily 0730–1630.

Useful Addresses
Australia: High Commission: *Parkes Pl., Parkes, Canberra; tel: 06-6261 3305.*
Canada: Honorary Consul: *14 South Dr., Toronto, Ontario M4W 1R1; tel: 416-978 2495; fax: 416-324 8239,* or see USA.
South Africa: Embassy: *Infotech Building, 1090 Arcadia St, Arcadia, Pretoria; tel: 012-342 4760.* **Air Botswana:** *tel: 011-447 6078.* **UK: High Commission:** *6 Stratford Pl., London W1N 9AE; tel: 0171-499 0031; fax: 0171-495 8595.* **Air Botswana:** *3rd Floor, 177 Tottenham Court Rd, London W1P 0HN; tel: 0171-757 2737.*
USA: Embassy: *3400 International Dr. N.W., Washington DC 20008; tel: 202-244 4990.*
Zimbabwe: High Commission: *22 Fifth Ave, Harare; tel: 04-729 551*

STAYING IN BOTSWANA

Accommodation
Comfortable hotels, motels and lodges are to be found at major centres, with standards ranging from simple to deluxe. Botswana is best-known, however, for its many luxury safari camps scattered throughout the country. Booking details are listed with the camps in the main text (see p.341–350). Reservations are essential for cheaper Parks Board campsites in Chobe National Park, Moremi Game Reserve, Nxai Pan National Park and Makgadikgadi Pan National Park. **Botswana National Parks Reservations Office**: *PO Box 20364, Boseja, Maun; tel: 661 265, fax: 661 264.* Reservations may also be made in person at the office, which is clearly signposted near the Police Station in Maun. Open Mon–Sat 0730–1230, 1345–1630; Sun 0730–1200.

Eating and Drinking
Bars and restaurants can be found in the main

towns, usually within hotels, but in other parts of the country, outside major hotels and lodges, food is generally basic. Most lodges and safari camps have licensed bars and restaurants.

Electricity

220–240 volts AC, 50 Hz, and 15 and 13 amp plug sockets are both in use.

Foreign Embassies in Botswana

Canada: see Zimbabwe.
Namibia: *BCC Bldg, 1278 Lobatse Rd, Gaborone; tel: 314 227.*
South Africa: *Kopanyo House, Nelson Mandela Dr., Gaborone; tel: 304 800/1/2/3.*
UK: *Queen's Rd, The Mall, Gaborone; tel: 352 841.*
USA: *Bodiredi House, The Mall (PO Box 90), Gaborone; tel: 353 982.*
Zimbabwe: *Plot 8895, Orapa Close, Gaborone; tel: 314 495/7.*

Opening Hours

Banks: Mon–Tues 0800–1430, Wed 0800–1200, Thur–Fri 0800–1430, Sat 0800–1045. **Post Offices:** Mon–Fri 0815–1300, 1400–1600, Sat 0830–1130. **Offices:** Mon–Fri 0730–1630, Sat 0730–1230. **Shops:** Mon–Fri 0830–1300, 1400–1700, Sat 0830–1300. **Petrol Stations:** most filling stations open daily 0600–2000, with some opening and closing an hour or two later. A few offer 24-hr service.

Postage

Gaborone's main post office is in The Mall. All counters attract big queues. Postal services are cheap but slow; airmail to Europe, for example, takes 1–3 weeks. There are post offices in all main towns, but there are no deliveries – residents and businesses use box numbers. There are fax and telex facilities available at larger post offices and new hotels.

Public Holidays

1, 2 Jan; Good Friday; Easter Monday; Ascension Thursday; 16 July (President's Day); 30 Sept (Botswana Day); 25, 26 Dec.

Public Transport

Air Botswana: *IGI Building, The Mall, Gaborone; tel: 04-351 921,* operates domestic services between larger centres, and occasionally has special packages offering flights, accommodation and sightseeing. Air charter companies fly light aircraft into lodges in the Okavango Delta and Chobe National Park, but this can be an expensive way to travel. Charter companies are based at Gaborone, Maun and Kasane airports.

Major **bus services** are operated between Gaborone and Francistown, Gaborone and Mahalapye, and Palapye and Selebi–Phikwe. Other routes are Ramatlabama–Francistown and Francistown–Nata-Kasane. Gaborone-based **Mahube Express**, *tel: 04-352 660,* operates a daily service along the Nata–Maun highway. For **rail** information, see p. 54.

Telephones

Botswana has automatic trunk and international dialling. There are no internal area codes. The telephone service is adequate, but there are very few phone boxes, and in remote areas, such as safari camps, radio is the usual form of communication. Overseas calls may be made from the Botswana Telecom office: *Khama Crescent, Gaborone* (open Mon–Fri 0915–1300, 1415–1630; Sat 0815–1130). Country code: *267.*

There are telephone boxes in major post offices. Telex, telegram and fax facilities exist at main post offices and major hotels.

LESOTHO

Capital: Maseru. **Language:** Sesotho and English are official languages. **Currency:** the Maloti (M), divided into 100 lisente. The Maloti is linked to the South African Rand, which is also accepted everywhere. US dollars and UK pounds are easily exchanged in Maseru. Major credit cards are accepted in larger hotels and some restaurants, but are not much use in smaller centres.

Passports and Visas

With the exception of those from Australia, Ghana, India, New Zealand, Nigeria, Namibia, Pakistan and South Africa, citizens of Commonwealth countries do not need a visa to enter Lesotho. Citizens of Denmark, Finland, Greece, Iceland, Ireland, Israel, Japan, Norway

29

and Sweden are also exempt. Visas must be obtained from a Lesotho Embassy or High Commission before entering the country.

Customs
Lesotho is a member of the Southern African Customs Union, which permits visitors to import personal possessions, one litre of spirits, two litres of wine and 400 cigarettes. However, if you arrive from one of the other member countries – and it is almost impossible not to – there are no duty-free concessions. The importation of alcohol from another customs union country is strictly forbidden. There are no limits on the amount of foreign currency or traveller's cheques which may be imported. Exportation of Lesotho money is restricted to M500. **Airport/Departure Tax**: M20.

Tourist Information
Lesotho Tourist Board: *Christie House, Maseru; tel: 313 760; fax: 310 108.* Information *Office: next to the Hotel Victoria, Kingsway, Maseru; tel: 312 896.*

Useful Addresses
South Africa: High Commission: *6th Floor, West Tower, Momentum Centre, 343 Pretorius St, Pretoria; tel: 012-322 6090.*
UK: High Commission: *7 Chesham Pl., Belgravia, London SW1 8HN; tel: 0171-378 8581/2; fax: 0171-235 5686.*
USA: Embassy: *2511 Massachusetts Ave N.W., Washington DC 20008; tel: 202-797 53533.*

Accommodation
Maseru has a few hotels of international standards and a number of reasonable independent restaurants. Small hotels and tourist lodges, many offering pony trekking and hiking, can be found in most districts. Prices and standards are reasonable, and while facilities may be spartan in some country lodges, cleanliness and hygiene will not have been sacrificed.

Eating and Drinking
Don't expect to find haute cuisine in Lesotho.

There are some reasonable restaurants in Maseru, but elsewhere it is a matter of taking pot luck. The most likely places to find adequate food are in small hotels and lodges. Generally, the hiking and pony trekking centres serve wholesome, tasty meals.

Electricity
220–240 volts AC, 50 Hz. Both 15 amp 2-pin (round) and 13 amp 3-pin (round) plug sockets are in use. Small hotels and lodges in remote areas may have their own generator and power may be switched off well before midnight.

Emergencies
Ambulance: *121;* Police: *123/124;* Fire: *122.*

Foreign Embassies in Lesotho
Ireland: *Christie House, Plot 856, Orpen Rd (P. Bag A67), Maseru; tel: 314 068; fax: 310 028.*
South Africa: *10th Floor, Lesotho Bank Centre, Kingsway, Maseru; tel: 315 758.*
UK: *Linare Rd, Maseru; tel: 313 961.*
USA: *Kingsway (PO Box 333), Maseru; tel: 312 666.*

Opening Hours
Shops and businesses: Mon–Fri 0800–1700; Sat 0800–1200. **Government Offices:** Mon–Fri 0800–1245, 1400–1630. **Banks:** Mon, Tues, Thur, Fri 0830–1500, Wed 0830–1300, Sat 0830–1100. **Post Offices:** Mon–Fri 0800–1630, Sat 0800–1200. **Petrol Stations:** filling stations are to be found in major towns and are usually open daily 0800–1800; some open 24 hrs. As elsewhere in southern Africa, fill up whenever you can.

Postage
Poste restante, available at the post office opposite the intersection of *Tonakholo Rd* and *Kingsway* in Maseru, is notoriously unreliable. Stamps may also be purchased in hotels.

Public Holidays
1 Jan; 11 Mar (Moshoeshoe's Day); 4 Apr (Heroes Day); Good Friday; Easter Monday; Ascension Day 1 May; 17 July (King's Birthday); 4 Oct (Independence Day); 25, 26 Dec.

Public Transport

Lesotho Airways; *tel: 324 507*, flies daily between Moshoeshoe I Airport, *18 km south of Maseru*, and Johannesburg. The only domestic service is between Maseru and Qacha's Nek on Mon, Wed and Fri.

There is a good network of long-distance **bus services**, but journeys can be long and uncomfortable. **Minibus taxis**, often stuffed to the gunwales with passengers, cover shorter distances. There are no passenger rail services in Lesotho.

Telephones

Telephone services are reasonably efficient. There is automatic trunk dialling between Lesotho and South Africa, and there are satellite connections with many parts of the world. International calls may be made from the public call office adjoining the post office in Maseru. Long-distance and international calls are expensive.

Country code: *266;* IDD: *00;* Operator: *100;* International Operator: *109;* Directory Enquiries: *151;* International Directory Enquiries: *159159.*

MOZAMBIQUE

Capital: Maputo. **Language:** there are 10 widely spoken local languages, including Shangaan, Tsonga, Swahili, Sena-Nyanga, Makua-lomwe and Shana, but the common tongue and language of government, spoken by nearly all, is Portuguese. In tourist circles, most people have at least a smattering of English. Elsewhere, you won't find it spoken. **Currency:** The Metical (plural meticais; Mt) is a highly unstable currency, with many thousands to the dollar or pound. It is totally useless outside the country and many places within Mozambique also prefer payment in US$ or SA Rand. Due to recent frauds, you may experience problems exchanging American Express traveller's cheques. Few places outside the major hotels accept credit cards.

Passports And Visas

All visitors must obtain a visa before arrival (you will be turned back at the border without one). If you have time, it is probably easier to get your visa in South Africa or Zimbabwe than in Europe or the USA. If you have no available embassy, contact the Empresa Nacional de Turismo (Mozambique Tourist Office); see Tourist Information/Useful Addresses, below.

Customs

You may be asked to declare all foreign currency and electronic equipment on arrival. If so, keep the declaration and any exchange receipts in case you are asked to produce them on leaving. **Airport/Departure Tax**: US$10 regional; US$20 international.

Tourist Information

Empresa Nacional de Turismo (Mozambique Tourist Office), *Av. 25 Septembre 1203, corner Av. Vladimir Lenine (CP614), Maputo; tel: 01-421 795, fax: 01-421 796.* This is the official tourist office for the entire country. The staff are willing, but a visit is a totally useless exercise as they have no information in any form, no brochures to hand out, no booking organisation, and virtually no English.

Other tourism associations include **Direcçao Nacional de Turismo (DINATUR)**; *tel: 01-420 596/420 147,* and the **Fundo Nacional de Turismo**; *tel: 01-420 856; fax: 01-430 978.*

Useful Addresses

South Africa: High Commission: *199 Beckett St, Arcadia, Pretoria; tel: 012-343 7840.* **Consulates:** *7th Floor, Cape York Building, 252 Jeppe St, Johannesburg; tel: 011-336 1819/22; fax: 011-336 9921* and *7th Floor, 45 Castle St, Cape Town; tel: 021-262 944/5; fax: 021 262 946;* also Durban and Nelspruit. **Mozambique National Tourist Company:** *3rd Floor, Noswal Hall, 3 Stiemens St, corner Bertha St, Braamfontein 2017; tel: 011-339 7281; fax: 011-339 7295.*

Swaziland: High Commission: *Princess Dr., PO Box 1212, Mbabane; tel: 43700.*

UK: High Commission: *21 Fitzroy Sq., London W1P 5HJ; tel: 0171-383 3800; fax: 0171-383 3801.*

USA: Embassy: *1990 M St, N.W., Washington DC 20036; tel: 202-293 7146; fax: 202-835 0245.*

Zimbabwe: High Commission: *corner L.*

31

Takawira and H. Chitepo Sts, Harare; tel: 04-90 837; fax: 04-732 8968.

STAYING IN MOZAMBIQUE

Accommodation
Maputo has a couple of superb, international standard hotels and a handful of pleasant establishments at a moderate price. Beira has couple of good hotels, and there are a few wonderful, very isolated lodges on the beach or on islands that are entirely supplied and accessible by air. Cheap hotels in Mozambique are not recommended. If camping, take everything with you, including a shovel for a toilet pit, and your own water.

Electricity
220V two-prong plugs. The service is reliable in any tourist areas.

Emergencies
Ambulance: *197* or (Maputo only) *tel: 493 924 or 430 214*; Police: *119* or *422 2001/2*; Fire: *198*.

Foreign Embassies in Mozambique
Australia: *794–9 Av. Julius Nyerere, Maputo; tel: 01-493 072.*
Canada: *1128 Av. Julius Nyerere, Maputo; tel: 01-492 623; fax: 01-492 667.*
Lesotho: *1138 Av. Kim Il Sung, Maputo; tel: 01-490 050.*
South Africa: *Av. Eduardo Mondlane 41, Maputo; tel: 01-491 614/490 059.*
Swaziland: *Av. do Zimbabwe 608, Maputo; tel: 01-492 451/491 721.*
UK: *310 Av. Vladimir Lenine, Maputo; tel: 01-420 111/2/5/6/7.*
USA: *193 Av. Kenneth Kaunda, Maputo; tel: 01-492 797* (consular department).
Zimbabwe: High Commission: *Av. Kenneth Kaunda 816/820 (CP 743), Maputo; tel: 01-499 404; fax: 01-492 239*; **Consulate:** *617 Rua Franciso Dechange, Almelda, Ponde Grea (CP 649), Beira; tel: 03-372 950; fax: 03-328 942.*

Opening Hours
Banks: Mon–Fri 0800–1100. **Offices:** Mon–Fri 0800–1230, 1400–1730. **Post Offices:**

Mon–Fri 0745–1200, 1400–1700, Sat 0745–1200. **Shops:** Mon–Fri 0900–1200, 1500–1800, some shops also open Sat 0900–1300. **Petrol Stations:** Mobil/BP stations are all open 24 hrs.

Postage
Postal service is extremely erratic. Use a special counter for the *Última Hora* (Express Mail) service which is sent on specific days via Johannesburg, Lisbon or Harare and takes about one week to reach its destination. If possible, wait and post things in South Africa or Zimbabwe, or, for anything of value, use one of the courier firms such as DHL.

Public Holidays
Jan 1 (New Year's Day); Feb 3 (Heroes Day); Apr 7 (Women's Day); May 1 (Workers' Day); June 25 (Independence Day); Sept 7 (Day of Victory); Sept 25 (Day of the Revolution); and Dec 25 (Christmas Day).

Public Transport
Maputo is well connected by **air** to Johannesburg and Harare, with a few long-haul flights to Europe (Portugal). There are limited domestic air services, mainly between Maputo, Vilhanculos (with connections for the island lodges) and Beira.

As distances are very long, the roads very bad, and security indifferent, travellers are not recommended to use local **buses** at present. However, there is a good **coach** service to South Africa and Swaziland; contact **Panthera Azul**; *tel: 01-494 238,* or Johannesburg; *tel: 011-337 7409*. The only passenger **rail** service is between Maputo and Johannesburg (p.54).

Colour section (i): Touring Southern Africa: on the open road; travelling by steam train; close encounters with a baboon.
(ii): Southern Africa is renowned for its wildlife (see pp.59–61): giraffe at sunset; lion; baboon.
(iii) Golden Gate Highlands National Park (p.97); game-viewing (p.21); inset, protea (p.122).
(iv): Cape Town (see pp.100–114): view from a cable car; inset, the Victoria and Alfred Waterfront.

Telephones

Service within the country can be difficult, but most towns of any size are connected to satellite and it is easy to make international calls. There are some public call boxes in the cities; or you can make calls from major post offices.

Country code: *258;* IDD: *00;* Operator: *100;* International Operator: *100;* Reverse Charge Calls: *108;* Directory Enquiries: *130;* International Directory Enquiries: *130.*

NAMIBIA

Capital: Windhoek. **Language**: English is the official language, but Afrikaans and German are widely spoken. There are also 11 other ethnic groups in Namibia, each with its own indigenous language and a variety of dialects. These divide roughly into two groups: the Bantu languages spoken by the Wambos, Hereros, Kavangos, Caprivians and Tswana; and the Khoisan languages spoken by the San and the Nama/Damara. **Currency**: the Namibian dollar (N$), divided into 100 cents. The currency is fixed to and equals the South African Rand, which is also legal tender. You may import any amount of foreign currency. Traveller's cheques and foreign currency can be exchanged at any commercial bank (throughout the country) and major credit cards are widely accepted. Most major towns have Bank Windhoek ATMs, where you can draw cash using Visa or MasterCard.

Note that credit cards are not accepted when paying for petrol. Only cash, credit cards, bank guaranteed cheques and South African traveller's cheques are accepted in the state-run rest camps; foreign currency is not accepted.

Passports and Visas

All visitors should have a full passport, valid for at least 6 months from date of entry. Visas are not required by travellers from any Commonwealth or EU countries, or by visitors from Angola, Brazil, Finland, Iceland, Japan, Norway, Russia, Switzerland or the USA. Other nationalities should check with the nearest embassy, or at the Namibian Tourist Offices in Johannesburg or Cape Town (see below) before travelling. No photos are required if visas are stamped in passports. Transit or single entry

Visitor's Visa: R20; multiple entry (issued from Windhoek): R50. Tourists are allowed to remain 90 days, business people 30 days.

Customs

There is no import duty for visitors from Botswana, Lesotho, South Africa and Swaziland. Duty-free allowances for those from other countries include personal effects, sporting and recreational equipment, 400 cigarettes, 50 cigars, 250 grams of cigarette or pipe tobacco, 1 litre wine, 1 litre spirits, and 50 ml of perfume. Visitors importing any goods over the legal limit are offered a choice between paying a flat-rate assessment of 20% of all goods up to a value of R1000 or having duty calculated on each item. Only hunting rifles may be imported (with a temporary import permit); all other firearms are strictly prohibited. **Airport/ Departure Tax**: none.

Tourist Information

Namibia Tourism: *Ground Floor, Continental Buildings, 272 Independence Ave, P. Bag 13346, Windhoek; tel: 061-284 2111/2178; 061-221 930.* **Air Namibia**: *TransNamib Building, Bahnhof St, Windhoek; tel: 061-298 1111;* reservations: *tel: 061-229 639.*

Useful Addresses

Canada: Honorary Consul: *122 Avondale Ave South, Waterloo, Ontario N2L 2G3; tel: 519-578 5932, fax: 519-578 7799*, or see USA below.

South Africa: Embassy: *Tulbagh Park, Eikendal Flat, Suite 2, 1234 Church St, Pretoria; tel: 021-343 3520.* **Tourist Office**: *209 Redroute, Carlton Centre, Johannesburg 2000; tel: 011-331 7055;* and *Ground Floor, Main Tower, Standard Bank Centre, Heerengracht, Cape Town 8001; tel: 021-419 3190.* **Air Namibia**: *1st Floor, Standard Bank Centre, Heerengracht, Cape Town 8000; tel: 021-216 685.*

UK: High Commission: *6 Chandos St, London W1M 0LQ; tel: 0171-636 6244.* **Tourist Office**: *6 Chandos St, London W1M 0LQ; tel: 0171-636 2924.* **Air Namibia**: *Beaumont House, Lambton Rd, Raynes Park, London SW20 0LW; tel: 0181-944 0188.*

USA: Embassy: *1605 New Hampshire Ave*

33

N.W., Washington DC 20009; tel: 202-986 0540.

STAYING IN NAMIBIA

Accommodation

Most small towns have a hotel of some sort, with a wider range available in larger centres. Throughout the country, there is an excellent range of first-class game lodges (the best are generally the private ones) and ranches offering accommodation in tented camps, bungalows or thatched lodges. Moderately priced guest farms and bed & breakfasts are an excellent alternative. Standards of cleanliness and efficiency tend to be high – given the German origins of this ex-colony. Campsites with caravan facilities can be found in most of the national parks and nature reserves. It is advisable to book ahead during school holidays (late Apr–mid May, mid June–mid July, mid Aug–mid Sept and early Dec–mid Jan).

Eating and Drinking

On the coast, particularly at Swakopmund, expect excellent fish dishes. Do not expect gourmet cooking outside Swakopmund and Windhoek. In the hinterland, the emphasis is on game and other meats – for every meal, including breakfast. Everywhere meals are biased towards heavy, Germanic-style portions and consistency. So beware: dieting is not something you hear much about in Namibia. Al fresco eating is popular – braais and picnics. South African and international wines are available and there is some excellent Namibian beer.

Health

The north and east of the country has malaria; never visit those areas without taking the proper precautions. Bilharzia is thought to exist in the Kavango River, so swimming there is not recommended. As anywhere else in Africa, the risk of contracting HIV is ever present. Take the necessary precautions. See also pp.20–22.

Electricity

220V, using 3-pin 15 amp sockets. Supply is normally reliable, but a torch may be useful for nights in the bush.

Emergencies

Ambulance: tel: 09264-203 2270. **Windhoek Municipal Ambulance Service**: tel: 061-61251; **Windhoek State Hospital**: tel: 061-303 9111. Or look in the telephone directory on the first page of each town. Police: 10111 (countrywide); Fire: tel: 09264-203 2270.

Foreign Embassies in Namibia

Australia: see Zimbabwe.
Botswana: 101 Nelson Mandela Ave, Klein Windhoek, Windhoek; tel: 061-221 941.
Canada: 111a Gloudina St, Ludwigsdorf, Windhoek; tel: 061-222 941.
New Zealand: see Zimbabwe.
South Africa: RSA House, corner Jan Jonker and Nelson Mandela Aves, Windhoek; tel: 061-229 765. **Consulate**: M&Z Building, 1st Floor, 8th St, Walvis Bay; tel: 064-87771/2/3.
UK: 116 Robert Mugabe Ave, Windhoek; tel: 061-223 022.
USA: Ausplan Building, 14 Lossen St, Windhoek; tel: 061-221 601.
Zimbabwe: Gamsberg Building, corner Grim and Kaiser Sts (P. Bag 23056), Windhoek; tel: 061-227 738; fax: 061-226 859.

Opening Hours

Banks: Mon–Fri 0900–1530, Sat 0830–1100. **Government Offices**: Mon–Fri 0800–1300, 1400–1630. **Post Offices**: Mon–Fri 0830–1300, 1400–1630, Sat 0830–1200. **Shops**: Mon–Fri 0800/0830–1700/1730, Sat 0800/0830–1300. **Petrol stations**: in most larger towns, petrol and diesel are available 24 hrs; in smaller towns, there is no set rule. Pumps should be manned during daylight hours (until 1800); services are erratic or non-existent at weekends. In hamlets, where fuel is evidently available, just ask if desperate. Rest camps have their own fuel. Always tank up before you leave and take a supply with you. Most good maps identify places where fuel is available.

Postage

Post offices keep normal business hours. Post is slow nationally and, by comparison, very fast indeed internationally. Post offices in big towns and cities, in other words Swakopmund and Windhoek, have poste restante services. Airmail post to Europe takes anything from 4 days to 2 weeks. Everything goes via Windhoek, so the further away you are, the slower the post. Remote areas are served by mobile post offices. Stamps for lightweight letters and cards cost 20c within Namibia, 25c to South Africa, 30c to Botswana, Swaziland or Zimbabwe, and 35c (air letters or postcards only) to Europe, North America, Australia or New Zealand. Anything bulkier should be weighed. Stamps are available from post offices, newsagents and in good hotels (above 4-star).

Public Holidays

1 Jan (New Year's Day); 21 Mar (Independence Day); Mar/Apr (Good Friday/ Easter Monday); 1 May (Workers' Day); 4 May (Cassinga Day); May (Ascension Day – 40 days after Easter); 25 May (Africa Day); 26 Aug (Heroes Day); 12 Dec (Human Rights Day); 25 Dec (Christmas Day); 26 Dec (Boxing Day).

Public Transport

With such huge distances between locations, it is often advisable to hire a car (often the only way to get to game parks, although ask advice from the destination because some do lay on transport). However, there is a good network of **long-distance buses**, which even link key South African cities with Swakopmund and Windhoek. **Minibus taxis** are the usual alternative and, generally devoid of comfort and overfilled with passengers, they have a high accident rate. For trains, see p. 54.

Telephones

Namibia has an excellent telephone system, with only a few remote areas still connected via an operator. Telecards for public phones are available from post offices and telshops, in denominations of N$10, N$20 and N$50. There is a mobile phone network, but it is not yet comprehensive and is largely confined to areas surrounding the country's main arteries. Many dialling codes are in the process of being changed. If you cannot get through, call Directory Enquiries. Cheap periods for local, national and international calls (South Africa only): Mon–Sat 2100–0700, Sat 1300–Mon 0700.

Country code: *264;* IDD: *09 + country code;* Operator: *1190;* International Operator: *1190;* Directory Enquiries: *1188;* International Directory Enquiries: *1193.*

VAT

General Sales Tax (GST) is levied at a rate of 8% on goods, 11% on services, 10% on beer; 5% on clothing, footwear and spare parts for motor vehicles; and 15% on spirits, wine, cigarettes, jewellery and semi-precious stones. Tourists may get tax exemption on luxury items such as jewellery or furs.

SOUTH AFRICA

Capital: Cape Town is the parliamentary capital; Bloemfontein the judicial capital; and Pretoria the administrative capital. **Currency**: Rand (R). 1 Rand = 100 cents. Exchanging currency or traveller's cheques can be a trying and tiresome business in South African banks, taking as long as 45 mins to complete the transaction, involving several departments and much use of rubber stamps. The easiest – and cheapest – way to obtains rands is to use your credit or cashpoint card in one of the ubiquitous ATMs (Standard and Barclays are both linked to international schemes). Major credit cards are widely accepted, though not at petrol stations. **Language**: South Africa has 11 official languages – English, Afrikaans, Ndebele, Northern Sotho, Southern Sotho, Swati, Tsonga, Tswana, Venda, Xhosa and Zulu. English is the main language of government and spoken almost everywhere.

Passports and Visas

Visitors must have a full passport, valid for at least six months beyond their intended stay. Visas are not required by citizens of Australia, Canada, Ireland, New Zealand, United Kingdom or the United States.

Customs

Duty-free allowances (available only to those over the age of 18) are: 400 cigarettes, 250 grams of tobacco and 50 cigars, 1 litre of spirits, 2 litres of wine, 50 ml of perfume and 250 ml of toilet water. Gifts worth up to R500 are allowed, in addition to personal possessions.

35

Unlimited foreign currency and traveller's cheques may be taken into the country but no more than R500 in notes may be imported or exported unless a permit has been obtained from the **South African Reserve Bank**, PO Box 427, Pretoria 0001; tel: 012-313 3911.

Currency exchange receipts should be kept; they may need to be produced if re-converting rands on departure. **Airport/Arrival Tax**: an arrivals tax of R60 is included in the fare paid by international travellers, R39 for a regional fare and R17 for a domestic ticket.

Tourist Information

Satour maintains tourist information centres at the international airports at Cape Town, Durban and Johannesburg and in some major cities. Local information centres managed by provincial or city authorities exist in many parts of the country, especially in larger communities and places attractive to tourists.

Satour Offices: 22 Gardiner St, Durban; tel: 031-304 7144; Tourist Rendezvous, Railway Station, Adderley St, Cape Town; tel: 021-21 6274; North State Building, corner Kruis and Market Sts, Johannesburg; tel: 011-331 5241.

Useful Addresses

Australia: High Commission: Rhodes Pl., State Circle, Yarralumla, Canberra, ACT 2600; tel: 62-273 2424. **SAA**: 5 Elizabeth St, Sydney NSW; tel: 2-223 4448. **Satour**: Level 6, 285 Clarence St, Sydney, NSW 2000; tel: 02-9261 3424; fax: 02-9261 3414.

Botswana: Embassy: Kopanyo House, Nelson Mandela Dr., Gaborone; tel: 304 800/1/2/3.

Canada: High Commission: 15 Sussex Dr., Ottawa, Ontario K1M 1M8; tel: 613-744 0330; fax: 613-741 1639. **Consulate**: Ste 2615, 1 Place Ville Marie, Montreal, Quebec H3B 4S3; tel: 514-878 9231/2. **Satour**: Suite 2, 4117 Lawrence Ave East, Scarborough, Ontario M1E 2S2; tel: 416-283 0563; fax: 283 5465.

Ireland: Embassy: 2nd Floor, Alexandra House, Earlsfort Centre, Earlsfort Terrace, Dublin 2; tel: 01-661 5553; fax: 01-661 5590.

Lesotho: High Commission: 10th Floor, Lesotho Bank Centre, Kingsway, Maseru; tel: 315 758.

Mozambique: High Commission: Av.

Eduardo Mondlane 41, Maputo; tel: 01-491 614/490 059.

Namibia: High Commission: RSA House, corner Jan Jonker and Nelson Mandela Aves, Windhoek; tel: 061-229 765. **Consulate**: M&Z Building, 1st Floor, 8th St, Walvis Bay; tel: 064-87771/2/3.

Swaziland: High Commission: The New Mall, 2nd Floor, Plasmall St, Mbabane; tel: 44651.

UK: High Commission: South Africa House, Trafalgar Sq., London WC2 5DP; tel: 0171-451 7299; fax: 0171-451 7204. **Satour:** 5–6 Alt Grove, Wimbledon, London SW19 4DZ; tel: 0181-944 6646. **SAA**: St Georges House, 61 Conduit St, London W1R 0NE; tel: 0171-312 5002 (also Alliance Air).

USA: Embassy: 3051 Massachusetts Ave N.W., Washington DC 20008; tel: 202-232 4400. **Consulates**: 333 East 38th St, 9th Floor, New York, NY 10016; tel: 212-213 4880; 200 South Michigan Ave, 6th Floor, Chicago, IL 60604; tel: 312-939 7929; and Ste 300, 50 N. La Cienega Blvd, Beverley Hills, CA 90211; tel: 310-657 9200. **Satour**: 500 Fifth Ave, 20th Floor, Suite 2040, New York NY 10110; tel: 212-730 2929 or 800-822 5368 (toll-free); fax: 212-764 1980; and Ste 1524, 9841 Airport Boulevard, Los Angeles, CA 90045; tel: 310-641 8444 or 800-782 9772 (toll-free); fax: 310-641 5812.

Zimbabwe: High Commission: Temple Bar House, corner Baker Ave & Angwa St, Harare; tel: 04-753 147/8/9. **Satour**: Offices 9&10, Mon Repos Building, Newlands Shopping Centre, PO Box HG1000, Harare; tel: 04-707 766/786 487; fax: 04-786 489.

STAYING IN SOUTH AFRICA

Accommodation

South Africa has a broad spectrum of accommodation, although there is a narrow choice of upmarket international chain hotels, the result of being beyond the investment pale during the apartheid years. Nevertheless, standards are high and prices generally reasonable across the range.

At the luxury end of the market, the pace is still set by the country's classics: the Mount Nelson Hotel in Cape Town, The Royal in

Durban, the Carlton in Johannesburg. But the country's real strength in this field lies in its wealth of small de luxe properties, often in wonderful historic buildings and beautiful settings. A number of home-grown chains – companies such as City Lodge, Holiday Inn, Karos, Protea and Southern Sun – cover the middle ground, and many of South Africa's larger communities have a hotel from one of these groups. Some places, especially the smaller towns, will have independent, locally-owned hotels, whose standards vary widely.

The widest choice comes from the rapidly expanding number of bed and breakfast establishments. These are mostly family homes – remote farmhouses, substantial colonial-style bungalows, country mansions and charming suburban townhouses – with accommodation for three or four overnight guests. Hospitality is usually expansive, the food exemplary. And there is the considerable advantage of meeting people with a profound knowledge of the locality. Another plus, in rural areas at least, is that guesthouses are fairly easy to find, thanks to an excellent signposting system. Self-catering is another expanding sector. Here, the options range from condominium-style properties, especially along the coast in Kwazulu-Natal, the Garden Route and around Cape Town, to furnished cottages, cabins and chalets. Municipal campsites are found in many communities.

Safari accommodation is in a class of its own. For the rich – and possibly famous – there are exclusive game lodges, such as those found along the course of the Sabie River, on the edge of the Kruger National Park, where standards are indulgent and game-viewing superb. Full service lodges exist in most National Parks, where you will also find self-catering chalets and cabins and tent and caravan sites.

Satour and the South African Automobile Association publish annual accommodation guides and lists. The other really useful local publications are the *Portfolio* brochures, with separate listings for top quality country hotels, guesthouses and bed and breakfasts. These are all available at local tourist offices and at Satour offices overseas. There are also listing guides to hotels, campsites and self-catering resorts

published by the AA in South Africa, available from good bookshops. For all central booking details, see pp. 407–408. All establishments are graded by star, according to the facilities available, and by colour (bronze, silver etc) for the far less tangible assets of efficiency, hospitality, ambience etc. Many supposedly 3-star hotels actually offer 5-star de luxe service (and prices), but do not have enough rooms, lifts or other physical amenities to reflect their true status.

Eating and Drinking

South Africans dispel the myth that a hot climate dulls the appetite. They eat often and they eat a lot. And while they produce some of the world's finest fruit and vegetables, they are notoriously carnivorous. The quality of meat is good, but bandsaw butchery produces some curious cuts, and the careless use of deep-freeze and microwave by some cooks produces dishes that present a real challenge to mastication.

Food in the good hotels, some of the guesthouses and major South African cities can be excellent – creative, beautifully cooked and presented, with an imaginative use of local ingredients from impala to butterbeans and traditional recipes (see p. 72–73). Step outside these pockets and standards are generally those of Britain about 30 years ago, with overcooked steaks (smothered in sticky barbecue sauce), mangled vegetables and slightly stale cakes laden with food colouring.

Breakfast, served between 0630 and 0900, is usually a full buffet, with a wide range of fresh, dried and/or canned fruit and fruit juice, cereals, cold meats, cheese, full fry-up, toast, a few fancy breads, and a bottomless supply of tea and coffee. It is good value and worth stocking up because lunch is more difficult to find, unless you want a full meal or sandwiches. Your choice here is likely to be restricted to ham, cheese, tomato, ham and cheese, ham and tomato, cheese and tomato and chicken mayonnaise. Or you can have it toasted. Dinner is normally served between 1900–2100.

Prices are generally low, with a remarkably small range between the lowliest steakhouse and the gourmet restaurants. Where you can find them, most foreigners can afford to eat well. Expect to pay no more than about R100

37

a head for a good three-course meal at a top restaurant.

Electricity

The standard power source in South Africa is 200/230 volts. Just to be different, Pretoria uses 230 volts and Port Elizabeth 200/250 volts. Plugs are usually 3-round pin; an adapter is needed for foreign appliances and this is not a configuration found on the universal travel adapters. They can be difficult to track down even in South Africa and, even then, you may find the occasional hotel (such as the Royal in Durban) which has non-standard wall sockets.

Emergencies

Ambulance: *1022*; Police: *10111*; Fire: *1022*.

Foreign Consulates in South Africa

Australia: *292 Orient St, Arcadia, Pretoria; tel: 012-342 3740;* and *14th Floor, BP Centre, Thibault Sq., Cape Town; tel: 021-419 5425.*
Botswana: *Infotech Building, 1090 Arcadia St, Arcadia, Pretoria; tel: 012-342 4760.*
Canada: *1103 Arcadia St, Hatfield, Pretoria; tel: 012-342 6923; fax: 012-422 3052;* and *Reserve Bank Building, 30 Hout St, Cape Town; tel: 021-235 240.*
Ireland: *Delheim Suite, Tulbagh Park, 1234 Church St, Arcadia, Pretoria; tel: 012-342 5062; fax: 012-342 4752.*
Lesotho: *343 Pretorius St, Momentum Centre, 6th Floor, West Tower, Pretoria; tel: 012-322 6090.*
Mozambique: *199 Beckett St, Arcadia, Pretoria; tel: 012-343 7840.*
Namibia: *Suite 2, Eikendal, Tulbagh Park, 1234 Church St, Colbyn, Pretoria; tel: 012-342 3520;* and *Main Tower, Standard Bank Building, corner Adderley St and Hertzog Blvd, Cape Town; tel: 021-419 3190.*
Swaziland: *Infotech Building, 1090 Arcadia St, Arcadia, Pretoria; tel: 012-342 5782;* and *Room 19, The Rand Central Building, 165 Jeppe St, Johannesburg; tel: 011-29 9776.*
UK (also New Zealand): *Greystoke, 255 Hill St, Arcadia, Pretoria; tel: 012-431 121;* and *91 Parliament St, Cape Town; tel: 021-461 7220.*
USA: *877 Pretorius St, Arcadia, Pretoria; tel: 012-342 1048; 11th Floor, Kine Centre, corner*

Commissioner and Kruis Sts; Johannesburg; tel: 011-331 1681; 4th Floor, Broadway Industrial Centre, Heerengracht, Cape Town; tel: 021-214 280; and *Durban Bay House, Smith St, Durban; tel: 031-304 4737.*
Zimbabwe: *798 Merton St, Arcadia, Pretoria; tel: 012-342 5125; 6th Floor, Bank of Lisbon Building, 37 Sauer St, Johannesburg; tel: 011-838 2156;* and *53/55 Fawley Towers, Cape Town; tel: 021-462 4349.*

Maps

There is a wide range of free maps of the country, regions and cities available from tourist information organisations. Most are as good as, or better than, anything on sale, other than the full A–Z city plans or detailed contour survey maps which are far more comprehensive than most tourists need. Newsagents and booksellers such as CNA, or the Automobile Association offices in main centres, are the best place to buy commercial maps.

Hiking trail maps are available from the National Parks shops.

Opening Hours

Banks: Mon–Fri 0900–1530, Sat 0830–1100; many branches, even in rural areas, have 24-hour Automatic Teller Machines (ATMs). **Businesses**: Mon–Fri 0800–1700, with an hour's break for lunch; a few work Sat morning. **Shops**: Mon–Fri 0800–1700, Sat 0830–1230, but shops and stores in major shopping centres and malls often stay open later, while some small towns operate half-day closing on Wed. A few shops in the cities, including some supermarkets, open on Sunday until 1300. **Bottle stores**: (liquor stores or off-licences) Mon–Sat 0900–1800. **Post Offices**: Mon, Tues, Thur and Fri 0830–1630, Wed 0900–1630, Sat 0800–1200. **Petrol stations**: mainly open daily 0700–1900, though many larger communities now have at least one 24-hour station.

Postage

South Africa has an efficient, though not speedy, postal service, and the scene inside some major post offices can be chaotic at times, with serpentine queues reaching out to the street. Post Restante facilities are available in main post offices.

Public Holidays
1 Jan; 21 Mar (Human Rights Day); Good Friday; Easter Sunday; Easter Monday; 27 Apr (Freedom Day); 1 May (Workers' Day); 16 June (Youth Day); 9 Aug (National Women's Day); 24 Sept (Heritage Day), 16 Dec (Day of Reconciliation); 25 Dec.

Public Transport
In a country the size of South Africa, it is not surprising, perhaps, that domestic **airlines** – some quite small – form the backbone of long-distance travel. Even light aircraft charter may be feasible if several people travel together. Major operators include: **Care Airlines**, *tel: 011-975 5830*; **Comair,** *tel: 011-921 0111*; **SA Express** (SAA's domestic wing), *tel: 011-356 1111*; **SA Airlink**, *tel: 011-973 2941*; and **Sun Air**, *tel: 011-397 2233/44*.

Long-distance **coaches** are the most popular and most practicable form of inexpensive public transport, and there is an excellent round-the-clock network of intercity routes. Reservations should be made at least 24 hours ahead. There are three main companies: **Greyhound Coachlines**; *tel: 011-333 2139* (information), *011-333 2130* (reservations); **Intercape**; *tel: 011-386 4444*; and **Translux Express**; *tel: 011-488 1350*.

For backpackers and budget travellers, the best way to get round the country is on the **Baz Bus**, *8 Rosedene Rd, Sea Point, Cape Town 8001; tel: 021-439 2323; fax: 021-439 2343* (twice-weekly; Cape Town–Johannesburg one-way R535). Set up specifically for travellers, this is a hop-on, hop-off service connecting most of the country's main tourist areas on a route that includes Johannesburg, the Drakensberg, Durban, Port St Johns, Port Elizabeth and numerous stops along the Garden Route to Cape Town. You may take as long as you like to do the journey and many backpackers' hostels will provide connecting transport.

The biggest supplier of public transport, both in town and long-distance, is a growing network of **minibus taxis** offering cheap fares in unreliable, overcrowded and, frankly,

dangerous vehicles, which are frequently involved in spectacularly tragic accidents. Local **metered taxis** are safer, but expensive, and can be hard to find. They do not cruise and ranks are few and far between; see details in each town.

Those with a romantic turn of mind will be attracted to South Africa's **railways** for long-distance journeys. Trains are slow, but on-board service and catering still retain the standards of the pre-jet age. See p.53.

Telephones
Public phones are few and far between, but the telephone system – both internally and internationally by satellite – is generally reliable. Phonecards for use in the blue public call boxes can be bought in pubs and newsagents. In cash kiosks, the minimum charge is 20 cents. The most expensive rate band is Mon–Fri 0700–1800 and Sat 0700–1300. The medium band is Mon–Fri 1800–2000, and the cheap rate is Mon–Fri 2000–0700, Sat 1300–Mon 0700.

Mobile phones are available for hire at all international airports, but they are not cheap, and although a mobile might seem a useful accessory for emergencies in remote areas, it is worth noting that these are often the 'dead' spots for transmission and reception.

Country code: *27*; IDD: *09 plus country code;* International Operator: *0900;* phone books carry a full list of international codes; Operator: *0020;* Directory enquiries: *1023;* International directory enquires: *0903.*

VAT Refunds
At the time of writing, VAT in South Africa is set at 14%, and is incorporated in the marked price of most goods and services. Foreign visitors can reclaim VAT on goods taken out of the country if they total more than R250 in value. For a refund at your airport or harbour of departure (or at a customs office), the documents you need are the original tax invoice (be sure to request this when you make purchases), VAT refund control sheet and your passport. You must be prepared to present the items you are taking away, so it is best to carry them separately as hand baggage, or to get to your

point of departure early enough to go through these formalities before you check in your luggage. When you first arrive in South Africa, you can pick up a leaflet giving details of the VAT refund process at the international airports in Johannesburg, Cape Town and Durban. For further information contact *PO Box 9478, Johannesburg 2000; tel: 011-484 7530.*

SWAZILAND

Capital: Mbabane. **Currency:** lilangeni, plural emalangeni (E). The lilangeni is pegged to the South African rand, which is widely accepted. US dollars and UK pounds are easily exchanged in Mbabane and at major hotels. Major credit cards are accepted at hotels and restaurants and there are ATMs at banks in Swazi Plaza, the main shopping centre in Mbabane. **Language:** SiSwati and English are both official languages.

Passports and Visas
Among the few nationalities requiring visas to enter Swaziland are citizens of Austria, France, Germany and Switzerland. They will not find it an onerous task: visas are freely available at border posts and at Matsapha International Airport, near Manzini.

Customs
Swaziland is a member of the Southern African Customs Union, with Botswana, Lesotho, Namibia and South Africa. Visitors from other countries may import duty-free 400 cigarettes, 50 cigars or 250 grams of tobacco; one litre of spirits, two litres of wine, 250 ml of toilet water, six cans of beer, plus new and used goods worth not more than R500. There are no duty-free allowances for residents of the Customs Union. There are no currency controls; travellers are advised to change emalengeni back into their own currencies before leaving Swaziland. **Airport/Departure Tax**: E20.

Tourist Information
Swaziland Tourist Office: *Swazi Plaza, between Commercial Rd and Western Distributor Rd (PO Box 338) Mbabane; tel: 44556; fax: 42774.*

Useful Addresses
Canada: High Commission: *130 Albert St,*

Ottawa, Ontario K1P 5G4; tel: 613-567 1480; fax: 613-567 1058.
Mozambique: Embassy: *Av. do Zimbabwe 608, Maputo; tel: 01-492 451.*
South Africa: Embassy: *Infotech Building, 1090 Arcadia St, Arcadia, Pretoria; tel: 012-342 5782;* **Swaziland Trade Mission**: *Room 19, The Rand Central Building, 165 Jeppe St, Johannesburg; tel: 011-299 776.*
UK: High Commission: *20 Buckingham Gate, London SW1E 6LD; tel: 0171-630 6611; fax: 0171-630 6564.*
USA: Embassy: *Suite 3M, 3400 International Dr., Washington DC 20008; tel: 202-362 6683.*

STAYING IN SWAZILAND

Accommodation
The area around Mbabane has a number of international chain hotels. There are numerous reasonably good and some not very expensive hotels in the Ezulwini Valley and other major centres throughout the country. There are also camping and caravan grounds, and self-catering cottages and cabins may be rented at nature reserves and wildlife sanctuaries. All accommodation within the parks is handled by **Big Game Parks of Swaziland**, *PO Box 234, Mbabane; tel: 44541; fax: 40957; e-mail: biggame@realnet.co.sz; website: http://www.realnet.co.sz/real/tour/biggame.html.*

Eating and Drinking
In addition to hotel restaurants, there's a fairly wide choice of eating places in Mbabane and Manzini, including a handful serving such ethnic cuisines as Chinese, Indian, Italian and Portuguese. Outside these centres you may have to travel some distance before finding a place to eat. At weekends it's a good idea to book a table for lunch or dinner in an out-of-town hotel dining room or restaurant.

Electricity
Current is supplied at 220 volt AC50 Hz and 15 amp round-pin wall sockets are used.

Foreign Embassies in Swaziland
Mozambique: *Princess Dr., PO Box 1212, Mbabane; tel: 43700.*

South Africa: *The New Mall, 2nd Floor, Plasmall St, Mbabane; tel: 44651.*
UK: *Allister Miller St, Mbabane; tel: 42581/5.*
USA: *Central Bank Building, Warner St, Mbabane; tel: 46441/5.*

Opening Hours
Banks: Mon–Fri 0830–1430, Sat 0830–1100.
Businesses and shops: generally Mon–Fri 0830–1700, Sat 0830–1200. **Post Offices**: Mon–Fri 0800–1600, Sat 0800–1100. **Petrol Stations**: many remain open 24 hours.

Postage
The main post office in Mbabane is on *Warner St* between *Market St* and *Allister Miller St*. A stamp bureau adjoins the post office.

Public Holidays
1 Jan; Good Friday; Easter Monday; 19 Apr (King Mswati III Birthday); 25 Apr (National Flag Day); 22 July (King Sobhuza II Birthday); 25, 26 Dec.

Public Transport
There are a few express **bus** services between major centres, and a reasonable cross–country network of local buses, although most of these services are slow and infrequent. **Minibus taxis** are cheap, but often crowded and can be dangerous. There are no regular passenger **rail** services in Swaziland.

The national airline, **Royal Swazi Airlines**; *tel: 86155*, operates scheduled services to Johannesburg, Maputo, Harare, Lusaka, Dar es salaam and Maseru from **Matsapha Airport**, *8 km west of Manzini*. Air charter facilities throughout Swaziland and adjacent territories are operated by **Scan Air Charter**; *tel: 844748*, and **Steffan-Air Charter Services**; *tel: 36531*.

Telephones
Swaziland has no area codes and some places do not yet have automatic exchanges. In these cases, calls must be made through the operator. International calls from Swaziland are expensive and the sound quality unreliable. Calls abroad may be made from the main post office in Mbabane. Country code: *268;* Operator: *90.*

ZIMBABWE

Capital: Harare. **Currency:** Zimbabwe Dollar (Z$), divided into 100 cents. Keep plenty of small bills as it can be difficult to change larger denominations. Visitors to upmarket hotels may be required to settle bills in hard currency or provide proof of exchange. Credit cards are widely accepted; US$100 bills are not, after a spate of forgeries. Many ATM machines are linked to the Cirrus network allowing you to withdraw money using a national bank card.
Language: There are two main local languages, Shona, which has a number of sub-dialects, and Ndebele, the majority language in the south-west of the country. English is the language of government and is widely spoken almost everywhere, to a greater or lesser degree.

Passports and Visas
All visitors should have a passport valid for at least 6 months, together with a return or onward ticket and sufficient funds to cover their stay (a credit card will usually suffice as proof). Citizens of Australia, Canada, Ireland, New Zealand, the UK and USA do not need a visa for stays of up to 90 days. South Africans do need a visa, available from their nearest consulate. Citizens of other countries should check before travelling. If your home country has no Zimbabwean representative, affairs are handled by the British Embassy or High Commission.

Customs
Duty-free: up to 5 litres of alcohol, of which no more than 2 litres may be spirits (over age 18); other goods to a value of Z$1000. Anything for personal use may be imported free of charge. **Currency**: you may import or export no more than Z$500 in currency (it is also totally useless elsewhere). You may import and export any amount of foreign currency, provided that you declare it on arrival, and may re-exchange currency on departure as long as you have proof that you changed it originally.

Two-Tier Payments
Quite a few parks, museums etc have a separate (and much higher) entrance fee for non-residents, calculated in US$. They will convert this back into Z$, but it is a lengthy process and

41

it is much easier to keep a fistful of small denomination US$ notes with you when travelling round Zimbabwe. At Victoria Falls, the rates jump quite alarmingly and many of the activities cost US$90–100 per person. More upmarket hotels will also usually quote prices in US$, but are happy to accept payment in any major currency or in Z$. In both these circumstances, the easiest option is to pay by credit card and let someone else sort it out. **Airport Departure Tax**: US$20 (airports only). This must be paid in US dollars. You can buy the stamp at all airports, banks and post offices.

Tourist Information
Zimbabwe Tourism Development Authority, *Three Anchor House, 54 Jason Moyo Ave (PO Box CY286), Harare; tel: 04-758 712/4 or 752 570; fax: 04-758 828.* **National Parks and Wildlife Resources Board**, *Makombe Building, Herbert Chitepo Ave (PO Box 8070, Causeway), Harare; tel: 04-705 661.*

Useful Addresses
Australia: High Commission: *11 Culgoa Circuit, O'Malley, ACT 2606; tel: 06-286 2281.* **Air Zimbabwe**, *South Pacific Express, Level 11, 456 Kent St, Sydney, NSW 2000; tel: 02-264 7346; and South Pacific Express, Ste 5, Level 7, City Arcade Tower Block, 207 Murray St, Perth, WA 6000; tel: 09-321 3751.*
Botswana: High Commission: *Plot 8895, Orapa Close, Gaborone; tel: 314 495/7.*
Canada: High Commission: *332 Somerset St West, Ottawa, Ontario K2P 0J9; tel: 613-237 4388/9; fax: 613-563 8269.* **Air Zimbabwe**, *Sita World Travel Inc., (Pyramid Travel), 110 Bloor St West, Ste 220, Toronto, Ontario M55 2W7; tel: 416-972 7515; and Sita World Travel Inc., Ste 1500, Pacific Center, 710 West Georgies St, Vancouver BC V7Y YAY; tel: 604-681 8955.*
Mozambique: High Commission: *Av. Kenneth Kaunda 816/820 (CP 743), Maputo; tel: 01-499 404; fax: 01-492 239.* **Consulate**: *617 Rua Franciso Dechange, Almelda, Ponde Grea (CP 649), Beira; tel: 03-372 950; fax: 03-328 942.*
Namibia: High Commission: *Gamsberg Building, corner Grim and Kaiser Sts (P. Bag 23056), Windhoek; tel: 061-227 738; fax: 061-226 859.*

South Africa: High Commission: *789 Mertons, Arcadia, Pretoria; tel: 012-342 5135.* **Consulates**: *Bank of Lisbon, 37 Sauer St, Johannesburg 2000; tel: 011-838 2156; fax: 011-838 5620 53/55; and 53/55 Fawley Towers, Cape Town; tel: 021-462 4349.* **Tourist Office**: *Upper Shopping Level, Carlton Centre, Commissioner St, Johannesburg 2000; tel: 011-331 3137; fax: 011-331 6970.* **Air Zimbabwe**, *Carlton Centre, Commissioner St, Johannesburg 2000; tel: 011-331 1541; fax: 011-331-6970; Johannesburg International Airport; tel: 011-970 1689; and Shop 6, Durban Bay House, 333 Smith St, Durban 4000; tel: 031-301 2671; fax: 031-301 0271.*
UK: High Commission: *Zimbabwe House, 429 The Strand, London WC2R 0SA; tel: 0171-836 7755; fax: 0171-379 1167.* **Tourist Office**: c/o Zimbabwe High Commission (see above). **Air Zimbabwe**, *Colette House, 52/55 Piccadilly, London W1V 5AA; tel: 0171-491 0009; fax: 0171-355 3326. Also Gatwick Airport, South Terminal; tel: 01293-502 086.*
USA: Embassy: *1608 New Hampshire Ave, N.W. Washington DC 20009; tel: 202-332 7100.* **Tourist Office**: *Rockefeller Center, Ste 1905, 1270 Ave of the Americas, New York, NY 10020; tel: 212-332 1090.* **Air Zimbabwe**, *Sita World Travel Inc., 767 Fifth Ave, GM Plaza Bldg, New York, NY 10153; tel: 212-980 8010; and Sita World Travel Inc., (Pyramid) Travel, 8135 San Fernando Rd, Sun Valley, CA9135; tel: 818-767 0039; and Sita World Travel Inc., Ste 202, 9001 Airport Blvd, Houston, Texas; tel: 713-943 2279; fax: 713-626 1905.*

STAYING IN ZIMBABWE

Accommodation
There is a good range of accommodation in the country and, thanks to the favourable exchange rate, many foreigners can afford to jump a notch or two in their expectations. There are several local chains, of which one, Zimbabwe Sun, now linked to Holiday Inn, is massively dominant, with hotels everywhere you might wish to stay. There is an increasing number of small, charming and remote game lodges, at a price, and the major towns have a selection of mid-range business hotels and scruffy cheap

hotels. There is relatively little accommodation for backpackers outside Harare, but campsites and National Parks rest camps are excellent value. Always book ahead during the school holidays (Apr–May; Aug–Sept; Dec–Jan) as these are very popular amongst locals.

Eating and Drinking
Don't expect haute cuisine, but the food is usually well-prepared, hygienic and copious. Most of the larger hotels do table-groaning buffets for breakfast and lunch (and some evenings) which are exceptional value for the hungry. Zimbabweans are keen carnivores, so vegetarians may encounter some problems.

Electricity
220/230V, 13 amp, with 3 square-pin plugs. UK plugs and equipment work without adapters. Some old properties may still have round-pin sockets. The power supply is usually reliable, but may fail occasionally in rural areas. Take a torch just in case.

Emergencies
Ambulance: *994*; Police: *995*; Fire: *993*; General emergencies: *999*. **Medical Air Rescue Service**: Harare: *tel: 04-737 086/739 642/3*; Mutare: *tel: 120-64647*; Bulawayo: *tel: 19-60341*; Victoria Falls: *tel: 113-4646*.

Foreign Embassies in Zimbabwe
Australia: *4th Floor, Karigamombe Centre, 53 Samora Machel Ave, Harare; tel: 04-757 774; fax: 04-757 770.*
Botswana: *22 Fifth Ave, Harare; tel: 04-729 551.*
Canada: *45 Baines Ave, Harare; tel: 04-733 881; fax: 04-732 917.*
Mozambique: *corner L. Takawira and H. Chitepo Sts, Harare; tel: 04-90 837; fax: 04-732 8968.*
Namibia: *31a Lincoln Rd, Avondale, Harare; tel: 04-47930.*
New Zealand: *8th Floor, Eastgate Centre, Greenbridge, Harare; tel: 04-759 221/6; fax: 04-759 228.*
South Africa: *Temple Bar House, corner Baker Ave & Angwa St, Harare; tel: 04-753 147/8/9; fax: 04-776 715. Consular Section: 1 Princess*

Dr., Newlands Shopping Centre, Highlands, Harare; tel: 04-776 712.
UK: *Corner House, L. Takawira St and Samora Machel Ave; tel: 04-772 990.*
USA: *Arax House, 172 Herbert Chitepo Ave; tel: 04-794 521; fax: 04-796 488.*

Opening Hours
Banks: Mon, Tues, Thur, Fri 0800–1500, Wed 0800–1300, Sat 0800–1130. **Offices**: Mon–Fri 0800–1300, 1400–1700; some commercial offices open Sat 0800–1200. **Shops**: Mon–Fri 0800–1700, Sat 0800–1200/1230; some supermarkets and grocers' shops stay open until 1900 in the evenings and open for a limited time on Sundays. **Post Offices**: Mon–Fri 0830–1600, Sat 0830–1130. **Petrol Stations**: many stay open 24 hrs.

Postage
Postage is reasonably reliable, but often very slow. Most locals use PO Box numbers as a postal address. For any urgent documents, use one of the private courier companies such as TNT or DHL which have offices in the major cities. Look in the local yellow pages.

Public Holidays
1 Jan (New Year's Day); Easter (4 days, Fri–Mon); 18 Apr (Independence Day); 25 May (Africa Day); 11 Aug (Heroes Day); 12 Aug (Defence Forces Day); 25 Dec (Christmas Day); 26 Dec (Boxing Day).

Public Transport
There is an excellent road north from Pretoria to the Zimbabwe border for motorists, but you may not be allowed to take a hire car into the country, and it may be better to look at public transport. Zimbabwe has excellent connections by **air** with South Africa and most other surrounding countries, as well as long-haul direct flights to many countries in Europe and the USA. The national carrier, **Air Zimbabwe**, Harare Airport; tel: 04-457 5111, central reservations: tel: 04-575 021; fax: 04-575 069, has regular flights to London, Frankfurt, the USA and South Africa, as well as domestic services. Other regional services are run by **Zimbabwe Express Airlines**, *1st Floor, Kurima House, 89*

Baker Ave (PO Box 5130), Harare; tel: 04-729 681/9 (admin), *729 681-9* (sales); *fax: 04-737 117*, and **SAA** (see p.39). For the wealthy, there are several companies offering private air charters, including **Bush Pilots**; *tel: 073-2567/2233, fax: 073-2612;* **Executive Air**; *tel: 04-304 601/304 610; fax: 04-304 328;* and **Southern Cross Aviation**; *tel: 013-4618; fax: 013-4609.*

Zimbabwe has several excellent long-distance **coach** companies operating both within the country and down to Johannesburg: **Express Motorways**, *Shop 2, corner Rezende St and Baker Ave, Harare; tel: 04-737 438/720 392, fax: 04-731 677;* **Blue Arrow**, *Chester House, Speke Ave (between 3rd and 4th Sts), Harare; tel: 04-729 514; fax: 04-729 572*, and *Swift Town Depot, 73a Fife St, Bulawayo; tel: 19-69673;* **Silverbird**, *Suite 109, Sheraton Hotel, Harare; tel: 04-729 771*. For **rail** services, including cruise trains to Victoria Falls, see p.54.

Telephones

Although the national telephone network is improving, it is still a pretty hit-or-miss affair and it can be easier to phone overseas via satellite than it is to get a landline to the next town. As the lines themselves are also often crackly and difficult to hear, locals use fax for anything of importance. Most hotels will be happy to send and receive faxes for you, and there are public machines at main urban post offices. A small but steadily growing mobile phone network uses GSM equipment, available for hire from Harare airport. There are limited numbers of working phone boxes in the larger towns.

Country code: *1419;* IDD: *110;* Operator: *0* or *967;* International Operator: *966;* Directory Enquiries: *962;* International Directory Enquiries: *965.*

Note

Homosexuality is an arrestable offence in Zimbabwe – a law that has the personal backing of President Mugabe, so is taken very seriously. Therefore, gay couples should be circumspect both in their behaviour and who they talk to.

44

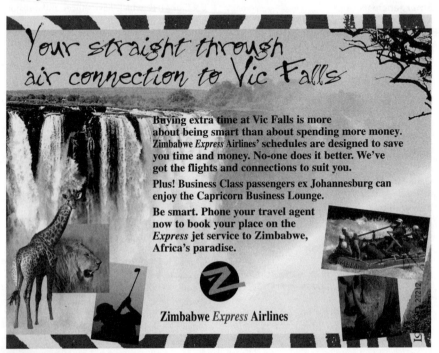

DRIVING IN SOUTHERN AFRICA

Car travel is one of the most enjoyable ways of seeing this vast region, with long, straight, almost empty roads that are a sheer pleasure to drive. Distances are often great, and it is worth planning well in advance and pre-booking accommodation where possible.

BASIC RULES AND REGULATIONS

All countries in this book **drive on the left** and **give way to the right**; the wearing of **seatbelts** is compulsory.

Importation of Vehicles

Private vehicles, caravans and trailers may be brought in temporarily to all countries in the Southern African Customs Union (see p.40), as long as they are licensed in their home countries and have correct number plates and country identification. You will need a triptyche (available from the AA) to cross any border without lodging high import duties. The International Certificate of Motor-Vehicles (Carnet de Passage) is recognised for temporary imports of cars from outside the Union.

Driving Licences

Always carry your licence with you. If you are asked for it and cannot produce it, you will be fined. If using an International Licence, also carry a copy of your national licence.

Botswana: Foreigners may use their national driver's licence for up to 6 months.
Lesotho: All foreign visitors require an International Driver's Licence.
Mozambique: All foreign visitors require an International Driver's Licence.
Namibia: All foreign visitors require an International Driver's Licence.
South Africa: All foreign visitors require an International Driver's Licence.

Swaziland: All foreign visitors require an International Driver's Licence.
Zimbabwe: You may use your national licence for up to 90 days. If it is not written in English, get a certificate of authority and validity, or a translation of the text with the bearer's photo attached. If in doubt, get an International Driver's Licence, valid for 1 year.

Third Party Insurance

Third party insurance is compulsory everywhere. In some countries, such as South Africa, it is included in the price of petrol. In others, such as Mozambique and Zimbabwe, you can buy cover at the border (payment in foreign currency only). This will be basic and it is strongly advised that you get full cover from a reputable broker, insurance company, the AA or RAC before leaving home. If hiring a vehicle, third party cover should be included within the compulsory car insurance payments.

Documentation

When driving in Southern Africa, you should carry with you an original or international driver's licence and vehicle registration documents. International registration letters denoting the country of origin must be attached to the rear of your vehicle. In Zimbabwe, towed vehicles must display 'T' plates.

RULES OF THE ROAD

Speed Limits

South Africa: 120 kph on freeways, 100 kph on rural roads, 60 kph in built-up areas, unless otherwise indicated. Speed traps occur frequently, day and night, along any section of road, operated by electronic timers, cameras and police 'pace cars'. It is an offence to fail to stop when signalled to do so. You will be banned instantly if caught doing more than 140 kph.

45

Botswana: 110 kph on open roads; 60 kph in built-up areas.
Lesotho: 120 kph on open roads; 50 kph in towns.
Namibia: 120 kph on tarred roads; 100 kph on gravel roads, 60 kph in town.
Mozambique: 120 kph on tarred roads; 50 kph at all other times.
Swaziland: 80 kph on open roads, 60 kph in built-up areas. A road tax of E1 is levied at the border.
Zimbabwe: 100 kph on rural roads, 60 kph in town.

Freeway Driving

When driving on freeways, there are a few rules to observe: don't stop on freeways, except in emergencies; don't stop on an entrance or exit road; never reverse or cross the centre island divide; and never overtake on the hard shoulder. In some cases, it is forbidden to drive at less than a certain speed – indicated by white figures on a circular blue background.

Mobile Phones

The cell phone is undoubtedly one of the most useful pieces of modern gadgetry for the motorist, as help can be summoned in emergencies. Long-distance travellers should consider hiring one; **Vodacom** have 24-hr desks at various major international airports. The South African network is extensive; Zimbabwe, Namibia and Botswana are growing rapidly; the other countries are still trailing behind. Sadly, nowhere is the net yet broad enough to reach the really remote rural areas, where a phone could literally be a lifeline. Pull over to the side of the road while using a mobile phone. It is not yet illegal to use a hand-held phone while driving, but the law in South Africa is due to change shortly. Whatever the case, it is not safe, particularly at high speed or in heavy traffic.

ROADS

Road Classification

National (N) roads (freeways) are generally shown on maps in blue, with the route number in white on a blue pentagon with a white border. Road signs are blue. Toll roads are marked by a large black T set with a yellow circle; a consequent black A within a yellow circle marks an alternative (free) road.

Regional (R) roads are divided into major provincial routes (equivalent to the British A roads), marked on the map in solid yellow, with the route marker as yellow digits within a green diamond, and minor provincial routes marked in solid red lines, with the route marker as yellow digits in a green rectangle. Untarred roads are marked by parallel red or black lines.

State of the Roads

South Africa: South Africa has Africa's best, most comprehensive network of roads. Many are currently being upgraded, and it may be that by the time you use this book their route will have altered slightly. All roads are tarred; the most important are being turned into dual carriageways or freeways (some with tolls). Gravel roads are well-maintained, only causing slight problems if very dry conditions throw up huge amounts of dust, or heavy rains cause flood damage. There are very few places where a 4x4 is needed; these are marked clearly in the text. Some roads, tunnels and bridges in South Africa have tolls. These vary according to route and vehicle type, but are never high. Ensure you have a good supply of change before setting out or plan a route that avoids tolls.
Botswana: there are some good surfaced main roads, but the rest are tracks and pistes.
Lesotho: there are some good surfaced roads, but many are fairly basic, and many are impassable in the rainy summer season. Much of the country is only accessible by bridle paths.
Namibia: the roads are generally good. Two-wheel drive is sufficient, except for parts of the Namib Desert, the Kaudom Reserve and Kaokoland, where four-wheel drive is required.
Mozambique: a major rebuilding programme means that the roads here vary from superb to diabolical, with nothing much in between. Main through routes (such as the Komatipoort–Maputo link, and most of the long coast road between Maputo and Beira) are now excellent. Elswhere, mines remain a dangerous hazard. They are being cleared from the roads (but not necessarily the verges), and flags should mark danger zones. Never travel roads unfrequented

by other drivers unless you can get reliable advice from locals, and never drive off the road except in villages and towns.

Swaziland: main roads are in good condition, most side roads are still gravel, but fairly well-maintained. Many of the roads are very mountainous, so check your brakes.

Zimbabwe: the roads are generally excellent. Most 'tourist' roads are tarred and the others are graded regularly.

DRIVING TIPS

Long Distance Driving

Distances here can be immense, so don't be too ambitious. Set a limit of no more than 500 km a day, even on good roads. Roads are often very straight and empty so it is easy to fall asleep at the wheel. Get up before dawn and leave early so that much of your travelling is done while it is still cool. Stop every 4 hours, stretch your legs, get some fresh air and a drink. In general, try and complete your journey by about 5pm. When your final destination is a game park, be through the main gate by 3pm to give yourself time to make camp before the 6pm curfew. Night driving is a possible option, but may not be safe; check the security situation before setting out. Be particularly careful about animals on the road at night. And don't think you can avoid speed traps because it's dark; you can't.

Untarred Roads

Many rural roads are untarred and require extra vigilance. It is more difficult to break effectively at speed, and you need to keep a sharp eye out for potholes and corrugations. It is often easier to take small corrugations at a slightly higher speed (40 kph). Try not to let more than one wheel go into a pothole at once, or the car will ground itself on the hummock in between. Keep your distance from the car in front, or its dust will leave you blind and choking. Never overtake if your vision is obscured, ensure that your lights, particularly those at the rear, do not become obscured by dust, and, if necessary, use them as you would for driving in fog.

Stuck in Sand or Mud

If the car gets stuck in sand or mud, do not attempt to accelerate. The wheels will spin and the car will sink even further. All the passengers should alight and, if the car is seriously embedded, all luggage should be taken out. Pack branches or stones, or, if you have it, sacking, behind the driving wheels; put the car into second gear and accelerate gently. With the wheels in the forward position, rev by slipping the clutch. The passengers should push – from the side, not the rear. It is sometimes easier to come out in reverse – but then you still have to get round the obstacle. Once the car is moving, don't stop to collect passengers until you have reached flat, hard ground. Deflating the tyres on the driving wheels improves traction, but only do this if you are sure you can re-inflate them.

Driving through Floodwater

If approaching a low bridge, ford or flooded section of road, slow down in order to test the strength and depth of the water. If necessary, get out and test it on foot. Never drive at speed; vision may be obscured by splashback, you could lose control of the car or spray water may swamp the engine. If water comes up over the bodywork, it's best not to continue. If you do cross, drive in the centre of the road (its highest point) in low gear. Never change gear while crossing; water may be sucked up into the exhaust pipes causing extensive damage to the pistons, connecting rods and crankshaft. Don't stop until you reach the other side. On emerging from the water, test your brakes. If they are soaked, they may be useless. Dry them by depressing the brake pedal and driving slowly.

Animals on the Road

This is a real danger in rural areas. Around villages, dogs run free and herds of cattle graze on the verges, while antelope can burst on to the road and literally leap into the windscreen. Take animal crossing signs seriously. If an animal suddenly appears in front of you, it will be panicking and, at night, probably blinded by your headlights. Your course of action will depend on your speed, the size of the animal, traffic conditions and the surrounding terrain. If you hit anything bigger than a dog head on, the collision will undoubtedly result in serious damage to your car and, possibly, yourself.

47

If you hit a dog or cat, you are not required by law to stop. If you hit a bovine animal (cow, horse, pig, sheep, goat or ostrich), by law, you must stop and ascertain the extent of the animal's injuries; its owner may expect to be compensated. If you hit a wild animal, you cannot remove it. In either case, you must report the incident to the police within 24 hours.

What to Take

It is sensible to keep the following items in your car, especially when driving long journeys: first-aid supplies; extra fuel; extra water; extra oil; a spare fanbelt; sacking and a small spade to enable you to get out of sand or mud; a full-use spare tyre, inflated, as well as the tools with which to change it (many hire cars are supplied with smaller temporary tyres designed for limited mileage at low speeds – not much use if you are on dirt road, right out in the bush); small change for tolls; emergency drinks and munchies; and some sort of rug, space blanket, or other means of keeping warm if broken down overnight

48

DANGERS

Dreadful Drivers

Sadly, the whole region has an appalling driving record, with the number of road accidents soaring over public holidays. A large number of cars are unroadworthy, while more and more buses belch great clouds of choking black smoke and, while you may be an excellent driver, many around you are not. Many southern African drivers have only ever had arbitrary driving instruction. Don't expect people to indicate before turning, or slow drivers to keep exclusively to the slow lane. Never presume that you can predict the car in front's sequence of future actions, or that fast drivers on multi-lane freeways will overtake exclusively on the right. People have been known to drink at the wheel, reverse on freeways and drive at night without lights. Overtaking on blind rises is very common, so apply even the most basic rules of driving safety with extreme vigilance. You also need to keep a wary eye out for small children popping out from nowhere, or even the odd elephant in the middle of the road.

Personal Security

Car-jackings and **thefts** are on the increase, particularly in the Gauteng area. It is absolutely essential that motorists acquire survival skills and take extra precautions.

1. Lock all doors and windows, particularly when driving in city traffic. When alighting, even for a moment, make sure you lock, and, if possible, alarm the car. If you must open a window, then open it a quarter of the way only.
2. Never leave valuables in view, either while driving or when parked. Lock them away in the boot or glove compartment.
3. Be wary of strangers approaching while traffic is stationary, and be extra vigilant when somebody tries to attract your attention by banging on your side of the car. Often an accomplice will open the passenger door and remove your belongings.
4. Be wary of stopping to help apparently injured people lying on or beside the road, particularly in areas where the roadside is scrubland or bushy. There may be concealed accomplices nearby. Check if there has been a genuine accident. Likewise, do not stop if an apparently distressed person flags you down. If you feel you ought to stop, slow down, but don't stop; keep the engine running and the car in gear; never get out, open the windows or unlock the doors until you are completely convinced it is safe to do so. At night, always keep the lights on high beam. If you are unsure, drive on and report the incident to the police. If you hit a pedestrian in an area obscured by scrub or bushes and are unsure of the situation, do not stop; drive on to the nearest police station, private house or telephone and report the incident.
5. When waiting in a queue or at the traffic lights, always leave a wide margin of space between yourself and the car in front, and never allow yourself to be blocked in on all sides. If the car behind you bumps into you, wait before jumping out to see what's happened. Car-jackings often occur when you get out to inspect the damage. If you do get out, lock your doors.
6. Never leave children alone in the car.
7. Never leave the key in the ignition while you are away from the car.
8. If you are followed, drive to the nearest police station, service station or private house

and ask for help. If you need to consult a map, do it at a service station or other public place.

9. Always have your keys ready in your hand as you approach your parked car.

10. When parking, always leave your car in a well-lit spot, attended parking areas or garages. If the car attendant requests a key, give him the car keys only, never the whole bunch.

11. When returning to your parked car, always check the back seat for hidden intruders and the immediate vicinity to see who, if anyone, is watching you.

12. Never pick up hitch-hikers.

13. If you are hijacked, never struggle. Hand over your keys immediately on request and, if possible, move away from the car. Remember, your car can be replaced.

POLICE

You will almost certainly encounter the police at some stage, especially if travelling outside South Africa, where road blocks are more common. These may be to check for vehicle safety, stolen vehicles, drunk drivers or speed traps. In Mozambique, they may simply be a little free enterprise by the local force. Westerners have a reputation for honesty and are rarely approached for bribes; if you are, play it as straight as possible without landing yourself in jail.

If you are arrested or involved in an accident, try to keep a friend with you as a potential witness, inform your embassy or high commission and get yourself legal representation as soon as possible. Never lose your temper. It only irritates people, who see shades of old imperialism. Be polite, but stand firm.

Drinking and Driving

It is an offence to drive while under the influence of alcohol or narcotics. In South Africa, the alcohol level in the blood must be less than 0.08g alcohol per 100ml of blood. In fact, checks are rare. If you are stopped, you can be breathalysed, but the results of such tests are not yet acceptable as evidence in court. You may also be asked to take a blood test. You may refuse to be breathalysed, but you cannot refuse the blood test. The penalty for driving under the influence is a fine of up to R24,000 and/or a prison sentence of up to 6 years. The penalty

is determined by the person's driving ability at the time of the offence.

ACCIDENTS AND BREAKDOWNS

If you have an accident, there are certain actions, which you must take by law if a person is killed or injured, or property is damaged:

1. Stop immediately. If you don't, you can be prosecuted, fined or imprisoned. You don't have to stop if only your car is damaged and injuries are to you alone. Where there is a collision, both drivers must report the accident to the police within 24 hours. The police do not need to be summoned to the scene of the accident, unless there has been a death, or injuries have been sustained by one party.

2. If someone has been killed or injured, it is an offence to move any of the vehicles from the positions in which they came to rest – unless they cause a complete obstruction or a law officer advises you to do so. If you have to move them, record the position of the wheels and direction of the front wheels, and find a witness to confirm this.

3. Give your name and address, and that of the vehicle's owner, and the vehicles' registration number to the police within 24 hours.

4. Do not have any alcohol or take any narcotic drug, unless a doctor says you may. The police may require you to be medically examined.

Making a Statement

Say as little as possible. You do not have to make a statement to the police, either at the scene of the accident or at the police station. If you do make a statement, you are entitled to write it yourself, and to receive a copy.

Evidence

Record the names and addresses of all those involved. Drivers are obliged by law to reveal these details. Record the details of the vehicles involved. Neither passengers nor witnesses are obliged to disclose their details. However, if a witness can be identified, and his evidence is crucial, he may be subpoenaed, and could be prosecuted if he then failed to give evidence.

Emergency Assistance

Local Automobile Associations provide the

49

same services as their counterparts in the UK or USA. They have reciprocal arrangements with numerous other motoring organisations, allowing members to have roadside repairs, accommodation and route planning advice, technical and legal services, and so on. If you are planning to drive in southern Africa, take out membership before you leave. AA Mayday provides emergency medical treatment or evacuation throughout Southern Africa.

South Africa: Johannesburg: *Denis Paxton House, Kyalami Grand Prix Circuit, Allendale Rd, Kyalami, Midrand 1685; tel: 011-799 1000.* **Cape Town**: *Shop 5, Parkade Mall, Strand St; tel: 021-419 6914.* **Durban**: *Shop 79, Upper Level, The Workshop, Commercial Rd; tel: 031-301 0340.* There are also branches in many other towns and cities. **Toll-free information and advice**: *tel: 0800-111 999.* **Emergency Numbers**: 24-hr **Emergency Breakdown Service** countrywide, *tel: 0800-010 101 (toll-free)*; AA Mayday **Emergency Medical Rescue**, *tel: 0800-033 007 (toll-free)*; **AA** membership, travel and legal, *tel: 011-466 6640.*

There are no AA offices in Botswana, Lesotho, Swaziland or Mozambique. South African AA cover also operates throughout Lesotho and Swaziland.

Namibia: Windhoek: *Carl List House 15, Independence Ave, Peter Müller St; tel: 061-224 201.* **Emergency Number**: *tel: 061-224 201.*

Zimbabwe: Harare: *57 Samora Machel Ave; tel: 04-752 779.* **Emergency Number**: *tel: 04-752 522.*

FUEL

Fuel is considerably cheaper than in Europe. Filling stations are reasonably plentiful along freeways, prolific in towns and cities, thin on the ground in rural areas. For opening times, see Country by Country, pp.28–44. Expect to be assisted by a petrol pump attendant, who will fill the car, pump the tyres, check the oil and water and wash the windows (a tip is advisable).

Very few filling stations take credit cards, so keep plenty of cash available. When travelling long distances, keep a spare can of petrol in the boot. Fill up on Saturday as a precaution, some small towns still observe strict Sunday closing.

PARKING

Most urban areas have metered parking bays, with a limited time allowed. Parking is free outside the times stated on the meter or road sign. Do not park on the right-hand side of the road, at or near a junction, or in such a way that road signs or pedestrian crossings are obscured. If you park obstructively or dangerously, leave a vehicle at the meter too long, or park in a restricted area, you may get a ticket or be towed away. Traffic wardens are vigilant and numerous, particularly in the city centres. Multi-storeyed and security parking lots are fairly common in the larger cities centres.

VEHICLE RENTAL

Car hire can be expensive, with hefty base rates doubled by a raft of extras, such as Collision Damage Waiver and insurance. They are higher still outside South Africa, where the roads are particularly punishing and new cars expensive. Shop around for deals. 4x4s are rarely necessary, but check the small print carefully as some companies and insurance policies specifically forbid you to take the car on to dirt roads. Not only is this virtually impossible, but it cuts out any serious game-viewing. Air-conditioning is advisable. Taking hire cars between South Africa, Lesotho and Swaziland is not a problem, but you will probably not be allowed to cross any other borders, especially into Zimbabwe or Mozambique.

Condition of the Car

Large international firms tend to rent out new or nearly new vehicles. Smaller, local firms may provide older, more battered cars than you are used to. Always check that the brakes and lights are working, and that you have a full-size spare wheel and tools before you accept the car. Also check it for existing damage and make sure this is marked onto the hire agreement to save potential arguments afterwards.

Kilometre Allowances

Most companies offer a baseline charge with a per kilometre fee. This can be advantageous for limited city driving, but is prohibitively expensive when travelling long distances. Shop around for deals, ideally offering unlimited kilometreage. An allowance of up to 350 km a day is usually as good (and slightly cheaper), assuming that you intend to stop for breath and sightseeing between the marathon journeys.

Payment

Payment is generally by credit card. A deposit may be required – payable when the contract is signed.

Requirements for Rental

You will need a valid driver's licence, provided the photograph is an integral part of the document, and provided it is in English. If your licence does not comply with this, you should obtain an International Driving Permit. A minimum age (23 or 25) is usually specified

Price Guide

Note that these prices are a rough guide only, based on South African prices in mid 1997. Other countries are roughly comparable, with the exception of Mozambique and Zimbabwe, which are slightly more expensive.

Standard rates: expect to pay a daily rental of about R75–R298, with an additional R0.81–R2.99 kilometreage charge, according to the category of car. Rates include third party liability. Collision damage waiver and theft loss waiver (covering 90% of costs) are optional. However, if they are not taken, a hefty additional deposit will be required. There are special rates for weekends, longer rentals or a daily allowance of kilometres. Cheaper cash rentals are possible on some categories of car. There is generally an airport surcharge of 2% at all state airports.

Smaller, local companies charge between R55–R65 per day plus R0.55–R0.65 per kilometre for a Group A car. For a minimum of 1–3 days (with 300 free kilometres per day), expect to pay around R159 per day. Insurance per day is extra: with excess, around R29 per day; full cover, around R59; collision damage and theft waiver per day, around R10. Most vehicles will have a radio cassette.

VEHICLE RENTAL IN SOUTH AFRICA

You can hire everything here from economy compacts to chauffeur-driven limousines, minibuses, 4x4s and even motorhomes (RVs), all in excellent condition. Budget Rent-a-Car, Imperial (Hertz in disguise) and Avis have offices countrywide, including all main airports, and (for a premium) allow you to hire from one and return at another. Many local firms offer a more limited service at cheaper rates.

Car Hire Central Reservations

In addition to those listed below, look at the classified section of the South African monthly travel magazine, *Getaway*.

Avis: *tel: 0800-021 111 (toll-free)*.
Budget: *tel: 0800-016 6622 (toll-free)*.
Imperial (Hertz): *tel: 0800-131 000 (toll-free)*.

Bicycles

Cape Town: Hopkins Cycle Hire, *133a Bree St; tel: 021-232 527*. Half-day, full day or weekly rentals. Also tours with professional guides. It is not safe to cycle in either central Johannesburg or Durban.

Campers

Britz: Africa, *Kempton Park 270, Tulbagh Rd, Pomona; tel: 011-396 1860*, also has depots in Cape Town, Harare, Durban, Windhoek and Johannesburg. Prices from R400 per day (with 200 km free per day, R1.40 per km above that) for a 2-person vehicle. Vehicles available to accommodate a maximum of 5 people.

4x4

Safari Rentals, *Cape Town 8012; tel: 083 225 1209*. Branches in Cape Town, Johannesburg and Port Elizabeth. Prices: (single cab, 2–3 people) daily rate from R485 per day with 100 km free, plus R1.95 per km). Individual packages available. Also minibuses, cars, bakkies and luxury buses.

Motorbikes

Cape Town: Sunshine Bikes, *313 Voortrekker Rd, Goodwood; tel: 021-592 1339*. Scooters from R95 per day, including 100 free km, R0.37 per extra km; 200cc motorbikes from R225 per day, including 200 free km, 45c per extra km. Also 400 or 500cc motorbikes. Deposit of R3000 required. Helmets (compulsory in South Africa) for hire also.

51

Johannesburg: **Superbike Safaris**, *Main Reef Rd* (inside the licensed testing grounds), *Langlaagte, Johannesburg; tel: 011-839 1660*. Motorbikes from R290 (Kawasaki KLR650) to R342 (BMW F650) per day for a minimum 3–7 days. Deposit required (R2000). International driving license essential. Motorbike self-drive only in South Africa and Swaziland. Vehicles can be dropped off at extra cost: Durban (R300), Port Elizabeth (R50), Cape Town (R450).

VEHICLE RENTAL IN BOTSWANA

Car Hire
Avis: Gaborone, *Sir Seretse Khama International Airport; tel: 313 093*, and *Sheraton Hotel; tel: 312 320;* **Francistown**, *Airport; tel: 213 901;* **Maun**, *Airport; tel: 660 039*.
Holiday Car Hire (Hertz): **Gaborone**, *168 Queens Rd, The Mall; tel: 353 970*, and *Sir Seretse Khama International Airport; tel: 303 255;* **Francistown**, *VIP Travel, Blue Jacket St; tel: 214 524*, and *Airport; tel: 215 258;* **Maun**, *Northern Air Building, opposite Airport; tel: 660 820*.

VEHICLE RENTAL IN LESOTHO
See South Africa.

VEHICLE RENTAL IN MOZAMBIQUE

Car Hire
Hertz and Avis both have offices, but it would be wise to book ahead as the number of cars on offer is not huge. You must return any car to the original hire point.
Hertz: Maputo: *Avenida 24 de Julho; tel: 01-331 72/3; fax: 01-426 077*. Branches also at *Hotel Polana* and *Mavalane Airport*. **Beira**: *Avenida Armando Tivane; tel: 03-322 315; fax: 03-322 415*.
Avis: **Maputo**: *Airport; tel: 01-465 140; fax: 01-465 493*. **Beira**: *Airport; tel: 03-301 263; fax: 03-301 265*.

VEHICLE RENTAL IN NAMIBIA

Car Hire
Avis: **Windhoek**: *Hotel Safari, Aviation Rd*, and

Airport; tel: 061-233 166 (also central reservations); **Swakopmund**: *Swakopmund Hotel and Entertainment Centre; tel: 064-402 527*. Several other offices around the country.

Campers
Camping Car Hire, *corner Edison and Mandume Ndemufayo Aves, Windhoek; tel: 064-237 756*.

4x4
Into Namibia, *Lepardi Centre, 90 Sam Nujoma Dr., Windhoek; tel: 061-253 591/2*.

VEHICLE RENTAL IN SWAZILAND
See South Africa.

VEHICLE RENTAL IN ZIMBABWE

Car Hire
Hertz, which is linked with the giant tour operator UTC, is the largest car hire company in the country, but other multi-national firms are also represented in major centres. There are a few cheaper local companies, with strictly limited service available in Harare and Bulawayo.
Hertz: Harare, *Beverley Court, Baker Ave; tel: 04-727 209*, and *Airport; tel: 04-575 206;* **Bulawayo**, *corner George Silikunda St and 14th Ave; tel: 09-74701*, and *Airport; tel: 019-27177;* **Victoria Falls**, *Zimbank Building; tel: 013-4267*, and *Airport; tel: 013-4297*. Also in Kariba, Masvingo, Mutare, Hwange and others.
Avis: Harare, *5 Samora Machel Ave; tel: 04-720 351/704 191;* and *Airport; tel: 04-50121;* **Bulawayo**, *99 Robert Mugabe Way; tel: 09-68571;* **Victoria Falls**, *corner Mallet Dr. and Livingstone Way; tel: 013-4532*, and *Airport; tel: 013-4668*.
Europcar/Echo Car Hire: Harare, *19 Samora Machel Ave (next to Jameson Hotel), Harare; tel: 04-706 484/5/9;* **Bulawayo**: *9a Africa House, Fife St; tel: 09-67925;* **Victoria Falls**, *Sprayview Motel; tel: 013-4958*, and *Airport; tel: 013-4344*.

Campers
Rent-a-Camper, *503 Memorial Building, 35 Samora Machel Ave, Harare; tel: 04-780 396*.

GREAT TRAINS

South Africa has a great many wonderful railway lines. Unfortunately, the national network of passenger trains, run by Spoornet, is less than comprehensive. Many small regional tracks, long out of use, have been closed or are derelict, while many routes are used only for freight. Even major intercity routes have as little as a single daily scheduled passenger service.

Most South Africans regard the railways as down-market and dangerous. Cape Town's efficient suburban network is popular by day, but should be avoided after dark, while the Johannesburg local services are only useful for commuters between the townships and the city centre, and are not safe for tourists at any time. However, there are few security problems on the long-distance services, and even if second class is not that comfortable, first class is cheap, safe, comfortable and spacious. Prices are more expensive than long-distance bus travel, but you can relax in the privacy of your compartment, drink in hand, watch the countryside roll by outside, go for a stroll, take dinner in an old-fashioned dining car, bathe on the move and curl up for a good night's sleep, ready to start your sightseeing as soon as you arrive in the morning. The downside is that trains are very slow. They are good for cross-country journeys to major destinations, but sadly there are simply not enough passenger services to make touring by train alone a viable option.

If you are considering using trains or buses, the *Thomas Cook Overseas Timetable* is indispensable. For more details of this publication, see p. 26 or p. 223.

SERVICES

Most services link Johannesburg and the coast. The **Trans-Karoo Express** runs between Cape Town–Pretoria via Kimberley (27 hrs; 1525 km) and is deemed a good second-best to the luxury of the Blue Train (at a fraction of the price). The **Trans-Natal** operates a daily service between Johannesburg–Durban, with stops including Ladysmith and Pietermaritzburg

(13½ hrs; 724 km). The **Algoa Express** (Johannesburg–Bloemfontein–Port Elizabeth return; daily; 20½ hrs; 1112 km) stops at Bloemfontein and Cradock amongst others. The **Amatola** (Johannesburg–East London; daily; 20 hrs; 1120 km) stops in Bloemfontein and Queenstown.

Elsewhere, cross-country links include the **Diamond Express** (Bloemfontein–Kimberley–Johannesburg–Pretoria; 11 hrs; out daily except Sat, return daily except Sat); the **Bosvelder** (Johannesburg–Louis Trichardt–Messina; daily; 14½ hrs); the **Trans-Oranje** (Cape Town–Durban; 30½ hrs, 2091 km; out Mon, return Wed), with stops including Kimberley, Bethlehem and Ladysmith.

There are also several cross-border services, which could be helpful for those not allowed to take hired cars across the frontier, such as the **Komati Express** (Johannesburg–Pretoria–Nelspruit–Komatipoort–Maputo return, daily to Komatipoort and three times a week to Maputo); the **Limpopo Express** (Johannesburg–Beit Bridge–Harare return: 13 hrs; out Fri, return Sun); and the **Bulawayo** (Johannesburg–Beit Bridge–Bulawayo; 10 hrs; out Tues, back Thur).

TICKETS

Book first- and second-class tickets at least 24 hours in advance, either at the stations or by telephone (reservations and enquiries): **Cape Town**: *tel: 021-405 3871;* **Durban:** *tel: 031-361 7621;* **Johannesburg:** *tel: 011-773 2944.* Order your bedding at the same time.

In the UK, you can obtain a Spoornet Rail Pass or make reservations for the Blue Train via Leisurail at *PO Box 113, Peterborough, PE3 8HY; tel: 01733 335599; fax: 01733 505451.*

For general information, contact **Spoornet**, *Room 1724, 222 Smit St, PO Box 2671, Joubert Park 2004; tel: 011-773 8920* (Mainline trains), *011-773 7621* (The Blue Train); *fax: 011-773 7643* (for all services).

Expect to pay R554 for a first-class return Pretoria (via Johannesburg)–Cape Town (R374

53

second-class). Ask about special deals: there is a cheaper rate if you share a first-class compartment; and tourists get a 25% discount on all first-class fares.

BOTSWANA

Botswana's only railway line runs from Lobatse, some 50 km from the South African border, to Ramokgwebane, where it crosses into Zimbabwe. The main stops for passenger trains are Gaborone, Mahalapye, Palapye, Serule and Francistown. There are no passenger services between Botswana and South Africa, but there is a daily train to Bulawayo in Zimbabwe. For information, contact **Botswana Railways**, *Station Rd, Gaborone; tel: 351 401/2.* Tickets are on sale at the station office (open Mon–Fri 0730–1300, 1400–1900, Sat–Sun 1400–1930).

MOZAMBIQUE

The only regular passenger service currently running is the South African-run **Komatipoort Express** service between Johannesburg and Maputo (see p.53). Serious attempts are being made to get the passenger service from Beira to Mutare in Zimbabwe operating again, along the once notorious Beira Corridor.

NAMIBIA

Namibia has a well-structured, fairly comprehensive, regular rail network, which provides access to most of the major centres and reserves. Check before any long journey that the train has a dining car or buffet service; if not, take your own supplies. Reserve a berth and bedding for overnight journeys in advance. Main scheduled passenger services: **Windhoek–Walvis Bay** (daily except Sat in both directions; 13 hrs); **Windhoek–Tsumeb** (out Tues, Thur, Sun, return Mon, Wed, Fri; 15–16 hrs). Other services: **Windhoek–Gobabis**; and **Swakopmund–Keetmansdorp** (2 trains changing at Windhoek, with a 13 hr wait).

TransNamib Rail, passenger services and general enquiries: *tel: 061-298 2032; fax: 061-298 2495.*

ZIMBABWE

NRZ (the National Railways of Zimbabwe) survive on freight services and a handful of extremely slow, but quite comfortable, cross-country, overnight passenger services, including **Harare–Mutare** (8 hrs; first-class single, Z$59; snacks available), **Harare–Bulawayo** (9½ hrs; first-class single, Z$102; snack bar) and **Bulawayo–Hwange–Victoria Falls** (12 hrs; first-class single, Z$102; dining car), which is considered to be one of the great train journeys of the world. Between them, these routes take in many of the country's more important tourist destinations. There are also regular cross-border services to South Africa and Botswana. Book at least 24 hrs in advance at the stations, especially if you require a first-class coupe (recommended), and buy a bedding voucher (Z$15) at the same time. Second class is perfectly safe, but uncomfortably spartan and often overcrowded. Take some munchies to supplement the spasmodic on-board catering.

Zimbabwe is also one of a tiny handful of countries in the world that still use steam for commercial operations. You are unlikely to travel behind a steam engine, but hang around Bulawayo station and shunting yard, and you will soon have your fill. Get permission from the station manager before taking photographs.

Information and bookings: **Bulawayo Station**, *off 13th Ave*, reservations: *tel: 09-322 210* (open Mon–Fri 0700–1600, Sat 0700–1300, Sun 0700–1300); tickets: *tel: 09-322 294* (Upper class open Mon–Fri 0715–1600, 1800–2050, Sat–Sun 0700–1300, 1800–2050; Economy Mon–Fri 0630–2050, Sat–Sun 0630–1430, 1700–2050).

Harare Station, *Kenneth Kaunda Ave, tel: 04-733 901.* Reservations: open Mon–Fri 0700–1600, 1900–2125, Sat 0700–1130, 1900–2125; Sun 1900–2125; tickets: Upper class open Mon–Fri 0700–1600, 1900–2125, Sat 0700–1130, Sun 0600–0800, 1900–2125; Economy Mon–Fri 0800–1300, 1400–2125 (local only after 1600), Sat 0800–1100, 1500–2125 (local only in pm), Sun 1400–2125.

CRUISE TRAINS

The Blue Train

The Blue Train is one of the most famous – and expensive – trains in the world. If you have the money, it really is worth the effort, particularly now that it has been upgraded once again and its standards are even higher than before. It is one of South Africa's finest tourist assets.

The service originated in the 1920s, when two express trains were introduced – the Union Limited (see below), operating between Johannesburg and Cape Town; and the Union Express, which made the return journey. The train was always luxurious, but in the 1970s it was improved even more, with the addition of air-conditioning, hot and cold running water and bathrooms with flushing lavatories. It is currently being refurbished to an even higher standard, and the food too is first-class, as is the wine cellar.

The Blue Train operates two scheduled services: **Pretoria–Cape Town** is a sybaritic 26-hr journey (1600 km), which runs 3 times a week; return fares are between R5000 for a luxury compartment, with shared toilet and shower, and R16,000 for a suite (prices based on one or two occupants per compartment include meals, drinks and bedding). It leaves Pretoria 0850 and arrives in Cape Town 1200 the following day. The less frequent (once a month) **Pretoria–Victoria Falls** service leaves Pretoria 0930 (Thur) and arrives in Victoria Falls 0900 (Sat). Luxury fare, return from R5400 per person sharing.

Reservations: PO Box 2671 Joubert Park 2044, South Africa; tel: 011-773 7631, fax: 011-773 7643, toll-free 0800-117 715. Pretoria: tel: 012-315 2436. Cape Town: tel: 021-405 2672. Durban: tel: 031-361 7550.

Rovos Rail

Neither as venerable or as well-known (yet) as the Blue Train, Rovos Rail is a privately run service, which is billed as the 'world's most luxurious train'. In fact, there are two trains, both sleeping a maximum of 68 passengers. Cabins are large, elegantly wood-panelled and immaculately furnished, with full amenities including private bathrooms and air-conditioning. There are two dining cars, a bar/lounge car and a glass-ended observation car. Where possible, the trains run under steam, and efforts are made to give passengers suitably scenic photo opportunities, or a ride on the footplate. The food and wine are both excellent and copious.

There are several regular routes: **Pretoria–Cape Town** (48 hrs, with sightseeing stops at Kimberley and Matjiesfontein; R4795); **Pretoria–Victoria Falls** (48 hrs, with a sightseeing stop in Bulawayo; R5595); **Pretoria–Komatipoort** (24 hrs; with an onward road connection to Skukuza for the Kruger National Park; R2295), with an onward connection on some departures to **Maputo** (23 hrs; R2295); **Cape Town–Knysna**, along the Garden Route, via George (24 hrs; R2875); and once a year, magnificently, the whole way from **Cape Town–Dar es Salaam** in Tanzania (US$7200), an 11-day trip, with plentiful sightseeing stops.

Bookings and information direct from Rovos Rail, or through most good travel agents or specialist tour operators. **Rovos Rail**, *Victoria Hotel, PO Box 2837, Pretoria 0001; tel: 012-323 6052; fax: 012-323 0843.*

The Union Limited

Those looking for a real taste of history should try the Union Limited steam train. Locomotives and carriages are all vintage stock acquired and accurately restored (the coaches date from 1912) by the Transnet Heritage Foundation.

There is a regular programme of trips from Cape Town. The classic is known as the **Golden Thread**, a 6-day tour of the Western Cape mountains, the Garden Route and the Little Karoo. Going over main, secondary and branch lines around the Cape, often using routes not open to other passenger trains, this is a magnificent 1750 km journey, which returns via Oudtshoorn. There are three classes of accommodation: the fairly basic 'standard vintage' (R2500 per person sharing), 'super first-class' (R3500 per person sharing) and, finally, top of the range suites (R10,000 per suite).

Other trips include: the **Union Limited Zambezi** – two 15-day trips a year to Victoria Falls (R8000); and an 8-day **Golden Flower** safari up the West Coast in spring – with added special outings to the Kalahari Gemsbok National Park. There are also various special packages; enquire at **Union Limited**, *3 Adderley St, Cape Town 8000; tel: 021-405 4391; fax: 021-405 4395*, or call **Thompsons**

Tours & Travel; *tel: 031-202 6130, fax: 031-213 203*, which offers steam-safari packages. Routes, dates and packages change yearly.

Shongololo Express

The **Shongololo Express** opens up huge tracts of South Africa and Namibia simply by ploughing through them, as you watch through the window of your compartment. Meals on board are traditional Cape Dutch, Malay, Oriental, central and southern African cuisine. A 16-day option does a huge loop through South Africa, taking in such highlights as the Kruger and Hluhluwe National Parks, Grahamstown, Oudtshoorn, the Garden Route, Cape Town, Stellenbosch and the Wine Route. There is approximately one train a month (trains leaving Jan, Feb, Apr, June, Aug, Sept, Nov Johannesburg–Cape Town; returning Jan, Mar, May, June, Aug, Oct, Nov Cape Town–Johannesburg). Fares: 16 days (high season) R8550 per person sharing a double compartment; low season R8140 per person sharing.

The second option is a 13-day trip to Namibia (Cape Town–Windhoek–Cape Town), taking in the Fish River Canyon, Sossusvlei, Luderitz, Swakopmund and Etosha Pan, amongst other locations, with excursions at the various points of interest. Fares: N$7150 per person sharing a double compartment (trains leaving Mar, June, Aug, Oct Windhoek–Cape Town; returning May, July, Sept, Nov Cape Town–Windhoek). Other options include a 5-day Cape Peninsula trip and a 6-day Botswana/Zimbabwe trip.

Shongololo Express, *10 Amelia St, Dunvegan, Edenvale 1610; tel: 011-453 3821; fax: 011-454 1262.*

Zimbabwe Rail Safaris

Zimbabwe's home-grown competition is another wonderful luxury heritage train, which uses historic locomotives and coaches from the Bulawayo Railway Museum to do the classic journey between Bulawayo and Victoria Falls. There are up to 4 scheduled departures each month, leaving Bulawayo on Sat, Victoria Falls on Tues, arriving the following day. There is a stop, with a game-viewing drive, at Hwange

National Park. It is also possible to leave or join the train in Hwange and pay only a percentage of the fare (40–60% dependent on which leg you are travelling). This is not quite as opulent as its more famous brothers, but is still remarkably comfortable and great fun. There are three classes of accommodation: Heritage is the most basic (single fare – US$395 per person); Ivory is the middle class (single fare – US$438 per person in a twin cabin; US$485 per person for a suite); Emerald is the top class and the only one offering en suite facilities (single fare – US$570 sharing a double bed, US$598 per person for twin beds).

For information and bookings, contact: **Rail Safaris**, *2c Prospect Ave, Raylton, Bulawayo, Zimbabwe; tel: 09-75575/64466 fax: 09-42217.* For UK information; *tel: 0181-544 0151;* for US information; *tel: 800-521 7242 (toll-free).*

There are also a number of delightful little day-trips by steam train on offer, in South Africa, Namibia and Zimbabwe.

The Banana Express

The Banana Express steam train is based at Port Shepstone on the Natal South Coast near Durban (see p. 161). There are two itineraries: a 90-min journey through the banana and sugar plantations to Izotsha and (when open) Imbube Zulu ethnic village (operates between 10–16 days per month on a variable schedule; phone to check or collect the up-to-date timetable from the tourist office); and a weekly (except during school holidays, when it is up to four times a week) day-trip to Paddock and the Oribi Gorge Nature Reserve. Advance booking is essential.

Tickets: R24 for Izotsha; R80 for Paddock and Oribi. For information and reservations: *tel: 039-682 4821* or *039-682 5003* (open weekdays 0830–1600, Sat 0900–1100).

The Outeniqua Choo-Tjoe

Further down the coast, in the Western Cape, the Outeniqua Choo-Tjoe is the most imaginatively named steam service in the country. It is also one of the most enjoyable, a narrow-gauge railway running through magnificent coastal and forest scenery in the heart of the Garden Route between George and Knysna.

For information: *tel: 0441-738 202.* Open Mon–Fri, and Sat in Dec; departs George 0930, returns 1700. Tickets, R45 return, R35 single, from George or Knysna Stations.

Shamwari Express

This runs from Johannesburg to the Shamwari Game Reserve in the Eastern Cape (see p. 184) and back. It is not a steam train, but a luxurious private coach, which is attached to the regular Johannesburg–Port Elizabeth service on Thur (departs 1400), and deposits the overnight traveller at Eagles Craig, the private station for Shamwari (arrives Fri 0730). Dinner, bed & breakfast R750 per person. For information: *tel: 011-773 8929, fax; 011-773 8562.*

Desert Express (Namibia)

The Desert Express is an overnight luxury train that runs between Windhoek and Swakopmund. Sleeper coaches, dining car and compartments are all 5-star. Prices per person (return): luxury double compartment – R1200; Comfort Class – R1000; Relax Class – R600. For information and bookings: *tel: 061-298 2370; fax: 061-298 2160.*

Victoria Falls Safari Train

This is the most recent addition to the list. Based at Victoria Falls Railway Station (next to the Victoria Falls Hotel) in Zimbabwe (see p.402), it is a super-smart lovingly restored train, using historic steam engines and coaches. There are two trips a day, both heading into Zambia (US$90 per person, including the cost of your visa, available on the border – remember that this may affect a single entry visa back into Zimbabwe). The morning trip (3½ hrs) stops for a 15-min photo call on the bridge, before heading through to Livingstone to the Railway Museum. In the afternoon (4½ hrs), it goes to Simonya, via the Moso-oa-Tunya Game Park, for superb views over the Falls. There are drinks and snacks on board and occasional full lunch or dinner specials. Details and tickets from all Victoria Falls travel agents or tour operators.

There are also certain 'hobby steam services' run by enthusiasts on an intermittent basis. These are very popular during tourist season so it is an idea to book well in advance.

The **Apple Express** is a steam train, and one of the few remaining narrow-gauge railways in the world (founded 1906). It operates intermittently month to month from Port Elizabeth, along the Langkloof to Thornhill Village, stopping at the Van Stadens River Bridge to let passengers off for photo opportunities as the train steams over the world's highest narrow-gauge bridge. R40 return, adults. Train leaves Humewood Station at 0930, returns at 1600. Duration of outward journey 2½ hrs, return trip 2 hrs. Timetables, which are not planned until the last moment, and reservations: *tel: 041-507 2333.* See also p.293.
Magaliesberg Express: Johannesburg–Magaliesberg–Johannesburg. Day-trips usually run twice a month (second and fourth weekend) between Easter and December. Departs Johannesburg Station 0815, arrives Magaliesburg about 1030; departs Magaliesburg 1600, arrives Johannesburg 1745. There are resort stops at Valley Lodge or the Magaliesburg Country Hotel in Magaliesburg (see p.216) Book in advance for lunch, swimming and so on. Tickets R58 adults. For timetable information and reservations: *tel: 011-888 1154.*

The **National Railway Museum**, *Hilton Ave, Hilton (near Pietermaritzburg), Kwazulu-Natal; tel: 0331-431857*, runs 6 steam train day-trips, using vintage coaching stock (one trip a month – phone for information). Destinations are Balgowan, Nottingham Road, Bainesfield Estate, Inchanga, Waterberg and Howick (prices vary depending on duration of trip, but start from R20. Some suggest optional lunch en route). See p.263. Natal-based **Umgeni Steam Railway**; *tel: 08362-80152*, runs the last Sun of every month between Kloof (near Durban)–Botha's Hill–Kloof (tickets R16; departures at 0900, 1130, 1530). In June, July, Aug, its route changes: Durban Station–Scottburgh–Durban Station (R30). Tickets for the Kloof journey available from Kloof Station or Computicket, and for the Scottburgh journey, only from Computicket. See also p. 161.

57

BACKGROUND

GEOGRAPHY

Australians or Americans find it relatively easy to understand the landscape of Africa – they consider it normal to drive 500 km for a weekend in the city, and can grasp the idea of a single farm the size of a small country. To Europeans, the sizes are mind-boggling – South Africa is five times the size of the UK, an eighth of the size of the USA, with an area of 1,228,376 sq. km and 2954 km of coastline; the Kruger National Park alone is the size of Wales or Israel. Then add the surrounding nations: Namibia, at 824,290 sq. km, is four times the size of Germany; Mozambique (801,590 sq. km) is nearly as big, with 2500 km of coast; Botswana (581,730 sq. km) is the size of France; while Zimbabwe covers 391,090 sq. km. Completing the map of the region, are tiny, mountainous Lesotho, about the size of Belgium, at a mere 30,355 sq. km, and Swaziland (17,363 sq. km). Together they add up to a vast area, but within this huge expanse, there are only a handful of cities with more than a million people. The entire population is around 75 million people, of which two-thirds live in South Africa. There are seemingly endless tracts of nothingness, a landscape of bushveld or desert scrub inhabited by nothing but the odd antelope or owl.

Landscape

In the far south of the region is the Cape coastal zone, where cool Antarctic winds create a lush Mediterranean climate, with warm, dry summers and cool, sullen winters, perfect for growing apples, peaches and grapes. The Cape Floral Kingdom has a staggering 23,000 native species of plants and flowers. Heading north, still on the coast, the warmer currents of the Indian Ocean and the damp humidity of the south-west monsoon nurture the flamboyant subtropical rain forests, cane fields and pineapple plantations of southern Natal and Mozambique. Heading inland a little way,

progress is dramatically blocked by a series of ragged mountain ranges, amongst them the Cedarbergs and Swartbergs, which sweep right along the south coast, cutting it off from the interior. Beyond these, the scenery, climate and vegetation all change dramatically to the arid scrubland of the Karoo Desert and the mountainous grasslands of northern Natal.

In the west, the dry Karoo stretches north into the parched, barren sands of the Kalahari, eventually joining the Namib in a vast and growing expanse of desert, at the same latitude as the Sahara, and just as hot and inhospitable. In the centre of South Africa, the land rises steadily to a huge, high plateau planted with miles of wheat and corn, its earth salted with gold and diamonds, uranium and chrome. North of Johannesburg, this eventually gives

South Africa

A large and complicated country, South Africa has three capitals, a legacy of the Act of Union between the British Cape, the Boer Free State and the South African Republic (ZAR), in 1910. The legislature is in Cape Town (former British capital); the administration in Pretoria (capital of the old Transvaal) and judiciary in Bloemfontein (capital of the Orange Free State).

The country is divided into nine provinces, along roughly tribal lines – Western Cape (capital, Cape Town), Eastern Cape (capital, Bisho), Northern Cape (capital, Kimberley), North-West Province (capital, Mmabatho), Gauteng (capital, Johannesburg), Northern Province (capital, Pietersburg), Mpumalanga (capital, Nelspruit), the Free State (capital, Bloemfontein) and Kwazulu-Natal (capital currently shared by Pietermaritzburg and Ulundi).

way to the African bushveld; the rolling plateau of grass and acacia as ideal for antelope and elephant as it is for the local long-horned, semi-wild cattle. Here the climate is mild and sunny in winter, hot and sunny in summer, the rain blasting down in short, drenching bursts accompanied by strobe lightning and crashing thunder. In the east, the line of mountains curves north as the Drakensburg and the Eastern Highlands of Zimbabwe run parallel with the Mozambique coast, creating a towering escarpment, which marks the southern end of the 4000 km African Rift Valley.

The whole area is split by a series of great rivers, the southern Fish River; the Gariep (Orange) and Vaal; which together formed the boundaries between Anglo and Boer territories; the Okavango, which eventually seeps into the desert sands in a spectacular wilderness flowering, making it one of the most important and beautiful wetlands in the world; Kipling's 'great, grey, green, greasy Limpopo River, all set about with fever trees', which marks the boundary between South Africa and Zimbabwe; and on Zimbabwe's northern border, the greatest of them all, the magnificent Zambezi, first explored by David Livingstone.

FLORA

It may not seem like it from a cursory glance, but southern Africa has probably the richest and most diverse vegetation in the world, with over 24,000 species catalogued to date. Botanists divide the globe into six 'floral kingdoms', from tropical rain forest to tundra. The Cape, from the Cedarbergs in the Western Cape to Port Elizabeth in the Eastern Cape, stretching inland for around 200 km, is one of the six. It covers 90,000 sq. km (0.04% of the earth's land surface) and is home to 8500 species of plant. There are more indigenous plant species on Table Mountain (1470) alone than in the British Isles (1443).

This almost infinite variety of wonderful Cape mountain plants – fine-leafed evergreens perfectly adapted to poor, sandy soil, hot, dry summers and cold, wet winters – is known collectively as *fynbos* ('fine bush'). There are three main families: wind-pollinated reeds *(restios),* which act as common ground cover; ericas

(ericaceae), similar to European heathers and well-known to most gardeners; and proteas *(proteaceae),* from the magnificent heavy-headed king protea, the national symbol of South Africa, through an enormous array of species, with massed florets and cushions of flowers to spiky red stems. Between these, smaller groups of legumes and bulbs include many species now common to horticulturalists, including freesias, pelargoniums, campanulas, lobelias, gladioli and strelizias, while the desert areas are ablaze with sheets of orange and pink mesembryanthemums and daisies *(asteraceae).*

Beyond these are the remains of the primeval forests, where the coastal zones are still crowned by giant yellowwoods and stinkwoods, while the inland tropical regions support mahogany, teak and ebony. Under them shelter the last remaining cycads and tree ferns, unchanged since the Jurassic era (150–200 million years ago). Between stretches mile upon mile of savannah grass and scrub, with shade from acacia and mopani, and, in the lowest areas, powdery yellow fever trees, or the giant, spongy baobabs.

FAUNA

If the flora is spectacular, the animal life of the region is even more so: about 160 species of mammal, over 900 species of birds, over 2000 species of fish, 115 species of snake (only about 30 of them poisonous), some 5000 species of spiders and scorpions, and almost uncountable numbers of other reptiles and insects.

Mammals

The first thing most visitors want to do is tick off the **'Big Five'**. Called this, not because of their size or even their rarity value, but because they are considered the most difficult to hunt. These are **elephant, buffalo, rhino, lion** and **leopard**. Rhinos (both the more placid white, which grazes open grassland, and the bad-tempered, bush-dwelling browser, the black) are highly endangered; leopards are reasonably common, but are solitary, nocturnal and live in wooded areas, so are very difficult to see; elephant, lion and buffalo are more easily seen, but you will probably have to go to the larger parks. Elephant and lion both need huge territories

59

and cannot be kept in the smaller game farms, except in very limited numbers, while buffalo, as carriers of foot-and-mouth, are barred from most of South Africa (except the Kruger and northern Natal), although widespread in Botswana, Namibia and Zimbabwe.

There are several other animals as exciting and even more difficult to see. **Cheetah** are the rarest and most graceful of the big cats, as well as the fastest animal in the world, clocking up speeds of over 110 kph over short stretches. **Cape hunting dogs** (also known as wild dogs) are now so rare that there are prizes for any tourist who manages to photograph one. Ungainly, largely nocturnal **hyenas** are far easier to hear than see, their eery whooping howl echoing for miles through the bush. **Hippos** are relatively easy to find, but the usual sighting is of a couple of beady eyes and some nostrils. The coup is to see one out of the water.

Then there are more common animals, which are nevertheless so beautiful, fascinating or funny that they are endlessly pleasing. Of these, the finest is probably the gentle, giant **giraffe**, covered in crazy paving, from its little furry horns all the long, long way to its hooves. The comedian of the pack is the knobbly **warthog**, which lives underground, rootles for tubers, wallows in mud, and runs with its tail up in the air.

The open grasslands usually house huge herds of black and white stripy **zebra**, always sleek and replete, the stripes on each as individual as a fingerprint; ungainly **wildebeest**, unkindly said to have been made up of spare parts, with 'the forequarters of an ox, the hindquarters of an antelope and the tail of a horse'; and gamin **impala**, with their dainty heads, huge, lustrous eyes and spindle-thin legs, which can leap up to 3m high or 9m long, and reach speeds of 96 kph when necessary.

Other common antelope include the heavy-set, closely related **blesbok, bontebok** and **tsessebe**, the massive cow-like **eland**, the gloomy, chestnut-red **hartebeest**, and the most magnificent of all, the glossy black **sable**, with its huge backwards-sweeping horns, found commonly only in northern Zimbabwe

and Botswana. The Kalahari desert is home to two of the prettiest species, the startlingly beautiful **gemsbok**, with its patterned face and horns like skewers, and the dainty **springbok**, ironically adopted as a symbol by South Africa's burly rugby players.

More difficult to spot are the small, shy, nocturnal antelope, who shun the open spaces in favour of the woods or rocks, such as the **bushbuck, duiker, grysbok, klipspringer, grey rhebok, steenbok** and, the smallest of all, the tiny red-gold **suni**. Larger antelope, such as lookalike **kudu** and **nyala** also lurk in dense bush, while shaggy **reedbuck** and heavy **waterbuck**, a white ring painted like a target on their rumps, prefer to remain near water.

Smaller creatures to watch out for include the **bat-eared fox**, 11 species of **mongoose, jackal, chacma baboon, vervet** and less commonly, **samango monkeys**. The night is given over to a whole new army of strange creatures, including the ant-eating **pangolin** and **aardvark**, the **aardwolf** and **honey badger**, the quill-covered **porcupine, bushbabies, genets, civets, spring hares** and small cats, such as the **caracal** (lynx) and **serval**.

Reptiles

Amidst the reptiles, the **crocodile** is king, with the **leguaan**, or **water monitor lizard** as crown prince. The villains are definitely the killer snakes, the short, fat, black and tan **puff-adder**, gaudy **gaboon viper**, bright-green, tree-dwelling **boomslang**, the **rinkhals** or **spitting cobra**, the olive-green **black mamba**, and brighter **green mamba**. The huge **python** (300–500cm long) is not poisonous, killing by squeezing or constriction.

Birds

Only about 300 of the 900-odd species of bird are seen regularly and identified easily. Many are 'LBJs' (little brown jobs), about 500 are shy and have only a very localised habitat, others are migrants, only here for part of the year. But there are more than enough birds to keep even the most ardent twitcher happy.

The easiest and often most rewarding birding is to be found in the open savannah grasslands, which are, happily, also the preferred habitat of many big game animals. Some of the largest and most spectacular birds in Africa roam the open spaces; some, such as the spiky **secretary bird**, **kori bustard** and the ungainly black and red **ground hornbill**, often content to walk, while the massive **ostrich** has long since lost the ability to fly. Snowy **cattle egrets** and little, brown **red-billed oxpeckers** follow the herds, and clumsy **guinea fowl** and **francolins** dart for cover in the bushes. Above them, the smaller branches are alive with smaller yellow-beaked **hornbills**, red-eyed, ring-necked or black-faced **doves**, and whole kaleidoscopes of flashing colour in the fabulous forms of the **hoopoe**, **purplecrested lourie**, **lilac-breasted roller**, **glossy** and **plumcoloured starlings**, brilliant yellow **weaver birds**, yellow, blue and violet **waxbills**, or irridescent **bee-eaters** and **sunbirds**.

Tucked into the forks or perched up high on larger branches are the **storks**, the raucous **hadeda ibis**, and the slowly-blinking, swivel-headed **owls**. The great raptors rest briefly before swooping – the **lammergeier** and **bateleur**, the **snake eagle** and majestic **African fish eagle**, and a whole range of smaller buzzards, falcons, kestrels, kites and goshawks. The clear-up crew of **vultures** and hideous, hunched **marabou storks** wait in the wings, squabbling over the rubbish dumps as they wait for fresher pickings.

The rivers and lakes are crowded with water birds, including **cormorants** and **darters**, many species of **heron**, **sacred ibis**, **African spoonbill**, **blue** and **crowned cranes**, **plovers**, **stilts**, **geese**, **ducks**, **teals** and **moorhens**. On the coast are many more, from salmon-pink **flamingos** to **pelicans**, **jackass penguins**, **terns**, **gulls** and **Cape Gannets**, while far offshore, the **albatross**, **petrel** and **sooty shearwater** live a storm-tossed life perpetually on the wing.

Sealife

Between them, Namibia, South Africa and Mozambique have over 6000 km of coastline, with every possible form of marine habitat, from the desert shore and icy Benguela current

in the south Atlantic, to coral reefs warmed by the gentle Mozambique current.

Common **deep-sea fish** include sardines, anchovies, herrings, hake, kingclip, flounders, sole, mackerel, bream, snappers, anglerfish, snoek, tuna and billfish (swordfish, marlin and sailfish). Southern right, humpback, sperm and killer **whales** all come inshore from late July–Oct, in addition to which there are seven species of **dolphin**, leatherback and logger-head **turtles**, about 60 species of **ray**, and 100 species of **shark**, including great white, hammerhead and ragged-tooth. Most exciting of all was the rediscovery of the extraordinary, prehistoric **coelocanth** (see East London pp. 176 and 177).

The coral reefs on the east coast are home to vast numbers of spectacular creatures, from the magnificent **corals** themselves, to **sponges**, **anemones**, translucent **jellyfish**, huge **rock cod** and **eels**, ugly little **scorpion-fish** and **stonefish**, and psychadelic **angel**, **butterfly**, **damsel** and **clown fish**. In the sandy shallows, **oysters** and **periwinkles** cling to the rocks, while **starfish**, **sea urchins**, **lobsters** and **prawns** scamper through the seaweed forests.

HISTORY

Most of the earliest remains of man, dating back nearly 6 million years, have been found in the East African Rift Valley, at sites such as the Olduvai Gorge and Koobi Fora, but the hunt for our origins actually began in South Africa. In 1924, a workman digging in a limestone quarry at Taungs in the Northern Cape found a fossilised skull (the 'Taung baby'). It had a humanoid brain and canine teeth, and walked upright. An adult was discovered in 1936, in the Sterkfontein Caves (see p. 216); the species was christened *Australopithecus africanus,* dated to roughly 2.5 million years BC, and trumpeted as the evolutionary 'missing link' between ape and man. Since then, several other species or sub-species, *Australopithecus robustus,* and the even earlier *Australopithecus boisei* and *Australopithecus afarensis* (c. 5.5 million years BC) have been found in Africa. Two million years ago, *Homo habilis* ('handy man') still lived partially in trees, walking awkwardly, but using his flexible hands

61

to craft and use crude tools. *Homo erectus* (1.6 million–250,000 years BC) was the first of our ancestors to adapt fully to walking upright, using speech and tools, kindling fire and travelling. Some of his earliest remains were excavated at Swartkrans, near Krugersdorp, in 1948.

Homo sapiens and Neanderthal man emerged only about 100,000 years ago, while *Homo sapiens sapiens* (modern man) dates back to around 40,000 BC. From then on, life grew rapidly more complex as peoples and cultures proliferated; man began to farm, created art, music, religion and weapons of war. At last, there is an almost continuous, if very fragmentary, record of human activity in southern Africa. And the people here were almost certainly the direct ancestors of the small, nomadic hunter-gathering San (see p. 70), a people characterised by their coffee-coloured skin, small, wiry frame with large buttocks, sharp features and almost oriental eyes.

The Black Invasion

From around 500 AD, the **Nguni people** began to drift south from West and Central Africa, colonising the continent as they went. There were many different tribes, but they were all loosely related, used interlinked languages, and had many other things in common. Physically, they were much larger and darker than the San, with rich, chocolate-coloured skin and broader features. They were pastoralists and farmers, planting small crops of millet and vegetables, herding cattle and goats, building complex villages, and only moving on when the land was exhausted. More importantly, they brought with them tools and weapons made of iron. In the inevitable confrontations which followed as the two groups battled for territory, the San were hopelessly outclassed. Many were killed, some were enslaved. The majority were forced out, away from the lush valleys and bountiful plains into the desert fringes, where they learned to eke survival from the sand. Over the next 1000 years, the Nguni spread right across southern Africa and the familiar tribes of today began to stake their territorial boundaries.

On the Mozambique coast, Arab traders arrived in about 700 AD, setting up the southern capital of Oman at Sofala, and trading for gold, ivory, tortoiseshell and slaves. Inland, one tribe, the Karanga-Rozwi (part of the modern Shona tribe), claimed dominance. Under their priest-king, who came to be known as the **Mwene Mutapa** (Great Plunderer), they raided, conquered and married, until they had built a powerful empire which covered all of modern Zimbabwe, much of Mozambique, some of northern South Africa, Botswana and southern Zambia. Their capital, at Great Zimbabwe (see pp. 393–395), is one of the most fascinating historic sites in Africa, a rare (but not unique) city of stone in a continent that was built of wood and mud. It was also a centre of enormous power and wealth, which caught the imagination of early traders, who sent highly embellished stories of treasure ricocheting round the globe.

The European Arrival

In 1488, the Portuguese navigator, Bartolomeu Dias, was sent south in search of the sea route to India. He crept round the coast of Africa as far as Mossel Bay before his nerve failed and he fled back to Europe. In 1492, the Spanish sent Christopher Columbus round the other way. He, too, failed – but did discover America. Finally, in 1497, another Portuguese mariner, **Vasco da Gama**, set sail, triumphantly reaching India on 20th May, 1498. The effect of his return was electric.

Within 10 years, Portuguese ships were regularly plying the route, stopping for supplies in Namibia, South Africa and Mozambique. By 1520, they had built small forts and trading posts at Sofala, on the Ilha da Moçambique and Ibo. Within 200 years, they had virtually wiped out the overland Silk Road and sidelined the Arabs at sea. At first, the majority of the land officially remained under local control and the Portuguese leased the plantations, but a series of judicious marriages with the daughters of the local chiefs soon gave them outright ownership. The Spanish and Portuguese signed a treaty splitting the world, giving the Spanish the Western Hemisphere, the Portuguese the Eastern. But the French, British and Dutch were also desperate to get in on the act and the

Europeans became embroiled in an increasingly bitter struggle amongst themselves for control of the trade routes.

However, almost everything was aimed at trading rather than settlement, until 1652, when the Dutch East India Company, concerned at the levels of scurvy and malnutrition amongst its crews, sent a young captain, Jan van Riebeeck, to set up a refreshment station in Table Bay. His mission was to provide passing ships with fresh water, vegetables, meat and repairs. His first action was to lay out a market garden; his second to build a fort.

Until that point, relations with the local Khoikhoi (see pp.70–71) had been friendly, with European iron, cloth and other trade goods offered in exchange for meat, milk and water. Van Riebeeck's station not only wiped out this lucrative trade, but his farmers annexed and enclosed traditional grazing lands, blocked off access to essential water supplies, and even introduced slaves from the east to work the farms. The Khoikhoi lost their lands, livelihood, many of their traditions and even, during a desperate outbreak of smallpox in 1713, their lives. The fort that Riebeeck built was necessary.

In 1795, during the Napoleonic Wars, Britain invaded the small Dutch colony. It was handed back at the end of the war, but retaken in 1806 when Napoleon escaped from Elba. The Congress of Vienna, in 1815, formally ceded the Cape Colony to Britain, who gained a valuable strategic naval base on the sea route to India and the East.

The Great Trek
As the 'Mother City' flourished, more and more Dutch settlers arrived, joined by a fair sprinkling of Germans and French Huguenots fleeing religious persecution. They were tough, stubborn survivors, prepared to work all the hours of the day to make a humble living. Most were also ill-educated and strongly puritan in outlook, seeing the world in simple terms of outright good and evil and regarding the 'heathen' Africans as literally sub-human. Belligerently anti-establishment, and allergic to any imposition of government, law and, above all, tax, they soon moved out of Cape Town, carving new farms and towns from the bush. As

soon as there was a degree of wealth and civilisation, however, the colonial government followed, simply annexing the new settlement. Each time some remained, but the most hardened of the Boers (the word means 'farmer' in Afrikaans) just packed up their ox-wagons and moved on. In this way, the white settlers leap-frogged their way across the country, ignoring any black claims to the land. By the early 19th century, all the land as far north as the Gariep (Orange) River, and east to the Great Fish River, was under white control. The Xhosa people glaring at them from the opposite bank were a very different proposition from those they had met till now, and were prepared to defend their lands to the death. As the British continued to annexe the newly colonised land, the line of the Fish River became a fortified frontier, with a row of carefully sited forts controlled from the new settlement of Grahamstown (pp.185–187). A series of eight bitterly fought Frontier Wars rocked the region for nearly a century before, inevitably, British fire power triumphed over the persistent Xhosa.

The Birth of the Zulu Nation
Meanwhile, the Xhosa were also under threat from the other side. In about 1809, with a rapidly growing population and a severe land shortage, a formidable Mthethwa ruler, Dingiswayo, in what is now central Natal, began to flex his military muscles and conquer his neighbouring clans. In 1815, he was succeeded by his adopted son, **Shaka**, and the history of Africa was changed forever.

Shaka belonged to a very minor clan, the **Zulus**. He was an extraordinarily intelligent, forceful young man, who bitterly resented both the subservient status of his clan and the bad treatment of his beloved mother, Nandi, over the years. His path to the throne was hotly contested, but, on succeeding, he promptly changed the name of the greater tribe and those of all its vassals to Zulu. With a new model army as innovative as Cromwell's, he stormed his way across the region in a sea of bloodshed, known to the Zulus as the *Mfecane* (literally meaning 'crushing'), and to the Sotho as the *Difaqane* (the same meaning, but with terrible connotations of defeat and conquest).

63

Many surrounding peoples were absorbed into the Zulu nation; some chose to flee. The northern Ngwane, under King Sobhuza, headed inland, defeating several Sotho and Nguni clans en route. When they reached the safety of the mountains, they stopped; their kingdom became known as Swaziland. Further west, the southern Sotho also fled to the mountains, creating the fortress kingdom of Lesotho. In the east, various Zulu, Swazi and Shangaan peoples moved into southern Mozambique, forming a kingdom that encompassed the modern provinces of Maputo, Gaza and Inhambane (later conquered by the Portuguese).

Meantime, one of Shaka's captains was caught stealing royal cattle. His son, Mzilikazi, fled north with a band of followers, conquering and absorbing people as they went. By the time they reached the area just north of modern Johannesburg, many felt that they were out of the great King's reach and chose to settle. Others, including Mzilikazi, were only content to stop once they had crossed the Limpopo into southern Zimbabwe. This flight was the foundation of the Ndebele nation.

In Zimbabwe, the empire of the Mwene Mutapa had crumbled from about the 16th century onwards, as rival heirs battled for a slice of the pie. There was still a Mwene Mutapa, but he was toothless, and the country had slid back into a series of tiny warring principalities. Mzilikazi carved out a kingdom covering nearly a third of modern Zimbabwe, which he supported by raiding the Shona cattle on the border. He was long-lived and successful, and left to his son, Lobengula, a powerful kingdom, ringed by whispers of great treasure.

In 1828, Shaka was assassinated by his half-brother, Dingane, who took the throne and continued the reign of terror. Not a corner of southern Africa was unaffected by the *Mfecane*. By 1834, the Boers in the Eastern Cape, resentful of the abolition of slavery, had had enough of British rule and were ready to resume their trek. With many thousands of Africans slaughtered by the Zulus and even more in hiding, the Boer scouts came back and reported, erroneously, that they had found great swathes of uninhabited and unclaimed land – a myth perpetuated by some of their descendants to this

day. By the time the Africans returned home, their land was in Boer hands.

The Zulu Wars

By 1938, the wagons of the trekboers had crossed the battlegrounds and reached the heartland of the Zulu kingdom, where they were less than welcome. One of the Boer leaders, Piet Retief, and a party, including his son, went to Dingane's capital, uMgungundlovu, to discuss land rights. That evening, the entire party was massacred. On 9 Dec 1838, a group of Voortrekkers, led by Andries Pretorius, swore revenge, taking a solemn vow that if God would allow them victory and vengeance, they would mark the anniversary as a holiday of thanksgiving forever. On 16 Dec, at Blood River (see p. 270), the Boers won a towering victory, without a single casualty. Over 4000 Zulus died. The 16 December is still a national holiday, renamed the Day of Reconciliation in the New South Africa.

The victorious Boers chased the remnants of the Zulu army south to destroy Dingane, who torched his capital and fled north of the Tugela River, where he opened negotiations for a land deal with British traders at Port Natal (Durban). The Boers did a deal with Dingane's brother, Mpande, annexing land in exchange for military support, creating the Boer Republic of Natalia and driving the King deep into the mountains, where he was eventually killed. Mpande took the throne; the British simply waited until the restless Boers had done the groundwork, moved north and annexed Natal.

In 1854, a party of Boers founded the Orange Free State in the area around the Gariep (Orange) and Vaal Rivers; in 1860, another created the more northerly South African Republic (ZAR). In 1873, the peaceful and long-reigning Mpande died, leaving his kingdom to his war-like son, Cetshwayo, who raided British-protected territory. This led to a new outbreak of war, which included such terrible battles as the famous Isandhlwana and Rorke's Drift (see p. 269). Cetshwayo was eventually defeated at Ulundi in 1879, and the British carved up his land amongst 13 minor Zulu chiefs – who promptly began a bloody civil war. In 1883, Cetshwayo was returned to his throne, but all future Zulu kings were powerless puppets. In 1887, all Zulu land was officially annexed to Britain.

Cecil Rhodes

Although Britain had officially recognised the independence of the two new Boer republics, the order was dramatically upset when the first diamonds were discovered on the frontier in 1869. In 1871, the British annexed Colesberg Kopje (now Kimberley) as the diamond rush reached full flood.

Later that same year, Cecil Rhodes, a rather weedy, young Englishman, son of a country vicar, arrived in South Africa for his health and made his way to the diamond fields, where he soon amassed a vast fortune. He was only one of a number of new diamond millionaires, including showman Barney Barnato, Lionel Phillips, Alfred Beit, Joseph Robinson, Julius Wernher, Solly Joel and Samuel Marks, but the rest were all content to be tycoons. Rhodes' ill health drove him to achieve; he was obsessed by the expansion of the British Empire, dreaming of building a railway from the Cape to Cairo through British territory all the way. He ploughed much of his personal fortune into politics, became an MP, and eventually became Prime Minister of the Cape Colony in 1890.

In 1877, with the Boers already furious at Britain's theft of the diamond fields, the Cape simply annexed the whole ZAR. In 1880, Paul Kruger led a victorious revolution (the first Anglo-Boer War), reclaimed internal self-government for the ZAR, and became its President. Nobody was totally happy with the solution. Kruger wanted full independence; Britain full control. The real crunch came with the discovery of gold on the Witwatersrand in 1886.

For the time being, Kruger and the ZAR seemed unassailable. Rhodes ploughed enormous wealth into, and gained even more out of, the Transvaal goldfields, but politically he looked further north and west.

The recent unification of Germany had created a new potential superpower, with the ability to threaten Britain's trading supremacy. Germany was actively looking for territory in Africa – British and German missionaries had

---

Shaka's Impis

More than anything else, Shaka is famous for his prowess as a military leader. He formed the young Zulu warriors into a formidable, highly disciplined fighting machine, making them train barefoot on thorns for hours to build up stamina and resistance to pain. Seeing the wastage caused by throwing spears, which often missed and could not be used again (unless the enemy chose to throw them back – not to be encouraged), he created the *assegai*, a lethal short stabbing spear, which brought the battle into close hand-to-hand conflict. Above all, he perfected the *impi*, a formation based on the horns of the ox, with the mass of troops in the middle and the fastest runners curved to the sides, ready to run round and encircle the enemy.

---

been working in the interior since the early 1800s. In 1884, Germany colonised the vast, sparsely populated German South West Africa (now Namibia). It was the trigger needed to alarm the British government into following Rhodes' dream. The Tswana King Khama III, sandwiched between the Germans and the Boers, was persuaded to ask for British aid and, in 1885, the British Protectorate of Bechuanaland (now Botswana) was created.

The situation north of the Limpopo was more problematic. Not only was this thought to be the mineral-rich mother lode, but it was in the hands of the powerful king, Lobengula. Rhodes sent emissaries to negotiate for the mineral rights. With a large helping of shady dealing and outright lying, he eventually managed to get a written concession. He took it back to Britain, using it as the basis (with more backhanders) for royal assent to the creation of a charter company, the British South Africa Company, which would colonise and run the country in the name of the Queen. In effect, Rhodes had bought himself a private kingdom.

Lobengula was furious, but it was too late. In 1890, a pioneer column of 600 men and 100 wagons headed north, eventually crossing right through Matabeleland to colonise Mashonaland (around present-day Harare), which had never been part of any agreement, as it was not even under Lobengula's rule. Within months, Rhodes' best friend, Dr Leander Starr Jameson, had also taken over the Manyika territory to the east and, within a year, Britain and Portugal signed a treaty formalising the border with Portuguese Mozambique along its present lines.

By 1893, while Lobengula protested ever more loudly and Queen Victoria sent back messages of peace, Rhodes and Jameson plotted to provoke the king and force a war. When, eventually, he was driven beyond endurance and massed his troops on the Mashona border, a second column was sent in from Bechuanaland to his rear, his armies were routed, and his capital at kwaBulawayo destroyed. Lobengula fled into the hills, where, it is said, he died (no one has ever found his tomb, or his supposed treasure). Matabeleland was incorporated as a province of the new country, named Rhodesia, after its founder.

With the land around them now firmly British, Rhodes turned his attention back to the Boer Republics, and tried to whip up a rebellion to depose Kruger amongst the *uitlanders* (foreigners) on the goldfields. In 1895, the uprising was announced and Jameson led a raiding party into the Transvaal to support the rebels. It was a total fiasco. The rebels were betrayed, rounded up and arrested. Jameson forgot to cut the telegraph lines, so by the time he came near enough to be any sort of threat, the Boers were waiting. He was captured and paraded through the streets. It spelt the end of Rhodes' political career in South Africa. In an odd sort of way, however, it worked. The Jameson Raid so infuriated the Boers that it led eventually to the outbreak of the Second Anglo-Boer War. It took years, enormous resources and thousands of lives, but at the end of it all the Witwatersrand goldfields were in British hands.

The Second Anglo-Boer War

This has been called the first modern war. It certainly ended forever the 'gentleman's' concept of big set-piece battles. It was here that hit-and-run guerilla tactics were used for the first

time by small bands of fast-moving Boer commandos. It was now that the British rid themselves of their heavy, horribly visible red wool jackets and took to khaki and camouflage. And it was here that Britain, to her shame, introduced the first concentration camps, to intern Boer civilians. This was also, in some senses, the first media war. For the first time, modern technology (in this case, the telegraph) managed to get news home and into print within hours, while daredevil reporters, such as the young Winston Churchill, gained instant fame and glory for their stories.

Hostilities began with a build-up of British troops along the Natal border. President Kruger demanded their withdrawal but was ignored, so, in 1899, he invaded Natal. The fighting was bitter and protracted, with Kruger's 'people's militia' – bush-hardened farmers in civilian clothes – running rings around a supposedly superior British force. The Boers knew the country, the climate, and were excellent horsemen, but they were eventually overwhelmed by sheer force of numbers, with a staggering 448,715 British troops outnumbering them by nearly five to one. The sieges of Ladysmith, Kimberley and Mafeking were lifted painfully and slowly, and the long slog to victory began for the British. Pretoria and Johannesburg both surrendered in 1900, but the Boers began a campaign of sabotage. In retaliation, the British rounded up all their women and children, and instituted a devastating 'scorched earth' policy – torching any possible shelter or source of food. By the end of the war, there were 136,000 Afrikaners in 50 white prison camps, and a further 115,700 Africans in 66 black camps; over 26,000 Afrikaner women and children and more than 14,000 Africans had died of disease and neglect. The work of an English philanthropist, Emily Hobhouse, in exposing this horror helped force through the Peace of Vereeniging (1902).

Boer rule was over. The British colonial government began to put the country back together, and, in 1910, an Act of Parliament, the Union of South Africa, officially bound the Cape, Natal, the Orange Free State and the ZAR into a single state. The black population was never consulted; only whites could be elected to the new Parliament, and English and Afrikaans became the official languages of government. At the end of World War I, when South Africa was given a League of Nations mandate to rule the former German territory of Namibia, this became, to all intents and purposes, another province of the country.

THE TWENTIETH CENTURY

If the 19th century was one of imperial expansion, the 20th has been an almost continuous nationalist struggle for freedom and equality throughout southern Africa.

The San and Khoikhoi were all but destroyed by the white colonists; the much larger and more belligerent black communities were never treated quite as badly, but their lands were stolen with impunity and the people forced into labour. The moves towards apartheid began in the Kimberley diamond fields in the 1870s, for purely practical reasons. The whites needed a plentiful source of cheap labour, but did not want to share the rewards, so they forced through a number of measures banning black ownership of claims.

The convenient concept of separate but equal development began to gain popularity amongst both the Boers and British. This assumed that all Africans were inferior both in education and civilisation and that, like children, it would take them a while to catch up. There was an eventual, theoretical goal of equality and reintegration. Meantime, they should be allowed to develop separately, at their own slow pace, and be given menial tasks suitable to their capabilities. Official segregation began with the first forced resettlement, which moved black people out of central Cape Town in 1901. In 1920, President Jan Smuts passed a Native Affairs Act, which established real political segregation, and soon afterwards, in both South Africa and Rhodesia, native reserves were set up. No African could buy or lease land outside these areas, and the best farmland was reserved for the whites, who made up a tiny proportion of the population. The next 30 years saw a slow but steady erosion of black rights throughout the entire region, with the exception of little Lesotho and Swaziland, which had managed to maintain a remarkable

degree of independence. In 1928, the South African Immorality Act banned mixed-race sex outside marriage. In Rhodesia, the Native Passes Act required all Africans to register, carry ID cards and get permission to travel.

The first stirrings of nationalism began early. In 1912, a group of mission-educated Africans set up the South African Native National Congress in the Eastern Cape and Natal. In 1913, Gandhi began his first campaign of non-violent non-cooperation on behalf of the Indians in Natal (see p. 288). In the 1920s, the Inkhatha Movement was founded by the Zulus, and, in 1923, the SANNC became the African National Congress. Also in the 1920s, the Bantu Voters' Association was born in Rhodesia, although there was no real strength here until the emergence of the Rhodesian African National Congress in 1945.

Apartheid

The real horror began in 1948, when the Afrikaner National Party won the South African election and party leaders, Hendrik Verwoerd and D.F. Malan, coined the phrase 'apartheid'. A flood of new laws brought in a hundred petty restrictions, from separate beaches, public benches and building entrances to white-only public lavatories. The 1949 Mixed Marriages Act and 1950 Immorality Act banned any sexual contact (including marriage) between people of different race. From 1952 onwards, black South Africans also had to carry a pass at all times, while the Group Areas Act set up completely separate towns for White, Black, Indian or Coloured (mixed race) communities. This was followed in 1970 by the Bantu Homelands Act, in which a series of nominally independent, cash-starved puppet states were set up for the different black tribes. All black South Africans became citizens of one of these homelands, aliens in white South Africa, without any possible political rights and vulnerable to deportation at any moment.

Namibia, ruled directly by South Africa, suffered under full apartheid. Botswana had managed to remain a British Protectorate at the time of the Union, so escaped the worst injustices. Lesotho and Swaziland were black-ruled under British protection, and Mozambique was

67

not so much governed as inhabited by the laid-back and muddled Portuguese administration, who seemed to have relatively few of the race prejudices of their neighbours. In Rhodesia, there was never an official policy of apartheid, but the reality was there, complete with heavy media censorship, a total lack of freedom of speech and increasing violence, torture, poorly explained deaths, disappearances and other attendant horrors.

Independence

For a while, in the 1950s, an attempt at federation between Northern (Zambia) and Southern (Zimbabwe) Rhodesia and Nyasaland (Malawi), made it seem as if life were about to become more tolerable for black Rhodesians. However, by 1963, it had become all too clear that the federation was a failure. The same year, the two most famous of the Zimbabwean nationalist movements were set up; ZAPU (the Zimbabwe African People's Union) led by Ndebele Joshua Nkomo and ZANU (the Zimbabwe African National Union) led at that stage by the Shona Ndabaningi Sithole.

In 1964, the federation broke up, with Zambia and Malawi gaining full independence. Botswana was also peacefully granted internal self-government in 1965, with full independence following in 1966, with Sir Seretse Khama as president. Only white-ruled Rhodesia was denied independence until it had a fully democratic, multi-racial constitution.

On 11 Nov 1965, amidst a growing tide of black protest, the Rhodesian government, under Prime Minister Ian Smith, made a Unilateral Declaration of Independence. A week later, a UN resolution condemned their action and imposed the first of an increasingly tough series of economic sanctions. South Africa became a clearing house for Rhodesian trade goods and, as the violence began in 1967, the arms trade. There were serious attempts to find a peaceful solution, in 1965, 1968 and 1972, but all collapsed when faced by the white intransigence. The violence grew steadily, escalating into outright civil war. In 1973, Zambia closed its border and both Zambia and Botswana offered homes to guerilla bases, training camps and refugee colonies.

War

In 1974, a left-wing coup in Portugal led to sudden independence for Mozambique, whose own nationalist movement, Frelimo, took power in 1975 as a hard-line Marxist Socialist government. They too offered support and bases to the Zimbabwean nationalists, and the rest of the Socialist world joined in, with Cuban, Russian and Chinese equipment, training and personnel. At the end of the year, after a series of internal squabbles between the various factions, the young, virtually unknown Robert Mugabe took control of ZANU.

Meanwhile, South Africa had refused to release its control of Namibia when asked in 1948, but while the first nationalist resistance groups were also formed here in the 1950s, nothing much happened until 1966, when the UN General Assembly formally terminated the South African mandate, and the South West African Peoples Organization (SWAPO) took up arms. In 1975, Angola gained independence and promptly gave Swapo a refuge and the support of the socialist world. South Africa suddenly found itself surrounded by enemies, with only Rhodesia as a buffer and ally. South Africa invaded southern Angola in an attempt to stamp out the Swapo camps, and Rhodesia and South Africa got together to fund and arm Renamo in violent opposition to Frelimo in order to destabilise Mozambique. Their efforts succeeded only too well, plunging the country into 20 years of horrendous civil war.

By 1977, the situation in Rhodesia was appalling and growing steadily worse, with the country nearly bankrupted by economic sanctions and the cost of waging an unwinnable war. Much of the country was at a virtual standstill, with travel only possible in military convoys or under armed guard. No farm was safe, towns along the eastern border were being mortared regularly, and thousands were dying as both the guerillas and the army attacked villages. Smith eventually agreed to talk to the more moderate black factions, and set up a deal with Bishop Abel Muzorewa for a new constitution, with shared power and separate voters' rolls. In 1979, the country's name was changed to Zimbabwe-Rhodesia and Muzorewa became Prime Minister. However, the compromise did not satisfy anyone and the war intensified, until nearly 1000 people were dying every month.

In Sept 1979, Britain's new Conservative government stepped in and set up multilateral talks at Lancaster House in London, chaired by the Foreign Secretary, Lord Carrington. It took months, but he cut through the posturing and delaying, eventually forcing through a settlement. Rhodesia reverted briefly to British control, and in April 1980, after the first truly democratic elections, Rhodesia became independent Zimbabwe, with Robert Mugabe as Prime Minister (soon to become executive President).

The South African Struggle

The struggle within South Africa took a very different form. The first violence began in the 1950s, with strikes by the African Miners' Union, and mass protests by the ANC Youth League. Violence erupted thanks to the overreaction of the police, but while the level of violence rose steadily for the next 40 years, it never developed into full-scale war.

In 1959, Robert Sobukwe persuaded breakaway members of the ANC to form the more militant Pan African Congress (PAC). In 1960, thousands of people burnt their pass books in protest at the pass laws. In Sharpeville, between Vanderbijlpark and Vereeniging, 69 died and 180 were injured when police fired on the crowd. The government panicked, declared a state of emergency, arrested Sobukwe, and banned both the PAC and ANC. Both organisations went underground, many of their leaders fled into exile; others remained and formed military wings, the PAC founding *Poqo,* and the ANC, *Umkhonto we Sizwe* (Spear of the Nation).

In 1962, remaining ANC leaders were rounded up and charged with treason and sabotage in the famous Rivonia Treason Trial. Most, including **Nelson Mandela** and Walter Sisulu, were jailed on Robben Island and the back of the struggle was broken. It was 10 years before the next generation, amongst them the charismatic Steve Biko, leader of the Black Consciousness movement, could regroup. Biko died in police custody in 1977.

In 1976, black schoolchildren began a boycott of the Afrikaans language, pouring out of the schools and onto the streets in mass protest. Television screens across the world were filled with images of police with dogs exploding tear gas and even firing live ammunition into crowds of dancing teenagers. Hundreds were killed or injured; others fled to ANC camps outside South Africa; tens of thousands were detained without trial and tortured. Horrendous factional violence broke out between Inkhatha and the ANC, with so-called traitors burnt alive, a car tyre filled with petrol round their necks. In 1977, the UN imposed an arms embargo on South Africa, to be followed in 1986 by economic sanctions.

New South Africa

The first cracks had already appeared in Fortress White South Africa. In 1984, a new constitution created three separate houses of parliament, giving Indians and coloureds the vote. The pass laws were repealed, and many of the more petty rules of apartheid were abolished. In 1986, Mozambiquan President, Samora Machel, was killed in a plane crash. His successor, Joaquim Chissano, desperate to revive a dying country, took a less dogmatic stance towards South Africa. In Namibia, SWAPO was becoming increasingly effective, while the arrival of large numbers of Cuban troops in 1988 embroiled South Africa in an unwanted war on the Angolan border. Most importantly of all, however, in 1989, F. W. de Klerk became President.

By 1 April 1989, a UN-supervised cease-fire was in place in Namibia. Elections were held in November, and in March 1990, Namibia gained its independence, with SWAPO leader Sam Nujoma as executive president. Funding to Renamo was cut off and talks between South Africa and Mozambique began in earnest. In Oct 1992, a peace treaty was signed by Frelimo and Renamo, setting up a joint interim government in the run-up to fully democratic elections.

In 1990, President De Klerk made a historic and astounding speech renouncing apartheid, legalising the ANC, the PAC and the Communist Party, and announcing the repeal of many discriminatory laws. Nelson Mandela was released from 27 years of imprisonment to

69

head further talks. In 1992, a referendum amongst white South Africans voted over-whelmingly to end apartheid. In 1994, the homelands were abolished and reincorporated into South Africa, which now held its first truly democratic elections. Nelson Mandela and F.W. De Klerk jointly accepted the Nobel Peace Prize. On 10 May 1994, with the eyes of the world watching, Nelson Mandela took office as President of the New South Africa.

Today, all seven nations of southern Africa are parliamentary democracies and members of the Commonwealth (including Mozambique, which was never a British colony). South Africa, Botswana, Namibia, Zimbabwe and Mozambique are all republics, with executive presidents; executive control of Swaziland still lies with King Mswati III, who is also the spiritual leader of his people; while Lesotho is ruled by a Prime Minister, with King Moshoeshoe II as head of state.

PEOPLE

During the handover of power, Archbishop Desmond Tutu made one of the most memorable statements in South African history:

'Let us be channels of love, of peace, of reconciliation. Let us declare that we have been made for togetherness, we have been made for family, that, yes, now we are free, all of us, black and white together, we, the Rainbow people of God!'

The country, from black to white and all shades in between, rushed to adopt his phrase, and now proudly proclaims itself the Rainbow Nation. It is remarkably apt, for South Africa and its neighbours are a true cultural melting pot, which, for centuries, has soaked up immigrants from literally all over the world.

The nearest thing to original indigenous people are the few remaining **San** (bushmen) living in the desert fringes of the Northern Cape, Namibia and Botswana. Small, wiry and hardy, they are known to have lived in the region for some 40,000 years and may have a claim (alongside the Australian Aborigines) to be the longest-surviving race on earth. They have spent most of their existence in the well-watered and food-rich central plains and mountains. It was only the arrival of the more powerful Nguni and Europeans, in the last

1500 years, which forced them out into their current precarious position. Some became slaves, others were killed, many died of epidemic European diseases, and still more gradually intermarried and were absorbed into the 'coloured' population. Today, there are around 60,000 left across the three countries, but very few are either full blood or leading a traditional lifestyle.

Nomadic hunter-gatherers, they have a simple material life, living in domed huts made of branches, grass and reeds. Traditionally, both men and women wear small front and back skin aprons on a beaded belt, with elaborate beaded headdresses, necklaces, bracelets and anklets. Originally, these would have been made of ostrich shell and seeds. Tortoise and ostrich shells are used as dishes and for storage, together with pouches and water bottles of springbok leather. The men hunt in groups, using wooden clubs, spears, bows, poison-tipped arrows, and snares. The gathering of roots and tubers, berries and fruit, particularly water-rich melons, is done by the women.

Some of the world's earliest artists, the San decorated any smooth slab of rock, overhang or cave, engraving the stone, or using natural paints such as carbon, iron oxide or yellow ochre mixed with blood or animal fat. Most paintings depict animals, though there are more abstract designs like handprints or phallic symbols, and more sophisticated hunting scenes. They are notoriously difficult to date. Some have been carbon-dated back thousands of years; the latest show 19th-century European soldiers.

The **Khoikhoi**, whose ancestors originated around the Central African lakes, were nomadic pastoralists, who arrived in the Cape about 2000 years ago. They lived in easily transportable huts of wooden lathes and reed mats. Both sexes wore carosses of animal skin, leather and copper rings on the wrists and ankles, and painted their faces. They were prepared to trade cattle but, when the Dutch arrived, they lost this lucrative business and found themselves barred from their traditional lands. Society began to disintegrate and the culture was nearly wiped out by smallpox in the early 18th century. The survivors gravitated to the farms. They called themselves Khoikhoi (meaning 'men of men'); the early Dutch settlers named them *Hottentots* (Stutterers), after the abrupt clicking sounds of their language. Most of the tiny number of survivors have intermarried with the San, their progeny becoming known as the **Khoisan**.

The next arrivals were the **Bantu** or **Nguni** people, who flooded south from West and Central Africa about 1000 years ago, and, today, make up the vast majority of the population. There are hundreds of tribes, clans and dialects, but, basically, they all belong to the same racial and linguistic group, and have many aspects of their culture in common. Amongst the most important groups are the closely related **Xhosa**, **Zulus** and the **Ndebele** (actually a breakaway Zulu clan, who live in both South Africa and Zimbabwe); the **Sotho** (in South Africa and Lesotho); the **Swazi** (in South Africa and Swaziland); the **Tswana** (in South Africa and Botswana); the **Shona** (in Zimbabwe); the **Venda** (in South Africa and Zimbabwe); the **Tsonga** and **Shangaan** (in South Africa and Mozambique); the **Ovambo** and **Herero** (in Namibia).

Traditionally, they are all pastoralists and subsistence farmers. Young boys look after the goats; the older boys herd the cattle; young men are warriors; older men become elders and advisors to the chief. The women grow maize, vegetables and some fruit, look after the chickens, do all the food preparation and cooking, and look after the children.

Religion is very important. These days, most people are Christian, but they often run this in tandem with traditional beliefs and ceremonies. There is little conflict – both are monotheistic. The Nguni god takes care of the big things; small tasks are left to the ancestors, who fulfill much the same role as the Catholic saints. People keep in touch with their ancestors through mediums, *sangomas*, who look after the spiritual well-being of the people, while *nyangas* (traditional herbal doctors) look after the physical body. The role is split in some societies, filled by the same person in others. Superstitious belief in witchcraft, fortune-telling and curses is still very strong.

Rituals punctuate the life cycle, with formal ceremonies to mark birth, naming, puberty, marriage, and so on. A boy's family must buy his bride, the *lobolo* (bride price), set in cattle, the traditional symbol of wealth. The bride's parents must furnish the couple's home with useful household objects and clothes.

In practice, very few people still live this way. Most of the men and many women work away, in the mines and factories, in offices or as servants, while the old people are left to bring up the children, who now have compulsory school each day. In South Africa, nearly 80% of the population is now urban, living an often dire existence, scrapping for work in the townships, although many still own a smallholding run for them by a relative. Lobolo is still paid, but in cash, while people are usually content with one wife (instead of the traditional polygamous household). Traditional dress has all but died out, except for dancers, special occasions, and a very few remote peoples.

The first **white settlers** arrived in quantities from the mid 17th century onwards. The Portuguese settled along the Mozambique coast. In South Africa, most of the immigrants were Dutch, with a smattering of French and Germans thrown in. By the time the British arrived in numbers in the early 19th century, they had become bush-hardened Afrikaners. The opening up of the diamond and gold fields led to a flood of immigrants from across the world, including significant numbers of Central European Jews.

The Dutch imported as slaves one of the smallest and most interesting communities in South Africa, the **Cape Malays**, of whom there are only about 12,000, most living in the Bo-Kaap district of Cape Town. More correctly they should be known as Cape Muslims or Indo-Africans, as most actually hail from Singapore, Sri Lanka, Madagascar and Indonesia. Malay refers to Malayal, the lingua franca amongst traders in the Dutch East Indies by early Dutch settlers.

Unusually, the Malays shipped to South Africa were highly skilled builders, carpenters and household servants, often more highly educated than their Boer masters. Over the centuries, they managed to retain their own

71

strong cultural identity and belief in Sufism (the mystical branch of Islam), even though their language and history were officially banned. The holy men, once freed, held underground classes and managed to buy up and free many others in the community, but they only moved into the Bo-Kaap en masse after the abolition of slavery in 1834, an event celebrated each year on the 1st–2nd January in the riotously colourful Coon Carnival. Astonishingly, they managed to hang on to their property through all the clearances and remained the only non-white community in any South African city. A ring of tombs, belonging to holy man Sheikh Yusuf (died 1699) and 25 of his followers, now form a 'sacred circle' around Cape Town, and are said to protect the city against natural disasters.

Kwazulu/Natal has a large **Indian** population, representing most of India's 65 main 'tribes', although the majority come from the south. Their ancestors were imported as cheap mass labour for the sugar cane and cotton plantations after the abolition of slavery. An overcrowded paddle-steamer, the SS *Truro*, arrived from Madras on 16 Nov 1860, carrying 342 indentured Indian workers (including 75 women and 83 children under 14), each of whom had been persuaded to sign a ruinous 5-year contract. Other, wealthier Indians followed and spread out across the region as traders. They were too successful and immigration was banned in 1913. The indentured labour scheme was only abolished in 1920, one of Mahatma Gandhi's earliest political triumphs.

Unlike Europe or North America, where anyone not of pure white origins is usually classed as black, people of mixed race in southern Africa have always been regarded as a separate race, the **'coloureds'**, accepted by neither black nor white. Over the years, they have formed a distinct cultural group, speaking English or Afrikaans as their first language, living and socialising apart from all other communities, usually working as skilled manual workers or on the railways. Officially, during the apartheid years, they were said to be the result of intermarriage between the Khoisan and Cape Malays – and undoubtedly some

were – but the sheer numbers make it totally obvious that many were also the offspring of white fathers and black mothers.

FOOD

At its best, South African cuisine is magnificent, a cauldron of exotic culinary influences, including Cape Dutch, French Huguenots, Germans, Malays, Indians, Portuguese, British and, of course, the Africans. At its worst, it is all too boringly bland and badly cooked.

Probably the most typical food comes from Africa itself and from the long, hot journeys of the early Voortrekkers, who had to shoot their food as they travelled and dry the leftovers for future use. The *braaivleis*, usually abbreviated to *braai* (pronounced 'bry') is a barbecue, an open-air feast of meat or fish (snoek is a particular favourite along the Cape coast), roasted over an open fire, embellished with exotic sauces, marinades, spices and herbs, salad, *mealies* (sweetcorn), bread and wine or beer. The meat is normally familiar beef, chicken or lamb, but may include more exotic animals such as ostrich, impala, warthog, eland or crocodile. Sizzling beside these will be the *boerewors*, highly spiced pork, mutton and beef sausage, flavoured with coriander, ginger, mace, cloves, nutmeg, thyme, fennel, rosemary, mint and red wine or vinegar. Leftover meat was traditionally salted, spiced and sun-dried as *biltong*, and these hard, chewy strips of meat are still popular as a snack, or even served as a garnish in haute cuisine cooking.

Also on the fire at many braais are bubbling three-legged iron pots *(potjies)* filled with nourishing stews of spinach, beans, pumpkin, tomatoes and onions, with perhaps some added meat, known as *potjiekos* (pronounced 'poykeykos'). Eaten with this is *pap*, a thick and filling porridge made from maize (introduced to the continent by 15th-century Portuguese sailors) or sorghum, which can be served at any consistency from thin porridge to mashed potato. These together make up the traditional – and enormously healthy – staple diet of all black Africans, packed with vitamins and carbohydrates, with virtually no added salt, sugar or fat. Additional protein was traditionally supplied by soured milk, mopani worms, grasshoppers, ants and edible beetles, fried or roasted and eaten by the handful.

Once settled, the Cape-Dutch colonists could eat a far richer and more varied cuisine, based not only on their European traditions, with thick soups, slow-cooked stews *(bredies)* of fat-tailed mutton or venison, *frikkadels* (meatballs) and breads, German-style sausages and French *konfyt* (preserved fruits), but also on the highly spiced curries served with *sambals* (chutneys) and *atjar* (pickles), rice-based *breyanis* (similar to the indian biriyani), and *sosaties* (marinated kebabs) familiar to their Cape Malay servants. Most famous of all is the mild Malay curry of minced lamb, dried fruit and egg custard, *bobotie*, which has become the South African national dish. More unusual vegetables include pumpkin (sometimes served as sugary fritters), butternut squash, *waterblommetjie* (water lily), or sweet potatoes glazed in orange caramel.

South Africa, Namibia and Mozambique also glory in magnificent seafood at affordable prices, with game fish from shark, tuna and kabeljou, to more delicate whitefish, such as kingclip, yellowtail, snoek (also pickled by the Cape-Malay) and a cornucopia of shellfish, including oysters, mussels, limpets, crayfish, perlemoen (abalone) and some of the world's finest and largest prawns. Inland, the mountain rivers breed delicious trout, while Lake Kariba, nearly as large as an inland sea, has a rich supply of freshwater fish, including delicious Kariba bream.

Puddings are anything but healthy or modest, with solidly wicked treats from *melktart* (Dutch milk tart), Cape brandy pudding (British-style steamed pudding dripping with brandy) or *koeksisters* (plaited doughnuts soaked in honey or fruit syrup).

DRINK

South Africans of all hues enjoy a drink and the usual choice is **beer** (lager). Loyalties are usually split between *Castle* and *Lion,* but one or two other brands such as *Ohlssons, Amstel,* Namibian *Windhoek,* or Zimbabwean *Zambezi,* are gaining popularity.

Traditional African beer is a thick, yeasty concoction known as *maheu*. Maize and sorghum are left to germinate in wet sacks, sun-dried, ground into flour, boiled into a thin porridge, strained through a woven grass tube and left to forment. The process takes up to ten days. The work is done by the women, the sediment is given to the ancestors. Traditionally, the beer is drunk from a communal clay or woven pot. In the beerhalls and shebeens, it is usually served in large plastic buckets. Officially, these are passed round – in practice, people just drink an awful lot.

South Africa is also one of the world's oldest and foremost producers of **wine**, first made here in 1659. The industry here is huge, producing over 500 million bottles and supporting over 300,000 jobs. The boycott of the apartheid years ensured that most South African wine was drunk at home, with relatively little sold to the rest of the world – and most of that was through one outlet, the massive, commercial KWV cooperative. The revelation of the last few years has been not only the enormous variety of wines produced in the smaller, exclusive vineyards, but their superb quality, as good as, or even surpassing many European, American or Australian rivals. The vast majority of the vineyards are in the Western Cape, with smaller concentrations along the Gariep River in the Northern Cape, and in Mpumalanga and Northern Province. A Wine of Origin (WO) label guarantees the location of the vineyard, the grape varieties and the year. For more details, see Cape Town–Worcester pp. 144–148.

There are indifferent local copies of all spirits and many liqueurs, all considerably cheaper than the imported, branded version, but best drunk with mixers and ice. However, KWV do produce some excellent **brandy** and a pleasant tangerine-flavoured **liqueur**, *Van der Hum.* Amarula Cream is another popular after-dinner drink, a cream liqueur made from the berries of the wild marula tree (also popular when formenting amongst wild animals, from baboons to elephants). The Afrikaners also distil a variety of home-made firewaters, known as *mampoer* or *witblitz* – indulge at your peril.

73

TOURING ITINERARIES

Half the fun of a journey lies in the planning, in the endless hours of day-dreaming before you set out. By dividing the region into key destinations and recommended routes, this book is intended to make it easy and pleasurable for you to plan your ideal tour. For those who like a little help in making up their minds, we have put together a few sample itineraries, given some easy-access listings of highlights and thought up a number of possible themes for those with special interests. You could use our suggestions as a blueprint for a trip, but you may well prefer to use them as a framework on which to hang your own personal adventure.

PRACTICAL HINTS

There are a few golden rules to remember when planning a trip:
1. Don't try to be too ambitious. The distances here are huge, and you will be doing an enormous amount of driving anyway. If you try and cram absolutely everything in to a split-second timetable, you will end up frazzled and unable to enjoy anything. If you do miss a few sights, you can always come back next year.
2. Be a little imaginative about your planning. Most visitors to southern Africa tread a very narrow path and although what they do see is lovely, they miss far more.
3. If you have limited time, look at the possibilities of combining air or even rail transfers and local car hire, which will save you days.
4. Always pre-book your first and last nights' accommodation, particularly if you are arriving in the evening or have an early morning flight out. Allow a full 'business' day at the start of your trip to double-check that all your long-distance arrangements have actually been made.

5. Unless you have accommodation pre-booked, plan to arrive at your overnight stop in time to find lodgings (usually by 4pm). Make the tourist information office your first call. Always pre-book in high season (Dec–Jan, Apr). In most cases, it is also a sensible security precaution not to be on the open road after dark.
6. Don't move on every night. You need to allow at least two nights in any game park. You also get tired and run out of clothes. Laundry breaks are essential on a touring holiday.
7. Keep a good, up-to-date road map in the car. South Africa, in particular, has embarked on a major programme of road-building and upgrading, and you may well find that roads have appeared from nowhere or numbers have been changed. Other countries are doing the same thing, but on a lesser scale. Don't ever set off on cross-country journeys without knowing where you are going. There are far too many possibilities of getting into serious trouble.

SUGGESTED ITINERARIES

Suggested overnight stops are in **bold** type.

CLASSIC TOUR

14 Days/21 Days
Most first time visitors to South Africa spend time in Cape Town, along the Garden Route and at Kruger National Park. This is a variation on that theme, also incorporating a little time in Pretoria/Johannesburg, a train trip, a cultural village and Sun City, the Vegas of the South.
Day 1: arrive Johannesburg, stay in **Pretoria/Johannesburg**, see pp.194–203 and 294–302.
Day 2: in **Pretoria/Johannesburg**, overnight train to Cape Town, see pp.100–114.
Day 3: on train, arriving in Cape Town.
Days 4, 5, 6: **Cape Town** area, see pp.100–114 (also Cape Town–Cape Point, pp. 115–122 and Cape Town–Worcester, pp. 144–148).
Days 7, 8, 9, 10: drive up the Garden Route, see Cape Town–Mossel Bay, pp.132–137, and Mossel Bay–Port Elizabeth, pp. 272–280.

Day 11: Fly Port Elizabeth–Johannesburg, Johannesburg–Skukuza, for **Kruger National Park**, pp. 239–245.
Day 12: in **Kruger**.
Day 13: in **Mpumalanga Drakensberg**, see Kruger–Phalaborwa, pp. 249–254.
Day 14: drive back to Johannesburg, see Johannesburg–Kruger, pp. 224–229; fly home.

Extension Week
Allow 1 extra day in Pretoria/Johannesburg, 1 extra day in the Cape, 1 extra day at Kruger.
Day 18: instead of flying home, drive to **Lesedi Cultural Village**, see p. 210.
Day 19: drive to **Sun City**, see pp. 318–320.
Day 20: in **Sun City**.
Day 21: return to Johannesburg, and fly home.

REGIONAL HIGHLIGHTS

With 1 or 2 days travelling between them, these circuits could easily be linked for a grand tour.

CAPE MEANDER

14 Days
This more gentle journey forms a stunningly beautiful loop through the Cape Peninsula, the Garden Route, the Karoo and the Winelands. The driving is easy, the scenery superb and the accommodation and food excellent.
Day 1: arrive Cape Town International Airport.
Days 2, 3, 4, 5: in **Cape Town** and **Cape Peninsula**, see pp. 100–114 and pp. 115–122.
Days 6, 7: drive Cape Town–Mossel Bay route, see p. 132–137.
Days 8, 9, 10: drive Mossel Bay–Plettenburg Bay (Mossel Bay–Port Elizabeth, pp. 272–280).
Days 11, 12: return to George and drive George–Worcester route, see pp. 332–336, including Oudtshoorn, see pp. 281–284.
Days 13, 14: Worcester–Cape Town route, see pp. 144–148, including Stellenbosch, pp. 313–316; overnight return flight from Cape Town.

THE GREAT EASTERN LOOP

21 Days
This is real Africa, incorporating dramatic mountain scenery, excellent game-viewing and unsurpassed cultural tourism.

Day 1: arrive Johannesburg.
Day 2: in **Johannesburg/Pretoria**.
Day 3: drive Johannesburg–Kruger route as far as **Hazyview**, see pp. 224–228.
Day 4: drive Kruger–Phalaborwa route, see pp. 249–254, either returning to Hazyview or continuing through to Letaba or Oliphants Camp within the Kruger National Park.
Days 5, 6: in **Kruger**, see pp. 239–245.
Days 7, 8, 9: drive Kruger–Hluhluwe route, via Swaziland, see pp. 246–248 and 379–387.
Days 10, 11: in **Hluhluwe-Umfolozi/St Lucia** area, see pp. 190–192.
Days 12, 13, 14: sections of the Hluhluwe–Kosi Bay route, returning to **Hluhluwe**, p. 188–193.
Days 15, 16, 17, 18: either drive Hluhluwe–Ladysmith and Ladysmith–Durban routes (pp. 264–271 and 255–263) and Pietermaritzburg (pp. 285–289) or do Hluhluwe–Durban in 2–3 days and have an extra 1–2 days on the beach.
Days 19, 20: select a resort along the Natal coast, see pp. 158–164 and 165–172, and have a couple of days serious sunbathing.
Day 21: fly from Durban–Johannesburg in time to connect with your overseas flight.

THE DESERT IN BLOOM

14 Days
This option takes a very long detour into some of the most remote areas of southern Africa as it heads south from Johannesburg to Cape Town through the Kalahari Desert. It is a tough journey involving huge amounts of driving. The itinerary below is the minimum time needed. It is inadvisable to travel it in summer, due to the heat. To see the flowers in all their glory, you need to travel in September.
Day 1: arrive Johannesburg.
Day 2: in **Johannesburg/Pretoria**.
Day 3: drive to Sun City, see p. 318–320.
Day 4: in **Sun City**.
Day 5, 6: drive to Mafikeng and pick up Johannesburg–Kimberley route, pp. 213–219.
Day 7: in **Kimberley**, see pp. 230–233.
Days 7, 8, 9, 10: drive Kimberley–Upington, see pp. 234–238, and Upington–Springbok, see pp. 323–331 (if you wish to travel the 4x4 trail and visit the Richtersveld, pp. 328–329, allow another week).

Days 11, 12: drive Springbok–Cape Town route, see p. 138–143.
Days 13, 14: in **Cape Town**, pp. 100–114, flying to Johannesburg for your flight home.

BEST OF SOUTHERN AFRICA

All places in these sections are listed in alphabetical order.

10 BEST ROUTES WITHIN SOUTH AFRICA

1. Bloemfontein–Cape Town, pp. 82–88.
2. Cape Town–Cape Point, pp. 115–122.
3. Cape Town–Springbok, pp. 138–143.
4. Cape Town–Worcester, pp. 144–148.
5. East London–Graaff-Reinet, pp. 177–180.
6. Hluhluwe–Kosi Bay, pp. 188–193.
7. Kruger (Skukuza)–Phalaborwa, pp. 249–254.
8. Ladysmith–Durban, pp. 255–263.
9. Ladysmith–Hluhluwe (the Battlefields route), pp. 264–271.
10. Mossel Bay–Port Elizabeth (the Garden Route), pp. 272–280.

10 BEST ACTIVITIES

These are some of the best places in which you can do these activities, although there are others.
1. **Canoeing** – Victoria Falls, Zimbabwe, p. 402; Okavango Delta, Botswana, pp. 349–350; Gariep River, Northern Cape, p. 131.
2. **Diving** – Sodwana Bay, Kwazulu-Natal, p. 192; Aliwal Shoal, Natal South Coast, p. 161; Mozambique coast, if you have your own gear and can dive without back-up, pp. 356–364.
3. **4x4 Driving** – Richtersveld, Northern Cape, South Africa, p. 328; Skeleton Coast and Namib-Naukluft, Namibia, pp. 374–376.
4. **Fishing** – trout: Drakensberg, Mpumalanga (pp. 255–263); Kwazulu-Natal (pp. 158–172, 188–193, 255–271); Lesotho (pp. 351–355). Lake fishing: Lake Kariba, Zimbabwe (p. 403). Saltwater and deep-sea fishing: East London (pp. 173–176); Port Elizabeth (pp. 290–293); Wild Coast (pp. 162–163); Durban (pp. 149–157); St Lucia (pp. 191–192); Mozambique coast (pp. 356–364).
5. **Golf** – a South African passion, with good courses everywhere; there is a particularly fine collection on the Natal South Coast, South Africa, pp. 158–164.

6. **Hiking** – all over the place, with up to 300 trails, but particularly the Cedarbergs in the Western Cape, pp. 140–141; the Wild Coast, pp. 162–163; Tsitsikamma Forest in the Eastern Cape, p. 279; and the Drakensberg (pp. 255–263) in Kwazulu-Natal; all in South Africa.
7. **Hot Air Ballooning** – Magaliesberg, Gauteng, pp. 216–217; Pilanesburg, North-West Province, pp. 320–321; both in South Africa.
8. **Riding** – pony-trekking in the Lesotho mountains, pp. 351–355.
9. **Surfing** – the Eastern Cape coast, particularly between Port Elizabeth and East London, but stretching right up to Durban; pp. 181–184 and 158–164.
10. **White Water Rafting** – Victoria Falls, Zimbabwe; p. 402; Gariep River, Northern Cape, South Africa, p. 131.

TOP 10 FAMILY ATTRACTIONS

1. **Croc World** – Natal South Coast, Kwazulu-Natal, see p. 161.
2. **East London**, beaches, activities, aquarium and museum – Eastern Cape, see pp. 173–176.
3. **Golden Mile Beachfront**, Durban – Kwazulu-Natal, see p. 156.
4. **Gold Reef City** – Johannesburg, see p. 203.
5. **Outeniqua Tjoe-Choo steam train** – Garden Route, Western Cape, p. 56 and p. 274.
6. **Ostrich Farms**, Oudtshoorn – Western Cape, South Africa, see pp. 281–284.
7. **Pioneer Museum and Willem Prinsloo Museum**, Pretoria – Gauteng, South Africa, see p. 302.
8. **Pretoria Zoological Gardens** – Gauteng, see p. 301.
9. **Sun City** – North-West Province, pp. 318–320.
10. **Table Mountain Cable-Car** – Cape Town, see p. 114.

TOP 10 GAME PARKS

1. **Chobe National Park**, Botswana; pp. 348–349.
2. **Etosha National Park**, Namibia; pp. 377–378.
3. **Greater St Lucia Wetlands Park**, Kwazulu-Natal, South Africa; pp. 191–192.
4. **Hluhluwe-Umfolozi National Park**, Kwazulu-Natal, South Africa; pp. 190–191.

5. Hwange National Park, Zimbabwe; pp. 399–400.
6. Kalahari Gemsbok National Park, South Africa/Botswana; p. 325.
7. Kruger National Park, Mpumalanga, South Africa; pp. 239–245.
8. Lake Kariba, several small parks, Zimbabwe; p. 403.
9. Okavango Delta, Botswana; pp. 349–350.
10. Pilanesburg National Park, North-West Province, South Africa; pp. 320–321.

TOP 10 HISTORIC PLACES

1. Cape Town and Cape Peninsula, Western Cape; pp. 100–122.
2. Graaff-Reinet, Eastern Cape; pp. 85–87.
3. Grahamstown and Settler Country, Eastern Cape; pp. 185–187.
4. Great Zimbabwe Ruins, Zimbabwe; pp. 394–395.
5. Kimberley, Northern Cape; pp. 230–233.
6. Natal Battlefields area, Kwazulu-Natal; pp. 264–271.
7. Pietermaritzburg, Kwazulu-Natal; pp. 285–289.
8. Pretoria, Gauteng; pp. 294–302.
9. Stellenbosch, Western Cape; pp. 313–316.
10. Ulundi/Eshowe area, Kwazulu-Natal; pp. 169–171.

TOP 10 NATURAL SPECTACLES

1. Blyde River Canyon, Mpumalanga; pp. 252–253.
2. Drakensberg Mountains, Kwazulu-Natal; pp. 255–263.
3. Fish River Canyon, Namibia; pp. 366–367.
4. Namaqualand flowers, Western/Northern Cape; p. 331.
5. Okavango Delta, Botswana; pp. 349–350.
6. Sossusvlei Dunes, Namibia; p. 375.
7. Table Mountain, Cape Town; p. 114.
8. Thabana-Ntlenyana Mountain, Lesotho; p. 354.
9. Victoria Falls, Zimbabwe; pp. 400–402.
10. Zambezi River, Zimbabwe; pp. 401–403.

EDITOR'S CHOICE

This is an unashamedly subjective list of my favourite things in southern Africa.

1. Cape Town (Western Cape, South Africa; see pp. 100–114) – simply one of the most beautiful cities in the world.
2. Cape Winelands (Western Cape, South Africa; pp. 144–148 and 313–316) – this is not Africa in any sense of the word; the area feels, acts and looks European, but the triumvirate of Stellenbosch, Paarl and Franschhoek are delightful towns in lovely surroundings, with plenty of history, superb food and luscious wine.
3. Graaff-Reinet (Eastern Cape, South Africa; see pp. 85–87) – this little Cape Dutch town is beautiful and historic, while in nearby Nieu Bethesda is the extraordinary Owl House.
4. Hluhluwe–Umfolozi National Park (Kwazulu-Natal, South Africa; pp. 190–191) – the game-viewing in the Natal parks is every bit as good as that at the Kruger. Most accommodation is a fraction of the price and the number of tourists per animal infinitely lower.
5. The **Kalahari** (Northern Cape, South Africa; see p. 325) – it is as powerful as the Nile to see the thin green lifeline of the Gariep River threading through the red dunes of the Kalahari during sunset.
6. The **Karoo** (Eastern Cape, South Africa; see p. 284) – compelling semi-desert; the vast area of the Eastern Cape around the Swartberg mountains is particularly stunning.
7. Maputo (Mozambique; pp. 356–364) – this city has taken a terrific beating and still bears very visible scars. It is desperately poor and run-down, but it is also beautiful, exotic and welcoming with a tremendous appetite for life.
8. Okavango Delta (Botswana; see pp. 349–350) – drifting past elephants by canoe through reedbeds and lily ponds. Nothing could be more peaceful or breathtakingly beautiful.
9. Township Tours (Soweto, Gauteng; see p. 203) – it is as shocking as a slap across the face and may be distressing, but even the smallest glimpse of township life puts all that beauty and luxury into perspective. It is also a chance to be part of a very different, very vibrant culture.
10. Victoria Falls (Zimbabwe; see pp. 400–402) – it is becoming a little like a Pepsi Max action-mad advertisement these days, with a frenzied round of rafting, bungee jumping and other activities, but the Falls are truly one of the wonders of the natural world.

77

BLOEMFONTEIN

This somewhat dour city, whose name means 'fountain of flowers', grew up around a spring which, at different times, provided water for Bushmen hunters, Sotho farmers and the Voortrekkers – to say nothing of vast herds of antelope and other game. In 1854, still no more than a village, it became the capital of the newly formed Boer republic of the Orange Free State, and in 1920, following the Act of Union, it became the judicial capital of South Africa. Modern Bloemfontein is a jumble of architectural styles, with imposing colonial edifices and low-rise Victorian emporia slumbering among an aggressive glitter of skyscrapers.

TOURIST INFORMATION

Tourist Office: *60 Park Rd, Park West, Bloemfontein; tel: 051-405 8489.* Open Mon–Fri 0800–1615, Sat 0800–1200. Keen and knowledgeable staff dispense free literature and maps. Especially useful is a self-guided walking tour leaflet detailing major sights in the city centre. **Satour**, *Sanlam Parkade, Charles St, Bloemfontein; tel: 051-471 362.* General information on all South Africa. This rather cheerless office is frequently closed; even when open, callers must ring a bell to gain admission.

ARRIVING AND DEPARTING

Airport
JBM Herzog Airport, *on the N8,* 10 km east of Bloemfontein; *tel: 051-332 901.* There are SAA services to Cape Town, Durban, George, Johannesburg, Kimberley and Port Elizabeth. Taxis offer the only transport between the airport and city centre.

By Car
Bloemfontein is by-passed on the N1, South Africa's major north–south route, but the city centre is well signposted and easy to reach from all directions. The main east–west route, the combined N8/R64, passes through the centre as two main one-way streets: *Zastron St* travelling east, and *Voortrekker St* going west. Street parking is plentiful and there is a big multi-storey Parkade on *Charles St.*

By Rail
Bloemfontein Railway Station, *Harvey St (M13); tel: 051-408 2946,* is a stop for trains serving Durban–Cape Town (the Trans Oranje), Johannesburg–East London (the Amatola), Johannesburg–Port Elizabeth (Algoa) and Bloemfontein–Kimberley–Pretoria (the Diamond Express). There is a taxi rank outside the station. *Maitland St,* directly opposite the station, leads to the city centre.

By Bus
Translux, *17 Cricket St; tel: 051-408 2262,* offer services to Johannesburg-Pretoria, East London, Durban, Port Elizabeth and Cape Town. **Greyhound** buses leave from *Shell Ultra on the N1* and serve Durban, Pretoria, Kimberley, Upington, Port Elizabeth and Cape Town; reservations are handled by **Rennies Travel**, *8 Elizabeth St; tel: 051-302 361.*

GETTING AROUND
Many of Bloemfontein's major attractions are in the city centre and are easily reached on foot. Attractions further out – **Franklin Nature Reserve**, **Naval Hill** and the **Military Museum** – can be reached by bus, although services stop early in the evening. All municipal bus routes (information: *tel: 051-405 8135*) pass through *Hoffman Sq.* **Taxis**: **Alfa Taxis**; *tel: 051-470 144;* **Bloem Taxis**; *tel: 051-333 776;* **Rosestad Taxis**; *tel: 051-511 022;* **Silver Leaf Taxis**; *tel: 051-478 888;* **Vrystaat Taxis**; *tel: 051-306 354.*

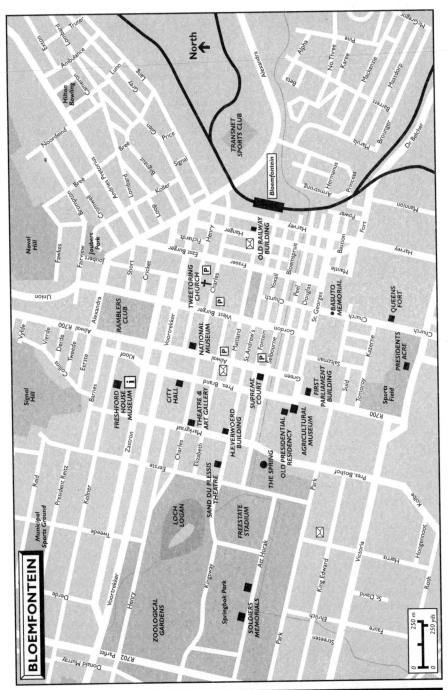

STAYING IN BLOEMFONTEIN

Accommodation

Bloemfontein offers a fairly good selection of accommodation in all price ranges. A comprehensive list may be obtained from the Publicity Association's tourist information office. Some moderately priced hotels are close to the city centre, with more expensive properties located around the western end of **King's Park**. Bed and breakfast establishments offer an expanding option in most areas. Accommodation may be harder to find at weekends featuring major cricket or rugby matches. Hotel chains in Bloemfontein include *CL, Hd*.

Top of the range is the four-star **Bloemfontein Hotel**, *Sanlam Plaza, East Burger St; tel: 051-430 1911; fax: 051-447 7102* (expensive), catering for business travellers, conference delegates and tourists.

Also centrally located is the **Halevy House Hotel**, *corner Charles and Markgraaf Sts; tel/fax: 051-480 271* (moderate–expensive), a 36-room property within strolling distance of theatres, rugby and cricket grounds. The **Holiday Inn Garden Court**, *corner Zastron St and Melville Dr., Brandhof; tel: 051-447 0310; fax: 051-430 5678* (moderate) has more than 100 rooms, modern facilities and is just 2 km from the city centre. **Die Herburg**, *12 Barnes St, Brandhof; tel: 051-430 7500; fax: 051-430 4494* (moderate) is also handy for the city centre, with 49 rooms and ample parking.

Best-known of the city's guesthouses is the **Hobbit House** (J.R.R Tolkien was born in Bloemfontein), *19 President Steyn Ave; tel/fax: 051-447 0663* (cheap), which has five guest rooms and was voted Satour Guesthouse of the Year in 1996. Among the newer bed and breakfast homes is **Plover Cottage**, *on the N1 at Riverside-Glen,* 15 km north of Shell Ultra City; *tel/fax: 052-142 236* (cheap–moderate). Rooms in this attractive thatched cottage are on the small side, but the hospitality compensates.

Campsites: **Dagbreek Caravan Park**, *Andries Pretorius St (M30); tel: 051-332 490,* offers accommodation in retired railway carriages as well as caravan pitches. **Reyneke Park**, *Petrusburg Rd; tel: 051-23 888,* has caravan pitches and chalets.

Eating and Drinking

If you are slogging round the city centre in the heat of the day, the **Middestad Sentrum** shopping mall, *Charles St,* is probably the best place to head for lunch, with three floors of department stores, shops and restaurants. You can study the menus as you stroll in the cool.

Away from the city centre, the **Mimosa Mall**, *off Zastron St,* near the Holiday Inn Garden Court, offers a good choice of eating places. The **Hard Rock Café**, *adjoining the Holiday Inn Garden Court, tel: 051-471 517/8* (budget–moderate) is rather more sedate than its counterparts elsewhere in the world, but offers an above-average HRC menu.

Schillaci's, *115 Zastron St; tel: 051-482 835* (moderate; reservations advised) is a popular Italian trattoria with alfresco dining. The **Porterhouse**, *Middestad Sentrum, West Burger St; tel: 051-448 3224* (moderate) specialises in seafood and steaks.

Traditional South African dishes are served at **Onze Rust**, *Boerekos, Landgoed, about 40 km south of the city on the N1; tel: 051-441 8717* (moderate). The house is the former residence of M. J. Steyn, president of the Boer Republic.

Communications

Main Post Office: *Hoffman Sq., corner Maitland and Fraser Sts.*

Money

All the main banks have branches in the city centre. A **Thomas Cook/Rennies Foreign Exchange** branch is located at *120 Voortrekker St; tel: 051-430 2361; fax: 051-430 6468.*

ENTERTAINMENT

The focal point of Bloemfontein's entertainment scene is the **Sand du Plessis Theatre Complex**, *Markgraaff St; tel: 051-447 7931,* which is the headquarters of the Performing Arts Council of the Free State and the principal venue for a continuing programme of drama, ballet, opera, musicals and symphony concerts.

Nightlife is confined to a scattering of bars and clubs, some offering live music. **Simply Red**, *St Andrew St, near Hoffman Sq.,* is the venue for blues and reggae fans. Other favoured spots are **The Boys**, *West Burger St,* and **Deja**

Vu, *Voortrekker St.* Two **multi-screen cinemas** are in **Mimosa Mall**, *next to the Holiday Inn Garden Court, off Zastron St; tel: 051-484 841* and at **Noorstad***; tel: 051-331 423.*

SHOPPING

The major shopping area in central Bloemfontein is in the streets bounded by the eastern end of *Voortrekker St* and *Selbourne St,* but the greatest concentrations of department stores and shops are to be found in the big shopping malls. **Middestad Sentrum**, *West Burger St*, has 76 stores and is said to cater for 12,000 shoppers daily. Other major malls are the **Sanlam Plaza**, *Maitland St;* the **Brandwag Shopping Centre** and **Mimosa Mall** – both just north of *Zastron St* at Brandwag; and **Noorstad**, *Eeufees Rd*, which has more than 50 shops, including Pick & Pay, Boardmans and Clicks. There are few opportunities or incentives for souvenir shopping here.

SIGHTSEEING

The best place for panoramic views of the city and surrounding areas is **Naval Hill**, *Union Ave*, on the city's north-eastern edge. Marked by a white horse carved during the Anglo-Boer War by men of the Wiltshire Regiment, the hill accommodates the **Franklin Game Reserve**, *Union Ave; tel: 051-405 8124* (open daily 0800–1700; free), which has a number of animal species, although no major predators.

A half-hour stroll along **President Brand St**, between *St George's St* and *Voortrekker St,* leads past Bloemfontein's most significant buildings. The humble **First Raadsaal**, *95 St George's St; tel: 051-479 610* (open Mon–Fri 1015–1500, Sat–Sun 1400–1700; R1) still has the thatched roof and cow-dung floor dating from 1848, when it was built as the city's first council chamber and school. It is now a small museum featuring life in the Boer republic. The other edifices are grandiose, built of mustard-yellow sandstone and designed to impose a solid authority on even the most casual observer. The **Old Presidency**, *corner President Brand and St George's Sts; tel: 051-480 949* (open Tues–Fri 1000–1200, 1300–1600, Sat–Sun 1400–1700; free) was built in 1885 as the official residence of the Free State presidents. The **National**

> ## *Emily Hobhouse*
>
> T he ashes of Emily Hobhouse, a member of the English aristocracy who supported Afrikaner independence, are buried at the foot of the **National Women's Memorial**. Appalled at conditions in the Boer concentration camps, she launched a campaign in 1901 to raise money to help the suffering civilians and to improve conditions in the camps. The war over, she worked with victims and established schools for Boer girls.

Afrikaans Literary Museum, *corner President Brand and Maitland Sts; tel: 051-405 4711* (open Mon–Fri 0800–1215, 1300–1600, Sat 0900–1200; free) is, as its name suggests, South Africa's major repository for the Afrikaans language and literature, housed in the Old Government Building, erected in 1908. The **National Museum**, *corner Charles and Aliwal Sts; tel: 051-479 609* (open Mon–Sat 0800–1700, Sun 1300–1800; R3), has extensive archaeological and zoological collections and a street of re-created 19th-century shops and houses.

Elsewhere, the lifestyle of Bloemfontein's colonial citizens is encapsulated in a collection of Victorian brassware, stained-glass and furnishings at **Freshford House**, *31 Kellner St; tel: 051-479 609* (open Mon–Fri 1000–1300, Sat–Sun 1400–1700; R1). The **National Botanical Garden**, *Rayton Rd; tel: 051-313 530* (open daily 0800–1800; Mon–Fri free, weekends and public holidays R4), has some 200 species of plants, including 50 types of tree, in a thriving 70-hectare garden, which also has a lake, bird-watching hide and tea kiosk.

Most poignant of all, the **War Museum and National Women's Memorial**, *Monument Rd; tel: 051-473 447* (open Mon–Fri 0900–1630, Sat 0900–1700, Sun 1400–1700; R1) is a graphic reminder of the folly and horror of the Anglo-Boer war, with a special section on the concentration camps. The memorial, sculpted by Anton van Wouw, is dedicated to the 26,000 Boer women and children who died in the camps.

BLOEMFONTEIN–
CAPE TOWN

This magnificent route south crosses great swathes of the Karoo, the KhoiKhoi's 'land of thirst', a silent region with a sense of timelessness. The towns themselves, in particular Graaff-Reinet and Colesberg, have fascinating architecture and museums. This is a vast, arid wilderness with unusual and beautiful vegetation, and a landscape peppered with flat-topped koppies of hard doleritic rock, the formation of which entrapped thousands of fossils – from enormous trees to strange amphibious creatures with mammalian features. The last section is through superb Cape mountain scenery and the heartland of the wine country. This is a long journey, with hours of driving between stops. Fuel stops are frequent (take detours to local towns and villages should you need to), but it is advisable to carry some food and water.

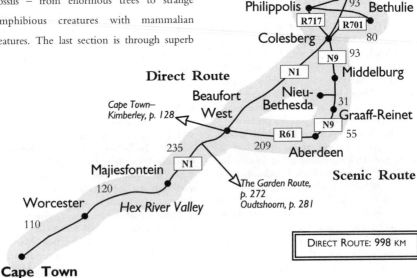

DIRECT ROUTE: 998 KM

ROUTES

DIRECT ROUTE

→ The fastest way to get from Bloemfontein to Cape Town is along highway N1 (bypassing Graaff-Reinet). Much of the scenery is stunning, particularly between Beaufort West and Victoria West. Take care, however – heavy lorries use this route and accidents are frequent, especially at night. Distance: 998 km; allow two full days.

SCENIC ROUTE

▶ Leave Bloemfontein on the R706 and head south for **Jagersfontein** (108 km). From Jagersfontein, retrace your steps through Charlesville (about 10 km), where you join the R704 to Trompsburg (37 km), then turn right onto the R717 and follow the signs to **Philippolis** (58 km). From here, the R717 continues south for 56 km to **Colesberg**.

Alternatively, turn back north from Philippolis along the R717; a short distance out of town, turn right onto an untarred secondary road signposted to Springfontein (47 km), cross over the N1 to join the R715 and head for **Bethulie** (about 45 km) at the far end of the **Gariep Dam**. The **Tussen-die-Riviere Nature Reserve** lies just to the east of Bethulie. From Bethulie, take the R701 and follow the signs to the N1 (48 km). From the N1 junction, this road continues round to join the R58 at the **Dam Wall**, from where it is 28 km to Colesberg. Take the N9 south from Colesberg to **Middelburg** (93 km), then continue south, over the Sneeuberg Mountains. After 56 km, turn right onto an untarred secondary road and follow the signs to **Nieu-Bethesda** (about 27 km from the turn off).

Return to the N9 and continue south to **Graaff-Reinet** (31 km from the turn off) and **Aberdeen** (55 km further on). From Aberdeen, take the R61 west to **Beaufort West** (209 km); this is a long, hot, tiring haul. Pack a lunch and take it easy, or leave early in the morning, when it is still cool. At Beaufort West, connect with the N1 once again. The Beaufort West to Matjiesfontein stretch (235 km) traverses a monotonous stretch of repetitive landscape. Beware of drowsiness, which induces frequent accidents. After 114 km, at *Prince Albert Rd*, the R328 connects south to Prince Albert, Oudtshoorn (see p.281) and the Garden Route (see p.272). From *Prince Albert Rd*, it is a further 111 km along the N1 to **Matjiesfontein**. Keep going south along the N1. About 90 km later, the road passes through the lovely **Hex River Valley** and over the Hex River Pass, beyond which is **Worcester** (about 30 km). From here, it is about 110 km to Cape Town (for more detail on the Winelands, see pp.144–148). Distance: 1372 km; allow four days.

TRAINS AND BUSES

The Trans Oranje departs Bloemfontein on Thur, travelling via Kimberley to Cape Town. Journey time approx. 20 hrs. OTT Tables 3515 and 3519.

Greyhound Citiliner and Translux both operate 2 daily overnight services calling at Colesburg and Beaufort West. Journey time: 12 hrs. OTT Table 3537.

JAGERSFONTEIN

Tourist Office: *Municipality, Market Sq.; tel: 051732, ask for 3* (open office hours).

The area's first diamond was found on Jagersfontein farm in 1870. Three years later, in 1893, came the discovery of the massive 971-carat Excelsior diamond. A rush of fortune hunters swamped the area and a small mining town sprang up almost overnight. The main reason to visit, however, is to see the **Mining Village**, *follow the signs from Market Sq.; tel: tourist information* (open Mon–Fri 0800–1300, 1400–1700; R3), an open-air museum on the rim of the local 'Big Hole' that is nearly 500 m in diameter and 500 m deep, and the source of the Excelsior diamond.

PHILIPPOLIS

Tourist Office: *Transgariep Museum, Voortrekker St; tel: 051772, ask for 157* (open Mon–Fri 0830–1700).

The central **Oranjehof Hotel**, *Voortrekker St; tel: 051772, ask for 8* (cheap), has a restaurant and bar. The **Waenhuis Guest House**, *26 Kok St; tel: 051772, ask for 157* (cheap), serves breakfast, lunch and dinner by arrangement.

Philippolis was founded in 1823 as a mission station for the Griqua. Visit the interesting **Transgariep Museum**, *Voortrekker St; tel: 051772, ask for 6* (open Mon–Fri 1000–1200; free), which outlines the town's history – and in particular that of its most famous resident, Griqua leader Adam Kok (see p. 235). Above all, come here for the stucco Karoo architecture. Look out particularly for an outstanding **Dutch Reformed Church**, **Adam Kok's home**, *Voortrekker St*, his **kraal** (see glossary, p.24), *Justisie St*, and his **kruithuis** (arsenal), on a hill west of town. Here too, the English philanthropist Emily Hobhouse established the first of 26 spinning and weaving schools for Boer girls after the Anglo-Boer War. April 6 is the date of the **Witblits Festival**; on this occasion the old distilling kettle is taken from the museum and put to good use, creating endlessly varied and alcoholic firewaters.

GARIEP DAM

The **Aventura Midwater Resort** *(Av), near the Dam Wall (follow signs from the N1); tel: 052172, ask for 45; fax: 052172, ask for 135* (cheap), is a good base for water sports enthusiasts; tennis and riding also available. Accommodation is in chalets, with **camping** and **caravan** sites.

Formerly known as the Hendrik Verwoerd Dam, this vast inland ocean, covering an area of 374 sq. km, when full, is the biggest stretch of inland water in South Africa. Formed by the Gariep (Orange) and Caledon Rivers, its role is to provide much needed water for irrigation and hydro-electric power. If the expanse of water is spectacular, then so is the dam wall (built in 1972), which is 914m long and 90.5m high. Around the shores are two important nature reserves.

The 11,237 hectare **Gariep Nature Reserve**; *tel: 052172, ask for 26* (open daily 0600–1900; R12 per car), protects a large expanse of virgin grassland and Karoo vegetation strewn with *koppies* (rocky outcrops) and massive boulders. Make enquiries about opportunities for sailing and swimming, game-viewing and bird-watching. There is accommodation in chalets (cheap–moderate). The second reserve is the huge Tussen-die-Riviere Reserve.

The 22,000 hectare **Tussen-die-Riviere Nature Reserve**; *tel: 051762, ask for 2803* (open daily 0800–1800; R12 per car), is an important wildlfe sanctuary in winter and a hunting preserve in summer. Its name means 'between the rivers' (Gariep and Caledon). A visit should include a detour to **Aasvoelkop**, near the Reserve's eastern boundary, to see some well-preserved San rock paintings. This Reserve provides opportunities for sailing, fishing and swimming, and there is simple, self-contained, self-catering accommodation for rent (cheap–moderate).

COLESBERG

Tourist Office: *Bank Sq., Murray St; tel: 051-753 0777* (open Mon–Fri 0830–1700).

ACCOMMODATION

The 2-star **Central Hotel**, *Church St; tel: 051-753 0734, fax: 051-753 0667* (cheap) is uninspiring, but does serve food and drink. Ask at the museum about a lovely self-catering cottage (cheap). **Campsite**: **Van Zyl's Vlei Motel and Caravan Park**, *6 km north of Colesberg on the Philippolis Rd; tel: 051-753 0589*, also offers food and drink (cheap). For good meals in pleasant surroundings, try the **Upstairs Restaurant**, *20 Church St; tel: 051-753 0646* (moderate; open Tues–Sat dinner).

SIGHTSEEING

This is perhaps *the* classic Karoo town: an isolated oasis of bleached-white buildings, some of them historic reminders of a pioneering past, in a rough landscape dominated by the 1707m high **Cole's Kop**, a natural landmark used for navigating by early travellers. Colesberg was established here, close to a waterhole on the route between Cape Town and Johannesburg, and has never expanded beyond its original boundaries. The settlement became a town in 1830, named after Sir Lowry Cole, Governor of the Cape (1828–1833). It flourished on trade with the interior and, as a result, developed into a rather fine settlement. Look out for the small Karoo block houses lining some of the streets, as well as the grander Victorian buildings clustering around its churches. The **Kemper Museum**, *Murray St; tel: 051-753 077* (open Mon–Fri 0800–1700, Sat–Sun by request; free) contains an interesting collection of local memorabilia, and a fascinating photographic exhibition on the Karoo nomads.

MIDDELBURG

Tourist Office: *8 Meintjies St; tel: 04924-21104* (open Mon–Fri 0800–1300, 1400–1630).

Accommodation options include the 2-star **Middelburg Hotel**, *Meintjies St; tel: 04924-21100; fax: 04924-21681* (cheap); the 1-star **Rosmead Hotel**, *Main St; tel: 0483-21426* (cheap); or the **Karoo Herberg Guesthouse**,

Meintjies St; tel: 04924-23310 (cheap). Chains: *Pa.* For meals, try **D'Huis Restaurant**, *10 Meintjies St; tel: 04924-24127* (cheap–moderate; open Mon–Sat 0700–1500, 1800–2200, Sun 0700–1500).

Founded in 1856 on the banks of the Little Brak River, and midway between the towns of Cradock and Colesburg, Middelburg is a pleasant market town and a centre for sheep farming. There are a number of fine old buildings. One, a Dutch Reformed school, now houses **Middelburg Museum**, *corner Bennie and vd Walt Sts; tel: 04924-21104 ext. 204* (open Mon–Fri 0930–1300, 1400–1630; free).

NIEU-BETHESDA

Tourist Office: see Graaff-Reinet (p.85), or call the Town Clerk at Nieu-Bethesda, *Muller St; tel: 04923-712* (open Mon–Fri 0900–1200).

Catered accommodation is limited. Ask at the tourist office about self-catering accommodation in cottages and farmhouses, or try the small **Stokkiesdraai Guest House**; *tel: 04923-711* (cheap), which offers light meals lunch and dinner, as does the **Village Inn**; *tel: 04923-667*.

Remote Nieu–Bethesda, tucked into a meandering river valley amongst the foothills of the massive Compassberg, is a delightful rural village pleasantly nurturing an old world calm. A handsome stone-built **Dutch Reformed church** dominates the centre, but the compelling reason to visit is the **Owl House**, *tel: 04923-642* (open daily 0900–1700; R5). Once home to an eccentric and reclusive artist called Helen Martins (born here in 1898), it is an odd attraction for so conservative a milieu: building and grounds are decorated inside and out with magnificent and disturbing sculptures.

GRAAFF-REINET

Tourist Office: *Old Library, corner Church and Somerset Sts; tel: 0491-24248* (open Mon–Fri 0900–1300, 1400–1700, Sat 0900–1200, Sun 1000–1200).

ACCOMMODATION AND FOOD

The best hotel in town by far is the charming, historic **Drostdy Hotel** *(Pf), 30 Church St; tel: 0491-22161; fax: 0491-24582* (moderate),

---

The Owl House

A native of Nieu-Bethesda, Helen Elizabeth Martins left home in 1915, had two short and deeply unhappy marriages, and returned home in 1935 to nurse her ailing parents, who died when she was about 50. Left alone, she began to decorate the family home – the famous Owl House.

Every available surface (including chair seats) is covered in glass, which Martins ground herself using an old mealie grinder. In a house devoid of electric lighting, the bold patterns she created, at once strange and beautiful, reflected mysteriously in the candle light with which she lit her evenings. Outside, huge, stylistically 'naive' concrete sculptures, in particular owls (there are also sphinxes, camels, human figures and other fantastical creations), litter the yard, many of them made with the help of her now famous assistant, Koos Malgas. The products of a reclusive, tortured, driven and undoubtedly talented mind, Martins's creations are powerful and disturbing.

By 1977, she was going blind and in desperate poverty. She committed suicide by drinking caustic soda. Thankfully, the Owl House was preserved.

85

which also offers substantial meals (moderate; open daily 0730–2015), including local specialities such as Karoo lamb. Second-best is the **Hotel de Graaff**, *Market Sq.; tel: 0491-24191; fax: 0491-24193* (cheap), whose restaurant offers table d'hôte, light meals and teas (cheap; open 0730–2015).

Amongst a rather uninteresting range of guesthouses, the best are the **Andries Stockenstroom Guest House and Dining Room**, *100 Cradock St; tel: 0491-24575* (cheap), which serves excellent, traditional table d'hôte meals (unlicensed; open Mon–Sat dinner); the **Kingfisher Lodge**, *33 Cypress Grove; tel: 0491-22657; fax: 0491-22657* (cheap), which has a swimming pool; and the **Karoopark Guest House**, *81 Caledon St; tel: 0491-*

22557; fax: 0491-25730 (cheap), which gives special rates for weekenders and tours.

Campsite: Urquhart Park, *3 km north of town on the Murraysburg road; tel: 0491-22136,* also has self-catering chalets, bungalows and rondavels (see glossary, p.24). For other self-catering accommodation, contact the tourist office. In particular, investigate the opportunities for 'farm holidays', which may offer catering, riding, mountain climbing, photo safaris, bird-watching, and so on.

For non-hotel restaurants, try the **Almar Steakhouse and Coffee Shop,** *30a Parsonage St; tel: 0491-910 029* (open Mon–Sat 0900–2200), or **Sout & Peper,** *90 Church St; tel: 0491-23403* (open 24 hrs for light meals and teas).

SIGHTSEEING

Graaff-Reinet is one of the finest towns in the South African hinterland, and the fourth oldest in the country. The quintessential Karoo settlement, with architecture every bit as fine as Stellenbosch, it is situated on a bend in the Sundays River at the foot of the Sneeuberg Mountains, and is surrounded by the Karoo Nature Reserve (pp.86–87). Founded in 1786, it was named after Governor van der Graaff and his wife Reinet, and flourished in the 19th century as the most important trading post in the interior and an outpost of white civilisation in a barren and 'untamed' country. It has retained much of its early character and, consequently, is a lovely place to stay. There are some outstanding museums, good accommodation and plenty of opportunities for hiking, hunting, golf, tennis and swimming, using the town as a base.

Today, much of its superb Cape Dutch architecture has been restored, and the town is now the proud home of some 200 historic monuments (obtain a walking map from the Tourist Office). In particular, walk along **Cradock** and **Parsonage Streets**.

The **Drosdty Hotel** (1806) was designed by the renowned architect Louis Thibault. Since he lived far away, in Cape Town, the local builders were left very much to interpret his designs as they thought best – hence its rather peculiar, if handsome, character. Behind it, now used as hotel bedrooms, **Stretch's**

Court is a complex of flat-roofed mid 19th-century Karoo cottages built for emancipated slaves. **Reinet House,** *1 Parsonage St; tel: 0491-23801* (open daily Mon–Fri 0900–1230, 1400–1700, Sat 0900–1200, Sun 1000–1200; R5) is a magnificent Cape Dutch mansion built (between 1806 and 1812) as the Dutch Reformed Parsonage. It now houses the local cultural museum and contains period furniture. Notice its stinkwood floors and yellowwood ceilings, and, in the yard, what has been proclaimed as the world's largest grapevine. Next door, **Urquhart House,** *tel: 0491-23801* (open daily Mon–Fri 0900–1230, 1400–1700, Sat 0900–1200; R2) is furnished as a Victorian dwelling. Have a look at the unusual entrance gable and the peach-stone kitchen floor. Opposite Reinet House, the early 19th-century **Old Residency,** *Parsonage St (details as for Urquhart House)* is another early mansion, which now houses the **Jan Felix Lategan Memorial gun collection**. The **Hester Rupert Art Museum,** *Church St; tel: 0491-22121* (open Mon–Fri 1000–1200, 1500–1700, Sun 1000–1200; R0.50), in the Dutch Reformed Mission Church (built 1821), contains an excellent collection of contemporary South African art. The **Old Library,** *corner Church and Somerset Sts; tel: 0491-24248* (open daily Mon–Fri 0900–1230, 1400–1700, Sat 0900–1200, Sun 1000–1200; R2 admission charge) houses a collection of fossilised reptiles that inhabited the Karoo area some 200 million years ago, San art, historic costumes, and the William Roe photography collection.

One of the finest silhouettes in town is provided by the **Dutch Reformed Church,** *Church St.* Other notable buildings include the **Town Hall,** *Church Sq.,* the **John Rupert Little Theatre,** *Parsonage St,* built as the Church of the London Mission Society, and the **Graaff-Reinet Pharmacy,** *24 Caledon St,* preserved today as a Victorian chemist's shop (still in use).

Practically surrounding Graaff-Reinet, the **Karoo Nature Reserve,** *8 km from town along the Murraysburg road; tel: 0491-23453* (game-viewing areas open daily, summer 0700–1900, winter 0700–1800; free permit at the gate) protects typical Karoo landscape and game,

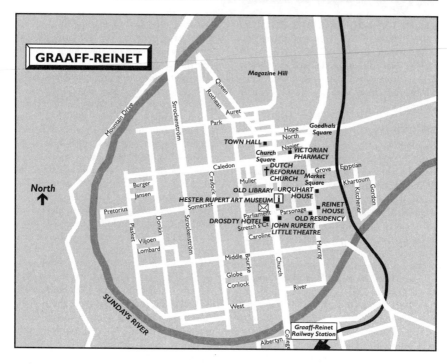

GRAAFF-REINET

including the endangered Cape Mountain Zebra. There are opportunities for walking, with short paths and overnight hiking trails (R2 fee, R15 overnight hut fee), and there is a 14 km drive (on a good tarred road; take the Murraysburg road, then turn left after 5 km from Graaff-Reinet) up to the bizarrely twisted rock formations of the **Valley of Desolation** (open 24 hrs; free), where there are magnificent views out over the Plains of Camdeboo (particularly fine at sunset).

Chalanie Tours; *tel: 0491-22893,* run minibus tours to the Valley of Desolation, the Karoo Nature Reserve, Nieu-Bethesda (see above) and other local points of interest. **Trails of the Camdeboo**, *tel: 0491-23046,* offer guided hikes, while **Sneeuberg Farm Trails**, *tel: 04923-749,* provide a network of guided and non-guided walks in and around the local mountains.

ABERDEEN

Tourist Office: *Grey St; tel: 049212, ask for 536* (open Mon–Fri 0900–1200).

Alternatives include the **Aberdeen Hotel**, *Hope St; tel: 049212-62* (1-star; cheap) or the **Homestead Guest House**, *21 Kerk St; tel: 049212 ask for 411* (cheap), which also provides excellent home cooking on request. **Campsite: Aberdeen Caravan Park**, *Andries Pretorius St; tel: 049212-14.*

Aberdeen, a hot little town marooned on the pancake-flat Plains of Camdeboo, is renowned only for its rich array of Victorian architecture. Pay it a visit and see the verandahed houses, the tin roofs, the turrets and the gables. This is an old world place, whose focus is the **Dutch Reformed Church**, one of the largest in South Africa, seating 2000 people.

BEAUFORT WEST

Tourist Office: *63 Donkin St; tel: 0201-51160* (open 0900–1700). An excellent office providing information on the whole central Karoo.

ACCOMMODATION

The excellent **Royal Hotel**, *Donkin St; tel/fax: 0201-3241* (cheap–moderate) and **Ye Olde**

Thatch Guest House, *155 Donkin St; tel: 0201-2209, fax: 0201-3714* (cheap) are both centrally located.

The **Karoo National Park** (see below) offers a variety of accommodation, including self-catering chalets with a pool, and a popular **campsite**.

SIGHTSEEING

Beaufort West, the largest town in the Karoo, straddles the highway, and is a favoured stopping point for drivers. Its busy streets are shaded by pear trees. There is a small **Museum Complex**, *Main St; tel: 0201-52308* (open Mon–Fri 0900–1700; R2), where the normal local history and antique furniture is joined by a vast array of awards presented to Dr Christian Barnaard, the first man to perform a heart transplant, and the town's most famous son.

The **Karoo National Park**, *5 km south, just off the N1; tel: 0201-52828;* reservations: *012-343 1991* (open daily 0630–2200, reception 0730–2000; R10), encompasses 46,119 hectares of virgin Karoo veld and much of the Nuweveld Mountains. The park supports 64 species of mammal, including mountain zebra, black rhino, leopard, lynx and huge herds of springbok; 194 species of bird, including 20 breeding pairs of black eagles and the rare blue crane; and 59 species of reptile. The park also has a small museum (open daily, 0800–1230, 1330–1800), a restaurant, basic accommodation, 4x4 and hiking trails (some hiking trails take more than a day; there are overnight huts).

MATJIESFONTEIN

Tourist Office: at hotel reception, see below.

ACCOMMODATION

Lord Milner Hotel, *Logan St; tel: 023-551 3011; fax: 023-551 3020* (moderate) is the best possible place to stay in this part of the Karoo. Excellent food is available at the hotel, while the **Laird's Arms** is the local pub.

SIGHTSEEING

Deep in the Karoo, Matjiesfontein began life in the 1880s as a health spa. The dry, crisp air was thought to be beneficial for those with weak chests. Certainly its founder, James Logan,

benefitted, and he was able to attract a wide range of glamorous, but similarly afflicted, guests – from Lord Randolph Churchill and the Sultan of Zanzibar to Cecil Rhodes. He developed Matjiesfontein as an international resort, built a magnificent dining room at its station (dining cars were not a feature of transKaroo trains), adorned the streets with real London lampposts and opened a mineral water factory. He piped water into town and sold it to the railways. His hotel still flourishes today. During the Anglo-Boer War, Matjiesfontein became the headquarters of the Cape Command. The original Matjiesfontein Hotel, now the Lord Milner Hotel, became the military hospital and its turret was used as a lookout post.

Nothing much has changed in the last century. A huddle of Victorian buildings with iron roofs line a single, short main street, still lit by Logan's original London lampposts. The recently restored, much balconied hotel, said to be haunted by armies of revelling ghosts, is the chief attraction and a very popular weekend venue. The hotel runs the **Matjiesfontein Museum**, *Station Buildings; tel: 023-5513011* (open daily 0800–1700; R3), which tells the story of this village's past.

HEX RIVER VALLEY AND THE HEX RIVER PASS

The Hex River Pass connects the Karoo with the Breede River Valley (see p. 334). The scenery is magnificent, as the high, dry central plains give way to the fertile, low-lying Western Cape. The original pass was built between 1874 and 1876, and was considered a magnificent feat of engineering when it opened. The railway pass is even more spectacular. The Hex River Mountains provide ample opportunity for hiking. The best locations to use as bases are, in the west, Ceres and Worcester (see p.338), where there is skiing in winter.

WORCESTER AND THE WINELANDS

See pp. 144–148.

CAPE TOWN

See pp.100–114.

BLOEMFONTEIN–EAST LONDON

This is a long drive south, both geographically and socially. It starts in Bloemfontein, at the heart of the Afrikaner Free State, and the first 173 km cross the prairie-like plains of the gold-rich highveld. At Aliwal North, on the border with the Eastern Cape, the scenery begins to change to the rocky wastes of the Great Karoo, while further south still, the road wanders into the rich, green pastures and rolling hills of the Settler country. The names change from Afrikaans to English and German, and eventually, at Bisho, to Xhosa, as the last leg of the journey is through the former homeland of Ciskei, one of the great power centres of black nationalism.

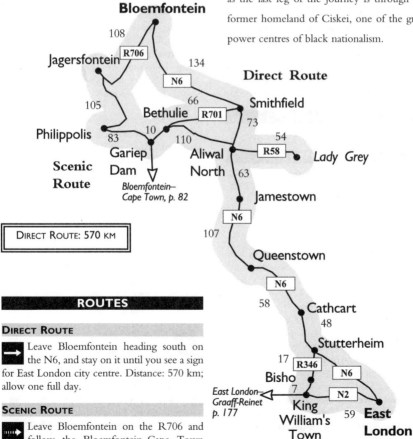

DIRECT ROUTE: 570 KM

ROUTES

DIRECT ROUTE

➡ Leave Bloemfontein heading south on the N6, and stay on it until you see a sign for East London city centre. Distance: 570 km; allow one full day.

SCENIC ROUTE

➡ Leave Bloemfontein on the R706 and follow the Bloemfontein–Cape Town route (see pp. 82–88) south through **Jagers-fontein** and **Philippolis**, past the **Gariep Dam** to **Bethulie** (305 km). From Bethulie, take the gravel road through the **Tussen-die-Riviere Nature Reserve** and Goedemoed (76 km) to join the N6 just north of Aliwal North. Alternatively, to remain on tarred roads, take the R701 from Bethulie to Smithfield and turn right on to the N6 to **Aliwal North** (139 km). Continue south on the N6 through Jamestown (63 km) to **Queenstown** (107 km), then take the N6 south through **Cathcart** (58 km) to Stutterheim (48 km). Turn right on to the R346, which leads through **Bisho** to **King William's Town** (24 km). From here, join the N2 for the last 59 km into East London.

TRAINS AND BUSES

The Amatola operates a daily train service from Bloemfontein to East London. Journey time: 12¾ hrs. OTT Table 3508. Translux run a bus service of this route, also calling at King William's Town (6½ hrs), daily except Thur. Journey time: 7 hrs 10 mins. OTT Table 3538.

GARIEP DAM

See Bloemfontein–Cape Town, p. 84.

ALIWAL NORTH

Tourist Office: *Old Tollhouse, Mitchell Rd, next to the Gariep River Bridge; tel: 0551-41791,* also at entrance to Spa, *De Wet Dr.; tel: 0551-2951.* Both branches open daily 0700–1700.

ACCOMMODATION AND FOOD

There are several small hotels in town, including the 2-star **Balmoral Hotel**, *Somerset St; tel: 0551-2453* (cheap) and the **Thatcher's Spa**, *Dan Pienaar Ave; tel: 0551-2772* (cheap), part of the spa complex. Just along the road, the **Umtali Motel**, *47 Dan Pienaar Ave; tel/fax: 0551-2400/7/8* (cheap) is a pleasant, rather old-fashioned country motel, with a pool, bar and restaurant. **Campsite**: there is a good caravan park at the spa (see below).

The best food in town is to be found at the **Pink Lady Steakhouse**, *Thatcher's Spa, Dan Pienaar Ave; tel: 0551-2861* (cheap–moderate), the **Balmoral Hotel**, or **Between Us Coffee Shop**, *Somerset St; tel: 0551-42458* (cheap).

SIGHTSEEING

Founded in 1849, on what was the Orange River and the border with the Afrikaner Orange Free State, Aliwal North was named after a famous battle in India three years earlier, when the British, commanded by Sir Harry Smith (by now Governor of the Cape, see p. 99) routed the Sikhs. It is a pleasant, flat, little town, with broad, shady roads and some fine old buildings. The chief point of interest is the large **Spa Complex**, *De Wet Dr.; tel: 0551-2951; fax: 0551-3008* (R10). Based on a series of hot sulphurous mineral springs (35°C), this has a huge array of amenities, including two indoor mineral swimming pools, three outdoor swimming pools (including a children's pool), tennis courts, children's playground, sauna, jacuzzi, sports facilities, from canoes to darts, an exercise centre and boats.

Elsewhere, the old Library is now home to the **Aliwal Museum**, *Smith St;* a charmingly ragtag collection of everything from old chemists' bottles to household crafts, Xhosa beadwork, 19th-century Afrikaner costume, local newspapers and a thriving medicinal and culinary herb garden. Allow time to rummage. Nearby, in an old church, the **Kerkplein Museum**, *Barkly St;* is another imaginative museum set up as a street scene, with homes, a photographic shop, a blacksmith's forge and many other possibilities, all lovingly furnished for accuracy. For information on both, *tel: 0551-2441* (open Mon–Sat 0900–1200 dependent on the availability of voluntary staff; free).

On the eastern edge of town, **Buffelspruit Nature Reserve**; *tel: 0551-2441/2951* (open daily 1000–1800 Oct–Apr, 1100–1730 May–Sept; R5 per vehicle) has a variety of game, including springbok, blesbok, ostrich, eland, black wildebeest, gemsbok and zebra.

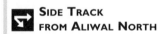

SIDE TRACK
FROM ALIWAL NORTH

Head east on the R58 for 54 km and you reach **Lady Grey**, a small town named after the wife of yet another governor, Sir George Grey. Tucked into a spectacular wooded valley between Witteberg Peak and Spioenkop, there are a number of pretty buildings. But the real reason to come here is to access the stunningly beautiful highlands, a mountainscape of grassland, scudding clouds and babbling brooks, perfect for riding and trout-fishing in summer and skiing in winter. There is a unique reverse railway line between Lady Grey and **Barkly East** (no services at present), with the train zigzagging up the mountain, while nearby **Rhodes** is gaining a reputation as an artists' colony. ⚑

QUEENSTOWN

Tourist Office: Stormberg Tourism: *Municipality Building, Owen St; tel: 0451-2265.* Open 0900–1300.

There are several hotels in Queenstown, but most are fairly uninspiring and you would do better at a local bed and breakfast, such as **Carthew's Corner**, *1 Park Ave, Blue Rise; tel: 0451-4112 (work)* or *81885 (home)* (cheap), or **Longview Lodge**, *9 Longview Crescent; tel: 0451-4143/ 4939* (cheap). Several others are in the surrounding area. **The Cottage**, *4 km north of town centre on the N6 to Jameson; tel: 0451-2435; fax: 0451-82514* (cheap) has self-catering cottages and backpackers' accommodation.

Founded in 1853 as a military outpost on the Xhosa frontier, and named after Queen Victoria, Queenstown has an extraordinary, defensive layout, its main streets all radiating from a central hexagon to allow covering fire in all directions. In fact, it was never attacked. The **Hexagon** is now a pleasant garden – its only military connection is the War Memorial. The town has a number of fine buildings, including the **Town Hall**, *Cathcart St* (1882); **Queens College**, a well-respected private school over a century old; and a particularly large stock of churches, of which the finest is the Anglican **Church of St Michael and All Angels**, *Robinson Rd* (1882).

Built originally as a school, the **Queens-town & Frontier Museum**, *Shepstone St; tel: 0451-5860* (open Mon–Fri 0800–1245, 1400–1600, weekends on request; free, donations welcome) has all sorts of exhibits, including a small natural history section, a collection of shells donated by its founder, a variety of household utensils and furniture, historic

telephones and medical equipment, and a reconstructed Frontiersman Cottage.

On the slopes of Madeira Mountain (1609m), on the north-west edge of town, the **Longhill Nature Reserve** and the **Lawrence de Lange Game Reserve** both have hiking trails, with a variety of small game and antelope and some spectacular local vegetation, including flowering aloes and cycads.

CATHCART

Tourist Office: *the Library, Main St; tel: 045-633 1022.* Open Mon, Wed, Fri 0930–1700, Tues 1400–1700, Thur 0930–1300, Sat 0830–1200.

The main hotel is the **Royal**, *Caernarvon St; tel: 045-633 1145* (cheap), which has been in business in various guises as long as the town. There are also several farm bed and breakfasts in the area; ask the Tourist Office for details. **Campsites: MOTH Caravan Park**, *Robinson Rd*, next to the golf course, pool and children's playground, and **Sam Meyer Park**, *Sam Meyer Dam, 1 km out of town on the East London road.*

Founded in 1856 as a military outpost after the 8th Frontier War against the Xhosa, Cathcart is not quite a one-street town, but it comes very close, and virtually all the buildings of note line the old *Main St*. Most imposing of all are the grand neo-classical **Library** (and Tourist Office), opened in 1885 as a Farmers' Store, and the art nouveau **Town Hall** (1905). The **CM Van Coller Museum**, *corner Cathcart and Main Sts; tel: 045-633 1737* (open Mon, Tues, Thur, Fri 1000–1200, Wed 1400–1600; free) is housed in the former library, a low stone building with a broad verandah and iron roof. Displays include an old shop and household items. The museum also has a craft shop and café (Fri).

BISHO

Tourist Office: Eastern Cape Tourism Board (Head Office): *Tourism House, Phalo Ave (PO Box 186) Bisho 5608; tel: 0401-952 115; fax: 0401-92756.*

The **Amatola Sun** *(SI), 3 Uppermount St, Bisho; tel: 0401-91111; fax: 0401-91330* (moderate–expensive) is a large international hotel with all the trimmings, from a pool and children's playground to a jogging track and thriving casino.

Bisho is extraordinary. It began life as one of many anonymous black townships, in this instance a satellite to King William's Town, only 7 km away. With the creation of the homelands, this area was divided, with the borders carefully avoiding any possible sign of white wealth. Bisho was suddenly thrust into the limelight as the capital of Ciskei. Even more astonishingly, with East London only 56 km away, it is now the capital of the Eastern Cape.

Most of the city is a broadening sprawl of poor grid housing, but the centre is taken up by a huge pink cement block, in which are housed all the relevant offices and shops. It is built around an echoing square, overlooked by a ring of dour stone leopards – said to smile only when a virgin enters the square! The only other building of note is the **casino** (see above).

KING WILLIAM'S TOWN

Tourist Office: *at the Library, Ayliff St; tel: 0433-23450* (open Mon–Fri 0830–1730, Sat 0830–1300).

ACCOMMODATION AND FOOD

The **Grosvenor Lodge**, *48 Taylor St; tel: 0433-21440, fax: 0433-24772*, is a comfortable 3-star family hotel (cheap–moderate). For a bed and breakfast with home comforts, try **Reflections Bed & Breakfast**, *8 Frere St; tel: 0433-21128; fax: 0433-21128* (cheap), a quiet 19th-century homestead with a large garden and pool, or **Webber's**, *21 New St; tel: 0824-934 616*. For other local bed and breakfasts, contact **East Cape Accommodation Network**; *tel: 0433-23369,* or the Tourist Office.

The best food in town is at **Sebastian's Restaurant**, *57 Market St; tel: 0433-21861* (moderate).

SIGHTSEEING

King William's Town, a settler town founded in 1835 by Sir Benjamin D'Urban, governor of the Cape, was an important military base during the Frontier Wars. It saw much military activity between 1850 and 1853 when it was the headquarters for no less than eight regiments. After 1861, many troopsmen settled in

Hubert the Hippo

In 1928, a hippo from St Lucia, in northern Natal, decided to go walkabout. Christened Hubert by an ever-more attentive press, it wandered along the coast for over three years, covering some 1000 km and gaining true celebrity status. Tragically, in 1931, it was shot by a farmer in the Eastern Cape – at which point they discovered that she was, in fact, Huberta. Stuffed for posterity, she is now in the Kaffrarian Museum, King William's Town, surrounded by her newspaper clippings.

the area, though it remained a British garrison headquarters until as late as 1914. One of the largest towns on this route, and probably the most attractive, King William's Town has several 19th-century churches and other interesting examples of colonial military architecture.

The **Kaffrarian Museum**, *3 Albert Rd, corner Alexandra Rd; tel: 0433-24506* (open Mon–Fri 0900–1245, 1400–1700; R1) is one of South Africa's best museums. It has an important natural history section containing what is thought to be the largest collection of African mammals in the world, with over 40,000 specimens. Pride of place goes to Hubert the Wandering Hippo (see above), stuffed and resplendent in a glass box. In a separate building next door, there are superb historic and contemporary displays on Xhosa culture. The **Missionary Museum**, *Berkeley St; tel: 0433-24506* (open Mon–Fri 0900–1300, 1345–1630; free), housed in a former church, explains the role of the missions in the development of South Africa.

Stephen Biko, the great nationalist leader who died in prison in 1977, is buried in the town. To find his grave, take *Cathcart St* towards Grahamstown; after the railway bridge, turn left under another bridge, then right to the cemetery. Park after the iron buildings, walk about 60m up the track; the grave is about 15m from the boundary fence.

EAST LONDON

See pp. 173–176.

BLOEMFONTEIN– HARRISMITH

There are two routes to choose when travelling between Bloemfontein and Harrismith. The more direct option takes you through the goldfields area to the north-east of the Free State capital. The landscape is relatively flat and dull, but there are several interesting towns en route. The other, more scenic route, heads due east to Ladybrand, then skirts the Lesotho border, becoming ever more beautiful as it moves into the Maluti Mountains and through the stunning Golden Gate Highlands National Park.

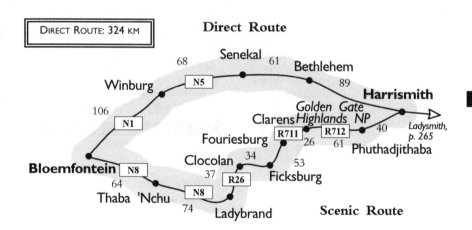

DIRECT ROUTE: 324 KM

Direct Route

68 Senekal 61 Bethlehem
Winburg N5 89
106 Harrismith
N1 Golden Gate
Clarens Highlands NP 40 Ladysmith, p. 265
Fouriesburg R711 R712
26 61 Phuthadjithaba
Clocolan 34 53
Bloemfontein N8 37 R26 Ficksburg
64
Thaba 'Nchu N8
74 Ladybrand **Scenic Route**

ROUTES

DIRECT ROUTE

From Bloemfontein, take the N1 north to **Winburg** (106 km). From Winburg, continue east on the N5 to **Senekal** (68 km), then **Bethlehem** (61 km) and Harrismith (89 km). Distance: 324 km; allow 4½ hrs, plus sightseeing time.

SCENIC ROUTE

Leave Bloemfontein, past the airport, on the N8 east to **Ladybrand** (138 km),

passing the casino city of **Thaba 'Nchu** along the way. From Ladybrand, take the R26 heading north-east, along the Lesotho border, through the small towns of **Clocolan** (37 km) and **Ficksburg** (34 km) to **Fouriesburg** (53 km). Turn off to the right here on to the R711 to **Clarens** (26 km), then turn right again on to the R712 along a spectacular route through the **Golden Gate Highlands National Park** to **Phuthadjithaba** (61 km). Continue along the R712 past the Sterkfontein Dam until it joins the N5. Turn right for the last few kilometres into **Harrismith** (about 40 km). From here, it is a short distance down the N3 to Ladysmith (see p. 265). Distance: 389 km; allow 1–2 days.

BUSES

Translux operate a daily service from Durban to Bloemfontein, which calls at Harrismith. Journey time: 5 hrs. OTT Table 3543.

WINBURG

Tourist Information: *Public Library, Town Sq., tel: 052-42361.* Open Mon–Fri 0800–1600.

Winburg was the first capital of the former Republic of the Orange Free State, founded in 1842. The name means 'victory town'; some say that this was the winner of a bitter squabble over which site to choose, others that it commemorates the Boer victory over the Ndebele King Mzilikazi in 1837. Today, it is a quiet little market town whose **Town Hall**, *The Square*, has African scenes painted on its interior walls. About 2.5 km south-west of the town, on the N1, stands the distinctive **Voortrekker Memorial**, a tribute to the five groups of Voortrekkers (led by Louis Trichardt, Hendrik Potgieter, Gert Maritz, Piet Retief and Pieter Uys), who got together to form their first government. In the grounds, the family home of former South African President J. M. Steyn is now a **Voortrekker Museum**, *on the N1*, portraying the daily routine of the Trekkers. One kilometre west of the town is a large **cemetery**, where early Voortrekkers are buried side by side with victims of the Anglo-Boer War concentration camp.

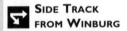

SIDE TRACK
FROM WINBURG

WILLEM PRETORIUS GAME RESERVE

PARK INFORMATION AND FACILITIES

Twenty kilometres north of Winburg on the Allemankraal Dam (well-signposted from the N1); *tel: 057-774 003.* Open 0700–1830, entrance gate open 0700–2230; licensed restaurant open Mon–Fri 0730–1600, Sat, Sun 0800–1600 (à la carte and takeaway). Admission (subject to change) R12 for car with up to 10 people, R12 for up to 10 additional passengers. No entrance charge for people staying in the chalets, or groups attending educational courses. Accommodation is available in four and five bed chalets (cheap). **Camping**: stands with power points available for caravans and tents.

SIGHTSEEING

Two distinct habitats, divided by the Sand River and the dam, attract different wildlife in the reserve. The hilly terrain with thick vegetation in the north harbours baboon, kudu, duiker, mountain reedbuck, bushbuck and hartebeest. The grassy plains to the south are home to zebra, springbok, eland and one of the world's largest herds of the rarer black wildebeest. Rhino and buffalo feed throughout the reserve. Within the reserve are also the well-preserved ruins of a stone-built Iron Age village, a small archaeological museum and a fully-equipped education and conference centre, where groups can attend environmental education programmes.

SENEKAL

Tourist Office: *tel: 014-331 2142.* Open Mon–Fri 0830–1300, 1400–1600.

ACCOMMODATION

Arizona Game Lodge, *15 km from Senekal on R707 off N5; tel/fax: 05848-2547* (moderate) is made up of wooden chalets or thatched cottages, each sleeping three. There are also caravan stands, a restaurant and bar, and the dam can be used for water skiing and fishing. **Camping**: the central **Municipal Caravan Park**, *Boer St; tel: 05848-2142*, has a pool and playground.

SIGHTSEEING

Senekal is a pleasant little town whose chief claim to fame is the wall (1929) surrounding the Dutch Reformed Church (1896) which, quite extraordinarily, is largely made up of petrified tree trunks found in the nearby Sand River Valley. Most are of coniferous trees, said to be at least a quarter of a million years old.

94

BETHLEHEM

Tourist Office: *Civic Centre, Muller St; tel: 01431-35732, after hours 31795.* Open Mon–Fri 0830–1630.

ACCOMMODATION

The fully-licensed 2-star **Park Hotel**, *23 Muller St; tel/fax: 058-303 5191* (moderate) has family rooms with bathrooms, air-conditioned de luxe rooms and luxury rooms in the Park Court block. For cosier alternatives, both **Franci's B&B** *(Pf), 38 Oxford St (off Church St); tel: 058-303 3550* (cheap) and the **Hoogland Guesthouse** *(Pf), 47 De Leeuw St; tel/fax: 058-303 3633* (cheap) are comfortable, welcoming homes with pleasant gardens. On the southern outskirts of town, the R26, the **Loch Athlone Resort**, *Commissioner St; tel/fax: 058-303 4981* (cheap) has self-catering chalets and 200 caravan and camping sites in a wooded setting beside the Loch Athlone Dam on the Jordan River. Its restaurant is in a replica ship, the *Athlone Castle*.

SIGHTSEEING

Set in a grain-producing region, against a backdrop of the Maluti Mountains, Bethlehem is an important commercial and industrial centre with a wealth of historic sandstone buildings. Devout Voortrekkers, arriving in the area on their way to Natal, named the river Jordan and the town that developed along its banks Bethlehem.

The town has good shopping, a variety of restaurants and musical, theatrical and operatic entertainment. An art market is held on the last Saturday of the month. Artefacts relating to the area's history are displayed at the former **Nazareth Missionary Church**, *Muller St.*

There are several good hiking trails in the vicinity, passing contented cattle and sheep grazing happily in a rocky countryside of glorious colours and contours.

Annual events include an agricultural show in March, an international hot-air balloon championship in May and a Wheat Festival in November.

THABA 'NCHU

Tourist Information: *tel: 051871-26.*

Built in traditional African style, the 116-room **Thaba 'Nchu Sun Casino and Holiday Resort** *(SI), within the Maria Moroka National Park; tel: 05265-2161, fax: 05265-2521* (moderate–expensive) overlooks the dam at the foot of the Thaba 'Nchu (the 'black mountain'). It has a spa, gym, pool, sauna, tennis courts and a children's games room. Entertainment includes a casino, movies, cabaret and dancing in Diamond Lil's Action Bar. The 30-room **Naledi Sun**, *tel: 05265-2100; fax: 05265-3757* (moderate), on the outskirts of town has a disco, 100 slot machines and a beer garden where local musicians perform.

The scattered homeland of Bophuthatswana stretched right into the Free State, and as with so many of the former homelands, the accommodation is the tourist attraction. The town itself is not too attractive, but mountain walking and wildlife-watching by day are followed by a sizzling nightlife, with casino games, cabarets and discos.

The **Maria Moroka National Park**, about 10 km south of town; *tel: 05265-2161,* is a delightful stretch of classic hill country, with a wide variety of less aggressive animals, such as eland, red hartebeest and other antelope, and a good selection of birds, including the rare blue korhaan. Guided game-viewing drives and hikes can be arranged on demand, and there are several mountain biking trails. The local women knit particularly fine Aran-style jumpers.

LADYBRAND

Tourism Information: *The Library, Main St; tel: 05191-40305.* Open Mon–Fri 0830–1630.

ACCOMMODATION

Set in park-like grounds, **The Railway Station** *(Pf), 37 Beeton St; tel: 05191-2290, fax: 05191-41168* (cheap) really is the former office and waiting room of the station building, cheerfully decorated with railway memorabilia. The same management also run **Cranberry Cottage Guesthouse** (cheap) next door, in a charming Victorian townhouse.

My Housy *(Pf), 17a Prinsloo St; tel/fax: 05191-41010* (cheap) is also delightful, but very different, owned by artists and flamboyantly decorated with their own work.

95

SIGHTSEEING

Only a few kilometres from the Lesotho border, Ladybrand is an attractive old town (1867), with several cherished sandstone buildings including the **Town Hall, Old Magistrates' Court** and **St Michael's Church**, grouped around the centre.

The **Catherina Brand Museum**, (open Tues–Sat 0900–1600; free) has examples of rock art, implements dating from the Stone Age and a replica of a discovery in a local quarry – a unique fossil, *Diathrognatus protozoon*, providing an evolutionary link between reptiles and mammals.

At **Modderpoort**, 11 km north of town, is a charmingly unusual **cave church**, founded by the Anglican Society of St Augustine in 1869. The cave also has a rich collection of **San paintings**.

CLOCOLAN

Tourist Information: *tel: 051993-224.*

With views of the Maluti Mountains, snow-capped in winter and orchards of cherry blossom in spring, this is a relaxing little town, tucked under Hlohlolane (the 'ridge of the battle' in Sotho), from which its name derives. **Camping**: **Municipal Caravan Park**, *about 1 km from the centre, tel: 051-943 0516*, on the banks of the Sleunmekaar Dam.

FICKSBURG

Tourist Office: *Highland Tourism Association, Old Post Office, Market St; tel: 05192-5547.* Open Mon–Fri 0830–1545.

ACCOMMODATION

Hotel Hoogland, *Market Sq., Voortrekker St; tel: 05192-2214, fax: 05192-2750* (cheap–moderate). The **Bella Rosa Guesthouse** *(Pf), 21 Bloem St; tel/fax: 05192-2623* (cheap), is a converted Victorian townhouse, which also serves excellent à la carte dinners. **Camping**: **Thom Park**, *corner McCabe and Bloem Sts; tel: 05192-2212*, is a well-appointed, shady camping and caravan site.

Out of town, the **Franshoek Mountain Lodge and Polo School**, *off the R26 north of Ficksburg; tel/fax: 05192-3938* (cheap) is well worth a bumpy dirt road drive (the lodge is

signposted) to stay amid spectacular mountain scenery and see polo ponies outside your window at daybreak. Activities on offer include trout fishing, rock climbing, locating dinosaur footprints, hiking, swimming, game drives and polo lessons.

Nearby, the **Nebo Holiday Farm**, *junction of S384 and S385, off R26; tel/fax: 05192-3947* (cheap) has a variety of self-catering chalets, a good restaurant and a pool, on a pretty sheep and cherry estate.

SIGHTSEEING

This industrial, commercial and agricultural centre bordering with Lesotho has retained its old-world charm, with some of its more important buildings, as well as private homes, created from locally quarried sandstone. These include the **Town Hall** (1897), the **Post Office**, and the **General Fick Memorial** commemorating the Boer hero of the Basotho Wars, after whom the town was named (1867). The history and culture of Ficksburg and the South Sotho people can be traced at the **General J. I. J. Fick Museum**, *Town Sq.;* free. During school hours, a collection of works by South African artists can be seen at the **S. H. Pelisier Art Gallery** at Ficksburg High School.

Asparagus is a major product of Ficksburg – growing and canning it – but what really puts the town on the map is its cherries. Massed blossom attracts busloads of visitors in spring and, in November, the annual **Cherry Festival** paints the town red as crowds celebrate the production of 90% of South Africa's crop. The **Cherry Trail** brochure includes several local orchards, farms and craft shops in the area. The 23 km **Imperani Hiking Trail** follows a circular route from the Meulspruit Dam over the Imperani Mountains, with several sandstone caves, some with San rock paintings, en route. Several farms in the area also have examples of rock art, which can be visited with farmers' permission (ask at the Tourist Office). Reaching these ancient works may sometimes involve a strenuous climb.

Rustlers Valley is about 15 km north of Ficksburg, on the R26, in the Witteberge Mountains. With one of South Africa's few outdoor pop festivals every Easter, and a two-week 'youth fest' at Christmas, this has become one of the rather extraordinary centres of hippy life South African style, although there is local concern about security at the site.

FOURIESBURG

Tourist Information: *PO Box 114, Fouriesburg 9725; tel: 058-223 0207.*

ACCOMMODATION

The 2-star **Fouriesburg Hotel**, *17 Reitz St; tel 058-223 0207, fax: 058-223 0257* (cheap–moderate) is small but comfortable and friendly, with a plain but pleasant dining room. **Camping: Meiringspoort Caravan Park**, *3 km from town; tel: 058-223 0067*, has chalets, caravan sites and space for tents, a pool and café.

SIGHTSEEING

Surrounded by flat-topped sandstone hills, Fouriesburg was the last stronghold of the Boer government during the Anglo-Boer War, and was almost entirely demolished for its pains. The results are a fairly unattractive modern town, with a few attractive old sandstone buildings, set amidst great hiking country. The **Meiringspoort Nature Park**, *2 km out of town*, is the start of the 60-km five-day **Brandwater Trail**, which takes in valleys, ravines, mountain views, rock art and caves – three of which are used as overnight shelters.

CLARENS

Tourist Information: *tel: 058-256 1411.* Leaflets of interest to tourists can be picked up in **This 'n That** convenience store.

ACCOMMODATION

In town, try the **Maluti Mountain Lodge**, *Steil St; tel: 058-256 1422* (cheap), which is a friendly hotel with comfortable chalet rooms, a pool, pub and good menu. The **Guinea Feather**, *tel: 058-256 1088*, also serves excellent meals. **Bokpoort Farm**, *8 km east of Clarens (towards the Golden Gate); tel/fax: 058-256 1181* (cheap) is a friendly backpackers' hostel, which also provides camping facilities.

SIGHTSEEING

This village with its bright gardens and shady nooks has a charmingly unplanned look, which appeals to artists and photographers and anyone who likes to just happen across craft and antique shops, art studios, galleries and tempting little restaurants. Founded in 1912, it was named after the Swiss village where President Kruger died in exile in 1904. Its most surprising tourist 'attraction' is **Cinderella's Castle**, *Naaupoort St,* built from about 55,000 beer bottles. Inside are various fairytale scenes, and a souvenir shop.

GOLDEN GATE HIGHLANDS NATIONAL PARK

PARKS INFORMATION AND FACILITIES

Park Information: *tel: 058-256 1471.* There is no entrance barrier so fees should be paid at the camp reception desks, which also handle all enquiries and bookings for the hiking trail and horses. The park is open daily 0600–2100. No charge for driving through the park. Visitors are asked to remain in their cars except at the viewpoints or on designated walking trails. Pets are not allowed in the park. Book accommodation as far ahead as possible through the **National Parks Board**, *PO Box 787, Pretoria 0001; tel: 012-343 1991; fax: 012-343 0905.*

Brandwag Rest Camp (cheap–moderate) is more of a comfortable lodge with well-equipped rooms, self-catering chalets, restaurant, bar, coffee shop, laundromat and facilities for tennis, bowls, table tennis and snooker. **Glen Reenen Rest Camp** (cheap) is less lavish, with self-catering accommodation in huts or rondavels, but also has a campsite, shop, filling station and natural swimming pool.

SIGHTSEEING

Nearly 12,000 hectares of unique scenery in the Maluti foothills make this park a fascinating place to explore on foot, by car, or on horseback. Curious rock formations, outcrops and sandstone cliffs in oranges and yellows, sculpted by wind and rain, are especially dramatic in the early morning and towards sunset, when the light tinges them deep gold.

Summer rain coaxes wildflowers into bloom. A good pair of binoculars can reveal a number of antelope species, black wildebeest, Burchell's zebra and other animals, and 140 bird

97

species, including the rare blue crane, black eagles and jackal buzzards.

The 26 km **Rhebok Hiking Trail** is a two-day circular hike. Book well in advance to overnight in a hut, and bring all essentials. Shorter nature trails from 1–5 hours need no reservations.

QUA QUA

Tourist Information: *Highland Development Office, Private Bag X826, Phuthaditjhaba; tel: 058-712 4444.*

ACCOMMODATION

Fika Patso Mountain Resort, *near Fika Patso Dam, 25 km south of Phuthaditjhaba; tel/fax: 058-789 1733/4* (cheap) is a delightful rural retreat, with 20 self-catering chalets, spectacular mountain views, a shop and restaurant.

SIGHTSEEING

Yet another tiny homeland, this time belonging to the Bakwena and Balokwa tribes, both part of the South Sotho language group, most of Qua Qua is a sprawl of houses, as villages have crawled across every available hill around the capital **Phuthaditjhaba** (formerly called Witsieshoek). The remainder of the area is now designated as the 21,000 hectare **Qua Qua National Park**; *tel: 058-713 4191.*

Within the park, the **Basotho Cultural Village**; *tel: 058-721 0300* (open Mon–Fri 0900–1600; Sat-Sun 0900–1700; R15) offers an entertaining glimpse of how the South Sotho people lived from the 16th century onwards. With a guide, you will meet the King, his messenger, his bodyguard, one of his wives, the village healer (or actors portraying them), and other characters grinding maize, rolling out mealie dough and playing the accordion – an import from Europe.

Huts are built and furnished according to the period each depicts, containing garments, cooking pots and animal skin 'beds'. The village's circular reception area displays paintings and crafts by talented local people and there is also a curio shop.

A two-hour herbal trail, accompanied by an ecologist and a traditional healer, can be followed by visitors interested in learning about grasses, roots, herbs, leaves and barks used for treating ailments. Four-hour guided pony rides in Qua Qua National Park, with refreshments at a Basotho family's home, can be booked at the Cultural Village.

There are also three excellent hiking trails, one of which, the **Sentinel Trail**, leads over the top of the Drakensberg to the Royal Natal National Park.

HARRISMITH

Tourist Office: *back of the Town Hall, Andries Pretorius St; tel: 05861-23525.*

ACCOMMODATION

There is little inspirational in town, although you could try the **Harrismith Inn**; *tel: 05861-21011*, or the **Sir Harry Motel**; *tel: 05861-22151*, both on *McKechnie St* (both cheap). Chains: Hd. **Camping**: **President Brand Caravan Park**, *Cloete St, 2 km from town on the Wilge River; tel: 05861-21061.*

Out of town, the **Rooikraal Inn** *(Pf), on the N3, 14 km north of Harrismith; tel: 05861-31527; fax: 05861-31661* (cheap), is a charming old sandstone farmhouse, decorated with antiques. **Mount Everest Game Reserve** *(Ce; see below); tel: 05861-21816, fax: 05861-23493*, has attractive self-catering chalets, log cabins, rondavels, permanent tents and two caravan parks (cheap).

SIGHTSEEING

This busy Eastern Highlands town, with a population approaching 90,000, is one of the oldest in the Free State, having been founded by and named after Cape Governor, Sir Harry Smith, in 1849. It is a gateway to the Maluti Mountains, the Natal Drakensberg and the Golden Gate National Park.

The town enchants visitors with its gardens (open daily sunrise to sunset), in particular the **Platberg Wildflower Gardens** in the Botanic Gardens, where one-fifth of all the flora of the Drakensberg can be seen. It is close to the **Platberg Nature Reserve** on the town's north-eastern outskirts. Trout fishing, hiking and mountain biking are enjoyed in this scenic wilderness area. It is closed on weekdays in winter, when hunting takes place.

Larger Than Life

Sir Harry Smith was one of those larger-than-life characters, blessed with tremendous physical energy, clear-sightedness and the nerve to make instant decisions and act on them.

A born leader and military strategist, he began his military career serving under the Duke of Wellington during the Napoleonic Wars. One day, while with the British Army in Spain, Smith, then a young captain, was confronted by a young married woman and her 14-year-old sister, seeking protection from the violence. Smith arranged for them to be taken to a place of safety, and within two years married the younger girl. Her name was Juana Maria de los Dolores de Leon, and she became a popular figure in English society.

Harry continued in the military, rising in rank and notching up mentions in despatches and commendations during campaigns in India, Europe and elsewhere. He was awarded a knighthood in 1842 after taking part as adjutant-general at the Battle of Maharajpur in India. He distinguished himself as a major-general in the East Indies in 1846, and the following year was created a baronet for his services in the Sikh War. The Duke of Wellington extolled Smith in the House of Lords after one of his military exploits. Six years later, in 1852, Smith was a pall bearer at the Duke's funeral in St Paul's Cathedral.

In 1847, Smith was appointed governor of the Cape of Good Hope and its dependencies, where he stirred up an instant hornets' nest by reaching an agreement with tribal chiefs to release their captives, massively extending the Cape Colony, and declaring himself, as Queen's representative, chief of the blacks.

The Boers in Natal, who were planning a mass exodus because of the British government's support of the natives, also received a visit from Sir Harry, who persuaded them to change their minds. But the Boer leader, Pretorius, took exception to a proclamation by Sir Harry extending British sovereignty between the Vaal and Orange Rivers, and expelled the British representative in Bloemfontein. Outraged, Smith assembled troops and went into the attack. The outcome, after two months of battling, was that the representative was reinstated.

Sir Harry was honoured by having a town, which originated as a military outpost, named after him. Ladysmith, where British and Boer troops fought during the famous siege, was named after his wife, as was Ladismith, in the Western Cape.

The couple had no children. Sir Harry died in 1860, Lady Smith in 1872. They are buried in England, near Smith's family home at Whittlesey, Cambridgeshire.

99

Harrismith was an important British base during the Anglo–Boer War (1899–1902). In the Botanic Gardens is a blockhouse erected by British troops to protect the town's water supply during the war.

The imposing sandstone **Town Hall**, built in 1907, is a National Monument. Near it is a fossilised tree, claimed to be 150 million or 250 million years old, depending on your source of information. Either way it is ancient.

During the Anglo–Boer War, a British soldier, Major John Belcher, scoffed at the height of the **Platberg** (2377 m) and was challenged to scale it in under an hour. He took them on, won, and donated a trophy for the **Berg Marathon**, one of South Africa's toughest cross-country races, still run every November as competitors pound up the mountain, along the summit and down the other side.

Mount Everest Game Reserve, *21 km north-east of Harrismith; tel: 05861-21816* (open daily 0600; R10 per person, R10 per car) is a private game reserve, with over 22 species of animal. Visitors to the 1000 hectare reserve's mountains, valleys and plains can hike and climb without restriction, but should keep a wary eye open for potential aggressors like ostrich and rhino. Horses and 4x4 vehicles can be hired, and fishing and swimming are available.

CAPE TOWN

Cape Town straddles the neck of the Cape Peninsula. Behind it, Table Mountain heads a chain of peaks which curve south, dip, rise, and fall away to Cape Point. To the west, the shore is battered by the full force of the Atlantic Ocean. Facing the city to the south-east is the wide, welcoming curve of Table Bay. Within its arms rests Robben Island.

This is the 'Mother City', the first city of the Old South Africa. It exported its culture throughout the country; it presided over the landing on these shores of slavery, racism, capitalism and colonialism. Port, parliament's seat, cultural HQ, city of rich suburbs and poor townships, it was also Nelson Mandela's prison for 27 years. In Cape Town, Dr Hendrik Verwoerd, the architect of apartheid, was assassinated, and here, on his release in 1990, Mandela proclaimed freedom for the blacks. Nowadays it is known for its sleepy charm and an incomparable landscape.

TOURIST INFORMATION

Tourist Office: *3 Adderley St; tel: 021-418 5214* (open Mon–Fri 0800–1800, Sat 0830–1500, Sun 0900–1300), provide assistance with accommodation and travel advice, as well as information on cultural activities, guide and car hire, tours and so on – ask for brochures on the various tourist 'routes' (wine, spring flowers, arts and crafts, antiques, fynbos, whales and bird-watching). **Branch:** *Shop 007, Tygerberg Valley Centre, Bellville; tel: 021-914 1786* (open Mon–Fri 0900–1730, Sat 0900–1330).

Western Cape Tourism Board (formerly Satour): *3 Adderley St; tel: 021-216 274* (open Mon–Thur 0800–1630, Fri 0800–1600) has information on other areas of the Western Cape and South Africa.

ARRIVING AND DEPARTING

By Air

Cape Town International Airport is 22 km from the city centre (on the N2). For information and arrival and departure updates: *tel: 021-934 0407* (open 0600–2200 daily). There are numerous scheduled flights to and from international destinations, including London, neighbouring countries, all major South African cities and various smaller places, such as towns on the Garden Route. The drive to the airport takes around 25 mins; allow more time during rush hour (0700–0830 citybound, 1630–1730 outwards). An **airport bus** links with Cape Town Station, adjacent to the tourist office, where there are taxis for hire and trains to the suburbs. The best option is to take a **taxi** from the airport (around R90 one way). Consider sharing; drivers generally do not object.

Airport Shuttle Services, *tel: 021-794 2772* (reservations); *021-794 4995* (information) run a 24-hour, 365 days a year, door-to-door airport transfer service. Pre-booking is essential (minimum 2 hrs before departure/arrival; for flights departing before 1000, no later than 1600 the previous day). The company also runs a minibus service to and from Cape Town Station (meet at the Intercape office) 1 hr–30 mins before flights (R60 per person, R70 for 2, R80 for 3). The timetable begins at 0515 and continues until the last flight of the day. Private cars with phones also available. **Welcome Shuttle**, *tel: 021-262 134*, operates a similar service between major hotels and the airport. Various chauffeured car services link the city centre and airport. **Nono's Chauffeur Service**, *tel: 081 211 1566*, provides luxury cars with phones, while **Rendezvous Cape**, *tel: 021-683 2503*,

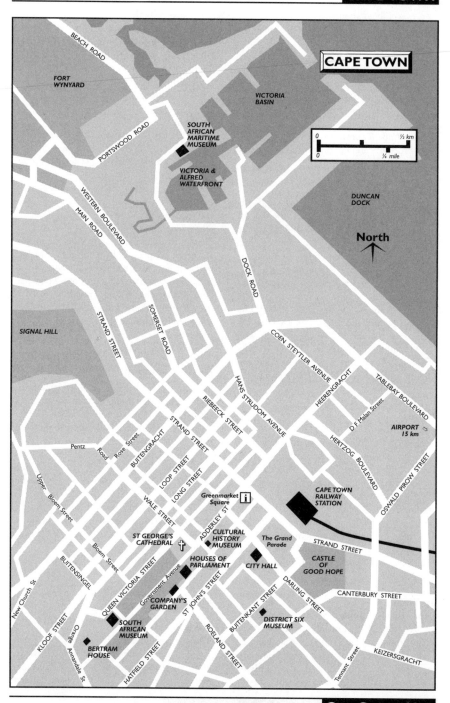

CAPE TOWN

VICTORIA
BASIN

FORT
WYNYARD

BEACH ROAD

PORTSWOOD ROAD

SOUTH
AFRICAN
MARITIME
MUSEUM

VICTORIA &
ALFRED
WATERFRONT

0   ½ km
0   ¼ mile

DUNCAN
DOCK

WESTERN BOULEVARD

MAIN ROAD

DOCK ROAD

North

SIGNAL HILL

STRAND STREET

SOMERSET ROAD

COEN STEYTLER AVENUE

HEERENGRACHT

TABLEBAY BOULEVARD

HANS STRUDOM AVENUE

D F Malan Street

RIEBEECK STREET

HERTZOG BOULEVARD

AIRPORT
15 km

OSWALD PIROW STREET

Pentz   Road   Rose Street

BUITENGRACHT

STRAND STREET

LOOP STREET

LONG STREET

Upper Bloem Street

WALE STREET

Greenmarket
Square

ADDERLEY ST

CAPE TOWN
RAILWAY
STATION

Bloem Street

ST GEORGE'S
CATHEDRAL

CULTURAL
HISTORY
MUSEUM

The Grand
Parade

STRAND STREET

BUITENSINGEL

HOUSES OF
PARLIAMENT

CITY HALL

CASTLE
OF
GOOD HOPE

New Church St.

QUEEN VICTORIA STREET

Government Avenue

COMPANY'S
GARDEN

ST JOHN'S STREET

BUITENKANT STREET

DARLING STREET

CANTERBURY STREET

KLOOF STREET

Orange

SOUTH
AFRICAN
MUSEUM

DISTRICT SIX
MUSEUM

Annandale St.

BERTRAM
HOUSE

HATFIELD STREET

ROELAND STREET

Tennant Street

KEIZERSGRACHT

101

supplies Mercedes-Benz cars with drivers to and from the airport.

The airport departure lounges are fully equipped with places for refreshments, newsagent, public telephones and car hire agencies, including **Avis**: *tel: 021-934 0808;* **Budget**: *tel: 021-934 0216;* and **Imperial**: *tel: 021-934 0213.* For city centre car hire, see p. 51. Western Cape Tourism Board's kiosk supplies maps, brochures and information about accommodation, tours and so on.

By Car

Cape Town is linked to the provinces and outlying areas by three main arteries: the N1 (to Johannesburg); N2 (to Durban); and N7 (to the north-west and Namibia). The Cape Peninsula is well served from the city centre by a magnificent coastal 'corniche' (principally the M6, M65 and M4), and is straddled by a series of connecting roads linking suburbs on the Atlantic Seaboard with False Bay. The Southern Suburbs are reached on *De Waal Dr.* (M3), or on *Eastern Blvd* which connects with the M3 at Hospital Corner, below Rhodes Memorial. Avoid travelling to the Southern Suburbs at rush hour 1630–1730, and into the city at 0700–0830.

By Bus

Bus Station: *Cape Town Railway Station, Adderley St*; for information, contact bus companies listed below. Enter the station beside the Tourist Office and pass through; buses park in the courtyard behind. Intercity buses operate an efficient, fast service between Cape Town and Johannesburg, Bloemfontein, Port Elizabeth, Durban, Windhoek and many towns en route. The three main buslines are **Greyhound**, *tel: 021-418 4310,* **Intercape Mainliner**, *tel: 021-934 4400,* and **Transcity and Translux**, *tel: 021-405 3333.*

By Train

Cape Town Railway Station: *Adderley St; tel: 021-405 2991.* Intercity trains run from Johannesburg and Durban to Cape Town. A far from comprehensive network of trains links the city with its suburbs and the outlying townships. Timetables are available at the station. **Mainline reservations**; *tel: 021-405 3871;* **price information**; *tel: 021-405 2847;* **Blue Train reservations**; *tel: 021-405 2672.* **The Union Limited**, *tel: 021-405 4391,* offer authentic steam rail tours from Cape Town on a variety of scenic routes (see pp. 53 and 55).

By Boat

Port: *Duncan Rd;* information: *tel: 021-405 3175;* for shipping enquiries: *tel: 021-405 2805* (also for berthing addresses and access). For the harbour entrance, take the V&A Waterfront access route from the seaward end of *Buitengracht St,* branch right at the roundabout and follow signs to the Port/Harbour. For passenger disembarkation, enter at J Main Gate, *Duncan Rd* (parking inside). Visitors can now also arrive dramatically by ocean liner, and dock in the shadow of Table Mountain. Many major cruise liners are now calling at Cape Town harbour: **P&O, c/o World Travel**; *tel: 021-252 470;* **Royal Viking Line**; *tel: 011-339 4865;* and **Orient Line, c/o American Express** (ship, the *Marco Polo); tel: 021-215 586.* Cruises sail once every 1–2 years.

GETTING AROUND

The city centre is based on a straightforward grid system – easy to follow with the mountain at one end and the ocean at the other. There is plenty of undercover and external **parking**, with multi-storey car parks at the V&A Waterfront (open 24 hrs; from R2.50 per hour; only useful for visits there), at the Gardens Centre, *Mill St* (open 0800–0100; free) and at the Parkade, *Strand St* (open 0600–1800; from R4.50 per hr). Once parked, the historic city centre is remarkably small and most sights are easily accessible on foot. It is not safe to walk around at night.

The best **maps** are available from book stores (see shopping) or the tourist office. The AA shop (see Country by Country, p. 38) also has a range of country and city maps.

Taxis

Taxis (non-minibus) are metered, but before you get in, make sure the driver knows where he is going and agree the price, or make sure that the meter works. Taxi touts hang about at

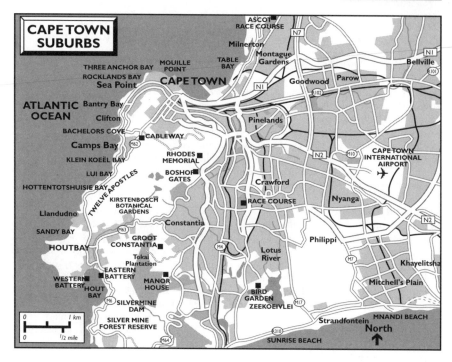

CAPE TOWN SUBURBS

ASCOT RACE COURSE
Milnerton
Montague Gardens
TABLE BAY
THREE ANCHOR BAY
MOUILLE POINT
ROCKLANDS BAY
Sea Point
CAPE TOWN
Goodwood Parow
Bellville
N7
N1
N1
N1
N1
R101
R102

ATLANTIC OCEAN
Bantry Bay
Clifton
BACHELORS COVE
CABLEWAY
Camps Bay
KLEIN KOEËL BAY
LUI BAY
HOTTENTOTSHUISIE BAY
Pinelands
RHODES MEMORIAL
BOSHOF GATES
KIRSTENBOSCH BOTANICAL GARDENS
Crawford
RACE COURSE
CAPE TOWN INTERNATIONAL AIRPORT
Nyanga
M62
M2
M10
N2
N2

Llandudno
Constantia
SANDY BAY
HOUTBAY
GROOT CONSTANTIA
Tokai Plantation
EASTERN BATTERY
WESTERN BATTERY
HOUT BAY
MANOR HOUSE
SILVERMINE DAM
SILVER MINE FOREST RESERVE
Philippi
Lotus River
BIRD GARDEN
ZEEKOEIVLEI
Strandfontein
SUNRISE BEACH
Khayelitsha
Mitchell's Plain
MNANDI BEACH
North
M63
M4
M7
M17
M6
M64
R310

TWELVE APOSTLES

0   1 km
0   ¹/₂ mile

103

ranks, in the railway station and in busy shopping centres – avoid them. Only take a recognised minibus or metered taxi; anything else opens you to a barrage of unpleasant possibilities, from being ripped off to having your luggage stolen. Most sights, shops and restaurants are happy to call you a cab; and there are ranks at the Gardens end of *Adderley St*, in *Greenmarket Sq.* and outside the main entrance to the *V&A Waterfront*. **Marine Taxi Hire**, tel: *021-424 0434*; **Unicab Radio Taxis**, tel: *021-448 1720*, **Sea Point Taxis**, tel: *021-434 4444*. Alternatively, take a **Rikki**, a small open vehicle, which offers a door-to-door service. Catch them outside the **Golden Acre Centre** in *Adderley St*, on main roads in the city centre, and on *Kloof Nek Rd* or *Kloof St*. Prices begin at around R1 a ride. Otherwise, tel: *021-234 888, 021-234 892* or *021-214 871*.

Minibus taxis prolifically, and dangerously, occupy the streets of the city. They are a quick, cheap way of getting about, but accidents are common. They are usually overcrowded and militant towards other road users. Major

pick-up points are the roof of the Cape Town Railway Station, and main stops on *Adderley St* (outside the Golden Acre shopping centre), on the *Grand Parade*, in *Strand St,* and anywhere along the main roads in Sea Point or Green Point. They announce themselves with vigorous hooting.

Buses

The city, suburban and peninsula bus service is slow and unreliable. The main terminals are outside the Golden Acre shopping centre, halfway down *Adderley St*, and the *Grand Parade*. **Golden Arrow Buses**; tel: *021-786 1377,* go from *Adderley St* to Sea Point, Camps Bay and the Kloof Nek area. From the *Grand Parade,* they generally head for the Southern Suburbs, and even go as far as Simon's Town. A **Waterfront Bus** service connects the tourist office in *Adderley St* and Sea Point (Peninsula Hotel in *Beach Rd* and *Sea Point Main Rd),* with Victoria Wharf shopping centre at the *Victoria & Alfred Waterfront*. The service operates at 10–15 min intervals.

Trains

A suburban railway line, with a regular train service on two main routes, connects the city centre with the Bellville, Stellenbosch and Strand areas, and with Simon's Town on the False Bay coast, stopping at Southern Suburb stations, Muizenberg, St James, Kalk Bay and Fish Hoek. The coastal run is lovely. There are no trains to the city's Atlantic Seaboard. It is generally safe during the day, but be vigilant and move into a crowded carriage if you feel threatened. Buy tickets at stations, and begin the journey from Cape Town Station.

Organised Tours

For tours of the Cape Peninsula, the winelands and other areas, you must either hire a car or join an organised coach or minibus tour, which can be arranged for you by the Tourist Information Centre or your hotel. Highly recommended are **Mother City Tours**, *tel: 021-418 2580*. Other established tour operators include **Hylton Ross**, *tel: 021-51 1178* and **Springbok Atlas Tours**, *tel: 021-25 1271*. **Green Cape Tours**, *tel: 021-797 0166*, specialises in the birdlife, flora and geology of the Western Cape. **One City Tours**, *tel: 021-387 5351*, introduces South African politics, history and sociology, with a fascinating 3–4 hr tour of the squatter camps and the townships, focusing on history, culture, art, food and drink, music and dance, religion, politics and language. **Jochen Beckert Tours**, *tel: 021-22 1849*, offers tailor-made golfing tours. For helicopter trips over the peninsula, **Court**, *East Pier, Waterfront; tel: 021-252 966* (open 0800–1800), offers a 10-min overview of mountain and city (R400 for 4 people; around R3000 for 1 hr trips to Cape Point). **Civair**, *East Pier, Waterfront; tel: 021-419 5182* (open 0900–sunset) has competitive prices.

Waterfront Charters, *tel: 021-253 804* or *021-254 292*, run daily boat trips around Robben Island (see p.105) and other Peninsula areas, whale-watching trips and sunset cruises. Other services include deep-sea fishing charters, diving charters and private yacht charters.

Bicycles

Mike Hopkins, *133a Bree St; tel: 021-232*

527. Road and mountain bikes at daily, weekly or weekend rates; from R45 per day.

Accommodation

Cape Town is booming as a holiday and business destination; book as early as you can, particularly over Christmas. **Captour's Hotel and Accommodation Booking Centre**, *3 Adderley St; tel: 021-418 5214*, provides details and helps with same-day hotel reservations (if available). Hotel chains include *CL, Hd, HI, Pa, SS, Rl.*

The **Mount Nelson**, *76 Orange St, Gardens; tel: 021-231 000, fax: 021-247 472* (expensive) is probably the most famous hotel in South Africa. In the heart of the city, beneath the mountain and surrounded by pretty gardens, the 'Nellie' is large, old-fashioned, gracious and very elegant – a local institution. Even if you can't afford to stay there, try one of its three restaurants or its excellent afternoon tea.

The city is sprouting new luxury alternatives almost every month. The **Table Bay** *(Sl), Quay 6, Waterfront; tel: 021-406 5000; fax: 021-406 5656* (expensive) is already being touted as one of the world's top hotels, although it is so new that its reputation is not yet proven. The location is magnificent. The **Victoria and Alfred**, *Pierhead, V&A Waterfront; tel: 021-419 6677; fax: 021-419 8955* (expensive) is well placed for excellent shopping, eating or simply lazing on the terrace admiring the view. Close to both the city centre and the Waterfront, and at the start of the Peninsula Route, the **Victoria Junction** *(Pa), Somerset Rd; tel: 021-418 1234; fax: 021-418 5678* (expensive) is marketed as a 'designer hotel', with minimalist industrial-style décor.

For something smaller and less pricey, the **Mijlhof Manor**, *5 Military Rd, Tamboerskloof; tel: 021-261 476, fax: 021-222 046* (moderate) is an early 18th-century farmhouse, converted into a charming, homely hotel, only 15 mins walk from the city centre.

The **Cape Town Inn**, *corner Strand and Bree Sts; tel: 021-235 116, fax: 021-242 720* (moderate) is smack in the city centre, which is convenient, but can be a disadvantage when trying to sleep. The somewhat ordinary **Townhouse**, *Corporation St; tel: 021-457 050; fax: 021-453 891* (moderate) is well located in the city centre and popular with tour groups, as well as politicians when parliament is in session. Those on a budget should try **Breakwater Lodge**, *Portswood Rd, Waterfront; tel: 021-406 1911, fax: 021-406 1070* (moderate), well-located for visits to the Waterfront; or the **Cape Swiss Hotel**, *corner Kloof and Camp Sts, Tamboerskloof; tel: 021-238 190, fax: 021-261 795* (cheap), near the city centre.

Many visitors with their own transport choose to stay a little way out of town on the Cape Peninsula (see pp.115–122), in Somerset West (p.133) or Stellenbosch (pp.313–316).

The many guesthouses in the suburbs provide an excellent alternative to the cheaper hotels. A **Guesthouse Hotline** is available in both the domestic and international airport lounges; a freephone service, it provides bookings and advice on suitable guesthouse locations. Otherwise, *tel: 0283-700 823*. Of the many guesthouses around, one of the best in the suburbs, and convenient for the city and for Constantia and Kirstenbosch, is **Medindi Manor**, *4 Thicket Rd, Mowbray; tel: 021-686 3563, fax: (021) 689 7386* (cheap), with en suite bathrooms, phone and TV in every room.

The **B&B Association**, *17 Talana Rd, Claremont; tel: 021-683 3505*, represents around 100 bed and breakfasts on the peninsula. Rates for double rooms with en suite bathrooms, TV and phone begin at R80 per person. The **Accommodation Hotline**, *tel: 021-757 130*, is a reservation service for bed and breakfast facilities in private homes and self-catering accommodation. Many people like to rent self-catering flats, cottages, seaside villas or mansions. All are available. **Captour** (see p.104) can provide details, otherwise call **Cape Holiday Homes**, *5th Floor, 31 Heerengracht, Lower Adderley St; tel: 021-419 0430*, or **Apartments and Homes**, *154 Main Rd, Sea Point; tel: 021-439 4126*, for details. Prices from around R400 to R8000 per day (for up to four bedrooms and private pool).

A hostelling information desk at the Tourist Office, *tel: 021-418 5202* (open Mon–Fri 0900–1700, Sat 0900–1300), has information

on Cape Town's **hostels**, discounted trips, pubs and so on, and makes reservations. The Go 25 Youth Card and ISIC Student Cards (R25) are sold here. Expect to sleep 4–12 to a room in bunk beds, with shared bathroom facilities and kitchens. Try **Albergo**, *5 Beckham St, Gardens; tel: 021-221 849*; **Bunkers**, *15 Graham Rd, Sea Point; tel: 021-434 0549*; **Green Elephant**, *57 Milton Rd, Observatory; tel: 021-448 6359*; or **Oak Lodge**, *21 Breda St, Gardens; tel: 021-456 182* (all very cheap: from R25 per person per night). A **YMCA**, *Burnham Rd, Observatory; tel: 021-476 217*, is an option open to both sexes. **Camping** and **caravanning** are options – most locations are rarely further than 40 mins from the centre (see Cape Town–Cape Point and Cape Town–Mossel Bay, pp. 115–122 and 132–137).

Eating and Drinking

In the city centre, those with money to spend might try **Leinster Hall**, *7 Weltevreden St; tel: 021-241 836* (expensive; open Mon–Fri lunch, Mon–Sat dinner). It is a 19th-century Cape house, with an excellent chef who dishes up super-smart South African food, from Knysna oysters to springbok. The **Cape Colony**, *The Mount Nelson Hotel, 76 Orange St; tel: 021-231 000* (expensive; open daily dinner only) has wonderful décor, a pretentious menu and excellent food, ranging from Thai to Cape specialities. **Restaurant Bukhara**, *1st Floor, 33 Church St; tel: 021-240 000* (expensive; open Mon–Sat lunch and dinner; closed Sun) is Cape Town's best Indian restaurant.

For snacks and light meals, **Melissa's**, *94 Kloof St; tel: 021-245 540* (moderate; open daily 0830–2000) is very stylish, while **Nino**, *52 Shortmarket St; tel: 021-247 466* (cheap–moderate; open Mon, Tues and Sat 0800–1800, Wed–Fri 0800–midnight) is noisy and busy with views of Greenmarket Sq.

Within the V&A Waterfront, the **Waterfront Café**, *V&A Hotel Pierhead, V&A Waterfront, Cape Town; tel: 021-419 6677* (moderate; open Mon–Sat 0700–2300, Sun 0700–2200) has spectacular views of Table Mountain and a bistro-style menu. The **Col'Cacchio**, *Seeff House, 42 Hans Strydom Ave, Foreshore; tel: 021-419 4848* (unlicensed;

105

cheap–moderate; open Mon–Fri lunch; daily dinner) has excellent pizzas with a range of toppings, including peri-peri prawns. The **Mama Africa Restaurant and Bar**, *178 Long St; tel: 021-248 634* (cheap–moderate; Mon–Sat lunch and dinner, with a late bar until 0300 at times; booking advisable) is wonderfully laid-back, with a menu including ostrich, Cape Malay lamb and fresh fish.

For traditional Cape Malay meals, try the **Noon Gun Tearoom**, *273 Longmarket St, Bo-Kaap; tel: 021-240 529* (cheap–moderate; unlicensed; open daily 0900–2300). Tea and traditional sticky cakes are available at all times. For a full meal, phone ahead and plan the menu of traditional curries and breyanies (see Food and Drink, Background, pp.72–73) with the proprietor. For Cape Dutch specialities, try the **Kaapse Tafel**, *Montreux Building, 90 Queen Victoria St; tel: 021-231 651* (moderate; open Mon–Sat lunch and dinner; booking essential), and for a taste of traditional Africa, in cheerful, friendly surroundings, head a short distance out of the centre to the **Africa Café**, *213 Lower Main Rd, Observatory; tel: 021-479 553* (cheap; open Mon–Fri lunch, Mon–Sat supper).

For seafood, there are plenty of options. Almost all of the better restaurants will have a 'catch of the day' – make sure it is that and not the frozen equivalent. Of the central choices, one of the best is **The Mussel Cracker**, *222 Victoria Wharf, V&A Waterfront; tel: 021-419 4300* (moderate; open daily lunch and dinner; booking advised), where roast tuna, fish bobotie and seafood casserole are just some of the specialities. There are plenty of other seafood options at the Victoria & Alfred Waterfront, while many people with transport choose to head out to Stellenbosch (see pp. 313–316) or the Cape Peninsula (pp. 115–122).

Communications

Main Post Office: *Parliament St; tel: 021-461 5670* (open Mon–Fri 0800–1630, Sat 0800–1200). The poste restante desk is situated in the main hall.

Public telephone facilities are available at **Pronto Phone**, *Tourist Office, 3 Adderley St; tel: 021-253 897* (open Mon–Fri 0800–1800, Sat 0830–1500, Sun 0900–1300). Also at *Shop 42,*

Thibault Sq.; tel: 021-419 2959 (open Mon–Fri 0800–1700, Sat 0830–1330, closed Sun). **Telinternational**, *263c Main Rd, Sea Point; tel: 021-434 2162* (open daily 0900–2200) has public phone booths and a fax and telephone message service.

Buy public telephone cards at the tourist office, at post offices and Telkom offices.

Money

Adderley St is home to several banks with exchange facilities and ATM machines, including the magnificent 19th-century Standard Bank, a tourist attraction in its own right. **Rennies/Thomas Cook**: *8th Floor, Safmarine House, 22 Riebeek St; tel: 021-418 5776, fax: 021-418 5849.*

ENTERTAINMENT

Tickets

Computicket; *tel: 021-214 715* (open Mon–Fri 0900–1700, Sat 0900–1600) is a city-wide agency, which handles tickets for theatre, cinema, opera, music and some film events such as the **Cape Town Film Festival**. **Branches**: *Victoria Wharf; Ground Floor, Gardens Centre, Mill St; Boardmans, Burg St* (closes Sat 1300); *Exclusive Books, Constantia Village; Baxter Theatre Complex, Main Rd, Rondebosch;* and the *Theatre on the Bay, Camps Bay.*

What's On Listings

The local daily press is best for listings; the morning daily *Cape Times* has a *Top of the Times* entertainment section on Fri; the *Tonight!* supplement of the afternoon daily, *The Argus*, and the *Weekend Argus* are also good. The national *Weekly Mail & Guardian* has city-by-city listings. *Cape Style* magazine, a glossy monthly, has an excellent, well-informed and up-to-the-minute listings section at the back. *What's On in Cape Town*, available from the Tourist Office, is very general.

Cinema

Mainstream new releases are distributed by Ster-Kinekor and Nu-Metro. There are multiplexes at the *V&A Waterfront* and at *Cavendish Sq.;* for listings see above.

106

There are also various independent venues, showing a mix of mainstream, art, foreign and retrospective films. These include the **Labia**, *68 Orange St, Gardens; tel: 021-245 927;* the **Baxter Cinema**, *Baxter Theatre, Main Rd, Rondesbosch; tel: 021-689 1069;* and the **South Africa National Gallery**, *Government Ave, Gardens; tel: 021-451 628.* The **BMW Imax Cinema**, *the BMW Pavilion, Waterfront; tel: 021-419 7364,* is unique in South Africa; a giant-format screen, with wraparound Imax digital sound.

There are three annual film festivals – the **International Film Festival** (Apr–May); the **Weekly Mail & Guardian Festival** (Sept) and the **French Film Festival** (Sept–Oct).

Performance
Theatre in Cape Town was, for a long time, in the backwoods. It's pulling itself out and fringe theatre, at least, is now better than ever. **CAPAB**, the resident classical ballet company, and **Jazzart**, an exciting low-key group marrying European and African rhythm, sound and music, are the front runners in the world of dance, backed up by international tours.

The main venues are: **The Baxter**, *Main Rd, Rondesbosch; tel: 021-685 7880,* an excellent venue with first-class local and international productions, musicals and recitals; the **Nico Malan Theatre Centre**, *DF Malan St, Foreshore; tel: 021-415 470* (switchboard); *021-217 839* (box office); or *021-217 695* (credit card bookings), home of CAPAB and the performing arts council, has two theatres, an opera house and, these days, Afrocentric leanings; the **Theatre on the Bay**, *Link St, Camps Bay; tel: 021-438 3301,* is a venue for revue, drama, farce or the fringe; the **Dock Road Theatre**, *Dock Rd, Waterfront; tel: 021-419 5522,* is a small intimate space for musicals and drama; and the **Agfa Amphitheatre**, *Waterfront; tel: 021-418 2369,* is used for dance.

Music
Classical music, opera, jazz, alternative and rock are all part of the Cape Town music scene.

Recitals by the **Cape Town Symphony Orchestra** are held in the **City Hall**, *Darling St; tel: 021-400 2230* (Thur, Sun 2000). The

Nico Malan and Baxter theatres (see above) are also important venues. **Josephine Mill**, *Boundary Rd, Newlands; tel: 021-686 4939,* is home to the **Nedbank Sunday Summer Concert Season** (Nov–Feb), which offers jazz, folk, classical and choral music. Open-air, hour-long evening concerts are held at **Kirstenbosch Botanical Gardens**, *Rhodes Dr., Newlands; tel: 021-762 1166* (Dec–Mar; bring a picnic).

The city has an excellent reputation for jazz. Serious aficionados go to **Blue Note (at Club Galaxy)**, *Cine 400 Building, College Rd, Rylands; tel: 021-637 9027* (open Thur–Sat, 2030–late; R10). The **Dock Road Café**, *V&A Waterfront; tel: 021-419 7722* (open daily 1800–late; from R10) offers intermittent jazz, while **Manenberg's Jazz Café**, *1st Floor, Dumbarton House, corner Adderley and Church Sts; tel: 021-418 1148* (open Mon–Sat 1100–late, Sun 1800–late; R10) is the best for Cape, Afro and improvised jazz. The 5-day **Cape Town International Jazz Festival** is in Feb.

Rock and alternative music are best at **The River Club**, *corner Liesbeeck Parkway and Station Rd, Observatory; tel: 021-448 6117* (open daily 2030–late; from R5); **The Purple Turtle**, *corner Shortmarket and Long Sts; tel: 021-262 277* (open Mon–Sat 1000–0200, Sun 1600–0100), a pub with places to eat and lounge, and **The Shebeen on Bree**, *25 Bree St; tel: 021-212 951* (open Tues–Sat 1600–late; from R5).

SHOPPING
Cape Town is a world-class shopping centre, filled with suitably expensive designer boutiques and galleries alongside the more mundane utilities.

Shopping Centres
The **Victoria Wharf Shopping Centre**, *Victoria & Alfred Waterfront, tel: 021-418 2369* (open daily; shops Mon–Fri 0900–2100, Sat–Sun 0900–1900) is Cape Town's newest and most central shopping venue, with a variety of shops from curios to fashion, restaurants and cinemas (see p. 112). The other good malls are a short distance out of town. **Cavendish Square**, *Southern Suburbs, tel: 021-643 050* (shops open 0900–1700; centre open until

0100) is perhaps the most prestigious, with specialist shops, restaurants, cinemas and undercover parking. **Constantia Village**, *Spansgemat Rd, Constantia; tel: 021-794 5065*, has a smaller mix of food shops, antiques, bookshops and clothing stores. With over 250 shops, 10 cinemas and 33 places to eat, the **Tyger Valley Shopping Centre**, *Willie van Schoor Ave, Bellville* (Exit 9/R302, off the N1), *tel: 021-948 5905* (open Mon–Thur 0900–1730, Fri 0900–1900, Sat 0900–1700) is the Western Cape's largest shopping mall, at the centre of the Northern Suburbs, and conveniently situated between Cape Town and the Winelands.

Markets

At the city centre, **Greenmarket Square**, *Burg St, between Long and Shortmarket Sts* (open Mon–Fri 0800–1700, Sat 0800–1400) is filled daily with bric-a-brac, curios and clothing. The **Grand Parade**, *Darling St* (open Wed, Sat 0800–1400) is a lively venue for fruit sellers, second-hand books, plants and fabrics. **Church Street Market**, *Church St* (open Mon–Sat 0800–1600), is filled with junk, antiques and collectables. For crafts, try **The Red Shed**, *King's Warehouse, Victoria Wharf Complex, Waterfront* (open Mon–Sat 0900–1800, Sun 1000–1800). Less frequently, and a short distance from the city centre, are the **Constantia Craft Market**, *Alphen Centre, Main Rd, Constantia* (open first and last Sat of each month 0900–1400), and **Craft in the Park**, *Rondebosch Park, corner Campground and Sandown Rds, Rondebosch* (open second Sat of each month 0900–1600). For antiques, **Groot Constantia Antiques and Collectibles Market**, *Groot Constantia Estate* (open Sat, Sun and public holidays) is best. **Green Point Stadium Market**, *Green Point Stadium, Fritz Sonnenberg Rd, Green Point* (Sun) is a huge and growing fleamarket for curios, clothing and bric-a-brac.

Antiques

The Main Roads in Kalk Bay and Simon's Town (see pp.120–121) are worth a visit, as are the various shopping centres. **Long Street** is dotted with small second-hand shops selling antiques, books, clothing and bric-à-brac; **Church Street** is for more serious shoppers.

Books

For new books and magazines, **Exclusive Books** has branches at *Constantia Village; tel: 021-794 7800, Cavendish Sq.; tel: 021-643 030*, and *Victoria Wharf at the Waterfront; tel: 021-419 0905*. **Wordsworth**, *Garden Centre, Mill St; tel: 021-461 8464*, is another good option. For antique and second-hand books, and Africana, **Clarkes**, *211 Long St; tel: 021-235 739*, is world famous.

Curios

African Image, *52 Burg St; tel: 021-238 385*, is an excellent source for gifts from across Africa. **Indaba**, *1 Harbour Café Annexe, Waterfront; tel: 021-253 639*, sells popular African crafts and curios.

Drink

Vaughan Johnson's Wine Shop, *Dock Rd, Waterfront; tel: 021-419 2121*, is the most comprehensive stockist of local wines, with daily tastings, advice on visits to vineyards and an export service.

Hiking and Camping Equipment

Cape Union Mart, *Victoria Wharf, Waterfront; tel: 021-419 0019*; and *150 Main Rd, Claremont; tel: 021-642 148*, is the best place for boots and climbing equipment, clothing and camping accessories.

Jewellery

Penny Murdoch, *50 Victoria Rd, Camps Bay; tel: 021-438 1600*; and *Shop 28, The Link, Claremont; tel: 021-643 860*, provides top quality bespoke jewellery. **The Jewel Tree**, *Protea Assurance Building, Greenmarket Sq.; tel: 021-230 747*, is the place for antique pieces.

SIGHTSEEING

The Victorians loved to embellish the outposts of the British Empire with buildings reminiscent of those back home. Cape Town's **City Hall**, *Darling St; tel: 021-461 7086* (open Mon, Wed, Fri 0900–0530, Tues 1300–1800, Thur 0900–1400, Sat 0900–1600; free), which faces onto the *Grand Parade*, is no exception. Built in 1905 and faced with Bath stone, it is a curious blend of the Italian Renaissance and British

Colonial architectural styles. Today it houses the office of the Mayor of Cape Town and the City Library, and symphony concerts are held here Thursday and Sunday evenings. Well restored, it provides a dignified backdrop to the daily cacophony of the Grand Parade flea-market nearby. The **Grand Parade** has always been a hive of activity for street sellers. But more importantly, it had long been a venue for public meetings – a role it lost during the years of repression. When an estimated 100,000 people gathered to hear Nelson Mandela speak from the City Hall's balcony after his release from jail in Feb 1990, it signalled freedom.

Nearby, South Africa's oldest European building is the **Castle of Good Hope**, *Darling St; tel: 021-469 1111* (open daily 0900–1500; R7.50). Built by slaves (1666) using Robben Island stone, its plan is a pentagon with protruding defensive corner bastions. The solid walls enclose various utilitarian structures, ranging from historic, graffiti-ridden, below-sea-level cells to armouries. At the heart of the castle is the 'kat', a massive wall which bisects the internal courtyard to allow the defence to retire into one part of the fortress if the other half were to be invaded. The castle has never been attacked, and in time the kat was built over – the famous baroque **Kat Balcony**, adorned with plaster reliefs by Anton Anreith (c.1785) is one of the city's loveliest structures. From it, proclamations and criminal sentences were read.

Under the Dutch, the Castle was the headquarters of the powerful Dutch East India Company, the Governor's residence and a fortress. Under the British, it became government headquarters. The council chamber and the state rooms house the **William Fehr Collection**, *tel: 021-469 1160*, of 17th- to 19th-century paintings (including many by Thomas Baines), decorative arts and furniture, much of it relating directly to the artistic, cultural and political development of the Cape Colony. There is also a military and maritime museum.

The residue of the William Fehr Collection can be seen at **Rust-en-Vreugd**, *78 Buitenkant St; tel: 021-453 628* (open Mon–Sat 0900–1600; free), a beautiful double-storeyed 18th-century mansion overlooking the city. The name means 'rest and joy'; it was built, at the time, on the edge of town for the State Prosecutor. Here you can see important 17th- to 19th-century paintings, sketches and etchings relating to the history of the colony. An adjacent herb and rose garden is a re-creation of an historic Dutch garden.

Government Avenue

Right at the heart of the city is the pedestrian, tree-lined Government Avenue (see p. 113), around which are clustered many of Cape Town's most important sights. At the top of *Adderley St,* facing the Houses of Parliament and the South African National Library, 13.2 hectares of the **Company's Garden**, *enter from Adderley, Victoria or Orange St* (open dawn–dusk; free) are all that survives of the original 18 hectare vegetable garden established by Jan van Riebeeck in 1652 for the provision of fresh fruit and vegetables to merchant ships on their way to the East. Today, this is a welcome area of green in a busy city, and a fine botanical garden, containing magnificent indigenous and exotic plants (see the City Tour, p. 113).

Cape Town is the seat of the country's legislative government, and its offices, the ponderous and dignified **Houses of Parliament** (completed 1884), *Parliament St and Government Ave,* designed to suit the tempo of another age, overlook the Company's Gardens. To attend parliamentary sessions (Jan–June, Tues, Wed, Thur at 1415), or for guided tours during the recess (July–Jan, Mon–Fri, hourly 0900–1300); *tel: 021-403 2460 or 021-403 2461;* or call at the public relations office V12 (use' the *Parliament St* entrance and ask for directions). Next door, the **Tuynhuis** was, at one time, the Company's Guest House. Built in 1770, and much altered since – most notably by Lord Charles Somerset in the Regency style – it is now the office of the President.

At the top of *Government Ave,* **Bertram House**, *tel: 021-249 381* (open Tues–Sat 0930–1630; R1) is home to the British Colonial House Museum. This late Georgian house is a typical example of early 19th-century Cape British domestic architecture, and is unique in Cape Town. Its Regency-style

Post Office Stones

In the 17th century, an extraordinary method of posting letters was originated along the South African Coast. Since Dutch and English navigators usually put in at Mossel Bay, Table Bay and one or two other key points for supplies of fresh meat and water, they began leaving letters under certain stones on the beach. Sometimes stones, onto which names of ships and their crew were chiselled, were brought along specifically for that purpose. This custom allowed sailors who were often away from home for years on end to get news of the outside world, and to send mail home with ships bound for Europe. With the arrival of Jan van Riebeeck, and the setting up of a victualling station at the Cape, the practice died out. Surviving stones can be seen in the Cultural History Museum in Cape Town (see opposite).

rooms contain, as a nucleus, the Anna Lidderdale Collection of furniture, ceramics and silver – illustrating the lifestyle of a patrician English family resident at the Cape.

Not far away, the **South African Museum**, *25 Queen Victoria St; tel: 021-243 330* (open daily 1000–1700; R3 for the museum, R6 for the Planetarium) is the country's oldest museum (1825). Dedicated to the natural sciences, it houses an array of stuffed animals, replica dinosaurs, sea shells and a Whale Well – a four-storey exhibition area in which the skeletons of three whales are suspended. It also has excellent examples of San rock paintings and engravings, along with numerous examples of traditional crafts from a variety of local peoples, including the San and Khoikhoi, and historic furniture, applied-art and silver from the history of white South Africans. The Planetarium is the place to explore the Southern Hemisphere's night sky.

The adjacent **South African National Gallery**, *Government Ave; tel: 021-451 628* (open Tues–Sun 1000–1700; free) houses a small international art collection. It also has one of the country's most comprehensive collections

of contemporary South African art (together with Pretoria's Art Museum) and is concentrating on establishing an historical African collection; this includes tribal and ethnic art (Ndebele, Fingo, Xhosa, Zulu beadwork), as well as urban and rural holograph art. The contemporary collections are becoming more comprehensive all the time, and a series of lectures, workshops and films contribute to a better understanding of South African culture.

Next door, the **Jewish Museum**, *84 Hatfield St; tel: 021-451 546* (open Tues, Thur 1400–1700, Sun 1000–1230; Dec–Mar Tues, Thur 1000–1700; free) is housed in part of South Africa's oldest synagogue, a building of curious Egyptian Revival design. The museum traces the history of Jewish communities in the Cape and contains items of religious and historical significance. The first ever service took place here in 1841, on Yom Kippur.

The first slaves brought to the Cape (1685), to work in the Company's Garden, were housed in what is now the Cultural History Museum, *49 Adderley St; tel: 021-461 8280* (open Mon–Sat 0930–1600, R5). Once known as the Slave Lodge (built 1679), a plaque on the traffic island in adjacent *Spin St* marks the site of the tree under which the last slaves were sold after the Second British Occupation of the Cape. In 1810, Louis Thibault converted the building into government offices; it later became the Supreme Court. It is now dedicated to the lifestyles of the country's various population groups, and includes domestic utensils, applied arts, coins, weapons, ceramics, stamps and textiles. There is an excellent collection of white South African furniture and applied-art objects (particularly silver), and a fascinating display covering world history and anthropology. A section on discovery and exploration includes models of many ships used by early Portuguese and Dutch traders and a display of post stones (see above).

Other Museums

Koopman's de Wet House Museum, *35 Strand St; tel: 021-242 473* (open Tues–Sat 0930–1600; R1) is a typical 18th-century (1701) patrician townhouse. Much altered, what exists now is largely the work of the Cape's most illustrious architect, Louis Thibault. Today, in rooms elaborately painted with *trompe l'oeil* effects, it houses a magnificent collection of Cape and European furniture and porcelain, blue-and-white VOC porcelain of the Dutch East India Company and Cape glass. It was put together by sisters of the de Wet family, which had occupied the house for most of the 19th century. At the time it was built, *Strand St* was the city's most fashionable thoroughfare.

The **Old Town House**, (begun 1755) *Greenmarket Sq.; tel: 021-246 367*, was originally the headquarters of the Burgher Council, which maintained law and order. Fire was an ever-present hazard and the city streets needed patrolling nightly by the Burgher Watch (the building is also known as the Burgher Watch House). Proclamations were read from its balcony to citizens summoned by a bell. Today, the building houses the magnificent **Michaelis Collection** of 17th-century Dutch and Flemish paintings. Open daily 1000–1700; free.

Not far away, on the slopes of Signal Hill, overlooking the city and the full expanse of Table Mountain from its situation in the so-called **Malay Quarter**, is the **Bo-Kaap Museum**, *71 Wale St; tel: 021-243 846* (open Mon–Sat 0930–1630; R1). Furnished as a typical Muslim family home of the late 19th century, it reflects the Islamic contribution to South African culture. The house itself is a fine example of those built locally in the late 18th and early 19th centuries to house European immigrant artisans. Most typically, they are single-storied with raised *stoeps* (verandahs). On the abolition of slavery, the Muslim 'Malays' moved in; most Europeans moved out, and the neighbourhood has remained predominantly Muslim ever since, the only non-white city centre community in South Africa to survive the enforced evictions of apartheid. **Tana Baru Tours**, *tel: 021-240 719* (Mon–Sat 1000–1200, 1400–1600; R45 per person) conducts excellent walks through the Bo-Kaap, making references to its history, culture, architecture and social life.

The **District Six Museum**, *25a Buitenkant St; tel: 021-461 8745* (open Mon–Sat 1000–1600, Sun by appointment; donation) charts the demolition of an area that was not so lucky.

Robben Island

This most significant and symbolically charged piece of land in South Africa lies 9 km off the coast of Cape Town. Long a place of banishment, its name derives from *robbe,* the Dutch word for seals, though English sailors knew it as Penguin Island. In the 17th and 18th centuries, political prisoners and criminals – high ranking exiles, Islamic holy men, pirates, murderers, Europeans, Khoikhoi, San, Chinese, Indians and slaves – were dumped there. In the 19th century, it was home to various African leaders who tried resisting the advance of the colonial frontier and, in the 1960s, those who opposed the state of oppression were detained here. Of these, the most famous was Nelson Mandela. In May 1991, the last political prisoners were released, and the prison shut its doors for ever in 1996. President Mandela said: 'It will never again be used as a prison, not if we can help it.' The island and a one sea-mile zone around it were declared a national monument, though its future is still uncertain. **Robben Island Museum Tours**; *tel: 021-419 1300,* operate 2½ hr guided tours of Robben Island (R80), including Nelson Mandela's cell. There are three departures daily, at 0915, 1145 and 1315, from *Quay 5, V&A Waterfront.* The ticket office opens 0730, and you must be prepared to queue. Alternatively, **Waterfront Charters**; *tel: 021-418 6436* (open office hours) will do the queueing for you, and throw in a sunset cruise to Clifton, but the price goes up to R150.

District Six was a buzzing multi-cultural and multi-racial urban neighbourhood extinguished utterly by apartheid ideology manifest in the Group Areas Act (see Background chapter, p.67). Its sprawling 18th- and 19th-century terraces of houses and shops at the foot of **Devil's Peak**, home to a wide mix of people from gangsters and hookers to poets and musicians, were condemned as a slum, and subsequently reserved for white ownership and development.

The flamboyant expressionist, Irma Stern, was one of South Africa's great pioneer painters. After her death in 1966, her home and studio were preserved by the University of Cape Town as the **UCT Irma Stern Museum**, *Cecil Rd, Rosebank; tel: 021-685 5686* (open Tues–Sat 1000–1700; R4). This houses a small collection of her own work, but Stern was also a discriminating collector. Here, too, is a wide range of treasures gathered on world travels – Congolese masks, oriental ceramics, 17th-century furniture, Greek artefacts, Coptic weavings, Zanzibar doors and the Buli Stool, one of only 20 known works by master Zairean carver, Buli.

Down to the Sea

The history of Cape Town's association with the sea is documented at the **South African Maritime Museum and Museum Ships**, *Dock Rd, Table Bay Harbour; tel: 021-419 2506* (open daily 1000–1700; R5). It contains information and exhibits on shipwrecks – a common sight around the Cape Peninsula even now – Table Bay Harbour, shipping lines, ship modelling and maritime archaeology. It also has a shipwright's workshop and two floating exhibits – the SAS *Somerset*, the only boom defence vessel preserved in the world, and the *Alwyn Vincent*, a steam tug built in 1959 for use in the Harbour, and the only one still in use in the Southern Hemisphere.

The **Two Oceans Aquarium**, *Dock Rd, Victoria & Alfred Waterfront; tel: 021-418 3823* (open daily 0930–2000; R24), houses more than 4000 creatures, representing over 300 species, many of which can be seen from a 'diver's eye view'. Huge tanks tower over the spectator, and in them are sharks, snoek, yellow-tail and other ocean fish. Seals and penguins can be seen from beneath and above the water, and there is a touch pool filled with starfish, sea urchins, chiton and winkles.

The **Victoria & Alfred Waterfront** itself is a growing city attraction, named after Queen Victoria and her second son, Prince Alfred, who, in 1860, inaugurated the construction of the breakwater for Cape Town's harbour. It is a unique marriage of working harbour and leisure centre, filled with shops, restaurants, bars, outdoor sitting areas and art spaces. It also has 3 hotels, a small theatre, cinemas, an aquarium and a maritime museum. Peninsula cruises and trips around Robben Island begin here, and, all the while, cargo arrives from abroad, tankers dock and seals cavort in the water under the jetties. **Waterfront Information Centre**, *Old Harbour, Market Sq.; tel: 021-418 2369* (open Mon–Fri 0930–1700); **Waterfront Information Kiosk**, *Victoria Wharf Shopping Centre; tel: 021-418 2369* (open Mon, Tues, Thur and Fri 0900–1900, Wed 0900–2100, Sat–Sun 0900–1900).

Churches

In the earliest days of the settlement, church services were heard on board Jan van Riebeeck's ship, the *Dromedaris*. Later, a shed in the Castle of Good Hope was converted into a church, and suitably adorned with gabled entrance and stone floor. Only in 1700 did the settlement acquire a proper church for Dutch Reformed services – the thatch-roofed precursor of the present (1841) **Groote Kerk**, *Adderley St; tel: 021-461 7044* (open Mon–Fri 1000–1400; free). This is the parent of the Dutch Reformed Church in southern Africa, and the oldest church in the country. It houses an elaborate wooden pulpit carved by Anton Anreith (1788) and the largest organ in the southern hemisphere, with 6000 pipes.

Not far away, the **Lutheran Church**, *96 Strand St* (enquiries at Church House, *19 Buitengracht St;* open Mon–Fri 0830–1300, 1330–1630; free) contains another magnificent pulpit by Anton Anreith (1784). Only in 1780 were the Lutherans allowed formalised services in their own church – which began life as a wine store. Next door, the **Martin Melck House**, named after the Melck family builders, was the parsonage (1781), and is now a nightclub. A rare surviving feature is the *dakkamer* – a room in the roof, with windows looking out to sea. On the other side of the church, the

City Centre Walking Tour

Start at the junction of *Adderley and Wale Sts*, under the gazes of General Jan Smuts and Queen Victoria. On your left are the **Cultural History Museum** and, beyond it, the gardens of the Houses of Parliament; on your right, **St George's Cathedral** and cathedral school. As you walk up leafy *Government Ave*, you will see on the left the **Houses of Parliament**; to the right, the **South African Library**, *Queen Victoria St; tel: 021-246 320* (open Mon–Fri 0900–1800, Sat 0900–1300; free), an irreplaceable national archive, which also houses many magnificent manuscripts, including a First Folio Shakespeare and 10th-century illustrated gospel. The Library's portico overlooks the **Company's Garden** and the statue of Sir George Grey, Governor of the Cape 1854–1861. Continue along the Avenue and an opening in the hedge to your left reveals the long, low formal garden facade of the **Tuynhuis**.

Alternatively turn into the Company's Garden and follow the main path past lawns and benches, aviaries and arbours, until you find a tearoom (open daily 0830–1730) near the statue of Cecil John Rhodes. The main path emerges into the **Delville-Wood Memorial Garden**, a wide, formal space adorned with ornamental pools, commemorating the World War I tragedy at Delville-Wood, in which some 13,000 South Africans died. It also contains 3 colonial war memorials. Directly ahead of you are the **South African Museum** and **Planetarium**. On the far left, at the end of the formal terrace, is the **National Gallery**. Facing the Gallery, turn right into *Paddock Ave*, which leads past the **Great Synagogue and Jewish Museum**, then bear right into *Avenue St*, rejoining *Government Ave* beside the classical-style **Little Theatre**. Turn left and carry on up the Avenue. Twin **Lion Gates** face each other; the left opening to the grounds of **Cape Town High School**, the right leading to the Orange Street Campus of the **University of Cape Town**. The Egyptian Revival-style building, which flanks the Avenue, was built in 1841 and is the oldest in the university. Just further on, the Avenue comes to an end facing the columned entrance to the **Mount Nelson Hotel**. On your right is **Bertram House**.

Turn right onto *Orange St*, then take the second left onto *Long St*. This aptly named road is synonymous with the identity of the city. From mountain to sea, it is flanked by a rich profusion of churches, mosques, shops, banks, offices and apartment blocks, cafés, restaurants and clubs of one description or another. Only one building, no. 185, now the **Palm Tree Mosque**, is a complete surviving 18th-century house – though many others are undoubtedly entombed within later shells. Number 185 was converted into a mosque (1805) by Jan van Boughies, a freed Malay slave – he planted the two palms which gave the mosque its name. Elsewhere, there are art deco shopfronts, cast-iron, double-tiered verandahs on Victorian rooming houses, and exuberant neo-classical buildings awash with brightly painted decorative plasterwork and other period details. Turn right onto *Wale St* to rejoin *Adderley St*.

113

Dutch Embassy was once the Sexton's House (1787). The charming little South African Missionary Society church, built in 1904 for the education of slaves and non-Christians, is now home to the **Sendinggestig Museum**, *40 Long St; tel: 021-236 755* (open Mon–Fri 0900–1600; free), dedicated to the history of the missions in South Africa.

The headquarters of the Anglican Church in South Africa is **St George's Cathedral**, *Wale St* (open Mon–Fri 0700–1800, Sat 0700–1200, Sun 0715–1130). First built in 1834, it was heavily rebuilt in 1901 by the heavy-handed British architect Sir Herbert Baker. Today, this Gothic Revival structure, more reminiscent of the English shires than of Africa, comes replete

> ## Cape Architecture
>
> Africa is rarely associated with fine architecture, but European involvement in the Cape for nearly 350 years has ensured both a rich historic legacy and the evolution of a distinctive style, adapted to local materials and conditions. The earliest settlers came from a society that built thatched wattle-and-daub houses on a timber frame. They built what they knew best, although in a simplified form – rectangular farmhouses, with a steeply pitched thatched roof. The front door was placed in the middle of the long side (sometimes with a back door directly opposite), with heavily shuttered windows on either side. Inside, a central hall was flanked by two rooms, one for sleeping, one for living. Floors were of polished dung or mud, inset with peach kernels. The walls were whitewashed for coolness, and the woodwork painted dark green (the only colour paint available). As wealth and families grew, wings were added to form a T- or U-shape. Eventually, a rear courtyard was added, with the kitchens, servants' quarters, barns and stables making up the other three sides. Next came a raised verandah along the front of the house. New materials were used, with floors and ceilings fashioned from highly polished local hardwoods, such as yellowwood or stinkwood. By the mid 18th century, there was sufficient money and fashion consciousness in Cape Town for leading citizens to add a simplified gable over the front door. Few of these were as elaborate as those in Holland, but they provided an elegant frame for decoration, which commonly included the family crest or the date of construction. The heyday of classic Cape Dutch architecture was short-lived, although some fine examples remain in Stellenbosch, the Cape Winelands and Graaff-Reinet. By the early 19th century, the British were in control, and they brought with them the newly fashionable two-storey Georgian townhouse, with its triangular pediment and flat roof. Very few have survived, but they did live on in the many small sugar-cube cottages, still to be seen in areas such as Bo-Kaap, Cape Town and country towns throughout the Karoo.

114

with stained-glass windows dedicated to Lord Mountbatten. During the apartheid years, under the auspices of South Africa's first black Archbishop, the flamboyant and heroic Desmond Tutu, its pews were packed, its sermons provocative and its walls a sanctuary from attack by the police or protestors.

Table Mountain
If there is a single sight which sums up Cape Town, it must be South Africa's best-known landmark, **Table Mountain**, which totally dominates the city and the bay. Its cloud-clothed bulk is linked via Kloof Nek to **Lion's Head**, which in turn is connected by a 'lion's' body to a rump with superb views, known as **Signal Hill**, from where the garrison kept watch for incoming ships, and where a cannon is still fired at noon each day.

This 700 million-year-old block of shale, sandstone and granite was known to the Cape's early Khoi inhabitants as Sea Mountain; its present name was awarded by Antonio de Saldanha, the first European to reach its 1082m summit in the 16th century. One of its most striking aspects is the beauty and diversity of its plant life: there are over 2600 species of indigenous plants in the Cape Peninsula, more than in the whole of the UK, and more than half of these are found on Table Mountain alone. Extensive networks of paths cross the mountain, and there are strenuous walks up its various gorges. Serious climbers should obtain advice from the **Mountain Club of South Africa**, *97 Hatfield St, Gardens; tel: 021-453 412*, or the **Hiking Federation of South Africa**, *tel: 021-964 156*. Others, with more leisurely intent, can find details of individual walks at the tourist office. The **Table Mountain Climb Company**, *606 Heerengracht Centre, Foreshore; tel: 021-419 2667* (open Mon–Fri 0830–1700) organises guided walks up the mountain, as does guide **John McDonnell**; *tel: 021-452 503* (open Mon–Fri 0800–2000). The famous **Table Mountain Cableway** is closed until late 1997 for upgrading and repairs.

CAPE TOWN–CAPE POINT

At the bottom of Africa, the Cape Peninsula is a spectacular combination of sea and mountain scenery. From Cape Town, where the ramparts of Table Mountain soar to 1082 m, a chain of peaks stretches south, only to fall into the sea at the tip of a beautiful, unspoiled natural wilderness, the Cape of Good Hope Nature Reserve. Dotted with beaches and seaside villas, and accessed through mountain paths and a magnificent corniche that follows the coastline, the peninsula is home to thousands of plant species occurring nowhere else in the world.

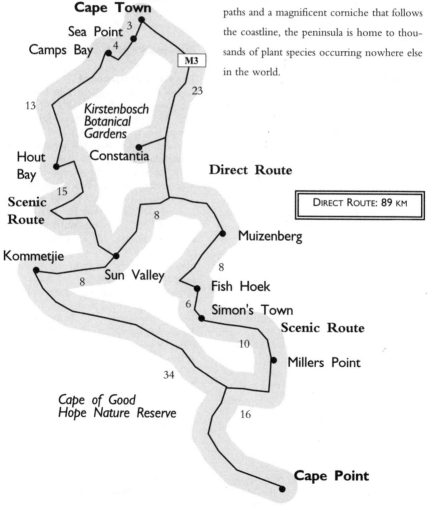

Cape Town

Sea Point 3

Camps Bay 4

M3

23

13

Kirstenbosch Botanical Gardens

Hout Bay

Constantia

Direct Route

115

DIRECT ROUTE: 89 KM

Scenic Route

15

8

Kommetjie

8

Sun Valley

Muizenberg

8

Fish Hoek

6

Simon's Town

Scenic Route

10

Millers Point

34

Cape of Good Hope Nature Reserve

16

Cape Point

ROUTES

DIRECT ROUTE

→ Leave the city on the M3, *De Waal Dr.,* signposted to **Muizenberg**. At its junction with the M42, turn right, then 2 km further on, left onto the Ou Kaapse Weg (M64) and continue over the Steenberg Mountains to Sun Valley. At the M65, go right to, and through, Kommetjie. Continue on to Scarborough, then carry on to the entrance to the **Cape of Good Hope Nature Reserve** (10 km) on the right. Distance: 89 km; allow 1 hr.

SCENIC ROUTE

⇢ From central Cape Town, turn left at the bottom of *Buitengracht St* (M62) on to the M6. This bypasses the Waterfront as *Port Rd,* before becoming *Western Blvd* as it passes through Green Point, *Beach Rd* in **Sea Point** and *Victoria Rd* as it passes through Bantry Bay, Clifton, **Camps Bay**, Bakoven and Llandudno; stay on it to **Hout Bay**.

For an alternative, quicker route to Hout Bay, avoiding summer congestion in Sea Point and Clifton, take *Buitengracht St* (M62) going south-west (towards the mountain), and its continuation, *Kloofnek Rd,* and proceed over the saddle of land connecting Table Mountain to Lion's Head. At the summit – note the view both ways – proceed down *Geneva Dr.* to Camps Bay, connecting with *Victoria Rd* at Bakoven. Go left and continue via Llandudno to Hout Bay.

On the approach to Hout Bay, go left, following signs to **Fish Hoek/Constantia** (M6) and, after a few hundred yards, branch right (still the M6) and follow the signs to Fish Hoek via Chapman's Peak. Continue on to **Noordhoek** along scenic *Chapman's Peak Dr.* At Sun Valley, turn right, connecting with the M64 Simon's Town/Fish Hoek, and continue until the sign M65 to Kommetjie/Ocean View, at which go right. Follow this road on to and through Kommetjie and Scarborough until, after 10 km, on the right, is the entrance to the Cape of Good Hope Nature Reserve.

On leaving the reserve, go right, rejoining the M65, which now becomes the M4, and continue on to Miller's Point, Boulders, **Simon's Town**, **Fish Hoek**, **Kalk Bay**, St James and **Muizenberg**. After Muizenberg, follow City/Stad signs, taking the M42 Ou Kaapse Weg/City turn off, off which, to the right, is the M3 which heads for the city centre. For **Constantia**, take the M41 Constantia/Wynberg turn off and follow the signs to Constantia and Groot Constantia. For **Kirstenbosch Botanical Gardens**, take the signposted suburban route through Bishopscourt (follow the brown signs). Further on, **Rhodes Memorial** is signposted to the left. Distance: 139 km; allow one day (more to do justice to Kirstenbosch and Constantia).

ACCOMMODATION

The Atlantic Seaboard

Top of the range, modern **The Bay**, *Victoria Rd, Camps Bay; tel: 021-438 4444, fax: 021-438 4455* (expensive), faces palm-fringed Camps Bay beach and has a pool for people-watching. Pricey, but well positioned, **The Peninsula**, *Beach Rd, Sea Point; tel: 021-439 8888, fax: 021-439 8886* (expensive), has suites with kitchen facilities. Beachfront **Fairways**, *The Fairway, Victoria and Fairway Rds, Camps Bay; tel: 0221-438 7060, fax: 021-438 2692* (expensive) is small (8 rooms) and exclusive. **Ellerman House**, *180 Kloof Rd, Bantry Bay; tel: 021-439 9182, fax: 021-434 7257* (expensive) is a charming former home of a shipping magnate. Elegant, luxurious and discreet, it has magnificent views out over a terraced garden (with pool) to sea and mountain.

Less expensive, the **Ambassador**, *34 Victoria Rd, Bantry Bay; tel: 021-439 6170, fax 021-439 6336* (moderate), rises from the rocks at Bantry Bay. Magnificent views from rooms and pool. The old-fashioned **Winchester Mansions**, *221 Beach Rd, Sea Point; tel: 021-434 2351, fax 021-434 0215* (moderate) is located across the road from the ocean and a beachfront promenade. **Hout Bay Manor**, *Main Rd, Hout Bay; tel: 021-790 4730, fax: 021-790 4952* (moderate) is at the foot of *Chapman's Peak Dr.*

The Atlantic Seaboard's best guesthouse is the **Cape Victoria**, *13 Torbay Rd, Green Point; tel/fax: 021-439 7721* (cheap). Its sun deck, roof terrace and pool are worth staying for, and there are mountain and sea views. In Bantry Bay, **Enchanted**, *12 Craigrownie Rd; tel/fax: 021-439 5566* (cheap) is quiet and comfortable.

Campsite: **Chapman's Peak Caravan Farm**, *Main Rd, Noordhoek; tel: 021-789 1225* (caravans). Close to the beach.

The Indian Ocean Coast

The Lord Nelson Inn, *58 St George's St, Simon's Town; tel: 021-786 1386, fax: 021-786 1009* (moderate) is a small, comfortable hotel, while the **British Hotel**, *90 St George's St, Simon's Town; tel/fax: 021-790 4930* (cheap) provides four handsome self-catering apartments with lovely sea and mountain views in central Simon's Town. Simon's Town also has plenty of guesthouses, bed and breakfasts and self-catering places – details from the Tourist Office. At Boulders, **Bosky Dell**, *5 Grant Ave, The Boulders; tel: 021-786 3906, fax: 021-786 1830* (cheap) has self-catering cottages with lovely views and private gardens right on the beach. The **Boulders Beach Guesthouse**, *4 Boulders Place, The Boulders; tel: 021-786 1758, fax: 021-786 1825* (cheap) is a gentle stroll from the beach, and there is separate accommodation for backpackers at the **Boulders Beach Guesthouse**; *tel: 021-786 1758, fax: 021-786 1825* (cheap) – dormitory and private rooms.

Further north, luxurious **Monoblet**, *15 Upper Kimberley Rd, St James; tel: 021-788 6525, fax 021-788 6546* (expensive) overlooks False Bay. Less pricey, **Shrimpton Manor**, *19 Alexander Rd, Muizenberg; tel/fax: 021-788 5225* (moderate) is handily placed for the beach. **Campsites**: **Oatlands Holiday Village**, *Froggy Pond, Simon's Town; tel: 021-786 1410, fax: 021-786 1162* (caravans); **Sandvlei Caravan Park**, *The Row, Muizenberg; tel: 021-788 5215* (caravans).

The Constantia area, dripping with historic Cape Dutch buildings, is home to some of the finest hotels in the Cape. Top of the range is the **Cellars-Hohenhort Country House Hotel** *(RC), 15 Hohenhort Ave, Constantia; tel: 021-794 2137, fax: 021-794 2149* (expensive), a superb country house hotel, set in magnificent gardens containing swimming pools, tennis courts and helipad. At **Constantia Uitsig**, *Spaanschematriver Rd, Constantia; tel: 021-794 6500, fax: 021-7605* (expensive), guests are accommodated in garden cottages on a private, working wine farm. Access to one of the best restaurants in Cape Town.

Other luxury hotels in the area include the **Alphen**, *Alphen Dr., Constantia; tel: 021-794 5011, fax: 021-794 5710* (expensive), an 18th-century manor house; the Southern Suburbs's **Vineyard Hotel**, *corner Colinton and Protea Rds, Claremont; tel: 021-683 3044, fax: 021-683 3365* (expensive), charmingly situated on the banks of the Liesbeeck River; and **The Andros**, *corner Newlands and Phyllis Rds, Claremont; tel: 021-797 9777, fax: 021-797 0300* (expensive), a small, intimate hotel in a 1930s mansion.

The **Constantia Lodge**, *Duntaw Close, Rhodes Dr., Constantia; tel: 021-794 2410, fax: 021-794 2418* (moderate) is within walking distance of Kirstenbosch.

EATING AND DRINKING

Sea Point

La Perla, *Beach Rd, Sea Point; tel: 021-434 2471* (expensive) is the best choice in Cape Town for lobster (reservations essential). The **San Marco**, *92 Main Rd, Sea Point; tel: 021-439 2758* (expensive; open Mon–Wed dinner, Sun lunch; reservations essential) is a famous old-fashioned restaurant with Mediterranean bent; the oysters and carpaccio are best.

Camps Bay

The Restaurant at the Bay, *The Bay Hotel, Victoria Rd, Camps Bay; tel: 021-438 4444* (expensive; open daily 0700–1030 breakfast, 1900–2230 dinner) has award-winning gourmet cuisine, while **Blues**, *The Promenade, Victoria Rd, Camps Bay; tel: 021-438 2040* (expensive; open daily 1200–2400), runs a close second. The **Bayside Café**, *51 Victoria Rd, Camps Bay; tel: 021-438 2650* (moderate; open Sun lunch, Tues–Sun dinner; reservations essential) is a popular seafront venue selling seafood and grills.

Hout Bay

One of the best places to eat seafood in the

117

Hout Bay area is the **Wharfside Grill**, *Mariner's Wharf, Harbour Rd, Hout Bay; tel: 021-790 1100* (expensive; open daily breakfast, lunch and dinner). Alternatively, try **Dunes**, *Hout Bay Beach, Hout Bay; tel: 021-790 1876* (moderate; open Sun breakfast, Tues–Sun lunch and dinner), which serves Mediterranean fare with a seafood emphasis. Other options include **Kronendal**, *Main Rd, Hout Bay; tel: 021-790 1970* (moderate; open daily, breakfast, lunch and dinner); or **Prinsenhof Restaurant**, *Groot Moddergat Estate, Main Rd, Hout Bay; tel: 021-790 6189* (moderate; open Tues–Sun lunch and dinner).

Noordhoek to Cape Point
Thorfynns at Monkey Valley, *Monkey Valley Beach Nature Resort, Mountain Rd, Noordhoek; tel: 021-789 1391* (cheap; open Mon–Sun 0800–2400, closed Mon lunch, Tues dinner; unlicensed). At Cape Point itself, overlooking the ocean from on high, **Two Oceans**; *tel: 021-780 9200* (cheap; open daily 0900–1800) has an extensive menu and is open for tea, snacks, drinks or meals.

Simon's Town
Seaforth, *Seaforth Beach, Seaforth Rd, Simon's Town; tel: 021-786 1659* (moderate; open daily lunch and dinner) offers good seafood right on the beach, while the **Black Marlin**, *Main Rd, Miller's Point, Simon's Town; tel: 021-786 1621* (moderate; open daily lunch, Mon–Sat dinner) has a menu ranging from ostrich fillet to Knysna oysters.

Fish Hoek to Muizenberg
Kalk Bay has a number of inexpensive, casual places to eat. **The Timeless Way Restaurant**, *101 Main Rd, Kalk Bay; tel: 021-788 5619* (cheap; open Mon–Sun lunch and dinner, Sat and Sun breakfast) produces traditional Cape cuisine, overlooking the harbour, while the **Brass Bell**, *Waterfront, Kalk Bay; tel: 021-788 5455* (cheap; open Mon–Sun 1100–2400) is an à la carte restaurant and pub at the water's edge.

In nearby Muizenberg, **Gaylord's Indian Cuisine**, *65 Main Rd, Muizenberg; tel: 021-788 5470* (cheap; open Mon dinner, Wed–Sun lunch and dinner) offers exotic North Indian

cuisine in a picturesque setting. **Shrimpton Manor Guesthouse and Restaurant**, *19 Alexander Rd, Muizenberg; tel: 021-788 1128* (moderate; open daily breakfast, lunch and dinner) is renowned for outstanding seafood and fresh fish. **La Mer**, *Muizenberg Station, Muizenberg; tel: 021-788 3251* (moderate; open daily for dinner) provides seafood with a sea view.

Constantia
Constantia Uitsig Restaurant, *Spaanschematriver Rd, Constantia; tel: 021-794 4480* (expensive; open Tues–Sun lunch and dinner, Mon dinner; reservations essential) is one of South Africa's top ten restaurants, set in a top vineyard, serving a mainly Provençal menu. Nearby, the **Cellars Restaurant**, *15 Hohenhort Ave, Constantia; tel: 021-794 2137* (expensive; open Mon–Sun breakfast, à la carte lunch, dinner; reservations essential) also offers excellent French/English cuisine and a broad-ranging wine list. At Groot Constantia, the **Jonkershuis**, *Groot Constantia Wine Estate, Constantia Main Rd, Constantia; tel: 021-794 6255* (moderate; open Mon–Sun 0900–1700) offers Cape Malay dishes, fresh linefish, curries and samplers of Cape cuisine, and the **Groot Constantia Tavern**; *tel: 021-794 1144* (cheap; open daily 1000–2200; weekends reservations essential) is a bustling wine tavern with cheese platters, smoked salmon and cold meats. **Peddlars on the Bend**, *Spaanschmatriver Rd, Constantia; tel: 021-794 7747* (moderate; open Mon–Sun 1100–2300) serves country fare; **Parks Restaurant**, *114 Constantia Rd, Constantia; tel: 021-797 8202* (moderate; open Mon–Sat dinner, Tues–Fri lunch) is excellent, with an eclectic à la carte menu; and **Pages in Thyme**, *60 Main Rd, Plumstead; tel: 021-797 2697* (moderate; open Mon–Sat) specialises in simple South African fare.

Southern Suburbs
The Wild Fig, *Courtyard Hotel, Mowbray; tel: 021-448 0507* (moderate; open daily lunch and dinner; reservations essential) serves excellent pastas, grills and inventive salads. **Jake's**, *5 Summerley Rd, Kenilworth; tel: 021-797 0366* (moderate; open Sun–Fri lunch, Mon–Sat dinner; reservations essential) is a successful,

bustling venue, whose food knows no particular nationality or style. **Obz Café**, *115 Lower Main Rd, Observatory; tel 021-448 5555* (open Mon–Sat lunch, daily dinner) is the coolest, trendiest café in the suburbs, with huge salads, crostini and a good wine list. **The Africa Café**, *213 Lower Main Rd, Observatory; tel: 021-479 553* (open Mon–Sat 1100–1500 lunch, 1830–2400 dinner) serves pan-African cuisine in a friendly, jazzy backstreet location.

SEA POINT TO HOUT BAY

Sea Point is Cape Town's Miami, a densely populated seaside suburb whose sea-facing apartment blocks look out towards Robben Island (see Cape Town, p.105). There's a small beach, a tidal pool (the largest sea water pool in the southern hemisphere) and endless rock pools filled with marine life. A seafront promenade is popular with walkers, joggers and rollerbladers. Busy in the summer, Sea Point's main road is known for its late, late restaurants and diners, its clubs and delicatessen.

Clifton is the next major stop. With four little sandy beaches (First, for trendies; Second, for teenagers; Third, for rich playboys; and Fourth, for families) divided by huge granite boulders, it has some of Africa's most expensive real estate. The steep hillside is layered with terraced apartments, while along the shore, at its foot, are pretty, early 20th-century wooden bungalows, where people holiday or weekend. The water is safe, if freezing; only the hardiest can endure more than about 10 mins. During summer, parking is hard to find. Go early, or take a taxi.

After Clifton, **Camps Bay** has a long, wide beach, prefaced by roadside lawns and dominated by the massive peaks of the magnificent **Twelve Apostles** behind. A dramatic flank of Table Mountain, topped by the cable station, is also visible. The sea is not safe here: it is very cold and has a strong backlash. Children should not swim alone. Camps Bay is popular with picnicking families, particularly at Christmas, while surfers use adjacent **Glen Beach**, just to the right. A variety of shops are handily situated across the road. There are cold showers and volleyball.

After Camps Bay, *Victoria Rd* continues on through Bakoven, then meanders along undeveloped coast to **Llandudno**, where the lovely, small beach has extremely cold water. It and its neighbour, Sandy Bay (Cape Town's only nudist beach; follow the signs), are dominated by a peak called **Little Lion's Head**. The powerful surf at Llandudno attracts surfers, and there is a resident surf lifesaving club. Both Llandudno and Sandy Bay are good places for picnics, but there are no shops or restaurants. To reach the beach at Sandy Bay from the car park, there is a 20-min walk on a rough gravel path. For up-to-date information on surf conditions, call **Surf Report**, *tel: 021-788 5965*. KFM Radio also offers a surf report at 0715 daily.

After Llandudno, **Hout Bay**. Cut wood *(hout)* taken from this area was used in the construction of many of Cape Town's earliest buildings. Principally known for its harbour and fishing fleet, Hout Bay is the centre of the snoek industry and crayfishing – and seafood is a staple of its many restaurants. The beach is a popular venue for windsurfers, hobie cats, paddleskiers and surfers, and is ideal for families. **Drumbeat Charters**, *tel: 021-438 9208*, run boat trips to **Duiker Island**, a seal and bird sanctuary where, during the summer, several thousand Cape Fur Seals can be seen. Inland, **The World of Birds**, *Valley Rd; tel: 021-790 2730* (open daily 0900–1900; R17) is one of the largest wild bird sanctuaries in the country, with over 450 species housed in walk-through sanctuaries designed to simulate natural habitats.

HOUT BAY TO CAPE POINT

The route from Hout Bay to Noordhoek and Kommetjie takes in one of the world's most spectacular scenic drives. An engineering feat completed between 1915 and 1922, the 10 km **Chapman's Peak Drive** is cut into dramatic cliffs dropping sheer to the ocean below. The final stretch of the drive looks down over 6 km Long Beach which, with the hulk of the wrecked ship, the *Kakapo*, was used in the movie, *Ryan's Daughter*. This is one of the loveliest views in the peninsula. The swimming is dangerous, though the powerful surf attracts surfers and windsurfers. Lifeguards are present only in season. The long sands are popular with walkers and horse riders. At the end of

119

Noordhoek beach, Kommetjie is a quiet seaside village whose beach is a favourite for surfers. The water, famously, is freezing. A shallow tidal pool provides safe swimming for children.

CAPE OF GOOD HOPE NATURE RESERVE

Tourist Office: *tel: 021-780 9100* (open 0700–1800 Nov–April, closes sunset, and 0700–1700 May–Oct; R5). Reserve admission, information and maps.

The Cape of Good Hope is the most southerly point of the Cape Peninsula not, as so many erroneously believe, of Africa itself. It is a protected area, a magnificent 7750 hectare reserve for indigenous flora and fauna, and one of the few places near Cape Town where wild animals can be seen in a natural wilderness. However, the low nutritional value of the indigenous vegetation means high numbers of animals cannot be maintained and this is not primarily a game reserve. Sightings can be elusive. Original game species reintroduced include the rare mountain zebra, eland and bontebok, and there are plenty of dog-faced chacma baboons.

The rich and varied indigenous flora is known as *fynbos,* and includes the protea family (see pp.59 and 122). Fynbos is remarkable for the restriction of different species to certain localities, often very small indeed, as a walk in the reserve will show. Some species only grow wild in one place in the whole world: here.

To the east, the reserve's coastline consists of high ground and mountains, their sheer cliffs dropping steeply into the warm waters of the Indian Ocean's False Bay. To the west, the land slopes downwards much more gently in a series of ridges to the wind-blown beaches and dunes pounded by the freezing Atlantic waves (oceanographers may say that the warm and cold currents meet not here but at Cape Agulhas). On a good day, the point elicited the remark, 'the Fairest Cape we saw in the circumference of the world', from Sir Francis Drake, although Bartolomeo Dias, who encountered it a few centuries earlier on a bad day, named it Cabo Tormentoso, the Cape of Storms. Both apply, and the ferocity of the winter weather is matched only by its beauty

and tranquillity in the summer. From the point there are outstanding views; perhaps you'll see the phantom ship, the 17th-century *Flying Dutchman,* which, over the centuries, has brought misfortune to mariners who've spotted her vainly trying to sail around the point and on to Batavia. You can easily spend a day at Cape Point. Drives are laid out throughout the reserve, and there is a restaurant, as well as wild, unspoilt places to picnic at **Buffels Bay** and **Olifantsbos**. Buffels Bay has a tidal pool for safe swimming. Look out for the remains of wrecks, some over a century old, littering the reserve's 40 km coastline, and for shells (particularly at Olifantsbos) and driftwood. The Reserve offers numerous magnificent hikes, including the **Kanonkop Trail** (4 hrs, with potential for swimming at Bordjiesrif) and 6-hr coastal **Groot Blouberg–Cape Point Trail**.

SIMON'S TOWN

Tourist Office: *Main Rd; tel: 021-786 2436* (open Mon–Fri 0900–1600, Sat 0900–1300, Sept–Apr).

Just before reaching Simon's Town proper, **The Boulders** (R3) is an area of huge, smooth granite rocks which stick out of the ocean and the sand, creating safe, shallow inlets. The most southerly of these little beaches (nearest the car park) is the most protected. Swimmers and sunbathers have to share water and sand with an inquisitive colony of delightful African Jackass Penguins. Normally resident on small islands off the coast between Namibia and Port Elizabeth, these penguins are listed as an endangered species, and only here, where, rather unusually, they've chosen to live under the full public gaze, are their numbers increasing. Interfere with them at your peril. This is an idyllic spot, which is why Cape Town crowds into it at weekends. Go early, or visit during the week.

The little port of **Simon's Town**, now the country's principal naval base, was named after Simon van der Stel, Governor of the Cape from 1691–1699, and was used as winter anchorage from 1741. In 1795, British troops made use of it on their way to the Battle of Muizenberg during the First British Occupation, and the Royal Navy made this its headquarters in 1814. In 1957, the SA Navy took over the dockyard.

Today, the town has a quaint turn-of-the-century colonial, if nautical, air and, so far, has managed to avoid slipping into the clutches of developers. Many of the buildings in the main street are over 150 years old. Narrow winding streets climb the hill behind, and there are magnificent views out over False Bay. The best introduction to the town and its surroundings is the **Simon's Town Museum**, *The Residency, Court Rd; tel: 021-786 3046* (open Mon–Fri 0900–1600, Sat 1000–1300), once the governor's residence (built 1777), later a court and prison. Other places to visit include the **Martello Tower**, the **South African Naval Museum**, *West Dockyard; tel: 021-787 4635* (open daily 1000–1600) and the **Warrior Toy Museum**, *St George's St; tel: 021-786 1395* (open daily 1000–1600), which houses a permanent collection of dolls, model cars, boats and trains. For tours of the **naval dockyard**, *tel: 021-787 3911*.

FISH HOEK TO MUIZENBERG

False Bay Tourist Office: *52 Beach Rd, Muizenberg; tel: 021-788 1898* (open Mon–Fri 0900–1700, Sat and Sun 0900–1200).

Fish Hoek is a popular seaside resort with a wide, safe beach and warm water. Fish Hoek Bay, with Fish Hoek on one side and Clovelly on the other, is much frequented by catamaran sailors and windsurfers. This is also one of the places in which Southern Right whales choose to calve annually in Aug and Sept. Fish Hoek has the distinction of being the only teetotal town in the country – a stipulation laid down in 1818 by Lord Charles Somerset, who also declared free fishing rights for all. Behind Fish Hoek, **Peers Cave** is the home of 'Fish Hoek Man', who lived in this rock shelter about 15,000 years ago. Peers Cave can be visited, though the walk up to it is long and arduous.

From Fish Hoek, the road passes Clovelly and Glencairn, with pretty beaches, and continues on to **Kalk Bay**. The name 'kalk' means 'lime': in the 17th century, shells were burnt to produce lime for painting houses. This small, picturesque fishing harbour – particularly busy during the June–July snoek season – is home to the brightly painted False Bay fishing fleet. Fresh fish is flung in heaps on the quay and

auctioned off in the harbour. The main road has a variety of antique and junk stores, craft shops and places to eat. Wander through the steep, cobbled back streets dotted with Victorian cottages and soak up the atmosphere. The mountain slopes above the town are pitted with deep caves and provide many good walks. Out in the bay, **Seal Island** is home to seals and birds and is one of the few breeding grounds of the great white shark. To view the sharks here or, even better, off Dyer Island on the south-east coast (near Gansbaai), call **White Shark Ecoventures**, *tel: 021-419 8204*. Experienced divers can view from the safety of a galvanised steel cage suspended in the water, others view from the boat's deck. There are endless possibilities for game and deep-sea fishing: **Bluefin Charters**, *tel: 021-783 1756*, **Adventure Safaris & Sport Tours**, *tel: 021-438 5201;* and **Game Fish Charters**, *tel: 021-790 4550*. Professional information can be obtained from **WP Deep Sea Angling Association**, *tel: 021-924 386*, and the **WP Shore Angling Association**, *tel: 021-557 8428*.

Continuing up the coast, **St James** is named after an early church built here in 1874. In the 19th century, this was a holiday resort for rich Capetonians. Magnificent villas overlook the bay and the little sheltered beach is characterised by brightly painted bathing boxes. A tidal pool provides safe swimming for children.

Close by is **Muizenberg**, a popular seaside resort, and once Rudyard Kipling's favourite swimming spot. Many of the millionaire randlords had holiday homes here: one is now the **Natale Labia Museum**, *192 Main Rd, tel: 021-788 4106* (open Tues–Sun 1000–1700; free), a satellite museum of the South African National Gallery, while **Rhodes's Cottage**, *Main Rd, tel: 021-788 1816* (open Tues–Sun 1000–1300, 1400–1700; free) is a memorial museum – Rhodes died here in 1902. Muizenberg's star has faded somewhat now, but nothing can change the view across its lovely beach, which stretches 35 km to Gordon's Bay at the far side of False Bay. Shallow and safe for bathing, there are no rocks and the warm breakers are good for surfing (**Surfer's Corner** is the local surfers' nursery). There are numerous species of shark, including the great white, but shallow water keeps them away from swimmers. Dolphins and seals play in the surf and whales come in to calve. Rows of colourful changing booths line the sand, and there is a pavilion, an esplanade and an amusement park.

CONSTANTIA

Originally a farm presented to Governor Simon van der Stel by Commissioner van Rheede in 1684, Constantia is a well-known wine-producing valley. There are many historic houses in the vicinity, and of these, **Groot Constantia**, van der Stel's own country house, is perhaps the best known. Able to boast that it's at the heart of the country's oldest wine estate, the Cape Dutch manor house, *off Constantia Rd; tel: 021-794 5067* (open daily 1000–1700; R2), is much restored. Rebuilt, probably by Louis Thibault and the sculptor Anton Anreith (see his magnificent stucco pediment on the winery), today it is a museum of farm life in the 1800s, with collections of mid 18th–century furniture and Japanese, Rhenish and Delft porcelain. The **Wine Museum** (same opening hours and ticket as the manor) in the old winery houses drinking and storage vessels from 500 BC to the 19th century. The complex has places to eat formally and informally, buy and taste wine, and hosts a monthly antiques fair. The short **Constantia Wine Route**, *tel: 021-794 5128*, comprises three wine estates – **Groot Constantia**, **Klein Constantia**, *tel: 021-794 5188* and **Buitenverwachting**, *tel: 021-794 5190*.

KIRSTENBOSCH

Kirstenbosch Botanical Gardens, *Rhodes Dr., Newlands; tel: 021-762 1166* (open daily 0800–1800 Apr–Aug; 0700–1900 Sept–Mar; R5, pensioners free Tues; free guided walks Tues, Sat 1100; eco-tours daily, hourly 1000–1600, R20; glasshouse tours daily 1000, 1200, 1400, 1600, R10; 45-min clubcar rides, 5 people max per car, 0900–1600, R10. Guides for groups by prior arrangement).

Cecil John Rhodes, who bequeathed the land to the nation, is directly responsible for the foundation of this superb botanical garden, one of the most important in the world, founded in

Proteas

Proteas, part of the **Fynbos** group of plants, appear in many and varied forms. In fact, they take their name (given them by the Swedish taxonomist Linnaeus) from the Greek 'old man of the sea', who was able to assume any form. Concentrated in southern Africa and Australia, there are more than 300 species in South Africa. They flower at various times of the year; good places to see them are the Cape of Good Hope Nature Reserve and Kirstenbosch Botanical Gardens. Some are rare, like the *Mimetes fimbrufolius,* found at Smitswinkel Bay, hard by the Cape of Good Hope Nature Reserve, others are more common, like the *Protea repens,* the sugarbush – the protea adopted as South Africa's national flower.

1913. Devoted almost exclusively to the indigenous flora of southern Africa, it now contains about 9000 of South Africa's 22,000 plant species. Plants selected for inclusion have horticultural potential, are of botanical interest, enjoy rare and endangered status, or are used for educational or scientific purposes. With 36 hectares of formal gardens, including a braille trail and fragrance garden for the blind, and nearly 500 hectares of wild *fynbos* and coastal forest on the eastern slope of Table Mountain, there are numerous walks, a popular restaurant (open breakfast, lunch and tea) and a Garden Shop selling plants and flora-related books. Musical concerts are held at Kirstenbosch every Sun in summer.

Rhodes Memorial

Off Rhodes Dr., Rondebosch (open daily 24 hrs). One of the most dramatically sited buildings in Cape Town, this memorial to Cecil John Rhodes was designed by Sir Herbert Baker and Francis Masey (1912) and built from Table Mountain granite. On the slopes beyond are rare fallow deer, zebra and wildebeest. A pretty stone tearoom is located next to the memorial; *tel: 021-689 9151* (open Tues–Sat 0930–1700, Sun 1700).

CAPE TOWN– CLANWILLIAM

From winelands to deserted beaches, parched landscapes, whales and pretty country towns, this route is hugely varied. Wild flowers, however, are its most spectacular attraction: each spring, thousands carpet the landscape to Namaqualand.

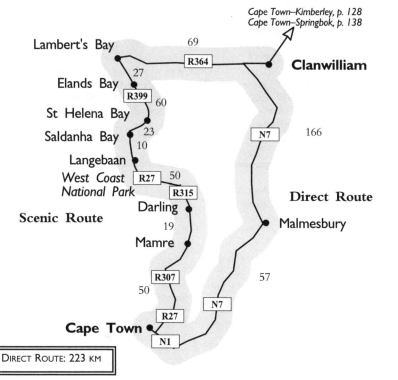

Cape Town–Kimberley, p. 128
Cape Town–Springbok, p. 138

Lambert's Bay   69
R364   Clanwilliam
Elands Bay   27
R399   60
St Helena Bay
Saldanha Bay   23   N7   166
10
Langebaan
West Coast   R27   50
National Park   R315
Darling   **Direct Route**
Scenic Route   19   Malmesbury
Mamre
R307   57
50
N7
R27
Cape Town
N1

123

DIRECT ROUTE: 223 KM

ROUTES

DIRECT ROUTE

Leave Cape Town on the N1. After 10 km, branch left on the Malmesbury turn off to the N7, and continue to Clanwilliam. Distance: 223 km; allow 2½ hrs.

SCENIC ROUTE

Leave Cape Town on the N1. After 3 km, branch left on to the R27 at the Paarden Eiland/Velddrif turn off. After 47 km, turn right on to the R307 and follow the signs to Atlantis and **Mamre**. From Mamre, continue along the R307 to **Darling** (19 km), then take the R315 back to the R27 (15 km). Continue north for 10 km, then branch left and

Darling's Flower Shows

Darling's annual **Spring Wild Flower Show**, *Darling Sports Ground* (third week Sept) lures about 15,000 spectators to the town. This event coincides with the spring flowering of over 1000 species of plants. The spectacle is extraordinary – though not unique to Darling. In this particular area, the flowers – daisies, bloupypies, arum lilies, nemesias – emerge two months after the first rains (last week of Aug) and disappear just a few weeks later (mid Sept–mid Oct). In the nearby Swartland and Sandveld (east of Darling), arum lilies and other flowers can be seen alongside the road July–Oct.

Near to Darling are a series of small, private reserves in which to witness the extravagant spring flower displays: the **Darling Flora Reserve**, *5 km south of town on the R307*; the **Tienie Versveld Flora Reserve**, *15 km on the R315 between Darling and the R27*; **Contreberg**, *closer to Mamre than Darling on the R307* (enter on foot only); **Waylands Farm**, *6 km from Darling on the R307* (enter by car and then walk); and **Oudepost**, *3 km from Darling on the R307* (enter by car or on foot). The **Duckitt Nurseries**, *3 km south of Darling on the R307; tel: 02241-2602/2606 or 2352* (open May–Nov first Sat of the month 0900–1200), is a large orchid nursery, whose **Orchid Show** (14–17 Sept) of cymbidium and phalaenopsis orchid plants and flowers (for sale or simply to view) coincides with the Spring Wild Flower Show. The **Flowerline**, *tel: 021-418 3705* (open daily 0800–1600 June–13 Oct, and from April Mon–Fri 0800–1630, Sat and Sun 0830–1600 for advance planning) provides details on the condition of the flowers day-by-day, accommodation, tours and special attractions in the flower regions. The **Spring Wild Flower Show** (14–17 Sept) is a key event – contact the tourist office for details. **Tailormade Tours**, *tel: 021-729 800 or 011-486 0975*, offers a variety of flower tours (prices from R1890 for 3 days per person sharing).

124

enter the **West Coast National Park**. Within the reserve itself, the road forks: to the left is pretty Churchhaven; to the right, **Langebaan** straddles the mouth of Langebaan Lagoon as it opens to Saldanha Bay.

An untarred route links Langebaan with the town of **Saldanha Bay**. From Saldanha Bay, head north on the R45 via Vredenburg to join the R399. After 10 km on the R399, branch left and follow the signs to **St Helena Bay**. Return to the R399, and continue through Velddrif to Laaiplek and Dwarskersbos, from which an untarred road proceeds north through Soutkuil to **Elands Bay**. Leaving Elands Bay, follow the signs to Leipoldtville. Just before you reach the town, take an untarred turning on the left, along the R365 to **Lambert's Bay** (28 km). The tarred R364 links Lambert's Bay with Clanwilliam (69 km).

MAMRE

Tourist Office: *Blaauwberg Municipality; tel: 021-576 1073* (open office hours).

Situated in a lush region once known as De Groene Kloof (Green Ravine), picturesque Mamre, like Genadendal near Caledon (see p. 134), began life in 1808 as a mission station. Run by the German Moravian Society, its activities were aimed at the remnants of the Khoikhoi, who had taken refuge in the area. The missionaries colonised a collection of abandoned 18th-century military buildings, and erected a **church** (1817), parsonage, school, **water mill** (now the museum) and the characteristic whitewashed, black-thatched cottages, which are still there today. The mission buildings can be viewed Mon–Sat 0900–1300; *tel: 021-576 1117; R5.*

DARLING

Tourist Office: *Pastorie St, Darling; tel: 02241-3361* (open Mon–Fri 0900–1600).

ACCOMMODATION AND FOOD

A number of small establishments offer simple, peaceful places to stay. The **Darling Guesthouse**, *Pastorie St; tel/fax: 02241-2385*, and **Old Buffers**, *9 Station Rd; tel: 02241-3008*, are amongst the best. Both cheap. Book well in advance during festival season.

There aren't many places to eat here, though **Zum Schatzi**, *6 Long St; tel: 02241-3095* (cheap; open Tues–Sun lunch and dinner) is a German restaurant. Darling is close to the **Swartland Wine Route** (see pp.139–140), some of whose wine farms offer lunch.

SIGHTSEEING

Laid out in 1853, and named after the retiring Lieutenant-Governor of the Cape, Sir Charles Henry Darling, this country town is the focus of the surrounding farms, which are noted for their dairy produce, peas, wool, export lupins and chincerinchees.

The **Darling Museum**, *Pastorie St; tel: 02241-3361* (open Mon–Sat 0900–1300, 1400–1600, Sun 1115–1300, 1400–1630; R2), otherwise known as the 'Butter Museum', outlines the history of the local dairy industry, the Darling Creamery once having been a key dairy co-operative. The museum also records the founding and development of Darling and its community, while its art gallery features the work of the many local artists living and working here. A **Darling Art Walk** (first weekend of every month; enquire at the museum) opens up their homes and studios. The **Hildebrand Monument** is a memorial to Field Cornet CP Hildebrand of the Boer Forces' Maritz Commando; Darling is the most southerly village to which a Boer commando penetrated during the Anglo-Boer War (1899–1902).

The **Darling Arts Festival** is held in the third week of September.

LANGEBAAN

Tourist Office: *corner Bree St and Main Rd, Langebaan; tel: 02287-22115* (open Mon–Fri 0930–1630, Sat 0900–1200).

ACCOMMODATION AND FOOD

Langebaan is not well equipped with first-class accommodation. However, one of the best places to stay on the West Coast happens to be here: **The Farmhouse**, *5 Egret St; tel: 02287-22062, fax: 02287-21980* (cheap) set on a hillside overlooking the lagoon. **Club Mykonos**, *2 Lietjieklip, Olifantskop, Langebaan; tel: 02287-22101, fax: 02287-22303* (cheap), a hotel, time-share and resort complex, is an ersatz recreation of a Greek island town. It's convenient and has a variety of places to eat. Otherwise, there are private homes to rent: **Cape Hiring Service**, *tel: 02287-22772;* **Freeport**, *tel: 02287-21277;* **Harveys Rental Agency**, *tel: 02287-21322;* **Langebaan Properties**, *tel: 02287-22409*. **Campsites:** the Langebaan Municipality runs four caravan and campsites; *tel: 02287-22115* (office hours).

The **Farmhouse**, *5 Egret St; tel: 02287-22062* (cheap; open daily lunch and dinner) is a hotel with a lovely terrace restaurant. For seafood cooked on beach braais (swim between courses), visit **Die Strandloper Seafood Restaurant**; *tel: 02287-22490*. From the R27, turn left at the Langebaan turn off and, 8 km later, turn right towards Mykonos. Die Strandloper is 200 yards on the left (cheap; open lunch and dinner; reservations essential). Take your own drink.

SIGHTSEEING

Langebaan is a very popular holiday spot, favoured by anglers, divers and swimmers, while the sailing conditions are the best anywhere on the coast (there is good mooring, a good slipway and a comfortable club house, with temporary membership available to visitors). The village straddles the shores of a lovely lagoon, discovered at the beginning of the 17th century. The first Europeans, aware of the area's potential as a sea haven, were finally discouraged from settling because of a fresh water shortage. Had this not been the case, nearby Saldanha may well have become the Mother City instead of Cape Town. The whole area flourished on the back of the whale industry – at the beginning of this century, this was the location of the biggest whaling station in the entire southern hemisphere.

The tidal, salt-water, plankton-rich lagoon penetrates the land for 17 km behind the Atlantic coast, from Saldanha Bay to the village of Geelbek. It is one of the world's most important wetlands and represents almost 42% of South Africa's salt marshes, much of it protected by the **West Coast National Park**; *tel: 02287-22144*. Enter from the R27, 120 km from Cape Town, or continue up the R27 for a further 22 km before turning left to Langebaan (a longer route). Open sunrise to sunset for access – Nature Reserve only open during the flower season Aug–Sept; out of season, R12.50 per car from the Langebaan entrance, free at the R27 entrance; during season, R18.75 per car from both entrances.

This important park, comprising 20,000 hectares of coastlands, was set up to preserve the landscape, flora and the prolific bird life that flocks here in the summer. It encompasses the entire lagoon, including the **Postberg Nature Reserve** beyond the pretty fishing hamlet of **Churchhaven**, on the peninsula arm protecting the lagoon from the sea (the extremity is closed to the public). In addition to magnificent displays of spring flowers, it boasts a variety of game, including black and blue wildebeest, bontebok and eland, and huge colonies of birds. The park is home to 50% of the total world population of a subspecies of the silver gull, houses 25% of the breeding population of the great crested grebe, almost 12% of the world population of the black oystercatcher, and provides pasture for thousands of waders which, breeding in the higher Arctic latitudes, migrate to Langebaan during the northern winter. There are four islands – **Malgas**, on which, over the years, Cape gannets, cormorants and penguins have produced a layer of guano more than 10 m thick; **Jutten**; **Marcus**; and **Schaapen**. Whales can be seen in **Plankies Bay**.

SALDANHA BAY

Tourist Office: *Oorlogsvlei, Van Riebeeck St, Saldanha Bay; tel: 02281-42088* (open Mon–Fri 0830–1300, 1400–1700).

ACCOMMODATION

Chains hotels include *Pa.* The **Mermaid's Guest House**, *6 Vondeling St; tel: 02281-44416, fax: 02281-41345*, and **Jane's Guest House**, *8 Beach Rd; tel: 02281-43605, fax: 02281-41522*, are both cheap, simple and comfortable, while the **Oranjevlei Guest Farm**, *on the R45 between Vredenberg and Saldanha Bay; tel: 2281-42261* (cheap) offers accommodation in a farm setting. Elsewhere, there are holiday flats

and cottages to rent – enquire at the Tourist Office. **Campsites**: **Saldanha Holiday Resort**, *Beach Rd, Saldanha Bay; tel: 02281-42247*; **Tabakbaai Holiday Resort**, *Diaz Rd, Tabakbaai, Saldanha Bay; tel: 02281-42248*.

There are plenty of places to eat at Saldanha. The restaurant at the **Mermaid Guest House** (see above) is excellent; open daily lunch and dinner.

SIGHTSEEING

Saldanha Bay is one of the world's great natural harbours. The water is deep enough for large ships, and it is safe and protected. If there had been enough freshwater, there is little doubt that this would have been the country's original main port. Its name commemorates a 16th-century Portuguese admiral, Antonio de Saldanha, who never even visited the area. The name was originally given to Table Bay, but was later moved to this town by the Dutch.

Saldanha is a very popular resort and there is a lot to do here. **Schaafsma Charters**; *tel: 02281-44235,* operate **boat trips** out to, and around, the islands of Malgas and Jutten to see the huge colonies of birds between Nov and Mar. It costs R65 per person or R600 per boat for the 3 hr round-trip to Malgas; R75 per person or R1000 per boat for the 5 hr trip to Malgas and Jutten. Ask them also about opportunities to go deep-sea angling to the submerged volcanic island of Mt Verna (500 nautical miles to the west of Lambert's Bay).

The town also has ample opportunities for sailing (Saldanha has a good slipway but poor mooring facilities), swimming, hiking and feasting on marine catch from oysters and prawns to perlemoen (abalone).

ST HELENA BAY

Tourist Office: see Saldanha Bay.

ACCOMMODATION AND FOOD

Accommodation in St Helena is simple. **Steenberg's Cove Hotel**, *Main Rd, St Helena; tel: 02283-61160; fax: 02283-61560* (cheap) has excellent sea views and a restaurant (open for breakfast, lunch and dinner). The **Paternoster Hotel**, *Paternoster; tel: 02281-752 703, fax: 02281-752 750* (cheap) is a simple, comfortable hotel about 20 km from St Helena, whose restaurant serves excellent seafood (book in advance). **Campsite: Boulevard Travelodge Caravan Park**, *Golden Mile, Britannia Bay; tel: 02284-773.*

To eat out, try **De Palm**, on the Main Rd (R27), 2 km after Steenberg's Cove Hotel – watch for the signs; *tel: 02283-61704* (open daily lunch and dinner), which has excellent, freshly caught fish in rustic surroundings with live jazz – evenings only.

SIGHTSEEING

St Helena Bay is something of an oddity. Historically, it is one of the oldest European reconnaissance points in the country (Vasco da Gama sailed into the bay in 1497, on St Helena's Day – his first stop in Africa). Its beautiful, beach-lined bay is today adorned with stinking fish factories. The fishing industry here is the largest in the country – snoek and crayfish are also in abundance. Few fishermen return home empty-handed. Visit the quay during the snoek season (May–July), collect shells on the beaches and dine on an exciting array of seafood. To the west of St Helena, **Britannia Bay** offers good swimming, surfing and windsurfing, as does the nearby fishing village of **Paternoster**.

ELANDS BAY

Tourist office: *Swartland and Sandveld Region, 95 Voortrekker Rd, Malmesbury; tel: 0224-22996* (open Mon–Fri 0800–1700).

Book well ahead when visiting during the flower season, as the **Eland Hotel**, *Elands Bay; tel: 0265-790* (cheap) only has 16 rooms. **Campsite: Dwarskersbos Holiday Resort and Camping Site**, *Dwarskersbos; tel: 02288-40110*, has 156 stands protected by the shade of the *kersbos* (candle trees).

Elands Bay is a tiny fishing village at the foot of the Bobbejaansberge (Baboon Mountain), at the mouth of the Verlorenvlei. People visit for two things: the surfing and the crayfish. Surfers congregate here in huge numbers at weekends, even though the water is cold. The rock formations at the foot of the mountain, as it plunges into the sea, are an ideal breeding ground for crayfish.

LAMBERT'S BAY

Tourist Office: *Kerkstraat (in the Sandveld Museum), Lambert's Bay; tel: 027-432 2335* (open Mon–Fri 0900–1300, Sat 0900–1300).

ACCOMMODATION AND FOOD

The quality and quantity of hotel accommodation generally decrease the further up the West Coast you go. Guesthouse accommodation is provided by the **Raston Gasthaus**, *24 Riedeman St, Lambert's Bay; tel: 027-432 2431; fax: 027-432 2422* (cheap). For ungraded holiday accommodation, contact **Cape Holiday Homes**, *tel: 021-419 0430*, or the local tourist office. **Campsite: Lambert's Bay Caravan Park**, *tel: 027-432 2238;* follow the signs as you enter town.

Chains hotels include *Pa.*

Alfresco dining is the order of the day at the informal **Bosduifklip Open-air Restaurant**, *Albina Farm, 4 km from Lamberts Bay; tel: 027-432 2735* (cheap; open daily lunch and dinner; book in advance), or **Muisbosskerm**, *5 km south of Lambert's Bay on the Elands Bay road; tel: 027-432 1017* (cheap; open daily lunch and dinner; advance booking essential), which provides freshly caught seafood cooked on the beach.

SIGHTSEEING

Lambert's Bay is a fishing community famous for locally caught crayfish. The **Sandveld Museum**, *Kerk Straat, Lambert's Bay* (open Mon–Fri 0900–1200, 1400–1600, Sat 1000–1100; R2) preserves antiques and memorabilia of the region. **Bird Island**, at the entrance to the pretty harbour, is a breeding ground for hundreds of Cape gannets, cormorants, penguins and other seabirds – yielding 300 tonnes of guano annually. Although you cannot visit the island, a blind has been erected for viewing. An excellent time to visit is during the flower season, when the wild veld flowers reach to the beach. A series of pans at **Steenbokfontein** and **Wagendrift**, about 8 km south of Lambert's Bay, are a favourite haunt of aquatic birds; bird-watchers take their binoculars.

CLANWILLIAM

See Cape Town–Springbok, pp. 138–143.

127

CAPE TOWN–KIMBERLEY

This route heads through some of the toughest, most arid and harsh sections of the Karoo. Only the hardiest should attempt it; for those that do, the rewards are great. The landscape, littered with fragments of doleritic rock and the occasional clump of trees, is magnificent. Drive slowly, wake at dawn for sunrise, stay up late and see the night sky. Unsullied by urban light, the skies are brilliant with stars not normally encountered elsewhere. It is a huge, sparsely populated region in which hotel accommodation is, on the whole, simple.

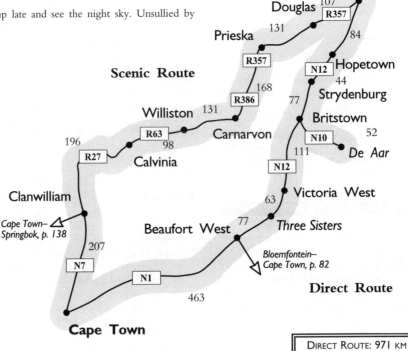

128

DIRECT ROUTE: 971 KM

ROUTES

DIRECT ROUTE

→ The most direct, and certainly the quickest, way to reach Kimberley from Cape Town is to head north on the N1 through Beaufort West, as far as Three Sisters (540 km), named after three significant hillocks which mark the landscape on the way north. There, branch left on to the N12 and continue to **Victoria West** (63 km), **Britstown** (111 km), **Strydenburg** (77 km), **Hopetown** (44 km) and, finally, Kimberley. Distance: 971 km;

allow a minimum of two days to do the journey safely.

SCENIC ROUTE

 The alternative route is far longer with greater distances between stops, but it is also more scenic, taking to remote country roads through the back of beyond. Leave Cape Town on the N7 and head north to **Clanwilliam** (207 km). From here, continue along the N7 for 75 km to Vanrhynsdorp, then turn left on to the R27 for **Calvinia** (121 km). From Calvinia, take the R63 through **Williston** (98 km) to **Carnarvon** (131 km), from where the untarred R386 heads north, joining the tarred R357 just 10 km before **Prieska** (Carnarvon to Prieska, 168 km). The section between Carnarvon and Prieska is fairly arduous. Make sure you have spares, extra water and fuel, and are able to repair a puncture. From Prieska, the R357 continues on to **Douglas** (131 km) and Kimberley (a further 107 km). In total, 1038 km; allow a minimum of four days.

TRAINS AND BUSES

The Trans Karoo has a daily service between Cape Town and Kimberley. The Trans Oranje operates the same route on Mon. Both journeys approx. 16½ hrs. OTT Table 3519.

Greyhound Citiliner has a Cape Town–Johannesburg service (Mon) via Beaufort West and Kimberley. Translux has the same service Tues, Thur, Fri, Sun. Journey time: 12 hrs. OTT Table 3541.

BEAUFORT WEST

See Bloemfontein to Cape Town, pp.87–88.

VICTORIA WEST

Tourist Office: *Municipality, 87 Church St; tel: 053-621 0026 (open weekdays 0800–1700).*

Hickman's Halfway House, *Church St; tel: 02042 ask for 129 (cheap)* is a simple, but reasonable hotel. Probably better value for money is the **Melton Wold Guest Farm**, *40 km from Victoria West on the Loxton Rd; tel: 02042 ask for 1430 (cheap–moderate)*, a lovely 19th-century farmhouse. **Campsite: Victoria West Caravan Park**, *Miggelstone Rd; tel: 02042-26.*

Victoria West, which takes its name from Britain's most famous modern queen, is a lovely Karoo town with a turn-of-the-century character. Founded in 1843, it was an important stepping stone on the way north for those joining the diamond rush. In the **Victoria West Museum**, *Church St; tel: 053-621 0413* (open Mon–Fri 0745–1300, 1400–1645; free) are some interesting exhibits, including Stone Age artefacts.

To the south (1 km on the Carnarvon road) is the **Victoria West Nature Reserve** (open daily dawn–dusk; for access, ask at the *Municipality, 87 Church St* for a key; free). Home to Burchell's zebra, eland, springbok, blesbok and gemsbok, there are several short walking trails.

BRITSTOWN

Tourist Office: *Municipality, Mark St; tel: 053-6712, ask for 3 or 053-675 0202 (open office hours).*

The only hotel in Britstown is the 2-star **Transkaroo**, *13 Market St; tel: 053-6712, ask for 27, fax: 053-6712, ask for 363 (cheap).* **Campsite: Britstown Caravan Park**, *Market St; tel: 5732-712.*

Britstown is a principal centre for sheep farming and associated industries – wool, mutton and karakul skins. It was named after Hans Brits, who accompanied David Livingstone on one of his journeys. He also owned the farm on which the town was founded in 1877, as a staging post on the route to the diamond fields. The **Municipality Museum**, *Holy Trinity Church, Market St; tel: 0536, ask for 3* (open Mon–Thur 0800–1700, Fri 0800–1430; free) is filled with interesting local history.

⤵ SIDE TRACK
FROM BRITSTOWN

DE AAR

To reach De Aar (52 km from the turn off), branch right at Britstown on to the N10.

Tourist Office: *Municipality Buildings, Voortrekker St; tel: 05363-60927 (open office hours).*

The Hopetown Diamond

In 1866, near Hopetown, Erasmus Jacobs, son of Daniel Jacobs, a farmer on the banks of the Orange River, picked up a pretty, shiny pebble to play with. A neighbour, Schalk van Niekerk, offered to buy it, but the family thought it worthless and gave it to him.

Van Niekerk took it to Colesberg for verification; it turned out to be a 21.25 carat yellow diamond, which became known as the *Eureka*. The first diamond found in South Africa, it was bought by Sir Philip Wodehouse, then Governor of the Cape, for £500; today, it can be seen in the **Kimberley Mine Museum**, see p.232.

In 1869, a Griqua shepherd found an even bigger diamond, the *Star of South Africa* (83.5 carats), which was also acquired by van Niekerk. This was eventually bought for £30,000 by the British Earl of Dudley. Needless to say, there was a rush of diamond prospectors, but gems proved elusive and gradually interest in Hopetown as a source of great, quick wealth dwindled – but not before diamond hunters had discovered rich deposits at Kimberley and Barkly West.

The Jacobs family received nothing and died impoverished and embittered.

Accommodation is sparse in De Aar; try the 1-star **Mountain View Hotel**, *Topaas St; tel: 05363-2223* (cheap). **Campsite: Oasis Caravan Park**, *Wenport St; tel: 05363-4381*.

De Aar is a famous railway junction; it is also South Africa's second largest, with about 92 trains passing through each day, amongst them a number of steam locomotives. If you are a railway enthusiast, then come to De Aar. Otherwise it lives up to its reputation: deadly dull and hot in summer, cold in winter. Pay a visit to **Olive Schreiner's House**, *Grundlingh St; tel: 05732-3535*. Now a restaurant, the famous author lived here between 1907 and 1913.

STRYDENBURG

Tourist Office: *Municipality, Liebenberg St; tel: 053682, ask for 16* (open office hours).

Try the 1-star **Excelsior Hotel**, *Church St; tel: 053682 ask for 106* (cheap). **Campsite: Strydenburg Caravan Park**, *Hopetown Rd; tel: 05762-16*.

At one time a staging post between Britstown and the diamond fields of Kimberley, Strydenburg is still little more. Sheep farming gives additional importance, while Brakwater, a large shallow pan just outside town, is an attraction during the rainy season, when flocks of flamingos fly in.

HOPETOWN

Tourist Office: *Municipality, Church St; tel: 053-203 0008* (open Mon–Fri 0730–1300, 1400–1600).

The 2-star **Radnor Hotel**, *25 Church St; tel: 053-203 0015* (cheap) is small and simple, but offers excellent hospitality.

It was the discovery here, in 1866, of the Eureka diamond, and in 1869 of the Star of South Africa (see above) that led to the great South African diamond rush. Hopetown became an instant tented city, as the fortune hunters rushed in, but disappointment followed as the early promise failed and few diamonds were found. Nevertheless, Hopetown prospered as its inhabitants took to supplying Kimberley. There was a slight resurgence of the diamond industry in 1917, when alluvial deposits were discovered along the banks of the Gariep River, but Hopetown's prosperity now depends on stock and fruit farming.

CLANWILLIAM

See Cape Town–Springbok, pp.138–143.

CALVINIA

Tourist Office: *Church St; tel: 0273-411 712* (open Mon–Fri 0830–1700 and Sat 0900–1200).

The **Hamtam Hotel**, *Church St; tel: 0273-411 512, fax: 0273-412 462* (cheap) is a cosy hotel, which also serves pub lunches.

Campsite: **Calvinia Caravan Park**, *Tuin St; tel: 0273-411 011.*

A large sheep farming centre, Calvinia is a fairly prosperous market town, with wide, dusty streets typical of the Karoo towns. The **Calvinia Museum**, *Church St; tel: 0273-411 043* (open Mon–Fri 0900–1300, 1400–1700; R1) houses local ephemera, together with a display on Abraham Esau, who formed a pro-British defense force amongst the local coloured population during the Boer War, and was shot for his pains. The small, curious museum is housed in Calvinia's former synagogue. The 2300 hectare **Akkerendam Nature Reserve**, just north of town, is a bird sanctuary with some pleasant hiking trails.

WILLISTON

Tourist Office: *Municipality, Herbst St; tel: 02052, ask for 3* (open Mon–Fri 0900–1200, 1300–1500).

Accommodation: try **The Williston Hotel**, *Lutz St; tel: 02052, ask for 5* (1-star; cheap).

Williston, a small dusty town in the middle of nowhere, is perhaps one of the region's most interesting places. Not only is it dominated by an extraordinary sandstone church, but it is the focus of an area famous for an architectural oddity: **corbelled houses**. The earliest date, perhaps, from the mid 19th century, but their form is remarkably similar to those built in the Mediterranean in megalithic times. Flat stones, piled on top of one another so that the structure is conical and beehive-like, create a simple, one-roomed dwelling which housed an entire family and their servants. Cool during the summer and warm in winter, these were the preferred dwellings of the early stock farmers, who were the first to settle permanently in the Karoo. On **Arbeidsfontein Farm**, *30 km east of town*, it is possible to visit and even, perhaps, stay in one of these stone beehives; ask at the Tourist Office for details.

CARNARVON

Tourist Office: *Municipality, Hanau St; tel: 02032, ask for 12* (open office hours).

There are two local hotels: the **Astoria**, *Victoria St; tel: 02032, ask for 110;* and the **Carnarvon**, *Pastorie St; tel: 02032, ask for 95* (both 1-star; cheap).

The terrain around Carnarvon is a one of flat-topped hillocks, the might and magnificence of the typical Karoo landscape dwarfing what Man has made. The town, a pleasant oasis, began life as a mission station (c. 1850). **Carnarvon Museum**, *Hanau St; tel: 02032, ask for 12* (open Mon–Fri 0800–1300, Sat–Sun by request; free) is interesting – see in particular the corbelled dwelling. Others are on nearby **Stuurfontein Farm** and at Williston (see opposite).

PRIESKA

Tourist Office: *Municipality, Victoria St; tel: 0594-61002* (open office hours).

Try the **Prieska Hotel**, *corner Steward and Church Sts; tel/fax: 0594-31129* (cheap).

In order to reach Prieska, travellers must cross the Gariep River. Originally a well-used river crossing frequented by pioneers heading into the interior, in 1878, a town was founded at the spot. It is a lonely remote area, known for its sheep ranches and vegetable and fruit farms. Mining is a key activity; Prieska is a centre for tiger's eye gemstones. Overlooking the town is an octagonal, British **fort**, built almost entirely of unpolished tiger's eye, used in the Anglo-Boer War.

On the river, **Die Bos** is a resort, where the locals go to swim in an effort to escape the intense summer heat.

DOUGLAS

The **Douglas Hotel**, *Church St; tel: 053-298 1029* (cheap).

Douglas, an agricultural centre originally founded in 1848 as a mission station, is famous, chiefly, for a series of **San rock engravings** on nearby Driekop Island in the Riet River, just east of town. To find them, take the Douglas–Kimberley road, turn off at the Plooysburg sign and continue for 8 km, before turning off the road to a marked parking area.

KIMBERLEY

See pp. 230–233.

CAPE TOWN– MOSSEL BAY

This route traverses the Hottentots Holland Mountains, sweeping east on to Mossel Bay and the Garden Route. Take the longer, coastal R44 skirting False Bay, and you will find first-class beaches, resorts, nature reserves, some of the world's great angling waters and your best chance of seeing whales from the shore.

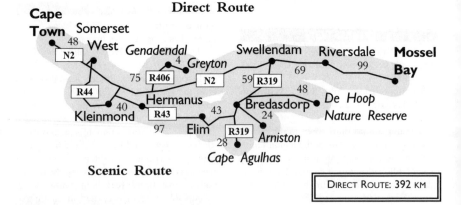

Direct Route

Scenic Route

DIRECT ROUTE: 392 KM

ROUTES

DIRECT ROUTE

Cape Town and Mossel Bay are linked by the N2. Distance: 392 km; allow 5 hrs.

SCENIC ROUTE

Leave Cape Town on the N2 towards **Somerset West**. Take the Strand turn off (48 km) and follow signs through Gordon's Bay to the coastal R44 through Betty's Bay and **Kleinmond**, which loops round to meet the R43 at Botriviervlei. For the side track to Genadendal and Greyton, join the N2 east towards Swellendam then branch left on the R406 (35 km).

For the main route, branch right at Botriviersvlei and follow the signs to **Hermanus**, then Gansbaai. Just before reaching Gansbaai, branch left through the hamlets of Strandskloof and Baardskeerdersbos to **Elim**. Much of this section is on slow gravel roads. From Elim follow the signs to the R319 Bredasdorp-Struisbaai/L'Agulhas and continue to Bredasdorp (43 km).

After side tracks to Cape Agulhas and Arniston, return to Bredasdorp and take the R319 north for 6 km, then branch right on to the untarred Bredasdorp-Malgas road. Just before Ouplaas, turn right for **De Hoop Nature Reserve** (10 km). Rejoin the Bredasdorp-Malgas road and cross the Breede River by pont (nominal charge), go through Malgas and turn left on to the R324 into Swellendam. From Swellendam the N2 heads through Heidelberg and Riversdale to Mossel Bay (168 km).

BUSES

Greyhound operates 2 trips a day to Mossel Bay via Somerset West and Riverdale. One is a daytime service, the other overnight. Translux has the same service, but the overnight bus only runs 4 times a week. Journey time: 5½ hrs. See OTT Table 3550.

SOMERSET WEST

Tourist Office: *11 Victoria St, Somerset West; tel: 021-851 4022* (open Mon–Fri 0830–1300, 1400–1630, Sat 0900–1200).

ACCOMMODATION

The **Erinvale Estate Hotel and Golf Club**, *Lourensford Rd, Somerset West; tel: 021-847 1160, fax: 021-847 1169* (expensive) is a restored Cape Dutch homestead, which provides an exceptional place to stay. Also at the top end of the market is the **Lord Charles**, *Old Stellenbosch Rd; tel: 021-551 040, fax: 021-551 107* (expensive), a large, elegant hotel with lovely gardens. Less grand are **Willowbrook Lodge**, *Morgenster Ave, Somerset West; tel: 021-851 3759, fax: 021-851 4152* (moderate), a country lodge on the banks of the Lourens River, and the atmospheric
    Van Riebeeck Hotel, *Beach Rd, Gordon's Bay; tel: 021-856 1441, fax: 021-856 1572* (cheap). For guesthouses, bed and breakfasts and self-catering cottages, contact the Tourist Office. **Golden Mile Accommodation**, *104A Da Gama St, Somerset West; tel/fax: 021-854 775*, is a locally-based accommodation agency. **Campsites: Hendon Park**, *Faure Marine, Gordon's Bay; tel: 021-856 2321;* **Voortrekker Park**, *Hofmeyer St, Strand; tel: 021-853 7316.*

EATING AND DRINKING

Somerset West has some of the Western Cape's most prestigious restaurants. The **Lady Phillips' Tea Garden**, *Vergelegen, Lourensford Rd, Somerset West; tel: 021-847 1346* (open daily 0930–1600 for teas and lunches; reservations advisable), is situated in the lovely grounds of an historic Cape Dutch manor house and winery, with alfresco lunches and snacks served on the **Rose Terrace** (Nov–Apr). **Drakes**, *Lord Charles Hotel, corner Faure and Stellenbosch Rds, Somerset West; tel: 021-885 1040* (open Mon–Sat dinner; reservations essential), is the small, elegant end of the Lord Charles Hotel's dining operation (see above). At the cheaper end is the **Garden Terrace** (open daily, breakfast, lunch and dinner). Also reasonably priced is **Chez Michel**, *41 Victoria Rd, Somerset West; tel: 021-851 6069* (moderate; open Tues–Fri lunch, Tues–Sat dinner; reservations essential).

SIGHTSEEING

Somerset West, a small resort town facing False Bay from the slopes of the magnificent Helderberg Mountain, developed at the beginning of the 19th century, and in 1820 was named in honour of the British governor, Lord Charles Somerset. Before that, it was the focus of the wine estate, **Vergelegen**, *Lourensford Rd; tel: 021-847 1334* (grounds open daily in season 0930–1600; R7.50), established by Governor Willem Adriaan van der Stel (1700), who was attracted by the area's natural beauty. The restored Cape Dutch house is now owned by the Anglo-American Corporation (open Mon–Sun 0930–1700). There are guided tours of the cellar and wine tasting (Mon–Sat 1030, 1130 and 1430) and guided walks in the grounds (*tel: 021-847 1342*, Tues and Sat by appointment).

In the foothills of the Helderberg Mountain, the **Helderberg Nature Reserve**, *off Lourensford Rd, Somerset West* (open summer, daily 0700–2000, winter 0700–1800; R2.50 per vehicle, R1 per person), is 245 hectares of natural *fynbos* and home to nearly 200 different bird species. There are places to walk, hike or climb (the information centre at the Herbarium has details) or picnic (there is also a restaurant). There are other hikes in the area: the famous **Boland Hiking Trail**, *tel: 021-886 5858*, is a 2–3 day hike to Stellenbosch and Franschhoek along the Hottentots-Holland range.

ROOIELS-KLEINMOND

Tourist Office: *Municipal Office, Main Rd, Kleinmond; tel: 02823-4010* (open Mon–Fri 0800–1300, 1400–1630, Sat 0900–1600, Sun 1100–1500).

ACCOMMODATION AND FOOD

Much of the best accommodation in this area is

bed and breakfast, including the **Drummond Arms**, *Anenome Rd, Rooiels; tel: 02823-28458* (cheap); the **Sandpiper Lodge**, *259 Hangklip Rd, Pringle Bay; tel: 02823-28607, fax: 02823-2832* (cheap); **Peter's Place**, *Betty's Bay; tel/fax: 02823-29527* (cheap); **Santos Lodge**, *Clarence Dr., Betty's Bay; tel/fax: 02823-29496* (cheap); and the **Strand Street Bed and Breakfast**, *Kleinmond; tel: 02823-3538* (cheap).

If you prefer a real hotel, **The Beach House on Sandown Bay**, *Sandown Bay, Kleinmond; tel: 02823-3130, fax: 02823-4022* (moderate) is first class. Its **Tides Restaurant** (moderate; open 1200–1400 lunch, 1930–2130 dinner) specialises in seafood.

SIGHTSEEING

From Gordon's Bay, the R44 hugs the coast, past **Koeëlbaai**'s spacious beach (a powerful backlash makes swimming dangerous) to **Rooiels**, a little settlement of holiday homes overlooked by spectacular cliff faces. Here, there are quiet little bays and the *fynbos* grows almost to the water's edge. Beautiful to look at, it's extremely dangerous to line fish from this shore. From Rooiels, the R44 cuts inland. After 5 km, a road branches right to **Pringle Bay**, where the coastline is broken with low rocks and sandy bays and the fishing is spectacular year-round. The R44 meets the coast again at **Silver Sands** and continues to **Betty's Bay**, a holiday village and former whaling station. Nearby **Verwoerd Beach** is one of the few places where paper nautilus shells are washed ashore during winter months. Here too, is the lovely **Harold Porter Botanical Garden**, *access from the R44 at Betty's Bay; tel: 02823-29311* (open daily 0800–1700; R2). After Betty's Bay comes **Kleinmond**. Within a 5 km radius of this small village, you can find every single type of natural habitat that exists anywhere in the whole of the Western Cape.

SIDE TRACK TO GENADENDAL AND GREYTON

Greyton Tourist Office: *The Library, Main Rd, Greyton; tel: 028-254 9414* (open Mon–Fri 1030–1230, 1330–1600, Sat 0930–1300, 1430–1600, Sun 1000–1200).

ACCOMMODATION AND FOOD

There is only one hotel, the original **Greyton Hotel**, *Main Rd, Greyton; tel: 028-254 9892, fax: 028-254 9862* (cheap), but there are several good guesthouses, including **Greyton Lodge**, *46 Main St, Greyton; tel: 028-254 9876, fax: 028-254 9672* (moderate), a charming collection of renovated cottages with an excellent restaurant (open for breakfast, lunch and dinner Tues–Sun); the **Post House**, *Main Rd, Greyton; tel: 028-254 9995, fax: 028-254 9920* (moderate), an historic building with a Victorian character (open for lunch and dinner); and the **Guinea Fowl Guest House**, *Dominee Botha St, Greyton; tel: 028-254 9550, fax: 028-254 9653* (moderate). For bed and breakfast, try **High Hopes**, *76 Main Rd, Greyton; tel/fax: 028-254 9898* (cheap), while hikers' accommodation is available at the **Oak Tree Hikers Loft**, *35 Oak St, Greyton; tel: 028-254 9820* (cheap). The **Houwhoek Inn**, *on the N2 between Grabouw and Bot River; tel: 02824-49646, fax: 02824-49112* (moderate) lies at the summit of the Houwhoek Pass.

For meals, head towards the **Greyton Country Restaurant**, *35 Oak St, Greyton; tel: 028-254 9449* (moderate).

SIGHTSEEING

The first Moravian mission station in South Africa was established at Genadendal (1792), today a pretty village with neat, early thatched cottages, church, watermill and groves of old oaks. The **Mission Museum**, *Hermut House, Church Sq.; tel: 02822-8582* (open Mon–Thur 0830–1300, 1400–1700, Fri 0830–1300, 1400–1530, Sat 1000–1300; R5), chronicles the mission's history. The **Genadendal Hiking Trail**, *tel: 02353-621* for bookings, winds through the breathtaking Riviersonderend Mountains. Close by is the picturesque village of **Greyton**. Only 80 mins from Cape Town, it is a popular, quiet retreat. Explore the old village with its restored buildings (bicycles can be hired – enquire at the Tourist Office), **Noupoort Gorge** with its streams and towering cliffs, or the 14 km **Boesmanskloof Trail** joining Greyton and McGregor. Greyton has a popular Saturday morning market. ⬛

HERMANUS

Tourist Office: *105 Main Rd, Hermanus; tel: 0283-22629* (open Mon–Fri 0800–1630, Sat 0900–1500, Sun 1100–1500); **Hermanus Accommodation Centre**, *Myrtle Lane, Hermanus; tel: 0283-700 004* (open Mon–Fri 0830–1700). Information and reservations for bed and breakfasts, guesthouses, self-catering cottages and apartments.

ACCOMMODATION AND FOOD

The **Marine Hotel,** *Marine Dr., Hermanus; tel: 0283-21112, fax: 0283-700 160* (moderate) has the best location in Hermanus itself, while the **Windsor Hotel**, *Marine Dr., Hermanus; tel: 0283-23727, fax: 0283-22181* (moderate) has great views of the sea and the whales. Outside Hermanus is the **Klein River Lodge**, 12 mins away at Stanford *(take the R43); tel: 0283-300 689, fax: 0283-300 987* (moderate). **Campsite: Onrus Holiday Camp**, *De Villiers St, Onrus; tel: 0283-61210* (caravans).

Hermanus is filled with informal places to eat. **Bientang se Grot**, *off Marine Dr., between Old Harbour and the Marine Hotel; tel: 0283-23651* (expensive; opening details on enquiry; reservations essential) cooks lavish seafood on a *braai* in a huge seaside cave. **Burgundy**, *Market Sq.; tel: 0283-22800* (moderate; daily lunch, Mon–Sat dinner; reservations essential) serves seafood, fresh-water fish, ostrich and a range of puddings.

SIGHTSEEING

Hermanus is one of South Africa's most fashionable summer holiday resorts, chiefly famous as a haven for the Southern Right Whale.

The Old Harbour was the focal point of the early village and its fishing industry. Now, as the **Old Harbour Museum**, *Marine Dr.; tel: 0283-21475* (open weekdays 0900–1300, 1400–1600, Sat 0900–1300; free) it forms part of the small museum complex, which depicts the history of fishing and whaling in the area. Hermanus offers some of the best whale-viewing in the country – a 12 km cliff path gives whale-watchers unlimited opportunities

to study them from just metres away. A **Whale Hotline**, *tel: 021-418 3705* or *0283-22629* (June–Dec) provides information on their daily whereabouts. At the new fishing harbour of **Westcliff**, there are charter and deep-sea fishing trips and fresh fish to buy, while the nearby lagoon offers boating, sailing, water-skiing, other water sports and angling at the lagoon's mouth. The long, wide sandy beach is popular with sun-worshippers, joggers and families. The water is safe – **Langbaai**, **Voelklip** and **Grotto** beaches are recommended, as are the clear natural pools in the caves at **De Kelders** (walk there along Die Plaat). On the southern side of Hermanus, tidal **Fick's Pool** is good for children. A weekend fleamarket sells local produce, clothing, bric-à-brac and shells. Walk or hike in the pretty **Fernkloof Nature Reserve**, *entrance from top of Fir Ave; tel: 0283-21122* (open daily; free). Africa's most southerly vineyard-cellars are here: **Hamilton Russell Vineyards**, *Hemel-en-Aarde Valley, R320, Hermanus; tel: 0283-23595* (open for free tastings and sales weekdays 0900–1700, Sat 0900–1300); and **Bouchard Finlayson**, *Hemel-en-Aarde Valley, R320, Hermanus; tel: 0283-23515* (open for free tastings and sales Mon–Fri 0930–1700, Sat 0930–1230).

ELIM

Elim, like Genadendal, began life as a Moravian mission (1824). The main street is lined with water furrows, fruit trees and rows of thatched cottages: this is one of the Western Cape's finest early streetscapes. The **Old Water Mill** (1833) is the country's largest wooden water mill. The thatched **Moravian Church** is open for services. The main local industry is drying flowers from the local *fynbos*.

BREDASDORP

Tourist Office: *Dirkie Uys St, Bredasdorp; tel: 02841-42584* (open Mon–Fri 0830–1630, Sat 0830–1300).

Bredasdorp is a pretty country town whose museum, the **Bredasdorp Shipwreck Museum**, *Independent St; tel: 02841-41240* (open Mon–Fri 0900–1700, Sat 0900–1300, 1400–1530, Sun 1030–1230; R2) reveals the

135

details of the local coastline's predilection for wrecking ships.

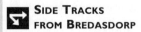

SIDE TRACKS FROM BREDASDORP

CAPE AGULHAS

Leave Bredasdorp on the R319, heading south to Cape Agulhas (28 km).

ACCOMMODATION

Accommodation here is simple. Try the **Agulhas Heights Guest House**, *639 High Level St, L'Agulhas; tel: 02846-56934, fax: 02846-56750* (cheap). **Campsite**: **L'Agulhas Caravan Park**, *Main Rd, L'Agulhas; tel: 02846-56015* (caravans).

SIGHTSEEING

Rounded Cape Agulhas is Africa's southernmost tip. Here, in the shadow of the country's second oldest lighthouse (1848), **Cape Agulhas Lighthouse**, *tel: 02846-56078* (open Mon 1000–1600, Tues–Sat 0930–1645, Sun 1000–1315; R5), the Indian and Atlantic Oceans officially meet, washing a coast of wide, sandy beaches, cliffs, caves and coves. The sea here is murderous: what Rudyard Kipling called the 'dread Agulhas roll' drowned many a seaman. Graves and wrecks litter the coast.

ARNISTON

From Bredasdorp, take the R316 to Arniston (Waenhuiskrans). Distance: 24 km.

ACCOMMODATION AND FOOD

Arniston Hotel, *Beach Rd, Arniston; tel: 02847-59000, fax: 02847-59633* (moderate) is well-known, with lovely views and a good restaurant, ensuring that it's a sought-after location. Nearby **Arniston Lodge**, *23 Main St, Arniston; tel/fax: 02847-59175* (cheap) offers guesthouse accommodation, while the **Arniston Seaside Cottages**, *tel: 02847-59772* (cheap) provide the best self-catering available.

Campsite: **Waenhuiskrans Caravan Park**, *tel: 02847-59620* (caravans).

SIGHTSEEING

A wrecked British troopship of 1815 gave its name to the little seaside village of **Arniston** (also called *Waenhuiskrans* – wagon-house cliff – after an enormous cave only accessible at low tide). Its chief attraction, apart from a cluster of 19th-century fishermens' cottages, is a long, magnificent beach.

DE HOOP NATURE RESERVE

North-east of Bredasdorp, the 36,000 hectare **De Hoop Nature Reserve**, *Bredasdorp-Malgas Rd, access just before Wydgelee (Ouplaas); tel: 028-542 1126* (open daily 0700–1800; admission R5 per vehicle, R2 per person – brochures and maps on entry) is important for the conservation of rare lowland *fynbos*. It is home to various animals, including the endangered bontebok and the Cape mountain zebra. The birdlife is prolific, with some 260 species recorded. There is an important wetlands here, and the entire coast is a **marine reserve,** one of the largest in Africa. There are hiking trails, picnic sites, walks, drives and a mountain bike trail. Accommodation is in self-catering cottages or on a campsite; *tel: 028-542 116.* Overnight visitors should report to the De Hoop office before 1600 on arrival.

SWELLENDAM

Tourist Office: *Main St, Swellendam; tel: 0291-42770* (open Mon–Fri 0900–1300, 1400–1700, Sat 0900–1200).

ACCOMMODATION AND FOOD

There are two relatively uninspiring hotels, the **Swellengrebel Hotel**, *91 Voortrek St, Swellendam; tel: 0291-41144, fax: 0291-42453* (moderate) near the town centre, and the **Carlton Hotel**, *23 Voortrek St, Swellendam; tel: 0291-41120, fax: 0291-41169* (moderate), which offers homely, country-style accommodation.

The best local accommodation is in a raft of charming guesthouses in historic homes, most notably the **Klippe Rivier Homestead**, *Klippe Rivier (3 km west of Swellendam – from the N2, take the R60 for 0.5 km, turn left and, after 1.8km, go left at the signpost); tel: 0291-43341, fax: 0291-43337* (moderate), the 19th-century family home of past Presidents Steyn and Reitz. Enquire at the Tourist Office about others. For dormitory-style accommodation, try the **Swellendam Backpackers Lodge**, *5 Lichtenstein St; tel: 0291-42648* (cheap), or **Waenhuis Backpackers**, *5 Buitekant St; tel: 0291-42281* (cheap). **Campsite: Bontebok National Park** (see below); *tel: 0291-42735* (caravans).

Zanddrift, *32 Swellengrebel St; tel: 0291-41789* (moderate; open daily except Thur, 0900–1600 breakfast, lunch and tea) is a pleasant restaurant in a reconstructed Cape Dutch farmhouse. **Gentleman & Jackal**, *132 Voortrek St; tel: 0291-41988* (cheap) offers pub lunches with a good wine list.

SIGHTSEEING

Laid out in the shadow of the Langeberg Mountains, Swellendam is a charming country town characterised by oak-lined streets and well-preserved historic buildings. The **Drostdy** (1747), the seat of the *landdrost* (the magistrate), is now the **Drosdty Museum**, and part of the excellent **Swellendam Museum Complex**, *18 Swellengrebel St, Swellendam; tel: 0291-41138* (open Mon–Fri 0900–1645, Sat 1000–1600; R5 entry to the whole complex), which contains a range of early buildings, including a **water mill**, the **gaol** and **Mayville** (1853), a furnished period homestead with a herb and rose garden. To the south (7 km), the **Bontebok National Park**, *take the N2 for 7 kms out of Swellendam; tel: 0291-42735* (open Oct–April 0800–1900, May–Sept 0800–1800; R12 for car plus first 4 people), is the home of hartebeest, steenbok, mountain zebra and the rare bontebok. There is a caravan park, places to swim and fish, and guided, or self-guided walks. Other small reserves are in the area; enquire at the Tourist Office for details.

RIVERSDALE

Tourist Office: *Civic Centre, Van den Berg St, Riversdale; tel: 02933-32418 ext. 236* (open Mon–Fri 0730–1630).

Royal Hotel, *Long St, Riversdale; tel: 02933-31100* (cheap). **Guesthouse: Sleeping Beauty House**, *3 Long St, Riversdale; tel/fax:*

Whales

Every year, between June and Nov, Southern Right whales migrate to the waters of the Western Cape to calve and nurse their young. Just a few metres offshore, there are unsurpassed whale-watching opportunities. Identify them by a V-shaped blow and lack of dorsal fin. These were the first of the large whales (about 15.5m long, they weigh 30–60 tonnes) to be protected, in 1935.

The population was virtually exterminated between 1790 and 1825, when over 12,000 were killed by open-boat whalers. Now the population is increasing at a rate of 7% annually. Today, the Southern Rights are fiercely protected: go within 300m in a vessel, and there's a heavy fine. Humpbacks also migrate throughout the region (May–Dec), and Bryde's whales are found further offshore all year round, as are Killer Whales (sightings are rare).

02933-31651 (cheap). There are also self-catering apartments and homes, and places to camp and caravan. **Campsite: Takkieskloof Tourist Resort and Caravan Park**, *Truter St, Riversdale; tel: 02933-32418, fax: 02933-33146*, will organise hiking trails; golf and bird-watching are also available.

Riversdale lies in the grassveld, between the Langeberg Mountains and the sea. To the north-east is the Klein Karoo and the interior, reached via Thomas Bains' **Garcia's Pass**, the R323 (see p.340). The sea is 42 km away to the south at **Stilbaai**. Riversdale is best-known for the **Julius Gordon Africana Collection** (furniture and paintings) in **Versfeld House**, *Long St, Riversdale; tel: 02933-32418 ext. 223* (open Mon–Fri 1000–1300; donations). There are plenty of hiking trails in the area: **Kristalkloof Hiking Trail** takes 2 days (20.9 km), and the **Sleeping Beauty Trail** takes 4 hrs (13 km); further information from the tourist office.

MOSSEL BAY

See Mossel Bay–Port Elizabeth, pp.272–280.

CAPE TOWN–SPRINGBOK

Magnificent scenery surrounds Cape Town on all sides. Within a 20 minute drive of the city, this route crosses through the Swartland and the Sandveld, entering a region of fertile wheatlands, fruit orchards and vineyards. Beyond, it enters the Olifants River Valley, an area of citrus plantations dominated by the towering mountain ranges of the Cedarberg. Further still, the route heads deep into Namaqualand, a largely semi-desert area of sunbaked, sandy plains and granite mountains, with truly spectacular displays of wild flowers.

138

DIRECT ROUTE: 539 KM

Springbok

67

Kamieskroon

45 — N7

Garies

62

Bitterfontein

67

21 — **Vanrhynsdorp**

Klawer

57 — N7

Clanwilliam — *Cedarberg Mountains*

Cape Town–Kimberley, p. 128 — 54

Citrusdal

45

30 — **Piketberg**

Moorreesburg

39

Malmesbury

52 — N7

Cape Town

ROUTE

Leave Cape Town on the N1 (in the direction of Paarl) and after 10 km, bear left on to the N7 and head for **Malmesbury** (52 km). Keeping to the N7, leave Malmesbury and continue north. After 32 km, the R311 branches off to the left and heads for **Moorreesburg**, just beside the highway. Return to the N7 and continue on to **Piketberg** (30 km) and then to **Citrusdal** (45 km), which lies just to the right of the N7. **Clanwilliam** is 54 km further on; the route heads north in the shadow of the magnificent **Cedarberg Mountains**, to the

right. Beyond Clanwilliam, the N7 continues on through **Klawer** (57 km), **Vanrhynsdorp** (21 km) and Bitterfontein (67km) after which, about 32 km later, it crosses the state border into the Northern Cape. **Garies** is 62 km from Bitterfontein, and **Kamieskroon** 45 km beyond that. This is the start of the huge district of Namaqualand. From Kamieskroon, it is 67 km to **Springbok**. This is the most direct route. Distance: 539 km; allow one day non-stop; at least two slow days with sightseeing.

BUSES

Intercape Mainliner run a bus service from Cape Town to Springbok (Tues, Thur, Fri, Sun); Transtate have a Fri service and Namaqualand Bus Service operates Mon–Fri. Journey time: 8¾ hrs. OTT Table 3553.

MALMESBURY

See p. 340.

MOORREESBURG

Tourist Office: *Municipality, corner Plein and Retief Sts; tel: 0264-32246* (open Mon–Fri 0830–1630).

The best option is probably the 3-star **Samoa Hotel**, *Central St; tel: 0264-31201; fax: 0264-32031* (cheap). Alternatively, try the **Lorelei Guest House**, *4 Church St; tel: 0264-32586* (cheap). **Campsite: Moorreesburg Caravan Park**, *Main Rd; tel: 0264-32246* .

Moorreesburg is a handsome market town at the heart of the fertile Swartland area – the grainbasket of the West Coast region. Wheat has been grown here since 1752, though the town itself only came into being in 1879. The **Art Gallery**, *Dirkie Uys High School, Heuwel St; tel: 0264-32253* (open Mon–Fri 0830–1500; free) has a good collection of South African art. The **Wheat Industry Museum**, *Main St; tel: 0264-31093* (open Mon–Fri 0800–1200, 1400–1700; R2) documents the exploitation of Moorreesburg's main source of wealth.

PIKETBERG

Tourist Office: *Municipality (the Library), Church St; tel: 0261-31126* (open Mon–Fri 0900–1830).

ACCOMMODATION

Noupoort Farm, on the north side of Piket-berg *(just off the N7, to the right, up Versveld Pass); tel: 0261-5754, fax 0261-5834* (cheap–moderate) is an extremely comfortable week-end retreat, a guest farm with accommodation

in cottages, a pool and excellent food. Catering or self-catering available. Also near Piketberg is **Dunn's Castle**, *take the R399 in the direction of Velddrif and follow the signs; tel/fax: 0261-32470* (cheap–moderate), a somewhat remote baronial mansion turned guesthouse, with huge log fires and incredible views. Dinner is by prior arrangement. **Campsite: Municipal Camp-site**, *Main St, Piketberg; tel: 0261-31674*.

SIGHTSEEING

Piketberg snuggles up against the slopes of the magnificent Piketberg Mountains, where tall sandstone cliffs reach up to a height of 1459m (at Zebraskop). Both town (founded 1835) and mountains take their name from the pike-armed guards posted here to secure a bulwark against the local Khoi in the 18th century. During that century, and the early 19th cen-tury, bands of Khoi and their mixed race followers made this area their home, using the surrounding mountains as a refuge (see pp.70–71). A single **cannon** at the local high school, *Simon van der Stel St*, is the reminder of those days. It was fired to warn of approaching Khoi.

The stone-built, daintily buttressed **Dutch Reformed Church** (1882) is worth more than just a glance, while the **Piketberg Museum**, *Hoog St; tel: 0261-31126, ext. 249* (open Mon–Fri 1000–1200; free) outlines the area's history.

CITRUSDAL

Tourist Office: *Sandveldhuisie, Church St; tel: 022-921 3210* (open Mon–Fri 0900–1630, Sat 0900–1200).

ACCOMMODATION

The **Cedarberg Hotel**, *66 Voortrekker St; tel: 022-921 2221, fax: 022-921 2704* (moderate) is situated in the valley of the Olifants River, surrounded by orange groves. **Van Meerhoff Lodge**, *Piekeenierskloof Pass (on the N7, south of Citrusdal); tel: 022-921 2570, fax: 022-921 2570* (moderate) offers chalets, meals and a location close to the wild flowers.

The Baths, *on a farm about 18 km south of Citrusdal (follow the signs from the centre); tel/fax: 022-921 3609*, is a private self-catering resort taking advantage of the local hot springs. There

139

are chalets, **campsites**, hot and cold swimming pools, spa baths and hiking trails. Enquire at the Tourist Office about other opportunities for renting self-catering cottages or chalets in the area. There are many.

EATING AND DRINKING

The **Van Meerhoff Restaurant**, *at the Van Meerhoff Lodge* (see above), *Piekenierskloof Pass; tel: 022-921 2570*, specialises in Cape cuisine (cheap–moderate; open daily lunch and dinner). **Craig Royston**, *on the N7, near the Citrusdal turnoff; tel: 022-921 2963* (cheap; open Mon–Sat 0900–1630, Sun 1000–1630) serves country-style lunches in an historic farm building. It also has a farm shop and wine tastings. The **Sandveldhuisie Tea Room**, *Church St; tel: 022-921 3210*, serves lavish teas (cheap; open same hours as the tourist office).

Some of the wineries on the Olifants River Wine Route offer meals. **Spruitdrift Co-op** offers snoek *braais* (barbecues) for 15 or more (lunch); advance booking is essential. At the **Klawer Co-op**, there are champagne breakfasts, picnic lunches and snoek or meat *braais* for a minimum of 10 people. Book in advance. During the wild flower season, **Trawal Wine Cellar** offers fish and traditional *braais* (by appointment only; 40–60 people).

SIGHTSEEING

As its name suggests, Citrusdal is a centre for orange growing and packing. There are hot baths – a hot spring (42°C) rises here – and San paintings can be visited nearby (ask at the Tourist Office for a map). In town, the **Citrusdal Museum**, *Church St* (open Mon–Fri 0900–1630, Sat 0900–1200; free) outlines the development of the town, with references to early San inhabitants as well as the pioneers. The **Sandveldhuisie**, a reconstruction of a typical Sandveld dwelling, not unlike a Scottish croft house, now houses the tourist office.

Most of the local wine estates and co-ops are part of the **Olifants River Wine Route** *(tel: 0271-33126* for maps and information) and are open for tastings and sales (see also Eating and Drinking, above). They include: **Cedarberg Cellars**, *tel: 027-482 2825* (open Mon–Fri 0830–1200, 1330–1730); **Goue Vallei Wines**,

tel: 022-921 2234 (open Mon–Fri 0800–1230, 1400–1700, Sat 0900–1230); **Klawer Co-op**, *tel: 02724-61530* (open Mon–Fri 0800–1700, Sat 0900–1200); **Lutzville**, *tel: 02725-71516* (open Mon–Fri 0800–1230, 1400–1700, Sat 0900–1200; cellar tours by appointment); **Spruitdrift Co-op**, *tel: 0271-33086* (open Mon–Fri 0800–1730); **Trawal Wine Cellar**, *tel: 02724-61616* (open Mon–Fri 0800–1230, 1400–1700); and **Vredendal Winery**, *tel: 0271-31080* (open Mon–Fri 0800–1300, 1400–1700, Sat 0800–1230).

Citrusdal is also an ideal base from which to visit the Cedarberg. Ask at the tourist office for information about mountain biking routes, walking and hiking routes, bird-watching, sky-diving and canoeing.

THE CEDARBERG MOUNTAINS

Tourist Information: For bookings and information, *tel: 027-482 2812; fax: 027-482 2406* (open Mon–Fri 0800–1300, 1400–1630; R3 per person to enter the Wilderness area, R5 to use a picnic site, R6 per person per day for hikes, R40 per day to use a campsite). Reservations for hiking and accommodation may be made 4 months in advance.

There is only one access route into the Wilderness Area, via the **Algeria Forest Station**, to which all visitors must report and where permits must be obtained before setting out on hikes. To get there from Citrusdal, take a tarred, then gravel, road heading north-west along the Rondegat River, or take the N7 going in the direction of Clanwilliam. After 27 km, branch right, over the Olifants River, and follow the signs. To get there from Clanwilliam, head south on the same roads for 26 km to the turnoff and follow signs as before.

Although there is accommodation in the Cedarberg in huts, bungalows or campsites (see p.141), you are generally free to sleep anywhere (except for caves containing rock art). **Climate:** winters are cold and wet, summers warm and dry. Most rain falls May–Sept, and it often snows in the higher parts.

In 1973, the **Cedarberg Wilderness Area** was designated a nature reserve, to protect 71,000 hectares of the spectacular Cedarberg mountain range. Here, in amongst the jagged peaks and the strange rock formations, are ancient, gnarled Cape cedar trees *(Widdringtonia cedarbergensis)* found nowhere else on earth. Some are thought to be nearly 1000 years old. By the 1840s, much of the Cedarberg's sweet-scented cedar forests had been wantonly destroyed by the timber industry, and only after 1876 was the situation brought under control. What you see now are the rare survivors. Here, too, is the unique white snow protea *(Protea cryphila);* while the rocket pincushion *(Leucospermum reflexum)* only grows wild in the northern Cedarberg, although it has become a common garden plant. Otherwise, the Cedarberg is mostly covered by typical *fynbos,* with heathers, proteas and flowering bulbs. There are also plenty of leopards. Farmers throughout the Western Cape are encouraged to allow the capture of problem animals in their territory, which are then set free here. You can also expect to see Cape wildcat, caracal, bat-eared fox, hyena and porcupines. Watch out for raptors, adders, puff adders and Cape cobras (wear sensible, high-sided walking boots). Hundreds of San rock paintings are in the area, dating back to anything between 300 and 6000 years.

Walks and Hikes

The Wilderness Area is divided up into 3 sections: North, Central and South. Numbers are limited to 50 people per day per section (minimum 2, maximum 12 per group). The **Kliphuis Forestry Campsite** is here. Hikes in this section range from easy (the **Pakhuis Stroll**; 7 km, 2 hrs) to strenuous (**Krakadoupas**; 12 km, 5 hrs; or **Algeria–Wuppertal**; 28 km; 2 days).

The **Northern** section is fairly isolated, rugged and stunningly beautiful; the true uniqueness of the Cedarberg is revealed here. The **Central** section, around the **Algeria Forestry Station**, is the most popular, with impressive and dramatic scenery and the easiest access to the Wilderness Area. The **Algeria Campsite** is luxurious, with a caravan site and places to braai (cheap; book well in advance).

The **Southern** section has the most startling scenery of all – the natural **Wolfberg Arch** rock formation, and the highest peak in the area, **Sneeuberg** (2027m). There are also numerous

San rock paintings. Probably the easiest to get to are those on Matjiesfontein, an easy walk from Kromriver, where you obtain permits and directions. Permits for admission to the various natural features are free if you are a guest. If not, they are obtainable at Algeria or on the farm itself (R4). **Campsites** (also bungalows) are at **Sanddrif**, *Dwarsrivier Farm; tel: 027-482 2825,* and **Kromrivier**, *Kromrivier Farm; tel: 027-482 2807.*

Tourist Office: *Main St; tel: 027-482 2024* (open Mon–Fri 0800–1630, Sat–Sun 0900–1300).

ACCOMMODATION AND FOOD

Strassberger's Hotel, *Main St; tel: 027-482 1101, fax: 027-482 2678* (cheap–moderate) has a pool, an excellent dining room and the separate **Reinhold's Restaurant**, which has an excellent menu, offering items such as springbok and Karoo lamb (moderate; open Wed–Sat 1900 dinner only). The **Olifants Dam Motel**, *7 km from Clanwilliam on the N7, opposite the dam; tel/fax: 027-482 2185* (cheap) offers a more basic alternative.

For bed and breakfast, **Saint Du Barrys Country Lodge** *(Pf), 13 Augsburg Dr.; tel/fax: 027-482 1537* (cheap), and **8 Visser Street** *(Pf), 248 Visser St; tel/fax: 027-482 2212* (cheap) are top of the range. **Marg-Will Farm**, *4 km from Clanwilliam on the Pakhuis road; tel: 027-482 2537* (cheap) is small and comfortable.

Bushman's Kloof Private Game Reserve; *tel: 027-482 2627; fax: 027-482 1011* (moderate–expensive) offers accommodation in private, self-contained lodges with terraces, a natural rock swimming pool and an extremely good restaurant. To get there, take the R364 east from Clanwilliam (about 30 km) and follow the signs to Bushman's Kloof. It is situated in the foothills of the Cedarberg Mountains, in the middle of an old San hunting ground. Both the plant and animal life are diverse, with gemsbok, eland, springbok, red and black hartebeest, Burchell's zebra, ostrich and eagles. Important San rock paintings are preserved here in caves and rock shelters.

Clanwilliam Dam Recreational Resort,

on the dam; tel: 027-482 2133 (cheap) has chalets and a campsite. For other self-catering establishments, enquire at the tourist office.

Given its size, Clanwilliam has plenty of places to eat and drink. The best are probably **Reinhold's Restaurant** (see p.141), and the **Pizzeria**, *Main St; tel: 027-482 2301* (open daily dinner only).

SIGHTSEEING

This is supposed to be one of the ten oldest towns in South Africa (settled c.1725); in fact, the area had been explored within 10 years of the arrival of the Dutch in 1652. Clanwilliam, founded in 1814, is a centre for the production of fruit, vegetables and *rooibos*, an indigenous Cedarberg bush, *Aspalanthus linearis*, which is a popular South African alternative to tea. Prepared and drunk in much the same way, it is free of tannin and stimulants, relaxing and rich in Vitamin C.

Clanwilliam has a pretty main street, a handful of elderly buildings and an old prison (1808), which now doubles as the **museum** and Tourist Office (for details, see above; free). Other fine buildings include the **Landrost's Court** (1808), *Visser St*, the **Dutch Reformed Church** (1864) and the **Anglican Church** (1866).

The 21 km-long **Clanwilliam Dam**, *about 2 km south-east of town (follow the signs from the Main St); tel: 027-482 2133* (open daily 0730–1730; R3.14 per person, R8.50 per vehicle, R17.50 to bring a boat) is a popular recreation spot for boating, waterskiing, swimming, angling, bird-watching and picnicking. On the eastern shore of the dam, the 54 hectare **Ramskop Wild Flower Reserve**, *well-signposted from Main St; tel: 027-482 2133* (open daily Aug–Sept; R7) has a mixture of Sandveld and *fynbos* plants, with over 200 specimens of indigenous wild flowers.

The wild flowers are a key attraction of this area (generally July–Sept, though the season lasts longer at the Ramskop Wild Flower Reserve). Annually, at the end of August, the Clanwilliam Wild Flower Society holds a 10-day **Wild Flower Show** in the old Dutch Reformed Church, with a landscape exhibition consisting of 360 species of flowers.

KLAWER

Tourist Office: *Klawer Hotel, Main St; tel: 02724-61032* (open same hours as hotel reception).

The **Klawer Hotel**, *120 Main Rd; tel: 02724-61032; fax: 02724-61098* (cheap) has a restaurant (open daily, lunch and dinner). Alternatively, try the **Kapel Guest House**, *5 km from Klawer on the Vredendal road; tel: 02724-61422* (cheap).

Situated on the N7 between Clanwilliam and Vanrhynsdorp, Klawer grew up around the railhead and takes its name from the wild clover that grows profusely here after heavy rain. Its only 'sight' is the **Klawer Co-op** wine cellars (see Citrusdal, p.140).

VANRHYNSDORP

Tourist Office: *Museum, Van Riebeeck St; tel: 02727-91552* (open Mon–Fri 0800–1300, 1400–1700).

The **Gastehuis Van Rhyn**, *1 Voortrekker St; tel: 02727-91429* (cheap) also serves excellent meals, tea and coffee. Alternatively, try the **Namakwaland Country Lodge**, *Voortrekker St; tel: 02727-91633* (cheap). **Gifberg Holiday Farm**, *29 km south of the town on the N7; tel: 02727-91555* (cheap) offers self-catering accommodation, with meals on request. Ask at the tourist information about other options. There are also private homes with rooms available during the flower season.

Vanrhynsdorp is at the hub of all the major spring flower routes in the district. At the **Kern Succulent Nursery**, *Voortrekker Rd; tel: 02727-91062* (open Mon–Fri 0800–1700; R5), there are succulents for sale at the largest succulent nursery in South Africa. There is also a succulent trail so you can see them in their natural habitat.

GARIES

Tourist Office: *Municipality, Main St; tel: 027-652 1014* (open Mon–Fri 0730–1230, 1400–1630).

The **Garies Hotel**, *Main Rd; tel: 027-652 1042, fax: 027-652 1141* (cheap) has a restaurant. For self-catering accommodation, try **Sarrisam Farm Accommodation**, *1 hr from Garies on the Hondeklipbaai road; tel: 02792, ask*

Flower-Watching In Namaqualand

When the first rains fall in early winter, out come the daisies, mesembryanthemums, aloes, lilies and a myriad of other flowers and wild herbs (about 4000 species in all). The flora here is nothing like that of the Cape Floral Kingdom (see pp.58–59). Here, climate, geography, geology and general topography have combined, over millennia, to provide unique conditions for the propagation and distribution of Namaqualand's floral displays. It is true to say that worldwide, wild flowers do not germinate like clockwork, year after year. But the adaptability of Namaqualand's flowers, combined with the ability of their seeds to lie dormant for a number of seasons, until optimum conditions for germination have been reached, ensures that unfavourable weather conditions do not exterminate them. From one year to the next, no area is ever the same as it was the year before, and will not be the same the following season. The blooming of Namaqualand's wild flowers is a truly remarkable phenomenon.

The rainfall and the absence of warm 'berg' winds determine the duration of the flower season. The best times to view them are generally 1100–1500 – the warmest hours of the day. In Namaqualand, they emerge at the end of July in the coastal regions, and last as long as the end of Oct in the mountainous areas. They turn their faces to the sun; the sun should therefore be behind you when viewing them. Call the wild flower hotline (see p.331) for information on where to find the 'best' displays, and obtain route maps from local tourist information offices en route, or from the Western Cape tourist office in Cape Town before leaving. Never remove plants, flowers or bulbs from the veld. This is strictly illegal.

---

for 2322 (cheap). **Campsite**: **Municipal Caravan Park**, *Main Road; tel: 027-652 1014, ask for the campsite.*

This small town, a good base from which to explore the surrounding countryside, is, in reality, nothing more than a main street flanked by buildings – church, houses and shops. At the north-eastern end of the main street is a turnoff to the west, leading to **Letterklip** (3 km). On this large conglomerate of huge boulders, the names of early Namaqualand travellers have been inscribed. Between 1901 and 1902, British soldiers had a fort here, accounting for the coats of arms chiselled into the rocks.

KAMIESKROON

Tourist Office: *Municipality, De Waal St; tel: 027-672 1627* (open Mon–Fri 0745–1245, 1345–1645).

ACCOMMODATION AND FOOD

The **Kamieskroon Hotel and Caravan Park**, *Old National Rd; tel: 027-672 1614; fax: 0257-672 1675* (cheap) also has a restaurant (open breakfast, lunch and dinner). Hearty farm food is available on request at **Arkoep Farm**

Accommodation, *14 km from Kamieskroon on N7; tel: 0257-672 1759* (cheap), a farm guesthouse a short way from town.

SIGHTSEEING

Spring flowers grow here in abundance each year, and flower-watchers flood in come the spring. A great cleft boulder 'crowns' a peak in the mountains known to the local Nama people as the 'Thamies' (jumble) – hence the name of the town. All around are popular walks and trails (some 3–5 days long) on unmarked routes (the Kamieskroon Hotel organises these – call for information).

To the west of the town is the 1000 hectare **Skilpad Nature Reserve**, *17.7 km north of Kamieskroon on along the Wolwepoort road, west of the N7;* contact the Kamieskroon Hotel for information; *tel: 027-672 1614* (open during the flower season 1 July–mid Oct, daily 0800–1700; R5). The Reserve (skilpad means tortoise, from the many found here) is one of the best places to view the spring flower displays.

SPRINGBOK

See Upington–Springbok, pp.330–331.

CAPE TOWN–WORCESTER

This verdant section of the Western Cape, centred on the four famous wine regions of Stellenbosch, Franschhoek, Paarl and Wellington, is cradled by spectacular mountain scenery, and punctuated by the ornate white-washed gables of Cape Dutch homesteads set in the midst of vineyards. In between, there are historic towns and villages to be explored, and provincial museums and gardens to be visited. This area is also unique in having a very wide selection of above-average places to eat.

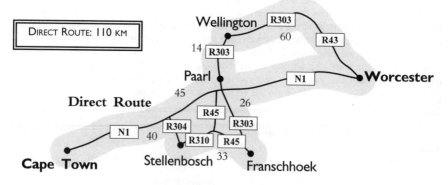

DIRECT ROUTE: 110 KM

Wellington · R303 · 60 · R43 · 14 · R303 · Paarl · N1 · **Worcester** · Direct Route · 45 · 26 · R45 · R303 · N1 · R304 · R310 · R45 · 40 · Cape Town · Stellenbosch · 33 · Franschhoek

Scenic Route

144

ROUTES

DIRECT ROUTE

➡ Take the N1 Cape Town–Worcester. The first section from Cape Town–Paarl (43 km) is motorway. For Stellenbosch, turn off at Exit 31 (then take the R304 for 15 km). For Franschhoek and Paarl centre, quit at Exit 55. For Franschhoek, then take the R45 (26 km). For Wellington, take the N1 to Exit 59, then follow the R303 for 16 km. Distance: 110 km; allow 1½ hrs.

SCENIC ROUTE

➡ For the first leg, Cape Town–**Stellenbosch**, see above. From Stellenbosch centre, take the R310 over **Helshoogte** (Hell's Heights). This route, a wide, high pass, treats you to magnificent views of the Simonsberg and Wemmershoek Mountains. After 17 km, turn right at the junction with the R45 towards Franschhoek-Villiersdorp, and follow it into **Franschhoek** (about 1 hr from Cape Town). This 16 km section makes up the famous **Franschhoek Wine Route**.

From Franschhoek, retrace your steps back along the R45 for about 9 km until the junction, on the right, with the narrow R303 Franschhoek–Paarl. Take the R303 for 13 km until you reach Suider-Paarl (South Paarl). Cross under Exit 59 of the Cape Town-Paarl section of the N1 and keep going into **Paarl** centre. From Paarl, the R303 continues for 14 km to **Wellington** (45 mins from Cape Town). For Worcester, continue along the R303 from Wellington for 35 km until the junction with the R43, then branch right for

Worcester which is a further 25 km on. Allow at least 2 days.

TRAINS AND BUSES

All Spoornet trains out of Cape Town stop at Worcester; some also stop at Wellington. Journey time: approx. 3 hrs. See OTT Tables 3518 and 3519.

Several bus companies operate between Cape Town and Worcester. OTT Tables 3537 and 3550. The Cape Town Metro runs a regular service to Stellenbosch, Wellington and Paarl. OTT Table 3526.

STELLENBOSCH

See pp. 313–316.

FRANSCHHOEK

Tourist Office: *66 Huguenot St, Franschhoek; tel: 021-876 3603* (open Mon–Fri 0900–1700, Sat 1000–1400, Sun 1000–1300). **Vignerons de Franschhoek**, *Huguenot Rd; tel: 021–876 3062* (open Mon–Fri 0900–1700, Sat 1000–1600, Sun 1000–1400) supplies excellent information on the Wine Route.

ACCOMMODATION AND FOOD

Hotel accommodation in Franschhoek is generally of a very high standard. The **Auberge du Quartier Francais**, *corner Berg and Wilhelmina Sts, Franschhoek; tel: 021-876 2151, fax: 021-876 3105* (expensive), is well-known and popular, as is its restaurant **Le Quartier Francais** (see below). Advance booking advised. The **Franschhoek Guest House**, *Main Rd, Franschhoek; tel/fax: 021-876 3386* (moderate) is well situated on the edge of town, while **La Cotte Inn**, *Huguenot St, Franschhoek; tel/fax: 021-876 2081* (cheap), is more central. There are bed and breakfasts and self-catering accommodation in cottages on farms in the locality; information from the tourist office.

For such a tiny town, Franschhoek has an extraordinary number of excellent restaurants, of which this is just a selection. **Le Quartier Francais**, *16 Huguenot Rd, Franschhoek; tel: 021-876 2151* (expensive; open Mon–Sat lunch, dinner, Sun lunch) is one of the best; the food is an innovative blend of Cape Malay and Provençal. Another excellent option, which is

dramatically situated high above Franschhoek, is **La Petite Ferme**, *2 km up Franschhoek Pass Rd, Franschhoek; tel: 021-876 3016* (expensive; open daily 1030–1630; booking essential), which specialises in country cooking. Also on the Pass Rd is the **Haute Cabrière Restaurant**, *tel: 021-876 3688* (moderate; open daily lunch, Fri–Sat dinner).

Of the wine estates also serving meals, **Boschendal**, *off the R310*, has the widest variety: **Le Café**, *in the old slave quarters; tel: 021-874 1152* (open daily 1000–1700) offers light meals and teas; **Boschendal Restaurant**, *tel: 021-874 1031* (open daily lunch; booking essential) offers a sumptuous buffet in elegant surroundings; and **Le Pique Nique**; *tel: 021-874 1031* (Nov–Apr; booking essential) offers French-style picnics in the grounds. Sample the house wines in Boschendal's **Taphuis**; *tel: 021-874 1252* (open Mon–Fri 0830–1630, Sat 0830–1230 May–Oct; Mon–Sat 0830–1630 Apr–Nov; Sun/long weekends 0930–1300 Dec–Jan). **Bellingham**, *tel: 021-874 1011*, offers light lunches during the season (Nov–Apr), as does **Cabrière Estate** (see above).

145

SIGHTSEEING

Known chiefly for its Cape Dutch farmhouses, wine and dramatic scenery, this district takes its name from the original Huguenot settlers who, escaping religious persecution in France, were granted land in 1688 at what became known as 'French Corner'. Some of the original (Huguenot) farms – La Bri, Bourgogne, Cabrière, Champagne, La Cotte, La Dauphine, La Motte, La Provence, La Terre de Luc – survive and are still associated with the wine industry, founded to a large degree on the expertise and traditions that the Huguenots brought with them from France. The history of the area, and of the Huguenots, is very well documented at the fascinating **Huguenot Memorial Museum**, *Lambrecht St; tel: 021-876 2532* (open Mon–Sat 0900–1300, 1400–1700, Sun 1400–1700; R2). It is housed in 18th-century **Saasveld House**, a gentleman's residence moved from its original location in *Kloof St, Cape Town*, and rebuilt here. Beside it, Coert Steynberg's **Huguenot Memorial** commemorates the 250th anniversary of the

Huguenots' arrival (1938). There are plenty of walks and trails in the Franschhoek area. The tourist office will organise the necessary permits and provide maps and advice.

The Franschhoek Wine Route

Following **Franschhoek's Wine Route** is an essential element of a day's visit to Franschhoek. The route, running through a valley under the towering peaks of the Franschhoek, Klein Drakenstein and Groot Drakenstein Mountains, is well-signposted and each estate easy to find. Of the 14 producers here, 12 are open to the public, specialising in Chardonnay, Semillon, Sauvignon Blanc, Cabernet Sauvignon, Shiraz and Pinot Noir. Some make a charge for tastings. Many of the wine estates are dominated by 18th-century Cape Dutch homesteads and, of those accessible to the public, one of the most notable is **Boschendal** (c.1746). The manor house is furnished with 17th- and 18th-century furniture; *tel: 021-874 1252* (open daily 1100–1700). For its various restaurants and wine-tastings, see Accommodation and Food, p. 145. There are tours of the vineyards (advance booking essential). Other key estates for wine-tasting include: **Bellingham**, *tel: 021-874 1011* (open Mon–Fri 0900–1700, Sat 1000–1230 Nov–Apr; Mon–Fri 0900–1600 May–Oct; R3 tasting charge for 6 different wines); **Cabrière Estate**, *tel 021-876 2630* (open for tastings R5, and sales Mon–Fri 0800–1700, Sat 1100–1300; Mon–Fri cellar tour and tastings 1100–1500, Sat 1100; R10); **La Motte**, *tel: 021-876 3119* (open Mon–Fri 0900–1630, Sat 0900–1200); and **L'Ormarins**, *tel: 021-874 1026* (open weekdays 0900–1630, Sat 0900–1230; R5 admission, free tastings).

Ask at the Tourist Office about the 5-km **Wine Walk** (maps available). For wine off-sales (and exports), visit **La Cotte Inn Wine Sales**, *35 Main Rd, Franschhoek; tel: 021-876 3775*. For winelands tours information, see p. 145.

PAARL

Tourist Office: *216 Main St; tel: 021-872 3829* (open Mon–Fri 0900–1700, Sat 0900–1300, Sun 1000–1300). The **Paarl Wine Route Office**: *also at 216 Main St; tel: 021-872*

The Huguenots

Of the many thousand French Huguenots who fled the religious persecution of Louis XIV in 1688, 200 came to the Cape. They are remembered today, chiefly, for the wine-making traditions inherited by the Cape's wine makers; by a proliferation of French surnames carried by many Afrikaans-speaking South Africans; and by a clutch of Franschhoek farms with names like La Provence. Franschhoek itself, is named after the settlers, and its pièce de resistance, apart from the quality of the locally-produced wines and food, is the **Huguenot Memorial and Museum** (p.145).

3605 (open Mon–Fri 0900–1600) supplies information and maps on the Wine Route and surrounding areas. Local events include the **Nouveau Wine Festival**, celebrating the harvest's first wines (1st weekend Apr), and the **Paarl Sparkling Wine Day** (1st Sat in Sept), which celebrates the local sparkling wine.

ACCOMMODATION AND FOOD

Grand Roche Hotel, *Plantasie St, Paarl; tel: 021-863 2727, fax: 021-863 2220*, (expensive) is sumptuously luxurious – sort of Hollywood meets the Huguenots. Less expensive, **Roggeland Country House**, *Roggeland Rd, Daljosaphat Valley, N. Paarl; tel: 021-868 2501, fax: 021-868 2113* (moderate) is a charming, small country house hotel. The **Zomerlust Guest House**, with its **Kontreihuis** restaurant, *193 Main Rd, Paarl; tel: 021-872 2117, fax: 021-872 8312* (moderate) is very stylish. Just out of town, **Mooikelder Manor House**, *Agter–Paarl Rd, N. Paarl; tel: 021-863 8491; fax: 021-863 8361* (moderate) is a delightfully friendly, antique-furnished Cape Dutch manor, once owned by Cecil Rhodes. There are numerous other bed & breakfasts, guest farms and self-catering cottages in Paarl and the surrounding area.

La Grand Roche's award-winning **Bosman Restaurant**, *Plantasie St, Paarl; tel:*

021-863 2727 (expensive; open Mon–Sun 0700–2100), supplies superb haute cuisine in elegant surroundings, with a staggeringly long wine list. Other options for serious wine buffs include **Rhebokskloof**, *Agter–Paarl Rd; tel: 021-863 8606* (expensive), a charming winery with a fine restaurant, offering a 7-course degustation menu; and KWV's **Laborie Restaurant**, *Taillefert St (off the R45 leading from the N1 into town); tel: 021-807 3095* (cheap–moderate; open daily lunch, dinner Tues–Sat), which has traditional and à la carte menus. Menus at **Roggeland Country House**, *Roggeland Rd, Daljosaphat Valley, N. Paarl; tel: 021-868 2501* (expensive; open lunch and dinner daily; reservations essential) reflect the Cape countryside, while **Wagon Wheels**, *57 Lady Grey St, Paarl; tel: 021-872 5265* (moderate; open lunch Tues–Fri; dinner Tues–Sat) is good for serious steaks, salad and seafood.

Pre-booked picnics can be arranged on the Wine Route at **Nederberg**, *tel: 021-862 3104*, while **Nelson's Creek**, *tel: 021-863 8453*, offers light lunches. Both are by appointment.

Set in the Berg River valley, and officially designated the country's third oldest town, Paarl takes its name from the huge, domed granite rocks towering over it, which glint in the rain like pearls. On the southern side is the hugely modernist **Taal Monument**, *tel: 021-863 2800* (open daily 0800–1700; free), dedicated to the glory of the Afrikaans language.

The first Europeans settled in the area in 1687 – 30 years after an explorer, Abraham Gabbema, discovered it brimming with hippo, rhino and zebra. Paarl itself was developed around 1720 along the length of a wagon road, which eventually became its main thoroughfare. Today **Main Street** is lined with Cape Dutch, Georgian, Victorian and art deco buildings. Many of the finest buildings can be seen on a 2 km walk from the Dutch Reformed **Strooidakkerk** (1805; 'thatched-roof church'), one of the oldest churches still in use in South Africa, to **Zeederberg Square**. Note the gabled vaults in the Strooidakkerk's churchyard. At no. 303, the **Oude Pastorie** (old parsonage) is now the **Paarl Museum**; *tel:*

021-872 2651 (open Mon–Fri 1000–1700; R2, Wed free), housing Cape Dutch furniture, silver, brass and copper. Also in town is the self-explanatory **Afrikaans Language Museum**, *11 Pastorie Ave, Paarl; tel: 021-872 3441* (open Mon–Fri 0800–1700; free, donations accepted). A section of it, the **Millwater Wildflower Garden**, is a showcase for indigenous flora. **Paarl Arboretum**, *Berg River Blvd* (open dawn–dusk) contains 700 species of exotic and indigenous trees. Paarl is, of course, also a major centre for the production of wine.

The Paarl Wine Route
Paarl's Wine Route is second to none. Full-bodied white and red wines, sherries and ports, can be tasted on this route, where 17 cellars and estates are open to the public. Look out for Sauvignon Blancs and Rieslings, and red cultivars such as Cabernet Sauvignon, Shiraz and Merlot. Some estates have their own restaurants, others are open for tastings (some make a charge), off-sales and cellar tours. Best-known are **Fairview**, *tel: 021-863 2450* (open weekdays 0800–1700, Sat 0800–1300; R3 charge for 6 tastings, no tours), which also makes well-known cheeses; **Backsberg**, *tel: 021-875 5141* (open weekdays 0800–1730, Sat 0800–1300; R3 charge for tastings; free cellar tours); and **Nederberg**, *tel: 021-862 3104* (open for free tastings and sales Mon–Fri 0830–1700, Nov–Apr 0800–1300), one of the most famous of all South African vineyards and winner of over 1000 awards, both nationally and internationally. The Cape Dutch homestead is one of the country's best known (1800). Cellar tours can be arranged by appointment (Mon–Fri 1030, 1430; free). Picnic lunches are available (see above), and this is the venue of the annual **Nederberg Wine Auction**, South Africa's premier wine auction (March).

Paarl is also the headquarters of the wine industry's controlling body, the **Co–operative Wine Growers' Association (KWV)**. Its sprawling 19 hectare premises – making brandies, ports, sherries, liqueurs and red and white wines – is thought to be the biggest anywhere in the world. The cellar complex is open for tours; *tel: 021-807 3008* (open Mon–Sat, bookings essential; R7 charge includes tastings).

147

Wine

There has been a renaissance of South African wine in the last 25 years and today, with international recognition, the Cape's finest are rated amongst the best from the New World. This is nothing new. With the first winelands established by Governor Simon van der Stel in Constantia and Stellenbosch, Cape wine makers were producing revered rivals to Europe's fortified wines and madeiras in the 18th and 19th centuries. The tradition of wine-making arrived with the Huguenot refugees from Catholic France, and today the industry is well-established. Regular sunny summers and winter rainfall ensure quality for nearly every vintage. In the coastal region – Constantia, Stellenbosch, Paarl, Franschhoek, Overberg and Swartland – the best vintages are aided by cool breezes. Others, inland, come from Robertson, Worcester, Tulbagh, Swellendam, the Klein Karoo and even the Gariep River valley in the Northern Cape. Best are Cape reds: those made from Cabernet Sauvignon; Pinotage – a hybrid of Pinot Noir and Hermitage (unique to the Cape); and Merlot. Of the whites, there are some notable Sauvignon Blancs, Sauvignon Blanc-Chardonnay blends and Chardonnays. The Cape has a great tradition of dessert wines; there are excellent ports (Allesverloren and Boplaas) and some good sparkling wines (Pongracz and Nederburg Kap Sekt). The key wine routes in South Africa are Stellenbosch, 41 km (35 mins), Paarl, 60 km (45 mins) and Franschhoek, 57 km (45 mins). The summer months, Nov–Mar, are the best time to visit them. The harvest is Jan–Feb.

South African Wines, by John Platter (about R42), is an essential guide to local wines, cellars, vineyards and wine makers. Available from all local bookshops.

WELLINGTON

Tourist Office: *Main St, Wellington; tel: 021-873 4604*, and **Wellington Wine Route Office:** *same address; tel: 021-873 4604* (open Mon–Thur 0800–1700, Fri 0800–1630, Sat 0900–1200).

The **Onverwacht Resort**, *Addy St, Wellington; tel: 02211-643 096; fax: 02211-32237*, has 50 fully-equipped cottages. Certain venues on the wine route provide lunch. **Bovlei**; *tel: 021-873 1567* (see Wine Route) offers a wine makers' lunch during the summer.

Wellington was founded in 1840, and named after the Duke of Wellington. It grew substantially following the opening of nearby Bain's Kloof Pass (p.340) in 1853. A few Cape Dutch homesteads have survived in the town: **Versailles** on *Main St* is a good example. For an overview of the town and its locality, visit the **Wellington Museum**, *Church St; tel: 021-873 4710* (open Mon–Fri 0900–1700; R2), with its collections of locally-collected Early, Middle and Late Stone Age implements and rock art, Huguenot artefacts and, oddly for provincial South Africa, a good collection of Egyptian antiquities. Today, Wellington is best known for its dried fruit industry.

The Wellington Wine Route

The **Wellington Wine Route** is small and compact. Cellar tours, tastings (both free) and a 'wine makers' lunch are on offer at the co-operative winery **Bovlei**, *tel: 021-873 1567* (open weekdays 0800–1230, 1330–1700, Sat 0830–1230; lunch 1200–1330). There are also tastings, tours and sales at **Jacaranda**, *tel: 021-864 1235* (open Mon–Sat 1130–1430, phone first; free); **Wamakersvallei Winery**; *tel: 021-873 1582* (open weekdays 0800–1230, 1400–1700, Sat 0830–1230; free); **Wellington Wine Cellar**, *tel: 021-873 1163* (open Mon–Fri 0800–1700; free tastings); and at historic **Welvanpas**, *tel: 021-864 1238* (open by appointment), the family home of the Retief family, one of whose ancestors was the Voortrekker leader Piet Retief. For details of tours, see Stellenbosch, p.313.

WORCESTER

See Worcester–Malmesbury, p.338.

DURBAN

Africa's favourite holiday resort, attracting more than 1.2 million visitors a year, Durban has crowded Indian Ocean beaches of different character, where you can choose between areas specialising in surfing, sailing, swimming, snorkelling, angling or simply sunbathing. The home of a large Indian population, it is also the nation's busiest port, with the second largest harbour (after Casablanca) on the African continent.

The city – South Africa's second largest – has all the ingredients of a world-class resort, including varied entertainment venues, a water park, harbour cruises, an aquarium and dolphinarium, snake park, a good choice of museums, an Indian Market, a 24-hour casino, and its own Golden Mile, which is a long mile indeed – a 6-km promenade of bars, night-clubs, cinemas, restaurants, shops and street vendors. For a family holiday in the sun, this is the place to come.

TOURIST INFORMATION

The Tourist Junction: *160 Pine St* (open Mon–Fri 0800–1700, Sat–Sun 0900–1400). The historic former Durban railway station is now an excellent tourism centre, housing **Tourism Durban**, *tel: 031-304 4934*, the city tourist authority; **Timeless Afrika**; *tel: 031-307 3800*, the marketing authority for most of KwaZulu-Natal province, including the Midlands, Thukela and Zululand; and a number of local tour and transport operators and accommodation offices, including the **National Parks**; *tel: 031-304 4934*; the **Natal Parks**

Boards; *tel: 031-304 4934;* and **Book-a-Bed Ahead**; *tel: 031-304 4934.* Free pamphlets on local attractions, amenities, leisure activities, galleries, museums, accommodation and restaurants are available, together with an accommodation service covering the whole of South Africa.

Branches: **Greater Durban Marketing Authority Beach Office**: *Ocean Sports Centre, Marine Parade (next to Sea World); tel: 031-322 608* (open daily); **Airport Kiosk**: *Domestic Arrivals Hall, Durban International Airport; tel: 031-420 400.*

ARRIVING AND DEPARTING

By Air
Durban International Airport, *off the N2, 16 km south of the city; tel: 031-426 111;* reservations: *031-611 111,* is an international gateway, served by SAA, British Airways and other international carriers, including the national airlines of Malawi, Mozambique, Swaziland and Zimbabwe, and by domestic airlines Airlink, Comair and InterAir. Daily flights link Durban with Cape Town, Johannesburg/Pretoria, Bloemfontein, Port Elizabeth, East London and Kimberley, with connecting flights to other South African centres.

An **airport bus service** runs to and from the **SAA Terminal**, *corner Smith and Aliwal Sts.* Air-conditioned, 24-hr, pre-bookable shuttle services between the airport and city are provided by **Durban Shuttle**; *tel: 083-305 2207* (cellphone), using buses (R15 per person); **Super Shuttle**, *4122 International Arrivals, Durban International Airport; tel: 031-469 0309/203 5407* or *083-777 3399* (cellphone), using micro-buses, and **Bullet Shuttle**; *tel: 031-831 519* or *083-775 8583* (cellphone).

By Rail
Station: *NMR Ave; tel: 031-361 7652/09* (enquiries); *031-361 7621* (mainline reservations).* There are daily services between Durban

149

and Johannesburg, stopping at regular points en route, as well as commuter trains to other resorts and beaches along the coast.

By Bus

Long-distance Bus Station: *next to Durban Station, NMR Ave.* There are coach services to all major and many minor towns in South Africa, with onward connections to neighbouring countries. **Greyhound Citiliner**: *tel: 031-309 7830* (credit card bookings); **Translux**: *031-361 7461/8333;* **Golden Wheels Intercity**: *tel: 031-292 894/285 032.* Services to Wild Coast – **U-Tours**: *tel: 031-368 2848* (depart Durban Station); **Umhlanga Tours**: *tel: 031-561 3777* (depart Hilcon Centre); services to Richards Bay and Empangeni – **Interport**: *tel: 0351-91791/4.*

By Car

There are good motorway connections north to Johannesburg on the N3, and along the coast in both directions on the N2.

GETTING AROUND

Like most South African cities, Durban is laid out on a grid, so navigating is easy. *Smith St* and *West St* are the main thoroughfares in the city centre, laid out parallel to the bay, which now houses the small boats marinas. The docks area is to the south-west, while the beach strip runs north-east to the Umgeni River Mouth, separated from the docks by a narrow peninsula, the Point. The city centre is easily walkable; the beachfront is 6 km long. You will need transport to connect the two, and to reach some of the more out of the way sights and beaches.

All the major car hire companies are represented, including **Avis**: *tel: 031-426 333;* **Budget**: *tel: 031-304 9023;* and **Imperial**: *tel: 031-373 731.* Durban has about a dozen public car parks. Handy for the central district are car parks off *Aliwal St,* between *Smith St* and *Victoria Embankment.* The *Rutherford St* car park is close to South Beach, while North Beach is served by car parks off *Point St* and near Victoria Park.

Public Transport

Getting around the city by bus is easy, so to avoid parking problems you can leave your car

in the hotel garage. The small yellow buses of the **Mynah Shuttle Service**; *tel: 031-307-3503,* operate various 'migration' routes between the city centre, North Beach, South Beach and suburbs within a 10 km radius. **Durban Transport** has many bus stops in and around the city, and runs a twice-weekly service to The Pavilion shopping centre. The 852 bus service leaves the beachfront Wed and Sat at 0900, leaving The Pavilion at 1330 (single: R5 from the Beachfront; R3 from the city; books of tickets from Durban Transport Management Board information office; *tel: 031-307 505).*

An amusing, if not particularly cheap, way to travel between the beach and the city centre is by *tuk-tuk,* an Asian-style motorised covered tricycle carrying up to six people. Durban is famous for its man-powered **rickshaw rides**. The brightly painted rickshaws and their strong Zulu pullers line up in *Marine Parade.* A trip of about 7 mins costs R7, with an extra R4 if, like most people, you have your photograph taken with your driver in his brilliant costume and elaborate head-dress. Introduced from Japan in 1893, there were some 2000 runners by 1904, providing the city's main form of public transport. There are few left today, and those that do remain are far more a tourist attraction than a viable form of transport.

Taxis do not cruise. **Mozzie Cabs**; *tel: 031-368 1114,* run short-distance trips between the beachfront and the business district. Among other taxi companies are: **Aussies**; *tel: 031-309 7888;* **Bunny Cabs**; *tel: 031-322 914;* **Eagle**; *tel: 031-378 333;* **Swift**; *tel: 031-325 569;* and **Zippy Cabs**; *tel: 031-202-7067.*

Tours

Details of walking tours introducing different aspects of Durban are available from the **Tourist Junction** (see p.149). The **Oriental Walkabout** takes in the Indian Quarter, Victoria St Market, some important mosques, a sari emporium and other sights; the **Historical Walkabout** covers sites relating to the city's development from the first white settlement (both daily 0945–1230; R25). The **Durban Experience** is a cultural walking tour (Tues only).

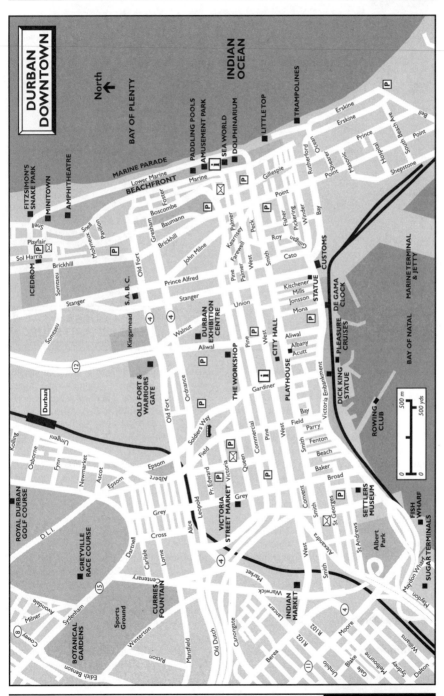

DURBAN DOWNTOWN

North

BAY OF PLENTY

INDIAN OCEAN

FITZSIMON'S SNAKE PARK
MINITOWN
AMPHITHEATRE

PADDLING POOLS
AMUSEMENT PARK
SEA WORLD
DOLPHINARIUM
LITTLETOP
TRAMPOLINES

MARINE PARADE
Lower Marine
BEACHFRONT

Snell
Playfair
Sol Harris
ICEDROM
Brickhill
Somtseu
Stanger
S.A.B.C.
Kingsmead

Molyneux
Pavilion
Old Fort
Gresham
Foster
Boscombe
Baumann
Brickhill
John Milne
Prince Alfred
Stanger
Walnut

Marine
Gillespie
Point
Palmer
Karmsey
Farewell
West
Pine
Palmer
Union
Pine
West
Aliwal

Erskine
Erskine
Prince
Rutherford
Ocean
Point Shearer
Point
Masonic
Hospital
Shepstone
Bell
Point
South Beach Ave

P

Gillespie
Peck
Fisher
Pickering
Winder
Bay
Smith
Roy
Cato
Kitchener
Mills
Jonsson
Mona
West
Albany
Acutt

CUSTOMS
STATUE
DE GAMA CLOCK
PLEASURE CRUISES
DICK KING STATUE
ROWING CLUB

MARINE TERMINAL & JETTY

BAY OF NATAL

DURBAN EXHIBITION CENTRE
THE WORKSHOP
CITY HALL
PLAYHOUSE

Durban

Kolling
Osborne
Fynn
Newmarket
Ascot
Umgeni
Epsom
Albert
ROYAL DURBAN GOLF COURSE
D.L.I.
GREYVILLE RACE COURSE
Grey
Cross
Dartnel
Carlisle
Lorne
Centenary
CURRIES FOUNTAIN
Sydenham
Sports Ground
Winterton
Mansfield
Ritson
Old Dutch
Canongate
BOTANICAL GARDENS
Avondale
Milner
Cowey
Edith Benson

Old Fort
Ordnance
Old Fort
OLD FORT & WARRIORS GATE
Soldier's Way
Field
Pr. Edward
Victoria
Queen
Commercial
Pine
Gardiner
Bay
West
Field
Parry
Smith
Fenton
Beach
Baker
Broad
Grey
VICTORIA STREET MARKET
Leopold
Alice
Warwick
Lancers
INDIAN MARKET
Market
Berea
Umbilo
Gale
Blake
Melbourne
Moore
Williams
Sydney
Dalton
Maydon Wharf
SUGAR TERMINALS
FISH WHARF
SETTLERS MUSEUM
Albert Park
St Georges
St Andrews
Alexandra
Convent
Smith
West

R102
R102

Victoria Embankment

500 m
500 yds
0

151

12
4
4
4
4
15
8
11

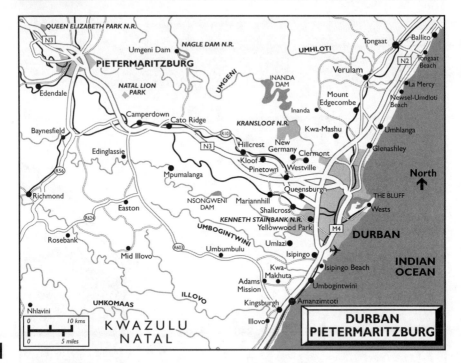

Several companies offer tours of the city and into other parts of KwaZulu-Natal and beyond. **Shaka Tours and Safaris**; *tel: 031-561 2860*, run bus tours of Durban city; **Strelitzia Tours**; *tel: 031-861 904*, offer scheduled and private minibus tours of the city. For a tour of the outlying townships, contact **Hamba Kahle Tours**, *Tourist Junction; tel: 031-305 5586.*

Harbour cruises with **Durban Ferry Services**; *tel: 031-361 8727*, depart from alongside the Maritime Museum at the Esplanade end of *Aliwal St*. Day cruises and 90-min evening tours are available with **Lynski Charters**; *tel: 031-561 2031*. Fishing charters are also offered. Other pleasure trips around the harbour and deep-sea cruises are available from the *Gardiner St Jetty*. For departure times, *tel: 031-305 4022.*

STAYING IN DURBAN

Accommodation

With at least 1.2 million people a year visiting the city, Durban has a wide choice of accommodation, much of it cheap–moderate, with houses, apartments, campsites and hostels amongst the options. There are several reservation agencies. **Book-a-Bed-Ahead**, *Tourist Junction; tel: 031-304 4934*, has 1600 places on its books. Hotel chains in Durban include *CL, Hd, HI, Ka, Pa, TC.*

The most venerable and famous hotel in the city is the large, venerable and luxurious **Royal**, *267 Smith St; tel: 031-304 0331; fax: 031-307 6884* (expensive), whose seven restaurants, four cocktail venues, 22 suites, 10 family rooms and 240 doubles have hosted royalty and countless celebrities in the hotel's century and a half of service. Set to give it a good run for its money, the art deco **Edward** *(Ka), 149 Marine Parade; tel: 031-373 681; fax: 031-321 692* (expensive), has recently been lovingly restored as a first-class hotel, right on the beachfront, with several wonderful restaurants and bar areas.

Right next door, and also newly restored, the old colonial **Balmoral**, *125 Marine Parade; tel: 031-374 392; fax: 031-375 962*, offers extraordinary value, with large airy, sea-facing rooms (cheap–moderate). The food doesn't match up but there are plenty of options within an easy walk.

As might be expected, there are several other large hotels facing the sea along this highly desirable stretch of real estate. The **Holiday Inn Garden Court** (Hd), *167 Marine Parade; tel: 031-373 341; fax: 031-329 885* (moderate) is one of three Garden Court properties in Durban, with 344 rooms all facing the sea. The **Seaboard Protea Hotel** *(Pa), 577 Point Rd, Marine Parade; tel: 031-373 601, fax: 031-372 600* (moderate–expensive) includes 42 family rooms with sea views (up to two children under 19 sharing with parents stay free, paying only for breakfast). The **Beach Hotel**, *107 Marine Parade; tel: 031-375 511, fax: 031-375 409* (cheap) has TV, telephone, tea and coffee-making facilities and air-conditioning in all rooms, a pool, bar and restaurant. Further out, the four-star **Holiday Inn Crowne Plaza** *(Hd), 63 Snell Parade, opposite North Beach; tel: 031-371 321; fax: 031-325 527* (moderate–expensive), has a health centre, sauna, pool, and offers extensive banqueting facilities.

In the suburbs, there are several excellent bed and breakfasts, amongst them **Sica's Guest House**, *19 Owen Ave, Westridge; tel: 031-812 768, fax 031-815 081* (cheap–moderate), an 1886 farmhouse set in 2 hectares of park-like gardens, with a pool; **Rainsgrove Lodge**, *220 St Thomas Rd, Berea; tel: 031-219 379* (cheap), also offering self-catering; and **Sommersby Bed and Breakfast**, *17 Claribel Rd, Morningside; tel: 031-238 667* (cheap–moderate).

Backpackers should try the **Durban Beach Youth Hostel** *(HI), 19 Smith St, Durban; tel: 031-324 945, fax: 031-324 551*, which has singles, doubles and dormitories, home-cooked meals, a bar, day and nightlife tours, and a free walking orientation tour. The hostel is close to the beach and Golden Mile, and guests can hire surfboards. Alongside the usual amenities are a laundry, swimming pool and free pick-up service from airport and stations. Alternatively, try the **Backpackers Club International**, *154 Point Rd; tel: 031- 320 541* (cheap), 200 m from the harbour, which also offers free collection from the airport and central Durban.

Campsites: there are caravan parks at *Grays Inn Rd; tel: 031-473 929* and *Ansteys Rd; tel: 031-474 061.*

Eating and Drinking

As well as a wide choice of ethnic restaurants, Durban has several places inviting guests to eat as much as they like for a set sum – a challenge for those with hearty appetites. There are also masses of fast-food outlets – burger bars, pizza houses, bistro 'supernosh' and outlets specialising in ribs, shellfish or steaks. Pub lunches – usually quite substantial – are also popular.

With a large Indian population, the city has plenty of restaurants offering authentic dishes from North and South India. Bunny chows are a Durban delight – a take-away curry mix served in a hollowed-out half loaf of bread. Italian, Portuguese, Continental, Mexican, African, Chinese, Polynesian, Indonesian, Japanese, Pakistani, French, American – all these cuisines and more can be found.

Wherever you go at lunchtime, there are easy-on-the-pocket items on the menu. Dinner dishes tend to be a little more expensive, but are almost always good value. Sunday roast lunch has become a regular date for many at some of Durban's restaurants.

Eating out is a regular feature of local life, and it is advisable to make a dinner reservation any night of the week. Some restaurants are fully licensed and some are licensed only for beer and wine. It is usually acceptable to BYO (Bring Your Own) drink if a restaurant has no licence, but it is best to check first as a few places do not allow alcohol.

Self-caterers should go to the **Victoria St Market** at the corner of *Queen and Victoria Sts; tel: 031-306 4021*. Their noses should lead them to the heady spices and curries at this original Indian market. There are about 90 stalls, where you can buy anything from fresh fish and halal meats to hand-rolled incense.

For a more formal taste of India, try **Aangan**, *86 Queen St, Durban; tel: 031-307 1366* (moderate), where Bombay chefs prepare vegetarian and meat dishes; the eat-as-much-as-you-like **Maharajah Restaurant**, *Palm Beach Hotel, 106 Gillespie St, Durban; tel: 031-373 451* (cheap), or the **Jewel of India**, *Holiday Inn*

153

Eastern Lifestyle

More than a million Indians live in Kwazulu-Natal, forming one of the world's largest populations of Indians outside the sub-continent. A large influx of Indians arrived in the province in the late 1860s, in response to the need for a strong labour force to work the sugar cane plantations (see Background, p.72). Most stayed on, bringing to Durban and other parts of Kwazulu-Natal a Hindu/Islamic culture that has considerable influence in the region. Tamil, Hindi and other Indian languages are still in use, especially among the older generation. Durban's Indian Quarter is around *Grey St*, centred on the Victoria St Market and the Juma Mosque, one of the largest mosques in the Southern Hemisphere. Tourists can take a look at the city's Eastern lifestyle by joining the Oriental Walkabout, held on weekdays.

A number of Indian festivals take place through the year, of which probably the most fascinating is the Hindu ritual fire-walking at Easter. Kavady Festivals, held by Hindus in their temples to appease the gods, are held in Feb and May, and in mid Dec, a huge chariot bearing an image of Lord Krishna is pulled along *Marine Parade* to the accompaniment of singing and chanting.

Crowne Plaza, Snell Parade tel: 031-378 168 (moderate–expensive), where live Indian music complements a choice of nearly 100 curries and tandooris.

For the European touch, the **Coimbra**, *130 Gillespie St, Durban; tel: 031-255 447* (moderate; closed Mon) specialises in traditional Portuguese cuisine, including chicken peri peri, seafood and steak, while the best French food in town is served at the **St Geran**, *31 Aliwal St; tel: 031-304 7509* (expensive; booking advisable). **Roma Revolving**, *John Ross House, Victoria Embankment; tel: 031-376 707* (expensive; booking advisable) offers Italian with a twist in a 31st-floor revolving restaurant.

Good seafood is available everywhere, but for the real specialists, try the large, bright **Langoustine-by-the-Sea**, *131 Waterkant Rd; tel: 031-837 324*, or the smaller **Lord Prawn**, *2nd Floor, Coastlands Building, West St; tel: 031-372 978* (both moderate–expensive). Several places also offer entertainment, including **Thatcher's**, *17 Boscombe Pl., Marine Parade; tel: 031-374 311* (moderate), an English-style pub with good food (including steak and seafood) and dancing to live bands (Tues–Sun); **Duke's Palace**, *60/64 Smith St tel: 031-379 756* (moderate–expensive), which serves pub lunches, Sun night family supper club and dining and dancing to the Duke's Combo; and **Cranky Frank's**, *corner Hunter and John Milne Sts; tel: 031-368 5337* (cheap–moderate; best to

book), a popular restaurant serving fish and other dishes, with live entertainment every evening.

In the 5-star hotels (see Accommodation), the **Royal Hotel** offers fine dining with a choice of elegant restaurants – the Royal Carvery, Royal Grill, Royal Steakroom and Palm Court, while the buffet at the Charthouse in the **Edward** has to be seen to be believed.

Communications

Main post office: *West St, Durban; tel: 031-305 7521*. Poste restante facilities.

At the **Telekom International Call Office**, *320 West St (First Floor)*, local and international calls can be made by ordinary metered phone or with a phonecard, charged at R0.40 per unit. Open Mon–Fri 0800–2200, Sat 1000–220, Sun 1600–2100.

Money

There are several banks with exchange facilities and ATMs on *Smith St* and *West St.* **Thomas Cook bureau de change**: *Rennies Travel, Ground Floor, Durban Bay House, 333 Smith St; tel: 031-305 5722; fax: 031-305 2497.*

ENTERTAINMENT

Subtropical Durban, with year-round summer weather (more or less) is Fun City for visitors from all over South Africa and beyond, and the entertainment scene is vibrant and varied. For their elders, there are a dozen or so casinos (most illegal) around Durban, while theatres, cinemas, concert halls, discos, clubs and pubs cater for many tastes.

The free publication, *What's On in Durban and KwaZulu-Natal,* is published six times a year. It lists main events and also contains maps of the beachfront area and major centres. A smaller monthly pamphlet, *Durban for all Seasons* (also free) covers the entertainment scene, museums, attractions and local events, and carries advertisements detailing 'adult-oriented' information.

There are five **theatres** within the impressive **Natal Playhouse**, *Smith St, Durban; tel: 031-304 3631,* a major venue for avant garde plays, dramatic, operatic, musical, dance and cabaret performances.

Most main shopping centres, including the Musgrave Centre, The Workshop, the Pavilion at Westville and the Sanlam Centre in Pinetown, have **cinemas**. There are seven at the Musgrave Centre alone, and another dozen at **The Wheel**, *between Gillespie St and Point Rd,* near the beachfront.

Several of the **casinos** are open 24 hours a day, among them **Caesar's Grand Casino**, *West St;* and **Durban Casino**, *West St.*

Live bands perform at some of the **pubs** and **clubs**. African music and African food are enjoyed at **Jam 'n Sons'**, *1st Floor, Belmont Arcade, 1 West St;* while **Franky's**, *45 Maritime Pl.*, introduces new bands and sometimes stages an African jazz evening or a nude show.

For youngsters, there are fun-fairs, water-parks, video arcades and a whole host of other daytime activities, including an **Ice Rink**, *Sol Harris Crescent, North Beach; tel: 031-368 3022.* Indoor go-karting with computerised lap times appeals not only to youngsters and their parents, but also to local businessmen and women, whose companies vie for the competitive edge at **Action Traction**, *Edwin Swales Dr.* **Kids' Fantasy Land**, *Sanlam Centre, Pinetown; tel: 031-722 655,* caters for tiny tots and children up to 10 years with ball ponds, bouncy castles and other delights. Pony and tractor rides and contact with young animals attract small holidaymakers to the **Children's Farm**, *Battery Beach, Durban; tel: 031-321 674.* A weekend

visit there may coincide with a magic show. Along the Golden Mile there are games arcades and street entertainments.

Popular annual **events** include: late **Jan–Feb:** Thursday concerts in World Symphony Series; **Apr:** Autumn Rose Show; **mid June:** Comrades' Marathon between Durban and Pietermaritzburg (see p. 287); **late Sept–early Oct:** German Beer festival; **Dec:** Catch a Million fishing competition; Bonsai Summer Show; Indian Festival of Chariots; Candles and Dolphins by Candlelight – five nights in mid Dec at Sea World; Christmas Carnival.

SHOPPING

Anyone who likes shopping will love Durban. You could visit a different modern shopping and entertainment complex every day for a week, spending hours (and mega-money) in sophisticated shops and boutiques, coffee shops, restaurants and cinemas.

Leather goods, hand-woven African rugs, designer gold and diamond jewellery, carved animals in ebony and other woods and beadwork are among items which visitors like to take home.

The major department stores are congregated along *Smith St* and *West St,* and there are several big malls, of which the closest to the city centre is **The Workshop**, originally Workshop No. 1 at the local railway works, with the girders to prove it. The 120 specialist shops are on two floors, with Victorian-style barrows selling goods at the lower level. **The Wheel**, near the beachfront between *Gillespie St* and *Point Rd*, has 140 shops, bars, restaurants and cinemas – and what is claimed to be the world's largest ferris wheel.

Just out of town, *off the N3 near Westville,* the glass-domed **Pavilion** is the East Coast's biggest shopping complex with cinemas, restaurants and some 180 shops offering fashions, food, jewellery, electronics, books, art and music. Other good shopping centres include the **Village Market**, *Jan Hofmeyr Rd, Westville,* and the **Musgrave Centre**, *near the Botanic Gardens.*

The city's many **markets** are fun to nose around. The **Indian Market**, *Victoria St,* is home not only to a huge array of Indian foods,

155

Dick King's Ride

An equestrian statue on Durban's Victoria Embankment depicts Dick King and his trusty steed, Somerset. In 1842, the pair made a speedy 950 km journey over rough terrain from Durban to Grahamstown, to get help for British troops besieged by Boers at the Old Fort, Durban. The ride took 10 days. On getting King's message, the British sent a frigate to Durban to free the garrison and the day was saved.

Nearby is an elaborate clock donated to the city to mark the 400th anniversary of Vasco da Gama's arrival off the coast. The 500th anniversary is in 1997.

fabrics and other beautiful souvenirs, but some of the most unusual African crafts available. It is worth a stroll just for the *muti* (traditional medicine) stalls. Durban has a range of fascinating markets where you can seek out beautiful and unusual gifts and souvenirs. Many are open daily.

Buskers entertain at the 500-stall **South Plaza Market**, *Durban Exhibition Centre; tel: 031-301 9900*, while the **Farepark Market**, *between West and Pine Sts; tel: 031-368 2190*, has crafts and collectables in rustic cabins and 100 stalls trade at the **Bazaar**, *opposite The Wheel; tel: 031-368 4361*, which also has a great many food stalls and video arcades.

Stalls selling anything from plastic hair slides to velvet set up shop in the **Church St Arts and Crafts Market**, *opposite Durban City Hall*. Finally, there is a thriving unofficial souvenir trade along the beachfront, near the rickshaws. At weekends, this grows into the large and lively **Point Waterfront Fleamarket**; *tel: 031-368 5436* (open Sat–Sun and public holidays), where street entertainers and seafood cafés' ethnic cuisines add to the atmosphere. It is one of a number of fleamarkets and antiques markets, most of which open monthly on a Sat or Sun.

Finally, those in search of real quality should look in the **African Arts Centre**, *8 Guildhall Arcade, 35 Gardiner St; tel: 031-304 7915* (open

Mon–Fri 0830–1700, Sat 0900–1300; free) a small outlet selling magnificent Zulu beadwork, basketry, pottery and telephone wire weaving, amongst a host of other options. Profits go towards promoting African art.

SIGHTSEEING

This area was 'discovered' on Christmas Day, 1497, by the Portuguese explorer, Vasco de Gama, who named the area Natal in honour of the season. Although sailors continued to call in search of a safe port, fresh water and food, the first permanent white settlement and trading post was only established here in 1824 by British Lieutenant Francis Farewell, who named the group of huts after the Governor of the Cape, Sir Benjamin d'Urban. Today, his settlement has grown into a major city with a sprawling population of nearly 4 million, one of the largest ports in Africa, and a hive of seaside frivolity.

The subtropical climate provides around 320 sunny days a year, and although humidity is high, the prospects for serious sunbathing have brought the holidaymakers flocking. Durban's **beaches** are protected by shark nets, and lifeguards are on duty daily 0700–1700. North Beach and the Bay of Plenty provide world-class surfing. Regular surfing competitions are held at Dairy Beach, and South Beach is popular with sunbathers. Unfortunately, there is a significant amount of petty crime, so leave valuables securely locked away.

A wide range of family entertainments has grown up along the Golden Mile. The best of them is **Sea World**, *Lower Marine Parade; tel: 031-373 536* (open daily 0900–2100, shark-feeding sessions Tues, Thur and Sun, 1230), an aquarium and dolphinarium with plenty to see, including seal, penguin and dolphin shows. With the focus on education, **Fitzsimon's Snake Park**, *Snell Parade; tel: 031-376 456* (open daily 0900–1630) demonstrates the importance of snakes in their natural environment. Visitors can watch the milking of snakes' venom and see other reptiles. The **Umgeni River Bird Park**, *Riverside Rd; tel: 031-579-4600* (open daily 0900–1700; includes birds' free-flying shows daily at 1100). The park has 3000 native and foreign birds of 400 species, in

156

a lovely setting of trees, rocks, gardens, water-falls and walk-through aviaries.

Water World, *between Snell Parade and Battery Beach; tel: 031-329 776* (open daily, hours vary according to season and weather; covers day's entertainment; R25, surcharge if you take your own picnic) provides great excitement on slides and chutes and looping water-propelled rides, while **Fun World**, *Marine Parade; tel: 031-329 776* (opening times vary according to season and weather) is an amusement park with daring rides, bumper cars and an aerial cableway.

There are also a number of more sober, and often very good museums, a couple of them in Durban's flamboyant neo-baroque **City Hall**, a close copy of Belfast City Hall in Northern Ireland. Allow plenty of time to study the array of stuffed creatures and the accompanying information at the **Durban Natural Science Museum**, *1st Floor, City Hall, Smith St; tel: 031-300 6211* (open Mon–Sat 0830–1700, Sun 1100–1700; free), where exhibits range from one of only five dodo skeletons in the world to the social life of the cockroach – a survivor from the age of the dinosaurs. **Durban Art Centre**, *2nd Floor, City Hall, Smith St; tel: 031-300 6238* (open Mon–Sat 0830–1700, Sun 1100–1700; free) contains works by noted South African and overseas artists, including Victorian and contemporary collections, and some atmospheric photographs. Seekers after African art should also visit the commercial **African Arts Centre** (see Shopping, p. 156).

Under the umbrella of the **Local History Museum** come five small museums, each dealing with a different aspect of Durban's history and culture. The **Old Court House**, *Aliwal St; tel: 031-300 6240* (open Mon–Sat 0830–1700, Sun 1100–1600; free) depicts the history of the early settlers and the colonial conflicts, with a collection of costumes, a sugar mill and old stores. The **KwaMuhle Museum**, *132 Ordnance Rd; tel: 031-300 6313* (open Mon–Sat 0830–1700, Sun 1100–1600; free) covers the city's 20th-century history from the standpoint of its non-white inhabitants. The **Old House Museum**, *31 St Andrews St; tel: 031-300 6520* (open Mon–Sat 0830–1700, Sun 1100–1600; free) is a careful reconstruction of an 1894

settler home, furnished in period. The **King's Battery Museum**, *Point Waterfront* (open Sat 0830–1700, Sun 1100–1600; R2) covers the role of Natal in World War II, and the **Port Natal Maritime Museum**, *Bayside end of Aliwal St; tel: 031-300 6320* (open Tues–Fri 1000–1600, Sun 1100–1600; R2) has a 1927 steam tug, a 1957 minesweeper and a host of ocean-going memorabilia. For security reasons, use the street entrance over the railway off *Victoria Embankment* (alongside Point Yacht Club) rather than the subway.

Also on the waterfront, learn how sugar is produced at the **Sugar Terminals**, *57 Maydon Rd, Maydon Wharf, Durban; tel: 031-301 0331* (four 75-min tours daily 0830–1515, no afternoon tour Fri; R6; booking essential), which are capable of storing more than half a million tons of raw sugar.

In the hilly suburbs behind the city centre, the **Killie Campbell Museum**, *corner Marriott and Essenwood Rds, Berea; tel: 031-207 3711* (open Tues, Thur 0800–1300 or for guided tours by appointment) is worth making the effort for. Housed at Muckleneuk, a magnificently designed and furnished sugar baron's mansion, it has one of the world's finest collections of African art and craft, including costumes, beadwork, pottery, basketry and weapons, together with a fine set of paintings by local artist, Barbara Tyrell, and a superb Africana library. Nearby, the **Durban Botanic Gardens**, *Sydenham Rd, Berea, Durban; tel: 031-211 303* (garden open daily 0730–1745 mid Sept–mid Apr, to 1715 rest of year; orchid house open daily 0930–1230 and 1400–1700; free) is 20 hectares of peace and beauty with tropical vegetation, flowering trees, scented garden, rare cycads and an orchid house, tea gardens and information centre.

Out of Town

Just south of Durban, reached by the Southern Freeway, the architecture and opulence of the **Temple of Understanding**, *Ambassador Rd, Chatsworth; tel: 031-433 328* (open daily for guided tours; free) cannot fail to impress. It was built by the Hare Krishna movement and also has a vegetarian restaurant (open daily 1100–2100).

DURBAN–EAST LONDON

From Durban south to Scottburgh is known officially as the Strelizia Coast; from Scottburgh to Port Edward, it becomes the Hibiscus coast. The name is all that remains of the many thousands of brightly flowering hibiscus bushes that once lined the road south. In reality, the area from Durban to Port Edward, on the Eastern Cape border, is more often simply known as the South Coast.

This is one of the most popular tourist areas in the country, a heavily built-up stretch of warm, subtropical beaches filled with family attractions. Cross the border into what actually used to be another country; most of the rest of the journey, along the aptly named

Wild Coast, is through the former homelands of the Transkei and Ciskei, past sprawling African towns and villages, with rutted side roads twisting down to tiny villages and remote hotels on some of the most stunning beaches in southern Africa. There have been some security problems in this area, and it is sensible to travel this section of the road only in daylight hours.

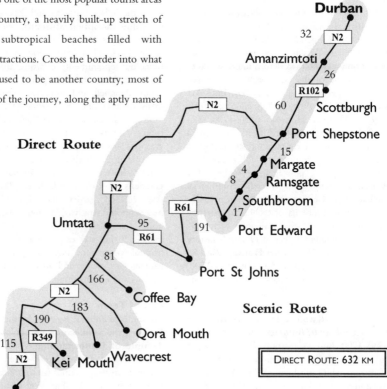

ROUTES

DIRECT ROUTE

➡ Leave Durban on the N2 freeway, heading west. This follows the coast as far as Port Shepstone, then turns inland through Umtata to East London. Distance: 632 km; allow one long day.

SCENIC ROUTE

▐ᴵᴵᴵᴵ➤ Leave Durban on the N2, heading west. The easiest way to travel this section of the route is to remain on the N2, coming off for small detours at any of the towns you wish to visit, such as **Amanzimtoti**, **Scottburgh** or **Port Shepstone**. However, it is also possible to travel along the parallel old road, the R102. From Port Shepstone, remain on the coast road, which now becomes the R61 through **Margate**, **Ramsgate** and **Southbroom** to **Port Edward**. The new South Coast Toll Road also connects Port Shepstone and Port Edward. Distance: Durban–Port Edward, 164 km; allow 2–3 hrs non-stop.

From Port Edward, remain on the R61. A bridge across the Umtamvuna River marks the provincial border with the Eastern Cape. The road loops inland round to Lusikisiki (160 km), then becomes gravel for the last 31 km down to **Port St Johns**. Leave Port St Johns on the tarred section of the R61, which climbs back out on the other side of the river valley to **Umtata** (95 km). From there, take the N2 towards East London. After 18 km, a tarred road on the left leads down to **Coffee Bay**. For the more adventurous, a meandering network of dirt roads leads through to **Qora Mouth**, **Wavecrest**, Kentani and the **Kei Mouth** ferry, where you can pick up the R349 and head back to the N2. However, the coast is split by a continuous series of creeks. Almost all the local roads are narrow, winding and gravel in a variable state of repair. Some may also involve fording streams or using ferries, others require long detours inland. None of these roads require 4x4, but they are very slow, the distances are long and driving is tiring.

The best option is to remain on the N2 and keep doing forays to the coast and back. If you do this, turn left at Idutywa for Nqabara and Qora Mouth, and at Butterworth for Wavecrest and Qolora Mouth. The N2 continues over the massive, spectacular **Great Kei River Bridge**, beyond which is the R349 to Kei Mouth and Morgan's Bay. It is 66 km from the bridge into East London. Distance: Port Edward–East London, 594 km on the N2; total distance: 786 km. It is possible to do it in two days, but it would be far better to allow at least four or five and chill out on the beach along the way.

BUSES

Translux and Greyhound both operate a daily service on this route. Journey time: 13¼ hrs. OTT Table 3546.

There is also a Durban–Margate service. Journey time: 2½ hrs. See OTT Table 3555.

THE SOUTH COAST

Tourist Offices: Amanzimtoti: *Beach Rd, Amanzimtoti; tel: 031-903 7498;* **Central South Coast Publicity,** *130 Scott St, Scottburgh; tel: 0323-21364;* **South Coast Publicity,** *Main Beach, Margate; tel: 039-377 7322.*

ACCOMMODATION AND FOOD

This is a long stretch of coast, lined with places to stay, mostly large self-catering apartment blocks or time-share resorts. Local Tourist Offices can provide comprehensive lists of these, while estate agents or the **Scottburgh Holiday Letting Service,** *PO Box 726, Scottburgh 4180; tel: 0323-20872/81303,* handle short-term rentals of the many private holiday homes dotted between.

There are several fine country house hotels towards the southern end of the strip, all of which have excellent restaurants. **Brackenmoor,** *Skyline Rd, Uvongo, near Margate; tel: 03931-75166; fax: 03931-75109* (cheap) has an elegant Edwardian feel, all billowing curtains and formal gardens. The flamboyant **Country Lodge,** *Southbroom; tel: 03931-78380; fax: 03931-78557* (moderate) has rooms in various African styles, from old colonial to Sheba, Queen of the Jungle, in a magnificent seaside cycad forest. The **Selborne Country Lodge & Golf Resort,** *Pennington; tel: 0323-51133; fax: 0323-51811* (moderate–expensive) and the

159

Golf Coast

Kwazulu-Natal must be one of the most golf-obsessed areas in the entire world, with no fewer than 63 golf courses in the province. Most are incredibly beautiful, from the sweeping mountain grasslands of the north, to the rugged skylines of the Drakensberg and the hot, sunny expanses of the coast, with 23 between Stanger on the North Coast (see p.168) and Port Edward on the South Coast. These wonderful courses prove a tourist magnet in themselves. There is a detailed brochure, available from all state tourist offices, which gives information on courses, golf resorts and specialist tour operators. For further details, contact **Golf Coast Promotions**, *PO Box 1253, Margate, South Africa; tel: 039-377 7322; fax: 039-377 6886.*

sprawling red-brick **San Lemeer Estate Hotel**, *Lower South Coast Main Rd, Southbroom; tel: 03931-30031; fax: 03931-30015* (expensive) both aim primarily at golfers, and are set on painstakingly manicured courses.

Lower down the price scale are several friendly, slightly faded seaside hotels, including the modern **Blue Marlin**, *180 Scott St, Scottburgh; tel: 0323-21214; fax: 0323-20971* (cheap), with a pool and sea views; the cosy, low-slung **Pumula Hotel**, *Umzumbe, 4 km south of Hibberdene village; tel: 039-684 6717; fax: 039-684 6303* (cheap), with pretty gardens, a pool and beach; and the 1950s-style **Marina Beach Country Hotel**, *Marina Dr., Marina Beach; tel: 039-313 0022; fax: 039-313 0070* (cheap), about 200m from the sea. **Widenham Holiday Resort**, *Cheltenham Rd, about 2 km south of Umkomaas; tel: 0323-30351/31472; fax: 0323-30923* (cheap) offers small brick-built self-catering chalets, an on-site restaurant and bar, spread through shady grounds 400m from the beach. **Margate Sands**, *Margate; tel: 03931-22543; fax: 03931-21541* (cheap) is a huge town-centre self-catering apartment block, on the beachfront.

Campsites: there are a great many camping and caravan sites along this coast. In Amanzimtoti, the **Amanzi Club Caraville** *(Ck), 55 Beach Rd; tel: 031-903 2366,* and the **H appy Days Club Caraville** *(Ck), 65 Beach Rd; tel: 031-903 3246,* are both large, cheerful resorts, with their own restaurants.

In **Scottburgh**, there are three excellent parks. The **Rocky Bay Caravan Park**; *tel: 0323-20546,* has self-catering log cabins, a recreation centre, pool and children's playground. Nearby, the **MacNicol's Bazley Beach Resort**, *on the edge of the Ifafa Lagoon; tel: 0323-98863/79,* goes one better, with two pools, *braai* parties, cream teas and a games room. **Scottburgh Municipal Caravan Park**; *tel: 0323-20291,* has its own 1 km beach frontage, swimming pools with a supertube, a children's mini-train and mini-golf.

The luxury hotels, particularly the Brackenmoor and the Country Lodge (see above) are the best places to eat. However, there are plenty of other possibilities. Crocodile inevitably features heavily on the menu at the **Crocodilian**, *Croc World, Old South Coast Rd; tel: 0323-20083* (moderate). In central Scottburgh, **The Hooded Thief**, *100 Scott St; tel: 0323-83454* (cheap) is a traditional pub, with a full menu and big screen sports action. **The Bistro**, *Ramsgate; tel: 03931-44128* (moderate) specialises in freshly caught line fish, while the **Trattoria La Terrazza**, *Outlook Rd; Southbroom, tel: 03931-6162* (moderate) serves good Italian food on the shore of the lagoon. There are also several **Spur Steakhouses** and branches of **Mike's Kitchen** scattered along the route.

SIGHTSEEING

There are so many little towns and villages

Colour section (i): De Hoop Nature Reserve (p.136); Chapman's Peak Drive on the Cape Peninsula (p.119).
(ii): Taal Monument, Paarl (p.147).
(iii): Durban seafront at night (p.149); East London beach at sunset (p.173).
(iv): Johannesburg (see pp.194–203): cityscape; Lesedi Cultural Village (p.210); inset, A Corner of Remembrance in Soweto (p.203).

along this stretch of coast, many merging along the fringes, that most people treat it as one large resort. All sites are easily accessible to anyone with a car. Sadly (except for passengers), the railway literally hugs the coast for much of the way, meaning that holidaymakers have to cross the tracks to reach the beach. Once there, however, all the beaches are excellent, with miles of fine gold sand. Some are on lagoons for safe bathing, and most have lifeguards in season, while shark nets offer protection from predators. Do keep a watchful eye out for smaller nasties such as jellyfish or sea urchins.

Inland, much of the route runs through enormous, rolling sugar cane fields; the Natal coast is one of the largest sugar-producing areas of the world. Further south, around South-broom and Ramsgate, the vegetation becomes lusher and greener, with large tracts of original forest interspersed by smaller property developments and more obvious money.

Known locally as 'Toti,' **Amanzimtoti** is an ever-expanding, rather downmarket resort – all ice-creams and beauty contests. It does have good beaches, and amongst the entertainments on offer, **Kinnear's Pleasure Boats**, *on the lagoon, opposite the railway station; tel: 031-903 3698*, hires out boats, from motor boats to pedaloes. **Funland**, *19 Beach Rd; tel: 031-903 6395* (open daily 0900–2330) is a catch-all play-pen, with dodgems, mini-golf and a four-storey video arcade. Just south of Toti, on the N2, is the large **Umgababa craft market**.

Just before reaching Scottburgh, turn right off the N2 to **Croc World**, *Old South Coast Rd; tel: 0323-21103* (open daily 0900–1700; feeding times 1100 and 1500; R12), the largest croc farm in Africa, with over 10,000 crocs, an excellent audio-visual presentation and tour, and bonuses such as an aquarium, children's bunny farm and playground, small museum, bird park with fish eagles and flamingos, Zulu dancing, a curio shop and excellent restaurant. **Scott-burgh** itself is one of the more popular family destinations, with a tidal pool and lagoon providing safe bathing, canoes for hire, a water slide, beach mini-golf and a mini steam-train.

Ten minutes walk from town, the **TC Robertson Nature Reserve** is a popular picnic spot, with over 180 species of bird and

10 km of hiking trails. Further south, the 2189 hectare **Vernon Crookes Nature Reserve**; *tel: 0323-42222* (open sunrise–sunset; R6) is an important remnant of coastal forest, with a wide variety of birds and small animals. To get there, take the South Coast freeway to the Park Flats/Umzinto fly-over, turn on to the Highflats/Ixopo road, continue for 12.5 km (3 km past Umzinto), turn off and follow the signs for a further 6 km to the park gate. There are 12 km of driving roads, various walking trails (use insect repellent as a guard against ticks) and accommodation in self-catering rondavels; book through the Natal Parks Board *(Nt)*. There are also over 300 species of bird, and, in season, magnificent displays of wild flowers, including orchids, lobelias and watsonias.

Umkomaas, *46 km south of Durban*, is home to one of South Africa's major dive sites, the **Aliwal Shoal**, a fossilised sand dune 3 km long and 300m wide, at depths of 5–30m, colonised by corals and an array of sponges. This far south, warm and cold water fish converge, and divers can expect to meet everything from angel fish to whales (in season) and dolphins, 11 species of shark (most seasonal), turtles, rays and eels.

The **Protea Banks**, *9 km offshore, reached from Shelley Beach*, are also a good diving area and there are several wrecks along the coast. Most dive operators in the area will arrange pick-ups from your hotel. They do courses, but if you are qualified, make sure you take your certificates. Contacts: **Andy Cobb Eco Diving**, *Winklespruit; tel: 031-964 239*; or **Widenham Dive Charters**; *tel: 0323-30351*, who also operate boat trips to the shoal (daily 1500–1600; R35; ages 12–60 only for diving).

Port Shepstone is home to the narrow gauge **Banana Express** railway (see p. 56) and has a small **Museum**, *near the beach; tel: 0391-21507* (open Wed, Thur 1200–1600; donation), covering local history, coastal shipping and early trade and industry. In **Shelly Beach**, the **Shell Museum**, *995 Marine Dr.; tel: 039-375 5723* (open High Season – Christmas, Easter, July and Sept – daily 0900–1700; Low Season Wed–Sun 1000–1600; R4) is a fascinating collection of over 40,000 shells from around the world, and things made from shells, some pretty, some truly tacky.

161

At Port Shepstone, turn inland for 21 km to the **Oribi Gorge**. All visitors must report to the office in the **Natal Parks Board Restcamp** *(Nt), tel: 0397-91644* (open 0800–1230, 1400–1630; R6). The rest camp also has self-catering chalets (with on-site cooks; bring your own food) and a campsite. Carved by the Umzimkulwana River, this lavishly beautiful valley is 24 km long, 5 km wide and 366m deep. A road runs right down to the bottom, or there are hiking trails for the more energetic. There is some small game, including leopards, monkeys and several species of antelope, and there are rich pickings for bird-watchers, but the real treat is in the scenery and the ancient forest, clinging precipitously to the cliff walls.

Back on the main road, *1 km south of the Uvongo Bridge*, the **Uvongo Bird Park**, *Main South Coast Rd; tel: 03931-74086* (open daily 0900–1700; R8) has walking trails leading past dams and aviaries containing a broad array of birds, from finches and lovebirds to parrots, cranes and hornbills. It also has a children's playground, picnic area and tea garden.

Heavily built-up **Margate** is one of the most popular family destinations, with a variety of freshwater and tidal pools, a beach and other entertainments. **Pleasureland**, *behind the Margate Hotel; tel: 03931-75864* (open daily 0900–1700; closed Fri out of season; rides R2.50 each) is an **amusement park** with funfair rides, while, for the more cerebral, there is a small **Art Museum**, *in the grounds of the Civic Centre complex, Dan Pienaar Sq.; tel: 039-377 7525* (open Tues–Fri 0900–1100, 1130–1300, Sat 1000–1300; free). **Southbroom** is one of the most upmarket of the little resorts. **Riverbend Crocodile Farm**, *National Road, Southbroom; tel: 03931-6204* (open daily 0900–1700, feeding time Sun 1500; R8) has only 200 reptiles, but is interesting, with guided tours, an art gallery, a shop selling bits of crocodile, and the **Crocpot Restaurant** (more crocodile and cream teas; lunch and tea only). Nearby, the **Barn Owl** craft market and farm stall has displays of Zulu dancing (Sun, 1500; free).

Follow the signs to the **Southern Cross Space Centre**, *4 km beyond Port Edward, on the right; tel: 03930-32891* (open Wed, Thur, Sun 1500, school holidays, Tues–Sun 1100 and 1500, guided tours only; R12), a museum and observatory with a variety of historic and modern astronomical equipment from antique telescopes to lasers. There are regular night observations and presentations.

PORT EDWARD TO UMTATA

ACCOMMODATION

Just beyond the Mtumvuma River Bridge, the **Wild Coast Sun** *(SI); tel: 0471-59111; fax: 0471-52924* (moderate–expensive) was set up to provide homelands gambling for eager South Africans. It is still the largest hotel on the Wild Coast, offering plenty of sporting activities, a casino, cinema and live evening entertainment.

Accommodation in Port St Johns could not be more different. The best is at **Lily Lodge**, *about 2 km west of town along the coast road; tel/fax: 0475-441 229*, a pretty, laid-back rest camp set in beautiful clifftop forest, with easy access to the beach below. Other options include **The Lodge**, *tel: 0475-441 171*, a cheap bed and breakfast near Second Beach; a few self-catering cottages at Ferry Point and at **Second Beach Holiday Resort**; *tel: 0475-441 245*; and several backpackers hostels, including the **Port St Johns Backpackers**, *Berea Rd*, and the **Wild Coast Guesthouse** (both cheap, no phones – just pitch up). Most offer space for camping.

If you are looking for something more formal, the **Umngazi River Bungalows**, *on the coast, about 20 km beyond Port St Johns (90 km from Umtata); tel: 0475-441 115* or reservations: *031-725 208/9; fax: 031-701 7006* (cheap), is one of the most luxurious hotels along the Wild Coast, with thatched cottages set amidst silky lawns. Amenities include tennis, a swimming pool, children's playroom with full-time nannies, mountain biking, water skiing, fishing, a private beach and boat trips.

SIGHTSEEING

Where the South Coast is all about energetic fun in the sun, the virtually undeveloped Wild Coast is about doing as little as possible in spectacularly beautiful surroundings. Most local hotels provide a range of land and water sports, but there are few formal sights. A last little remnant of the Natal good life has crawled across the Mtumvuma River, thanks to the Wild Coast Sun, which has brought with it gambling, golf and the **Wild Coast Waterworld**; *tel: 0471-53024* (open daily 0900–1700) offering a positive feast of watery entertainment, including windsurfing, speed boats, aquabikes, aqua scooters, waterskiing, motorboats, canoes, paddle skis, boogie boards and river cruises.

Virtually opposite the hotel, the **Mzamba Craft Village**; *tel: 039-305 1083/4* (open daily 0800–1600) is a hive of activity with small craft workshops surrounding a huge souvenir-fest.

Nothing very much happens for a long distance, as the road crosses rolling hills, liberally peppered with multi-coloured villages, until the turn off for the coast and **Port St Johns**. Towering cliffs, the 'Gates of Port St Johns', loom over the Mzimvubu River estuary, the third largest river outlet in South Africa, creating an entry to Port St John worthy of Cecil B. de Mille. Long cut off from the world by politics, this enchanting little town, named after a Portuguese ship, the *São João*, wrecked on this shore in 1552, was founded as a trading post in 1846, and grew into a proper town when the British added a fort in 1878. Today, the town has become the latest 'in' place on the hippy trail. Bemused locals are being joined by increasing numbers of sarong-clad, long-haired, dope-smoking Europeans, who chill out for months on end at a growing collection of laid-back travellers' hostels. Locals and visitors alike seem very happy with the arrangements and the sunsets.

Port St Johns has a fantastic setting, surrounded by the river, cliffs, forest, dunes and open sea, with perfect golden beaches and a number of pretty old colonial buildings. The small **museum**, *Golf Course Dr.; tel: 0475-441 265* (open Mon–Fri 0800–1630; free), a satellite of the Umtata Museum, housed in the old Freemasons' Hall, has displays on Xhosa tradition and local natural history. Other activities on offer include fishing and surfing, bird-watching, boat-hire and hiking, and there are arts and crafts for sale on Second Beach.

Shorter treks in the area include a 4½ hr trip to visit some self-sufficiency farmers on the Mugwa Plantation (take your own food). More importantly, this is the western end of the **Wild Coast Hiking Trail**, which runs the full

length of the Wild Coast. It takes about five days to reach Coffee Bay and up to 15 days to walk the whole thing to Kei Mouth; for information and permits, contact the **Dept of Agriculture and Forestry**, *P. Bag X5002, Umtata 5100*. Continue south along the coast from Port St Johns and there are two small nature reserves, the **Silaka Nature Reserve**, *4 km south of Port St Johns;* and the 772 hectare **Hluleka Nature Reserve**, *30 km south of town*. Both have self-catering accommodation, walking trails through the coastal forest, game including zebra, wildebeest and blesbok, and a wide variety of birds. For information and reservations for both, *tel: 0471-24322*.

UMTATA

Tourist Office: *corner York Rd and Victoria St; tel: 0471-312 885/6*. Open Mon–Fri 0800–1630. **Wild Coast Central Reservations**, *corner York and Elliot Sts; tel: 0471-25346; fax: 0471-25344*, handles hotel bookings for most of the properties in the area.

The **Holiday Inn Garden Court** *(Hd), National Rd, 5 km from the city centre; tel: 0471-370 181; fax: 0471-370 191* (cheap–moderate) is probably the best place in town, with the **Umtata Protea Hotel** *(Pa), 36 Sutherland St; tel: 0471-310 721/2; fax: 0471-310 083* (cheap–moderate) coming a close second. For a decent meal, try the Italian **La Piazza**, *Sissons St; tel: 0471-310 795* (cheap) or **Jim's Place**, *corner Leeds and Craster Sts; tel: 0471-310 995* (cheap–moderate) for a seafood option.

Once capital of the Transkei, and still the only town of any size in the region, Umtata is an unlovely and unloved city made up of mini-skyscrapers and government buildings, a few part-worn colonial buildings and a Victorian stone Anglican Cathedral. Since the government moved away, the Parliament Building has been used for offices and conferences. The **National Museum**, *corner York Rd and Victoria St, opposite the tourist office; tel: 0471-312 427* (open Mon–Thur 0800–1630, Fri 0800–1600; free) is generally poor, but is worth a stop for the magnificent Xhosa beadwork. The **Umtata Community Arts Centre**, *Durban Rd; tel: 0471-310 158*, is also dirt-poor, but remarkably vibrant, producing a

163

Nelson Mandela

Nelson Rolihlahla Mandela was born on 18 July 1918, into a humble family in a small village near Umtata. He earned places at the all-black University of Fort Hare, then at the University of the Witwatersrand, before setting up South Africa's first black law practice, with Oliver Tambo (former ANC leader). Drawn further into politics, in the 1950s, he became head of the militant wing of the ANC, *Umkhonto we Sizwe* (Spear of the Nation). In 1963, after a massive show trial at Rivonia, near Johannesburg, he and most of the other ANC leadership were jailed for treason. He spent 27 years in prison on Robben Island, becoming an international symbol of the Struggle. Released on 11 Feb 1990, he headed the ANC delegation in talks to dismantle apartheid, for which he received the Nobel Peace Prize, with former President F.W. de Klerk. On 10 May 1994, he was sworn in as South Africa's first black president.

steady stream of traditional and new drama, dance, classical, gospel and African music, as well as fine art and sculpture. As yet, little of it is likely to take London or New York by storm, but the imagination, inventiveness and public popularity are inspiring in the face of terrific difficulties and a severe shortage of cash.

UMTATA TO EAST LONDON

Tourist Office: *Kei Bridge; tel: 0438-890 030/50.* Open daily 0830–1800. The old Transkei borderpost has now been transformed into the main Tourist Office for the Wild Coast area, with efficient, friendly staff, a plentiful supply of leaflets, and a small craft shop.

There are around a dozen small, delightful getaway resorts along this stretch of coast. Architectural styles vary, with some thatched, some tiled and some old colonial with corrugated iron roofs, but most are made up of pretty self-contained cottages sprawled across shady gardens and dunes, with private beaches and river or lagoon frontage. Most provide or will arrange a variety of activities, including riding, swimming, fishing (beachfront and deep-sea), boating, golf, canoeing and a games room with anything from snooker to video games. All are cheap–moderate, and have their own dining rooms and bars, serving, amongst other things, spectacular seafood.

Those near Coffee Bay include **Anchorage Hotel**; *tel/fax: 0471-340 061*, the **Ocean View Hotel**; *tel: 0471-442 005; fax: 0471-311 425*, and the **Hole in the Wall**; *tel: 0471-25344; fax: 0431-312 715*. Further south, accessed via Butterworth or the Kei River

Ferry, are **Wavecrest**; *tel: 0474-3273; fax: 011-421 7393;* reservations: *0800-123 630;* the **Kob Inn**; *tel/fax: 0474-4421* and, standing together at Qolora River Mouth, the charming colonial **Trennery's**; *tel: 0474-3293*, and **Seagulls**; *tel: 0474-3287*. All are fairly inaccessible, so ask for detailed directions on how to get there when booking. More accessible but less attractive, just south of the Kei River, is the larger modern block-style **Kei Mouth Beach Hotel**; *tel: 043-841 1017* (cheap).

Qunu, *34 km west of Umtata on the East London road*, was the birthplace of Nelson Mandela (see above). His former home is now a vacant plot, but fans can visit his old school and plans are in progress for a museum and cultural village. Just beyond the town, on the left, is the simple house that he still uses as his holiday home. There is little obvious to see along the rest of the journey – unless you count the sunlight playing like fire on the foam–tipped waves, the wind whipping the fine white sand into plumes of smoke. Or the 800 species of marine life, including dolphins and turtles, or the 130-something species of bird, or the huge tracts of primeval hardwood coastal forest. Or the beaded Xhosa women, their faces painted white with clay, their backs doubled under perilous loads of firewood. This is the heartland of the Xhosa kingdom and the formerly independent Transkei homeland. It is also largely unspoilt countryside on a pristine coast. Enjoy it while you may.

EAST LONDON

See pp. 173–176.

DURBAN–HLUHLUWE

Head north out of Durban; the first section of your journey is through holidayland, a built-up ribbon development of hotels and resorts. Beyond Stanger, however, the buildings vanish and the coast changes abruptly to wild and spectacular dunes, lashed by crashing waves.

Inland, the hills are heavily laden with blood as the route threads its way through the historic heart of Kwazulu (the place of the Zulus) to the royal capitals of Dingane and Shaka. Please note that the northern sections of this route are malarial and prophylactics should be taken (see p. 22).

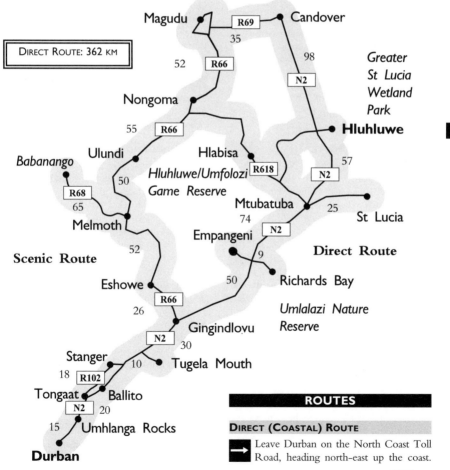

DIRECT ROUTE: 362 KM

Magudu — R69 — Candover
35

52 — R66

98

N2

Greater
St Lucia
Wetland
Park

Nongoma

55 — R66

Hluhluwe 165

Ulundi   Hlabisa
Babanango Hluhluwe/Umfolozi R618   57
           Game Reserve   N2
50
R68   Mtubatuba
65   74   25
Melmoth   St Lucia
              Empangeni N2
52
Scenic Route   Direct Route
9

Eshowe   50   Richards Bay
        R66
26   Umlalazi Nature
        Gingindlovu Reserve
    N2   30
Stanger 10 Tugela Mouth
18 R102
Tongaat Ballito
    N2 20
15 Umhlanga Rocks
Durban

ROUTES

DIRECT (COASTAL) ROUTE
Leave Durban on the North Coast Toll Road, heading north-east up the coast.

ROUTES

This is a new, fast freeway, still under construction along some stretches. On those, it links to the old N2. If you wish to avoid the tolls, the other sections of the N2 still run parallel for much of the way. This is free, more attractive, but significantly slower (for route as far as Gingidlovu, see Scenic Route below). After 165 km, there are turn offs to Empangeni and Richards Bay.

A further 66 km on, at Mtubatuba, you reach a crossroads with the R618. Turn left for the **Hluhluwe-Umfolozi Game Reserve** (about 22 km from the turn off to the gate); turn right for St Lucia and the southern end of the Greater St Lucia Wetland Park (29 km from the turn off).

Continue north on the N2 for about another 53 km and there is another crossroads, on to gravel roads. The left turn again leads to the Hluhluwe-Umfolozi Game Reserve (about 30 km from the turn off), the right turn leads to Hluhluwe village (about 4 km). For all these, and the game parks of Maputaland, see Hluhluwe–Kosi Bay, pp.188–193. Distance: 362 km; allow: 4½–5 hrs non-stop.

SCENIC (INLAND) ROUTE

▶ Leave Durban on the old N2 road, which heads north hugging the coast to **Umhlanga Rocks** and **Ballito**. Turn inland here, through the cane plantations, to **Tongaat**, to pick up the Old Main Road, the R102 to **Stanger**.

From Stanger, continue along the R102 until it links up with the old N2 and follow this until you meet a turning on the right on to the R111 to **Tugela Mouth**. Return to the old N2 and continue to **Gingindlovu** (155 km from Durban), then turn left and head inland on the R66 through **Eshowe** (26 km) and **Melmoth** (52 km) to **Ulundi** (about 50 km).

Just north of Ulundi, a dirt road leads off to the right to the western edge of the Hluhluwe-Umfolozi Game Reserve. For a better road, continue north on the R66 for about 55 km to Nongoma and turn right onto the R618, which leads down through Hlabisa to the game reserve (about 50 km, of which only the first section is tarred). Once within the park, either branch left and take the smaller dirt road, which connects

with the N2 directly opposite the Hluhluwe village turn off, or continue south along the R618 to Mtubatuba and the N2 (see Direct Route).

If you wish to miss out Hluhluwe-Umfolozi Game Reserve, and remain on good tarred roads, you will need to do a large loop. Continue north from Nongoma along the R66 to Magudu (52 km), turn right onto the R69 to Candover (35 km), then turn right onto the N2 and head south to the Hluhluwe crossroads (98 km). Distance: 523 km; allow at least three days.

BUSES

Greyhound Citiliner have a weekend service from Durban to Johannesburg, calling at Ballito (40 mins), Richards Bay (2hrs 20 mins) and Empangeni (3hrs 10 mins). See OTT Table 3544.

UMHLANGA ROCKS

Tourist Office: *Chartwell Dr.; tel: 031-561 4257.* Open daily 0830–1300, 1400–1630; closed weekends in low season.

ACCOMMODATION

There are several large hotels and self-catering resorts lining the beachfront, including, at the top end of the market, the 3-star colonial-style **Oyster Box Hotel**, *2 Lighthouse Rd; tel: 031-561 2233; fax: 031-561 4072 (moderate),* which takes its name from the first cottage built in the area in 1869; the 5-star **Beverly Hills Sun** *(SS), 54 Lighthouse Rd; tel: 031-561 2211; fax: 031-561 3711 (expensive);* **Breakers Resort**; *tel: 031-561 2271; fax: 031-561 2722* (moderate); and the 3-star **Cabana Beach**, *10 Lagoon Dr.; tel: 031-561 2371; fax: 031-561 3522* (moderate), whose family suites come complete with kitchenettes.

For a wide range of self-catering properties, contact **Umhlanga Accommodation**, *Shop 24, Sanlam Centre, corner Chartwell Dr. and Lighthouse Rd; tel: 031-561 2012; fax: 031-561 3957.*

SIGHTSEEING

Only 18 km north of Durban, Umhlanga (meaning 'place of the reeds') is a thriving, trendy holiday resort, and is a less crowded alternative to the city centre.

Since the 1950s, the **Natal Sharks Board**, *Umhlanga Rocks Dr., off the M12; tel: 031-561 1001* (open Mon 1200–1500, Tues–Fri 0900–1500, first Sun of every month 1400; R10) has operated protective nets or electronic barriers on 42 beaches between Port Edward and Richards Bay, designed to keep the 16 species of shark found in Natal waters away from the swimming beaches. At their headquarters, visitors can see a spectacular audio-visual presentation and a display hall (open Mon–Fri 0800–1600) with replica sharks and – what must surely be one of the most bizarre tourist attractions in the country – a shark dissection (open Tues–Thur 0900, 1400, and 1st Sun of each month 1400). There are also 2-hr boat trips to watch staff service the shark nets (advance booking essential). **Lynski Charters**, *26 Manaar Rd, Umhlanga Rocks; tel: 031-561 2031; fax: 031-465 8764*, also offer deep-sea fishing trips and coastal tours.

UMHLANGA ROCKS TO STANGER

Tourist Office: Dolphin Coast Publicity Association; *Ballito Dr., Ballito; tel: 0322-61997; fax: 0322-61997*. Open Mon–Fri 0830–1230, 1400–1630, Sat in school holidays.

ACCOMMODATION

Shortens *(Pf), about 500m from the Compensation exit on the N2, between Ballito and Umhlali; tel: 0322-711 403; fax: 0322-71144* (moderate) is a charming colonial country house hotel (1903) and restaurant, in lush gardens bordering the Umhlali Country Club. Nearby, **Holland Farm** *(Pf), Esenembi Rd, between Umhlali and Ballito; tel: 0322-918 663; fax: 0322-918 831* (moderate) is a luxurious Cape Dutch-style guesthouse with a pool and fine views, on a flower farm.

On the seafront, several fine bed and breakfasts include **Lalaria** *(Pf), 25a Dolphin Crescent, Shaka's Rock; tel: 0322-525 5789; fax: 0322-525 8869* (cheap); **Nalsons View** *(Pf), 10 Fairway Dr., Salt Rock; tel/fax: 0322-525 5726* (cheap); and **Seascape** *(Pf), 3 Sheffield Dr., Sheffield Beach, Umhlali; tel: 0322-525 8527;*

fax: 0322-525 8687 (cheap–moderate). For self-catering, contact **Ballito Accommodation**, *22 Sandra Rd; tel: 0322-62141; fax: 0322-63486*.

Campsites: the **Dolphin Caravan Resort**, *Compensation Beach Rd, Ballito; tel: 0322-62187*, also has self-catering cottages, a pool, games room and a beach with lifeguards.

SIGHTSEEING

These next 80 km are named the **Dolphin Coast**, after the bottlenose dolphins who come close to shore to surf the huge waves. It is a beautiful stretch of coast, lined by small seaside villages – although most are now growing together into a continuous stream of cottages and cafés – picture-book perfect beaches and, for those who care to look, fascinating history.

Ballito is the largest of the towns along the coastal strip, named, extraordinarily, after a brand of Italian silk ladies' stockings. It has no 'sights', but does lay on a wide range of water and land sports. A little way north, **Shaka's Rock** was said to have been Shaka's favourite

Shaka Zulu

Born in 1787, Shaka was the son of a minor Zulu chief, who grew up at Dingiswayo's court. When, in 1815, Dingiswayo was murdered by a rival clan, the Ndwandwe, he became king, changing the name of the whole tribe to that of his clan, the Zulus. Shaka proved to be a military genius, transforming his army into a deadly fighting machine, developing new tactics, such as the terrifying *impi*, with the the main army attacking in a curved bull-and-horns formation, while troops from the rear circled round to enclose the enemy. He also replaced the traditional javelin-style throwing spear with the less wasteful short stabbing *assegai*, and created ruthless military discipline amongst his forces. By the time he was murdered in 1828, by his half-brothers, Dingane and Mhlangana, the Zulu empire was one of the strongest ever seen in Africa.

167

coastal resort. He threw his enemies off the cliff here, while any Zulu warrior wishing to prove his manhood could do so by leaping off voluntarily. A little further on, the women were hard at work making salt in the tidal pools at **Salt Rock**.

There is a small crocodile farm, **Crocodile Creek**, *on the D809, Greylands, near Tongaat; tel: 0322-23845* (open Sun–Fri 1000–1700, feeding daily 1500; R12).

Inland, set in rolling hills wrapped in smooth green cane fields for the last 100 years, **Tongaat** is the oldest Indian community in South Africa, formed by the indentured cane cutters brought in to man the 19th-century plantations. At **Hulett's Maidstone Mill**; *tel: 0322-24551* (open Tues, Wed, Thur 0900, 1100 and 1400; tours last 1½ hrs; booking essential) an audio-visual presentation and tour shows how sugar is made from raw cane. The little town has a fine collection of old buildings, including two beautiful temples, the **Vishwaroop Temple** and the huge **Juggernath Puri Temple**, dedicated to Vishnu and built in 1901, as a replica of one in Puri, India.

The **Hazelmere Resources Reserve**, *about 4 km south of town, on the Verulam road; tel/fax: 0322- 332 315*, is a nature reserve and bird sanctuary surrounding a small dam, with water sports, fishing, camping and caravan sites.

STANGER

ACCOMMODATION

On the coast, about 7.5 km south of Stanger; **Prince's Grant**; *tel: 0324-482 0005; fax: 0324-482 0040* (moderate; no children under 12) is an elegant little country house hotel overlooking a magnificent golf course leading on to the dunes.

SIGHTSEEING

Stanger was Shaka's capital, a royal town of some 2000 beehive huts, whose layout was so confusing it became known as KwaDukuza ('place of the lost person'). According to tradition, all public meetings were conducted under a large, shady *indaba* (meeting) tree, in this case, an old *mkuhla* (Natal mahogany) tree, still living next to a supermarket in *Roodt St*.

On 22 Sept 1828, Shaka's half-brothers, Dingane and Mhlangane, murdered the king under a large fig tree and then torched the town. A very European-looking **memorial**, *Couper St*, marks the site of his grave. Behind it, the **Dukuza Interpretive Centre**, *Couper St; tel: 0324-22762* (open Mon–Fri 0820–1600, Sat–Sun 0900–1600; free) has a display on the life and wars of Shaka, some traditional Zulu crafts and a small shop.

Plans are also underway to open a new **museum**, *opposite the memorial on Couper St; tel: 0324-23091*, which will include displays on local Zulu history, the sugar industry and the Indian role in the plantations.

STANGER TO ESHOWE

ACCOMMODATION

Gone With The Wind comes to Natal at **Mine Own Country House** *(Pf), on the R102, 4 km north of Gingindlovu; tel: 0353-30162; fax: 0353-301 025* (cheap), an antebellum-style country guesthouse in beautiful gardens on a sugar plantation. About 3 km out of Gingindlovu, **Inyezane**; *tel: 083-255 7345; e-mail: inyezane @dbn.lia.net* (cheap) is an extraordinary bush backpackers' hostel/1970s acid-trip type of place, with a range of private and dormitory accommodation, the usual options for bushwalks and historic sightseeing, together with a whole range of craft classes, music weekends and mud baths.

SIGHTSEEING

In the mid 19th century, the Tugela River formed the boundary between British Natal and Zululand. In 1878, the British, commanded by Sir Bartle Frere, prepared for war, building a series of forward observation posts and supply depots, amongst them, **Fort Pearson**, *on a bluff overlooking the river,* (follow signs from the R111; open access). The views are excellent, there is an informative board on the Anglo-Zulu Wars, and it is possible to trace the layout of the fortifications and tented camp. Nearby, there is a group of British war graves.

A steep footpath leads down 2 km to the river bank and the **Ultimatum Tree** (also accessible by road). Military preparations in place, the British asked for a meeting with King Cetshwayo, which was held under a shady tree on 11 Sept 1878. Here, they made a series of eleven totally impossible demands, asking that the king disband his army, allow in the missionaries and give up his sovereignty. When he refused, they had an excuse to invade Zululand, and did so on 11 Jan 1879. The tree itself is now a dead stump, but its son is flourishing next door, and a third generation is also growing in reserve.

A signed turning leads to the small **Harold Johnson Nature Reserve**; *tel: 0324-61574* (open access) with picnic areas, walking trails, bird-watching, and limited open space for camping and caravanning, with lovely views of the Tugela River Mouth.

Across the river, at **Gingindlovu** (meaning 'swallower of the elephant'), Cetshwayo built his first capital in 1860, naming it in honour of his decisive victory over his brother, Mbulazi, in their struggle for the throne. On 4 July 1879, Lord Chelmsford, at the head of around 3000 men, marched against the main Zulu army of up to 20,000 warriors near here. Thanks to modern weaponry, it was a rout, with only three British fatalities, and up to 1500 Zulus dead. Pausing only to burn down the Zulu town, Chelmsford marched onto Ulundi, only to find the king and his army had fled, leaving the capital deserted. The military power of the Zulus had been broken. On 28 Aug, King Cetshwayo was captured and his kingdom became part of the British empire. He was eventually returned to the throne, dying in 1884 as a puppet ruler.

He is buried nearby in the magnificent 1620 hectare indigenous **Nkandla Forest** ('place of exhaustion').

ESHOWE

Tourist Office: *Osborne Rd, tel: 0354-41141.* Open Mon–Fri 0800–1600, with a satellite office at Fort Nongqayi.

At **KZN Kaleidoscope**, *PO Box 116, Eshowe 3815; tel/fax: 0354-42348*, registered tour guide Henry Bird offers excellent guided tours of the Zululand historic sights (R80 per hour; R500 per day, plus R2.50 per km if he provides transport).

ACCOMMODATION

The **George Hotel**, *Main St; tel: 0354-74919; fax: 0354-41434* (cheap) is a pleasant 25-room hotel, with a restaurant, 3 bars, pool and backpackers' lodge. There are also several bed and breakfasts, including **Forest Lodge**, *128 Main St; tel: 0354-74079; fax: 0354-41908* (cheap). **Campsite**: **Eshowe Caravan Park**, *Saunders St, near the Dhlinza Forest; tel: 0345-41141.*

SIGHTSEEING

Eshowe, whose musical name means 'the sound of wind in the trees', is one of the prettiest towns in Kwazulu-Natal, with flower-lined streets set high in the hills, surrounded by primeval forest. In its time, it's been a royal town, home to Shaka, Mpande and Cetshwayo (who was born and died here). It was he who invited in the first Norwegian missionaries in 1860. After his defeat, the little settlement went on to become the British regional military headquarters and, eventually, capital of British Zululand (1887–1897).

In 1883, the solid mud-brick **Fort Nongqayi** was built to house the native Zulu peace-keeping force, the Nongqayi. It is now home to the **Zululand Historical Museum**, *Nongqayi Rd; tel: 0354-41441* (open daily 0900–1600; free, donations welcome), which has displays on local history, the role of the missionaries, Zulu and European household items, memorabilia of King Mpande and a superb display of Zulu beadwork. It also houses the furniture of John Dunn (see, p.172).

The **Vukani Museum**, *Osborn St; tel: 0354-75274* (open Tues, Thur 0900–1300, or by special request for tours; R3, R5 with tour) has the world's largest collection of traditional Zulu arts and crafts. Set up originally as a famine relief scheme by a local missionary, the Vukani Association collected and sold high quality Zulu basketwork overseas. At the same time, this magnificent collection was gradually built up. The tours are particularly good, with a vivid picture of the people emerging from the many uses they find for different baskets and pots.

With a name meaning 'a grave-like place of meditation', the 200 hectare **Dhlinza Forest** *(Nt; open sunrise–sunset; free)* is a magnificent

169

remnant of the towering indigenous forest that once carpeted the region. There are some small antelope and bushpigs, but the birds are particularly special, with rare species including the spotted thrush, green coucal, trumpeter hornbill and purple-crested loerie. Above all, it is a delight to walk through the trails in the forest itself. Every second year, the *Forest Noel*, a large community nativity play, is performed in an open glade.

Four kilometres out of town, off the *KwaMondi Road*, near the original mission, **Martyr's Cross** commemorates the death, in 1877, of Eshowe's first Christian martyr, Maqhamusela Khanyile. There are superb 360° views from the hill on which it stands.

ESHOWE TO ULUNDI

Tourist Office: *Library, Reinhold St, Melmoth; tel: 03545-2082.* Open Mon, Tues, Thur, Fri 0900–1200, 1330–1630.

About 7 km north of Eshowe, the R230, on the right, heads towards Empangeni. About 26 km on, one of Shaka's homes, Kwa-Bulawayo (the place of killings), overlooked the Nkwalini Valley. Shaka and his mother had suffered during his childhood because of his illegitimacy, and he used this area to slaughter all their persecutors. The **Coward's Bush** then became the official execution ground for any warriors returning home without their spears (that is, defeated in battle).

A growing number of **Zulu cultural villages** are scattered across the grassy hills on this leg of the journey. Few people will want to visit more than one, but to experience that one properly, you need 24 hours. All of them offer roughly the same structure, with a tour of the resident Zulu village, demonstrations of beadwork and food, a talk with a *sangoma* (spirit healer) and a drink of the acrid Zulu beer. The finale will be a vigorous, soul-stirring dance display. All of the cultural villages also provide accommodation, usually in a choice of ultra-comfortable beehive huts (complete with en suite bathrooms, flush toilets and electricity) or more conventional rooms.

Shakaland *(Pa), Norman Hurst Farm, Nkwalini, 14 km north of Eshowe on the R68; tel: 035-460 0912; fax: 035-460 0824* (open daily, tours at 1100 and 1230; advance booking essential; R95 including lunch) was created as the TV set of Shaka's childhood home for the blockbuster series, *Shaka Zulu* (1985). This is the largest and most commercial of the cultural villages, offering a 3 hour 'Nandi Experience' (named after Shaka's beloved mother) that is often crowded with coach parties day-tripping from Durban.

Nearby, **Pobane**, *3 km from the R68 along the Goedetrouw Dam turn off, 15 km from Eshowe, tel: 035-460 0720,* does take individual tourists, but caters largely for groups and school parties.

A little further along the R68 towards Melmoth, the R34 turns right towards Empangeni. About 4.5 km along this road is the turn off to the third of the local cultural villages, **KwaBhekithunga**, *Stewart's Farm; tel: 03546-644; fax: 03546-867* (tours by appointment), whose beehive huts are scattered around a central thatched lodge, with a bar, pool and handicrafts centre.

About 46 km north of Eshowe, a giant wagon wheel marks the turning to the right on to the D256. Follow this for 12 km to the entrance of the last – and best – of the cultural villages, **Simunye**; *tel: 0354-600 912; fax: 0354-600 824.* With transport by ox-wagon or on horse-back, this is tucked far from anywhere into a steep river, with accommodation either in beehives or a stunning rock lodge built invisibly into the cliff. **Melmoth** itself is a little colonial country town, surviving largely on eucalyptus trees.

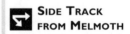

SIDE TRACK
FROM MELMOTH

BABANANGO

Tourist Office: *Justice St, next to the Courthouse; tel: 0358-350 001.*

ACCOMMODATION

Babanango has a clutch of three delightful country guesthouses: **Hall's Habitat** *(Pf), Babanango Village; tel: 0358-350 035; fax: 0358-350 010* (cheap); the **Babanango Valley Lodge**, *on the D139, 4 km from the village, off the R68; tel: 0358-350 062; fax:*

0358-350 160 (moderate); and **Eagle's View Country House**, *on the D139, 15 km north of Babanango, overlooking the Umfolozi River; tel: 0358-350 054* (moderate), which has en suite rooms in the colonial-style house, as well as rustic cabins and campsites on a 2400 hectare game farm.

SIGHTSEEING

There is relatively little in this tiny village, *65 km north-west of Melmoth on the R68*, apart from truly breathtaking mountain scenery. This is a place to hike, ride or get out the binoculars, with excellent bird-watching and some small game.

Continue north from Melmoth for about 18 km then turn left on to the R34 for about 6 km to **Mgungundlovu** ('the place of the great elephant') in the Mfolosi Valley. This was the capital of Dingane (c.1795–c.1843), who murdered his half-brother, Shaka, in 1828 and seized the throne. In 1838, he invited Piet Retief and a party of 101 Boers here, supposedly to negotiate a treaty and land deal. That night, during a celebratory feast, he massacred the entire party. The Afrikaners swore a solemn vow of retribution (see Background, p.64) and totally demolished Dingane's army at Blood River (see Ladysmith–Hluhluwe, p.270). In 1839, Dingane abandoned and burned the city, and in 1840 he was overthrown by his half-brother, Mpande, and fled to Swaziland. The core of the city has now been rebuilt as part of a **museum**; *tel: 03545-2254* (open daily 0800–1700; R5) and there is an obelisk **memorial** to Piet Retief and his followers. Retief's grave is signposted nearby.

Many members of the Zulu royal family, including Dinizulu (1884–1913) and Senzangakhona, father of three kings – Shaka, Dingane and Mpande – are also buried in the vicinity, at **eMakhosini** ('the place of kings').

ULUNDI

Tourist Office: *Legislature Buildings; tel: 0358-874 2038.* Open Mon–Fri 0730–1630.

ACCOMMODATION

The **Holiday Inn Garden Court** *(Hd),*

Princess Magogo St; tel: 0358-21121; fax: 0358-21721 (moderate) has the best accommodation and food in town.

SIGHTSEEING

Originally founded by Cetshwayo in 1873, the existing town of Ulundi is much newer, purpose-built as the capital of the Kwazulu homeland. Since reintegration, it has remained joint capital of Kwazulu-Natal with Pietermaritzburg. It is also the home of the Zulu monarchy, restored in 1951, with a great deal of local influence and no real power. The current king, Goodwill Zwelithini, is highly revered, while his premier minister, Mangosotho Buthelezi (also royal, a grandson of King Dinizulu) is a major force in South African politics, as leader of the dissident Inkhatha Freedom Party, still agitating for greater autonomy or even independence.

The **Legislative Assembly**; *tel: 0358-202 101* (viewing by appointment only) is an uninspiring modern building, but inside are a series of beautiful tapestries depicting the history of Kwazulu.

About 10 km from town, on the gravel road leading to the Hluhluwe-Umfolozi National Park, **Ondini** (meaning 'the heights') was the actual site of the royal capital. After careful archaeological excavations, the royal enclosure has been rebuilt, and is on show, together with a traditional kitchen garden, museum with audio-visual displays, and a craft market, at the **KwaZulu Cultural Museum**, *King Cetshwayo Highway; tel: 0358-791 223* (open Mon–Fri 0930–1700; R5).

GINGINDLOVU TO HLUHLUWE

Tourist Offices: *Town Board Offices, Hely Hutchinson St, Mtunzini; tel: 0353-401 421* (open Mon–Fri 0900–1200); *Turnbull St, Empangeni; tel: 0351-21131* (open Mon–Fri 1000–1600, alternate Sats 0900–1300); *Small Crafts Harbour, Richards Bay; tel: 0351-788 0040* (open Mon–Fri 0800–1600, Sat-Sun 0800–1200).

Heading north, the Zululand coast becomes more and more beautiful, but most people speed through this stretch of the route to get to

171

Art or Craft?

In most places, their work is still sold as curios or crafts, but like many African peoples, the Zulus never learned the concept of art for art's sake. Instead, all their artistic expression was bound into their everyday lives, in superbly decorative cooking pots, baskets and beaded clothing. Today, the true artistic value of the finest pieces is finally being recognised and Zulu art has become highly collectible. There are several types of work to look out for.

The finest **baskets**, so tightly woven into elaborate designs that they are entirely waterproof and last for decades, are said to come from the Hlabisa district, west of Hluhluwe. **Beadwork** began as personal ornamentation, using local shells and seeds. Glass beads were introduced by 19th-century missionaries, although the gaudier plastic variety have now largely taken over. Most beading is now done purely for the tourist trade; one of the most entertaining little presents is a 'Zulu love letter'. During the last century, with many of the men working away on the mines, and few people able to read, the women used to sew their longings into colour-coded messages – pink for poverty, green for jealousy or love-sickness, blue for faithfulness, red for tears and desire, yellow for wealth and stripes for doubts; white is for love and purity, black for grief and loneliness.

Zulu **pottery** is very simple in many ways, with bulbous bowls decorated by a single row of etched designs. They are elegant but, as fire-baked earthenware, also extremely fragile and, sadly, difficult to transport. **Hardwood bowls, platters** and the inevitable **salad servers** are excellent buys, but can damage the environment if trees are cut indiscriminately. As part of an ongoing programme of community-based tourism development, the Natal Parks Board are providing wood from clearing programmes or natural wastage free to local carvers in some areas.

the real riches beyond. There are a couple of worthwhile stops, however.

About 18 km north of Gingindlovu, on the Umlalazi river estuary, the little coastal town of **Mtunzini** ('a place in the shade') was the home of John Dunn, a 19th-century hunter and trader, who was the only white man to become a Zulu chief. He also accumulated 49 wives and 119 children along the way. It is an ideal do-nothing destination, with excellent coast and river-fishing, about 300 species of bird, a host of other interesting flora and fauna – and lots of people called Dunn.

The 1028 hectare **Umlalazi Nature Reserve** (Nt), 2 km east of town; tel: 0353-401 836, has self-catering log cabins, camping and caravan sites, and walking trails through the mangrove swamps and dune forests. Nearby, a boardwalk trail leads through a rare southerly grove of **Raffia Palms**, home to a breeding colony of equally rare palmnut vultures.

Empangeni is a busy little industrial town, surrounded by huge eucalyptus plantations, with several small game reserves, totally eclipsed

by those to the north. The **Empangeni Art and Cultural Museum**, Turnbull St; tel: 0351-925 196 (open daily 0900–1300, 1400–1600; R1.50) in the Old Town Hall, has collections of contemporary, traditional Zulu and pioneer arts and crafts.

Built as a bulk export harbour for the Natal coal fields, **Richards Bay** is a huge modern port with a soulless modern town, growing rapidly into a major centre of heavy industry. It is useful as the local business centre, but has little to recommend it to tourists, apart from the rather unusual tours offered by **Richards Bay Minerals**; tel: 0351-903 444; fax: 0351-903 442 (always book ahead), who are mining valuable titanium and zirconium from the huge coastal sand dunes. Although they are rehabilitating the dunes as they pass, they gained nationwide notoriety during their recent failed bid to mine the dunes within the St Lucia National Park.

HLUHLUWE

See pp. 189–190.

EAST LONDON

Straddling the mouth of the Buffalo River, East London is South Africa's fourth largest port and a popular seaside resort, with a warm climate, magnificent hinterland and beaches, and some of the best surfing in South Africa. From its unhappy beginnings as a supply harbour during the Frontier Wars to the hard years of sanctions and factory closures, sandwiched between the former homelands of Ciskei and Transkei, it's been a place of gritty courage and resourcefulness. Now, investors are returning; foreign tourists are stopping over; and holidaymakers are back in droves. East London is a good base from which to explore both the Sunshine Coast (south to Port Elizabeth, pp. 290–293) and the Wild Coast (north to Kwazulu-Natal, pp. 162–163).

TOURIST INFORMATION

Tourist Office: *Old Library Building, 35 Argyle St; tel: 0431-26015* (open Mon–Fri 0830–1630, Sat 0830–1100). After hours, information on hotels, resorts and bed and breakfasts is supplied by a 24-hour hotline; *tel: 0431-26034.*

ARRIVING AND DEPARTING

By Air
East London Airport: 10 km south-west of the city centre; *tel: 0431-462 267.* There is an information desk, taxis are plentiful, and the major car hire companies are represented here: **Avis**; *tel: 0431-461 344;* **Budget**; *tel: 0431-461 084;* **Imperial**; *tel: 0431-462 230.* The **Little Red Bus** is an airport shuttle service; *tel: 082-569 3599.* East London is linked by air to all other major South African countries.

By Train
Main Station: *Station St; tel: 0431-442 020.* **Spoornet:** *tel: 0431-442 719.* East London is on the line north to Johannesburg, with stops at Stutterheim, Cathcart, Queenstown, Burgersdorp, Bloemfontein and Kroonstad. There is also a train from East London to Cape Town.

By Bus
Translux; *tel: 0431-442 333,* links East London with Cape Town, Johannesburg, Durban, Bloemfontein, King William's Town, Port Elizabeth and Kroonstad. Buses depart from the railway station. **Intercape**; *tel: 0431-25508,* runs services between East London and Kenton-on-Sea, Port Alfred, Alexandria and Port Elizabeth. Services depart from Orient Beach. **Greyhound**; *tel: 0431-55327,* provides services to Johannesburg, Bloemfontein, Pretoria, Durban and Cape Town, as well as numerous, smaller centres. **Minilux**; *tel: 0431-413 107,* links with King William's Town, Grahamstown, Port Alfred and Port Elizabeth.

GETTING AROUND
East London is spread out, and it is not possible to visit all the sites and beaches without some form of transport. An **urban bus service** is run by the **Amatola Regional Council**, *60 Cambridge St, East London; tel: 0431-21251, ext. 274,* for bus timetables.

Taxis: Herman Taxis; *tel: 0431-438 076;* **Komani Taxis**; *tel: 0431-331 175;* **Moeba Taxis**; *tel: 0431-338 884;* **Smith Taxis**; *tel: 0431-439 918.*

STAYING IN EAST LONDON

Accommodation
There is plenty of accommodation in and around East London. A full list is available from the Tourist Office, and several accommodation agencies deal with holiday cottages and apartments, including **Wildcoast Holiday Reservations**, *Old Library Building, 35 Argyle St; tel:*

173

0431-436 181; fax: 0431-436 188; and **Coastal Accommodation**, *2a Chamberlain Rd, Berea; tel/fax: 0431-486 090.*

Hotels include the 3-star **King David** *(Pa), 27 Inverleith Terrace; tel: 0431-23174, fax: 0431-436 939* (moderate), and the smaller 2-star **Esplanade Hotel**, *Beachfront; tel: 0431-22518, fax: 0431-23679* (cheap). Overlooking Beacon Bay, the **Blue Lagoon**, *Blue Bend Pl., Beacon Bay; tel: 0431-474 821; fax: 0431-472 037* (cheap) is a large time-share and self-catering resort, with family-sized apartments, a gym, pool and 2 restaurants. Further out are **Gonubie Mouth**, a scenic resort with a magnificent beach, and comfortable **Gonubie Hotel**, *141 Main Rd, Gonubie; tel: 0431-404 010, fax 0431-404 012.* Chain hotels include *CL, Hd, Pa, SS.*

St Andrew's Lodge, *14 St Andrews Rd, corner Gately St, Selborne; tel: 0431-435 131, fax: 0431-439 009* (cheap) is a centrally located bed and breakfast. The **Loerie Hide**, *2b Sheerness Rd, Bonnie Doon; tel/fax: 0431-353 206* (cheap) overlooks the riverine forest, forming part of the Nahoon River ecosystem, close to the Nahoon Reed and a short drive from the city centre.

Forty-five minutes (28 km) from the city, **Crawfords Cintsa Beach Lodge,** *from the N2 (going north) take the Cintsa Mouth East turnoff; tel: 0431-385 000; fax: 0431-385 401* (cheap–moderate) is a charming guesthouse overlooking Cintsa Bay, with self-contained, thatched, whitewashed cottages, swimming, fishing, sailing, surfing and golf.

Budget travellers are catered for by the **Backpackers Hostel**, *128 Moore St; tel: 0431-23423* (cheap). **Campsite: Gonubie Resort and Caravan Park**, *North Transkei Rd, Gonubie* (19 km from East London); *tel: 0431-404 000.*

Eating and Drinking

The best places to eat and drink are **Movenpick**, *Orient Beach Complex; tel: 0431-21840* (moderate; closed Sat); **O'Hagan's Irish Pub & Grill**, *Aquarium Complex, Esplanade; tel: 0431-438 713* (moderate; open daily from 1200); **Settler's Restaurant 'n Sports Bar**, *Spar Centre, Gonubie; tel: 0431-*

405 438 (cheap; open daily 1100–2300); the **Office Pub & Grill**, *King's Entertainment Centre; tel: 0431-438 026* (cheap; open daily 1130–2300); and **Hunter's Jetty and Sportsman's**, *Latimer's Landing; tel: 0431-438 410* (moderate; open daily lunch and dinner).

Communications

Main Post Office: *Oxford St; tel: 0431-433 855.*

Money

Several major banks have branches with ATMs and exchange facilities on *Oxford St.* **Rennies/ Thomas Cook**: *Caxton House, 33A Terminus St; tel: 0431-21375; fax: 0431-26890.*

ENTERTAINMENT

East London has a wide range of cultural and sporting events throughout the year. Highlights include: **Feb**: **Surfers Marathon** – an 18 km beach and road run; *tel: 0431-431 926;* **May–June**: the **Gonubie Festival** – flea-market, road and cycling races; *tel: 0431-472 760;* **Dec**: a huge **Christmas Carnival**, attracting stallholders from all over the country.

Theatrical performances are held at the **Guild Theatre**, *Dawson Ave; tel: 0431-430 704,* **The Playhouse**, *Derwent St, Cambridge; tel: 0431-352 511,* and the **Arts Theatre**, *Paterson St; tel: 0431-26957.* There is a **multiplex cinema** at the *Vincent Park Centre, Devereux Ave; tel: 0431-58122.*

SHOPPING

There are several large shopping centres, of which the best is probably the **Vincent Park Centre**, *Devereux Ave, Vincent; tel: 0431-726 9732.* More specialist shopping centres worth a visit include the **Lock Street Gaol** (built as South Africa's first women's prison; 1880), and the waterfront **Latimer's Landing**.

Two of the best **antique** shops are **Antiques & Things**, *11 Chamberlain Rd, Berea; tel: 0431-52182,* and **The Collector**, *24 Curries St, Quigney; tel: 0431-439 479.* The most prolific of the city's **curio** shops are **Umzi Wethu**, *110 Moore St, Quigney; tel: 0431-433 069,* and **Africa**, *Shop 3, Lock Street Gaol; tel: 0431-430 798.*

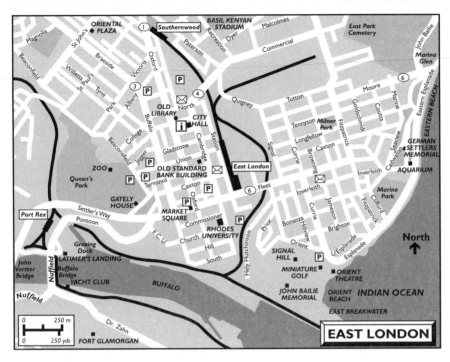

EAST LONDON

North
↑

INDIAN OCEAN

EAST BREAKWATER

EAST LONDON

For less formal shopping, try the **Lock Street Gaol Fleamarket**, *Fleet St; tel: 0431-26015* (Sat) or **Court Crescent Beachfront Fleamarket**; *tel: 0431-351 660* (Sun 0900–1300).

SIGHTSEEING

East London's finest attractions are alive. The **Aquarium**, *Esplanade; tel: 0431-342 209* (open daily 0900–1700; R6.50) has a large variety of fish species and marine animals, including Jackass penguins and seals (twice daily seal shows, 1130 and 1530; feeding at 1030 and 1500; fish feeding daily, 1030 and 1500).

In the 35 hectare **Botanical Gardens**, *Queen's Park, Beaconsfield Rd; tel: 0431-21171* (open daily dawn to dusk; free), the Buffalo River thorn, *Umtiza listeriana*, is found in its only natural habitat, amongst other indigenous trees and shrubs.

Within the gardens, the **Zoo** (open daily 0900–1700; R6.50; pony rides for children 1000–1630) is home to a variety of antelope, snakes, monkeys and birds.

Museums

The **East London Museum**, *319 Oxford St; tel: 0431-430 686* (open Mon–Fri 0930–1700, Sat 0930–1200, Sun 1100–1600; R2.50) is one of South Africa's foremost natural history museums. It is home to the world's only Dodo egg; a stuffed coelacanth (see feature box p.176) *Latimeria chalumnae*; discovered in the Chalumna Mouth in 1938; and an exhibition of Xhosa artefacts and Southern Nguni beadwork. Built in 1878 as a residence for the city's first mayor, the **Gately House Museum**, *1 Park Gates Rd; tel: 0431-22141* (open Tues–Thur 1000–1300, 1400–1700, Fri 1000–1300, Sat, Sun 1500–1700; donations) has a good small collection of Cape furniture. The **Anne Bryant Art Gallery**, *St Mark's Rd; tel: 0431-24044* (open Mon–Fri 0900–1700, Sat 0930–1200; free) is an Edwardian building, containing an interesting collection of contemporary South African art. The **City Hall**, *Oxford St, tel: 0431-342 235* (open by appointment) has recently been extensively restored; its Victoria Tower resembling London's Big Ben, commemorates Queen Victoria's 60 years on the British throne.

Fort Glamorgan, *Bank St, West Bank; tel: 0431-311 610* (open by appointment; free) was built in 1849 to provide quarters for troops at the time that the harbour was founded. Built in 1895, the **Hood Point Lighthouse**, *West Bank; tel: 0431-443 056* (open Mon, Wed, Fri 1400–1600, Sat 0900–1100; free) has traditional 'keyhole' windows, consoled upper gallery and steel upper structure. Nearby, the **Waterworld and Funpark**, *West Bank; tel: 0431-474 265*, offers a variety of water slides to children. Out of town, **Calgary Museum of Transport**, *13 km from East London (take the N6 to Stutterheim); tel: 0431-387 244* (open daily 0900–1630; R3) houses a fine collection of restored horse-drawn vehicles and an original gypsy caravan.

Beaches

East London has beaches for every age and style. Outdoor living and active sports are possible nearly all year round, so mild is the climate and so warm the water swept south by the Mozambique Current. Fronting the city, 2 km-long **Orient Beach** is one of the country's safest. It has an esplanade, water tube, mini-golf, the Orient Theatre complex, umbrellas, beach chairs and tents for hire. Next, **Eastern Beach**, *opposite Marina Glen*, has a sheltered childrens' playground and a miniature train. The wild, white expanses of **Nahoon Beach**, which easily rivals Sydney's Bondi Beach, are the most popular, particularly amongst surfers who head for **Nahoon Reef**, off Nahoon Point. To the south of the city, **Kidd's Beach** is popular with anglers, board sailors and surfers.

Out of Town

For nature-lovers, East London offers walks and trails in reserves, through rich forest, veld and woodland, around dams and along rivers: the Nahoon, Mpongo, Bridle Drift, Fort Plato and Cape Henderson. At Gonubie Mouth, the **Gonubie Mouth Nature Reserve**; *tel: 0431-404 000* (open Mon, Wed and Thur 0730–1300 and 1400–1630, Sun 1030–1300 and 1400-1630; free) features a coastal wetland with over 160 species of bird, excellent, safe bathing, a wide, white beach, facilities for surfing,

---

The Coelacanth

Fossil records show that the coelacanth first appeared more than 300 million years ago. Amongst the first fishes to have toothed jaws and horny, overlapping scales, they once existed in great numbers, but were thought to have been extinct for nearly 65 million years when a living example was discovered in 1938 near East London, to universal astonishment. Unlike other creatures, they had hardly evolved over this period, although the 1938 example, at about 1.5 m long, was larger than almost all extinct types known from fossils. They are thought to be predators with habits similar to those of large rock-cods. It is not known how many are surviving, but over 30 have now been caught, and at least one has been caught on film in its natural environment.

---

boating and rock, river and deep-sea fishing. The Umtiza Forest, in the **Umtiza Nature Reserve**, *15 km from East London; tel: 0431-463 532* (office open 0800–1630, trails dawn to dusk daily – a self-help kiosk is available to assist you) is a wonderful place to walk, with its unique Umtiza trees, ancient cycads and the monkeys chattering overhead. It offers three short day-trails. The **Strandloper Hiking Trail** (3 days, 65 km); *tel: 0431-841 1188*, along the beach between Kei Mouth and East London retraces the footsteps of the early Khoikhoi inhabitants of the area (known as *Strandlopers* to the Afrikaaners). Hutted accommodation is available in addition to the various seaside resorts through which the trail passes.

The Tourist Office produces an excellent booklet listing a wide range of outdoor activities available for adults and children in and around the city. **Township tours**: **Kai Safaris**; *tel: 0431-366 494;* **Amatola Tours**; *tel: 0431-430 471.* **Horse-riding**: **Welcome Stables**, *Igoda Beach; tel: 0431-462 521.* **Diving**: **Gonubie Dive School**; *tel: 0431-404 701;* **Ocean Diving Academy**; *tel: 0431-403 101/53332.* **Deep Sea Fishing**: *tel: 0431-25151 or tel: 0431-352 604.*

EAST LONDON– GRAAFF-REINET

Until 1994, this area was simply an extension of the Western Cape, both geographically and politically. During the apartheid years, it became the patchwork meeting point of white South Africa and two black 'homelands' – the Transkei and the Ciskei. Since then, with all boundaries rearranged, it has become part of the Eastern Cape. As a holiday area it is not well-known, but it is rich in possibilities. From the dramatic cliffs and dunes of the coast and the resort bustle of East London (see pp. 173–176), the route stretches inland through neat settler towns, green

mountains and across the arid expanse of the Great Karoo, coming to rest at Graaff-Reinet, the Karoo's most important historic town. The old frontier territories along the way were the scene of many dramatic conflicts between the Xhosa and white settlers. Today, the area is best known as one of the most politically active in South Africa, its intellectual hub at the black University of Fort Hare, providing the nation with many of its greatest leaders, including Nelson Mandela and Steve Biko.

177

DIRECT ROUTE: 408 KM

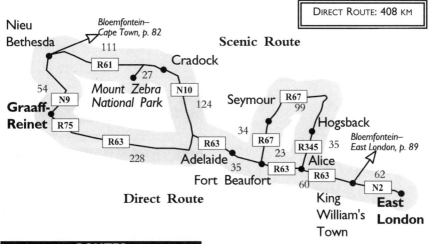

Bloemfontein– Cape Town, p. 82

Scenic Route

Bloemfontein– East London, p. 89

Direct Route

ROUTES

DIRECT ROUTE

➡ Leave East London on the N2 to King William's Town (62 km), then turn left

on to the R63. This heads west through Alice (60 km), Fort Beaufort (23 km) and Adelaide (35 km). From Adelaide it is 43 km to Eastpoort and the junction with the N10. Turn

Fort Hare University

A college for the higher education of black students was first proposed in 1878. By 1914, the missionary-funded and taught SA Native College had a constitution and 20 students (18 males and 2 females). By 1923, Professor Z. K. Matthews had earned its first ever degree, and in 1926, Gertrude Ntlabati became the first woman to graduate. Amongst those it was to send out as future leaders were Oliver Tambo, Nelson Mandela, Mangosuthu Buthelezi, Robert Sobukwe (PAC founder), ANC leader Govan Mbeki and other African leaders, including Robert Mugabe.

In 1946, it became the University of Fort Hare. In 1959, it was subjected to segregationist Bantu education policies. Admission was restricted to Xhosa speakers from the Transkei and the Ciskei, and to the Sotho from the Cape Province. This ruling set in train more than 30 years of protest. Throughout the 1960s this was sporadic, as ANC- and PAC-aligned organisations came to life and were quickly repressed. But under the leadership of Steve Biko's Black Consciousness-aligned SA Students Organisation, it came to a head. In 1976, students protested in solidarity with the Soweto school childrens' uprising against the use of Afrikaans in schools. Protest continued throughout the 1980s, as did violent intervention, and only in 1990 was a black chancellor appointed. Today, the new leadership has strong anti-apartheid credentials and is preparing itself for a future in which society is democratic, non-racial and non-sexist.

left (south) for about 12 km, then turn right on to the R63, which leads through Somerset East and Pearston for 149 km to a junction with the R75. Turn right for the last 24 km into Graaff-Reinet. In total, 408 km; allow 6 hrs.

SCENIC ROUTE

Leave East London on the N2 to **King William's Town** and **Bisho** (62 km), then turn left on to the R63 towards **Alice** (60 km). Return in the same direction and after about 6 km, turn left onto the R345 and follow the signs to **Hogsback** (35 km). Continue on the R345 from Hogsback towards Cathcart (37 km). Just before you reach Cathcart, the R345 meets the R67. Branch left at the junction and take the R67 to **Seymour** (62 km). From there, keep on the R67 to **Fort Beaufort** (34 km). Turn right onto the R63 and continue through **Adelaide** (35 km) to Eastpoort, and turn right onto the N10 to **Cradock** (124 km). Leave Cradock heading north on the N10, then branch left after about 6 km on to the R61. Fifteen kilometres from Cradock, branch left again onto an untarred road to the **Mountain Zebra National Park** (12 km). After that, return to the R61 and head for the N9. At the junction (72 km), continue straight across on to

the untarred road signed to **Nieu Bethesda** (27 km). This loops round from the village to return you to the junction with the N9 (23 km), 31 km north of Graaff-Reinet. Distance: 641 km; allow two days minimum.

BUSES

Translux operate a service from East London to Graaff-Reinet via Cradock, daily except Tues and Thur. Journey time: 7 hrs. OTT Table 3551.

KING WILLIAM'S TOWN/ BISHO

See Bloemfontein–East London, pp. 91–92.

ALICE

Alice is a quiet country town situated in the Tyumie Valley below the Amatola Mountains. Named after one of Queen Victoria's daughters, it is most famous as the home of **Fort Hare University**, the first black university in South Africa, founded in 1916 out of the mission-run Lovedale College (see feature box above). This was the alma mater of many, now famous, black leaders, including Nelson Mandela whose book, *The Long Walk to Freedom*, chronicles his years spent here, as well as the role it played in plunging him headlong into the 'Struggle'.

On campus, the **De Beer Centenary Art Gallery**; *tel: 0404-22011* (open Mon, Wed, Fri 0900–1200; Tues, Thur 1300–1400; free) has an excellent collection of contemporary black art.

HOGSBACK

Tourist Office: *Stormhaven Crafts, Main Rd; tel: 045-962 1050* (open daily 0900–1300).

There is plenty of accommodation in the area, with hotels, lodges, holiday bungalows and a campsite. The best place to stay is the **Hogsback Inn**; *tel: 045-962 1006, fax: 045-962 1015* (cheap–moderate), an historic wayside inn, which serves good country cooking. The **King's Lodge**, *Main Rd; tel: 045-962 1024, fax: 045-962 1058* (cheap–moderate) is comfortable, and snug in winter (it gets very cold here), with a restaurant that provides excellent Cape cuisine. Self-catering options include the **Hyde Park Cottages**, *Dinwiddie Lane; tel: 045-962 1069* (cheap), prettily situated on the edge of the forest, and the rondavels of **Hogsback Arminal Mountain Lodge**, *Main Rd; tel: 045-962 1005* (cheap–moderate), which look out over the Tyumie Valley.

Amatola means calf in Xhosa; the line of the lush, gentle Amatola Hills supposedly resembles a row of calves. Deep within them, the hill village and resort of Hogsback is set in a cool, green forest, whose trees hide most of the buildings straggling along a 3 km-long main street. It is a lovely spot – quiet, isolated and, possibly, one of the country's least developed tourist destinations. All around there are places to walk, hike or just amble. Trails lead to waterfalls, such as the magnificent Madonna and Child Falls, the Bridal Veil, the Swallowtail and the Kettle and Spout – and there are opportunities for riding or trout fishing in local dams and streams. A local curiosity is a craft favoured by the Xhosa locals: animals moulded from unfired clay – buy them at the roadside.

SEYMOUR

Accommodation: **Ntloni Lodge**, *Mpofu; tel: 0401-952 115* (moderate) is a fully staffed self-catering establishment. Chains: *Pa* (Katberg).

The little town of Seymour is located just to the south of the heavily forested Katberg. Along with Fort Beaufort (see below), it is an ideal base from which to visit two nature reserves: Mpofu and the Katberg Forest.

Mpofu, *access via the R67, halfway between Seymour and Fort Beaufort; tel: 0401-952 115* (open daily 0700–2100; R10 per vehicle, R2.50 per person) is made up of forest and grassland in the foothills of the Katberg. There are riding and hiking trails (see the Katberg Forest trails with which these are linked), San paintings, places to swim and plenty of game, including bushpig, leopard, caracal and grysbok.

The **Katberg Forest** straddles the uplands, offering wonderful views over the surrounding countryside. Strangely, this reserve is not visited as frequently as others, so there are opportunities for solitary game-viewing (vervet monkeys, baboon, bushpig, leopard, caracal and bushbuck). There are hiking trails – including the **Katberg Trail** (2 days), linked with the Mpofu Nature Reserve.

FORT BEAUFORT

Tourist Information: at Fort Beaufort Historical Museum (see below).

There are two 2-star hotels here (both cheap); the **Savoy Hotel**, *Durban St; tel: 04634-31146, fax: 04634-32082*, in town, with a pool, and the **Yellowwoods Hotel**, *18 km along the Adelaide Rd; tel: 046-684 0708, fax: 046-684 0701*.

Active in the Frontier Wars, Fort Beaufort, like many other towns in this region, began life as a military stronghold (1822), taking its name from the English Duke of Beaufort, father of the colonial governor Lord Charles Somerset. In 1851, it withstood a full-scale attack by the Xhosa army – only its location on a narrow peninsula between the Kat and Brak Rivers saved it from destruction. The original fort (1857) still exists; known as the **Martello Museum**, *Bell St*, it is currently closed. The **Fort Beaufort Historical Museum**, *44 Durban St; tel: 04634-31555* (open Mon–Fri 0830–1300, 1400–1700, Sat 0830–1300; R2), housed in the old officers' mess (1830), contains collections of military uniforms, guns and badges.

179

ADELAIDE

Tourist Office: *Library, Market Sq.; tel: 046-684 0034* (open weekdays 0900–1300, 1400–1700, Sat 0900–1230).

The **Adelaide Century Lodge**, *Market Sq.; tel: 046-684 1058* (cheap).

Adelaide is a large village situated below the Winterberg Mountains. Named after the wife of British King William IV, it began life in 1834 as a military post, but today is the hub of a farming community. It has an interesting museum, **Our Heritage Museum**, *Queen St; tel: 046-684 0290* (open Mon–Fri 0800–1300, 1400–1700; R2), with collections of glassware, settler furniture, silver and ceramics, housed in the 19th-century former parsonage of the Dutch Reformed Church.

CRADOCK

Tourist Office: *Market Sq.; tel: 0481-2383* (open Mon–Fri 0830–1700).

ACCOMMODATION

There are two small hotels, the 2-star **New Masonic Hotel**, *Stockenstroom St; tel: 0481-3115; fax: 0481-4402*, and the 1-star **Victoria Manor**, *Voortrekker St; tel: 0481-1650; fax: 0481-711 164* (both cheap).

The best accommodation in town, however, is in **Die Tuishuise**, *36 Market St; tel: 0481-711 322, fax: 0481-711 164* (cheap). Nominally a bed and breakfast (although other meals can be arranged), this is actually a whole street of 14 old cottages, all lovingly restored and individually furnished in period. A tour is as good as any museum, and your room charge buys you a whole house.

SIGHTSEEING

Cradock is a large Karoo town in the same league as Graaff-Reinet and Colesberg. A visit will be well rewarded. It began life in 1814 as a frontier settlement, taking its name from the Cape's then governor, Sir John Cradock. By 1873, it had become a town of considerable size, and it is from that period that it derives its character. The Dutch Reformed Church (1867) is a replica of London's 18th-century St Martin's-in-the-Fields. Today, it is a busy market town and a centre for farming. There are two small museums. The **Great Fish River Museum**, *87 High St; tel: 0481-4509* (open Tues–Fri 0800–1300, 1400–1600; R2) has 19th-century English, Voortrekker and Boer rooms. The **Olive Schreiner House**, *9 Cross St; tel: 0481-5251* (open Mon–Fri 0800–1245, 1400–1630; free) was the home of one of South Africa's favourite writers between 1867 and 1870.

MOUNTAIN ZEBRA NATIONAL PARK

Park Information: *27 km west of Cradock; tel: 0481-2427/2486,* or Pretoria booking office, *tel: 012-343 1991* (open daily Oct–Apr 0700–1900; May–Sept 0730–1800; R8). This 6536 hectare reserve straddles the Bankberg Mountains, providing sanctuary for one of the world's rarest mammals, the distinctive Cape mountain zebra. At only 1.2m high, it is the smallest of the zebra, with large ears, narrow stripes and a plain white belly. It has now been saved from extinction and there are over 200 in the park.

This is one of the most interesting and beautiful parks in South Africa. Not only is the scenery magnificent, but as a haven for over 200 species of bird (including the black eagle, the rare booted eagle and eagle owls) and other indigenous mammals, including eland, blesbok, springbok, black wildebeest, red hartebeest, kudu, mountain reedbuck, grey rhebok, duiker, steenbok, leopard and the caracal (or lynx), there is much to see and do. In addition to game-viewing and bird-watching, there are driving routes, nature trails and day walks (some are quite tough). The popular **Mountain Zebra Hiking Trail** (25.6 km) offers three days of hiking in the rugged Karoo landscape. The reserve also has riding stables, self-catering accommodation in two-bed chalets, a restaurant, a shop, swimming pool, and caravan and camping site. Reserve overnight accommodation well in advance.

NIEU BETHESDA AND GRAAFF-REINET

See Bloemfontein–Cape Town pp. 85–87.

EAST LONDON– PORT ELIZABETH

Between the cities of East London and Port Elizabeth, this route meanders along the coast of the Eastern Cape. It straddles the Great Fish River, the official eastern frontier of the Cape Colony in the 18th century, and crosses pretty farmland surrounding old settler villages, which gives way to dense forest near the coast. There are large reserves, open stretches of wild landscape (much of it never settled) and a lovely coastline.

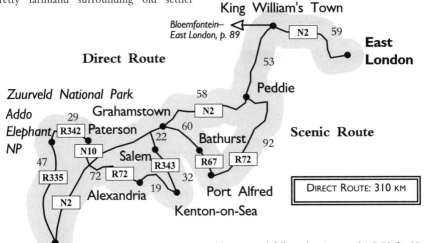

King William's Town

Bloemfontein–
East London, p. 89

Direct Route

N2 59

East London

53

Peddie

Zuurveld National Park
Addo 29 Grahamstown 58 N2
Elephant R342 Paterson 60
NP 22 Bathurst 92 **Scenic Route**
N10 Salem R67 R72
47 R343
R335 72 R72 32
N2 Alexandria 19 Port Alfred
Kenton-on-Sea

DIRECT ROUTE: 310 KM

181

Port Elizabeth

ROUTES

DIRECT ROUTE

➡ The direct route from East London to Port Elizabeth is via the N2, the main stop on which is Grahamstown (see p.185). Distance: 310 km; allow 3–4 hours.

SCENIC ROUTE

▶ For a longer, more scenic route, taking in mountains and coast, leave East London on the N2 to **King William's Town** (59 km) and on to **Peddie** (53 km). Turn left, towards the sea, and follow the signs to the R72 for 25 km. Turn right on to the R72 and follow it as it hugs the coast, across the mouth of the Great Fish River, whose valley is filled with dense euphorbia, milkwood and wild thorn, to **Port Alfred** (92 km from Peddie). At Port Alfred, the R67 branches north to **Bathurst** – from where it is about 60 km to **Grahamstown** (still on the R67). At Grahamstown, rejoin the N2 and continue in the direction of Port Elizabeth. After about 11 km, branch left and follow the signs to **Salem** (11 km on the R343) and on to **Kenton-on-Sea** (a further 32 km), where you should turn right, back on to the R72. Continue for 19 km to **Alexandria**. From Alexandria, continue along the R72 for 51 km until the junction of the N2 and N10.

Shamwari Game Reserve is just off the N2 near this junction. Cross the N2 and follow the N10 north to Paterson, then branch left onto the R342 and head for the **Addo Elephant National Park** (about 29 km). From Addo, the R335 leads south to Port Elizabeth (47 km). Take at least one day for this route; the scenery alone is worth slowing down to admire and the local history is fascinating.

BUSES

There are 3 daily bus services from East London to Port Elizabeth, one of which calls at Port Alfred and Port Alexandria. Journey time: 4 hrs. OTT Table 3546.

KING WILLIAM'S TOWN

See p. 92.

PEDDIE

Tourist Information: see Grahamstown (p. 185).

Named after Colonel John Peddie of the 72nd Regiment, the town began life as an eight-point earth fort built in 1835. In May 1846, the garrison was attacked by an army of 9000 Xhosa warriors. Defending were a small white contingent and Amafengu tribesmen, who had incurred the wrath of the Xhosa by befriending the settlers. From the mid 19th century, a town developed around the fort (no longer extant), and is now a largely black village, alive with music and chat, small fruit and vegetable stalls and carts selling everything from soft drinks to roast corn cobs. For a tiny taste of real Africa, stop here.

PORT ALFRED

Tourist Office: *Market Building, East Bank; tel: 0464-41235* (open Mon–Fri 0830–1300, 1400–1600, Sat 0830–1200).

ACCOMMODATION AND FOOD

In Port Alfred itself, the **Kowie Grand Hotel**, *corner Grand St and Prince's Ave; tel: 0464-41150, fax: 0464-43769* (cheap) is comfortable and spacious, while **The Halyards**, *Royal Alfred Marina; tel: 0464-42410, fax: 0464-42466* (moderate) is a pleasant modern development right on the harbour front, with a

good à la carte restaurant, **The Charthouse**. There are also plenty of self-catering apartments and guesthouses (details from the Tourist Office). Chain hotels include *Pa, SI*.

Out of town, at the Fish River Mouth, just 15 mins from Port Alfred, the **Fish River Sun** *(SI); tel: 0405-661 101, fax: 0405-661 115,* is a complete resort, with enough entertainment to keep you occupied for days. Also within easy reach is **Kariega Park** (see Kenton-on-Sea, p. 183). **Campsites**: **Riverside Caravan Park**, *Mentone Rd, Port Alfred; tel: 0464-42230;* **Willows Caravan Park**, *off the R72; tel: 0464-245 201.*

Dunes, *8 Sandawana, West Beach Dr.; tel: 0464-245 296,* offers à la carte meals, lunch and dinner, while the **Country Kitchen Restaurant**, *5 Southdowns Rd; tel: 0464-43465,* is good for no-nonsense home-style cooking.

SIGHTSEEING

Port Alfred is a tidy little coastal resort on the Kowie River estuary. The **Kowie Museum**, *Pascoe Crescent, East Bank; tel: 0464-42179* (open Tues–Fri 0930–1230, Sat 0930–1200; R2) has the usual blend of local history, with personal files on all the 1820 Settlers, but this place is really all about boats, with a marina, boat cruises, canoe trips and fishing charters. Just off the coast is one of South Africa's most colourful reefs, with a range of sponges, soft and horny corals (contact **Kowie Dive School**; *tel: 0464-244 432).* Ask at the Tourist Office for information about hikes and trails in the area (including overnight trails with huts) and opportunities for riding. **Kowie Anchorage**, *tel: 0464-245 275,* in the Small Boat Harbour of the Marina, offers canoes and pedaloes for hire, river fishing and cruising boats, skiing, and offshore cruise and fishing charters. **The Fish River Sun** (see Accommodation and Food) has a casino and facilities for playing golf, tennis, bowls and riding.

BATHURST

Tourist Office: see Port Alfred.

ACCOMMODATION AND FOOD

The **Pig and Whistle Inn**, *Bathurst; tel: 0464-250 673; fax: 0464-250 688* (cheap) is one of the oldest hostelries in the country (founded in 1831). Both hotel and pub, with a restaurant, it is very well-known throughout South Africa, and one of the main reasons people visit Bathurst.

SIGHTSEEING

Bathurst is a small, low white town, named after Earl Henry Bathurst, British Colonial Secretary in 1820. The town has several national monuments, including both the Anglican and Wesleyan churches, Bradshaw's water-driven wool mill and the settler fort. There is also an excellent **Agricultural Museum**, *corner Trappes and Show Ground Rds; tel: 0464-250 853* (open Tues–Sun 0900–1600; R5). Two kilometres from the town, on the top of Baillie's Beacon, a **toposcope** marks the spot from which the settlers staked out their farms. You can still see the triangles fanning outwards in the shape of the fields. This area is famous for pineapples, its biggest crop. At **Summerhill Farm**; *tel: 0464-250 833*, easily identified by its giant pineapple, there are farm tours and sales.

GRAHAMSTOWN

See pp. 185–187.

SALEM

Tourist Office: see Port Alfred, p.182.

Salem is a small, pretty 18th-century town which saw most action during the Frontier Wars, when its larger houses doubled as forts. In season, ferociously contested cricket matches adorn the pretty village green.

SALEM TO ALEXANDRIA

Tourist Office: *Municipality Building, Kenton-on-Sea; tel: 0464-82418* (open weekdays 1400–1630, Sat 0830–1230).

ACCOMMODATION

The exclusive **Kariega Park**, *on the R343 between Kenton-on-Sea and Salem; tel: 0461-311 049; fax: 0461-23040* (moderate) is a private game reserve, where you sleep in self-contained log cabins surrounded by bush. Almost next door, the **Happy Haven Inn**, *Salem Rd, 14 km from Kenton-on-Sea; tel: 0464-311*

802, *fax: 0464-311 803* (moderate) is well-placed for the views, and has a restaurant and tea garden. Other amenities include squash, sauna and gym. Most of the accommodation in Kenton itself is self-catering or b&b; details from the tourist office.

SIGHTSEEING

The two most interesting sights in this area are both along the road from Grahamstown, before you reach Kenton-on-Sea. The **Thomas Baines Nature Reserve**, 12 km from Grahamstown; *tel: 0461 28262* (open daily 0700–1900; admission R4.45 per vehicle, R2.20 per person) is a remarkable stretch of bush country that protects, amongst other creatures, the white rhino, bontebok and impala. The private 660 hectare **Kariega Game Park**, *14 km north of Kenton-on-Sea on the Grahamstown road; tel: 0461-311 049* (see Accommodation) has a wide variety of game (but not Big Five), birds and hiking trails. Game-viewing drives and guided walks in the area can be arranged through **Dias Tours**; *tel: 046-654 0215*.

Sandwiched between the Bushmans and Kariega Rivers, both of which are navigable for miles upstream, by boat or canoe, **Kenton-on-Sea** has excellent, sandy beaches, safe swimming and a small boat marina, where berths may be hired for private small craft.

ALEXANDRIA

Tourist Office: *Municipality, Voortrekker St; tel 046 653 0056* (open Mon–Thur 0800–1530, Fri 0800–1500).

Alexandria has limited accommodation. The **Heritage Lodge**, *Voortrekker St; tel: 046-653 0024, fax: 046-653 0735* (cheap) is the best local bed and breakfast, while its **Gordons Country Restaurant** supplies excellent lunches, teas and dinners.

This is the home of Africa's largest shifting sand dunes. Here too, there are settler cottages and churches, and a nearby coastline which offers surfing, sandskiing, swimming and angling. Pay a visit to **Leopard's Kloof**, a private reserve and farm, which offers a number of scenic hiking trails, night drives, river trips and deep-sea cruises.

About 40 km beyond Alexandria, off the

183

184

The War of the Axe

Between 1779 and 1878, the Cape Government and the Xhosa tribes fought a series of nine bitter Frontier Wars along the eastern border of the Cape Colony. The long, drawn-out conflict began when the trek farmers, who had rapidly dispersed east and north-east of the south-west Cape, came face to face with Xhosa cattle-keeping tribes living in the Zuurveld area, between the coast and the line formed by the Bushmans and Upper Fish Rivers. By 1844, Double Drift was a neutral zone along the Fish River, enforcing an uneasy truce between the Xhosa and British. When the British reneged and built a fort here, the Xhosa started raiding.

One story says that a Xhosa man stole a British axe and the local ruler, Sandile, refused to turn him over for trial; another that a Xhosa warrior was manacled to a British officer taking him in for cattle rustling. The only way his friends could release him was to chop the officer's arm off with an axe. Whichever version is true, the incident sparked the start of what is known as the Seventh Frontier War (1846–47).

N2, is the most exclusive private game park in the Eastern Cape – the only place in the province where you can see the Big Five. The 10,000 hectare **Shamwari Private Game Reserve**; *tel: 042-851 1196; fax: 042-851 1224* (moderate–expensive) was an old farm, which has been carefully re-stocked. The scrubby landscape can making spotting difficult, but the guided game drives and walks usually produce good sightings. Around 300 species of bird have been spotted. Accommodation is in the original farm buildings, including the gracious **Longlee Manor** (1860).

ADDO ELEPHANT PARK

Tourist Office: *at the main camp reception*. 72 km north of Port Elizabeth; *tel: 0426-400*

556; fax: 0426-400 196 (park open daily 0700–1900, information open daily 0700–2000; R20 per vehicle). Accommodation *(NP)* in chalets (cheap) and campsites, with a restaurant (open daily 0800–2100) and a shop for self-catering supplies.

Enormous herds of elephants once roamed across the Eastern Cape, their migration leading right down the coast, from Natal to the Cape Peninsula, adapting freely to savannah and the thick coastal forests. An animal without predators, they met their match in man, as towns cut the ancient paths, forests were felled indiscriminately, the open grassland was planted with crops and the elephants were shot, not only for sport and ivory, but as a farmyard pest. By 1931, the Eastern Cape was down to its last 11 elephants.

This 11,718 hectare reserve was created solely to protect the tiny herd and the last surviving Cape buffalo. Today, there are around 170 elephant here, together with numerous other species, including the eland, kudu, red hartebeest, bushbuck and Cape buffalo, 21 endangered Kenyan black rhino, and even a local rarity, the flightless dung-beetle. Birdwatching, with walking tours and hides is also available.

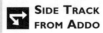 **SIDE TRACK FROM ADDO**

ZUURVELD NATIONAL PARK

Attached to the Addo Elephant National Park, the **Zuurveld National Park**, *tel: 0426 400 581;* (open daily dawn to dusk; admission charge), reached via the R335 just north of Addo, spreads over a vast area of bush, steeply wooded kloofs and rolling downs. Home to a variety of animals, including kudu, Cape mountain zebra and leopard, there are walks and horses to hire. The simple **Zuurberg Inn**, hard by the entrance to the Zuurberg National Park; *tel: 0426-400 583* (moderate) offers the area's only accommodation.

PORT ELIZABETH

See pp.290–293.

GRAHAMSTOWN

The lush, gentle countryside of this green Eastern Cape is the traditional homeland of the Xhosa people. The first Settler farmers began to drift into the area in the 1770s. They, like the Xhosa, were pastoralists and required extensive grazing for their cattle. The first war over the surrounding territory was fought in 1778, beginning a period of conflict which was to last for over a century. Grahamstown was founded in 1812 as a military base, but grew into a thriving market town. Over the years, it has been salted with a good sprinkling of private schools, and one of South Africa's most eminent universities. It is also famous for its annual arts festival, the largest in the southern hemisphere.

TOURIST INFORMATION

Tourist Office: *Church Sq.; tel: 0461-23241* (open Mon–Thur 0830–1300, 1400–1700, Fri 0830–1300, 1400–1600, Sat 0900–1100).

ARRIVING AND DEPARTING

By Air
There are daily scheduled flights to East London (150 km away) and to Port Elizabeth (127 km away). Private and charter aircraft can land at the small local airport, *tel: 0461-29073*, 31 km from the centre.

By Train
Station: *Roberts St; tel: 0461-269 203*. There is only one third-class train service Mon–Fri from Grahamstown, which connects at Alicedale with the Algoa train operating to and from Johannesburg. See OTT Table 3508.

By Bus
There is no local bus station. Contact bus companies or the Tourist Office for drop-off locations and times. Grahamstown is connected with Cape Town, Durban, Umtata and East London along the N2 by bus companies, **Greyhound**, *tel: 011-333 2130;* **Intercape**, *tel: 011-386 4444;* and **Translux**, *tel: 011-488 1350*. A Greyhound bus service operating between Port Elizabeth and Johannesburg also stops at Grahamstown. (OTT Table 3538).

GETTING AROUND
The historic centre is compact and most sites are easily accessible on foot. There is plenty of on-street parking.

STAYING IN GRAHAMSTOWN

Accommodation
Grahamstown's most expensive hotel is **St Aiden's Court Hotel**, *Milner Court; tel: 0461-311 188; fax: 0461-311 140* (moderate). The country-style **Cathcart Arms Hotel**, *5 West St; tel/fax: 0461-27111* (moderate) has 2-stars, while the **Settlers' Inn**, *below the 1820 Monument; tel: 0461-27313; fax: 0461-24951* (moderate) has three stars and a fine view over the town. Chain hotels include *Pa*.

One of the most comfortable and upmarket guesthouses in town is **The Cock House**, *10 Market St; tel: 0461-311 295, fax 0461-311 287* (moderate), with a good pub and restaurant (open Mon–Sat). Comfortable and central, **Oak Lodge**, *95 Bathurst St; tel: 0461-29122* (cheap) is within walking distance of all the main monuments. **The Hermitage**, *14 Henry St; tel: 0461-311 503* (cheap) is a luxury bed and breakfast housed in an 1820s English-style villa, while the comfortable **Historic Cottages**, *1 Scott's Ave; tel: 0461-28936* (cheap) is at the heart of town. For further information, contact the **Bed & Breakfast Association**; *tel: 0461-28001*. The **Backpackers Barn**, *4 Trollope St;* *tel: 0461-29720* (cheap) provides basic, clean

185

accommodation for those on a budget. **Campsite**: **Grahamstown Caravan Park**, *off Grey St; tel: 0461-306 072.*

Eating and Drinking
Grahamstown offers a wide variety of places to eat. Top of the range are the **Cock House** (moderate; see Accommodation) and **Il Tinello**, *at the St Aiden's Court Hotel; tel: 0461-311 188* (moderate), which is good for seafood and Cape dishes. Further down the scale, the **Copper Kettle**, *7 Bathurst St; tel: 0461-24358* (cheap) is good for light suppers, while students head for **The Rat & Parrot**, *New St; tel: 0461-25002* (cheap), which serves pub food.

Money
There are a couple of banks with exchange facilities and ATMs on *Church Sq.*

Little happens here for much of the year, but for ten extraordinary days every July, thousands of artists, performers and fans pour into this small, sleepy town for the second largest arts festival in the world (only Edinburgh is bigger). Alongside the official programme of music, dance, art and literature, there are simultaneous jazz, fringe and children's programmes. For information and bookings, contact the **Grahamstown Festival**: *PO Box 304, Grahamstown 6140; tel: 0461-492 3010.*

Founded by Colonel John Graham in 1812 as the military headquarters of the Cape's troubled eastern frontier, Grahamstown commanded a chain of small forts along the Fish River. By the mid 19th century, many of the original 1820 Settlers had abandoned their unprofitable and insecure farms and moved into town under the protection of guns. Until the lure of the gold and diamond fields proved too strong, Grahamstown flourished becoming, for a short time, the second city of the Colony.

Its rich legacy of fine architecture is evident in a walk around Grahamstown's broad, tree-lined streets, past imposing public buildings and charming Victorian shops and houses. Triangular **Church Square** began life as the military parade

ground between Colonel Graham's house and the officers' mess. In the centre towers the spire of the Anglican **Cathedral of St Michael and St George**, built as a parish church in 1824 and elevated to a Bishopric in 1852. The Lady Chapel was finally completed in 1952. Nearby, the **War Memorial** has an inscription specially composed by Rudyard Kipling.

In 1835, Major Selwyn designed the **Drostdy Gate**, *Drostdy Rd,* which was eventually built by the Royal Engineers in 1841, and now forms the pedestrian entrance to Rhodes University. There are also numerous fine restored buildings in *MacDonald St, Hill St* and the old artisans' quarter of **Artificers Square**, *corner Bartholomew and Cross Sts.*

In 1850, the Gothic Revival **Methodist Commemoration Church**, *High St,* with its fine organ and stained-glass windows, was dedicated in triumphant thanks for the Settlers' survival during their first, tough 25 years. Their 50th anniversary, in 1870, was celebrated by the **Settler Memorial Tower**, now part of the City Hall. Work on the **City Hall** itself began in 1877. On *Bedford Rd,* the **Bible Monument** marks a brief moment of friendship between the local Boers and British Settlers in 1837.

Several separate museums make up the **Albany Museum Complex**, *Somerset St; tel: 0461-22312.* The **History Museum** (open Mon–Fri 0930–1300, 1400–1700, Sat–Sun 1400–1700; R5) has an excellent display on southern Nguni lifestyles and traditions alongside a detailed history of the 1820 and later British settlers, with a fine collection of domestic utensils, furniture and applied arts, and a large collection of 18th and 19th century South African art. The **Natural Sciences Museum** (open Mon–Fri 0930–1300, 1400–1700, Sun 1400–1700; R5) covers all the natural sciences, from botany and geology to zoology, together with early human archaeology. The **Observatory Museum**, *Bathurst St* (open Mon–Fri 0930–1300, 1400–1700; Sat 0900–1300; R5) has a working camera obscura, and displays on the early diamond industry and Victorian South Africa. **The Provost Prison**, *Lucas Ave* (open Mon–Sat 1000–1700; free) is a 19th-century military gaol currently housing a craft shop. Above the town, **Fort Selwyn**,

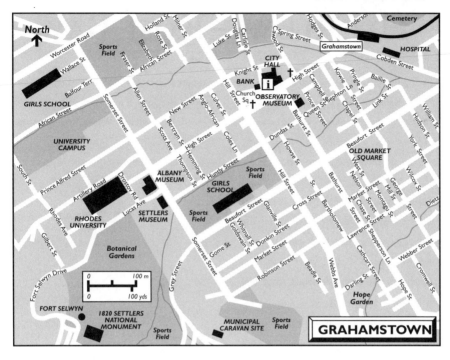

Gunfire Hill, (open by appointment; free), a small but efficient fort built in 1836, saw several battles against Xhosa forces. Next to it, in 1974, the townsfolk built the **1820 Settlers Monument**, *Gunfire Hill; tel: 0461-27115,* as an arts centre and official home of the Grahamstown Festival.

Several other museums are in the town. The **JLB Smith Institute of Ichthyology**, *Somerset St; tel: 0461-311 002* (open Mon–Fri 0830–1300, 1400–1700; free) is one of the world's largest collections of fish, with pride of place taken by three odd, prehistoric coelacanths (see East London, p.176). The **National English Literary Museum**, *87 Beaufort St; tel: 0461-27042* (open Mon–Fri 0900–1230, 1430–1630; donations) is a repository for South African literature in English, while its satellite, the **Eastern Star Gallery**, *4 Anglo African St; tel: 0461-27042* (open Mon–Fri 0830–1300, 1400–1630; free) covers printing techniques. Its name comes from *The Star* newspaper, which had its earliest roots in Grahamstown. The **International Library of African Music**,

Prince Alfred St; tel: 0461-318 557 (open Mon–Fri 0830–1245, 1400–1700, by appointment; donation) has over 200 traditional instruments as well as a large library of recordings.

There are plenty of outdoor activities in the Grahamstown area – angling, mountain biking, hiking, rock-climbing, bird-watching, riding, golf and tennis. The dams around the city provide opportunities for canoeing, sailing and wind-surfing. The Tourist Office has details, as well as information about guided city walks and guided wildlife and ecology tours. These include visits to the **Andries Vosloo Kudu Reserve** (part of the **Great Fish River Reserve Complex**; *tel: 0401-952 115,* whose game population includes leopard, African rock python, warthog and over 225 species of bird), the **Ecca Pass Flower Reserve** (with plenty of interesting trails; *tel: 0461-312 386),* the 1005 hectare **Thomas Baines Nature Reserve**; *tel: 0461-27909,* **Addo Elephant Park**, home to over 300 elephant (see p. 184), the **Mountain Zebra Park** (see p. 180) and the **Gannahoek Game Ranch**.

HLUHLUWE–KOSI BAY

The remote area of Maputaland, in the far north of Kwazulu-Natal on the Mozambique border, is one of the most beautiful in South Africa, a stretch of magnificent coast lined by towering dunes. Massive turtles drag themselves ashore to lay their eggs on isolated silver sand beaches, while offshore coral reefs teem with multi-coloured life. Inland are some of the richest 'Big Five' game parks in southern Africa. Best of all, much of the area is unknown and underdeveloped, with few other tourists around to spoil the perfect peace. The route does involve quite a bit of dirt road driving, but a 4x4 is only necessary within Kosi Bay Nature Reserve. Those planning to spend a lot of time in the Natal Parks (both in this area and the Drakensberg, see pp. 255–263) should ask for a Golden Rhino

188

Passport (R250, or R125 after 1st August), an annual pass allowing unlimited access to Natal Parks Board properties. Alternatively, you can buy a book of 20 entry tickets for a 25% discount. Note that this area is malarial and prophylactics should be taken (see p. 22).

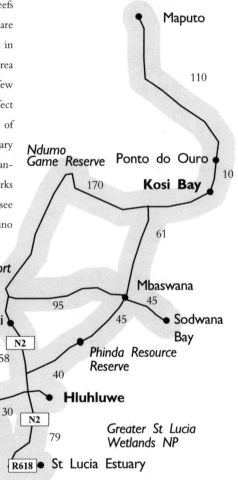

DIRECT ROUTE: 350 KM

ROUTE

From Hluhluwe village, head due west for 30 km, crossing the N2, to reach the **Hluhluwe-Umfolozi Game Reserve**. To reach the southern section of the **Greater St Lucia Wetland Park**, head south on the N2 for 46 km and turn left onto the R618 for 29 km. To reach False Bay and the central section of the Greater St Lucia Wetland Park, head due east (away from the N2) for 8 km.

For the **Phinda Resource Reserve**, return to the N2 for 18 km, then turn right on the Ngwenya-Sodwana exit and follow the signs for about 20 km to the gate. Keep going past the Phinda entrance and this road eventually comes out at Mbaswana, where you turn right for **Sodwana Bay** (90 km from the turn off). Beyond Sodwana Bay and Mbaswana, there is a road leading up past **Lake Sibaya** and the **Maputaland Marine Reserve** to connect with Kosi Bay, but it is in poor condition and should only be attempted in a 4x4 (for the alternative, see below).

To reach the far north from Hluhluwe village, return to the N2, turn right and head north. At Mkuzi village (58 km), turn right and head south on the dirt road for 9 km to the turn off for the **Mkuzi Game Reserve**. It is 16 km from the turn off to Mantima Camp. Return to the N2 and keep going north for another 20 km, then turn right along the southern edge of the **Pongolapoort Dam** through Jozini. From here, a dirt road leads east through Mbaswana to Sodwana Bay (120 km).

For the far north, remain on the tarred road for another 80 km, until a turn off on the left leads to the **Ndumo Game Reserve** (about 25 km further). The main road carries on past the southern boundary of the Tembe Elephant Park (currently closed to the public) to Ngwanase, where the tar ends. Turn right and follow the signs for **Rocktail Bay**. Continue straight on for **Kosi Bay**. Beyond Kosi Bay, a poor gravel road crosses the Mozambique border at Ponto do Ouro and connects up to Maputo (about 120 km; see p.356–364). There is no faster or more direct route. Distance: about 350 km (not including any side trips; allow one day for driving; preferably allow a week to explore the area).

HLUHLUWE VILLAGE

Tourist Office: *15 Main St; tel: 035-562 0353.* Open Mon–Fri 0830–1630, Sat 0900–1300.

ACCOMMODATION

The top accommodation in the area is at **Phinda Game Reserve** (see p.191), but under the same ownership, **Zululand Tree Lodge** *(Cv), 3 km from Hluhluwe; tel: 035-562 1020; fax: 035-562 1032* (expensive) is a worthy alternative, with stilted rooms in the forest on a private 1500 hectare reserve. **Zulu Nyala Lodge** *(Pf), follow signs from the southern Maputaland turn off, off the N2; tel: 035-562 0169;* reservations; *tel: 011-484 1560/1; fax: 011-484 2893* (expensive) is one of the largest and most well-equipped lodges in the area, with 35 stone-and-thatch rooms, a pool, tennis courts, game-viewing, bird-watching, walks and boat tours on its private reserve. Landless, but still excellent **Bushlands Game Lodge**, *Hluhluwe; tel: 035-562 0144; fax: 035-562 0205* (moderate) offers luxury treehouse rooms, connected by elevated wooden walkways at a more affordable price. **Bonamanzi,** *10 km north of Hluhluwe village; tel: 035-562 0181; fax: 035-562 0143* (cheap–moderate) is a private 4200 hectare game park (not Big Five), offering self-catering accommodation from basic treehouses to luxury lodges with a private cook.

SIGHTSEEING

Dumazulu Cultural Village, *about 10 km south of Hluhluwe village; tel: 035-562 0144* (tours and dance displays at 0815, 1100 and 1515; 1800 including dinner – 20 people minimum; R50; R45 for traditional lunch after the 1100 show) is one of the best of the Zulu cultural villages in the country – certainly amongst those easily accessible to day visitors. Its slightly rough and ready atmosphere, right out in the bush, provides an authenticity lacking in some more polished performances and the thundering dance (the name means 'thundering Zulu') shakes the ground, stirring the dust and the senses in equal measure. There is limited basic accommodation on site (cheap).

With Hlabisa, just north of Hluhluwe, considered to be the home of the finest basketry in

189

Rhinos

There are two species of Rhino in Africa: the larger, more docile grass-eating **White Rhinoceros**, *Ceratotherium simum* (180 cm; 2300 kg), named not for its colour, but for its square jaw (from the Afrikaans word 'wydt', meaning wide-mouthed); and the small, more aggressive, bush-dwelling browser, the **Black Rhinoceros**, *Diceros Bicornis* (160 cm; 850 kg), which is a slightly darker charcoal-grey, with a pointy hook-lip.

Contrary to opinion in the Far East, where rhino horn is revered as an aphrodisiac, it contains no magic ingredient, only the same mild analgesic found in human fingernails. In spite of this, the horn (actually made of heavily compacted fibre) fetches enormous sums on the black market, and both species have nearly been driven to extinction by poachers. At their lowest point, in the 1890s, it was estimated that there were only about 20 white rhinos left, most in the Hluhluwe-Umfolozi area. It was this that led to the creation of the first game parks. Thanks to **Operation Rhino**, a successful breeding and relocation programme in the 1960s, these few remaining rhinos became the ancestors of all the other rhinos in sub-Saharan Africa. There are now estimated to be around 7000, with 1800 in the Hluhluwe-Umfolozi area.

Zululand, **Ilala Weavers**, *on Ngweni, about 1 km north-east of Hluhluwe Village; tel: 035-562 0630/1*, with a gallery at the local airport, *Zebra Rd*, is the main shopfront for some 1200 Zulu men and women producing the finest possible traditional crafts. An excellent shopping stop. The truly extravagant may like to attend Hluhluwe's annual **game auction** (June), where upwards of 600 animals are sold by the Natal Parks Board for translocation, as a way of controlling numbers within the parks without resorting to culling.

HLUHLUWE-UMFOLOZI NATIONAL PARK

Parks Information and Accommodation: open daily 0500–1900 1 Oct–31 Mar, 0600–1800 1 Apr–30 Sept; Hilltop Camp office open daily 0700–1900, other camp offices open daily 0800–1230, 1400–1630; admission R6 per person and R25 per car. The accommodation within both sections of the park is run by the **Natal Parks Board** *(Nt);* reservations; *tel: 0331-471 981; fax: 0331-471 980.*

Hilltop Camp, *Hluhluwe, tel: 035-562 0255; fax: 035-562 0113* (moderate) is a very comfortable upmarket lodge, with a large variety of chalets surrounding a central block with a good restaurant, bar and shop. Other accommodation is in attractive self-catering bush camps, each with a cook/caretaker, although you must provide the food. These range in size from **Mpila**, which sleeps up to 70, and has a petrol station and camp shop, to **Gqoyeni** or **Munyawaneni**, which sleep only eight.

Night drives and two walks a day with an armed guide (no children under 12) are available through the parks office. There are also several self-guided walking trails and designated picnic spots. Elsewhere, due to the presence of lions, visitors are not allowed out of their vehicles.

In Umfolozi, a 24,000 hectare area is set aside between Mar and Nov for 4-day hikes accompanied by an armed ranger. On the 'easier' option, packs are carried by donkey; on the more basic, you tote your own; cooking is done over a fire, and accommodation is in your own tents. A minimum group of 8 people is needed for a booking (up to 6 months in advance); *tel: 035-550 1261.*

SIGHTSEEING

Originally two separate reserves, now linked by an 8 km wide corridor, Hluhluwe (named after a thorny liana) and Umfolozi (literally 'river of fibres') are two of the oldest wildlife sanctuaries in Africa, established in 1897 (the other is neighbouring St Lucia). Today, they make up a vast 96,000 hectare complex that offers a broad range of habitats, from rocky hillside to open savannah grass and thick woodland, supporting a rich variety of game, with some 86 species of mammal. This is big five country, with a particularly high concentration of rhinos. For twitchers, there are also around 425 recorded species of bird.

PHINDA GAME RESERVE

The **Phinda Resource Reserve** *(Cv), about 30 km north of Hluhluwe village; tel: 011-803 8421; fax: 011-803 1810* (very expensive) is one of the premier private game parks in southern Africa, a 17,000 hectare big five game reserve on the Mzinene River, sandwiched between Mkuzi and St Lucia. After a massive programme of restocking, the game-viewing is good and the service better, with game-drives, bushwalks, canoeing and sundowner cruises included in the price. For an additional fee, guests may also go on sightseeing flights over the Maputaland coast, snorkelling picnics, scuba safaris and deep-sea fishing trips.

There are currently two main lodges, the hilltop **Mountain Lodge**, with rooms peering through treetop foliage on the steep slopes and magnificent views from the pool deck and verandah, and the heavily wooded, much flatter **Forest Lodge**, which has extraordinary, beautiful Japanese-style glass cabins scattered amongst the trees. A third, **Rock Lodge**, is currently under construction.

GREATER ST LUCIA WETLANDS RESERVE

Tourist Office: *corner Katonkel and McKenzie Sts, St Lucia; tel: 035-590 1143.* Now covering 38,682 hectares, the Greater St Lucia Wetlands Reserve is growing all the time, as more and more pieces of the jigsaw are fitted together: Mapelane, the St Lucia Game Reserve, False Bay Park, Sodwana Bay National Park, Cape Vidal State Forest, Sodwana State Forest, St Lucia Marine Reserve (stretching 5 km out to sea), the Maputaland Marine Reserve, and the Mkuzi Game Reserve. All sections are open daily 0500–1900 1 Oct–31 Mar, 0600–1800 1 Apr–30 Sept; admission R6 per person. Unless otherwise stated, all accommodation listed is run by Natal Parks Board *(Nt;* cheap). Bookings for cabins and lodges should be made through central reservations, bookings for campsites should be made direct to the telephone number listed below.

Between Apr–Sept, the parks board run a series of 4-day **hiking trails**, starting from Mission Rocks, with two nights camping at Bhangazi and two nights wilderness camping. There are also opportunities for canoeing and snorkelling. For reservations; *tel: 035-590 1233.*

ACCOMMODATION AND SIGHTSEEING

Mapelane, *on the south bank of the Umfolozi River estuary; tel: 035-590 1407; fax: 035-590 1343,* is 50 km from the Kwambonambi turn off on the Empangeni-Mtubatube road; access not recommended for low-slung vehicles. This is the most southerly of the St Lucia camps, with ten 5-bed staffed, self-catering log cabins and 44 camping and caravan sites (no fuel or food available). There are ski boat and surf fishing areas; licences are obtainable from the office for musseling and crayfishing. The area is safe for swimming, and there are walking trails and over 200 species of bird.

The **St Lucia Game Estuary Reserve**, *25 km east of Mtubatuba; tel: 035-590 1340; fax: 035-590 1343,* has good access roads. At the heart of one of southern Africa's most important wetland systems, this park is one of the busiest tourist areas on the Maputaland coast, based on an ancient, 40 km-long lake, whose shores touch coastal dunes, marshlands, coastal forest, mangrove swamps, lily pans and, inland, bushveld and grassland. The lake and estuary, which connects it to the open sea, contain thriving colonies of about 2000 crocodiles, 800 hippos, and black fin and Zambezi River sharks (not recommended for swimming). But the birds are the stars, with over 450 species, including large colonies of pelicans and flamingoes, goliath and other herons, fish eagles and three species of kingfisher. There are several walking trails near the water. The **Santa Lucia**; *tel: 035-590 1340,* is an 80-seater launch, which runs 2-hr guided tours of the lake (daily at 0830, 1030 and 1400; R35). Near the jetty is a small ecology museum and **Crocodile Centre**; *tel: 035-590 1386* (open daily 0700–1730, feeding time Sat 1500) with live crocodiles of every species found in Africa. There are three campsites, of which **Sugarloaf** is the only one with electricity and a pool; it is also extremely pretty.

191

Outside the park, **St Lucia** village is a hive of activity, with several small hotels and restaurants catering to the local holiday trade. The good **Maputaland Guest House**, *1 Kabeljou St, St Lucia; tel: 035-590 1041* (cheap) also operates day and overnight trips from St Lucia to local game reserves and other coastal reserves, including Lake Sibaya and Kosi Bay (R85–350, to include meals). One of the most pleasant of the larger properties is the **Boma Hotel and Cabanas**, *McKenzie St; tel/fax: 035-590 1330* (cheap), which offers a variety of hotel rooms and self-catering accommodation. **Deep-sea fishing** boats and **diving** trips and equipment are available for hire from the **St Lucia Fishing Den**, *McKenzie St, St Lucia; tel: 035-590 1450*.

Twenty kilometres north of Mtubatuba, a turning off the N2 leads to the small **Charters Creek** and **Fanies Island** camps, with cottages (bring your own food) and campsites, used mainly by fishermen. There are walking trails, bird-watching and boats for hire, but swimming is not safe.

The access road to **False Bay Park**, *on the north-western shore of Lake St Lucia*; accommodation bookings; *tel: 035-562 0425*, leads east from Hluhluwe village. This 2247 hectare section of sand forest along the banks of Hluhluwe River is best visited in Dec–Apr, when hundreds of rare pink-backed pelicans arrive to nest. At other times, there is basic hut and camping accommodation, with birding, fishing, boating, limited game-viewing and hiking on offer.

The **Marine Reserve** is a long, thin strip of land stretching up the coast from Cape Vidal in the south right the way up to the Mozambique border, and 5 km out to sea. It is a natural wonder, encompassing the world's largest forested sand dunes, mini-mountains of gold and the world's most southerly coral reefs. There are few access points – this is for nature. The only accommodation is at **Cape Vidal**, *35 km north of St Lucia Village, past the Crocodile Centre; tel: 035-590 1404*, where there are three camps with log cabins, a camping and caravan site near the beach, surrounded by dense coastal forest and high dunes, and two small fishing camps on Lake Bhangazi.

Inland, the 34,644 hectare **Mkuzi Game Reserve**, *signposted 35 km north of Hluhluwe;* tourist information: *tel: 035-573 1120;* campsite reservations: *tel: 035-573 0003*, sprawls across the foothills of the Lebombo Mountains, all dusty earth, fever trees and fossils. Over 100 km of dirt roads provide an excellent network of game-viewing drives, with animals including all the major species except lion, and a particularly large number of black rhinos. There are also four hides near pans (waterholes), which attract large concentrations of game, and two near Nsumo Pan specifically for bird-watching, with over 400 species in the park. Guided day walks and night drives are available. There is a small cultural village and craft market at KwaJobe, in the north of the reserve. Accommodation includes several small self-catering lodges, cottages, tented camps and a caravan and camping site with game guards and cook/caretakers in attendance. Just outside the north gate to the park, **Ghost Mountain Inn**; *tel/fax: 035-573 1025* (moderate) is a pleasant small hotel, with a full restaurant and pool.

The main access road to **Sodwana Bay National Park**; *tel: 035682-1502*, actually leads through part of Mkuzi. This beautiful coastal park has dune forests, lakes, walking and birding on offer, but what people really come for – in increasingly huge numbers – is the water. With easily accessible coral reefs, this is one of the most popular dive sites in the country. Spearfishing licences are available from the camp office. The camp also has a bait shop, dive shop, and organises night turtle tours in breeding season (Dec–Jan). There are log cabins and a huge camping and caravan site in the park camp, as well as two smaller campsites and a full-service lodge, the **Sodwana Bay Lodge**; reservations: *tel: 031-304 5977; fax: 031-304 8817* (moderate), with accommodation in thatched huts on stilts. The Lodge also organises dive courses.

THE FAR NORTH

The road to the far north begins beside the **Pongolapoort Dam**, a massive white elephant built to irrigate the Makatini Flats and create a new area for intensive farming of sugar, fruit, rice and coffee. In fact, political events

---

Beach Etiquette

Only certain types of vehicles are allowed onto the beaches, and you will need a permit (available from the parks offices) before driving on the beaches at Umlalazi, Mapelane, Cape Vidal, Sodwana and St Lucia. Here are a few guidelines:

1. Make sure your vehicle is in good repair, you have a full tank of fuel, a spare tyre and repair kit. There is no one to bail you out if you run into trouble.
2. Deflate your tyres to about 1 bar pressure.
3. If possible, avoid bathing beaches, but always be alert for small children.
4. Never drive on the beach during high tide and never drive above the high tide mark; this causes erosion and can crush turtles' nests.
5. Avoid driving on the ecologically sensitive dunes, salt-marshes or mud-flats.
6. Do not use bright lights at night as it may disturb nesting turtles.
7. Do not litter, or leave fish hooks unattended.
8. Keep clear of skiboat landing or recovery areas.

---

overtook the scheme which has never come into fruition, leaving behind a huge, extremely beautiful lake. There are plans to develop it for tourism, but nothing much has happened yet. The nearest centre, **Jozini**, is a largely black town, humming with people and street stalls. The atmosphere is great, but there is nothing specific to see. From here, a road stretches right across the province back to the coast and **Lake Sibaya**, actually only 15 km north of Sodwana Bay. Originally a saltwater lagoon, which lost its access to the sea, this is the largest natural freshwater lake in southern Africa, covering an area of 77 sq. km. As with other sights in the area, **Baya Camp** is a small self-catering camp; reservations: *tel: 0331-946 698; fax: 0331-421 948* (office open 0700–1200 1400–1600 Mon–Sat, 0700–1400 Sun; cheap) with fishing, bird-watching and hiking as the main activities.

North of Jozini, the road reaches nearly to the Mozambique border before curling round towards the coast, past the **Ndumo and Tembe Game Reserves**. The 10,000 hectare **Ndumo Game Reserve**; reservations: *tel: 0331-946 698; fax: 0331-421 498*, is an enchantingly pretty wooded area, with huge mature trees set back from a large lake, surrounded by open grass. There is some good game-viewing, with a particularly large rhino population and good colonies of hippos and crocodiles, but the birdlife is quite extraordinarily wealthy, with 413 species noted. There is a small parks camp with self-catering huts and

camping and caravan sites, but the best place here, for those who can afford it, is the wonderful **Ndumo Wilderness Camp** *(Wd)*, reservations: *tel: 011-884 1458; fax: 011-883 6255* (expensive), a small, very exclusive permanent tented camp on stilts above the reed beds and river.

Note that the neighbouring **Tembe Reserve**, set up to provide a safe haven for Mozambique's elephants, is not currently open to the public.

KOSI BAY

On the coast, **Kosi Bay Nature Reserve** is a magnificent area of remote forested dunes, mangrove swamps, four coastal lakes, coral reefs, fine, white gold sand and sapphire waves. And if that is not enough, there are 250 species of bird, hiking trails, canoeing, and in season, huge leatherback and loggerhead turtles haul themselves up the beaches to lay their eggs.

There are three small self-catering thatched lodges and a campsite; reservations: *tel: 0331-946 698; fax: 0331-421 498*, while the **Kosi Bay Lodge**; *tel: 082-447 5125* (moderate) provides full-service hotel accommodation. Just south of the park is the very exclusive, gloriously remote **Rocktail Bay Lodge** *(Wd), Maputaland Coastal Forest Reserve;* reservations: *tel: 011-884 1458; fax: 011-883 6255* (expensive), whose wood and thatch treehouses are tucked into a forgotten valley next to a deserted turtle beach, in the most magnificent surroundings.

JOHANNESBURG

Some people think Johannesburg is the capital of South Africa. Many others think that it should be. It is certainly livelier, more cosmopolitan, commercial and authoritative than the country's three official capitals put together. It is also one of the fastest growing cities in the world – and one of the most dangerous.

Because of its industrial background, romantics call it 'the City of Gold'. To others it's 'Chicago on the Veldt' or even 'Murder Capital of the World'.

The truth is that Johannesburg – actually the capital of the Gauteng Province – is a vibrant, modern city; multicultural, multi-ethnic, whose pragmatic inhabitants are slowly coming to terms with the aftermath of the Big Bang that ended apartheid. Dangerous? Yes, if you have the misfortune to live in one of its insalubrious ghettos, or, as a tourist, fail to observe common sense precautions (see pp. 24 and 48).

TOURIST INFORMATION

Johannesburg Publicity Association: Main Office: *the Rotunda Bus Station, Leyds St, Braamfontein; tel: 011-337 6650* (open Mon–Thur 0800–1900; Fri 0800–1600; Sat–Sun 0900–1400). **City Centre**: *Ground Floor, North State Building, corner Kruis and Market Sts, Johannesburg; tel: 011-336 9461* (open Mon–Thur 0800–1700; Fri 0800–1600; Sat 0900–1200). **Johannesburg International Airport:** *International Arrivals Hall; tel: 011-970 1220*

(open Mon–Thur 0730–1630; Fri 0730–1600; Sat–Sun 0800–1300). All three offices have a useful selection of information on accommodation, attractions, entertainment and dining.

ARRIVING AND DEPARTING

Airport
Johannesburg International Airport, 25 km east of the city, *accessed by R21 or R24 highways; tel: 011-356 1111* (general), or *011-975 9963* (flights). This airport is simply too small these days and, as a result, is not the world's most user-friendly. The international arrivals hall can get very congested; it can be something of a struggle to fight your way through the regiment of taxi and hostel touts and good, honest folk meeting friends and relations. You cannot avoid it if you want to change money, rent a cell phone, obtain tourist information or refreshment. If you want to rent a car, find a chemist or the toilet, you must battle along the sloping corridor leading to the domestic arrivals hall. Banking and currency exchange services operate from two hours before to two hours after the arrival and departure times of international flights. The airport post office is located between the international and domestic arrivals halls (open daily 0800–2200).

Satour and the **Johannesburg Publicity Association** share a large and unmissable mock-up of a Cape Dutch homestead in the international arrivals hall, and between them offer a good range of brochures and maps. You will have to pay for some of Satour's literature, including their very useful accommodation guide.

Adjacent to the Satour information office is a pillar-mounted toll-free telephone, giving direct access to a central reservations office operated by the **South African Hostels Association**. A panel beside the telephone gives advice on making a reservation and finding transport to the hostel of your choice.

An **airport shuttle bus** service; *tel: 011-*

194

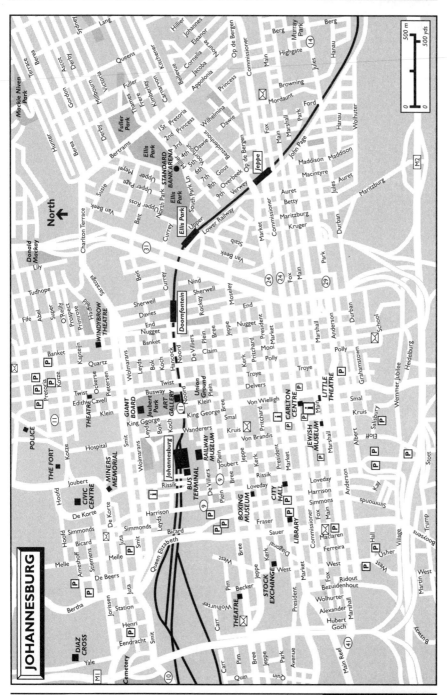

JOHANNESBURG

500 m
500 yds

195

394-6902/3, operates between the airport and the **Rotunda**, *Leyds St, Johannesburg* (daily 0500–2200). The **Magic Bus**; *tel: 011-884 3957*, operating a similar timetable, shuttles between the airport and major hotels in the Sandton area.

The recognised taxi service is **Airport Link**; *tel: 011-646 0160*. Some of the larger hotels operate minibus shuttles to and from the airport – at a price. In the interest of personal safety, beware of minibus taxi touts, although anyone sporting an official airport identity card should be reliable, and probably cheaper than other options. You should not expect to share a minibus taxi with strangers.

By Bus

All of the many long-distance coaches serving Johannesburg from every corner of South Africa, and most of the surrounding countries, arrive and depart from the **Rotunda**, *Leyds St, Braamfontein*. For information and reservations, contact **Greyhound Citiliner**; *tel: 011-333 2130;* **Intercape**; *tel: 011-333 5231;* or **Translux Express**; *tel: 011-774 3333*. There is a **taxi** rank just outside the station and it is strongly advised that you use one, even for short journeys. This is a known trouble spot, where muggers wait for naive newcomers with heavy luggage.

By Rail

Main Station: *De Villiers St;* *tel: 011-773 5878*. This cavernous building harks back to the days when there was a regular network (or was perhaps built with one in mind, which never materialised). There is an information office on the concourse. For information: *tel: 011-773 5878;* for reservations: *tel: 011-773 2944*.

Johannesburg is connected by **long-distance trains** to all the major cities in South Africa, as well as anywhere else along the lines. There is generally only one train a day in each direction, usually travelling overnight. **Metro-politan trains** serve commuters in the suburbs and townships to the east and west of the city, and are not really suitable for tourists. The **taxi** rank is a short walk from the station, on the far side of the road, under the railway bridge.

By Car

There are excellent road connections with the rest of the country, and fast motorway ring roads right round and through the city to allow easy access.

GETTING AROUND

Johannesburg is a big and expanding city, and its many attractions are scattered widely. **Municipal buses** operate from *Vanderbijl Sq.;* *tel: 011-838 2125*, but are not practicable for sightseeing. Services are most frequent during the morning and evening rush hours (Mon–Fri), operating on an hourly basis at other times and ceasing altogether at 1900. Buses to Sandton leave from the corner of *Kruis and Commissioner Sts* and are operated by **Padco**; *tel: 011-474 2634* (daily, more or less hourly, 0630–1715).

Taxis are plentiful, but may not be hailed and are not cheap. There are ranks near the Carlton and Johannesburg Hilton hotels downtown and by the Rotunda further north. Leading companies include **King Taxis**; *tel: 011-486 0042*, and **Rose's Taxis**; *tel: 011-725 3333*.

Apart from using your own car (always drive with the doors locked), your best option is to take a guided tour of the city (see Sightseeing, p.202).

Car Parking

There are half a dozen multi-storey car parks dotted around central Johannesburg. Closest to the Carlton Centre are those at the *corners of Marshall and Von Weilligh Sts, Marshall and Eloff Sts* and *Commissioner and Kruis Sts*. South of the Carlton Centre, there are car parks *off Eloff St, between Harris and Salisbury Sts,* and at the *corner of Troye and Anderson Sts*. Another car park lies at the western end of *Anderson St,* where it turns into *Ridout St*.

STAYING IN JOHANNESBURG

Accommodation

The city and its suburbs offer a wide range of accommodation in all categories and price ranges. Most visitors are drawn to the north-west suburbs – such as Randburg, Rosebank

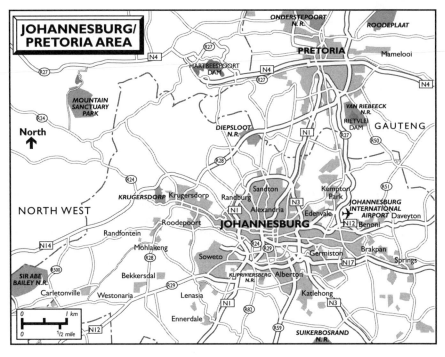

JOHANNESBURG/
PRETORIA AREA

North ↑

and Sandton – which are livelier and safer than central Johannesburg, especially at night. There maybe spot shortages of hotel beds if a conference or some other specific event is taking place, but the problem can usually be solved by upgrading or downgrading your requirements a notch or two, or moving on to another area. Chain hotels include: *CL, F1, Hd, HI, Hn, Hy, Ic, Ka, Pa, SI, SX.*

With 170 rooms, old-world courtesy and potted palm ambience, the **Carlton** *(TC), corner Main and Kruis Sts, Johannesburg; tel: 011-331 8911; fax: 011-331 3555* (expensive) is Johannesburg's grande dame. It manages to retain the authority of the best hotel in town, even though most social activities have moved elsewhere and downtown security is such that the hotel provides an escort if you wish to explore the adjoining Carlton Centre shopping mall.

Handy for downtown and the northern suburbs, the 4-star **Parktonian All Suites Hotel**, *120 De Korte St, Braamfontein; tel: 011-403 5740; fax: 011-403 2401* (expensive) has 294 rooms and is a favourite for business and other functions.

One of the newest hotels in the metropolitan area – and the first development by an international chain since the ending of apartheid – is the **Park Hyatt Johannesburg** *(Hy), 191 Oxford Rd, Rosebank; tel: 011-280 1234: fax: 011-280 1238* (expensive). Built in contemporary style, its public rooms and corridors adorned with original works of art – many by indigenous artists – the 270-room hotel has direct links with Rosebank's attractive complex of shopping malls and squares surrounded by boutiques and restaurants. In the centre of Sandton, attached to the huge Sandton Centre, the **Sandton Sun** *(SS), Fifth St, Sandton; tel: 011-780 5000; fax: 011-780 5002* (expensive) is equally large, luxurious and very convenient. If you prefer something smaller and more exclusive, the **Cullinan Hotel** *(SX), 115 Katherine St, Sandton 2146; tel: 011-884 8544; fax: 011-884 8545* (expensive) is a privately-owned luxury complex built in French colonial-style. It has 70 double rooms and 52 suites, some of which are self-catering, and a colonnaded verandah serving temptingly expensive morsels.

The airport area is served by a cluster of chain hotels, including the three-star **Holiday Inn Garden Court Johannesburg Airport** *(Hd), 6 Hulley Rd, Isando, Kempton Park; tel: 011-974 8097; fax: 011-974 8097* (expensive), only 1 km from the terminal, with 330 air-conditioned rooms, restaurant and pool. The nearby **Formula 1** *(F1); tel/fax: 011-392 1453*, (cheap–moderate) offers basic but comfortable accommodation.

In the outer suburban reaches, the **Karos Indaba** *(Ka), Hartebeestpoort Dam Rd, Wittkoppen, Sandton,; tel: 011 465 1400; fax: 011-705 1709* (expensive) is handy for the Western By-pass and the Sandton Fourways shopping mall, almost halfway to Pretoria. A self-contained estate of thatched chalets and low-rise buildings, the hotel is a popular conference venue, with a resort ambience. The **City Lodge Randburg** *(CL), corner Main Rd and Peter Pl., Bryanston West, Cramerview; tel: 011-706 7800; fax: 011-706 7819* (moderate) offers 122 comfortable rooms in a discreet and secure location. Its restaurant serves breakfast only, but there is a good choice of eating places nearby. The **Fleet Street Guest House**, *101 Fleet St, Ferndale; tel: 011-886 0790; fax: 011-789 6601* (cheap) offers bed and breakfast in 10 air-conditioned double rooms, and is handily placed for Randburg and Sandton.

Guesthouse reservations may be made with the **Bed and Breakfast Association**, *PO Box 91309, Auckland Park; tel: 011-482 2206.*

The **Explorers Club**, *9 Innes Rd, Observatory; tel: 011-648 7138*, is a reputable backpackers' hostel. **Backpackers Underground**, *Rockey St, Yeoville; tel: (011) 648 6132*, is another small, friendly hostel offering budget accommodation. There are also 6 hostels with *HI* affiliation in the city.

Eating and Drinking

As might be expected in a big, cosmopolitan city, Johannesburg has a wide and varied choice of places to eat and drink, though the greatest selection, again, is in the northern suburbs. That said, however, there are a number of reputable restaurants offering a range of cuisines in the central district. For snacks and fast food in this area, the best place to head for is the **Carlton Centre**. The lounge bar in the **Carlton Hotel** is a comfortable oasis, where you can enjoy a surprisingly inexpensive snack and drink.

A complete listing of restaurants in the areas around Johannesburg and Pretoria is given in the free 64-page monthly publication *Hello Gauteng*, available at tourism information offices.

The best-known establishment for traditional South African fare is the **Anton van Wouw Restaurant**, *111 Sivewright Ave, Doornfontein; tel: 011-402 7916* (expensive). Located in the home of the late Anton van Wouw, sculptor, painter, gardener, cook and bon viveur, it has elegant décor and is a favourite with theatre-goers from the Alhambra Theatre next door. The *pièce de résistance* on an adventurous menu of fish, meat, game and poultry dishes is Strandloper Potjie, a kind of Afrikaans paella consisting of langoustines, prawns, kingklip, mussels, calamari and mushrooms.

You do not have to attend a show to visit **Ovations**, the restaurant and bar at the Alhambra Theatre, *109 Sivewright Ave; tel: 011-402 6174* (moderate). The menu is good, the service unhurried but efficient. Across the street from the Alhambra is **Gerhard's**, *128 Sivewright St; tel: 011-402 1010* (expensive), a traditional German restaurant with open fireplaces, pressed steel ceilings and Baltic deal floors. Among the specialities is a game schnitzel enhanced with beef marrow and served with a red wine sauce and rösti.

Part of the Market Theatre complex (see Entertainment, p.199), **Gramadoelas**, *corner Bree and Wolhuter Sts, Newtown; tel: 011-836 6960* (moderate–expensive) is an atmospheric restaurant specialising in Cape Malay cuisine. Its opulently decorated interior – a treasure house of African art, calabashes, antique fittings and fixtures, with tables lit by paraffin lamps – has been the setting for dinners attended by such celebrities as President Mandela, Al Gore, David Bowie and Hillary Clinton.

Top of the city's many Indian restaurants is

198

the **Taj Palace**, *corner Bree and Mint Sts, Fordsburg; tel: 011-836 4925/6* (expensive; reservations essential at weekends). Its five chefs – two from Northern India, three from Pakistan – produce a classical menu, which includes seven chicken dishes and eight varieties of Tandoori bread. The food is strictly Halal and alcohol is not allowed.

Among the few restaurants serving African cuisine are **Ivaya**, *42 Hunter St, Yeoville; tel: 011-648 3500*, and **Café Afrika**, *Shop 2, RSA Building, corner Jorissen and Melle Sts, Braam-fontein; tel: 011-403 1745* (both moderate).

The best areas to find a wide selection of eating places and bars are the suburban shopping centres. For example, the maze of malls and squares at Rosebank, bounded by *Oxford Rd* and *Jan Smuts Ave*, and *Biermann* and *Bolton Aves*, presents an overwhelming choice – everything from takeaways to haute cuisine in surroundings ranging from stand-up bars to discreet alfresco corners.

Paros, *1st Floor, Rosebank Blvd* (behind the Park Hyatt Johannesburg Hotel); *tel: 011-788 6211* (moderate) is a friendly Greek restaurant with an impressive array of specials. Unless you have a truly gargantuan appetite, beware the lamb kleftiko – it is delicious, but could serve two people, with enough left over for a picnic lunch! In Sandton, **Linger Longer**, *Wierda Rd (off Johan), Wierda Valley; tel: 011-884 0465* (expensive) offers some of the finest dining and most innovative French cuisine in South Africa. For a very different experience, **Carnivore**, *Muldersdrift Estate, off DF Malan Dr.; tel: 011-957 2099* (moderate) offers a meat feast of game, with everything from crocodile to warthog available from the barbecue, while vegetarians can munch pizza and salad.

Sandton's **Fourways Mall**, at the intersection of *Witkoppen and William Nicol Hwy*, has a number of pubs, cafés and restaurants under one gigantic roof, while the **Randburg Waterfront**, the leisure and retail complex built around a man-made lake, has about 60 eating establishments, many with outdoor dining facilities.

Communications

Main Post Office: *Jeppe St, between Von Brandis and Smal St Mall; tel: 011-805 0395* (open Mon–Fri 0830–1630; Sat 0800–1200). Poste restante services are based here. The post office in *Rissik St,* opposite City Hall, is usually less busy.

Money

Most major banks in the city centre, Sandton and other northern surburbs have exchange facilities and ATM machines. Sandton City Shopping Centre has a banking mall with representatives of all the major banks and a Rennies/Thomas Cook office. Locals recommend that you don't change money downtown because of the risk of mugging when you leave the bank.

The **Rennies/Thomas Cook foreign exchange**, *95 Kerk St, Johannesburg 2001; tel: 011-333 0460, fax: 011-337 4456*, has heavy-duty security.

ENTERTAINMENT

Much of Johannesburg's nightlife takes place in bars and restaurants of one kind or another, but there are several excellent theatres and concert halls offering the most vibrant arts scene in the country. However, finding out exactly where a particular event is being held might be something of a challenge. Local information sources are extraordinarily coy about venues, frequently offering no more than a telephone number and a female first name, even for something as innocent as an evening of chamber music.

Entertainment listings appear in the *Tonight* section of *The Star* newspaper, which also publishes a monthly supplement, *MTN Gateway*, which is freely available to visitors arriving at Johannesburg International Airport. The *Weekly Mail & Guardian* newspaper also has good listings. Entertainment reservations of all kinds may be made through **Computicket**; *tel: 011-331 9991*. There are Computicket offices in the Carlton Centre; the Firs Mall, Rosebank and in Sandton City.

The **Market Theatre**, *next to Museum Africa, Bree St; tel: 011-832 1641,* is the city's leading venue for live drama, musicals and comedy, and a famous name, as home of some of the most politically challenging drama of the apartheid years. It is a complex of four theatres,

199

an art gallery, shops and a coffee bar. The **Alhambra Theatre Complex**, *109 Sivewright Ave, Doornfontein; tel: 011-402 6174*, is three theatres in one. Performances include large-cast plays, revues and vocal groups.

The **Civic Theatre**, *Loveday St, Braamfontein; tel: 011-403 3408*, is a complex of five theatres neighbouring Johannesburg's Civic Centre. Productions include world-class performances of dance, comedy, drama, opera and music of all kinds.

Other major theatres are the **Black Sun Theatre**, *corner Rockey and Raymond Sts, Yeoville; tel: 011-728 3280*; the **Alexander Theatre**, *Stiemens St, Braamfontein; tel: 011-339 3461*, and the **Windybrow Theatre Complex**, *Nugget St, Joubert Park; tel: 011-720 5217*.

Johannesburg City Hall, *Rissik St*, is frequently used as a venue for performances by the **National Symphony Orchestra**. Tickets are available from Computicket, or at the door. Solo recitals, performances of chamber music, contemporary song, jazz, poetry, satire mime and drama are staged in seasonal soirées at **Longnor House**, *49 St Patrick Rd, Houghton; tel: 011-487 1800*. Sponsored open-air concerts are held on the first Sun of every month at **Johannesburg Zoo**, *Jan Smuts Ave, Saxonwold; tel: 011-646 2000*. The concerts are free but there is a charge of R10 for admission to the zoo.

Bertie's Big Easy Theatre Restaurant and Bar, *Randburg Waterfront, Republic Rd, Ferndale; tel: 011-789 4300*, presents live supper shows Tues–Sun and public holidays from 2130. The restaurant is open 1100–0200. **Tate's Coffee Shop and Theatre Café**, also at *Randburg Waterfront; tel: 011-789 4949*, opens daily 0800–0200 and presents live cabaret seven evenings a week.

Artificial though it is, the **Randburg Waterfront**; *tel: 011-789 5052*, has been compared – by the developers, at least – with internationally known waterfronts of the stature of Cape Town and San Francisco. Well, maybe... However, it is a major leisure venue, with ten cinemas, video arcades, pubs, shops, a Pick 'n Pay supermarket, restaurants, a musical fountain – even banks and a flea market with 360 stalls. Visitors can rent rowing boats and pedaloes,

windsurf or learn scuba-diving. The car park is immense.

South Africa's distinctive jazz is performed in a number of locations, notably at **Kippies**, *Market Theatre Complex, Bree St; tel: 011-834 3741*, and **206**, *206 Louis Botha Ave, Orange Grove; tel: 011-483 1282*, which hosts jazz and raves.

The *Weekly Mail & Guardian* lists popular discos and dance clubs. As in many cities worldwide, these come and go, but among the most firmly established are **Dawson's Hotel**, *117 President St, Johannesburg; tel: 011-337 5788*; the **House of Tandoor**, *Rockey St, Yeoville; tel: 011-487 1569*; **Dylans**, *Rockey St, Yeoville; tel: 011-468 0125*; and the **Hard Rock Café**, *New Thrupps Centre, Oxford Rd, Ilovo; tel: 011-447 2583*, one of several trendy hangouts in the New Thrupps Centre.

Cinema listings can be found in *The Star, Weekly Mail & Guardian* and other local newspapers. Modern multi-screen cinema complexes are located in most shopping malls.

SHOPPING

One-stop shopping is a feature of Johannesburg life. Major shopping centres in the city centre include the **Carlton Centre**, between *Commissioner and Main Sts*, and the **Smal Street Mall**, a sadly unsafe pedestrian link between the Johannesburg Sun and Towers Hotel and the Carlton Hotel.

The **Rosebank Shopping Complex**, *off Oxford Rd*, north of the city, covers an area four blocks square and includes half a dozen major shopping malls and centres. The **Rooftop Market** at the *Rosebank Mall, Cradock St; tel: 011-788 5530* (open Sun) has more than 450 stalls offering a wide range of clothing, gift items, antiques and collectables, as well as an array of African crafts and curios.

Sandton has three major malls clustered around the Sandton Sun and Towers Hotel. **Sandton City Shopping Mall**, *tel: 011-783 7413*, and **Sandton Square**, *tel: 011-784 2750*, have a host of speciality shops as well as art galleries, delicatessens, restaurants and banks. **Village Walk**, *corner Maude St and Rivonia Rd; tel: 011-783 4620*, is an attempt to emulate the ambience of a European village, with an

The Randlords

Modern South Africa was forged by the discovery of diamonds in Kimberley and gold on the Witwatersrand – discoveries that brought immense wealth and power to a few, extreme poverty and misery to many.

Thousand of fortune-hunters from all parts of the world rushed south when the first discoveries were announced. They were content to work their claims, scratching and scrabbling under the scorching South African sun and nursing their fevered dreams. A few – a couple of dozen men, mostly from Europe – took a cooler, more measured and ruthless approach. They staked and worked claims, of course, but they also supplied the goods and services the others needed to survive. Wheeling and dealing, ducking and diving, they gained control of the diamond fields, and, from 1886, went on to take charge of the gold mines in the north.

The Randlords, as they were dubbed by British newspapers, led the lives of merchant princes, living in large, ostentatious mansions, building up art collections, setting up foundations and scholarships – and laying the political foundations that brought about the harsh oppressions of apartheid.

The chief player in this Byzantine drama was Cecil John Rhodes, whose vision of a block of British territory from the Cape to Cairo made him the darling of Victorian capitalism – until 1896, when discovery of his complicity in the ill-fated Jameson Raid forced him to resign as Prime Minister of the Cape Colony.

Others who flaunted themselves on South Africa's gold- and diamond-studded stage were the showman and entrepreneur Barney Barnato, Alfred Beit, Solly Joel, Samuel Marks, Lionel Phillips, Joseph Robinson and Julius Wernher. A later member of the cast was Ernest Oppenheimer, whose family still controls the international diamond market.

201

open-air crafts market, jewellery and accessory boutiques, music and book stores, restaurants, cinemas and four floors of underground car parking. The **Hyde Park Shopping Centre**, *Hyde Park, off Jan Smuts Ave*, also houses some delightfully chic – and expensive – shops.

Fleamarket World, *off Marcia and Allum Rds, Bruma; tel: 011-786 0776* (open Tues–Fri 0930–1800, Sat 0830–1800, Sun 0900–1800) is as much a tourist attraction as a market, pulling in more than 2.5 million visitors a year. Its weekday count of 320 stalls swells to more than 620 at weekends and there are 15 restaurants to feed hungry shoppers and sightseers. A great place for souvenir-hunting and African entertainment.

The **Jo'burg Market** is held in *Mary Fitzgerald Sq.*, near the Market Theatre, *corner Bree and Wolhuter Sts; tel: 011-832 1641* (open Sat 0900–1600). Stalls sell African arts and crafts, jewellery and fashion goods. The

Michael Mount Organic Market, *corner Culross and Main Rds, Bryanston; tel: 011-706 3761* (open Thur and Sat 0900–1300) has 110 stalls offering produce and craft articles, and there is a shady tea garden for shoppers. A night market is held monthly (open Tues nearest full moon 1700–2100).

In the bad old days, Fordsburg was bulldozed flat and its Indian inhabitants evicted. Now they are back with a colourful – and aromatic – neighbourhood of 300 shops. **Oriental Plaza**, *Main Rd, Fordsburg; tel: 011-838 6752*, sells herbs, spices, brassware and brilliantly coloured fabrics.

And finally, take a look at the extraordinary **African Herbalist Shop**, *14 Diagonal St, corner Twist and Koch Sts*, opposite Johannesburg Art Gallery; *tel: 011-838 7352* (open Mon–Sat 0730–1700), a *muti* shop, where advice and traditional African medicines are dispensed. Guided tours are available.

SIGHTSEEING

Best place for an overview of what you will be up against when touring Johannesburg is the **Top of Africa**, the observation deck on the 50th floor of the Carlton Centre, *Commissioner St; tel: 011-331 6608* (open daily 0900–2330). Some 200m above street level, the deck gives a spectacular view of the city and its surroundings, and on a clear day you can see as far as the **Magaliesberg**, a mountain range 80 km to the north-west.

Guided Tours

Guided coach tours of the city and environs are organised by **Springbok Atlas**; *tel: 011-493 3780*, **Welcome Tours**; *tel: 011-328 8050*, and **Magari**; *tel: 011-453 5635*. For a walking tour, try **Historical Walks of Johannesburg**; *tel: 011-673 8409*. **Gold Reef Guides**; *tel: 011-496 7100*, can provide a personal guide. Visits to a working gold mine must be booked in advance; contact **Gold Mine Tours**; *tel: 011-498 7100*. To visit Soweto – and other locations – contact **Jimmy's Face to Face Tours**; *tel: 011-331 6109*.

Bill Harrop's Original Balloon Safaris, *PO box 67, Randburg 2125; tel: 011-705 3201/2; fax 011-705 3203*, presents an exotic opportunity to view the Magalies River Valley and Haartebeespoort Dam area from a hot-air balloon. A minibus collects passengers – before dawn – from hotels in Johannesburg and Sandton, and transports them to the launch site. Flights, lasting up to 90 mins, are followed by a champagne brunch and take place daily, weather permitting; about R800 per person charge.

Museums and Galleries

Any tourist's first stop should be at the excellent **Museum Africa**, *121 Bree St; tel: 011-833 5624* (open Tues–Sun 0900–1700; R2). Collections from a number of museums (now closed) have been gathered under the substantial roof of a vast, former market warehouse in the revitalised **Newtown Cultural Precinct**, which also houses the Market Theatre Complex (see p.199). Eventually, it is hoped the consolidated collections will present the full multi-cultural canvas of South Africa's history.

Meanwhile, there are sections on geology, San rock paintings, traditional African art and costume, and the history of Johannesburg. A small, but realistic display depicts conditions in a gold mine, while another shows the home life people had to endure in the townships and squatter camps. A more cheerful section traces the development of kwela and other township music. The **Bensusan Photography Collection** covers the story of image recording from pinhole camera to CD-Rom, backed up by a powerful photographic exhibition of South African life.

Nearby, the **South African Breweries' Centenary Centre**, *Becker St, Newtown Cultural Precinct; tel: 011-836 4900* (open Tues–Sat 1100–1800; R10) tells the story of that other great South African love – beer – and how people have brewed it across the globe and through the centuries. Visitors get the chance to sample some of the breweries' products.

Designed by Sir Edward Lutyens and opened in 1915, the **Johannesburg Art Gallery**, *Klein St, Joubert Park; tel: 011-725 3130* (open Tues–Sun 1000–1700; free) houses a strong collection of South African and international art, with works by El Greco, Van Gogh, Henry Moore, Picasso and Rodin.

The **Bernberg Fashion Museum**, *corner Jan Smuts and Duncombe Aves, Forest Town; tel: 011-339 7170* (open Tues–Sat 0900–1300, 1330–1700; free) covers two centuries of women's fashions, jewellery and accessories, displayed in an authentically furnished Victorian house.

Military hardware on show at the **South African National Museum of Military History**, *Hermann Ekstein Park, Erlswold Way, Saxonwold; tel: 011-646 5513* (open daily 0900–1630; R2) includes fighter aircraft, tanks and artillery from both world wars, and there are sections on the conflicts in Angola and Namibia.

The **South African Transport Museum**, *Old Concourse, Johannesburg Railway Station Complex, De Villiers St; tel: 011-773 9118* (open Mon–Fri 0730–1545; R2) houses a remarkable collection of model trains, as well as displays on all aspects of the development of transportation in South Africa.

The City Nobody Wanted

Old white South Africa – the South Africa of segregation – had a problem. On one hand, it wanted the blacks kept out of the way and out of sight. On the other, it needed their labour, especially for menial domestic jobs and unattractive work at slave-labour rates of pay.

Committed to the notion of 'separate development', the Nationalist government passed the Native Urban Areas Act in 1923. The idea was to prevent black people from moving into the cities by setting up special townships for them miles away.

In the 1930s, farmland on the south-west fringes of Johannesburg was purchased by the city council, who wanted to develop a city for 80,000 Africans. Little happened until 1944, when the first areas were laid out. Officially, it was known as the South Western Townships, but it wasn't long before the people who lived there started calling it Soweto, an abbreviation with an oddly authentic African ring.

From the start it was the city nobody wanted. The white administration, who would have preferred not to have it there at all, provided the barest of amenities. For the residents, it was an uncomfortable location, lacking adequate utilities and far from the city centre, where work was available.

But Soweto grew. It grew from the hopes of the thousands of dispossessed Africans who poured in – not only from other parts of South Africa, but also from countries as far away as Malawi and Zambia. Today, its population is a guestimated 3.5 million.

Soweto has always been at the vanguard of African political aspirations. Nelson Mandela lived here as a young activist and lawyer (tour guides will point out his old home), and Winnie Mandela still has a grand home not far away.

The city has witnessed – and continues to witness – dreadful violence and stark contrasts between privilege and deprivation. But there is a vibrancy, a creativity and, above all, an amazing racial tolerance that makes Soweto the City of Hope.

203

Other Major Attractions

Gold Reef City, *off Xavier Rd, 8 km south of the city centre via M1 (signposted)*; tel: 011-496 1600 (open Tues–Sun 0930–2300; R20, free after 1700 weekdays) has become one of the most popular tourist attractions in South Africa. Built around the shaft of what was once the richest gold mine in the world (with underground tours), this theme park–cum-living museum recaptures the riotous times of Johannesburg's gold-rush era. There are reconstructed streets with pubs and restaurants. Live demonstrations include the pouring of liquid gold into bullion. The Gold Reef City International Dancers entertain with traditional tribal and miners' gumboot dances. And there are a few rides for gentle thrills.

At the opposite end of town, the

Johannesburg Zoo, *Herman Ekstein Park, Jan Smuts Ave, Parktown*; tel: 011-646 2000 (open daily 0830–1730; R10) is set amongst beautiful gardens. The 55 hectare zoo houses some 300 species of animal, many endangered, and is also used as a venue for open-air art exhibitions and concerts.

The **University of Witwatersrand Planetarium**, *Yale Rd, Milner Park*; tel: 011-716 3199 (presentations Fri 2000, Sat 1500, Sun 1600 in English; Sat 2000 in Afrikaans) offers a great introduction to the astronomy of the southern skies, and an opportunity for northern hemisphere dwellers to locate the Southern Cross. There are also no fewer than 26 small specialist museums at the university, some of the more interesting covering palaeontology, medicine, zoology, music and art.

JOHANNESBURG– BLOEMFONTEIN

From the industrial satellites to the south of Johannesburg, this route leads to the vast open prairie-like vistas of the Free State, visiting communities on the banks of the Vaal River and towns built on gold. It is not one of the most inspiring routes in the book, but there is more of interest along the way than first meets the eye.

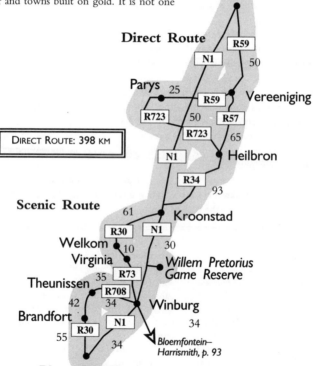

Johannesburg

Direct Route

R59

N1

50

Parys 25

R59 **Vereeniging**

R723 50 R57

R723 65

DIRECT ROUTE: 398 KM

N1 Heilbron

R34

93

Scenic Route 61 Kroonstad

R30 N1

Welkom 10 30

Virginia Willem Pretorius

Theunissen 35 R73 Game Reserve

R708

42 34 Winburg

Brandfort N1 34

55 R30

34 Bloemfontein–
Harrismith, p. 93

Bloemfontein

204

ROUTES

DIRECT ROUTE

Leave Johannesburg heading south on the N1 and stay on it until you see a signpost for Bloemfontein town centre. Distance: 398 km; allow 6 hrs.

SCENIC ROUTE

From central Johannesburg, take De Villiers Graaf Hwy and the Southern Bypass to the R59, which leads directly to **Vereeniging** (50 km). Continue along the R59 through Sasolburg and under the N1 to **Parys** (25 km). From here, take the gravel R723 south-east, back under the N1, to

Heilbron (50 km). If you wish to miss Parys and avoid the gravel road, the R57 heads due south from Vereeniging to Heilbron. Take the R34 south-west from Heilbron through **Kroonstad** (93 km) to Odendalsrus and turn left on to the R30 to **Welkom** (61 km). **Virginia** is 10 km south of Welkom on the R73.

From Virginia, continue south on the R73 to the junction with the N1. Turn left and head north for about 15 km for the turn off to the **Willem Pretorius Game Reserve** (signposted; see p.94). Turn right to go straight to **Winburg**, where you can connect to the Bloemfontein–Harrismith route (see pp. 93–99). At Winburg, turn right onto the R708 to **Theunissen** (34 km), then turn left and head south on the R30 to **Brandfort** (42 km). From here, continue south on the R30 for 55 km to Bloemfontein. Distance: 445 km; allow 1–2 days.

TRAINS

The Algoa train and the Amatola run daily from Johannesburg to Bloemfontein via Kroonstad. Journey time: 7 hrs. The Algoa departs at 1430 and the Amatola departs at 1245. See OTT Table 3508.

BUSES

At least four buses a day run from Johannesburg to Bloemfontein, mainly in the afternoon. They follow various routes – most go via Kroonstad and Welkom, although some go through Parys. Journey time: 6 hrs. See OTT Table 3537.

VEREENIGING

Tourist Office: Vaal Tourism Committee, *tel: 016-503 009.*

ACCOMMODATION

The 4-star **Riviera International Hotel and Country Club**, *Mario Milani Dr.; tel: 016-222 861, fax: 016-212 908* (expensive) is a spacious 100-room waterside hotel, with excellent sports facilities including an 18-hole golf course.

Club Koppisol Holiday Resort *(Ce), De Deur, 8 km north of Vereeniging; tel: 016-556 1112, fax: 016-556 1155* (cheap–moderate,

depending on the season) has self-catering chalets and a caravan park in a country setting with a pool, entertainment, a games room and supermarket.

SIGHTSEEING

Vereeniging, south of Johannesburg, was founded by Randlord Sammy Marks (see Pretoria, p.302) to exploit massive local coalfields. Its mines were soon joined by several large power stations, a huge steel mill and other heavy industry. It achieved fame as the site of the peace talks which ended the Anglo-Boer War in 1902, although the treaty which bears its name was actually signed on Laing's Nek Pass (see Johannesburg–Ladysmith, p.222).

Although Vereeniging is an industrial city, it has parks and riverside sites for such activities as swimming, water skiing, hiking, bird-watching, golf and horse riding. Art galleries and studios in the **New Vaal Meander**, offering a variety of arts and crafts, are open on the first weekend of every month, Sat 0900–1700, Sun 1130–1700. An annual **Art Festival** takes place Aug–Sept. Just west of Vereeniging is the infamous township of **Sharpeville**, where, on 21 March 1960, huge crowds gathered to burn their pass books in a protest against apartheid. Police badly overreacted and fired into the crowds, killing 69 and wounding 178. The shock wave of revulsion that swept around the world first brought the Struggle to international attention. The day is now commemorated by a South African public holiday, Human Rights Day.

PARYS

Tourist Information: *tel: 0568-2131.*

ACCOMMODATION

Mimosa Gardens, *Boom St, Parys; tel: 0568-2312, fax: 0568-76636* (cheap) has pleasant 4–6 bed self-catering bungalows along the banks of the Vaal River. In peak season (Dec–mid Jan), minimum booking is for 10 nights. Caravan stands available, with concessions for seniors, and a restaurant on site.

SIGHTSEEING

Nobody could even remotely regard Parys as a large, frenetic city, yet it was named after the

French capital. For some reason, the 19th-century surveyor involved at the planning stage saw the Vaal River as Africa's answer to the Seine, and visualised a metropolis like Paris developing on its banks.

The wide Vaal River, flowing fast after summer rains over its flat, rocky bed, is dotted with wooded islands and sustains a diversity of birdlife. The pretty highveld town attracts many visitors with its gardens, shady picnic spots and largely uncommercialised ambience. The river's islands provide hideaways for un-obtrusive angling and ideal water for skiing, rowing, sailing, canoeing and motor boating. There is also a trip boat – it doesn't operate when the river is in spate; at other times tickets for short trips are sold on board.

A suspension bridge in Parys's north-east corner leads to **Golf Island**, a 62 hectare property with a nine-hole golf course. There are campsites and caravan parks in the area, and across the road from the river, people can cool off on a twisting water chute and enjoy a beer on the terrace.

The **Mimosa Holiday Resort** (see above; open to day visitors; admission R10 per car plus R8 per adult) has rowing boats (R5 for 30 mins), a swimming pool (open Sept–Easter), licensed restaurant, trampoline and recreation hall with squash and badminton courts.

HEILBRON

Tourist Information: *tel: 01614-22014.*

Founded in 1872, and capital of the Free State Republic for a single week in May 1900, the town has its history and heritage outlined in the **Riemland Museum**, housed in an old Jewish synagogue. A monument honours British soldiers who died in the Anglo–Boer War, and there is a memorial to the women and children who died in the local concentration camp.

Driving between vast fields of sunflowers, wheat, maize and grazing cattle, it is difficult to imagine the bloodshed in the battle which raged between the Voortrekkers and Ndebele warriors in 1836. The site of the most vicious battle, **Vechtkop**, fought on 16 Oct 1836, is 25 km south of the town, marked by a monument and small battlefield museum.

KROONSTAD

Tourist Information: *Old Town Hall, Cross St; tel: 0562-22601.*

ACCOMMODATION

Kroon Park Holiday Resort, *Louw St, Kroonstad; tel: 0562-31492, fax: 0562-31941* (cheap) provides a choice of self-catering apartments and chalets, a campsite and caravan park in a riverside setting with lawns and willows. The resort has an Olympic-size pool, putting green and licensed restaurant. Boats can be hired on the Vaal River. **Verblyden Guest House**, *Debsie Farm, by the N1, Kroonstad; tel/fax: 0562-24031* (cheap) is a cheerful farm which permits pets, and is convenient for the highway and several 4x4 trails.

SIGHTSEEING

Established on either side of the Vals River in 1855, Kroonstad was named by an esteemed Voortrekker leader, Sarel Celliers, after his horse, *Kroon*, who is believed to have drowned in a local stream. A **statue of Celliers** by Coert Steynberg stands in the *Main St*. It depicts him in a dramatic pose on a gun carriage, while taking the Blood River Vow stands (see Background p. 64). His life and the history of the area, including the discovery of gold, are depicted in the **Sarel Celliers Museum** in *Steyn St.*

Other fine old buildings in the town centre include the **Old Post Office**, with prison cells in its backyard, the **Old Town Hall**, *Cross St*, and the **Old Market Building** – the latter two are National Monuments. The imposing **Dutch Reformed Church**, *Cross St*, is worth a look, as is the monument in the grounds to the 1838 Burghers. Modern South African art is displayed in **St Patrick's Cathedral**.

Like many of the other towns on this route, Kroonstad had a turn at housing the Free State Government, from 13th March–11th May, 1900. It later became the site of a huge British concentration camp, whose cemetery remains in the industrial area.

WELKOM

Tourist Information: *Clock Tower, Stateway; tel: 057-352 9244.*

A **Rennies Travel/Thomas Cook for-eign exchange** is located at *Shop 11, Sanlam Plaza, corner Buiten St and Stateway; tel: 057-353 3041.*

ACCOMMODATION

The 3-star **Welkom Hotel**, *283 Koppie Alleen Rd; tel/fax: 057-51411* (cheap–moderate) offers smoking or non-smoking rooms, a pool and sauna. The large **Welkom Inn**, *corner Tempest Rd and Stateway; 5 km from the airport; tel: 057-357 3361, fax: 057-352 1458* (moderate) is also 3-star, with 120 rooms and 28 suites. **Camping**: **Sirkel Caravan Park**, *281 Koppie Alleen Rd; tel: 057-53987.*

SIGHTSEEING

Welkom was laid out in 1947 and likes to present itself as a garden city and an attractive residential neighbourhood, with wide roads, plenty of trees, and bizarrely, no traffic lights (robots). Instead, it has a couple of dozen roundabouts, otherwise known as traffic circles or rotaries, and because traffic filters into these, there are few 'stop' signs. It also has all the trappings of prosperity – busy shopping malls, a thriving theatre and entertainment scene, green parks, an airport and a lively business centre. But at heart, Welkom is all about gold. This is an industrial town sitting squarely on top of some of the largest gold deposits in the world. **Underground mine tours** are popular with visitors (ask at the Tourist Office for details and bookings). Welkom claims to have the world's deepest wine cellar, 857m below the earth's surface in the **St Helena Mine**.

Industry tends to banish birdlife, but water pumped up from the deep underground mines has settled in evaporation dams and shallow pans, attracting over 200 species of bird, includ-ing several species of seagull, flocks of pink flamingos, ibis, Egyptian geese and marsh owls. The **Theronia Pan**, within the city, attracts thousands of waterbirds and is also the home of the Flamingo Yacht Club, which has a clubhouse, restaurant and picnic grounds. Other good bird-watching sites are **Flamingo Pan**, *off the R30 west of town*, and **Witpan**, *Oppenheimer Park, 4 km south-east.*

Entertainment from pop to opera, ballet,

drama and music recitals is staged at the **Ernest Oppenheimer Theatre**, *Civic Centre*, named after Sir Ernest Oppenheimer who was the power behind the planning of the Welkom garden city project. Four splendid tapestries hang in the foyer, and art exhibits are regularly staged in the hallway.

The **Goldfield Racetrack** at Welkom is a national motor racing venue, and the **Welkom Air Show** is an annual event in late Oct or early Nov. Crafts made by handicapped people can be seen at the town's hospital, also named after Oppenheimer.

VIRGINIA

Tourist Information: *Library, Virginia Gardens; tel: 057-212 3111.*

The 2-star 30-room **Tikwe Lodge**, *corner Highlands and Valley Dr.; tel: 057-212 3306, fax: 057-212 5059* (cheap–moderate) offers peaceful accommodation beside the Sand River, with a small game farm nearby. Nearby, and run by the same management, the **Virginia Park Holiday Resort** (cheap) has self-catering cottages and rondavels, camping and caravan sites, and a pool.

The Sand River flows through the centre of this garden town, giving it a holiday air, with people swimming, boating, water skiing, fish-ing or hiking along a riverside trail. Virginia is also a hard-working town, having grown fast since gold was struck in the 1940s. **Under-ground goldmine tours**, which may include mine dancing displays, are available at **Harmony Goldmining Co** and **Western Holdings** (ask the tourist office for details and bookings).

WILLEM PRETORIUS GAME RESERVE

See p. 94.

WINBURG

See p. 94.

THEUNISSEN

Tourist Information: *tel: 017-52-101.*

In the heart of the maize-growing region, Theunissen lies in the shadow of towering grain elevators. Cellar tours are available at the

207

Gold

Gold is virtually indestructible, malleable and pure. Much of the gold worn as personal ornamentation has been recycled from something else. Extracting it is a painstaking business. It takes an average 100,000 ounces to produce just one ounce of gold, yet it is so common in prosperous parts of the world, east and west, that almost everyone possesses some.

It has been used for adornment since the stone age, but its real value shot skywards when the gold standard was adopted as an international benchmark of currency in the late 19th century.

The timing could not have been better. In 1886, George Harrison picked up a stone on a farm in the Witwatersrand and marvelled at the traces of gold on it. As a miner, he knew what he was holding. But it was a fluke find that happened to turn up on the surface. All the worthwhile gold reefs were far below the surface.

It did not take long for hordes of prospectors and adventurers, their eyes agleam with avarice, to invade the region from near and far. One of the greatest gold rushes of all time had begun. Shanty towns mushroomed and South Africa's economy rocketed.

Men swarmed in to provide the hard physical labour up to 900m below the surface, and bars and brothels were set up to service the influx. The god-fearing Boers were dismayed by the rape of their resources by foreign interlopers and by the debauchery which accompanied the miners. Fortunes were made, and the biggest fortunes of all were made by those who had the resources to move in at once with mining machinery and start hacking the deeply hidden gold out of the ground. These were the diamond kings of Kimberley – Cecil Rhodes, Barney Barnato and a few other 'Randlords' (see p. 201).

The precious metal continues to be mined. Mine headgear stands silhouetted against the sky and spoil heaps form great walls across the goldfields. Nearly 40,000 tons of gold have been hauled out of South Africa's mines, though annual production has decreased in recent years.

In the new South Africa, workers are not so easily exploited. Thousands of lives have been lost in more than a century in appalling mining accidents, and today's workers demand better pay and conditions. Output is down and, no doubt, profits too, but the Republic still produces about a quarter of the world's gold. And even the slagheaps are being re-mined using new techniques, to squeeze out the last remnants of the gold and other trace metals.

208

Goldfield Wine Estate, *north of town, on the Welkom road*, which also grows 26 species of cycad. The **Erfenis Dam Nature Reserve**, *tel: 057-724 211, on the R708 between Theunissen and Winburg, 10 km from Theunissen*, is a 3200 hectare dam and popular local fishing spot. Campsites, ablutions and *braai* are provided. Game can be seen in the 400 hectare nature reserve.

BRANDFORT

Tourist Information: *tel: 051-403 3436*.

Much of Brandfort's history is associated with the Anglo-Boer War. Established in 1865, a concentration camp was set up near the town in 1901, occupied by 1022 women and children. Conditions were so bad that 375 of them became ill and died. A memorial commemorates them. The first aircraft in South Africa was built here by M.L.J. Weston, who flew it for the first time in Kimberley on 18 June 1911. The last version of his engine is on display in Bloemfontein.

More recently, Mrs Winnie Mandela spent a period in Brandfort under house arrest.

BLOEMFONTEIN

See pp. 78–81.

JOHANNESBURG–GABORONE

This route leads from the sophistication of Johannesburg's northern suburbs, through the gentle foothills of the Magaliesberg mountains, and on into the bushveldt country of the North West Province. Cotton, tobacco and citrus are the chief crops in this area, while underground resources yield chrome, platinum, granite and tin. The Magaliesberg are pretty, green and lush, but as the Botswana border nears, temperatures become more torrid, and the terrain drier and more desert-like.

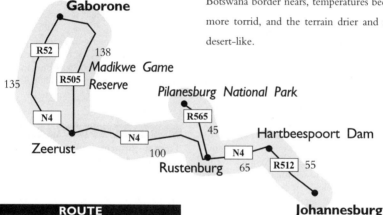

209

ROUTE

From central Johannesburg, take the M27 (it starts from *Bree St* as *Queen Elizabeth St)* and head north through Braamfontein, where the highway becomes *Jan Smuts Ave.* Continue along this route for 11 km, then turn left onto *Republic Ave.* After a further 2.5 km turn right onto the R512 *(Hans Strijdom Ave).*

About 30 km from central Johannesburg the road passes the **Lion Park**. After intersecting with the R28, the R512 continues past Lanseria Airport and, after a further 12 km, passes the entrance to **Lesedi Cultural Village**. After Lesedi, the highway, now very rural in character, passes **Hartbeespoort Dam**, crosses the R560 near Kosmos, then intersects with the N4. Turn left (west) on to the N4 for 65 km to **Rustenburg**. Keep going on the N4 for a further 100 km to **Zeerust**, the last South African

Johannesburg

DIRECT ROUTE: 355 KM

town before the border. From Zeerust there are two routes to Gaborone. The N4 continues west for 63 km to Lobatse in Botswana by way of the Skilspadsnek/Pioneer Gate border post (open daily 0700–2000). Gaborone is 72 km from Lobatse. The alternative route from Zeerust is to head north on the R505, passing through **Madikwe Game Reserve**, before crossing the border at the Kopfontein/ Tlokweng post (open daily 0700–2200). The distance from Zeerust to the border is 121 km, and Gaborone is a further 17 km from Tlokweng. There is no more direct route.

Distance: 355 km; allow 5 hrs without stops; 1–2 days with sightseeing (more if including stops at Lesedi and Sun City).

JOHANNESBURG TO HARTBEESPOORT DAM

The first section of the drive is through the ever-expanding urban sprawl of Johannesburg's northern suburbs. As you finally reach real countryside, the **Lion Park**, *30 km north of Johannesburg on the R512; tel: 011-460 1814* (open daily 0800–1630; R20) is home to some 60 lions, who are fed daily 0900–0930. There are also ostriches and a number of antelope, including gemsbok, impala and wildebeest. Traditional African life is on show in the Ndebele village.

The **Lesedi Cultural Village**, *Honeydew, 42 km from Johannesburg on the R512; tel: 01205-51394; fax: 01205-51433* (open daily) offers a much more detailed and imaginative tour of South Africa's 'Rainbow Nation'. 'Lesedi', a Sotho word meaning 'place of light', was given spiritual significance by Moshoeshoe, the founder of the Southern Sotho nation. As refugees from many nations joined him during the terrible Mfecane wars, Moshoeshoe greeted each new day with the words, 'Ke bona lesedi' – 'I see the light'. This cultural village, on the edge of the Magaliesberg mountain range, is endeavouring to extend the Sotho king's vision of hope to the peoples of the new South Africa – and to introduce white South Africans to the culture of their African neighbours.

Three programmes are offered at Lesedi. The **Monati Lunch Experience** (daily 1130–1400; from R125 per person) involves a walk through two homesteads followed by a feast, singing and dancing. The **Boma Evening Experience** (daily 1630–2130; from R145 per person) involves a walk through four homesteads and an extended fireside feast under the stars. **Homestay** (with accommodation in one of 16 twin rooms with private bathrooms; R620 per person sharing, R765 single) includes dinner, bed and breakfast, and all cultural activities.

Guests are escorted to each homestead by a *Makhosi* – a diviner-healer – who instructs them on protocol and introduces them to the chief.

Those spending a night at the village will be introduced to members of the chief's family and settled into a hut built in the traditional style, but furnished to the standards of western comfort. After visiting tribal homesteads and learning about the traditions of the Pedi, Sotho, Xhosa and Zulu nations, guests join a parade of singers and musicians and make their way to the *boma* – the village centre – for a surprisingly tasty traditional meal of meat stew, beans, maize porridge, spinach and pumpkin. And as they eat, the singing and dancing begins. Everyone joins in.

The people who live here are no theme park performers. They are real members of the tribal groups they represent, living out real, working lives in each of the four homesteads that make up the village. With members of their families – among them some very young children – they raise and herd cattle and goats, grow crops, brew beer from maize and sorghum, and carry out the daily tasks of a traditional community. The experience is one few visitors will ever forget.

HARTBEESPOORT DAM

Tourist Information: Publicity Association, *PO Box 106, Brits 0250; tel: 01211-582 274; fax: 01211-582 203*. **North West Tourism Council**, *Borekelong House, Lucas Mangope Hwy, Mmabatho 8681; tel: 0140-843 040; fax 0140-842 524*, open Mon–Fri 0830–1630. A glossy brochure published by the council includes information on accommodation of all grades throughout the province.

ACCOMMODATION

There are a number of small hotels, guesthouses and bed and breakfast homes scattered between the towns of Brits, Hartbeespoort and Kosmos, which is the most up-market of the three. The **Magaliesburg Park Country Club**, *Farm de Rust, Brits; tel: 01207-71315; fax: 01207-71373* (expensive) is a three-star resort on the banks of the Magalies River, with 123 self-catering rooms and a restaurant. The **Mount Amanzi Lodge**, *Old Rustenburg Rd, Hartbeespoort; tel: 01211-530 541; fax: 01211-530 510* (moderate–expensive) is another popular resort, with attractively thatched buildings, offering

165 self-catering rooms and the back-up of a restaurant. The **Village Lodge**, *59 St Monica St, Schoemansville, Hartebeespoort tel/fax 01211-530 786* (moderate; non-smoking) is a traditional bed and breakfast lodge in tranquil surroundings.

SIGHTSEEING

Surrounded by the rolling green hills of the Magaliesberg, **Hartebeespoort Dam** is a popular haven for city-dwellers from Johannesburg and Pretoria, both less than an hour's drive away. The lake, created by damming the Crocodile River, covers 1620 hectares and offers boating, angling, swimming, walking and bird-watching. The **Hartebeest Cableway**; *tel: 01211-30706*, takes 6 mins to cover a 2.3 km trip to a viewpoint high above the dam.

RUSTENBURG

Tourist Office: *Town Hall Building, Plein St; tel: 0142-943 194; fax: 0142-20181* (open Mon–Fri 0830–1630, Sat 0900–1300). On the ground floor of Town Hall Building, opposite the entrance to the town museum. Helpful and friendly staff will produce a list of local hotels, guesthouses and bed and breakfasts, but can give no indication of prices and cannot deal with reservations. A restricted restaurant list is included in the brochure, *Rustenburg – Another Glorious Day in Africa.* Attractions and major hotels in and around the city are well-signposted.

ACCOMMODATION

There are two or three moderately priced hotels, mostly catering for business travellers, in the centre of Rustenburg, but the choice widens if you are prepared to drive up to 20 km beyond the outskirts, where several resorts hope to pick up the overspill from nearby Sun City.

In town, try the **Bergsig Lodge**, *7 Peperboom Ave, Safari Gardens, Rustenburg; tel/fax: 0142-33343* (cheap–moderate), a bed and breakfast offering air-conditioned accommodation with private entrances. Further out, but owned by the municipality, the **Rustenburg Kloof Holiday Resort**, *7 km south-west on the Donkerhoek Rd; tel: 0142-971 352; fax: 0142-20181* (cheap) is magnificently set, close to a rocky gorge which forms part of the **Rustenburg Nature Reserve**. Accommodation is in fully-equipped chalets and there is a caravan park, as well as a heated pool, tennis, volley ball, indoor games and walking trails. Almost next door, but totally secluded, the more upmarket **Karos Safari Hotel**; *tel: 0142-971 361; fax: 0142-971 220* (moderate–expensive) has 119 rooms overlooking the gorge. The **Olifantsnek Country Hotel**, *16 km south on R20; tel: 0142-92208; fax: 0142-92100* (moderate) has single and double rooms and chalets in delightfully wooded surroundings.

Campsites: Ananda, *8 km south-west of Rustenburg on the Donderhoek Rd; tel: 0142-973 875;* **Cynthiana**, *5 km south of Rustenburg on the R30; tel: 0142-92361.* Both also have budget-priced rooms and chalets.

EATING AND DRINKING

The most interesting restaurant in the area is **Omaruru** (expensive) at the Karos Safari Hotel (see Accommodation above). Omaruru is a twin dining car built for South African Railways and Harbour, and in service from 1923 to 1978. It was brought out of retirement by Karos in 1985 as a static restaurant. Dishes dedicated to classical express trains throughout the world are served in the restrained elegance of wood panelling, bevelled mirrors and brass lamps. There are a number of fast-food cafés in the centre of town, especially in the shopping area at the junction of N4 and R30. **Mike's Kitchen**, *Van Staden St; tel: 0142-26676*, and **O'Hagan's Irish Pub**, *Van Staden St; tel: 0142-973 903*, are both open daily.

SIGHTSEEING

A busy, sprawling market town, Rustenburg lies on the western edge of the Magaliesberg. It is the third oldest white settlement in the old Transvaal Province, founded when trekkers first moved into the area in the mid 1800s. On the western outskirts of the town are two platinum mines, said to be the world's largest. Rustenburg's associations with the old Boer republic are marked by a **statue of Paul Kruger**, *Plein St,* in front of the Town Hall, and a **statue of Andries Hendrik Potgieter and Andries Pretorius**, *Reformed Church Sq.,*

211

which marks the spot where the two Voortrekker leaders reached a reconciliation, averting civil war. Most exhibits in the **Rustenburg Museum**, *Town Hall, Plein St; tel: 0142-973 111* (open Mon–Fri 0830–1630, Sat 0900–1300, Sun 1500–1700; R3) cover aspects of early Boer life with photographs and artefacts. Pride of place goes to the original flag of the ZAR. Iron Age archaeological finds are also displayed.

Located on the northern slopes of the Magaliesberg and encompassing the spectacular Rustenburg Kloof (gorge), **Rustenburg Nature Reserve**, *Donkerhoek Rd; tel: 0142-31050* (open daily 0800–1800; R10) has a number of antelopes, leopards, black-backed jackals and hyenas. Hiking and camping available.

SIDE TRACK
FROM RUSTENBURG

Seven km west of Rustenburg on the N4, turn north on to the R565 to reach **Pilanesburg National Park** and **Sun City**, 45 km from town.

Boekenhoutfontein, signposted as **Krugerhuis**, *19 km from Rustenburg on the R565; tel: 083-263 0928/9* (open daily 1000–1700; R5) is Paul Kruger's farmstead, with three dwellings, a schoolhouse and farmyard. Family furnishings and artefacts are displayed. Guided tours start in the 1862 Pioneer House and take in the original farm cottage (1840), the main homestead (1872), built in Eastern Cape style, and the 1890 schoolhouse, with a cow-dung floor.

Ten km further along the R565, the small town of **Boshoek** has a post office, two supermarkets and two petrol stations. The **Sundown Ranch Hotel**, *Rustenburg/Boshoek Rd; tel: 0142-733 121; fax 0142-733 114*, has a three-star Satour rating, 101 rooms, restaurant and ladies' bar. **Struthio**, *on the R565 on the northern outskirts of Boshoek; tel: 0142-733 245* (open daily 0830–1700; R10) is an ostrich show farm, with guided tours, tea garden and curio shop.

ZEERUST

Tourist Office: *Town Clerk, Town Hall, Box 92, Zeerust 2865; tel: 01428-21081.*

The best accommodation in town is at the **Abjaterskop Hotel**, *Rustenburg Rd; tel/fax: 01428-22008* (moderate), which has a three-star Satour rating, a restaurant, ladies' bar, swimming pool and 19 rooms.

Often blisteringly hot – even in winter the temperature rarely falls much below 30°C – Zeerust is a bustling, but not very interesting, crossroads town. It is best known as the major community in the Marico Bushveldt – the land made famous by the writer Herman Charles Bosman – and for the production of *mampoer*, the local firewater distilled from apricots, peaches and other fruit. The Marico Bushveldt, which extends north of Zeerust towards the Botswana border, has a great variety of indigenous trees and plants, and an abundance of game and birds. A number of dams in the area have facilities for angling and other watersports.

From Zeerust, the R49 heads south to Mafikeng and Mmabatho to join the Johannesburg–Kimberley route (pp. 213–219).

MADIKWE GAME RESERVE

On the R505, 90 km north of Zeerust; operated by North West Parks Board, *tel: 01466-55960/3; fax: 01466-55964.* Established in 1991 as a joint venture between the state, local communities and the private sector, Madikwe, flush up against the Botswana border, is now the fourth largest game reserve in South Africa, with an area of 75,000 hectares. All Big Five live here, together with a host of other animals, including the rare wild dog, cheetah and brown hyena, and over 250 species of bird. Accommodation is provided in a guesthouse and two lodges with luxury air-conditioned chalets, operated by concessionaires. New lodges are being planned. The **Madikwe River Lodge** *(Pf/LH); tel: 014778-891/2; fax: 014778-893* (expensive) is a luxury game lodge, with thatched chalets and river views.

GABORONE

See pp. 341–345.

JOHANNESBURG–KIMBERLEY

Two quite different alternatives are presented on this journey. The first, fast but relatively unexciting journey, heads straight along the N12, fringing the border between North West Province and the Free State for much of the way, with two or three major cities and a number of reasonably sized towns spaced out along the route. The other option strikes through the remote heart of the North West Province, almost touching Botswana at historically evocative Mafikeng before swinging south across hot, flat savannah bushland to the diamond territories of the Vaal River, once the frontier between British South Africa and the Boer Transvaal.

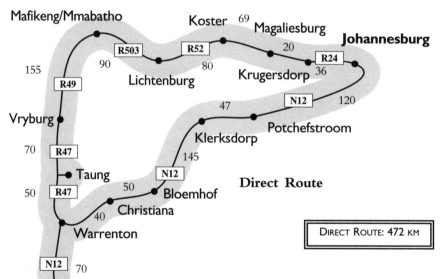

Scenic Route

Direct Route

DIRECT ROUTE: 472 KM

city's system of freeways. Within minutes of leaving the city centre, you can be speeding south towards **Potchefstroom**, **Klerksdorp**, **Bloemhof** and **Christiana** to enter the Northern Cape at **Warrenton**, just north of Kimberley. Distance: 472 km; allow 6 hrs.

ROUTES

DIRECT ROUTE

▶ The N12 forms Johannesburg's Southern Bypass and is easily reached from the

SCENIC ROUTE

▶ From the Carlton Centre in central Johannesburg, take *Commissioner St* west.

This is the start of the R24. Keep going along the same road for 36 km to **Krugersdorp**, for another 20 km to **Magaliesburg**, then for a further 69 km to Koster. At Koster, take the R52 to **Lichtenburg**, then turn on to the R503 to **Mafikeng/Mmabatho**.

From Mafikeng, the R49 curves gently south-eastwards through Stella to **Vryburg** (155 km), from where the R47 continues due south past **Taung** to connect with the N12 at Warrenton. Follow the N12 south to Kimberley. Distance: 640 km; allow two days.

TRAINS

The Trans Karoo (departs 1230) and The Diamond Express (departs 2040) run from Johannesburg to Kimberley, calling at Krugersdorp, Potchefstroom, Klerksdorp, Bloemhof and Warrentown. Journey time: 10½ hrs. OTT Table 3519.

There is also a train on Fri from Johannesburg to Kimberley via Mafikeng and Vryburg. Journey time: 15 hrs. See OTT Tables 3517 and 3520.

BUSES

At least one bus a day leaves Johannesburg for Kimberley via Klerksdorp, with bus companies Greyhound Citiliner and Translux. Journey time: 6½ hrs. See OTT Table 3541.

POTCHEFSTROOM

Tourist Information: *Carnegie Library Building, corner Potgieter and Kerk Sts; tel: 0146-299 5130; fax: 0148-294 8203* (open Mon–Fri 0745–1300, 1345–1630).

North West Tourism Council, *1st Floor, Royal Building, 44 Lombard St; tel: 0148-293 1611; fax: 0148-297 2802.*

ACCOMMODATION AND FOOD

'Potch', as the city is known locally, is a university centre, so there are times – notably at the beginning and end of an academic year – when there is a rush on accommodation.

There are a couple of reasonable hotels, including the central **Kings Hotel**, *25 Potgieter St; tel: 0148-297 5505* (moderate) and the 3-star **Elgro Hotel**, *60 Wolmarans St; tel/fax: 0148-297 5411* (moderate–expensive), which

has 103 rooms. However, the city's guesthouses probably provide the best accommodation. At the top end of the range, **Oudrift**, *about 4 km from the town centre at the northern end of Kerk St, Noordburg; tel 0148-297 4939; fax 0148-297 1272* (moderate) is an elegant, Mediterranean-style villa, with additional accommodation in well-furnished rondavels in the riverside grounds.

Pine Grove Manor *(Pf), Plot 464, Vyfhoek tel: 0148-297 4129; fax: 0148-297 6689* (cheap–moderate) is a 5-room guesthouse, with bar, restaurant and pool, set in lovingly tended gardens. **Smilin' Thru Chalets**, *Brakfontein tel: 0568-2123; fax 0568-2129* (cheap–moderate) is a game farm and resort with 1–2 star self-catering chalets on the banks of the Vaal River. Amenities include bar, restaurant, pool, hiking and sports facilities.

There are a few eating places in the area around the intersection of *Potgieter* and *Kerk Sts*, but Potchefstroom is not well blessed with catering establishments.

SIGHTSEEING

Potchefstroom ('stream of the chief Potgieter') was founded in 1838, when the Voortrekker leader Andries Potgieter decided to settle with his people on the banks of the Mooi River. As the original capital of the Zuid Afrikaanse Republiek, the place where the constitution of the Transvaal was written and the ZAR flag was raised for the first time, it holds a special place in Afrikaaner history.

Potchefstroom Museum, *corner Gouws and Wolmavans Sts; tel: 0148-299 5020* (open Mon–Fri 1000–1300, 1400–1700, Sat 0900–1300, Sun 1430–1630; free) houses art, cultural and historical exhibitions and displays the only surviving ox wagon from the Battle of Blood River in 1838 (see p. 270). The **Old Fort and Cemetery** (freely accessible), are the ruins of a fort where the Boers besieged British troops for 95 days during the first Anglo-Boer War. The British dead were buried in the adjacent cemetery.

Totius House Museum, *Church St; tel: 0148-299 50047* (open Mon–Fri 1000–1300 1400–1600, Sat 0900–1300, Sun 1430–1700; free) is the 1904 home of J.D. du Toit, poet, theologist and translator of the Afrikaans Bible. **Goetz/Fleischack Museum**, *New Market Sq., tel: 0148-299 5031* (open Mon–Fri 1000–1300 1400–1600, Sat 0900–1300, Sun 1430–1700; free) is the restored home of magistrate Andreas Marthinus Goetz, who served on the bench 1870–1881. It is furnished in Victorian style.

The **Dutch Reformed Church**, *opposite the City Hall, Church St*, is the oldest existing church building north of the Vaal River and is a national monument. The cornerstone was laid on 26 Dec 1859 by the first minister, Dirk van der Hoff, whose bust, by the sculpter Coert Steynberg, stands at the main entrance.

KLERKSDORP

Tourist Information: *Plant House, Municipal Gardens; tel: 018-462 3919.*

ACCOMMODATION

Most accommodation in Klerksdorp is in bed and breakfasts and guesthouses, although the 2-star **New Kemonate Hotel**, *149 Kafferskraal, Ventersdorp/Klerksdorp Rd; tel/fax: 018-462 6650* (moderate) has 30 rooms, restaurant, bar and pool. **Acacia Guest House and Restaurant**, *30 Austin St; tel/fax: 018-86563* (moderate–expensive) offers luxurious accommodation in 11 air-conditioned en suite bedrooms with their own garden entrances, while the **North Hills Country House**, *Brady Ave; tel/fax: 018-468 6416* (moderate) is a private game park with suites, some non-smoking accommodation, and a restaurant offering European cuisine. **Rose Cottage Country House** *(Pf), 4 Sport St, Flamwood; tel: 018-85403; fax: 018-83291* (cheap) is a charming guesthouse with lavishly appointed rooms and a full meal service.

SIGHTSEEING

Named after the area's first magistrate, Jacob de Clerq, Klerksdorp was founded in 1837 when twelve Voortrekker families settled on the banks of the Schoonspruit. The discovery of gold in 1865 brought thousands of prospectors and today, Klersksdorp is still the centre of a prosperous agricultural and mining area, producing gold and uranium.

The **Klerksdorp Museum** is in a grand sandstone building erected as a prison in 1891.

Exhibits portray life in the prison alongside displays on archaeology, geology and social history. **The Old Cemetery** contains the graves of British soldiers who fell in the Anglo-Boer War and of 986 children who died in the city's concentration camp. For the energetic, the **Ou Dorp hiking trail** is a 12 km meander through the old part of the city, settled by the original Voortrekker families, also taking in the remains of several prehistoric kraals.

On the outskirts, **Goudkoppie**, contains old mining shafts dating from the 1880s and inscriptions carved into rock by British soldiers who camped there during the Anglo-Boer War.

BLOEMHOF

This small country town, *145 km south of Klerksdorp; 47 km north of Christiana*, grew up around the frontier ferry across the Vaal River and the inevitable diamond workings along its banks. Today, it is dwarfed by the massive **Bloemhof Dam**, one of the largest in South Africa, with a dam wall 4.27 km long and 35.2 m high, its lake covering a massive area of 22,270 hectares.

Along its shores are several small nature reserves, including the **Bloemhof Dam Nature Reserve**; *tel: 01802-31706*, along the northern bank, nearest the road, and the **Sandveld Nature Reserve**, *10 km north-west of Bloemhof on the R34; tel: 01802-31701*, a magnificent expanse of dry thornveld with numerous animals, including gemsbok, white rhino and kudu.

CHRISTIANA

Tourist Information: *Town Clerk, Robyn St; tel: 0534-2206/7/8.*

ACCOMMODATION

There is really only one place to stay in Christiana – at the **Aventura Vaal Spa**, *tel: 0534-2244; fax: 0534-2354* (cheap–moderate), a large family resort with 82 one- and two-bedroom self-catering chalets, mineral baths and a small game reserve.

SIGHTSEEING

Christiana was founded hurriedly in 1870 by

215

the Transvaal government, which wanted to establish ownership of the diggings after diamonds had been found in the Vaal River. It was named after the daughter of M. W. Pretorius, first president of the Zuid Afrikaanse Republiek. The **Diggers' Museum** at the Spa displays diamond mining equipment and photographs.

From here on, the road south towards Kimberley roughly follows the line of the Vaal River. At several points along the journey, small diamond claims are still being worked and it is possible to watch the open mining in progress.

KRUGERSDORP

Tourist Information: Westour (Western Gauteng Tourism Association), *tel: 011-412 2701; fax: 011-412 3663.*

ACCOMMODATION

The 3-star **Auberge Aurora**, *off Pappegai St, Rant En Dal, Krugersdorp; tel: 011-956 6307; fax 011-956 6089* (expensive) is a tranquil country house hotel surrounded by restful gardens, with seven luxury rooms. Just out of town, the **Kromdraai Guest Farm**, *Kromdraai, Krugersdorp; tel: 011-957 0220; fax: 011-957 0230* (moderate–expensive) has en suite rooms furnished with Cape Dutch antiques, and offers guests the possibility of horse riding or hiking.

In Sterkfontein, **Brennan's Country Accommodation**, *Sterkfontein; tel: 011-956 6021; fax: 011-956 6356* (cheap–moderate) offers non-smoking bed and breakfast or self-catering facilities in a secluded location with panoramic views, near game reserves and the Sterkfontein Caves.

SIGHTSEEING

In Dec 1880, 4000 Boers gathered on the farm of Paardekraal, near the Vaal River. Each solemnly laid a stone on a cairn which eventually stood 3m high. On the top, they raised the flag of the ZAR. It was a symbolic act of defiance against British rule, which led almost directly to the outbreak of the first Anglo–Boer War. Seven years later, the farm was chosen as the site of a new administrative centre for the local goldfields. The town that grew up was

named Krugersdorp, after the President. It is still a major mining centre, which also became the first in the world to produce uranium as a by-product of gold.

The **Sterkfontein Caves**, *on the R563, Hekpoort Kromdraai Rd, Krugersdorp North; tel: 011-956 6342* (open Tues–Sun 0900–1600; admission charge) were discovered in 1896 by an Italian looking for gold. What he uncovered, however, proved to be one of the world's most significant prehistoric sites. In 1936, the first skull of *Australopithecus africanus*, an ape man from 2.5 million years ago, was found here by Dr Robert Broom. In 1995, scientists researching other bones found in the cave identified another missing evolutionary link, in the 3.3 million-year-old 'Littlefoot', who appears to represent the point at which man came down from the trees and began to walk upright. A collection of fossils is displayed in the Robert Broom Museum. The caves contain six massive chambers. Local Africans believe the waters of a deep underground lake can cure blindness and other ailments.

The **South African National Railway and Steam Museum**, *Randfontein Rd, off R28; tel: 011-888 1154* (open first Sun of the month) has a number of old locomotives.

MAGALIESBURG

Tourist Information: *tel: 0142-771 432.*

ACCOMMODATION

There is a good selection of accommodation nearby, mostly in small hotels and guesthouses. Classical music concerts are staged monthly at the **Mount Grace Country House Hotel**, *Magaliesburg; tel: 0142-771 350; fax: 0142-771 202* (expensive), a delightful, thatched hotel, which is a popular weekend escape for rich Johannesburgers. It was a finalist in the 1996 Satour Hotel of the Year Award. No children under 12. The more affordable **Magaliesburg Country Hotel**, *41 Main Rustenburg Rd; tel/fax: 0142- 77 1109* (moderate) has 3-stars, 20 rooms and accommodation on a dinner, bed and breakfast basis.

Hartley's Victorian Guesthouse, *Main Rustenburg Rd; tel: 0142-772 301; fax: 00142-774 506* (moderate) is a bungalow inn, built in

1876, which offers Victorian picnics, walks and bird-watching.

SIGHTSEEING

Magaliesburg town centre is a place of sprawling low-level buildings – stores and workshops – in a hotchpotch of architectural styles, but the outlying areas and surrounding hilly countryside form an attractive and popular weekend destination. The range of hills, named after a local 19th-century chief, Magali, stretch nearly 120 km to Rustenburg, taking in the Hartbeespoort Dam (see Johannesburg–Gaborone, pp. 210–211). Much of the area is protected nature reserve offering excellent hiking and bird-watching, with some 230 species, including 250 breeding pairs of Cape Vultures. Magaliesburg is also the country terminus of the **Magaliesburg Express**, *tel: 011-884 1154*, an historic steam train which makes the run from Johannesburg Station twice a month (see p. 57).

LICHTENBURG

Tourist Information: *Town Clerk, Box 7, Lichtenburg 2740; tel: 01441-25051.*

ACCOMMODATION

There are few accommodation options in this crossroads town at the heart of North West Province. The central, 2-star **Hotel Elgro**, *6 Scholtz St; tel: 01441-2 3051; fax: 01441-23055* (cheap–moderate) is within walking distance of shops and other amenities and has 58 rooms, restaurant, bar and pool. The pretty **Little Dreams Guesthouse**, *16 Swart St; tel: 01441-42111; fax: 01441-22100* (cheap) offers continental or cooked breakfast and rooms with en suite bath or shower.

SIGHTSEEING

The discovery of a magnificent gem on Elandsputte Farm in 1926 started the world's greatest diamond rush, and within 12 months 100,000 prospectors were on the diggings, spread along the course of a dried-up river. Today, the route followed by the diggers is a popular walking trail through a number of small villages. In town, the **William Annandale Art Gallery**, *Public Library, Melville St,* houses a

valuable collection of paintings by well-known South African artists.

Operated by the National Zoological Gardens, the **Lichtenburg Game Breeding Farm**; *tel: 01441-22818* (open daily; admission charge) was set up as part of an augmented breeding programme for endangered animals. The farm has 40 different rare species from all parts of the world.

MAFIKENG/MMABATHO

Tourist Offices: **Tourist Bureau**, *Mafikeng Museum, Martin St; tel: 0140-810023* (open Mon–Fri 0800–1600, Sat 1000–1230). This single-room office at the museum entrance has a helpful staff, but printed information is sparse. You can obtain lists of accommodation and eating places, while maps of the area and booklets dealing with Mafikeng's role in the Anglo-Boer War are on sale.

North West Tourism Council, *Borekelong House, Lucas Mangope Hwy, Mmabatho; tel: 0140-843 040/1–8; fax: 0140-842 524* (open Mon–Fri 0830–1630). This is the council's administrative headquarters, but advice and printed material on the entire province may be obtained in the reception area.

GETTING AROUND

The twin cities of Mafikeng and Mmabatho, a new city built as capital of the former 'independent homeland' of Bophuthatswana, lie mainly on opposite sides of *Voortrekker St* (the R52), which links Lichtenburg and the Botswana border, 25 km north.

Most visitors to Mmabatho make straight for **Megacity**, a gigantic shopping centre about 8 km from the centre of Mafikeng – the junction of *Main St* and *Voortrekker St*. Otherwise, Mmabatho consists mainly of industrial estates, offices and government administrative blocks. Most of Mafikeng's attractions are associated with the historic siege and are within walking distance of each other, in and around the city centre.

ACCOMMODATION

The **Mmabatho Sun Casino Hotel** *(SI)*, *Lobatsi Rd; tel: 0140-891 111; fax: 0140-891 746* (expensive); and the **Molopo Sun Hotel**

217

(SI), Dr Mokgobo Ave, off University Dr.; tel: 0140-24184/9; fax: 0140-23472 (expensive) are both large and very comfortable, set up like most of their sister hotels to provide gambling in the former homelands. Cheaper, but equally bland, the **Protea Hotel** *(Pa), corner Station Rd and Martin St; tel: 0140-810 177* (moderate) is in the city centre, close to the museum and other attractions.

The **Ferns Guesthouse**, *12 Cooke St; tel/fax: 0140-815 971* (expensive), offers bed and breakfast accommodation in 12 en suite chalets set around a swimming pool. Dinner can be arranged. No children under 12.

Out of town, the **Manyane Game Lodge**, *5 km from Mafikeng on the Zeerust road (R27); tel: 0140-816 075/5; fax: 0140-816 0020* (cheap–moderate) has self-catering chalets.

EATING AND DRINKING

Megacity in Mmabatho has a good selection of fast food and cheap–moderate eating places. Mafikeng has a **Steers** steakhouse, *Station Towers, Hatchard St* (moderate), and an **O'Hagan's Irish Pub and Grill**, *Tillard St* (moderate). **Letatsi**, in the Molopo Sun Hotel (see above) has a wide selection of surprisingly inexpensive snacks and light meals, and the **Ditha Restaurant**, in the same hotel, is a good choice for a moderately priced lunch or dinner.

SIGHTSEEING

First colonised by Boer mercenaries, who got land in exchange for service from two Baralong chiefs, the town of Mafikeng (meaning 'the place of boulders') was properly founded by Sir Charles Warren, leader of a British expeditionary force in 1885, as part of British Bechuanaland (now Botswana). It was near here that Jameson launched his ill-judged and ill-fated raid on the Transvaal (see p. 66) that led, eventually, to the outbreak of the Second Anglo-Boer War.

It was the Siege of Mafeking, which began on 14 Oct 1899, lasting a horrific 217 days until 17 May 1900, that placed the little town firmly in the pages of history. It remained the capital of British Bechuanaland until Botswana's independence in 1965. When Bophuthatswana was established as one of apartheid's homelands in

1977, Mmabatho, a new city based on a former township, was designated as capital and Mafikeng was relegated to suburban status. A final flurry of fame came shortly after the political handover in 1994, when the hard-right Afrikaaner AWB, led by Eugene Terre-Blanche, tried and failed to start an armed insurrection here.

Now back within the fold of the new, democratic South Africa, North West Province has decided that the older city, with a history involving all racial groups and encompassing more than the siege and the founding of the Boy Scout movement deserves the premier status, and Mafikeng is back on top.

Mafikeng Museum, *Martin St; tel: 0140-816 102* (open Mon–Fri 0800–1600, Sat 1000–1230; free) tells the story of the region in general and the city in particular from centuries before the Anglo-Boer War. There are also fascinating exhibits of traditional herbal medicines and remedies, while one room is devoted to railway transport, and other sections deal with the characters and events that helped shape the city's history. Inevitably, however, it is the informative section on the Siege of Mafikeng that will be of most interest to visitors. Artefacts ranging from commemorative mugs and siege bank notes to photographs, weapons and documents bring the whole episode into sharp focus.

Mafikeng Cemetery, *corner Carrington and Carney Sts*, contains the graves of British soldiers and members of the British South Africa Police and Town Guard who died during the siege. One row of crosses placed very close together marks the trench used as a mass grave for the men who died there during an attack in 1899. Another group of crosses honours the dead of the Irish Sisters of Mercy, who arrived in Mafikeng in 1899 to run a school and found themselves involved in nursing and other tasks associated with the siege. **St. Joseph's Convent**, which they occupied 1899–1968, is at the *Voortrekker St* end of *Victoria St*.

The **Mafeking Club**, *corner Robinson and Tillard Sts*, built in 1894, still bears the marks of damage caused by a shell during the siege. On the opposite side of *Tillard St*, is the **Masonic Lodge**, in which Boer prisoners of war were held before being shipped off to the island of St

The Trap That Caused a Siege

It was one of the most famous chapters of British Imperial history: a force of less than 1000 British troops gallantly holding out against an army of up to 8000 Boers, who had besieged a hot, dusty little town in the middle of Africa.

The siege was, in fact, originally a trap set by the British commander, Col. Robert Baden-Powell, with the aim of pinning down the Boers. At first, it worked wonderfully, with commanders, Generals Cronje and Snyman and Commandant Botha, realising too late that they could neither take the well-defended town nor retreat from the challenge.

However, while it was of strategic value for two months, the war progressed and Mafeking became irrelevant, except for its publicity value. It dragged on for seven months, while Baden-Powell and 1708 whites (including about 700 troops), and 7500 Africans (about 2000 of them refugees, the rest Barolong tribespeople) were boxed up in a town which covered an area of about 1000 square metres. Pundits agree that it would not really have made much difference if they had surrendered.

However, Baden-Powell, who was the very model of an English soldier-aristocrat, was obsessed by his command. He armed a black militia and young boys, whom he formed into a cadet corp (thereby founding the Boy Scout movement). When rations were tight for the whites, he simply took the black rations and let the Africans eat horse food; eventually he took all food rations away from the 2000 black refugees.

By the time the siege was eventually lifted, 354 members of the Barolong volunteer force were dead – more than twice the total British dead – and many had died of disease and starvation.

The British, and Baden-Powell in particular, emerged from the siege covered in glory and medals, amidst public euphoria. It is only recently with the release of his journals and other official papers that the true story has been told.

219

Helena. The **Anglican Cathedral**, was built of Zimbabwe stone by Sir Herbert Baker, as a memorial to those who died during the siege.

STELLALAND

Tourist Office: **Stellaland Tourism**, *60 Market St, Vryburg; tel: 05391-782 200; fax: 05391-3482.* The office can provide information on resorts, farm holidays, agricultural tours and hunting opportunities.

The 2-star **International Hotel**, *43 Market St, Vryburg; tel/fax: 05391-2235* (moderate) offers bed and breakfast accommodation in 34 rooms. The **Taung Sun** *(SI), R47, Taung Station; tel: 01405-41820; fax: 01405-41788* (expensive) is a definite step up, a luxurious hotel and casino, with 39 rooms, restaurant, cinema and entertainment facilities.

The western region of North West Province is known as Stellaland. On this route, you are in the area from the small community of Stella to just south of Taung. Extensive cattle ranches, and the fact that Vryburg is home to the largest cattle sales in the southern hemisphere, have earned the area its nickname, 'Texas of South Africa'.

There is relatively little to see, but people have been here for thousands of years. The small community of **Taung** hit the headlines in 1924, when a workman digging in a limestone quarry found the fossilised skull of a prehistoric baby. The Taung Baby, as the skull came to be known, had small canine teeth like those of modern humans, a brain with humanoid characteristics, and it walked upright. It was the first known example of *Australopithecus africanus*, one of the 'missing links' between ape and man (see also Background, p.61). Visitors to Taung today may visit the **Taung Heritage Site**, where a monument to the discovery of the skull has been erected.

KIMBERLEY

See pp.230–233.

JOHANNESBURG– LADYSMITH

This route south from the goldfields of Gauteng crosses the south-western corner of Mpumalanga on its way to the coalfields of northern Kwazulu-Natal. It is a journey through a troubled history, in territory long fought over by the Zulus, Sotho, and Swazi; the Boers and the Zulus; the British and the Zulus; and the British and the Boers. The southern section of the route also covers some magnificent scenery, across the vast mountain grasslands which connect the Natal and Mpumalanga Drakensburg.

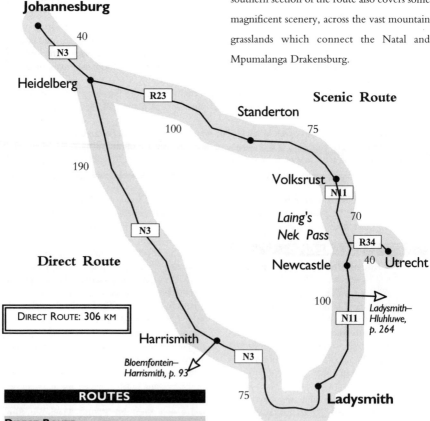

DIRECT ROUTE

➡ Leave Johannesburg on the N3 motorway, which forms the city's Eastern Bypass and is accessed by the main ring road. The N3 continues south to Durban. For Ladysmith, turn off at Sand River Valley and join the N11 for the last few kilometres into town. Part of the road (between Heidelberg and Harrismith) is a toll road. For Harrismith, see p. 98. Distance: 306 km; allow 4 hrs.

SCENIC ROUTE

➡ Leave Johannesburg on the N3, which reaches **Heidelberg** after 40 km. Continue south on the N3. Shortly after leaving the town, turn left onto the R23 and follow it for 100 km to **Standerton**, and another 75 km to **Volksrust**. From Volksrust and take the N11 south over **Laing's Nek Pass**. After about 40 km, a turning to the left, on the R34 leads to **Utrecht** (30 km). From here, there is a gravel road direct to **Newcastle** (40 km), but it is probably easier to return to the N11 and continue south. From Newcastle, remain on the N11 for a further 100 km to Ladysmith. After 32 km, a turning on the left, the R621, leads to Dundee and the heart of the Battlefields Area, see Ladysmith–Hluhluwe, pp. 264–271. Distance: 425 km; allow one day with stops.

TRAINS AND BUSES

The Trans Natal operates a train service from Johannesburg to Ladysmith via Standerton, Volksrust and Newcastle. Journey time: 8 hrs. OTT Table 3510.

Greyhound Citiliner run a daily bus service from Johannesburg (depart 1000) to Ladysmith via Standerton, Volksrust and Newcastle. Journey time: 6¼ hrs. OTT Table 3552.

HEIDELBERG

Tourist Information: *Public Library, corner Verwoerd and Ueckermann Sts; tel: 0151-3111.*

The **Heidelberg Guest House**, *29 Van Der Westhuizen St, Heidelberg; tel: 0151-95387, fax: 016-349 5387* (cheap) is a century-old former parsonage, offering double rooms with bath. The **Suikerbosrand Gasthuis**, *31 Pretorius St, Heidelberg; tel/fax: 016-341 7651* (cheap) provides rooms in a newly restored 1910 home.

The little town, founded in 1861, has more museums, albeit small ones, than one would expect, considering its size – and they are a diverse bunch. Domestic gadgets and household items from past ages, antiques and an art collection, can be seen at the **Museum and Cultural Information Centre**; *tel: 0151-*

2892. Old agricultural implements are displayed at the **Diepkloof Farm Musem**; *tel: 0151-2181.* The **Dynamite Museum**; *tel: 011-606 3206*, demonstrates the importance of explosives in South Africa's development and history. Early bicycles, motorcycles, cars and other vehicles are exhibited at the **Motor Museum**; *tel: 0151-6303.*

STANDERTON

This little town took its name from a farmer called Adriaan Stander, who worked the land on which it was established in 1876. During the Anglo-Boer War, a big bridge was blown up in the area and it was the site of heavy fighting and a siege, with 350 British troops trapped in town. Standerton then became a British garrison town until World War I. It is now an industrial centre and home to a major power station.

VOLKSRUST

Tourist Information: *Library, Joubert St, Volksrust; tel: 01773-2141.* Open Mon–Fri 0745–1300, 1400–1630.

The **Horseshoe Hotel**, *5 km from Volksrust on Standerton road; tel: 01773-2160, fax: 01773-51263* (cheap) has fully-catered cabins.

In 1881, Boer troops rested here to get their breath back after the battle at Majuba. Seven years later, when the Transvaal government decided to build the town, they named it Volksrust (Folks' Rest). During the second Anglo-Boer War, 772 Afrikaaner women and children died in the local concentration camp, a horrifying statistic commemorated in a major memorial (1918) in the town centre. A second memorial, on *Voortrekker St*, was erected in honour of those who fought in the 1881 war.

Just south of Volksrust on the N11, the **Majuba Battlefield** was the scene of the major deciding battle of the first Anglo-Boer War. Having made several futile attempts to cross Laing's Nek pass (see p. 222), on 27 Feb 1881, the British Commander, General Sir George Pomeroy Colley, led a troop of 554 men on an all-out assault of the 760m high Majuba Hill, which overlooked the pass and was under the control of Boer commandos. By morning, he and 91 other British soldiers were dead, a

221

further 134 were wounded. There were only two Boer fatalities. It was the final straw in the British efforts to break through the cordon. There are British and Boer memorials and a small museum on the battlefield.

A short way further along the N11, between Volksrust and Newcastle, is **Laing's Nek Pass**. At the top, a parking area with a diorama details the Langsnek Battlefield, where various British attempts to break through to the Transvaal failed. There are several graves and memorials at the summit. A signpost to **O'Neil's Cottage** indicates the home of Eugene O'Neil, which served as a makeshift hospital for British forces during the battle of Majuba. Following the disastrous British defeat, the peace treaty ending the war and recognising the independence of the Transvaal, was signed here on 23 March 1881.

UTRECHT

Tourist Office: *Civic Centre, Kerk St; tel: 03433-3041.* Open Mon–Fri 0900–1200.

The **Balele Mountain Lodge**, *5 km north of Utrecht on the Wakkerstroom road; tel/fax: 017-730 677* (cheap–moderate) has five partly-serviced chalets accommodating up to 24, and a caravan park. Activities include horseriding, trout fishing and hiking.

Originally the town, founded in 1853 and named after Utrecht in Holland, was an independent Boer republic, merging into Transvaal in 1860 and remaining part of it until 1902. It was heavily involved in the fighting in the Zulu and Anglo-Boer Wars before settling down to concentrate on coal-mining and agriculture. Contact the Tourist Office for details of **coalmine tours**.

A **museum**; *tel: 03433-3041* (open Mon–Fri 0730–1230, 1315–1600, weekends by appointment; phone Tourist Office), in a former parsonage, depicts life in the small town and the history of its Dutch Reformed Church. British soldiers are buried in the old part of the town's cemetery. In front of the **Dutch Reformed Church**, a marble plaque is the only memorial to a Russian soldier, Capt. Leo Powkrowsky, who fought with the Boers and was killed on Christmas Day 1900, when his men attacked the British garrison.

Several local buildings have been declared national monuments, including the Dutch Reformed Church, Old Drostdy and the Town Hall. Other fine buildings include the colonial-style Rothman House, Shaw House and Uys House (former home of the Afrikaner hero, Dirk Uys).

NEWCASTLE

Tourist Office: *Town Hall, Scott St; tel: 03431-53318.* Open Mon–Fri 0900–1600, Sat 0930–1130.

ACCOMMODATION

The **Majuba Lodge**, *corner Victoria St and Volksrust Rd; tel: 03431-55011; fax: 03431-55023* (moderate) offers comfortable chalets and a swimming pool. In its grounds, **Lawrie's**, *25 Victoria Rd; tel: 03431-26119* (moderate), is one of the nicest restaurants in town, in a turn-of-the-century manor house. The **Keg and Cannon**, *96 Allen St; tel: 03431-52307, fax: 03431-52308* (cheap) is an atmospheric English-style pub and restaurant, also offering accommodation. On its walls are pictures of old Newcastle and battle scenes from the Zulu and Anglo-Boer Wars. Chain hotels include the 2-star **Valley Protea Hotel** *(Pa), Ingogo Station Rd (off N1); tel: 03434-721 800, fax: 03434-746* (cheap), which offers colonial country comfort in the foothills of the Drakensbergs, and the 3-star **Holiday Inn Garden Court** *(Hd), corner Victoria and Hunter Sts; tel: 03431-28151, fax: 03431-24142* (moderate).

Campsite: **Municipal Caravan Park**, *Amcor Dam; tel: 03431-81273.* Rough camping is also permitted on some of the surrounding farms with hiking trails; ask the Tourist Office for details.

SIGHTSEEING

The cosmopolitan town, suitably dependent on coal and heavy industry, is 'twinned' with no fewer than twenty-five sister towns and cities around the world, all called Newcastle. The town grew from a small settlement known as Post Halt Two, a stop-over point for wagons and post-chaises. Hotels and places to eat were set up as the town formed a connection to the Orange Free State and the Transvaal. Today,

222

Newcastle is the largest conurbation in northern Natal, and even has a small airport with daily flights to and from Johannesburg and Durban.

It was the invasion of this Newcastle by the Boers on 15 Oct 1899 that led, five days later, to the first battle of the first Anglo-Boer War – the battle of Talana (see p. 269), and it was from here that General Colley headed out for the disastrous battle of Majuba (see p. 221).

It also played a part in the second Anglo-Boer War. Near Newcastle, remains of trenches dug by Boer soldiers can still be seen at **Botha's Pass**. General Sir Redvers Buller captured the Pass on 8 June 1900, enabling British troops to advance into the Orange Free State. **Fort Amiel**, *Memel Rd; tel: 03431-27211* (open Mon–Tues, Thur–Fri 0730–1600, Sat 0900–1300), a military base from 1867 to 1902, now houses the Newcastle historical and military museum, which includes a section on Rider Haggard, who used to live in the town.

Carnegie Museum, *Old Carnegie Library; tel: 03431-27211* (open Tues and Thur 0900–1300, Fri 1100–1600, Sat 0900–1200) has a collection of traditional and contemporary landscape paintings by South African artists, together with local crafts, including Zulu beadwork and ceramics.

Tours of the massive **Iscor** steelworks; *tel: 03431-47095*, are possible, but must be pre-arranged. Demonstrations of pottery making are available in the factory shop at **Mother Earth Pottery**; *tel: 03431-56622*. Purchases can be made there.

Every Sept an International Village event is held, emphasising the diversity of races living in the town, reflected in the cuisine, cultural events and crafts. There are numerous hiking trails in the mountains around the town, most privately owned and operated, ranging from easy day walks to heavy-duty two day hikes. For a full list and information on where to get permits and make bookings, contact the tourist office.

LADYSMITH

See pp. 265–266.

223

JOHANNESBURG/PRETORIA–KRUGER/SKUKUZA

The first section of this route heads east across the Highveld and some of South Africa's most forbidding industrial landscapes. All this changes as you begin to climb towards the grandeur of the Drakensbergs, through the vast eucalyptus and pine forests and magnificent mountain scenery of Mpumalanga, eventually toppling off the eastern escarpment to the lowveld bush and superb wildlife of the Kruger National Park. The area is stuffed full of some of the best accommodation that South Africa can provide, from bed and breakfast to luxury lodges; do your homework carefully and select exactly what you like.

224

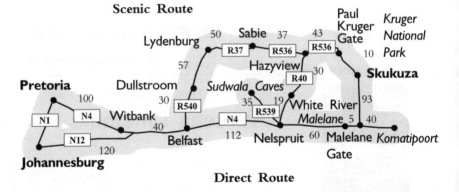

DIRECT ROUTE: 354 KM

ROUTES

DIRECT ROUTE

➡ Leave Johannesburg on the N12 or Pretoria on the N4, heading east. These join at Witbank and continue as the N4 the whole way to **Nelspruit**. In Nelspruit, turn north on to the R40 through **White River** (19 km) to **Hazyview** (30 km), then turn right on to the R536 to the Paul Kruger Gate (43 km). Skukuza is 10 km from the gate within the Kruger National Park. If you arrive in good time, an alternative is to continue through Nelspruit on the N4 for 65 km to Malelane Gate, and drive up to Skukuza through the park (93 km; allow 3 hrs). For all details of the Kruger National Park, see pp. 239–245. Distance: 354 km; allow 4½ hrs non-stop.

SCENIC ROUTE

▶ Leave Johannesburg on the N12 or Pretoria on the N4, heading east. These join at Witbank and continue on as the N4.

Stay on this for a further 76 km to **Belfast** (140 km from Pretoria). It is possible to do this first section of the route more slowly, via Cullinan, which is interesting (see p. 302), and the high-veld industrial towns of Bronkhorstspruit, Witbank and Middelburg, but your best bet is to get through them as fast as possible and allow plenty of time for the delightful route beyond Belfast.

From Belfast, take the R540 north to **Dull-stroom** (30 km) and **Lydenburg** (37 km), then turn right on to the R37, which heads east over the **Long Tom Pass** to **Sabie** (50 km). From Sabie, take the R536 through **Hazyview** (37 km) to the Paul Kruger Gate (43 km). Skukuza is 10 km beyond the gate. Distance: 367 km; allow one day (start early to make camp before the gates shut).

TRAINS

The Komati runs from Johannesburg, through Belfast and Nelspruit, to Skukuza. Journey time: 9¾ hrs. OTT Table 3503.

BUSES

Translux operate a bus service to Skukuza from Johannesburg via Nelspruit on Mon, Wed and Fri. Journey time: 9 hrs. Greyhound Citiliner run a daily service to Nelspruit. Journey time: 4¾ hrs. See OTT Table 3547.

NELSPRUIT

Tourist Information: Nelspruit Publicity Association, *Shop 5, Promenade Centre, Louis Trichardt St; tel: 013-755 1988/9; fax: 013-755 1350* (open Mon–Fri 0800–1700, Sat 0900–1600). Located in the city's attractive pedestri-anised shopping precinct, the office has a friendly and informative staff who will dispense information on accommodation, dining and attractions. A pay telephone is available for making reservations.

The **Mpumalanga Tourist Authority**, shares the Nelspruit Publicity Association office; *tel: 013-752 7001, fax: 013-752 7013*, and is the official state tourist board.

ACCOMMODATION

Nelspruit has some good accommodation, including a number of hospitable bed and breakfasts, but relatively few people stay here, preferring the magnificent hills surrounding White River and Hazyview. Nelspruit's most central accommodation is in the 3-star **Hotel Promenade**, *Louis Trichardt St, opposite Promenade Centre; tel: 013-753 3000; fax: 013-752 5533* (moderate). Formerly the town hall, the building adds a Mediterranean touch to the city centre, with its red-tiled roofs and clock tower. It has 73 rooms – some non-smoking – and a full range of facilities. The one-star **Town Lodge Nelspruit**, *corner Gen. Dan Pienaar and Koorsboom Sts; 013-741 1444; fax: 013-741 2258* (cheap–moderate) is primarily a business hotel with 106 rooms, some non-smoking. Other chains include: F1.

For something less anonymous, try the **Shandon Lodge** *(Pf), 1 Saturn St; tel/fax: 013-744 9934* (cheap), a Victorian-style bed and breakfast on the hill overlooking the town, or head out a bit further to the **Rest Country Lodge** *(Pf), Uitkyk Rd, off Ferreira St, 9.5 km from city centre (signposted); tel/fax: 013-744 9991/2* (moderate), one of the area's newest guesthouses, offering well-furnished two-storey cottages whose private sun decks have superb views across the foothills of the Drakensbergs. Dinner by arrangement.

Campsites: Nelspruit has two caravan parks. **Polka Dot**, *Johannesburg Rd (N4); tel: 013-752 5088*, offers chalets and cottages for rent; **Rippling Waters**, *White River Rd (R40); tel: 013-752 7847*.

EATING AND DRINKING

There is a reasonable selection of eating places dotted around the city centre, many of them familiar chains, with alfresco dining available around the Promenade Centre area. **Villa Italia**, *corner Louis Trichardt and Paul Kruger Sts; tel: 013-752 5780* (moderate), is a spacious Italian restaurant with an eclectic menu.

There are two moderately priced steak-houses: **Arkansas Spur**, *Louis Trichardt St; tel: 013-753 3478*, and **Black Steer**, *Brown St; tel: 013-755 3780*. Reliable family fare can be found at **Mike's Kitchen**, *Promenade Centre; tel: 013-752 7758*, and **O'Hagan's**, *corner Gen. Dan Pienaar and Piet Retief Sts; tel: 013-741 3584*. Both moderately priced.

225

SIGHTSEEING

The capital of Mpumulanga and commercial hub of the lowveld, Nelspruit is a large, modern town with wide tree-shaded streets. Conveniently placed on the N4, with road links in all directions and served by Rovos Rail and the Blue Train May–Sept (see pp.54–55), the city has good facilities, but is primarily a business and shopping centre, and not a tourist attraction in its own right.

The **Nelspruit Historical Trail** (route brochure available from Publicity Association) is a 1-hr walk winding from the Promenade Centre to the Civic Centre, *Nel St*. Features include a restored ox wagon in the library gardens, *corner Louis Trichardt and Brown Sts*.

Rock paintings, vervet monkeys, antelopes and a diversity of birds may be seen in **Nelspruit Nature Reserve**, *Andries Pretorius St, south of the Civic Centre* (open daily; free). There are several walking trails which can be covered in 1–6 hrs.

The biggest attraction in the immediate area is **Lowveld National Botanical Gardens,** *intersection of R40 and R37, north side of the Crocodile River, 6 km outside Nelspruit; tel: 013-752 5531* (open daily 0700–1630; R5). With a broad collection of lowveld vegetation on view, the gardens encompass one of the most comprehensive cycad collections in the world. Maps for a 2-hr Crocodile River trail are available at the entrance gate.

The **Promenade Centre** is Nelspruit's shopping Mecca, with a wide variety of shops, stores and market stalls, where you can buy craft items, leather goods and souvenirs. **Flea markets** trade at *Prorom Sq.*, (Fri); *Promenade Centre* (Sun); and **Hall's Gateway** (Sat–Sun).

⤳ SIDE TRACKS FROM NELSPRUIT

From Nelspruit, the N4 heads east to Malelane (63 km), Komatipoort (64 km) and the Mozambique border (open 0600–1800). From Nelspruit to Maputo (see pp. 356–364), it is 238 km. Make sure you leave in plenty of time if driving through. It is not sensible to travel the Mozambique section after dark. The area is rapidly increasing in popularity as another access point to the Kruger National Park, but there is also terrific scenery, often stunningly dramatic, sometimes mountainous, sometimes crossing flatlands adorned with sugar canes or banana plantains.

MALELANE

Malelane is a dusty country town, best known as the south-eastern entrance to Kruger National Park. The **Buhala Country House Hotel** *(Pf), 10 mins drive from the Malelane Gate (follow signs from the main road); tel: 013-790 4372; fax: 013-790 4306* (moderate–expensive) is a delightful small lodge on the southern bank of the Crocodile River, with impeccably furnished rooms and a broad verandah with built-in game-viewing. It offers dinner, bed and breakfast and the food is superb. No children under 12. The **Malelane Sun Intercontinental** *(Ic), also on the river, close to the Malelane Gate; tel: 013-790 3304; fax: 013-790 3303* (expensive) is a much larger hotel, with 99 luxury chalets, two presidential suites, a paraplegic room and full range of facilities.

KOMATIPOORT

Komatipoort is a further 45 km east along the N4. If you are planning an overnight stop before crossing into Mozambique, Hectorspruit would be the better choice. **Gazebo Game Lodge**, *394 Lowhills; tel/fax: 013-790 4526* (moderate) offers dinner, bed and breakfast in six rooms, with full range of amenities and activities. The **Izinyoni Lodge** *(Pf), 1742 Seekoeiweg; tel/fax 013-790 4555*, is a pleasant bush lodge-style bed and breakfast in the Marloth Nature Reserve, overlooking the Crocodile River and Kruger National Park. Lunch and dinner available. **Campsites: Komatipoort Caravan Park**; *tel: 01313-50213*, or **Crocodile Bridge Restcamp**, within the Kruger (see p. 242).

SUDWALA CAVES

The magnificent **Sudwala Caves**, *35 km north-west of Nelspruit, off the R539; tel: 013-*

733 4152 (open daily 0830–1630; tours last 90 mins) are carved out of dolomitic rocks over 2000 million years old. They have been inhabited since the Stone Age; their last tenants a group of 19th-century Swazi warriors led by Somquba, the son of King Sobhuza I. Having stolen some of the king's cattle, the group fled into the caves while another royal son, Mswati, laid siege outside. His attempts to smoke them out failed because of natural air vents, but Sombuqa was eventually killed. The caves are named after one of his lieutenants, Sudwala, who took over command of the frightened band.

The caves are thought to be nearly 30 km in length, although they have never been fully explored. The regular tours only go in about 600m, but even this small section is a wonderland of giant chambers, fantastic stalagtites and stalagmites. There is a 6-hr tour each Saturday for the enthusiastic (book in advance).

Next door, the small **Owen Museum** has a collection of somewhat tired but very large concrete dinosaurs, set in a lovely natural forest.

WHITE RIVER

Tourist Office: *corner Peter Graham and Kruger Park Sts; tel/fax: 013-750 1723.*

ACCOMMODATION

Like most small towns on the edge of the Kruger National Park, White River is geared up for tourists and has a good selection of accommodation.

The area's best-known hotel, with an international reputation, is the 4-star **Cybele Forest Lodge**, *off the R40; tel: 013-750 0511; fax: 031-750 2839* (expensive). This prestigious property is the ultimate mountain hideaway, with superb food, six double rooms and six suites (some with private pools) set among 125 hectares of gardens, timber plantations and meadows. The larger, 4-star **Pine Lake Sun** *(SS), main Hazyview Rd (R40); tel: 013-751 5036; fax: 013-751 5134* (moderate) has 67 rooms, a suite and extensive facilities, all in a tranquil, lakeside setting.

There are also two charming guesthouses in the vicinity: **Igwala Gwala Country Lodge** *(Pf), follow signs from the R40; tel: 013-750 1723; fax: 013-750 1999* (cheap–moderate), where garden apartments sprawl through delightful grounds, and the thatched, 'cottagey' **Kirby Country Lodge** *(Pf), Jatinga Rd, off the R538; tel: 013-751 2645; fax: 013-750 1836* (moderate), which does dinner, bed and breakfast, in a woodland setting next to the White River.

The **Hotel Bundu**, *Nelspruit Rd (R40); tel/fax: 013-758 1221* (cheap) has self-catering chalets and cottages and a caravan park, as well as hotel accommodation, on 290 hectares of unspoilt bush.

Campsite: Municipal Caravan Park, *in the town centre; tel: 01311-31176.*

SIGHTSEEING

Known as the nut capital of South Africa, White River is the centre of a flourishing citrus, fruit and timber producing area, where several dams provide popular fishing spots. Bougainvillaea, date palms and jacaranda trees line the streets of this attractive little town, which has become one of the best shopping areas on the tourist beat. This is a good area in which to look for souvenirs.

A thriving colony of over 60 local artists sell their work at the **Artists' Trading Post**, *Christie's Village Mall, Theo Kleyhans St; tel: 031-751 1053*. Other good buys are the huge bags of macadamia, pecan and cashew nuts sold by the street vendors.

Out of town, visitors are welcome to tour the cellars of the **Rottcher Wineries**, *Nutcracker Valley, off R40 about 3 km south of White River; tel: 031-751 3884* (open Mon–Sat; free), where unusual orange and ginger liqueurs are sold in hand-painted stoneware jugs.

To the north, en route to Hazyview, there are two excellent craft centres. The **Sibelala Tourist Centre**, *2 km north of White River, on the R40; tel: 013-751 1777*, sells crafts, safari clothes, books and home-made jams and cheese. It also has a nursery with a wide range of indigenous plants and bonsai trees. Its finest point however is the **Bag-dad Café**, which is not only one of the best restaurants in the area (moderate; booking advised in the evening),

227

but also produces excellent takeaways and picnic hampers.

Continue north and you reach **Kraal Kraft**, *14 km north of White River, on the R40; tel: 013-758 1228*, a huge curio shop with a restaurant, small museum and African village.

HAZYVIEW

See Kruger–Phalaborwa, p. 250.

BELFAST

Set amid arable and sheep and cattle grazing country, Belfast was originally founded as a trading post on the new Johannesburg to Delagoa Bay Railway. The town was named after the Northern Ireland capital, around 1890, by an anonymous, homesick Irish immigrant. It has the honour of officially being the coldest spot in South Africa. There are good trout fishing opportunities in the area.

The **Belfast Hotel**, *103 Vermooten St, tel/fax: 01325-30461* (cheap) is a small hotel, with games room and curio shop.

DULLSTROOM

ACCOMMODATION

The 2-star **Dullstroom Inn**, *corner Teding Van Berkhoit and Oranje Nassau Sts, Dullstroom; tel: 01325-40070, fax: 01235-40278* (cheap) has 11 rooms and an old English-style pub. There are also two luxurious country house hotels in the neighbourhood, both run by the same management, mainly catering for the Johannesburg and Pretoria weekend trade. **Critchley Hackle Lodge** *(Pf), Teding van Berkhout St; tel: 01325-40145; fax: 01325-40262* (moderate) has a definite tartan theme in its stone cottages built around a small fishing lake.

Walkersons *(Pf/LH), 10 km from Dullstroom on the Lydenburg road; tel: 01325-40246; fax: 01324-40260* (expensive) is a cosy stone and thatch lodge overlooking woodlands and a lake on its own large mountain estate, with excellent walking, birding, wildflowers and small game to add to the thrill of the rod and fly.

SIGHTSEEING

In spite of various rude comments, quiet little Dullstroom was actually named after a Dutch

merchant, Wolterus Dull, who raised funds for the Boers after the first Anglo-Boer War. These days, it is a pretty town, with the highest railway station in southern Africa (2076m) and one of the coldest climates.

It is best known as a popular trout fishing centre, with a **Trout Festival** every October.

LYDENBURG

Tourist Information: *50 Kantoor St; tel: 01323-2121*. A kiosk with accommodation cards and other tourism information stands outside the public library, *corner Viljoen and Voortrekker Sts*, near an ox wagon and pony trap.

ACCOMMODATION

Morgan's Hotel, *14 Voortrekker St tel: 01323-52165* (cheap) is a rather drab 1-star country hotel with a restaurant, ladies' bar and pool tables. The **Longtom Guesthouse**, in a farm on the edge of town, *tel: 01323-2749* (cheap) is a comfortable, friendly guesthouse and a better bet.

Campsite: **Uitspan Caravan Park**, *Viljoen St; tel: 01323-2914*, also has self-catering rondavels.

SIGHTSEEING

Lydenburg was founded in 1850 by Andries Potgieter, the oldest surviving town in Mpumalanga. It later spent time as an independent republic, before joining the Transvaal in 1860. It has a number of fine old buildings, including the **First Church and School**, now restored. The war memorial here honours those who lost their lives in the two world wars, the Korean conflict 'and the current fight against terrorism'. This Lowveld agricultural centre in a valley surrounded by hills and commercial forests is another trout anglers' Mecca.

The **Gustav Klingbiel Nature Reserve**, *3 km east of Lydenburg on the R37*, has small game and a hiking trail, but is most interesting for its archaeological traces of medieval villages and terraces. In 1957, a boy called Ludwig von Bezig found the broken pieces of seven stylized pottery heads. After careful reconstruction, six were found to be human and one animal. They have been dated to the 6th century, but their origin is totally unknown as they are unlike anything else in southern Africa.

The originals are in the South African Museum, Cape Town, but there are replicas in the **Lydenburg Museum**, *at the entrance to the Gustav Klingbiel Nature Reserve; tel: 01323-2121* (open Mon–Fri 0900–1200, 1400–1615, Sat–Sun, 1000–1600; R7), which has a broad range of fascinating material on pre-white South Africa.

LONG TOM PASS

This dramatic 57 km mountain pass takes its name from the 155 mm Long Tom field guns of the Anglo-Boer War. Drive through the pass at a steady speed so that you see every hill and boulder, every rock, shadow and contour of this heart-lifting sight. A board marks the highest point – 2150 m above sea level.

It is well worth parking at the **Siyachubeka Centre**, near the summit, where a replica of one of the cannons is on display at the spot where the originals were last in action, mounted strategically to pick off the British forces on the veldt below. Visitors can absorb the panoramic view at leisure and study information boards mounted in half a dozen shady enclosures. The panels outline the history of the conflict and give details of local events and general items of interest.

Local families have set up stalls offering a variety of beautifully-crafted works in wood, stone and clay. There are superbly carved wild animals and birds, and attractive stylised creatures, stone hippos, containers planted with bonsai trees . . . and prices start at R6.

SABIE

Tourist Office: *Main St; tel: 013-767 3492.* Open Mon–Fri 0900–1600, Sat 0900–1300.

ACCOMMODATION

Chain hotels include: *Pa.* There are numerous small, charming guesthouses in the vicinity. Amongst the most popular are the **Sabie Town House** *(Pf), Power St; tel: 013-764 2292, fax: 013-764 1988* (cheap), which has views over Sabie River Gorge, and the **Hill-watering Country House** *(Pf), 50 Marula St;*

tel: 013-764 1421; fax: 013-764 1550 (cheap), which has mountain views; dinners by arrangement.

The **Fern Tree Park**, *3 Main St; tel/fax: 013-764 2215* (cheap–moderate) provides self-catering accommodation in former miners' cottages.

Campsite: **Jock of the Bushveld Bungalows and Caravan Park** *(Ce), behind the Wimpy, in the town centre; tel: 013-764 2178,* has well-appointed self-catering cottages and chalets, as well as hostel accommodation, caravan and camp sites and a pool.

SIGHTSEEING

Sabie was founded as a result of pure luck, when, in 1880, a holidaying hunter idly fired at a rock, broke off a chip and revealed – gold. It now thrives on timber and tourism. The deep stands of eucalypt and pine, which supply half South Africa's timber requirements, replaced the many indigenous tree species which once graced the local hills.

The **Cultural and Historical Forestry Museum**, *Fort St; tel: 013-764 1243* (open Mon–Fri 0900–1600, Sat 0900–1300) has hundreds of interesting exhibits and much information on the industry. The local **Church of St Peter** was built by Sir Herbert Baker in 1913. The town also has a variety of good craft and souvenir shops. Most people use it as a base for outdoor activities, such as hiking, riding, mountain biking and white water rafting on the Sabie River.

The area is also famous for its many waterfalls, of which the 56 m **Mac Mac Falls**, 11 km north, off the R532 to Graskop (see p. 251), are the most famous, named supposedly by President Burgers because of the astonishingly high number of Scottish prospectors working along the river. There are souvenir sellers, a natural swimming pool and picnic site, together with several short walking trails.

Others within a short drive north include the 68 m **Lone Creek Falls**, the 70 m **Bridal Veil Falls** and the smaller **Horseshoe Falls**.

SKUKUZA

See Kruger National Park, pp. 240–245.

229

KIMBERLEY

Clean-cut, modern Kimberley belies its rough-and-tumble beginnings. In 1871, tens of thousands of fortune-hunters rushed to the New Rush diggings on the border of the northern Cape and the ZAR to dig for diamonds, turning Colesberg Kopje into the world's largest hand-dug hole and creating a shanty town that was to become the very symbol of wealth and power. However, today's city has not forgotten its past; behind the modern shopping centres and office blocks are many reminders of the days when South Africa's future was decided in what was little more than a huddle of tin shacks.

TOURIST INFORMATION

Tourist Office, *Public Library, Chapel St*; *tel: 0531-827 298; fax: 0531-827 211* (open Mon–Fri 0800–1700, Sat 0830–1130). The office is in the foyer of the public library, with a good display of leaflets and maps. A list of guesthouses, bed and breakfast accommodation and hotels is available and reservations may be made through the office, but staff prefer visitors to see accommodation for themselves first. A list of restaurants is also available, while details of local attractions, museums and guided tours are given in the free booklet, *Kimberley – The City that Sparkles.* A tourist's guide to the Northern Cape costs R15.

ARRIVING AND DEPARTING

By Car
Although geographically isolated, Kimberley is on the N12, one of the major roads between Cape Town and Johannesburg, and also has a good connecting road to Bloemfontein.

By Bus
Greyhound buses leave from the offices of their local agent, **Northern Cape Bus Service,** *5 Elliot St; tel: 0531-811 062,* while **Translux** services leave from the railway station. **Greyhound, Translux** and **Intercape** services all call at the *Shell-Ultra City, Transvaal Rd;* for central booking, see p. 39.

By Train
Station: *Florence St; tel: 0531-288 2631* (reservations), *0531-288 2060* (information). Kimberley has excellent rail connections, as a major stop on the Johannesburg–Cape Town route. Services include both the Blue Train and Rovos Rail. For more information, see Great Trains, pp. 53–55.

GETTING AROUND

Although the city centre is reasonably compact, it would be worthwhile spending a little time studying a street map. There is a streak of English eccentricity in the layout, and Kimberley is peculiar in that street names are painted on the kerbs at intersections. This might suit anyone driving an ox-cart, but is less convenient for the motorist. Few of the sights are within easy walking distance. Some of Kimberley's most significant historic sites can be seen from the **Kimberley Tram,** a restored 1914 tram that trundles hourly on a 5-min trip between the Mine Museum car park and City Hall, *Market Sq.* (daily 0900–1600; R6). Other attractions are contained within a 2 sq. km area of the city centre, but fierce temperatures, especially in the summer, will make one's air-conditioned car a more attractive option than slogging around on foot.

Guided tours of Kimberley and its surroundings, as well as day trips to archaeological and rock art sites and Anglo-Boer War battlefields of the Northern Cape, can be arranged through the Kimberley Tourist Information Office (see above) or **Diamond Tours Unlimited**; *tel: 0531-29834.* Bird-watching,

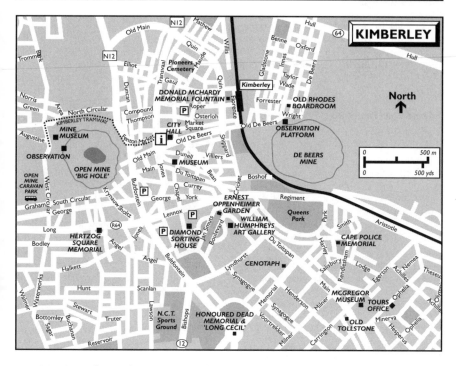

canoeing, river rafting and sunset game walks and drives are also available.

ACCOMMODATION

Accommodation is unlikely to break the bank in Kimberley. The city has less than a dozen hotels and motels, none of them expensive, and a plethora of budget priced guesthouses and bed and breakfastss. Top of the range are the uninspiring but comfortable **Holiday Inn Garden Court** *(Hd), 120 Du Toitspan Rd; tel: 0531-31751; fax: 0531-821 814* (moderate), the city's largest hotel with 130 rooms, five suites, a bar, swimming pool and sauna; and the **Diamond Protea Lodge** *(Pa), 124 Du Toitspan Rd; tel: 0531-811 281; fax: 0531-811 284* (cheap–moderate), a centrally located 2-star establishment with 34 rooms – some non-smoking – ladies' bar and pool. The 3-star **Hotel Kimberlite**, *162 George St, West End; tel: 0531-811 968; fax: 0531-811 967* (moderate), a kilometre or so from the city centre, is faintly reminiscent of a barracks block, but does have a restaurant and bar.

Of the various guesthouses, the best are probably the Edwardian **Pembury Lodge**, *11 Currey St; tel: 0531-24317* (cheap–moderate), which also has one of the best restaurants in town (book ahead), and the **Egerton House** *(Pf), 5 Egerton Rd, Belgravia; tel: 0531-811 150; fax: 0531-811 785* (moderate), in a historic house listed as a national monument. Other options in town include **Babsie's B & B**, *100 Lawson St; tel: 0531-813 338* (cheap); **Cosmos Guest Rooms**, *12 Jacobson Ave; tel: 0531-861 3795* (cheap); the **Hadida Guest House**, *8 Howie Rd; tel: 0531-861 2323* (cheap); and the **Van Gass Guest House**, *59 Milner St; tel: 0837-012 555* (cheap), which offers bed and breakfast or self-catering. **Long Court Guest Flats**, *102 Long St; tel: 0531-33391* (cheap) provide fully-equipped self-catering apartments. The **Langberg Guest Farm** *(Pf), on the N12, 21 km south of Kimberley; tel/fax: 0531-821 001* (cheap) is a Karoo cattle and game farm, with charming rooms in the converted stables (dinner by appointment).

Campsites: Big Hole Caravan Park,

West Circular Rd, right next to Kimberley's famous Big Hole; tel: 0531-806 322, offers caravan and tent pitches; day visitors R5 per vehicle plus R5 per person; **Kimberley Caravan Park**, *Hull St; tel: 0531-33582*, also has sites for caravans and tents.

EATING AND DRINKING

Two of Kimberley's watering holes, both dating from the city's diamond rush days, have achieved international renown. The **Star of the West**, *corner North Circular and Barkly Rds, near the Kimberley Mine Museum; tel: 0531-26463* (budget–moderate) is one of South Africa's oldest bars, opened in 1873. It still retains the combined atmosphere of an English Victorian pub and a Wild West saloon, with live music and *braais* on the patio at the rear. Snacks and full-blown meals are available. The food is not great, but the atmosphere makes up for it. Across town, the **Halfway House Hotel**, *corner Du Toitspan and Egerton Rds; tel: 0531-25151*, has a truly comforting drive-in bar – actually not much different from a car park – the result of a licence granted so that Cecil Rhodes and friends could enjoy a drink on horseback. Today's visitors are also offered cheap–moderate priced snacks, pub lunches and dinner. Then there are the steakhouses – the **MacRib**, *corner Lennox Rd and Jones St; tel: 0531-814 485* (moderate), which is better than its name might suggest, with a good choice of quality dishes and quick friendly service; and the **Safari Steakhouse**, *Market Sq., opposite City Hall; tel: 0531-824 621* (moderate), a well-deserved favourite with local residents, with low lighting and game trophy heads mounted on the walls giving the place an authentic old Africa feel. The food is good, too.

Another popular eating place is **Umberto's**, *Old Mutual Centre, Jones St; tel: 0531-823 741* (cheap–moderate), where snacks and full meals are served all day from breakfast to dinner; some tables are alfresco.

SIGHTSEEING

The **Big Hole and Kimberley Mine Museum**, *Tucker St; tel: 0531-31557* (open daily 0800–1800; R10) is the city's major attraction, and the only real reason most people

stop in Kimberley. This is the very spot where hundreds of men toiled to dig the world's biggest hole, while Cecil Rhodes, Barney Barnato and a few other crafty entrepreneurs plotted and schemed to gain control of the diggings and eventually the world diamond market. No longer worked and half full of water, the Big Hole is now the centrepiece of a wonderful open-air museum, with more than 40 restored homes, shops, offices, dealing rooms, a church, ballroom and Barnato's Boxing Academy, all carefully furnished and dripping with fascinating old photographs and newspaper cuttings. A unique collection of uncut diamonds and cut 'fancies' – diamonds of different colours – is on show in the De Beers Hall. There are replicas of some famous diamonds, but '616', the world's largest uncut diamond, and 'Eureka', the 21.25-carat yellow stone which was the first discovered in South Africa, are real. Other sections include a shed containing old sorting machines and, near the hole, visitors have a chance to try sorting.

The **Africana Library**, *Du Toitspan Rd; tel: 0531-806 247* (open Mon–Fri 0800–1245, 1330–1630; free), opened in 1887, features a wrought-iron gallery, spiral staircase, chandeliers and antique furniture, and houses a wealth of literary treasures, including Dr Robert Moffat's own copy of his translation of the Old Testament into Setswana. The **Duggan-Cronin Gallery**, *Egerton Rd; tel: 0531-32645/6* (open Mon–Fri 0900–1700; Sat 0900–1300, 1400–1700, Sun 1400, 1700) is home to an incomparable collection of 8000 photographs of South Africa's indigenous people taken by Alfred Martin Duggan-Cronin between 1919 and 1939. Take some of costumes with a pinch of salt; he travelled with his own leopard skin to dress subjects in. The work of more recent photographers, including Aubrey Elliot, Jean Morris and Alice Mertens, is also on show.

The magnificent **McGregor Museum**, *2 Egerton Rd; tel: 0531-32645/6* (open Mon–Sat 0900–1700, Sun 1400–1700) was built by Cecil Rhodes in 1897 to serve as a sanatorium, but was soon turned into a luxury hotel when he and his cronies tired of having sick people around. Rhodes occupied two rooms on the ground floor during the Siege of Kimberley,

232

KIMBERLEY

Hard Facts

The Big Hole was in production for little more than 40 years, but by the time it closed in 1914, it had produced diamonds weighing a total of 14,504,566 carats (2722 kg). In the process, 22.5 million tonnes of ground were excavated and the open-cast working reached a depth of 240 m. Today, the hole is 215 m deep. The water in it is 41 m deep and the depth from surface to water is 174 m.

from 15 Oct 1899 to 16 Feb 1900. It was a time of enormous hardship, with some 3000 women and children sheltering from heavy bombardments in the mine tunnels, while Rhodes turned the mine-machine shops to making shells and artillery. The museum now features a fascinating display on the siege, together with natural history exhibits, a collection of 19th-century furniture and a Hall of Religions. The original home of the McGregor Museum, of which it is now a satellite, is the building housing the **Alexander McGregor Memorial Museum**, *Chapel St; tel: 0531-32645* (open Mon–Fri 0900–1700, Sat 0900–1300, Sun 1400–1700), which dates from 1907. The museum, whose name honours an early mayor of the city, houses displays on the history of the Northern Cape, geological specimens from all over the world and a small costume collection. The **William Humphreys Art Gallery**, *Civic Centre, Jan Smuts Blvd; tel: 0531-811 724/5* (open Mon–Sat 1000–1300, 1400–1700, Sun 1400–1700) is one of the best in the country, now concentrating on traditional and contemporary works by black and white South African artists. The core collection also contains 16th- and 17th-century Dutch and Flemish Old Masters and British and French paintings collected by William Benbow Humphreys, MP (1889–1965). Although the town as a whole is not attractive, Kimberley's diamond wealth was used to create a number of architectural gems, of which the finest are the charming 1889 Roman-Corinthian style **City Hall**, *Market Sq.*; the 1882 **Dutch Reformed Church**, *Hertzog Sq.*; and the Pall Mall-Colonial grandeur of the 1882

Kimberley Club, *Du Toitspan Rd*. Not surprisingly, the diamond magnates also did themselves proud in the homes they built. **Dunluce**, *10 Lodge Rd*, built by John Orr in 1897, is now part of the McGregor Museum. The **Oppenheimer House**, *7 Lodge Rd*, was built for Sir Ernest Oppenheimer in 1907 and is the birthplace of Harry Oppenheimer. The Tourist Office produces a walking tour guide that includes many other historic buildings.

Cecil Rhodes commissioned the **Honoured Dead Memorial**, *Memorial Rd*, to commemorate those who died during the Siege of Kimberley. Designed by Herbert Baker, it carries an inscription written by Rudyard Kipling. At its base is **Long Cecil**, a field gun made during the siege in the De Beers workshops. **The Diggers' Fountain**, *Ernest Oppenheimer Memorial Gardens, Jan Smuts Blvd*, by Herman Wald, represents five miners holding a diamond sieve. In 1911, John Weston kept a plane in the air for a record-making 8 mins 30 secs and Kimberley, inspired by his achievement, founded South Africa's first school of aviation. The **Memorial to the Pioneers of Aviation**, *Oliver Rd, 3.5 km from the airport tel: 0531-32645* (open Mon–Sat 0900–1300, 1400–1700; Sun 1400–1700) consists of a monument, reconstruction hangar and replica Compton Paterson Biplane.

Out of Town

Another big hole marks the spot where Kimberley's first diamonds were found in 1869 – in the mud walls of a farmhouse. The farmhouse is long gone, but **Bultfontein Mine**, *Visitors' Reception Centre, Molyneux Rd; tel: 0531-829 651/32259* (surface tours – no children under 8 years – Mon–Fri 0900, 1100; underground tours – minimum age 16, reservations essential – Mon–Fri 0800) is still operational and open to the public. A small museum stands on the site of the ten-day **Battle of Magersfontein**, *off N12 near Spytfontein, 32 km south of Kimberley; tel: 0531-32645/6)*. In Dec 1899, this was the scene of some of the fiercest fighting in the Anglo-Boer War, between 12,500 British troops and 8200 Boers, costing the lives of 239 Britons and 87 Boers. Photographs of the battle, together with uniforms, weapons and documents, are on display.

233

SIGHTSEEING

KIMBERLEY–UPINGTON

Minerals – manganese, asbestos, tiger's eye, iron and diamonds – are responsible for the prodigious wealth of this dry, almost unbearably hot, isolated region of South Africa. This route traverses the awe-inspiring territories of Bushmanland and Griqualand West, passing romantic natural landmarks, such as the Asbestos Mountains and the Roaring Sands. This is a raw country; accommodation is generally simple, the inhabitants tough but hospitable, and the trip exhilarating.

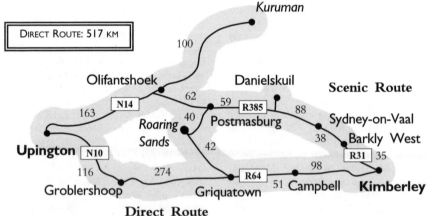

DIRECT ROUTE: 517 KM

Kuruman

100

Olifantshoek

Danielskuil

Scenic Route

62

59

R385

88

Sydney-on-Vaal

N14

163

40

Roaring
Sands

Postmasburg

38

Barkly West

42

R31   35

Upington   N10

98

116

274

R64

51 Campbell   Kimberley

Groblershoop

Griquatown

Direct Route

234

ROUTES

DIRECT ROUTE

From Kimberley, take the R64 going west to **Campbell** (98 km) and **Griquatown** (or Griekwastad; 54 km). Kudu constantly cross this road and are a real danger to speeding traffic; keep your speed down to a safe maximum 60 kph. From Griquatown, continue west on the R64 to **Groblershoop** (252 km). Just before Groblershoop, there is a turning to the Roaring Sands (see p.236). At Groblershoop, turn right onto the N10 north to Upington (116 km). Distance: 517 km; allow at least one long day.

SCENIC ROUTE

Leave Kimberley on the R31 and head for **Barkly West** (35 km). Stay on the

R31, which bypasses **Sydney-on-Vaal** (38 km), until you reach **Daniëlskuil** (88 km). From Daniëlskuil, retrace your route back along the R31 for 9 km, branch right onto the R385 and head for **Postmasburg** (50 km), from where there is a side track to the **Roaring Sands** (p.236). From Postmasburg, continue along the same road; 5 km beyond the town, it reverts to gravel. Continue for 56 km until you reach the N14, then branch right and head for **Olifantshoek** (6 km). From Olifantshoek there is a side track to **Kuruman** (see p.237). Return to Olifantshoek and stay on the N14 the whole way to **Upington** (263 km). Distance: about 725 km; allow a slow three days.

CAMPBELL

Located in what is quaintly known as 'the valley of the wild garlic', Campbell is a village on the old missionary and trade route to the interior. Its single main street is still evocative of the past, with numerous surviving elderly buildings, including the restored **mission church** of the London Missionary Society (1831).

GRIQUATOWN

Tourist Office: *2 Moffat St; tel: 05962, ask for 19* (open Mon–Fri 0900–1700).

The **Louis Hotel**, *Main St; tel: 05962, ask for 84* (1-star; cheap). **Campsite: Griquatown Caravan Park**; *tel: 05962-19*.

Once the capital of Griqualand, this small settlement in the shadow of the Asbestos Mountains is best known as a mission station of the London Missionary Society (1803). It was founded in an effort to mend the dissolute ways of the local Griqua population, who settled here in 1800 under the leadership of Adam Kok (see opposite). While many of their descendants moved on when they found work in the diamond mines, others are still here. Although officially classed as 'coloured' during the apartheid years, some managed to prosper, even to hang on to their property. The old mission house, birthplace of David Livingstone's wife, Mary Moffat, is now the **Mary Moffat Museum**, *Voortrekker St; tel: 05962, ask for 180* (open Mon–Fri 0800–1700; free). Today, Griquatown is famous for its gemstones, including jasper and tiger's eye. For a full range, visit **Earth Treasures**, *Moffat St; tel: 05962, ask for 121* (open Mon–Fri 0730–1700; free). **San engravings** can be seen at Pannetjie, 5 km from Griquatown.

GROBLERSHOOP

Tourist Office: *Oranje St; tel: 05472, ask for 38* (open Mon–Fri 0830–1600).

Grootrivier Hotel, *Main St; tel: 05472, ask for 14* (2-star; cheap). **Campsite: Buchuberg Dam Caravan Park**; *tel: 05472-1422* (cheap).

A busy market town, Groblershoop occupies the site of the original pump station used to supply water from the Gariep River to the surrounding valley. Not much happens here, although the **Buchuberg Dam** (take the R32 from town; turn off after 1 km and head east for 34 km) is a popular place to swim, fish and go boating.

The Griqua

The word Griqua is a simplification of Xurikwa, the original name of the Khoikhoi people, whose traditional lifestyle altered on arrival of Europeans. Enslaved, freed, stripped of their land, subject to alien diseases such as smallpox and the effects of alcohol, they became a sub-caste of mixed blood people, who called themselves 'Bastaards'. In the 18th century, they were cattle raiders and adventurers, settled in the area around Piketberg in the western Cape. Early in the 19th century, a freed slave, Adam Kok, former cook to the Governors of the Cape, led them north to settle around Klaarwater, where they drew in other displaced people of all races, from fragmented Tswana clans to army deserters. They settled large areas of the Northern Cape, near the Gariep River, managing to remain independent until the 1860s, when diamonds were discovered in their territory. What has become known as Griquatown was their sanctuary, the first town north of the Gariep River, and the capital of their independent state, Griqualand West, until absorbed by the British Empire.

235

BARKLY WEST

Tourist Office: *Campbell St; tel: 053-531 0671* (open Mon–Fri 0830–1600).

There are two hotels: the **Grand Hotel**, *Campbell St; tel: 053-531 0642* (1-star; cheap), and the **Queens Hotel**, *Campbell St; tel: 053-531 0514* (1-star; cheap). You would probably do better to stay in Kimberley (see p. 231). For bed and breakfast, try the pleasant **Melkvlei Guest Farm**, *23 km from Barkly West on the Postmasburg Rd; tel: 053-561 0014* (cheap).

On the banks of the Vaal River, and once known as Klipdrift, Barkly West is the site of the Northern Cape's first diamond diggings, and Africa's first diamond rush (to **Canteen Kopje**, now a nature reserve) in 1869. A cairn marks the spot. In 1870, the diggers, declaring independence from the Transvaal, proclaimed the short-lived Klipdrift Republic. It was annexed by Britain a year later and, in 1873, became Barkly West in honour of the Governor, Sir Henry Barkly. The old toll house stands beside a stone bridge (1884) across the Vaal. River diggings still attract prospectors, particularly when the river is at its lowest and its bed is revealed (June–Nov). Diamonds and gemstones are still found and sold here, so if you want to experience a little of the atmosphere of a prospecting town of the past, come on a Saturday when the shops and the bars are busy.

SYDNEY-ON-VAAL

The **Sydney-on-Vaal Game Lodge;** *tel: 053-561 0081; fax: 053-561 0085* (moderate) offers luxury accommodation in a restored lodge, dating from the diamond digging days. To get there, follow the Sydney-on-Vaal/Vaalbos National Park signs from the R31.

At Sydney-on-Vaal, the diamond boom tent town of Sydney Village (1896) offers opportunities for diamond panning (contact **Guildford Safaris**; *tel: 053-561 0081*). Here, too, is the 26,000 hectare **Vaalbos National Park**; *tel: 053-561 0088* (open all year, dawn–dusk; R20 per vehicle), where the vegetation of the Karoo and the Kalahari meet. There are over 26 species of mammal, including buffalo, black and white rhino, giraffe, springbok and eland. Chalet accommodation is available within in the park (cheap).

DANIËLSKUIL

Tourist Office: *Town Council Offices, Barker St; tel: 0598-30013* (open Mon–Fri 0830–1700). **Accommodfation: Commercial Hotel**, *Rhodes Ave; tel/fax: 0598-30019* (1-star; cheap). **Campsite: Piet Human Caravan Park**; *tel: 053872-30013* (cheap).

This is 'Daniel's Den', named by missionaries after a 6m conical sinkhole in the ground, used by the Griqua as a prison. Local legend has it that if you could survive 24 hours down there with the resident snakes, you were declared innocent. No one has ever been down to search for bodies or test the theory. Asbestos and marble are mined here, as are diamonds – 26 were found in the first 2 hours of prospecting in 1960. Call **Mount Carmel Safaris**, *tel: 0598-*

30564, to reserve places on hunting and photographic safaris, for game drives, farm holidays in the area and access to hiking trails. From Daniëlskuil, it is possible to head north to Kuruman (see p.237), along the R31 (87 km).

POSTMASBURG

Tourist Office: *Municipality Offices, Springbok St; tel: 0591-30343* (open office hours).

The **Postmasburg Hotel**, *37 Main Rd; tel/fax: 0591-71166*, (2-star; cheap) has a very popular beer garden, as does the **Oasis Motel**, *1 Kromme Ave; tel/fax: 0591-72182* (cheap). **Campsite: Postmasburg Caravan Park**, *Blink Klip St; tel: 0591-30343*.

Originally a trading post (founded in 1892) marooned in the vast grass-covered, thorny dolomite plain of the northern Cape, Postmasburg became wealthy when a nearby meercat burrow was transformed (1918) into **'the big hole'**. The Postmas Diamond Mine was worked successfully until 1935; the huge Kimberlite pipe (about 45m deep, with surface area of 1.4 sq km) is now filled with water and stocked with fish. There are **ancient mine workings** in the Gatkoppies (visit by appointment only; refer to the Municipality offices). According to archaeological evidence, these were created in about 700AD by the Khoikhoi, who mined a glittering black iron oxide called specularite for personal adornment.

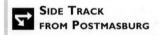

SIDE TRACK
FROM POSTMASBURG

THE ROARING SANDS

From Postmasburg, take the southbound untarred R309 and at the second junction (after about 5 km), branch right, following the signs to Bermolli (about 14 km). Keep going in the same direction. About 9 km beyond Bermolli, branch right and head over the Bergenaarspad Pass (about 4 km), then turn left and head for **Witsand** (Whitesands) and the **Roaring Sands** (about 8 km). An alternative, more direct, route to Witsand and the Roaring Sands leads off the direct route, from the R64 between Groblershoop and Griquatown.

About 10 km from Griquatown, branch left onto an untarred road and follow the signs to Witsand (about 32 km).

There is self-catering accommodation at the **Witsand Tourist Resort**; *tel: 0591-72373.*

Marooned in the middle of an ocean of red Kalahari sand, these 100m high snow-white dunes emit a strange, almost human, moan when disturbed by air. It is thought that the sand was once red but since it accumulated over water, exerting pressure on the water supply, the iron oxide vanished, and with it the red colour. In the dry conditions, and having been freed from the red oxide, wind movement through the loosely-packed sand causes the eery roar. Kick the sand, or even run your hands through it, and the sound effects are the same. The driest months are May–Oct; avoid the area if it's been raining.

Look out for 'fulgurites'. These are lumps of sand grains fused together when lightning strikes the dunes. Fulgurites of up to 2m long are not unknown. 🔺

OLIFANTSHOEK

Tourist Office: *Lanham St; tel: 059512, ask for 2* (open Mon–Fri 0830–1200).

The **Kalahari Hotel**, *Van Riebeeck St; tel: 059512, ask for 7* (1-star; cheap). **Campsite: Olifantshoek Caravan Park**; *tel: 059512-2.*

Founded in 1897, the little town of Olifantshoek is named after the elephant, whose tusks paid for the ground on which it stands. This is a centre for iron mining. **Meerlust Farm**, *about 50 km north-west of the town*, has a rich collection of San rock paintings.

SIDE TRACK
FROM OLIFANTSHOEK

From Olifantshoek, turn right on the N14 for 100 km to arrive at Kuruman.

KURUMAN

Tourist Office: *corner School and Voortrekker Sts; tel: 05373-21001* (open Mon–Fri 0830–1700, Sat 0900–1200). From Olifant-shoek, take the N14 north for 98 km.

ACCOMMODATION

There are two central choices: the 3-star **Eldorado Motel**, *Main Rd; tel/fax: 05373-22191* (cheap), or the **Grand Hotel**, *Beare St; tel/fax: 05373-21148* (cheap), close to the 'Eye' (see below). **Kamdebo Guest House**, *Seodin Rd; tel: 05373-21450* (cheap) offers comfortable bed and breakfast. **Campsite: Kuruman Caravan Park**, *6 Voortrekker St; tel: 05373-21479.*

The remote **Korannaberg Private Nature Reserve**, *130 km from Kuruman on the Kalahari Gemsbok National Park Rd; tel: 05375-215* (moderate–expensive) provides a luxurious way to experience the true vastness of the desert fringe, with comfortable 3- and 5-star accommodation, excellent food and a wide-ranging programme of game drives and walks.

SIGHTSEEING

Kuruman is the gateway to the hot, dry North West, an area of red and grey dunes, grasslands and thorny scrub. Known to the Tswana as *Gasegonyana* (place of the little calabash), the town is a lush oasis in the dusty Kalahari, located around the romantic **Eye of Kuruman**, a massive spring which pours 20 million litres of water a day into a deep, clear pool. The force of the water never weakens, even during severe droughts. Robert Moffat set up the area's first London Missionary Station here (1821), and the little settlement duly became known as Fountain of Christianity.

The **Kuruman Moffat Mission** is now a **museum**, *Hotazel Rd; tel: 05373-21352* (open weekdays 0800–1700, Sun 1500–1700; R5); the church (1838) is still in use. Just out of town, the 1400 hectare **Kuruman Nature Reserve**; *tel: 05373-21095* (open Sat–Sun 1400–1700; R10) has a few white rhino and several species of antelope. Take the Kahtu road for about 2 km, then follow the signs.

Some 40 km from Kuruman (take the southbound R31 Kuruman–Daniëlskuil; follow the signs and obtain permission from **Wonderwerk Farm**; *tel: 0598-30680)* are the **Wonderwerk Caves**, where some of

The Moffat Mission

In 1817, the London Missionary Society sent Robert Moffat (1795–1883) to Cape Town. He began work in Namaqualand, went to Bechuanaland, and then, in 1821, to Kuruman. In 1819, he married and, with his wife Mary, under hugely difficult circumstances, perservered in his attempts to convert the locals. By 1829, they had succeeded with two – his total tally was only eight. Most usefully, Moffat learned and preached in Tswana – one of the earliest publications in Tswana is his catechism (1831). He also translated the Bible, printing the Tswana edition on his own press. Moffat met David Livingstone on the Vaal River (1841); in 1845, his daughter, Mary, married the great explorer, who used Kuruman as a base from which to explore the hinterland and spread the gospel. Meanwhile, Moffat's son carried on with the mission at Kuruman, resigning in 1879 due to ill health.

South Africa's most magnificent San etchings are preserved. ▨

UPINGTON

Tourist Office: *Library Building, Mutual St; tel: 054-26911* (open office hours).

Upington offers 2-star **Oranje Hotel**, *Scott St; tel: 054-24177*; the 3-star **Upington Protea** *(Pa), 24 Schroder St; tel/fax: 054-25414* (moderate); and the 2-star **Oasis Protea** *(Pa), 26 Schroder St; tel/fax: 054-311 125* (cheap). There are also several bed and breakfasts, including the well-appointed art deco style **Chateau Guesthouse**, *9 Coetzee St; tel: 054-27504; fax: 054-27064* (cheap). **Campsite: Die Eiland Holiday Resort**, *Palm Ave; tel: 054-311 553,* has chalets and shady pitches for tents and caravans, right beside the river. The **Le Must Restaurant**, *11 Schroder St; tel: 054-24971* (moderate) is a charming restaurant, with good food in pretty surroundings. The **Gariep Lodge**, *40 km east of town on the Olifantshoek Rd, tel: 054902-919 812* (moderate) is a delightfully informal scattering of chalets and tented rooms

on the Kalahari dunes, in a private game reserve beside the river. Self-catering is available or traditional food is provided around the *braai*. Activities include fishing, riding, canoeing, hiking and game-viewing.

Upington is the north's metropolis. Founded as a mission station on the banks of the Gariep River, it has a lovely river frontage, and is the centre of a prosperous fruit and wine producing area. Many Koranna (mixed race Griqua and Tswana) managed to retain their land in this area and, against all the odds given the severity of the old Group Areas Act (see p.67), still farm nearby – as indeed they do at Keimoes (see pp. 325–326). Upington has one or two other odd claims to fame: it has the world's longest avenue of date palms (1 km); and its airport has the longest runway in the southern hemisphere (5 km). This is used for landspeed trials and is listed as a possible emergency landing strip for the space shuttle. Upington has two interesting **monuments**: a camel and rider *(Police Station)* commemorates the early Camel Corps used to patrol the desert border; a donkey *(beside the museum)* celebrates the crucial role of the donkey in opening up the area. The **Kalahari Oranje Museum**, *Schroder St; tel: 054-26911* (open Mon–Fri 0930–1230 and 1400–1700; free), housed in the old mission station's church (1875), has some interesting physical and photographic displays on the history of the Northern Cape. The **Orange River Winery**, *Industrial Rd; tel: 054-25651* (open Mon–Fri 0730–1700, Sat 0800–1200 for sales and tastings) is the second largest in the southern hemisphere.

The **Spitskop Game Reserve**, *13 km north of town on the R360; tel: 054-22336,* open daily dawn to dusk; R7) is filled with game, including springbok, zebra, gemsbok, hartebeest, eland and steenbok. There are excellent walks and simple accommodation, even if the game, as used to guns as cameras, is somewhat shy. **Cannon Island**, in the Gariep River, is covered with vineyards, and is the home to a thriving catfish industry. Locals are happy to show you around; ask at the Tourist Office.

For other sights reached from Upington, including the **Kalahari Gemsbok Park** and the **Augrabies Falls**, see pp. 325–327.

KRUGER NATIONAL PARK

Kruger National Park, one of the oldest and largest in the world, straddles South Africa's Northern and Mpumulanga Provinces, while its eastern boundary is the Mozambique border. The game-viewing here is magnificent, and even though some purists talk of over-crowding and zoos, it is extremely easy to get away into remote areas, where you hardly see another car. As well as the many popular animals and birds, the park is home to countless numbers of insects, including the malarial mosquito, which means most visitors must undergo a course of prophylactics, lasting from a week before they go to six weeks after they leave the park (see p. 22).

TOURIST INFORMATION

National Parks Board, *643 Leyds St, Muckleneuk (PO Box 787), Pretoria 001; tel: 012-343 1991; fax: 012-343 0905* (open Mon–Fri 0800–1545); and *44 Long St (PO Box 7400, Rogge Bay) Cape Town 8012 ; tel: 021-222 810; fax: 021-246 211* (open Mon–Fri 0900–1645). These offices are concerned mainly with general inquiries and accommodation reservations. Information on the Kruger and other national parks is also available on the board's worldwide website, *http://www.africa.com/satour/*.

Specific information on the park's geography, flora and fauna, as well as literature and maps, is obtainable at the park's gates, and at information centres at **Skukuza Letaba** and **Berg-en-dal** camps.

ARRIVING AND DEPARTING

By Road
The park is a comfortable five-hour drive from

Johannesburg and Pretoria by way of the N4/N12 (see Johannesburg–Kruger, pp. 224–229). There are eight entrance gates. **Numbi** and **Paul Kruger** (the main entrance and easiest access to Skukuza) are within easy reach of White River and Hazyview. **Crocodile Bridge** and **Malelane** are in the south, off the N4. In the central section, near the Mpumalanga/Northern Province border, **Orpen Gate** is 50 km east of Klaserie, at the intersection of the R40 and R531; **Phalaborwa Gate** is a mere 2 km from the town of Phalaborwa. In the far north, the two most remote gates are **Punda Maria**, accessible from Louis Trichardt and Thohoyandou on the R524; and **Pafuri**, close to the borders of Mozambique and Zimbabwe, on the R525, 139 km east of Messina.

Gates are open daily 0530–1830 Nov–Feb, 0530–1800 Mar and Oct, 0600–1730 Apr, 0630–1730 May–Aug, 0600–1800 Sept. Admission: R20 per person per day.

239

By Air
There are daily flights from Johannesburg to Skukuza, operated by **Comair**, *PO Box 7015, Bonaero Park 1622; tel: 011-921 0222; fax: 011-973 1659*, and Phalaborwa, operated by **SA Airlink**, *PO Box 7529, Bonaero Park 1622; tel: 011-394 2430; fax: 011-394 2649*. **Avis** operates car rental facilities at Skukuza; *tel: 01311-65651*, and Phalaborwa; *tel: 01524-5169*. All private lodges will arrange transfers from the nearest airport. Most rest camps and game lodges have small airstrips, which can accommodate private or chartered planes and helicopters. **Jetair Tours**, *PO Box 259, Lanseria 1748; tel: 011-659 1574/5; fax: 011-659 2498*, operate all-inclusive luxury fly-in safaris to many of the luxury lodges, from Lanseria Airport near Johannesburg and Pretoria (the small and private planes airport).

By Rail
See pp. 53–57.

GETTING AROUND

There are great benefits to be had from doing an organised game drive with a professional ranger, but these are expensive, and self-drive game-viewing in a normal family car is perfectly feasible in the Kruger.

Self-Drive

The park has an excellent network of over 2600 km of roads. Main access roads are tarred, the rest are all gravel, but are perfectly safe for ordinary cars, except under the most rare and extreme climatic conditions. Open vehicles, motorcycles and bicycles are banned from the park for safety reasons.

Speed limits are 50 kph on tarred roads and 40 kph on gravel, but with so much to see, there is no need to hurry. If you do, you will probably miss most of the excitement. Remember that allowing for game-viewing stops, a trip of 50 km could take well over two hours, even on tar. A central corridor road runs north–south right through the park, and you can spend several days moving camps to find different habitats and concentrations of animals.

Plan ahead. Excellent, cheap guides, visitors' maps and field guides are available at the park entrances and camp shops, and it is worth consulting these to plot a route and find out what you are likely to see. Ask reception about recent sightings. Most people returning from a game drive are happy to report on their findings.

Even if you have just eaten a hearty South African breakfast and plan an early lunch, take something to eat and drink. There are only a few places where visitors are allowed out of their cars, so make sure you have everything you need before setting out. See that essentials are in the car, not the boot. Check that the car has enough oil and water and that tyres – including the spare – are correctly inflated.

Petrol is available at Crocodile Bridge and Orpen gates, and at all major rest camps. It is a good idea to make sure the tank is full and replenished whenever possible. Diesel is available at Berg-en-dal, Crocodile Bridge, Letaba, Lower Sabie, Mopani, Olifants, Orpen, Pretoriuskop, Punda Maria, Satara, Shingwedzi and Skukuza.

If your car does suffer a breakdown, it may be some time before help arrives. Walking out to raise the alarm is not a viable proposition. Stay in your car, flag down anyone passing and ask them to send assistance. Emergency services and workshops are maintained by the South African Automobile Association (AA) at Skukuza, Satara and Letaba camps.

Guided Game-Viewing

This is the only option in the many private game reserves surrounding Kruger, most of which include guided drives and walks as part of the all-in package, and don't allow any self-drive on their land. However, it is also possible to do guided drives and walks within the park proper and these have many advantages, such as the attention of expert trackers and rangers, who can fill in all sorts of fascinating background detail on the flora and birds, as well as the animals. Ask at reception in the main camps. Several Nelspruit-based tour operators run day trips into the park for those staying outside (see pp. 225–226).

There are also seven hiking trails within the park. The Parks Board runs 2-day, 3-night hiking trips, staying at the same remote bush camp each night (usually in basic huts), and doing day hikes accompanied by an armed ranger. Space is strictly limited and you must book months in advance.

SKUKUZA

This is the Kruger's operational and administrative headquarters, *17 km from Paul Kruger Gate, on the Sabie River, in the southern part of the park,* and also the largest rest camp in the park. It is huge, with up to 3000 people at any one time, and most of the facilities you would expect in a small town – including an airport, post office, bank, launderette, police station, garage and filling station, a doctor's consulting room and dispensary, a large supermarket-cum-souvenir shop, library and information centre, open-air cinema and plant nursery.

ACCOMMODATION

Unless your visit to the Kruger has been arranged as part of a tour operator's package, reservations for accommodation within the

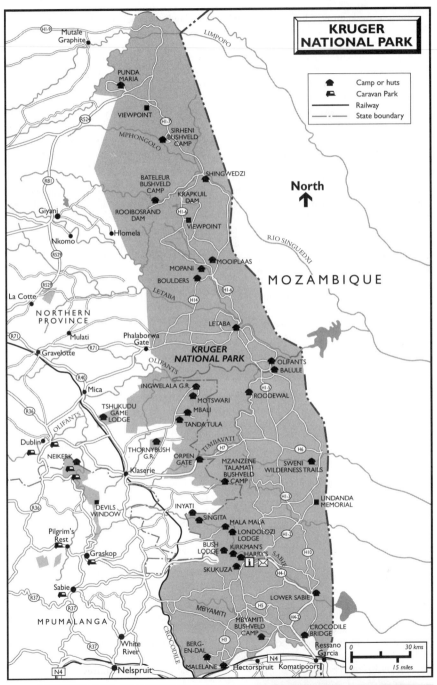

241

park must be made through the National Parks Board, preferably by fax or telephone, or online on the board's website (see Tourist Information). The busiest times of the year are Dec–Jan, when South African schools are closed, Easter and July–Aug.

Accommodation ranges from rondavels, huts, cottages and chalets to furnished tents, camping and caravan sites, all spotlessly clean and maintained to high standards. All units are serviced daily and bedding, soap and towels are provided. Many have either air-conditioning or fans. Most are self-catering, with private kitchens and *braaivleis* sites, while the main camps have full restaurant/cafeteria service. Some huts share communal kitchens and bathrooms. Visitors staying in units without private cooking facilities must provide their own utensils, crockery and cutlery if they intend preparing their own meals. Basic utensils, crockery and cutlery may be hired in some camps. The camps are fenced, but there are regular visitors, including small antelope, monkeys and baboons, so never leave windows or doors open, or food lying out in the open.

242

Skukuza, inevitably, has the widest choice of accommodation, but its thoughtful layout, thankfully, goes some way towards preventing an urban ambience. Try and get accommodation along the river, where you have built-in game-viewing from your front door.

At the top of the range are five 'sponsored' cottages, capable of accommodating 4–8 people. Sponsored accommodation is privately owned property, maintained and let by the National Parks Board, and equipped and furnished to a high standard.

Then there are two-bedroom cottages, each sleeping 4–6, with air conditioning, a fully-equipped kitchen and lounge/dining room, or verandah-cum-living room. Huts have 2–3 beds, with air-conditioning, bath and/or shower and refrigerator. Some have basic cooking facilities, others are not equipped with utensils, crockery or cutlery.

Two- and four-bed tents are furnished with wardrobe, fan, table and chairs, refrigerator and electric light. Tents stand on concrete floors under a shade net and have barbecue facilities, but no utensils, crockery or cutlery.

Similar, though not such wide choices, of accommodation are to be found at **Berg-en-dal**, *10 km from the Malelane Gate;* **Crocodile Bridge**, *at the south-east entrance to the park, 13 km from Komatipoort;* **Letaba**, *50 km from Phalaborwa Gate;* **Lower Sabie**, *on the bank of a dam in the Sabie River;* **Mopani**, *45 km north of Letaba;* **Olifants**, *in the east-central region of the park, 82 km from Phalaborwa Gate;* **Pretoriuskop**, *9 km from Numbi Gate;* **Punda Maria**, *in the Kruger's northernmost part,* **Satara**, *42 km east of Orpen Gate,* and **Shingwedzi**, *in the north-eastern part, close to the Mozambique border.* Of these, the most attractive are Olifants and Letaba, while Lower Sabie probably offers the best game-viewing. Berg-en-Dal, Pretoriuskop and Mopani have swimming pools.

Five smaller camps offer more primitive facilities. **Balule**, *on the southern bank of the Olifants River, 11 km from Olifants rest camp,* has six rustic three-bed huts and 15 sites for tents and caravans. The camp has neither shop nor restaurant, and there is no electricity. **Malelane**, *3 km from the Malelane Gate,* has one 3-bed hut and four 4-bed huts, with air-conditioning and refrigerators, basic cooking utensils, crockery and cutlery. There are also camp sites. The camp has electricity, a communal kitchen and barbecue facilities. **Maroela**, *about 4 km from Orpen,* is a small camping area overlooking the Timbavati River. No electricity, but a communal freezer is available. **Orpen**, *at the Orpen Gate,* is a peaceful little camp, with some of the amenities found in the larger rest camps – including electricity and a shop. Accommodation is in six-bed sponsored cottages and two- and three-bed huts, with fan, refrigerator and communal ablutions. **Tamboti**, *4 km from Orpen on the Orpen-Satara road,* has 2- and 4-bed furnished tents on wooden stilts overlooking the Timbavati River. No cooking utensils, crockery or cutlery.

Caravan and camping sites are available at Balule, Berg-en-dal, Crocodile Bridge, Letaba, Malelane, Maroela, Lower Sabie, Pretoriuskop, Punda Maria, Satara, Shingwedzi and Skukuza. All camps, except Balule, Malelane and Maroela, have caravan sites with plug-in power.

There are **launderettes** at Berg-en-dal,

Crocodile Bridge, Letaba, Lower Sabie, Mopani, Olifants, Pretoriuskop, Satara, Shingwedzi and Skukuza.

Four private camps – **Jock of the Bushveld**, **Nwanetsi**, **Roodewal** and **Boulders** – are only available for en bloc booking by small groups.

The most convenient places to stay for those wishing to stay outside the park and make day visits are Hazyview (see p. 250), White River (see pp. 227–228) and Phalaborwa (see p. 254).

The Big Five

The Big Five – the African animals visitors most want to see – are buffalo, elephant, leopard, lion and rhino (see p. 59). According to the latest population estimate, the Kruger National Park contains about 14,230 buffalo, 7800 elephant, 1000 leopard, 2000 lion, 1900 white rhino and 220 black rhino.

EATING AND DRINKING

There are restaurants and cafeterias at Berg-en-dal, Letaba, Lower Sabie, Mopani, Olifants, Pretoriuskop, Punda Maria, Satara, Shingwedzi and Skukuza. Daily mealtimes: breakfast 0700–0900, lunch 1200–1400, dinner 1800–2100. Light snacks – sandwiches, rolls, pies, beer, wine and soft drinks – are available between these times at the cafeterias.

There are also more than a dozen picnic sites, each with barbecue facilities and toilets. Most offer soft drinks for sale and some also have snacks. Picnic sites are shown on the park's *Visitor's Map*.

Groceries, fresh meat, vegetables, alcohol, crockery, cutlery and utensils may be purchased at shops at Berg-en-dal, Crocodile Bridge, Letaba, Lower Sabie, Mopani, Olifants, Orpen, Pretoriuskop, Punda Maria, Satara, Shingwedzi and Skukuza. Shops open daily 0800 to 30 mins after gate closure times.

Communications

There are public telephones at all entrance gates and rest camps. A post office at Skukuza is open Mon–Fri 0800–1300, 1400–1630; Sat 0800–1200. Skukuza also has a police station, which is signposted from outside the camp gate.

Money

There is a branch of the Volkskas Bank, with an autoteller machine located at Skukuza.

SIGHTSEEING

The Kruger is 350 km long and up to 60 km wide – about the same size as Israel – covers 21,497 sq. km and contains a staggering 147 species of mammal – including the Big Five –

507 species of bird, 114 different types of reptile and 49 species of fish. There are even 230 varieties of butterfly. The area is mainly between 300m and 1200m in altitude and is watered by several major rivers – the Crocodile, Sabie, Oliphants, Timbavati, Letaba, Luvuvhu and Shingwedzi – most of which flow west–east off the escarpment towards the Mozambique coast. Other watering holes provided by bores make sure that periods of drought don't prove too damaging to the wildlife, and help concentrate the animals at easily visible locations. There are nine ecosystems within the park, each with different soils, micro-climates, vegetation and inhabitants, although few of the larger mammals are too specific in their requirements. Together, they make up a broad spectrum of typically African bushveld, of the sort found far more commonly to the north, in Zimbabwe and Zambia. Stretches of open grass savannah are interspersed by rocky koppies, open acacia woodland and, where there is sufficient water, denser forests of hardwood trees. Kruger is also a paradise for botanists, with around 336 species of trees alone, including marula and wild fig, mopane, mahogany, ebony and ironwood, baobab and fever trees, plus innumerable species of grasses, flowering plants and bushes. In very general terms, the ground is slightly higher and more heavily wooded in the west, sloping downwards and getting dryer as it gets closer to the coastal plain. It also gets significantly hotter and dryer in the north.

Private Game Reserves

The western edge of the Kruger is fringed by a

243

How To Spot Game

The best season for viewing is winter or early spring (July–Sept) when the rivers are dry, vegetation is sparse and animals stay near the water holes. Summertime (Dec–Apr), however, is the breeding season, so you have a chance of seeing the animals with their young. This is also the season for migratory birds.

Always move slowly and stay alert. Even elephants and giraffes are astonishingly well camouflaged in their natural habitat and can fade into obscurity a few metres from the road. Don't be afraid to query what you think is a rock or branch, it may be a shaded rhino or antelope horn. Stop now and then, especially near water. When stationary, you often notice things not otherwise visible, and it probably will not be long before something turns up, if you have the patience to wait.

The best times for viewing are between dawn and 1000, and from 1600 to dusk, but not all animal life comes to a sleepy stop at noon. Some species, especially elephant, hippo, giraffe and zebra, remain alert in the heat of the day.

Most animals seem indifferent to the presence of vehicles and it is amazing how close you can get, although female elephants may charge if they feel their calves are threatened, and lone bulls can be cranky. Buffalo and black rhino have notoriously short tempers, while you should never get between a hippo and the water. As a general rule, it is best to.stop and let the animals come to you rather than upsetting them by moving in too close.

Never stand up or wave your arm out of the window – it disrupts the silhouette and alarms the animals. And never, never try feeding or stroking any wild animal, however placid or cuddly it looks.

244

series of private game reserves, of which the largest and most important are, from south to north, the 60,000 hectare **Sabi Sands**, **Timbavati**, which is particularly famous for its white lions, **Klaserie**, **Umbabat** and **Manyeleti**. Each of these is split into a host of small properties, many of them, particularly in Sabi Sands and Timbavati, owned and operated by some of the world's finest lodges. All fences are down and game wanders freely between the different private reserves and the main park. The great benefit of staying here, apart from sybaritic five-star pampering, is that you are allowed off the roads in the private reserves and have a much better chance of seeing most, if not all, of the Big Five during a 2–3 night stay.

Luxury Lodges
The luxury lodges are all small, few sleeping more than about 20 people, in beautifully designed chalets, filled with magnificent furniture and art, scattered through bush and lavish gardens, around a swimming pool. Meals are usually held outdoors, or around a campfire in the boma, and the atmosphere is more house

party than hotel. Game drives are held morning and evening, and there are usually plenty of other options, including night drives, guided walks and hides. Anyone with a special interest, such as a keen birder, will be catered for. None of the camps are fenced and animals can and do wander freely through the buildings to graze on the lawns. All the lodges insist that anyone walking around after dark is accompanied by an armed ranger.

The larger properties may have several small lodges scattered through different locations (such as on the river, up a hill, or in the forest), some at different prices. Get details of all and specify which you require when booking. Few have actual addresses, or even telephones. Booking is done via Johannesburg offices.

Sabi Sands
Sabi Sabi *(Pf), PO Box 52665, Saxonwold 2132; tel: 011-483 3939; fax: 011-453 3799,* has a 10 km frontage on the perennial Sabie River, where hippo and crocodile can be seen. The reserve has three lodges – the River Lodge, on the bank of the Sabie River, with 21 chalets

and 2 suites, one of which is a tree-house; the Bush Lodge, overlooking a water hole, with 22 chalets and 5 suites; and the atmospheric Selati Lodge, which uses oil lamps in place of electricity – and the tented Nkombe Camp. Renowned for lion sightings, Sabi Sabi is also noted for its environmental awareness walking trails and visits to secluded hides overlooking water holes and the river. An unusual feature at Sabi Sabi is the ranger training programme, which has been extended to guests keen to live and learn the life of a game ranger for a few days.

Londolozi *(Cv/Pf/Rx/SL), PO Box 1211, Sunning Hill Park 2157; tel: 011-803 8421; fax 011-803 1810,* straddles the Sand River, attracting a wide range of species to the area, although it is particularly famous for its leopards. It has three lodges – the most lavish Main Camp (8 chalets and 2 suites), Bush Camp, which has 8 chalets built on to the natural rock, and the magnificent Tree Camp, whose 6 stilted, thatched chalets are tucked into the forest canopy.

MalaMala, *PO Box 2575, Randburg 2125; tel: 011-789 2677; fax: 011-886 4382,* offers the Big Five with five-star facilities and is reputed to be South Africa's most expensive – and one of Africa's best – game lodges. Main Camp consists of luxury chalets overlooking the Sand River. Kirkman's Camp has guest rooms surrounding a picturesque old farmhouse, and is less expensive. Harry's Huts, in a lovely riverine forest, is the cheapest option.

Ulusaba *(Pf), PO Box 239, Lonehill 2062; tel: 011-465 6646; fax: 011-465 6649,* is one of the most dramatic properties, with two delightful lodges. The Rock Lodge is built vertically amongst the giant boulders of a granite koppie, and the Safari Lodge is built on wooden platforms in the forest canopy. Each has 10 rooms. Neither is suitable for anyone with mobility problems.

Exeter Lodge *(Pf), tel/fax: 013-735 5140.* Booking, *tel: 011-884 6438; fax: 011-783 1631.* This is one of the smallest and most intimate of the lodges, with only 10 thatched chalets set amongst the trees, while meals are served on a stilted game-viewing deck overlooking the Sand River.

Idube *(Pf), PO Box 2617, Northcliff 2115, Johannesburg; tel: 011-888 3713; fax: 011-888 2181,* uses its surroundings to create a bush garden around the natural rock swimming pool and 9 thatched chalets, with outdoor showers as an option to the full en suite facilities.

Inyati, *PO Box 38838, Booysens 2016; tel: 011-493 0755; fax: 011-493 0837,* is one of the most overtly comfortable of the famous lodges, its 9 chalets fitted with wall-to-wall carpets and private gardens, while the central facilities include a gym, elegant dining room and covered viewing platform.

Timbavati

Thornybush Game Reserve, *PO Box 798, Northlands 2116; tel: 011-883 7918; fax: 011-883 8201,* has several lodges on the property. The Thornybush Game Lodge is a single thatched lodge building with 16 rooms, overlooking the Monwana River, although guests can opt to spend the night sleeping under the stars. Serondella has colonial-style thatched cottages, while N'Kaya has African-style ethnic architecture, and Chapungu is again colonial-style, with airy rooms opening on to a wide verandah.

Motswari Game Lodge, *PO Box 67865, Bryanston 2021; tel: 011-463 1990; fax: 011-463 1992,* can accommodate up to 30 visitors in thatched rondavels, with en suite bathrooms. Its sister lodge, **M'Bali**, is an East African-style tented camp overlooking a 3 km stretch of water.

Manyeleti

Honeyguide Tented Camp, *Safariplan, PO Box 4245, Randburg 2125; tel: 011-483 2734; fax: 011-728 3767,* in the Manyeleti Game Reserve, offers luxurious accommodation and excellent game-viewing from a vehicle or on a three- or four-day hike, with accommodation in bush camps.

Interspersed between the luxury destinations are some cheaper rustic camps offering the same game-viewing opportunities, but even these are likely to cost upwards of R500 a night. Good hotels outside the reserves are significantly cheaper, as is the Parks Board accommodation (see above).

245

KRUGER (SKUKUZA)– HLUHLUWE

Southern Africa's scenic variety is encapsulated in this route – from the game-rich scrublands of the Kruger National Park and the grandeur of the Drakensbergs to the humid lowveld and on to the wild, sparsely-populated wetlands of Kwazulu-Natal's northern coast. Most South Africans choose to drive through Swaziland, which is by far the more interesting option. Whether visitors go this way may depend on their visa; remember that you will need a multi-entry visa to re-enter South Africa. The alternative is long, but there is some interesting scenery along the way. Neither route is particularly fast or direct.

Swaziland Route

ROUTES

SWAZILAND ROUTE

Leave Skukuza on the main road to Paul Kruger Gate (10 km), then take the R536 to Hazyview (43 km) and turn left on to the R40 through White River (36 km) and Nelspruit (19 km) to **Barberton** (45 km). From Barberton, continue south on the R40 over the

Saddleback Pass to Bulembu Borderpost into Swaziland (open 0800–1600). Continue on to Pigg's Peak (21 km). It is also possible to head south through the park and leave via Numbi Gate, to join the R538 to White River, or Malelane Gate, to join the N4, turn left towards Komatipoort (see p.226), then right on to the R570 and enter Swaziland via Jeppe's Reef borderpost (41 km; open 0700–1800), from where it is 40 km to Pigg's Peak.

From Pigg's Peak, head south towards Mbabane (64 km). From here, follow the main road through Manzini (50 km), Sipofaneni (47 km), Big Bend (35 km) and Nsoko (37 km) to Lavumisa Borderpost (34 km; open 0700–2200). From the border, it is 9 km to the N2. Turn left (south) on to the N2 and keep going for about 80 km. There will be a turn off to Hluhluwe village, Phinda and St Lucia on your left, and to the Hluhluwe-Umfolozi National Park on your right. Distance: 580 km; allow three days. It is possible to do this in one day if you start very early and are ready to cross the border as soon as it opens. However, the roads within Swaziland are very steep and winding, the driving tiring, and it would be a crying shame to miss some of the most beautiful scenery in Southern Africa. For Swaziland, see pp.379–387.

SOUTH AFRICAN ROUTE

Follow the route above until you reach **Barberton** (153 km). From here, take the R38 south-west over Bothasnek and Nelshoogte Passes to **Badplaas** (63 km). Turn south on the R541 to Lochiel (36 km), then left on to the N17 to Warburton (31 km). Then take the R33 south via Amsterdam (54 km) to **Piet Retief** (52 km). Here, you can pick up the N2, which heads south-east for a further 221 km, past the Pongolapoort Dam to the Hluhluwe turn off. Distance: 610 km; allow one long day.

BARBERTON

Tourist Office: *Market Sq., Crown St; tel: 013-712 2121.* Open Mon–Fri 0800–1300, 1400–1630, Sat 0830–1200. Information on the town and Mpumulanga in general. A leaflet giving details of Barberton's attractions and accommodation is available, and the office can also provide details of hiking trails in the area.

ACCOMMODATION

There are a couple of small hotels and about a dozen bed and breakfasts. The clean and comfortable **Phoenix Hotel**, *20 Pilgrim St; tel: 013-712 4211,* (cheap) is a typical country hotel, pub and restaurant. The **Fountain Baths Guest Lodge**, *48 Pilgrim St; tel: 013-712 2707* (cheap) offers bed and breakfast rooms and self-catering cottages at the former public baths and pool, built in 1885. **Camping**: self-catering chalets are also available at **Barberton Caravan Park**, *General St; tel: 013-712 3323.* Out of town, those in need of a little luxury should try the **Komati River Lodge**, *in the Songimvelo Nature Reserve; bookings tel: 011-789 6860; fax: 011-789 0739* (moderate–expensive).

SIGHTSEEING

Today, Barberton is a sedate little town, perched picturesquely on the slopes of the Makhonjwa Mountains. But its pretty streets of colonial-style buildings and a genteel Victorian tea garden belie its lively beginnings. The town is named after Graham Barber and his cousins Fred and Henry Barber who, in June 1884, discovered a gold reef so rich it was said to have sparkled in the sun. Their find sparked off a wild gold rush, and later that month the local mining commissioner officially named the town by smashing a bottle of gin over a rock.

With some 1400 prospectors flooding in, Barberton became a riotous place, and by 1886, there was a saloon for every 15 inhabitants. Cockney Liz, the most notorious of the town's many prostitutes, danced on a billiard table every midnight, auctioning herself to the highest bidder. Within a few years it was clear that mining here was going to be hard work and less rewarding than the Witwatersrand reefs. The circus moved on, but enough people remained for the fledgling town of Barberton to survive. Perhaps the town's most enduringly famous gift to the world was the Barberton daisy, first exported to Kew Gardens in London in 1884, and now adding colour to garden borders around the world. Barberton's story is told in the **museum**, *Pilgrim St* (see above). The museum and several old houses which open to the public do so on a rota system, with two open at any given moment. It is impossible to

247

pin down times in advance; ask the Tourist Office for details on arrival.

A number of restored buildings from Barberton's pioneer days may be seen on a walk around the streets. These include the 1886 **Stopforth House**, the 1904 **Belhaven House** and 1890s **Fernlea House** (all open to the public, see above); the **Kaap Gold Fields Stock Exchange** (the first in South Africa), opened in 1887, the 1887 **Globe Tavern** and the **Lewis and Marks Building**, the first two-storey building in the province. There is also a **British blockhouse** from the Anglo-Boer War and a **Masonic Temple**, built in 1884. The overhead **cableway** was built in 1939 to transport asbestos 20 km from the Havelock Mine in Swaziland; since the collapse of the asbestos industry it is no longer in use. A statue of **Jock of the Bushveld**, Sir Percy Fitzpatrick's legendary canine character, stands in front of the **Town Hall**, *General St*.

Just outside town, the 2-km **Fortuna Mine Walk** leads through a 600m tunnel carved out by an old mine (take a torch). The surrounding rocks are estimated to be a staggering 4200 million years old. The hopefully named **Eureka City**, *in the hills 15 km north-east of Barberton*, is a ghost town originally built to house workers in the Golden Quarry Mine on the Sheba Reef. Also nearby is the 56,000 hectare **Songimvelo Nature Reserve**, its habitats stretching from lowveld savannah to mountain moorland at almost 2000m. This is an excellent place for hiking and riding, and the game-viewing is good, even if it doesn't quite match up to the splendours of neighbouring Kruger. It does not have the Big Five.

SWAZILAND

See pp. 379–387.

BADPLAAS

Tourist Information: Middleveld Tourism Association, *PO Box 242; tel/fax: 017-843 2088*.

Badplaas marks the start of the Middleveld, an area of temperate climate and scenic beauty in south-east Mpumulanga. Hiking, fishing, bird-watching and wildlife observation are the principal activities in the area.

> ## *Best-seller Jock*
>
> Percy Fitzpatrick arrived from England in 1884, aged 22. He became a transport rider in the Eastern Transvaal goldfields, accompanied on his journeys by his beloved bull terrier, Jock. His account of their adventures, *Jock of the Bushveld*, first published in 1907, was an instant success and is still widely read. It has never been out of print. Fitzpatrick went on to an illustrious double career in mining and politics. He was knighted in 1902. The statue of Jock in Barberton is one of several memorials to Fitzpatrick and his pet in Mpumalanga.

The **Aventura Badplaas** *(Av)*, *Main Rd; tel: 017-844 1023; fax: 017-844 1391* is the area's major accommodation option (cheap–moderate), with 159 self-catering units and a full range of facilities, including restaurant and bar. There are also extensive pitches for caravans and tents. The resort's main features are mineral spring baths, cool pools and a hydro spa. There are a few bed and breakfast homes and guest farms between Badplaas and Carolina.

PIET RETIEF

There are two budget priced hotels: the **Imperial Hotel**, *Church St; tel: 013-434 251; fax 013-435 0815*, and the **Central Hotel**, *corner Church and du Toit Sts; tel: 013-434 344; fax: 013-435 0617*. **Campsite: Municipal Caravan Park**, on the N2 *(Church St)* at the southern end of the town; *tel: 013-432 619*.

The largest town in southern Mpumalanga, Piet Retief is really only suitable as a refreshment stop on the way to or from Swaziland or northern Kwazulu-Natal. It was founded in 1882 on land bought from the local Swazi chief and named after the Boer leader massacred by Dingane in 1838 (see p.64). The Dutch Reformed Church was built in 1921 by Gerard Moerdijk, the architect responsible for the Voortrekker Monument in Pretoria.

HLUHLUWE

For details of northern Kwazulu-Natal, see Hluhluwe–Kosi Bay, pp. 188–193.

KRUGER-PHALABORWA

Skirting the eastern edge of the Mpumalanga Drakensbergs, this is one of the most scenically spectacular driving routes in South Africa. It starts in the heart of the Kruger National Park (see p. 239–245), then climbs steeply up the edge of the escarpment through small, historic gold rush towns and vast forests of pine and eucalyptus to introduce travellers to awesome natural creations, including vast

panoramic views, a host of waterfalls and the spectacular, 30 km-long Blyde River Canyon. It is also possible to do the first part of this trip, to Pilgrim's Rest and the Blyde Canyon, as part of a loop including Lydenburg and Sabie (see pp. 228–229). To explore the area properly, consider staying at Hazyview instead of within the park.

Direct Route

249

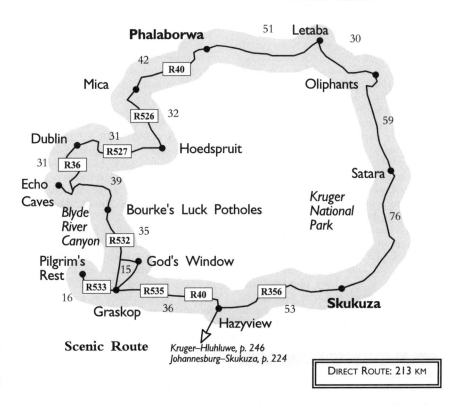

Phalaborwa · 51 · Letaba · 30
42
R40
Mica · Oliphants
R526 · 32
59
Dublin · 31
R527 · Hoedspruit
31 · R36
Satara
Echo · 39
Caves · Blyde · Bourke's Luck Potholes · Kruger National Park · 76
River · 35
Canyon · R532
Pilgrim's · God's Window
Rest · 15
16 · R533 · R535 · R40 · R356
Graskop · 36 · 53 · Skukuza
Hazyview

Scenic Route Kruger–Hluhluwe, p. 246
Johannesburg–Skukuza, p. 224

DIRECT ROUTE: 213 KM

ROUTES

DIRECT ROUTE

The most direct route from Skukuza to Phalaborwa is right through the centre of the Kruger National Park. However, if you drive within the legal speed limits (maximum 40 kph), you will be on the road for at least 6½ hrs, even without allowing time for game-viewing. In other words, to get the most out of this route requires an overnight stop within the park, probably at Satara or Oliphants (see pp. 242–243). Distance: 213 km.

SCENIC ROUTE

From Skukuza, head west and leave the Kruger National Park via the Paul Kruger Gate (10 km) and continue along the R356 for 50 km to **Hazyview**. Turn right on to the R40, then left onto the R535 to **Grasskop** (36 km). From here, the R533 winds westwards, climbing steadily to **Pilgrim's Rest** (16 km). Retrace your route to Grasskop, then turn north onto the R532. Just outside Grasskop, turn off onto the R534 for a 15 km loop road up to the stunning viewpoint known as **God's Window**. The R532 continues north to **Bourke's Luck Potholes** (35 km from Grasskop). For the next 39 km, the road winds along the edge of the **Blyde River Canyon Nature Reserve**, with several viewpoints over the canyon to the right, eventually linking with the R36. Turn left and almost immediately right for the access road to the **Echo Caves**. Return to the R36, turn left and continue north over the Abel Erasmus Pass and through the J. G. Strijdom Tunnel to Dublin (31 km). From here, take the R527 east to **Hoedspruit** (31 km). Turn left and continue north on the R526 for 32 km to Mica, then turn right and strike east on the R40 to **Phalaborwa** (42 km). Those planning to stay within the park should aim to be at the gate by 4pm at the latest, as it is a further 50 km to Letaba and 80 km to Oliphants Camp. Distance: 346 km; allow two days.

HAZYVIEW

Tourist Information: *Blue Haze Centre; tel: 013-737 7414.*

Hazyview's name has a lot to answer for; the address is well-known, but few people ever notice the town itself. There really isn't much to see; it is a small country town with a few shops catering for locals – and over 3500 tourist beds provided by a range of hotels, lodges, time-share properties, guesthouses and bed and breakfasts in the vicinity.

The most entertaining of the large hotels in the area is the 4-star **Casa do Sol**, *Sabie Rd; tel: 013-737 8111, fax: 013-737 8166* (expensive), a Mediterranean village complex, with rough plastered walls, brick-paved 'streets', plazas with fountains and cool, shady cloisters, all set in a small game reserve. Dinner and breakfast, served by waiters dressed variously as Arabs or French artists, are included in the price of the sumptuously-furnished double rooms and suites. The food is as imaginative as the surroundings. Even more luxurious is the smaller hideaway **Highgrove House** *(Pf), on the R40 between Hazyview and White River; tel: 013-764 1844; fax: 013-764 1855* (expensive), set amidst avocado and banana plantations. The eight garden suites all have log fires, and some have private pools and saunas. The food is good enough to make gourmets drool. Chains include Pa, Ka.

At a less rarified price level, **Hippo Hollow** *(Pf), off the R535 (Sabie road) near the junction of the R40; tel: 013-737 7752, fax: 013-737 7673* (cheap–moderate) is a wood and thatch lodge with self-catering chalets along the banks of the Sabie River near a hippo pool, surrounding one of the best restaurants in the area. The down-to-earth 3-star **Hotel Numbi**, *Main St; tel: 013-737 7301, fax: 013-737 7525* (moderate) has twenty family rooms, a couple of doubles, a caravan park and a reasonable restaurant, serving steaks and burgers at sensible prices. **Laughing Waters**, *on the R536 between Hazyview and Sabie; tel: 013-737 8144; fax: 013-737 8173* (cheap) is a friendly and comfortable guesthouse, with a pool, sauna and games room, set in beautiful gardens on a lemon farm. Dinner by arrangement. **Kruger Park Backpackers**, *junction of the R40 and road to Numbi Gate; tel: 013-737 7224* (cheap) provides basic dormitory accommodation and organises budget tours of the park and other local attractions.

GRASKOP

Tourist Office: *corner Oorwinning and Louis Trichardt Sts; tel: 013-767 1316; fax: 013-767 1798.* Open Wed–Sat 0900–1700. This small office at the entrance to the municipal tourist park, with adjoining shop, restaurant and café, has information on attractions and accommodation in town and throughout the Lowveld region. Cottages and bed and breakfast accommodation may be reserved here.

ACCOMMODATION AND FOOD

A favourite refreshment and overnight stop for travellers, Graskop owes more to its surrounding attractions than to any intrinsic charm of its own. It is nevertheless a pleasant little town – three blocks in each direction downtown – with three small hotels, a dozen or so establishments offering chalets, cottages and bed and breakfast and a couple of caravan/camping parks. The recently renovated **Graskop Hotel** *(Pf), Main St; tel: 013-767 1244* (cheap–moderate), is the most centrally placed of the local hotels (if anywhere can be less than central in a town this size), with jazzy ethnic furnishings, a pool and its own crafts studio. The **Blyde Lodge**, *Louis Trichardt St; tel: 013-767 1316* (cheap–moderate) is a quieter option, with rooms and chalets tucked away from through traffic. Other alternatives include the **Summit Lodge**, *Market St; tel: 013-767 1058* (cheap), about 500m out of town on the R532, and the **Log Cabin Village**, *Louis Trichardt St; tel: 013-767 1974; fax: 031-767 1975* (cheap–moderate), a small development close to the town centre with one- and two-bedroom self-catering units.

Campsites: **Municipal Tourist Park**, *Louis Trichardt St; tel: 031-767 1091* (cheap) has bungalows and flats as well as caravan and camping sites. Pitches are also available at **Panorama Rest Camp**, *Kowyns Pass Rd, 1 km east; tel: 031-767 1126* (cheap).

Graskop has about a dozen eating places, including several pancake houses – mostly located along *Louis Trichardt* and *Main Sts* – all cashing in on the nationwide success of **Harrie's**, *Louis Trichardt St; tel: 013-767 1273*, the first place in South Africa to do savoury crêpes. This is a good stop for lunch or tea, but demand can be high during summer weekends, so you might consider eating a little earlier or later than usual. The **Blyde Lodge** (see Accommodatoin) has a quiet bar and a roomy, discreet restaurant (cheap–moderate).

SIGHTSEEING

Founded in 1880 as a gold mining settlement, the only sightseeing opportunity in Graskop is a 12 km **walking trail** that takes in places mentioned in *Jock of the Bushveld*. The Tourist Office provides maps. The town's main tourism appeal lies in its shops, which offer a cornucopia of quality souvenirs, gifts and craft articles.

PILGRIM'S REST

Tourist Office: *opposite Royal Hotel, Main St; tel: 013-768 1296; fax: 013-768 1113* (open Mon–Sat 0930–1245, 1315–1630). Much of the space in this large information centre, located in an old general store, is given over to an exhibition of gold mining equipment and implements. It also dispenses information on local and regional attractions and accommodation, but does not handle reservations. A single ticket giving admission to all the town's museums may be bought here; R5.

ACCOMMODATION

The village's pride and joy is the **Royal Hotel** *(Pf), Main St; tel: 013-768 1100; fax: 013-768 1188* (moderate). Built in the mining pioneer-style that pervades Pilgrim's Rest, the single-storey, tin-roofed hotel has a surprisingly ornate interior and is a museum-piece in its own right. The hotel bar was originally a Catholic chapel in Lourenço Marques (now Maputo), Mozambique. In 1882, it was dismantled and reassembled at the Royal, after being transported by ox wagon. The hotel reception area is today the central reservations point for local campsites and self-catering cottages as well as hotel rooms. **District Six Miners' Cottages**; *tel: 013-768 1211; fax: 013-768 1113*, is a group of self-catering cottages near the village's historic cemetery.

Campsite: the **Pilgrim's Rest Caravan Park**, *at the western end of the village, near the Blyde River; tel: 013-768 1367.*

More luxurious accommodation is available

251

Privatisation

Huge changes can be expected on this route during the lifetime of this edition. Shortly before going to press, a deal was announced between the Mpumalanga Tourist Authority, the Mpumalanga Parks Board, the Dolfin Group, a private company which owns, amongst other things, the United Touring Company (already the largest tour operator in both Kenya and Zimbabwe), and Block Hotels. In a R400 million investment agreement, UTC have been given exclusive long-term rights to the management of the Blyde Canyon and Pilgrim's Rest and are planning far-reaching developments, including new hotels, organised tours and hikes within the canyon, an aqua centre, helicopter rides and a host of other activities. More details in the next edition; meanwhile, ask the local Tourist Offices what is up and running.

at the **Mount Sheba Hotel** *(Pf), Lydenburg Rd (R533), 20 km west of Pilgrim's Rest; tel: 013-768 1241; fax 013-768 1248* (expensive). This stone and thatch hotel, with 25 suites, stands in a remote valley surrounded by a private nature reserve, including large areas of magnificent hardwood forests filled with tree ferns and cycads. Activities include swimming, hiking, tennis and squash. Nearby, the **Inn on Robbers Pass** *(Pf), Lydenburg road (R533); tel/fax: 013-768 1491* (cheap–moderate) is a cosy inn with good food, accommodation in cottages and spectacular mountain views.

It is not difficult to find somewhere to eat in Pilgrim's Rest. Cafés, restaurants and bars are strung all along *Main St*, with a close concentration neighbouring the Royal Hotel.

SIGHTSEEING

Strung along a steep hillside, Pilgrim's Rest is truly quaint – a living museum that would surely be recognised by its founders, although it must be cleaner, neater and quieter, even on the busiest of high season days, than it was during its gold rush beginnings.

Gold was discovered in nearby Pilgrim's Creek in 1873 by Alex 'Wheelbarrow' Patterson, who owed his nickname to the fact that he kept everything he owned in a wheelbarrow. The village is said to have been named by William Trafford, who saw the settlement as the end of his personal search for wealth. More fanciful folk shift the apostrophe to the end of the first word and claim the name was given by early diggers who called themselves 'The Pilgrims' because they were on a permanent odyssey for spirits – the kind that come in a bottle. Nearby Whisky Creek was named after a wagonload of spirits bound for the mining camp that overturned into the stream.

Today, the whole village of Pilgrim's Rest is a national monument, and it is a joy to wander through the carefully preserved galvanised iron cottages. Several are open as museums, all easily accessible on foot. Among these are the **Alanglade House Museum**, the exquisitely furnished home of a former mine manager; the **Diggings Museum**, where visitors can see gold panning demonstrations; the **Dredzen Shop Museum**, a store stocked with goods used a century ago, and the **House Museum**, a typical timber and corrugated iron dwelling.

The **Pilgrim's Rest Cemetery** is also worth a trip. It stands above the settlement in the area known as District Six, a puzzling choice since the access road is so steep bearers had to work in relays to carry coffins there, and the ground in which the graves were dug is almost solid slate. Legend has it that the cemetery was founded when an unknown thief was shot dead by diggers and buried where he fell. The Robber's Grave is still there, inscribed as such, and on a north–south line to mark the tomb of a sinner.

BLYDE RIVER CANYON

Tourist Information: Escarpment Information and Craft Centre, *Monsoon Gallery, R527, near Dublin; tel: 01528-35114*. Open daily 0900–1700. A commercial enterprise rather than a local authority tourism service, this centre offers large regional maps illustrating tourist destinations, regional features and resource information covering the Central Lowveld region. You can also buy textiles, ceramics, basketware, artefacts and books in the gallery.

ACCOMMODATION

So far there is remarkably little accommodation – and even fewer dining choices – in the area of the **Blyde River Canyon Nature Reserve**, but there will certainly be improvements shortly (see feature box opposite).

The **Aventura Swadini** *(Av), on the Blyde River, just north of Bourke's Luck Potholes, near Mariepskop; tel/fax: 01528-35141,* and the **Aventura Blydepoort** *(Av), near the Blydepoort Dam; tel/fax: 013-769 8005,* both offer cheap–moderate self-catering accommodation in one- and two-bedroom chalets, together with camping and caravan sites. The originally decorated **Berlyn Peacock Tavern** *(Pf), Berlin Waterfall Road, 8 km north of Graskop; tel/fax: 013-767 1085* (cheap) provides comfortable accommodation, good food and friendly hospitality, amidst an explosion of colour.

At the northern end of the Canyon, **Trackers**, *north of Aventura Swadini; tel: 01528-35033* (cheap) offers chalet and lodge accommodation, with opportunities for climbing, hiking, canoeing, fishing and game-viewing, while the **Echo Caves Country Inn**, *near the intersection of the R532 and R36 (signposted); tel: 01323-80015* (cheap) is a comfortable bed and breakfast with 11 rooms and a reasonable range of amenities.

Campsite: Manoutsa Park, *on the banks of the Olifants River, just north of the J.G. Strijdom Tunnel, R36; tel: 01528-35125,* has 200 pitches for tents and caravans, a restaurant, grocery shop and a large swimming pool.

SIGHTSEEING

The 26 km Blyde River Canyon was carved to depths of 350–800m by the Blyde River over a period of around 60 million years. Today, it is preserved by the 26,000 hectare Blyde River Canyon Nature Reserve. At the southern end are several stunning viewing points on a loop road, the R534, including **Panorama Falls**, **The Pinnacle**, overlooking the 30m Pinnacle Rock, **Wonder View** and, most spectacular of all, **God's Window**. On a clear day, it presents an incredible view across the Lowveld and the Kruger National Park to the coast of Mozambique, about 150 km to the east. Even in the all-too-common mist, the cloud swirling below is dramatic. At the northern intersection of the R534 and R532, tracks lead to the 150m **Berlin Falls** and the 92m **Lisbon Falls**.

The southern end of Blyde River Canyon proper is marked by **Bourke's Luck Potholes**, *off the R532; tel: 013-768 1215* (open daily 0700–1700). Standing at the confluence of the Blyde and Treur Rivers, the potholes are a geological phenomenon created over thousands of years by swirling, pebble-bearing flood waters. They are named after Thomas Bourke, a 19th-century surveyor who discovered gold here, but as he was working for a mining company, he personally received none of the rewards. The Visitor Centre (open daily 0730–1645) contains a small eco-museum, and there are walking trails, accessible to disabled and blind visitors, across the rivers and along the banks.

Beyond here, the road skirts the rim of the canyon and, again, there are a number of superb viewing points, the best of which overlooks the **Three Rondavels**, three conical peaks named after their resemblance to the traditional African thatched hut, and the **Blydepoort Dam**.

At the northern end of the canyon, the **Echo Caves**, on the R36, *4 km south of the junction with R532, near Mogaba village* (open daily 0800–1700; R12) are a huge complex of tunnels and caverns, whose stalactites echo when tapped. The largest cavern is 100m long and 45m wide. Stone Age artefacts found in the caves are displayed in the nearby **Museum of Man**, housed in a painted San rock shelter.

HOEDSPRUIT

Tourist Information: Central Lowveld Tourism Association, *Public Library; tel/fax: 01528-31678.*

Fort Coepieba Motel, *R40; tel/fax: 01528-31175* (budget), offers bed and breakfast in chalets and has an à la carte restaurant, ladies' bar and swimming pool. A favourite dining and drinking place for locals, live bands perform most evenings.

Loerie Guesthouse, *85 Jakkals St; tel:*

River of Happiness

The name of the Blyde River arose out of an incident in 1844, when a party of Voortrekker men left their women and children encamped on the escarpment to seek a route to the coast. When they failed to return a month later, the women, fearing their men had lost their lives, decided to turn back. They named the river beside their campsite the Treur (the River of Sorrow).

A few days later, on the banks of another small river, they met their menfolk, safe and well. In their joy, they named the new river the Blyde – the River of Happiness.

01528-33990 (budget) is a small but luxurious bed and breakfast home offering optional lunch and dinner.

This is an uninspiring village, largely maintained by the local airforce base. However, it does have one huge draw. The **Hoedspruit Cheetah Project**, *on the R40; tel: 01528-31633* (open Mon–Sat 0830–1600; R20) is a breeding station and study centre for the magnificent cheetah, the fastest animal on earth and rapidly becoming one of the rarest. They also have some dark-coated king cheetahs and other endangered species such as white rhino, Cape hunting dogs and a variety of vultures. Tours last around 2 hrs. At the **Swadini Reptile Park**, *R527; tel: 01528-35203* (open daily 0800–1700), reptiles of all kinds are on display, including the 2m-long Green Iguana, a rare lizard from South America.

PHALABORWA

Tourist Office: *Hendrik van Eck St, next to Kruger Park Gate; tel: 01524-85860; fax: 01524-85870.* Open weekdays 0730–1700, Sat 0800–1200. This small, friendly office has information on local tours and activities, as well as accommodation and dining. At the time of writing, a new tourist centre was due to be built on the corner of *Hendrik van Eck St* and *President Steyn St.*

ACCOMMODATION

Phalaborwa has a good selection of accommodation. **Allin's Travel Lodge**, *35 Palm Ave; tel: 01524-5805/6/7; fax: 01524-5808* (cheap–moderate) has motel-style units with kitchenettes, and a small restaurant serving breakfast and an à la carte dinner. The **Hans Merensky Country Club**, *Koper St; tel: 01524-5931; fax: 01524-85309* (cheap–moderate) is best-known as one of the finest country clubs and golf courses in Southern Africa, but it also offers excellent bungalow accommodation in attractive surroundings and has an à la carte restaurant. The **Impala Protea Inn** *(Pa), 52 Essenhout St; tel: 01524-5681/2; fax: 01524-85234* (moderate) is close to the town centre, set among attractive gardens. Breakfast and pub lunches are served in the **Flying Oliphant** and dinner in the **Guinea Fowl** restaurant.

Daan and Zena's Guest House and Pottery Studio, *15 Birkenhead St; tel: 01524-86049; fax: 01524-86049* (cheap) offers informal bed and breakfast or self-catering accommodation, with walls cheerfully hand-decorated in Zena's distinctive style.

SIGHTSEEING

This is a prosperous, if unexciting town, thanks to the rich deposits of copper, iron and phosphate that are mined in the area. The real reason for coming here is the Kruger National Park, only 3 km away, but there are a couple of interesting sights. The **Palabora Copper Mine**, *Koper St; tel: 01524-802 342* (guided tours every Fri 0900; booking essential) is the largest open cast copper mine in Africa. Ore extraction has created the Open Pit, nearly 2 km across and more than 720m deep, and a tourist attraction in its own right. The pit may be viewed any time from a special look-out point.

The emphasis at the **Foskor Museum**, *16 Tombotie St; tel: 01524-892 019* (open Mon–Fri 1000–1230, 1400–1600; free) is also on mining, but there are also displays on local archaeology and ethnography. There is an interesting **archaeological site** just inside the Phalaborwa Gate of the Kruger National Park (follow the signs).

LADYSMITH–DURBAN

Drakensberg literally means 'Dragon Mountains' after their saw-toothed peaks. To the local Zulus, they are the *uKhahlamba*, the 'barrier of spears'. The Natal Drakensberg are some of the most scenically spectacular mountains in southern Africa. This winding route explores the wild and lovely countryside before emerging into the rolling meadows of the gentle Midlands and heading south to Durban through the lyrically named Valley of a Thousand Hills.

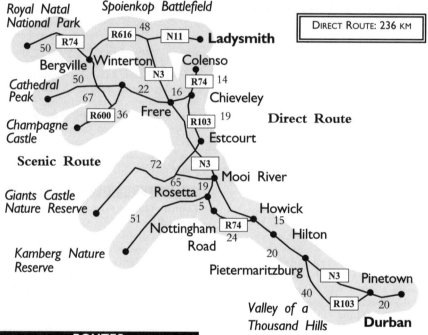

DIRECT ROUTE: 236 KM

255

DIRECT ROUTE

➡️ Leave Ladysmith on the N11, heading west, then turn south on to the N3, a major freeway which strikes right through the heart of Kwazulu-Natal, leading straight into Durban. It is an excellent road, offering distant views of the Drakensburg for much of its length. It skirts most communities on the way, but there are frequent exits. The central section, through the Midlands, is a toll road. Distance: 236 km; allow 3–3½ hrs.

SCENIC ROUTE

➡️ Leave Ladysmith on the N11 heading west. At the junction with the N3, go straight across and take the R616 past the **Spioenkop Dam and Battlefield** to **Bergville** (48 km). Turn right onto the R74 for 30 km, then left onto the approach road to the

Royal Natal Park (20 km). Retrace your route to Bergville and continue south on the R74 for 3 km, then turn right. After 16 km, turn right again for the road up to **Cathedral Peak** (31 km from the crossroads). Return to the crossroads and turn right for 13 km (the last few are on a good gravel road), then turn right and take the R600 up to **Champagne Castle** (23 km). Return to the crossroads, and continue straight along the R600 to **Winterton** (15 km).

From Winterton, turn right on to the R74 for 22 km to Frere, cross the N3 and continue along the R74 to **Colenso** (30 km), also passing'**Chieveley**, the **Bloukrans Battlefield** and the **Clouston Field of Remembrance**. Backtrack along the R74 as far as Chieveley (14 km), then turn left on to the R103 and head south to **Estcourt** (19 km). Leave Estcourt and head south on the R103 for 5 km to visit Fort Durnford, backtrack a short distance and turn west towards Giants Castle. After 36 km, turn left on to a 12 km stretch of gravel road, then right for the last 19 km to the **Giant's Castle Nature Reserve**. Return to the gravel road, turn right and follow signs to **Mooi River**.

From Mooi River, take the R74 south-west to **Rosetta**, from where a signed gravel road leads west to **Kamberg Nature Reserve** (70 km). A gravel road continues south-west skirting the feet of the Drakensberg to Himeville and Underberg. Side roads off it lead up to Sani Pass and the Lesotho Border (4x4 only), and to the southernmost sections of the Drakensberg. However, to follow this route, return to Rosetta and turn right on the R74 and head south to **Nottingham Road** (5 km), **Howick** (24 km), **Hilton** (15 km) and **Pietermaritzburg** (see pp.285–289). From here, take the N3 south for 15 km to Cato Ridge, then take the R103 south. This leads through the Valley of a Thousand Hills to reach Pinetown and the outskirts of Durban (35 km). Distance: with mountain side trips; expect to do 600 km plus; allow: 2–3 days.

BUSES

Translux run a bus service from Ladysmith to Durban on Tues, Thur and Sun. Journey time: 3 hrs. OTT Table 3543.

SPIOENKOP

This small hill was the site of one of the bloodiest, most chaotic and unnecessary battles in the entire Anglo-Boer War. On the night of 23 Jan 1900, when 1700 British troops attacked this small rocky hill, the few Boers on top retreated. Next morning, the much larger Boer army counter-attacked, with terrible losses, and eventually pulled back, believing the British impregnable. On the British side, however, a lack of support, artillery and even confusion over command led to a massacre, with 243 dead and over 500 wounded. The next night, the remaining British withdrew, not knowing that the Boers had done the same thing. At daylight, two Boer scouts found the hill deserted. Nothing had been achieved, apart from horrendous bloodshed, while hindsight showed that the road it overlooked was grossly underguarded and could have been taken with little effort. There are a number of military graves and monuments on the battlefield, which is now part of the **Spioenkop Nature Reserve***; tel: 036-488 1578* (open access; R6), surrounding a small dam. There are several walking trails, riding, swimming and tennis available as well as caravan and camping sites.

BERGVILLE

Tourist Office: Drakensberg Publicity Association; *tel: 036-448 1557*, covers the whole northern Drakensberg region.

The pleasant village of Bergville, on the banks of the Tugela River between Spioenkop Dam and the huge Woodstock Dam, has no specific sights, except an **Anglo-Boer War Blockhouse**, in the courthouse grounds.

Colour section (i): Old De Beers diamond building, Kimberley (p.232); Kruger National Park; inset, an elephant at Kruger (see pp.239–245).

(ii): Bourke's Luck Potholes (p.253); Blood River Battle Site (p.270).

(iii) Drakensberg Mountains (pp.255–263); George (see pp.273–274): Dutch Reformed Church; and inset, the old Slave Tree.

(iv): Pretoria (pp.294–302): Sammy Marks Square; inset, the Voortrekker Monument.

PRETORIA STATE THEATRE

The 2-star **Sandford Park Lodge**, *off the R616 to Ladysmith (follow the signs from the main road); tel: 036-448 1001; fax: 036-448 1047* (moderate) began life as a coaching inn in 1850. It is comfortable and friendly, with wonderful views and a country house ambience. **Campsite**: **Bergville Caravan Park**, *on the R74, south of town; tel: 036-438 1273*. In the Drakensberg foothills are two family resorts: the 2-star owner-run **Cavern Berg Resort**, *Bergville; tel: 036-438 6270, fax: 036-438 6334* (cheap–moderate; price includes full board); and 3-star **Little Switzerland Resort**, *Bergville; tel 036-438 6220, fax: 036-438 6222* (moderate), which offers sports facilities, a fitness centre and games room. Both have pools and will arrange riding, fishing and hiking.

ROYAL NATAL NATIONAL PARK

Parks Information and Facilities: **Visitors' Centre**, *about 1 km from the main gate; tel: 036-438 6303* (centre open 0800–1630; park open daily 0500–1900 Oct–Mar, 0600–1800 Apr–Sept; R6). This excellent centre has a shop and copious amounts of information, also supplying detailed topographical maps of the park, maps and fishing and hiking permits.

For advance accommodation bookings, contact **Natal Parks Board**; *tel: 0331-471 981*. Clearly signed within the park, the **Royal Natal National Park Hotel** *(Nt); tel: 036-438 6200; fax: 036-438 6101* (moderate) is a pleasant, friendly hotel in a superb setting. Self-catering accommodation in 1- to 3-star chalets, cottages and bungalows is positioned below the Amphitheatre at **Tendele**; *tel/fax: 036-438 6411* (cheap), and there are campsites at **Mahai** and **Rugged Glen** (ask for directions at the office). Just outside the park, the **Mont-aux-Sources** *(Ka); tel/fax: 036-438 6230* (expensive), is the smartest of the local resorts.

In 1906, some 8000 hectares at the foot of Mont-aux-Sources were proclaimed the Natal National Park. In 1947, King George VI, Queen Elizabeth and Princesses Elizabeth (now the Queen) and Margaret visited the area and 'Royal' was added to the name. In 1950, the park was extended by the inclusion of the Rugged Glen Reserve. Today, this beautiful

park is one of South Africa's leading tourist attractions. Botanists can seek up to 1000 plant species. Bird-watchers may spot rare vultures and eagles among the 180 bird species. Duiker, bushbuck, reedbuck, baboon, hare, wildebeest and small cats such as the rare caracal may be sighted. Trout anglers are in their element in the park's myriad streams. Hikers and climbers can be as energetic as they choose, with a couple of dozen hikes of varying lengths and degrees of difficulty to choose from.

However, many visit it purely for the incredible mountain scenery, notably the vast wall of the Amphitheatre, a sheer basalt cliff 4 km wide, in the shape of a half-moon, at the park's southern boundary, with the 3165m Sentinel and the 3047m Eastern Buttress standing guard at either side. Between them rise several rivers, including the Tugela River, which almost immediately cascades over several small falls before plunging a startling, sheer 614m. Altogether, their combined height of 948m make these the second highest waterfalls in the world (after the Angel Falls). Other rivers born on the Mont-aux-Sources include the Elands, which flows into the Vaal, and the Western Khubeda River, which later becomes the mighty Gariep (Orange) River. The hiking trail to the source of the Tugela River is fairly straightforward, but there is a challenging central section which involves climbing two chain ladders to negotiate a sheer 30m rock face.

Another popular walk, above the Mahai Campsite, leads to the **Cannibal Cave**, which gained its gruesome reputation when refugees from the Mfecane (see p.63) were trapped here and forced to resort to eating their companions to survive. According to legend, they gained a taste for the practice and spent the next 20 years preying on surrounding villages until hunted down by the Zulus.

CENTRAL DRAKENSBERG

Tourist Office: *tel: 036-488 1180* (open first weekend each month 0900–1600). There is a national parks office at **Mike's Pass** (open daily 0700–1900).

The **Cathedral Peak Hotel**, *42 km west of Winterton; tel/fax: 036-488 1888* (moderate) is a pleasant 3-star hotel, whose thatched stone

257

chapel is a popular venue for weddings. In the next valley, **Champagne Castle Hotel**, *32 km west of Winterton; tel: 036-468 1063; 036-438 6101* (moderate) offers similar accommodation. **Campsites**: there is a small campsite opposite the parks office and rough camping is allowed in several surrounding caves; for information, contact the Natal Parks Board (see p.408).

Winterton is a small agricultural village whose **museum**, *beside the Library; tel: 036-488 1620* (open Wed, Fri 0900–1200, 1300–1600, Sat 0900–1200) has displays on the natural history of the Drakensberg, and a replica amaZizi village. From here, the Cathedral Peak road is the next access point into the high Drakensberg. This is a stern landscape of high jagged peaks, such as the Bell (2930 m), the Inner and Outer Horns (3005 m), and Cathedral Peak itself (3004 m). The area is said to have been one of the last mountain strongholds of the San and there are a number of fine rock paintings, including some which show red-coated European soldiers. Some of South Africa's finest modern art is available at the **Ardmore Studio and Gallery**, *on the D275, 5 km from the Champagne Castle road; tel: 036-468 1314* (open Mon–Sat 0900–1630), a magnificent ceramics studio shared by around 40 artists

Dragon Peaks, near Winterton, next to the Cathedral Peak Hotel, is the home of the **Drakensberg Boys' Choir School**. Founded in 1967, the school has achieved an international reputation, with a repertoire including classical, contemporary and African songs. School concerts attract capacity audiences and early booking is essential; *tel: 036-468 1012.*

COLENSO

Tourist Office: *tel: 036-222 113.*

Founded in 1855, on the banks of the Tugela River, Colenso was named after the Bishop of Natal (1853–83). During the Anglo-Boer War, this area was the scene of several major battles. General Buller was headquartered in the town until he lost the disastrous Battle of Colenso on 15 Dec 1899, one of many abortive attempts to lift the siege of Ladysmith (see p.267). The site of his HQ is now the **Clouston Garden of Remembrance and war cemetery** (open daily). The

Blaauwkrantz Monument in the town centre harks back to an earlier war, as a memorial to the Voortrekkers massacred by Zulus. The **Robert E Stevenson Museum**, *Old Toll House (1879), next to Bulwer Bridge* (open Mon–Fri 0800–1800, obtain the key from the Police Station next door), near the monument, traces the history of Colenso with collections of badges, medals, weapons, photographs and personal items. Outside are a 19th-century tractor and two locomotives.

South of Colenso, on the R103 to Estcourt, are several Anglo-Boer War sites, including **Chieveley military cemetery**, *along a dirt road past the railway station* (open access). Amongst the soldiers buried here is Freddy, the son of British General Lord Roberts, who was fatally wounded in the Battle of Colenso. The **Armoured Train Cemetery**, *off the R103 near Frere* (signposted) is chiefly famous as the place where Winston Churchill, then a war correspondent working for a British newspaper, later to become Britain's most famous prime minister, was captured by Boer forces in 1899, after they derailed his train. Taken to Pretoria as a prisoner, he made a headline-grabbing escape.

ESTCOURT

Tourist Office: *Fort Durnford (see below); tel: 0363-23000.*

Farmhouse bed and breakfast is available at **Klipfontein**, *Frere, Estcourt; tel/fax: 0363-24518* (cheap). This industrial town is a livestock centre known for its dairy produce and bacon factory. **Fort Durnford**, *Kemps Rd; tel: 0363-23000* (open 0900–1200, 1300–1630 Mon–Thur, 0800–1200, 1300–1545 Fri, weekends by appointment; free, but donations welcomed) was built in 1874 against the possibility of Zulu attack. It's now a museum, with a section on military history and collections of birds' eggs and fossils on the upper floor, while the ground floor is devoted to the area's social and economic history. In the grounds is a reconstructed Zulu homestead.

GIANT'S CASTLE NATURE RESERVE

Tourist Information: *Main Camp Office; tel: 0363-24718* (open daily 0500–1900 Oct–Mar,

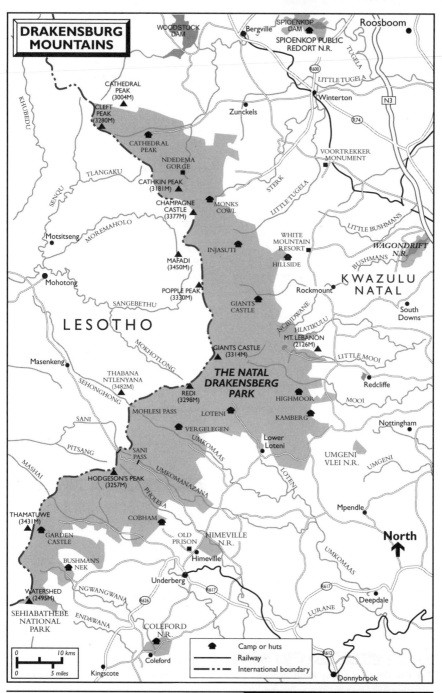

DRAKENSBURG
MOUNTAINS

WOODSTOCK DAM

Bergville

SPIOENKOP DAM

SPIOENKOP PUBLIC REDORT N.R.

Roosboom

LITTLE TUGELA

TUGELA

R600

CATHEDRAL PEAK (3004M)

CLEFT PEAK (3280M)

KHUBEDU

Zunckels

Winterton

N3

R74

CATHEDRAL PEAK

NDEDEMA GORGE

TLANGAKU

VOORTREKKER MONUMENT

SENQU

CATHKIN PEAK (3181M)

CHAMPAGNE CASTLE (3377M)

MONKS COWL

STERK

LITTLETUGELA

LITTLE BUSHMANS

MAFADI (3450M)

INJASUTI

WHITE MOUNTAIN RESORT

HILLSIDE

WAGONDRIFT N.R.

BUSHMANS

Motsitseng

MOREMAHOLO

Mohotong

SANGEBETHU

POPPLE PEAK (3330M)

GIANTS CASTLE

Rockmount

KWAZULU NATAL

South Downs

LESOTHO

MOKHOTLONG

GIANTS CASTLE (3314M)

NCIBIDWANE

HLATIKULU MT. LEBANON (2126M)

LITTLE MOOI

259

Masenkeng

THABANA NTLENYANA (3482M)

SEHONGHONG

THE NATAL DRAKENSBERG PARK

REDI (3298M)

HIGHMOOR

Redcliffe

MOOI

SANI

MOHLESI PASS

LOTENI

KAMBERG

Nottingham

PITSANG

VERGELEGEN

UMKOMAAS

Lower Loteni

UMGENI VLEI N.R.

UMGENI

MASHAI

SANI PASS

UMKOMANAZANA

PHOLELA

LOTENI

HODGESON'S PEAK (3257M)

Mpendle

THAMATUWE (3431M)

COBHAM

GARDEN CASTLE

OLD PRISON

HIMEVILLE N.R.

North

UMKOMAAS

BUSHMAN'S NEK

Himeville

WATERSHED (2495M)

NGWANGWANA

Underberg

R626

R617

R617

Deepdale

SEHLABATHEBE NATIONAL PARK

ENDAWANA

COLEFORD N.R.

LURANE

0   10 kms
0   5 miles

Camp or huts
Railway
International boundary

Coleford

R612

Kingscote

Donnybrook

0600–1800 Apr–Sept; R6). This is one of the highest and most remote of the Drakensberg reserves, reached by a less than perfect dirt road. It is accessible in an ordinary car, but negotiate the rock-strewn, potholed road with care, and consider postponing your visit in wet weather. Also take food and water, as you can only get chocolate bars or basic groceries in the reserve. The ride may be bumpy, but it is also beautiful and worth the effort. It would be a pity to miss seeing the peaks and valleys, grassy plateaux and gorges, rocks and caves of the 34,000 hectare reserve, surrounded by several dramatic peaks, including the basalt cliffs of the Giant's Castle (3314m) and Injasuti (3410m), South Africa's highest mountain.

Giant's Castle has many of the Drakensberg's finest San rock paintings, with up to 5000 paintings in about 50 caves. There are more than 500 in the **Main Cave** alone, and over 700 in **Battle Cave**, some depicting fighting (R6 admission to both caves). Beside Main Cave is the **Bushman Site Museum** (open daily 0900–1500), where a recording describing the San's culture and lifestyle is played, and models of a San family are displayed.

The other big draw of Giant's Castle is the wildlife, with 12 species of antelope including the tiny sure-footed klipspringer, and a magnificent array of birds. The rare **lammergeyer** (bearded vulture) may be sighted from a hide, *tel: 0363-24616* (open daily May–Sept; R30; minumum per party of R180). A maximum of 6 people are allowed in per day, so advance booking is essential. The vultures are fed in the early mornings at weekends.

There are numerous hiking trails within the park, and the parks board runs escorted 40 km, three-day hikes each weekend. They also have horses for hire, from guided rides by the hour *(tel: 0363-24435),* to overnight treks for experienced riders. Parks accommodation is in several small camps, with a range of possibilities, from comfortable cottages to basic trail huts; all self-catering. To book accommodation, long-distance treks or rides, contact the **Natal Parks Board**; *tel: 0331-471 981.*

MOOI RIVER

Tourist Office: *Gateway Reservations and Real Estate, tel: 0333-32450.* Open office hours. There is an excellent Midlands Meander brochure, available from all local Tourist Offices and many other outlets.

The **Swiss Manor House**, *Hidcote Rd; tel: 0333-32733, fax: 0333-1329* (cheap) is a guesthouse with 10 double rooms (no children under 13) and a full Continental restaurant. Self-catering accommodation is available at **Devon Farm Cottage**, *Giant's Castle Rd, Mooi River; tel/fax: 0333-32639* (cheap–moderate). **Campsite**: **Riverbank Camping and Caravan Park**; *tel: 0333-32144.*

The Kwazulu-Natal Midlands are gently rolling hills, covered in emerald meadows and white picket fences, horse stud farms and exclusive private schools full of rich children in neat blazers. It is also dotted with country inns, potteries, weavers, art studios and the occasional herb garden or cheese-making establishment, which have got together to market themselves as the **Midlands Meander**, an arts and crafts route where people can browse and buy direct from the originators. Mooi River is at the most northerly point of the route, in the heart of dairy and stock-breeding country. Mooi River, the waterway, is a trout fishing venue. Mooi River, the town, is known for its pottery and is also a polo-playing centre. The museum at **Rohde House**; *tel: 0333-31766* (open 1000–1230 Mon, Tues, Fri, 1400–1630 Thur, closed Wed, weekends and public holidays) has displays on dairying and polo, and photographs of Bruntville, the local black township.

ROSETTA

There is little to cause a pause in Rosetta. **Mother Goose**, *Old Main Rd; tel: 0333-37021,* is a waterside tea garden and gift shop, with many items under R15. Breakfast, lunch and tea are served.

SIDE TRACK
FROM ROSETTA

Tourist Office: *Main St, Underberg; tel: 033-701 1571.* Look for the *Sani Saunter* brochure, for a round-up of local activities.

All the nature reserves and parks locally have cheap self-catering accommodation,

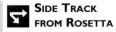

most bookable through the **Natal Parks Board** *(Nt); tel: 0331-471 981.* Each of the local towns has a small country hotel, of which the best are the town centre **Himeville Arms**, *Main St, Himeville; tel: 033-701 1305* (cheap) and the mountain-top **Sani Pass Hotel**, *22 km from Underberg, on the Sani Pass road; tel/fax: 033-702 1320* (cheap–moderate). There are also numerous bed and breakfasts. **Campsites:** camping and caravan sites at **Cobham**, *tel: 033-722, ask for 1831;* **Himeville**, *tel: 033-702 1036;* and **Loteni**, *tel: 033-722, ask for 1540.*

From Rosetta, a signed gravel road leads west for 70 km to the **Kamberg Nature Reserve** (open daily sunrise–sunset; R6 per person). Set in the Drakensberg foothills, there are a number of walking trails, one of which is specially designed for people in wheelchairs. The trout hatcheries are open to the public, and fishing rods can be hired.

Other small National Parks reserves in the area include Loteni, Cobham, Coleford and Garden Castle. All have the possibility of excellent fishing and wonderful, remote mountain walking. They are accessed by a gravel road, which continues south-west skirting the feet of the Drakensberg to **Underberg** and **Himeville**. Side roads off it lead up to **Sani Pass** and the Lesotho Border (4x4 only), as well as the southernmost sections of the Drakensberg.

Underberg is the main local business centre, but has little specific to recommend it. In high, cool Himeville, there is a small **museum**, *opposite Himeville Hotel; tel: 033-702 1184* (open 1000–1200 Wed, Fri, Sat, Sun; free, donations welcomed), with local history, costume, agricultural implements, San rock art and trout fishing displayed in the last loop-holed fort to be built in Natal (1900). It later became a prison and other prison buildings are also included. ▲

ROSETTA TO HOWICK

This is one of the busiest sections of the Midlands Meander. To do it properly, keep the wallet handy, to buy anything from leather satchels to pots of herbs. The atmosphere is pure Beatrix Potter, where the hotels have thatched roofs and chintz curtains. Amongst the best are **Rawdon's Hotel** *(Pf), Old Main Rd, Nottingham Rd; tel/fax: 0333-36044* (cheap–moderate), a low, thatched 'little England' country house hotel with charm and elegance and 25 rooms; **Thatchings**, *Curry's Post Rd, Nottingham Rd; tel: 0333-36275, fax: 0333-36276* (moderate), a guesthouse set in 135 acres, including trout dams; and the **Granny Mouse Country House** *(Pf), Balgowan; tel: 033-234 4071; fax: 033-234 4429* (moderate), which offers magnificent service and hospitality to those not afraid of small stuffed animals in frocks.

HOWICK

Tourist Office: *Fallsview; tel: 0332-305 305.*

ACCOMMODATION

Old Halliwell Country Inn, *Curry's Post Rd, Howick; tel: 0332-302 602, fax: 0332-303 430* (moderate–expensive) is a luxurious 4-star (silver) hotel built in the 1830s, with 15 double rooms. There is bed and breakfast accommodation at **Harrow Hill Guest Farm**, *Karkloof Rd, Howick; tel/fax: 0332-5033* (budget). The farm is 4 km from Howick on a tarred road.

SIGHTSEEING

Howick was built as a river crossing on the Umgeni River, just above the dramatically beautiful **Howick Falls**, where the river makes a single drop of 95 m. There is a lovely Gorges Walk laid out along the canyon rim, and a number of attractive old houses are scattered through the village, including the Victorian colonial **Howick Museum**; *tel: 0332-306 124* (open 0900–1200, 1400–1530 Tues–Fri, 0900–1300 Sat, 1000–1600 Sun), which presents the town's early history and its agricultural background. Medical and dental equipment is on display, and there is a collection of military badges. Nearby, **Crafts Southern Africa**, *Old Agricultural Hall, Morling St; tel: 0332-305 859,* is an arts and crafts market and art gallery.

The 650 hectare **Umgeni Nature Reserve**, *just out of town on the Karkloof road, tel: 0332-30393* (open daily sunrise–sunset; office open 0800–1630) has several hiking trails through lovely countryside, with a broad range

261

of flora, animals, birds and, less enticingly, spiders. It also has campsites, limited self-catering cottage accommodation and a conservation education centre with a high reputation. The **Midmar Public Resort and Nature Reserve** *(Nt), 8 km west of Howick off the R103; tel: 0332-302 067/8* (open daily sunrise–sunset; office open 0800–1230, 1400–1630; R6 per person) is set on a large and attractive reservoir. There is caravan and camping accommodation, together with chalets and cottages; advance accommodation bookings through Natal Parks Board; *tel: 0331-471 981*. Activities include fishing and watersports, such as sailing, power boats, jetskiing and water skiing. There are also nature trails, an open-air museum, a 1000 hectare game park, with zebra, rhino and antelope, and a bird sanctuary. The neighbouring **Midmar Historical Village**, *tel: 0332-302 067*, has a variety of irresistible rides – barge cruises on the dam, steam train trips and horse-drawn carriage rides – as well as a number of historic buildings. Live music from the bandstand, an arts and crafts hall and a living museum add to the holiday atmosphere.

At the **Touchwood Flower Farm**, *off the R617 near Bulwer, about 5.5 km from the N3's Interchange 99; tel: 0332-302 215* (open daily except Mon 1000–1700), visitors may stroll among the roses and other blooms and see the enticing displays in the dried flower shop. Lunches are served (booking advisable) with salads grown at the farm. The farm's own spring water and bread and cakes made from its stone-milled flour are served.

HILTON

There's a choice of several places to stay in and around Hilton, including the 3-star neo-Tudor **Hilton Hotel**, *Hilton Rd, Hilton; tel: 0331-433 311, fax: 0331-433 722* (expensive), which also has one of the best restaurants around; the **Cumbria Lodge**, *25 St Michael Rd, Hilton; tel/fax: 0331-434 339* (cheap), a comfortable bed and breakfast with sauna and pool; and the 2-star **Crossways Country Inn**, *2 Old Howick Rd, Hilton; tel/fax: 0331-433 267* (moderate).

Hilton marks the southern end of the Midlands Meander. One of South Africa's most exclusive boy's schools is here, but for tourists,

the real draw is the **Natal Railway Museum**, *Hilton Station; tel: 0331-431 857* (open 0800–1600 Mon–Fri, 0830–1330 Sat, occasional Sun). Its collection includes 12 steam locomotives and 14 passenger coaches and wagons, some built nearly 100 years ago. Many items of railway paraphernalia are on show, two model railways are set out, and there is a souvenir shop for steam enthusiasts. With luck your visit may coincide with the monthly steam train excursion to Howick (see p. 261).

PIETERMARITZBURG

See pp. 285–289.

PIETERMARITZBURG TO DURBAN

ACCOMMODATION

The **Rob Roy Hotel**, *Rob Roy Crescent, Botha's Hill; tel: 031-777 1305, fax: 031-777 1364* (moderate), has pitched roofs, a turreted tower, spacious rooms, magnificent views and a reputation for fine cuisine. **Cloud 9**, *27 View Hills Rd, Crestholme; tel/fax: 031-773 412* (moderate) offers luxury apartments, each with balcony, canopied king-size bed, large corner bath and fully-equipped kitchen. Guests can self-cater or have meals served. Closer to the city, in Pinestown, the 2-star **Pinedene Inn Hotel**, *65 Kings Rd, Pinetown; tel: 031-701 0130, fax: 031-701 0759* (moderate) has 28 air-conditioned double rooms and a bar.

SIGHTSEEING

This last stretch south is a lovely drive past the romantically named **Valley of a Thousand Hills**, with superb views of table-top mountains, green hills, dams and the Umgeni River valley. This is also the route of the punishing annual **Comrades' Marathon** (see p. 287).

It is also an area popular with Durban day-trippers, with plenty of entertainment laid on. **Intabamningi**, *Old Main Rd, Drummond; tel: 0325-34392* (performances daily 1100, 1500; R7) has Zulu dancing, crafters' workshop, shops selling curios and crafts and cave hiking. **PheZulu Traditional Zulu Village**, *Old Main Rd, Botha's Hill; tel: 031-777 1000* (open daily 0900–1600, performances at 1000, 1130,

The Birth of Aviation

South Africans point out that the world's first controlled heavier-than-air flight was at Howick, near Pietermaritzburg in Kwazulu-Natal, some 30 years before Orville and Wilbur Wright's success. The event is not perfectly documented, but it is known that Goodman Household piloted a flimsy glider as it was launched from the 350m Karkloof precipice some time between 1871 and 1875. The primitive aircraft soared about 100m into the air before striking a tree and plunging into a lake. Goodman's mother feared her son's tampering with the unnatural would incur the wrath of God. She made him abandon his experiments, and the glider was consigned to a rubbish dump. It was an ignominious start to a method of transport that was to become so important in the development of South Africa.

On Monday, 26 Aug 1929, Major Allister Miller, flying a Gipsy Moth biplane, took off from Cape Town on a 4-hr flight to Port Elizabeth. His cargo: five green mail bags. At Port Elizabeth, the bags were divided between two other aircraft, one flying to Johannesburg, the other to Durban. The Durban-bound plane, piloted by 'Caspar' Caspareuthus, arrived two hours ahead of schedule. Captain Graham Bellin's Johannesburg flight, hampered by strong headwinds, ended at Bloemfontein, and his mail bags had to travel the rest of the way by train. It was another uncertain milestone, but Union Airways had at least got off the ground. Dogged by bad luck and financial hardship, however, the airline lasted less than five years. In Feb 1934, the government took over the company and absorbed it into the newly-formed South African Airways. By the start of World War II, SAA had developed extensive domestic services, and had negotiated a circular route linking Angola, the Belgian Congo and Kenya with South Africa. In 1945, the airline launched its first intercontinental trunk route – the 'Springbok Service' between Johannesburg and Bournemouth in southern England.

Since then SAA has continued to expand its links into Europe, Australia, Asia and North and South America, but it still maintains an Historic Flight Section, run on a voluntary basis by aviation enthusiasts who are dedicated to the restoration and preservation of vintage aircraft. The section's fleet of historic aircraft – a Junkers JU52, two Harvards, two restored DC-4s and two DC-3s – is used for charter and pleasure flights.

263

1330 and 1530; R25) offers one of the least authentic, but most energetic displays of Zulu dancing and drumming, together with a small village tour, crafts gallery and curio shop. The ticket also gives admission to the neighbouring **Assegai Safari Park**, *5 Old Main Rd, Assigai, Botha's Hill*, (same tel and opening times) where crocodiles and other creatures can be seen.

The other attractions are shops, such as the **Barn Owl Pottery**, *122 Old Main Rd, Botha's Hill; tel: 031-777 1987*, which has a wide range of items made on the premises, and the **O'Donnell Gallery**, *32 Old Main Rd, Botha's Hill; tel: 031-765 7123*, run by a painter, John O'Donnell, adept at capturing South Africa's vivid colours, and his wife, Leonie, who works in oils, pottery and fabric media. For a wide range of shops selling hand-painted plates, earrings of stained-glass and African and Indian

textiles and ceramics, try the **Heritage Market**, *off the Old Main Rd, Hillcrest, 20 km from Durban;* a purpose-built 'Victorian' shopping centre with colonial-style shops, tea rooms and restaurants, set in lavish rose gardens.

Pinetown, on Durban's outskirts, also has a variety of places to eat, including seafood restaurants, and interesting shops. **Pineville Craft Village**, *corner Stapleton and Old Main Rds, Pinetown; tel: 031-725 149*, has turn-of-the-century shops, demonstrations of craft-making, and a craft market every Sat and on the last Sun of the month. **Pinetown Museum**, *Pinetown Library; tel: 031-719 2038 or 2160* (open 0900–1700 Mon–Thur, 0900–1600 Fri, 0900–1200 Sat) has exhibits from the early Stone Age to modern times. A display of traditional Zulu dress and a hand-worked tapestry depicting the town's past, present and future are also of interest.

LADYSMITH–HLUHLUWE
THE BATTLEFIELDS ROUTE

Over the last half of the 19th century, the Zulus, Boers and British were all colonising new lands, and it was inevitable that their expanding territorial claims would result in bitter confrontations. It was on the grassy mountains of northern Kwazulu-Natal, at the meeting point of the three territories, that many of the most famous and bloody battles were fought during the Anglo-Zulu Wars of 1879 and the Anglo-Boer Wars of 1880–81 and 1899–1902. This route is almost all about military history, but is surprisingly interesting for everyone. Major battlefields on other nearby routes are also included on the map.

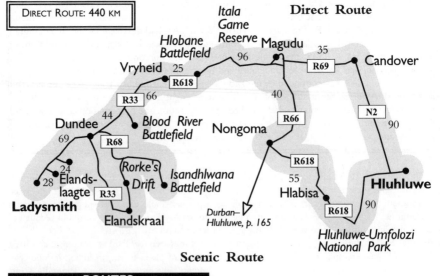

ROUTES

DIRECT ROUTE

Leave Ladysmith heading north on the N11. After 23 km, turn right on to the R602 to Glencoe (48 km), where you turn right again on to the R33, which leads through Dundee to Vryheid (74 km). From here, turn right on to the R618 for 30 km, then branch left on to the R69, past the Itala Game Reserve. After 121 km, turn left on to the R66. A couple of kilometres on, at Magudu, turn right on to the gravel R69, which heads due east for 35 km to join the N2 at Candover, then turn right. If you wish to remain on the tar, keep going north on the R66 for 18 km to meet the N2. Turn south and follow it south for 75 km to the Hluhluwe crossroads (see p. 189). Distance: 440 km; allow: one day.

SCENIC ROUTE

▪▪▪▶ Although this follows roughly the same line as the direct route, many of the sites are remote hills or fields, reached by minor roads. It is impossible to create a continuous route between them and, even if you can see the next, you may have to drive a frustrating 40 km to get there.

Leave **Ladysmith** on the N11 heading north. After 23 km, branch right on to the R602. **Elandslaagte** is on your right, about 5 km from the turn off. Continue along the R602. About 20 km on, a gravel turning on the right leads to **Wasbank**. Return to the R602 and continue on to Glencoe, then turn right to **Dundee**. Leave Dundee on the R33, heading east towards Vryheid. About 7 km on, turn right on to the R68 towards Nqutu and Melmoth. Remain on this for about 70 km, then watch for signs on your right to the **Isandlwana Battlefield**. Retrace your route up the R68 for about 49 km to Vant's Drift, then turn left on to a dirt road. Follow this until you reach a T-junction and turn left again. This leads past **Fugitive's Drift** to the **Rorke's Drift Battlefield** (42 km from Dundee). On leaving here, keep going left and the road loops round through **Elandskraal** to join the R33. Turn right and head north, past Helpmekaar battlefield, to Dundee.

Once again, leave Dundee on the R33 heading east. After about 42 km, a gravel turning on the right leads to the **Blood River Battlefield** (about 16 km). Return to the R33, turn right and continue east to **Vryheid** (50 km). Leave here on the R618, heading east. After about 25 km, you pass the flat-topped hills of the **Hlobane Battlefield** on your left. About 5 km further on, turn left on to the R69 and follow it for about 40 km to Louwsberg. Turn left again here and follow the signs for the **Itala Game Reserve**. Return to the R33, turn left and continue east for about 56 km to the junction with the R66. Turn right and head south to Nongoma (about 40 km), where you can pick up the Durban–Hluhluwe route to do the Ulundi area battlefields (see pp. 165–172). For this route, leave Nongoma on the R66, still heading south. Just out of town, turn left on to the R618, which drops down through **Hlabisa**

to the **Hluhluwe–Umfolozi National Park** (about 55 km). Turn left within the park for Hluhluwe village, or keep straight on for Mtubatuba and St Lucia (see p.191). Distance: expect to cover over 700 km; allow 4–5 days.

LADYSMITH

Tourist Office: *Town Hall, Murchison St; tel: 0361-22992.* Open Mon–Fri 0800–1600, Sat 0800–1300. Leaflets and brochures; self-guided walking tours of Ladysmith; and details and bookings for battlefield tours.

ACCOMMODATION AND FOOD

The slightly faded **Royal Hotel**, *128 Murchison St; tel/fax: 0361-22176* (cheap) is the town's original establishment, which housed the press corps during the Siege. A little further along the road is the rather smarter **Crown Protea** *(Pa), 90 Murchison St; tel: 0361-22266; fax: 0361-26458* (cheap–moderate). There are also several good bed and breakfasts, of which the best, centrally located in atmospheric old houses, are **Peaches and Cream**, *4 Berea Rd; tel: 0361-310 954* (cheap), and **Bullers Rest**, *61 Cove Crescent; tel: 0361-22847* (cheap). About 6 km out of town, the **Blockhouse B&B**, *Windsor Dam Rd; tel: 0361-324 091* (cheap) is filled with antiques. **Campsite: Municipal Caravan Park**, *Harrismith Rd; tel: 0361-26050* (follow *Poort Rd* north to get there).

The best food in town is at the **Guinea Fowl Restaurant**, *corner Alfred and Murchison Sts; tel: 0361-28163* (moderate), which serves everything from burgers to seafood; the intimate **Ristorante Theodorico**, *Old Mill Centre, Queen St; tel: 0361-27506* (moderate), offering steak and seafood; and the **Victor Victoria Pub**, *Oval Shopping Centre, Keate St; tel: 0361-311 051* (cheap), which has pub food in a house built for Queen Victoria's Diamond Jubilee and used as a hospital during the Siege.

SIGHTSEEING

Ladysmith was and is a fairly ordinary country town, set in a shallow bowl, almost entirely surrounded by low hills. Founded in 1847, this Boer farming settlement and trading post on the Klip River, was named after the Spanish wife of Governor Sir Harry Smith (see p.99).

265

Throughout most of its existence, virtually nothing has happened here. Yet for 118 bloody days, it was the focus of the world, as the Boers pinned down and bombarded the British army. It is easy to see how Ladysmith was besieged to such devastating effect, with the surrounding artillery able to pound every street of the town and choke any possible access through the narrow passes. It is well worth spending a few hours soaking up the stories. The best way to understand the siege is from high ground. Start on **Convent Hill**, which has an excellent lookout point from which to see the layout. All the siege sites are signposted, and a Tourist Office leaflet provides details of the smaller sights.

Right in the town centre is the Victorian stone **Town Hall**, *Murchison St*, built in 1893, and topped by an imposing, but still scarred clock tower. This proved to be a perfect aiming point for the Boer guns, who refused to believe that it was being used as a hospital and shelled it several times. The patients were moved to the Dutch Reformed church and, later, to a special camp a short distance from town. In front of the town hall are two British 6.3 Howitzer RML guns, nicknamed 'Castor' and 'Pollux', which saw action during the Siege, and a replica Boer Long Tom. Only four of these massive guns were made, each weighing 7 tons and firing 97-pound (43 kg) shells. Their sheer power and massive reach were instrumental in many Boer successes, striking terror into the hearts of the British. All four were destroyed to stop them falling into British hands.

Next door, the old Market Hall, used during the siege as the civilian rations depot, has now been turned into the **Siege Museum**, *Murchison St; tel: 0361-22231* (open Mon–Fri 0800–1600, Sat 0900–1300; R2, which also gives entry to the Cultural Centre). One of the best small museums in South Africa, it gives a graphic and often chilling account of the siege, with enough technical detail for the most finickety military historian, together with a wealth of social detail to enthrall even those who normally loathe war stories.

Behind the Town Hall car park, the new **Cultural Centre**, *25 Keate St; tel: 0361-22231* (open Mon–Fri 0800–1600, Sat 0900–1300; R2, which also gives entry to the Siege

Museum) is housed in a charming Victorian home. This is designed to showcase Ladysmith's various ethnic cultures, with historic exhibits alongside a small art gallery, arts and crafts centre and amphitheatre, used for cultural events. Above all, it contains the town's gallery of 'heroes', including World Boxing Champion, Sugarboy Malinga, Springbok rugby player, André Joubert, artist Lalitha Jwahirilall, and Ladysmith Black Mambazo, the magnificent band who shot to fame when they played with Paul Simon on his album, *Gracelands*.

A little further out, the comfortably neo-Gothic **All Saints Anglican Church**, *65 Murchison St; tel: 0361-24960* (open Tues–Fri 0830–1230; or ask for the key at the office next door; free, but donations welcome) was built in 1882. This too was damaged when the porch and south-east corner were destroyed by a Long Tom from Pepworth's Hill on 20 Nov 1899. Inside, it is very much a military church, lined with memorial tablets listing those who died in the Siege and the Relief, and commemorative stained-glass windows. The Prince of Wales presented the Regimental Standard to the Natal Carbineers in 1925. The **MOTH Museum**, *Egerton Rd; tel: 0361-23762/25236* (open by appointment; free) has a fascinating small collection of local military memorabilia.

Unlike the black South Africans, many of whom fought actively in the Anglo-Boer War, unsung and largely unnoticed by history, most of Natal's large Indian population did not fight. Thanks to Mahatma Gandhi, however, they played a heroic role, dodging bullets as stretcher-bearers to bring the wounded to safety and treatment. Gandhi himself was with Bullers relieving forces and a 3m bronze statue of him, cast in Bombay, now stands in the gardens of the Hindu **Vishnu Temple**, *Forbes St; tel: 0361-333 202* (see also p.288). Nearby, also in the former Indian quarter, is the Muslim **Soofi Mosque**, *Mosque St,* completed in 1969.

Out of Town
Wagon Hill, *5 km south of Ladysmith,* is part of a ridge extending into Caesar's Camp, together known commonly as the Platrand. This was one of the few areas of high ground controlled by the British, and a key defensive area, lined by

The Siege of Ladysmith

The siege began with the devastating British defeat at Nicholson's Nek on 30 Oct 1899. The British forces fled south into what they thought was the haven of Ladysmith. On 2 Nov, Boer troops took up positions on a ring of hills totally surrounding the little town. Inside the 30 km perimeter were some 20,000 people, of whom 12,500 were soldiers, others refugees from the fighting in northern Natal. The Boers made one abortive attempt to storm the town, but, when repulsed, decided to settle down and starve the British into submission. Luckily for the townsfolk, they were well-stocked with rations, including 4000 cattle. Life was extremely hard, with constant shelling by the Boers, which inflicted surprisingly little damage but wore down the nerves. Food did grow scarce and was carefully rationed. Deteriorating sanitation and a baking summer sun were the biggest problems. By the end of the siege, disease was killing up to 28 people a day. When the relieving forces finally broke through, they found 2800 people sick and wounded, and 3037 soldiers and 54 civilians dead. Eventually, on 28 Feb 1900, it simply took too many troops, which the thinly-stretched Boer army could not afford, to maintain the siege and stave off the 53,000 troops, commanded by General Sir Redvers Buller, who were fighting ferociously to break the cordon. Bullers was a remarkably inept general, responsible for bungles and massacres, but even he triumphed by sheer weight of numbers. The rest of the war was effectively lost while the Boers battled for Ladysmith.

a series of earthwork forts. Constantly under long-distance attack, it was the site of only one pitched battle, when Boer commandoes unsuccessfully stormed the hill on 6 Jan 1900. Several memorials stand up here, by far the largest (and most carefully sited), the modern **Burgher Memorial**, commemorating the 781 Natal Boers who died during the war, 310 of whom are buried in the crypt. Designed by Samuel Pauw and Peter Semra'd, and unveiled in 1979, it has seven vast stylised stone hands, rather like upraised spanners, each pointing to a group of Natal battlefields and enscribed by the names of those who died there. The **Blockhouse Museum**, *6 km from Ladysmith off the Harrismith road; tel: (0361) 24091* (by appointment), is an exact replica of a British blockhouse, with a small collection of Zulu and Anglo-Boer War artefacts.

One of the more entertaining ways to spend a day and get a break from military history is on the **Umbulwane Mountain/Township Tour** (ask the Tourist Office for details and bookings). Accompanied by a *sangoma* (traditional spirit healer), this takes in the traditional culture and Anglo-Boer War history of Umbulwane Mountain before heading into the local township for a taste of black South Africa, finishing with a *braai* and a drink in a shebeen. Cost: R100 for the standard 6 hr tour and meal;

R30 plus drinks for the Saturday Taverns Tour, a blinding pub crawl through the town centre pubs and township shebeens.

LADYSMITH TO DUNDEE

On 21 Oct 1899, as defeated British forces struggled south from Nicholson's Nek and Dundee, the small village of **Elandslaagte**, *on the R602* (open daily; free) was the site of a last ditch attempt to re-open the railway long enough to support the retreat. About 20 km on, in **Wasbank**, **Tactile Handcrafts**, *tel: 0346-511 678,* is an exclusive carpet and tapestry shop and workshop, with each piece individually created to abstract modern designs. Nearby, the road signposted to Newcastle/Collings Pass leads to the **Maria Ratschitz Mission**, *36 km from Dundee, tel: 0346-511 722,* currently being restored. Founded by Trappist monks on the slopes of Hlatikulu Mountain in 1886, it was named after a young girl, Maria, from Ratschitz, Czechoslovakia, who drowned in her local river. The church, built in 1909, has beautiful stained-glass and painted murals.

DUNDEE

Tourist Office: *Civic Gardens, Victoria St; tel: 0341-22121, ext. 262.* Open Mon–Fri 0900–1645, Sat 0900–1200. Branch: *Talana Museum,*

Guided Visits

The official **Battlefields Route**, from Estcourt in the south to Volksrust in the north, then eastward to Dundee, Utrecht, Vryheid and Ulundi, covers eleven towns, over 50 battlefields, and museums, war graves and memorials. Maps, guides, tapes and tours are all available to help you follow the route on a self-drive basis, while informative Walk and Talk tapes are available for individual sites. However, each area also has specialist guides, who can be hired to accompany you to the sites of your choice, and there are also regular scheduled tours. It is much better to do this area with a qualified guide, who can describe the period, the details of the battles and the characters who took part. The best of them, including Evan Jones in Pietermaritzburg, Pam McFadden in Dundee, Henry Bird in Eshowe, and David Rattray at Fugitive's Drift (see below), can make an abandoned trench hum with life. Contact: The Secretary, **Battlefields Route**, *Private Bag 2024, Dundee 3000; tel: 0341-22121; fax: 0341-22376.* Other Natal battlefields are included on the routes from Johannesburg–Ladysmith (pp.220–223), Ladysmith–Durban (pp.255–263) and Durban–Hluhluwe (pp.165–172).

on the R33; tel: 0341-22654. Open Mon–Fri 0800–1600, Sat–Sun 1400–1600.

ACCOMMODATION AND FOOD

Of the hotels in town, the small **Royal Hotel**, *61 Victoria St; tel: 0341-22147; fax: 0341-81376* (cheap) is the best. For atmosphere and hospitality, however, it is probably better to look at one of the 28 local bed and breakfasts, such as the **Kamnandi Guest House**, *91 Victoria St; tel: (0341) 21419/21423* (cheap) or **Clara's**, *24 Melville St; tel: 0341-21704* (cheap), which are charming old town houses. Details and bookings through the Tourist Office. Out of town, the most famous accommodation in the area is **Fugitive's Drift Lodge**, *15 km from Rorke's Drift, near Dundee; tel/fax: 0346-421 843* (moderate; booking essential). This is a very comfortable lodge, set on a 2000 hectare natural heritage site beside the Buffalo River, between Rorke's Drift and Isandlwana. It has an extensive library of Africana, but most importantly, the owner, David Rattray, is one of the great experts on the history of Natal, and is rapidly becoming world-famous for his magnificent story-telling.

Other good options include the family-run **Balbrogie Country House**, *1 km from the N11 between Ladysmith and Dundee, Wasbank; tel/fax: 0346-511 352* (cheap), which offers bed and breakfast and evening meals on request in a charmingly restored Victorian farmhouse, set in superb gardens; and **Penny Farthing**, *30 km*

south of Dundee on the road to Helpmekaar; tel: 0346-421 925 (cheap–moderate), a reconstructed Voortrekker farmhouse on a working farm. A very different atmosphere is provided by the **Isibindi Eco-Reserve**, *9 km from Rorke's Drift; 54 km from Dundee off the Greytown road (R33); tel/fax: 0346-421 620* (moderate). This bush lodge has accommodation in luxury beehive huts, with meals in a central stone-and-thatch building, and campsites down near the river. The setting is great, on a clifftop overlooking the Buffalo River on a small private game reserve. Attractions include a traditional Zulu village, abseiling, white-water river rafting, game walks and bird-watching. **Campsite**: the **Dundee Caravan Park**, *Union St, off the Ladysmith road; tel: 0341-22121 ext. 247,* also has a few self-catering rondavels.

There are several pleasant places to eat in town. The most upmarket is **Edwards Restaurant**, *The Mews; tel: 0341-22585* (moderate), where flickering candlelight complements the food. A louder, brighter ambience is provided by the **Buffalo Steakhouse**, *5 King Edward St; tel: 0341-24644* (moderate). Just out of town, **Farmer's Brewery**, *Hattingspruit, on the R621; tel: 0341-81735/6* (cheap–moderate) serves its own beers and German-inspired dishes. The **Miner's Rest Tea Shoppe**, *at the Talana Museum, Vryheid Rd; tel: 0341-21704* (open Tues–Sun, 0900–1600; cheap) serves light meals and teas.

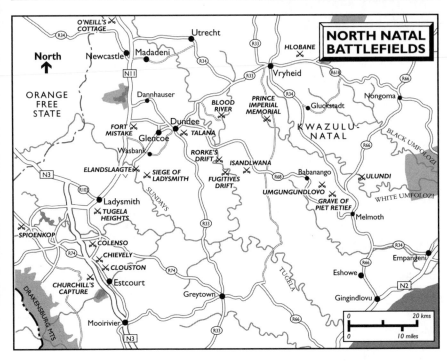

SIGHTSEEING

In 1864, Thomas and Peter Smith, from Dundee, Scotland, found high-grade coal on their farm, and a very small 'coal rush' created a viable community. In 1879, Dundee became the British headquarters for the Second Invasion of Zululand and in 1882, when the first larger commercial mine went into operation, the Smiths' neighbour, George Sutton, laid out this quiet market town in the foothills of the Biggarsberg Mountains. Coal is still important in the area, but it has long been eclipsed by the extraordinary history that has raged across the surrounding hills.

There are relatively few sights actually in town. The small **MOTH Museum**, *corner Beaconsfield and Wilson Sts; tel: 0341-21250* (open on request; ask at the cottage; free, but donations welcomed) contains a crowded jumble of fascinating military memorabilia dating back to 1879. The 1922 **Dutch Reformed Church**, *corner Beaconsfield and Wilson Sts; tel: 0341-23051*, was designed by

Gerard Moerdyk, with a sculpture by Anton von Wouw on the clock tower and the grave of the Boers who died at the Battle of Talana. The 1898 Anglican **Church of St James**, *Gladstone St, opposite the Old Court House; tel: 0341-22482*, has a memorial to the Natal British who died during the Anglo-Boer War.

However, one sight, just out of town, casts all the others into the shade. The **Talana Museum**, *3 km from Dundee on the Vryheid road; tel: 0341-22654* (open Mon–Fri 0800–1600, Sat 1000–1600, Sun 1200–1600; R3) is one of the finest country museums in South Africa. With the expanding collections now housed in some 10 buildings, around Peter Smith's original cottage, it has lively and informative displays on the development of Dundee, early mining, the coal industry, glass (another important local industry), the local stone age site of **Nkupe Cave**, Zulu history and rural life and crafts, including blacksmith's and carpenter's workshops and a coachhouse with wagons, farming and transport. A new Iscor Hall of Mining opens in early 1998, and dramatically vivid exhibitions on the Zulu and Anglo-Boer Wars help bring these to life.

This was also the site of the very first battle of the second Anglo-Boer war. With the conflict imminent and inevitable, 4000 British troops were sent to Dundee to protect the precious coal fields. War was declared on 9 Oct 1899; on 20 Oct, 14,000 Boer soldiers attacked the British camp on Talana Hill. The battle was fierce, but the British eventually won, with 51 British and 145 Boer casualties. Two days later, they retreated. The farm buildings (now the museum) were used as a dressing station during the battle. A footpath leads up the hill to the camp, where many of the gun emplacements and forts are still visible.

ANGLO-ZULU BATTLEFIELDS

About 80 km south-east of Dundee, off the R68, **Isandlwana**, *tel: 0342-710 634* (open Mon–Fri 0800–1600, Sat–Sun 0830–1600; R5) provides the opening chapter in one of the most tragic and heroic episodes in South African history. The British and Zulus were at war, but on 22 Jan 1879, neither side had any intention of fighting that day. The 20–25,000-strong Zulu army was waiting for the 23rd (after the full moon); the British commander, Lord Chelmsford, believed they had found the main Zulu army elsewhere and had ridden off to investigate, leaving only 1774 men with little ammunition at a temporary base. At about 11am, a British patrol stumbled over the Zulu army. Their hands forced, they attacked the unprepared camp immediately. Two hours later, 1329 British and over 1000 Zulu soldiers lay dead. The Zulus picked up 800 Martini Henry rifles, later used to devastating effect.

The remaining British soldiers fled across the Buffalo River at **Fugitive's Drift**, where many more were killed. By 3.15pm, the first two men stumbled into Rorke's Drift and raised the alarm. **Rorke's Drift**, *42 km from Dundee off the R68; tel: 0346-421 687* (open Mon–Fri 0800–1600, Sat–Sun 0830–1600; R5), named after James Rorke who set up a trading post here in 1849, was by now a Swedish mission, which had been commandeered as a military storehouse and hospital. It had a tiny garrison of 139 soldiers, 35 of them

hospital patients. They desperately began to fortify their surroundings, using even maize sacks and biscuit boxes to build walls. They had a little over an hour before King Cetshwayo's brother, Dabulamanzi, led the attack at 4.30pm, and 4000 Zulu warriors swept down the hill. For 12 hours, the tiny band fought off wave after wave, retreating slowly through the burning buildings until, eventually, at 4am, the exhausted Zulus withdrew. Lord Chelmsford and the main army arrived at 7am. Casualties included nearly 600 Zulus and only 17 British. A staggering 11 Victoria Crosses were awarded to the defenders, more than in any other single engagement in history. The rebuilt hospital now houses an excellent interpretation centre.

Next door is the **ELC Art and Crafts Centre**, *tel: 0346-421 627* (open Mon–Fri 0800–1630, Sat–Sun 1000–1500; free), a wonderful studio, managed by the Evangelical Lutheran Church in Southern Africa. Artists are given training and materials and produce a broad range of works, from paintings and prints to beautiful handprinted or silk-screened textiles, carpets, tapestries and stoneware pottery. Many of their works now grace museums.

A few kilometres down the road, Elandskraal is a pretty Germanic village with an old-fashioned local **Trading Store** selling everything from milk and plastic buckets to traditional pots to local tribespeople, who often gather on the verandah wearing their traditional beads and blankets.

BLOOD RIVER

In 1838, after the massacre of Piet Retief (see p.64) by Dingane, Andries Pretorius led an army of vengeance of 464 men and 64 wagons off to extract the Boers' revenge. On 9 Dec 1838, when stopped at Danskraal, they all made a solemn covenant with God that if He delivered their enemies and vengeance, they would celebrate the day forever. On the 15th December, they circled their wagons into a D-shaped formation between the Ncome River and a large ditch. Next morning, hidden in the mist, they were surrounded by a massive army of over 10,000 Zulus, who attacked three times but were driven off by rifle fire. When Pretorius eventually led a mounted charge, the

Zulus fled, trapping their own reserve. The Boers won a resounding victory, with 3000 Zulus dead and only 3 Boers injured, none fatally. Renamed Blood River, the battlefield site, *48 km east of Dundee; tel: 0346-321 695* (open daily 0800–1700; R2.50) has a small interpretation centre, a large concrete wagon erected as a monument to the Vow, and a D-shaped ring of 64 bronze wagons.

VRYHEID

Tourist Office: *Municipality, Hoog St; tel: 0381-812 133*. Open Mon–Fri 0730–1300, 1330–1600.

ACCOMMODATION AND FOOD

The cosiest accommodation in town is in the bed and breakfasts and guesthouses, of which the **Villa Prince Imperial**, *20 Deputation St; tel/fax: 0381-802 610* (cheap) and the **Oxford Lodge**, *corner Kerk and Deputation Sts; tel: 0381-809 280; fax: 0381-5673* (cheap) are probably the best. Just outside the centre, the 2-star **Stilwater Protea Hotel** *(Pa), 6 km from town on the Dundee Rd, tel: 0381-6181; fax: 0381-808 846* (cheap) is a modern business motel with a pool. **Campsites**: there are two local caravan parks, in town at the **Vryheid Caravan Park**, *Utrecht St; tel: 0381-812 133, ext. 260*, or a little way out at **Klipfontein Dam**, *5 km south of Vryheid on the Melmoth road; tel: 0381-4383*. The best restaurant in town is the Italian **Sergio's**, *139 Landrost St; tel: 0381-802 939* (moderate).

SIGHTSEEING

By 1884, the trek Boers had reached this remote corner of northern Kwazulu-Natal, deep in the heart of the Zulu kingdom, and were looking for farmland. They made a deal with Dinizulu, son of King Cetshwayo, to throw their modern fire power behind him, defeat his rival Zibhebhu, and secure his throne. In exchange, he gave them enough land to create a tiny independent Republic, which they named Vryheid (Freedom). Only 4 years later, they joined the ZAR. There are three little **museums**, all on *tel: 0381-812 133,* and all open Mon–Fri 0730–1600; free.

The **Lukas Meijer House**, *Mark St*, was built in 1884 in Cape Dutch revival style, as the home of the President of the short-lived republic. It is beautifully furnished in period and also has exhibits on the banking and printing of the republic, local mining and Zulu crafts. Opposite, the **Old Carnegie Library**, *corner Landrost and Mark Sts*, built in 1906–9, houses the local Boer history collection, with a fascinating range of personal items from old photographs and clothes to family bibles and artefacts made by Boers imprisoned on St Helena during the Anglo-Boer War. The **Nieuwe Republiek Museum**, *Landrost St*, was built in 1885 to serve as the republic's council chambers and government offices, with the fort and prison cells added two years later. Exhibits inside tell the story of the republic.

Three major battles of the Anglo-Zulu War were fought nearby at **Ntombe Drift** (12 Mar 1879); **Hlobane** (28 Mar 1879); and **Kambula** (29 Mar 1879).

ITALA GAME RESERVE

Parks Information Office: Ntshondwe Camp; *tel: 0388-75105; fax: 0388-75190.* Gates open daily 0500–1900 Oct–Mar, 0600–1800 Apr–Sept; office open daily 0700–1930. Entry R6 plus R25 per vehicle.

Ntshondwe Camp: *tel: 0388-75239* (moderate) is a charming game lodge between a rocky koppie and a waterhole, with views over the open grasslands, self-catering cabins, restaurant and a small supermarket. There are also several small bush camps. **Camping**: there are facilities for tents, but not caravans.

This is one of the least known but most beautiful game parks in South Africa. At least a quarter of its 29,653 hectares are made up of spectacular golden grassland. The rest, tumbling down into the Pongola River valley, is a mix of rocky kopjes, bushy thickets and wooded valleys. Bought as overgrazed farmland in the 1970s, the regeneration here has been spectacular, while careful restocking has provided it with all the major species except lion. The rangers provide a variety of day and night game drives, walks, bird-watching and fishing, and there are three-day hikes (Fri–Tues), camping rough for those with excess energy; *tel: 0388-75348*, for details and bookings.

271

MOSSEL BAY–PORT ELIZABETH (THE GARDEN ROUTE)

From Mossel Bay to St Francis Bay, there is an endless natural garden of mountains, cliffs, forest, lakes, rivers and varying seashores, the spectacular scenery and majestic landscape marred only by the almost continuous ribbon of development along the coast. This is the Garden Route, one of the most famous and sought-after holiday areas in South Africa. To find its true flavour, in the dark forests behind the resorts, requires a little ingenuity and a lot of time.

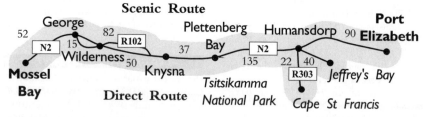

Scenic Route

George 82 Plettenberg Humansdorp 90 Port Elizabeth
52 15 R102 37 Bay N2
N2 Wilderness 50 Knysna 135 22 40 R303 Jeffrey's Bay
Mossel Bay Direct Route Tsitsikamma National Park Cape St Francis
Scenic Route

DIRECT ROUTE: 396 KM

ROUTES

DIRECT ROUTE

For the most direct route from Mossel Bay to Port Elizabeth, follow the N2 the whole way. Distance: 396 km; allow 6 hrs.

SCENIC ROUTE

The scenic route also follows the N2 from Mossel Bay to **George**, but veers inland between George and **Knysna**. Known as the Passes Route, this section is one of the country's most scenic drives (82 km), traversing a series of magnificent passes. From George, take the R102 to Knysna, and set aside a whole day if you want to stop and picnic en route. You will rejoin the N2 about 10 km before Knysna, then follow the N2 right through to

Port Elizabeth, calling at Plettenberg Bay, Tsitsikamma National Park and Humansdorp. Allow 3 days.

BUSES

There are several daily bus services that cover this route. Journey time: 5–6 hrs. OTT Table 3550.

MOSSEL BAY

Tourist Office: *Market & Church Rds, Mossel Bay; tel: 0444-912 202* (open Mon–Fri 0900–1700, Sat 0900–1300).

ACCOMMODATION AND FOOD

There is a reasonable variety of accommodation in this popular resort town. Hotels include the **Cape St Blaize Hotel**, *3 Matfield Rd; tel:*

MOSSEL BAY–PORT ELIZABETH

0444-911 069, fax: 0444-911 426 (cheap); **Ocean View Hotel**, *94 Bland St; tel/fax: 0444-3711* (cheap); and the **Hartenbos Hotel**, *Port Natal Rd, Hartenbos; tel: 0444-951 503, fax: 0444-951 024* (cheap). Chain hotels include *HI, Pa*. Amongst the guesthouses, some of the best are the **Old Post Office Tree Guest House**, *Market St; tel: 0444-913 738, fax: 0444-913 104* (moderate); the **Huijs te Marquette**, *1 Marsh St; tel/fax: 0444-913 182* (moderate); and, a little way out, the **Penrose Guest House**, *5 Amy Searle St, Great Brak River; tel: 04442-3748* (cheap). Backpackers should head for **Mossel Bay Backpackers (HI)**, *1 Marsh St, Mossel Bay; tel/fax: 0444-913 182* (cheap). There are also numerous self-catering apartments and homes (enquire at the Tourist Office). **Campsites: Dias Beach Caravan Park**, *on the beachfront; tel: 0444-951 740*; **Santos de Bakke Park**, *George Rd, Mossel Bay; tel: 0444-912 915.*

Mossel Bay sole, coastal oysters and mussels are specialities of this seaside town. Situated on the beach, **De Bakke Restaurant**, *George St; tel: 0444-912 321* (moderate; open daily 0900–2230), has live entertainment. **Tidals Waterfront Tavern**, *The Point, Marsh St; tel: 0444-913 777* (cheap; open Sun, Mon and Tues 0900–1600, Wed, Thur, Fri and Sat 0900–2200) is a trendy seaside pub, while **Baruch's Coffee Shop**, *8 Liberty Centre, Bland St; tel: 0444-912 343* (cheap; open weekdays 0900–1700, Sat 0800–1400) serves al fresco coffees and light meals.

SIGHTSEEING

In 1488, Bartholomeu Dias, looking for the sea route to the East, became the first European to set foot on this shore. Vasco da Gama arrived in 1497, and, in 1500, Pedro d'Ataide left an account of his visit in an old shoe hung onto a milkwood tree. The tree still stands – letters left there were collected by passing seamen and delivered. The tree is preserved as part of the **Bartolomeu Dias Museum Complex**, *Market St; tel: 0444-911 067* (open Mon–Fri 0900–1700 and Sat 1000–1300; donation expected), which documents the area's history in a series of small museums (maps of the complex are available at the museum reception).

The **Granary** (open Mon–Fri 0815–1300, 1400–1645) is a reconstruction of an 18th-century original, which functions today as the museum's information centre. The **Culture Museum** (open Mon–Fri 0900–1300, 1400–1645, Sat 1000–1300) documents the history of the area's inhabitants, from the Khoisan to the present. The **Maritime Museum** (open Mon–Fri 0900–1645, Sat–Sun 1000–1600) houses a replica of Dias's caravel. **The Shell Museum and Aquarium** (open Mon–Fri 0900–1645, Sat 1000–1300, Sun 1400–1700) houses Africa's largest collection of shells. Also part of the museum complex, the **Padrão** is a replica of Vasco da Gama's original stone cross, while **Munrohoek** is a collection of Mossel Bay's oldest cottages (c.1830), which now house an arts and crafts centre. They overlook Munro's Bay, the site of Dias' first landing. The freshwater spring which first drew him here, the **Aguada de São Bras** (watering place of St Blaize) still flows over a rock face into a little dam – as described by Gaspar Corea in 1512.

In spite of all this history, modern Mossel Bay is primarily an industrial centre and busy summer resort, with swimming, surfing, boating and fishing, a harbour accessible by both commercial and leisure craft and some fine beaches beyond the factories.

GEORGE

Tourist Office: *124 York St; tel: 0441-863 9295* (open Mon–Fri 0745–1700, Sat 0900–1200).

ACCOMMODATION AND FOOD

The most luxurious hotel at George is the **Fancourt Country Estate**, *Montagu St; tel: 0441-708 282, fax: 0441-707 605* (expensive), an exclusive resort with a world-class golf course. Chain hotels include *HI, Pa*.

There are also several good bed and breakfasts in the area. **The Shamrock**, *4 Kus Rd, Glentana; tel/fax: 0441-791 392* (cheap–moderate) is a luxurious, pretty beachside homestead, just 20 km from George. In the same class, **The Waves**, *Beach Rd, Victoria Bay; tel/fax: 0441-711 785* (cheap–moderate) and **Land's End**, *The Point, Victoria Bay; tel: 0441-713 168, fax: 0441-750 068* (cheap–moderate)

2273

273

MOSSEL BAY • GEORGE

are both at the water's edge, well situated for fishing and surfing. Backpackers should head for the **George Youth Hostel** *(HI), 29 York St; tel: 0441-747 807; fax: 0441-746 054* (cheap).

For traditional South African food, try **De Oude Werf**, *53 York St, George; tel: 0441-735 892* (moderate–expensive; open daily 0900–1530, 1600–2200; closed Sat out of season). **Red Rock**, *Arbour Rd; tel: 0441-733 842* (moderate; open Mon–Sat dinner) specialises in seafood, pizza and steak, while the **Wine Barrel**, *Multi Centre, corner Market and Meade Sts; tel: 0441-734 370* (cheap; open Mon–Fri lunch, Mon–Sat dinner; closed Sun), is a family restaurant with daily specials. Out of town, the **Highlands Lodge Longwood Club**, *Waboomskraal via Outeniqua Pass; tel: 0441 81765* (moderate; open Mon–Fri dinner, Sun lunch; booking essential), has wonderful views.

SIGHTSEEING

George is the principal town on the Garden Route, with an airport and scheduled flights from the major cities. Named after (Mad) King George III of Britain, it straddles a coastal terrace 8 km from the sea, in the shadow of the Outeniqua Mountains and two high peaks, **George Peak** (1370m) and **Cradock Peak** (1583m). At George, there is clearer comprehension of the route's name: the town's setting is part parkland, part garden, with a profusion of trees and flowers and a balmy climate.

The **George Museum**, *Courtenay St; tel: 0441-735 343* (open Mon–Fri 0900–1630, Sat 0900–1230; free), housed in the old Drostdy, outlines the town's history. It also has the country's largest collection of gramophones, and an exhibition of indigenous timber and its use in South Africa. The handsome **Moederkerk**, *Meade St*, is George's oldest church (1842). Nearby, the **Church of St Peter and St Paul**, *Meade St*, is the oldest Roman Catholic church in South Africa (1843). The Anglican **Cathedral of St Mark's** (consecrated 1850), is another venerable building. Apart from an array of interesting memorials, there is stained-glass by Kempe, Geoffrey Webb and Sir Hugh Easton. Across the road from the cathedral, **Bishop's Lea** was designed by the architect Sir Herbert Baker.

In front of the **King Edward VII Library**, *York St*, is a venerable oak (planted 1811) with a sad history. Known as the **Slave Tree**, slaves once were bought and sold here. The old chain embedded into its trunk, and the old lock attached to it, are the evidence.

Of George's other attractions, the **Crocodile Park**, *York St; tel: 0441-734 302* (open daily 0900–1700, feeding daily at 1500; R10) has over 2000 crocodiles, while the **Bado Kidogo Exotic Parrot Farm**, *Geelhoutboom Rd; tel: 0441-707 415* (open Tues–Sun 0900–1800; R8) has over 147 different bird species. The **George Golf Club**, *CJ Langenhoven Rd; tel: 0441-736 116*, has one of the Cape's finest courses and is a popular venue. Gary Player designed the **Fancourt Golf Course** (see Accommodation, p.273); *tel: 0441-708 282*, whose use is restricted to hotel guests and members.

There are plenty of **hiking trails** in the surrounding area. Contact the **Outeniqua Nature Reserve**, *Witfontein, George; tel: 0441-708 323*, for the range within their control. Best are: the **Doring River Trail** (15 km, 6 hrs; permit required); the **Tierkop Trail** (17.5 km and 12.5 km, 2 days; permit required); the **George's Peak** and **Cradock's Berg Trail** (17.2 km and 19 km respectively, 10 hrs; self-issue permit at Witfontein); the **Cradock Pass Trail** (12.5 km, 6 hrs; self-issue permit at Witfontein); the **Langasem Trail** (5 km, variable duration; no permit required). For the famous **Outeniqua Trail**, see Knysa (p.277).

George is the base of the **Outeniqua Choo-Tjoe**, *Transnet Heritage Foundation; tel: 0441-738 288*, an old, narrow-gauge steam train which crosses magnificent landscape on its runs between George and Knysna (Mon–Sat, departs George 0930, arrives Knysna 1200, departs Knysna 1415, arrives George 1700; book in advance at George or Knysna railways stations; R45 return).

For coach tours of the Garden Route, contact **Outeniqua Coach Tours**, *tel: 0441-744 940*, or **Springbok Atlas**, *tel: 0441-741 710*. **Garden Route Tours**, *tel: 0441-707 993*, offer a range of tours, including trips from George to Port Elizabeth. **EcoBound**, *tel: 0441-735 881*, offer a variety of tours into the

Little Karoo and along the Garden Route, emphasising off-the-beaten-track locations. **Outeniqua Adventure Tours**, *tel: 0441-711 470*, offer an extremely comprehensive variety of coastal and inland tours and will arrange trips around events (such as the Knysna Forest Marathon), or based on special interests such as hiking, bird-watching or cycling. To see the area from the air, **Scenic Aire**, *George Airport Terminal; tel: 0441-769 405* (flights daily sunrise to sunset, weather permitting; 20, 40 or 60-min duration) offer trips by aeroplane or helicopter.

From George, the N12 leads north over the Outeniqua Mountains to Oudtshoorn, the **Cango Caves** and the **Klein Karoo** (see pp. 281–284), which most people include as part of the Garden Route.

WILDERNESS

Tourist Office: *Leila's Lane, Wilderness; tel: 0441-877 0045* (open Mon–Fri 0830–1800, Sat 0900–1400).

ACCOMMODATION AND FOOD

The 2-star **Fairy Knowe Hotel**, *Wilderness; tel: 0441-877 1100, fax: 0441-877 0364* (moderate) has riverside views. Chain hotels include *Hd, Ka, Pa*. Amongst the best guest-houses are **Lakeside Lodge**, *midway between George and Knysna on the N2; tel/fax: 04455-31844* (cheap), on the edge of Swartvlei, and **Villa Sentosa**, *3 km from the N2 Hoekwil turnoff; tel: 0441-877 0378, fax: 0441-877 0747* (cheap), spectacularly situated on a rise with views over mountain, sea and lakes. There are also plenty of bed and breakfasts in Wilderness. Top of the range are **Moontide Guest Lodge**, *Southside; tel: 0441-877 0361, fax: 0441-877 0124* (cheap), well situated for most of Wilderness's attractions, and **The Pink Lodge**, *45 Die Duin; tel: 0441-877 0263, fax: 0441-877 1839* (cheap), on the beach. Other comfortable options include **Hildesheim**, *Church St, Hoekwil; tel: 0441-850 1115, fax: 0441-850 1144* (cheap), with chalets situated on a rose-growing farm, and **Samland Gaste Haus**, *Hoekwil; tel: 0441-850 1082, fax: 0441-850 1168* (cheap) at the heart of the region's lake district. For details of self-catering cottages and apartments, contact the Tourist Office.

Campsite: Lakes Holiday Resort, *on the N2, 1 km from Wilderness on the Port Elizabeth road; tel: 0441-877 1101.*

With a variety of restaurants and coffee shops to choose from, **Watneys Restaurant and Tavern**, *Pine Lake Marina, Swartvlei; tel: 04455-32151* (cheap) is laid-back and casual, as is **Tom's Tavern**, *Wilderness Shopping Centre; tel: 0441-877 0353* (cheap–moderate), which offers seafood, steak and a range of other dishes, including Indonesian specialities. On the N2 between Wilderness and George, **Drie Valleyen Country Kitchen**, *tel: 0441-877 1995* (moderate) has a diverse menu.

SIGHTSEEING

Wilderness, on the edge of the Touw River Lagoon just as it enters the Indian Ocean, is really a collection of small hamlets straddling a series of lakes. On the approach from George, the panorama is magnificent, the beaches wide and sandy. This is a first-class resort, which has remained untainted by development because the landscape around it is protected.

The famous **Wilderness National Park**, *tel: 0445-31302*, is just 4 km from Wilderness itself, accessible from the N2. This 10,000 hectare reserve encompasses 28 km of coastline, four lakes, five rivers and two estuaries. It is home to three distinct eco-systems: the coastal and montane *fynbos (Cape macchia)*; the evergreen Afro-montane forests; and a wetlands. Visit the area Apr–Oct to see the ericas, aloes, red hot pokers, George lily, wild dagga and pelargoniums in full flourish. The highlight of any visit is the day-long **Kingfisher Hiking Trail**, where it is possible to see five of South Africa's ten species of kingfisher. The park, whose wetlands is internationally recognised, is home to over 250 species of birds, including over 79 species of waders and water birds. There are numerous opportunities for water sports – swimming, sailing, waterskiing, power boating – and you can hire canoes and rowing boats from the park's restcamp, the **Ebb and Flow Rest Camp**, *tel: 0441-877 1197*, which also has simple accommodation – a caravan and camping site – and supplies information about trails, bird-watching and other activities. Wilderness is also well situated for access to the

275

Outeniqua Trail (see Knysna, p.277). For river cruises and guided walking trails in the park, contact **Kingfisher Ferry**, *tel: 0441-877 1101*. For forest, beach and wine tours, contact **Wilderness Connection Eco-tours**, *tel: 0441-877 1104*.

KNYSNA

Tourist Office: *40 Main St; tel: 0445-21610* (open Mon–Fri 0830–1800, Sat 0900–1500).

ACCOMMODATION AND FOOD

Some of the country's best hotels are situated at Knysna. At **Belvidere Manor** *(Pf), Duthie Dr., Belvidere Estate; tel: 0445-387 1055, fax: 0445-387 1059* (expensive) accommodation is in guest cottages at the lagoon's edge, surrounding a historic mansion (1834). Eat at its first-class restaurant. **Falcon's View Manor** *(Pf), 2 Thesen Hill; tel: 0445-826 767, fax: 0445-826 430* (expensive) provides elegant accommodation in a 19th-century mansion, while the **St James Club** *(Pf), The Point, Main Rd, Knysna; tel: 0445-826 750, fax: 0445-826 765* (expensive) provides luxury with an edge to it. Out of town, **Portland Manor** *(Pf), from the N2, take Rheenendal Rd (between Knysna and Sedgefield); tel: 0445-4804, fax: 0445-4863* (moderate) is a historic house (1864) set in a 200 hectare estate of orchards, game park and indigenous forest. Chain hotels include *HI, Pa*.

There are also some excellent guesthouses in the area. Top of the range are **Yellowwood Lodge**, *18 Handel St, Knysna; tel: 0445-825 906, fax: 0445-24230* (moderate), which has magnificent views of the lagoon and the Heads, and **Point Lodge**, *from the N2 take 'The Point' turnoff 3 km west of Knysna; tel: 0445-21944, fax: 0445-23455* (cheap) tranquilly situated at the water's edge. Others to look out for are **Ai Due Camini**, *30 George Rex Dr., The Heads; tel: 0445-825 339, fax: 0445-24620* (cheap) at the eastern head of the lagoon, above the protected swimming area, and **Ocean View Lodge**, *Brenton-on-Sea; tel/fax: 0445-810 063* (cheap), with magnificent views out over Buffalo Bay and the Indian Ocean.

Of the bed and breakfasts, the most luxurious are **Camelot**, *28 Lower Duthie Dr., Belvidere Estate; tel/fax: 0445-387 1393* (cheap),

The Olive Press, *37 Lower Duthie Dr., Belvidere Estate, Knysna; tel/fax: 0445-871 360* (cheap), both with views of the lagoon, and **Narnia Farm Guest House**, *off Welbedacht Rd, Eastford, Knysna; tel: 0445-21 334, fax: 0445-22881* (cheap), with a view of the Heads and the Outeniqua Mountains.

Excellent self-catering locations include the **Knysna River Club**, *Sun Valley Rd, Knysna; tel: 0445-826 483, fax: 0445-826 484* (cheap) on the lagoon, and the **Old Drift Forest Lodges**, *Old Cape Rd, 5 km from Knysna; tel/fax: 0445-21994* (cheap), deep inside the indigenous forest, close to the Knysna River. The **Knysna Hostel** *(HI), 42 Queen St; tel: 0445-22554* (cheap) caters for backpackers.

At the top end of the food range, **Bon Apetit**, *George Rex Dr., tel: 0445-24048* (moderate; open daily dinner only) is unbeatable. Also worth a visit is **Pink Umbrellas**, *14 Kingsway, Leisure Island, Knysna; tel: 0445-22409* (moderate; open daily 0900–1700, and Wed, Fri, Sat and Sun dinner), which serves excellent snacks and afternoon teas alongside fuller meals. More moderately priced are the **Main Street Café**, *51 Main St, Knysna; tel: 0445-825 553* (cheap; open daily for light meals from 0700) and, for a quick drink or a light, lazy meal, **Crab's Creek**, *on the lagoon – take the Belvidere/Brenton Rd; tel: 0445-387 1043* (cheap; open daily lunch, dinner; pub open all day).

At the *Long Street Jetty*, which pokes into the lagoon in front of the town, the **Oyster Tasting Tavern**; *tel: 0445-826 941* (moderate; open Mon–Thur 0800–1700, Fri 0800–1600, Sat–Sun 0900–1500) is open for sampling and buying Knysna's most famous product.

SIGHTSEEING

At the heart of the Garden Route, Knysna curls round a large, almost circular lagoon, connected to the Indian Ocean by a narrow channel through steep twin portals of sandstone known as **The Heads**. The setting is a picture postcard meeting of mountain, lagoon, forest and sea, with added decoration by man.

A key attraction at Knysna is the little 19th-century, Gothic-style **Belvidere church** (open daily 0900–1700) – as you enter Knysna, turn off at White Bridge towards Brenton/ Belvidere. Constructed of stone and modelled on 12th-century Norman architecture, its builder was Thomas Duthie, son-in-law of George Rex, one of Knysna's earliest pioneers. **Millwood House**, *Queen St; tel: 0445-825 066* (open Mon–Fri 0800–1700; donation) is Knysna's other main attraction. Originally erected at Millwood village during the 1880s gold rush, the building was dismantled and brought to Knysna when Millwood was abandoned. It now forms the centre of a local history museum, which also takes in the old gaol, the Parkes Cottage and Parkes Shop. The ghost settlement of **Millwood** itself (about 35 km inland) is also worth a visit. Centred on the Bendigo Mine, the population mushroomed within 6 weeks of the discovery of gold; within five years it had been abandoned.

Knysna's other attractions are varied. The **Outeniqua Choo-Tjoe** (see p. 274) calls here. The 17-km long **lagoon** is a favoured spot for swimming, water-skiing, sailing and other water sports. For **cruises** in the lagoon, *tel: 0445-21693* (1 hr or 1½ hr trips four times daily during the summer, weather permitting), or hire a live-in cabin cruiser from **Lightley's Holiday Cruisers**; *tel: 0445-871 026* (provides accommodation for 2–8 people).

The Knysna Forest has shrunk dramatically thanks to the predations of furniture-makers and the spread of holiday homes, but it is still one of the largest surviving tracts of rare coastal forest, with some magnificent old hardwood trees (yellowwood, ironwood and stinkwood), up to 800 years old. It is a glorious, dark wilderness with superb bird-watching. There are plenty of hiking trails, forest walks, mountain bike, horse or canoe trails in the area – particularly in the Outeniqua Mountains, separating the Wilderness from Knysna, where there is an abundance of forests, rivers, lakes and lagoons. The **Outeniqua Trail** itself is, perhaps, the most famous: 90 km over 5 days. Look out for animals such as elephant and grey rhebok, and forest birds like Knysna loeries and black eagles. Permits from the **Department of Water Affairs and Forestry**, *Demar Centre, Main Rd, Knysna; tel: 0445-825 466* (open Mon–Fri 0730–1300, 1345–1600).

George Rex

Mystery has always surrounded the origins of George Rex (1765–1839), Knysna's most illustrious past resident. Local legend has it that he was the legitimate son of Prince George (later King George III of Britain) and Hannah Lightfoot, a Quaker, said to have been married legally in 1759. This child was their first. However, when Prince George ascended the throne, he was obliged to take a royal consort and therefore, assuming these legends were true, George, the son, became an embarrassment.

In 1797, he was packed off to the Cape and there allowed to become a marshall of the Vice-Admiralty Court. In 1803, he moved to Knysna and, in due course, became the largest landowner in the district; it is said living on a crown grant of £1000 a year. He lived in splendid state until his death. The mystery of his identity died with him.

277

PLETTENBERG BAY

Tourist Office: *Victoria Cottage, Kloof St, Plettenberg Bay; tel: 04457-34065* (open Mon–Fri 0830–1700, Sat 0900–1200).

ACCOMMODATION AND FOOD

There are three first-class hotels in Plettenberg Bay. **The Plettenberg Hotel** *(Pf/Rx/LH/SX), 40 Church St, Look Out Rocks, Plettenberg Bay; tel: 04457-32030; fax: 04457-32074* (expensive) has chic design, dramatic sea views and a first-class restaurant. Just as exclusive and luxurious is **Plettenberg Park**, *take the Robberg Rd towards the airport, then follow the signs; tel: 04457-39067, fax: 04457-39092* (expensive). Just outside town, **Hunter's Country House** *(Pf/LH/SX), off the N2, 10 km west of Plettenberg Bay; tel: 04457-7818, fax: 04457-7878* (expensive) is archetypical olde-English, with roaring log fires, chintz, thatch, sherry, excellent service and fine dining. Marginally less expensive, the **Beacon Island**, *Plettenberg Bay; tel: 04457-*

31120, fax: 04457-33880 (moderate) is excep-
tionally well located on a promontory overlooking magnificent beaches, while the new
Redbourne Lodge, *Piesang Valley, Plettenberg
Bay (from the N2 take the Piesang Valley turnoff);
tel/fax: 04457-33954* (moderate) overlooks the
Country Club golf course.

Those in search of a guesthouse should try
luxurious **Crescent Country House**, *Country
Crescent, Piesang Valley Rd, Piesang Valley; tel:
04457-33033, fax: 04457-32016* (moderate),
which is minutes from the sea, or **Forest Hall**,
*turn off the N2 at 'The Craggs' sign; tel: 04457-
48869, fax: 04457-48883* (cheap), set in 90
hectares of private seaside nature reserve.

There are also numerous bed and breakfasts
in the area. Best of all are **Cottage Pie**, *16
Tarbet Ness Ave, Plettenberg Bay; tel/fax: 04457-
30369*; **Four Seasons Guest House**, *33 Cutty
Sark, Plettenberg Bay; tel/fax: 04457-32619*; and
Ravens View, *17 Raven Pl., Plettenberg Bay;
tel: 04457-30245, fax: 04457-34006*. Excellent
value are **Wavebreak**, *37 Maplin Dr., Plettenberg Bay; tel/fax: 04457-31890*, and **Weldon
House**, *N2 and Piesangs Valley Rd, Plettenberg
Bay; tel: 04457-32437, fax: 04457-34364*. All
cheap. **Albergo for Backpackers** *(HI), 8
Church St, Plettenberg Bay; tel: 04457-34434*
(very cheap) is located in the centre of town.

For further information on hotels, guesthouses and bed and breakfasts, self-catering
accommodation in cottages and apartments and
an extensive list of camping and caravan sites,
contact the tourist office.

Much of the best food in the area is found
in the top hotels – **Hunters Country House**,
the **Plettenberg Park**, and the **Plettenberg
Hotel** (all open daily for breakfast, lunch and
dinner; reservations essential; see accommodation for details). For seafood, try the **Islander
Seafood Grill**, *Wild Waters Park (8 km from
Plettenberg bay on the N2 to Knysna; tel: 04457-
33815* (moderate; open daily 1300–midnight).
The **Blue Bay Café**, *Lookout Centre, Main Rd,
Plettenberg Bay; tel: 04457-31390* (moderate;
open daily 0900–1500, 1900–2300), and **The
Med Seafood Bistro**, *the Village Sq., Main Rd,
Plettenberg Bay; tel: 04457-33102* (moderate;
open Mon–Sat 1830–2130) both serve seafood,
steaks and light meals.

278

SIGHTSEEING

Plettenberg Bay – 'Plett' to the locals – is one
of South Africa's most upmarket resorts, filled
with luxurious holiday homes and hotels.
There's plenty to do here, and at Christmas and
school holidays the crowds flock in. Over 20
km of beach are on offer, with holiday homes
and hotels straddling the low hills between the
Robberg Peninsula to the west and Lookout
Beach to the east, looking down over a sandy
sweep called Millionaire's Row. This in turn
links with Beacon Island and Central Beach.
The beaches are safe, the swimming and surfing
good and there are shells to collect (best at
Shelley, **Robberg** and **Lookout Beaches**;
only take those that are already dead and
empty).

Whale-watching is particularly good in
season. As always, the Southern Right Whale is
most prolific, though Humpback, Bryde's and
Killer Whales are not uncommon. Best viewing
areas are at Kranshoek, Robberg Nature
Reserve, Signal Hill, Lookout Point, Keur-
boomstrand, Nature's Valley and Storms River.
For the whales' daily whereabouts, call the hotline; *tel: 04457-33743*. For horse-riding safaris,
Equitrailing, *tel: 04457-30599*, offers half-day
rides or mini trails of up to 2 hours, while
Southern Comfort Western Horserides,
tel: 04457-30306, offers rides through forest
and open grasslands. For blackwater tubing,
forest tractor rides, mountain bike trails, clay
pigeon shooting and guided hiking trails, contact **Storms River Adventures**, *tel: 042-541
1609*. Deep-sea fishing and pleasure cruises are
provided by **Chembe Charters**, *tel: 04457-
31498*, and for information about rock, surf and
estuary angling, call **Plett Sports**, *tel: 04457-
31230*. For scuba diving, *tel: 04457-31130*.
Day tours along parts of the Garden Route are
offered by **Execubreak Tours**, *tel: 04457-
31890*, **Kingfisher Tours**, *tel: 04457-9719*,
and **Plett-a-Way**, *tel: 04457-32598*.

TSITSIKAMMA

Tourist Office: see Plettenburg Bay.
National Parks Board; *tel: 021-222 810*.

ACCOMMODATION

The **Tsitsikamma Forest Inn**, *Darnell St; tel:*

042-541 1711, fax: 042-541 1669 (cheap) is a large hotel situated within tranquil forest surroundings. For something smaller, try the **Tsitsikamma Lodge**, *10 km east of Storms River Bridge on the N2; tel: 042-750 3802, fax: 042-750 3702* (moderate), situated deep within the Tsitsikamma Forest. **Hog Hollow Country Lodge**, *16 km east of Plettenberg Bay on the N2 towards Nature's Valley; tel/fax: 04457-48879* (cheap) is an ideal rustic retreat on the edge of indigenous forest. At Storms River Mouth, the **Tsitsikamma National Park**; *tel: 021-222 810*, rents out serviced seaside chalets, cottages and apartments close to swimming spots and other recreational facilities, and also have 45 **camping and caravan sites** located in different areas around the reserve.

SIGHTSEEING

The Tsitsikamma area is one of the most panoramic on the Garden Route, with a Khoikhoi name meaning 'the place of sparkling waters', which refers to the Indian Ocean washing the rugged foothills of the Tsitsikamma Mountains.

The chief attraction of this area is the huge **Tsitsikamma National Park**; entrance to the **De Vasselot Section** at Nature's Valley from the N2, 30 km from Plettenberg Bay, and to the **Storms River Mouth Rest Camp**, 42 km further on (33 km on the N2, then right at the Storms River turnoff, 9 km to the Mouth). The Park stretches for 80 km from the village of **Nature's Valley**, just east of Plettenberg Bay, to the mouth of the Groot River in the east, and encompasses 5 km of ocean and 700 sq. km of **Tsitsikamma State Forest Reserve**. The land is largely covered by dense, impenetrable forest containing a huge variety of tree species, which provide a home to a variety of animals, including leopard, bushpig, vervet monkeys and otters.

There are excellent hikes – the best-known is the famous 48-km **Otter Trail** (named after the rare Cape clawless otter), running between Nature's Valley and Storms River Mouth. There are four rest camps on this route, which weaves its way through mountain gorges, waterfalls, tidal rivers and coastal forest. Obtain a permit (R200 for 5 days, 4 nights) and book

at least 12 months in advance; *tel: 042-541 1607.*

HUMANSDORP

Tourist Office: *24 Du Plessis St; tel: 0423-51361* (open Mon–Fri 0800–1300, 1400–1600).

Bed and Breakfasts: Pontac Guest House, *1 Nieshout Crescent; tel: 0423-51463*, **Loubser Guest House**, *5 Assegai St; tel: 0423-51588*, and the **Rose Garden Guest House**, *20 Protea St; tel: 0423-52458*, are best. To stay on a farm, try **Stalle Lodge Guest Farm**, 8 km from Humansdorp on the Cape St Francis Rd, branch left for 2.5 km on the Paradise Beach Rd, then follow the signs; *tel: 0423-52381*, or **Osbosch Lodge Cattle Farm**, 11 km from Humansdorp on the Cape St Francis Rd, then branch left for 3 km; *tel: 0423-940976*. All cheap. **Campsite: Ben Marais Caravan Park**, *Park St, Humansdorp; tel: 0423-52429*.

The **Tavern Inn**, *Alexander St; tel: 0423-51233* (cheap) offers pub food, while **Le Chameleon**, *Voortrekker Rd; tel: 0423-910 262* (cheap) does light lunches.

The countryside begins to open up here, the mountains disappear and the weather is appreciably warmer. Humansdorp presides over a more familiarly African landscape. This is the area's main commercial centre, but the town has little to offer, other than a small local history **museum**, *Bureau St; tel: 0423-910 625*. The chief attraction of the area is its surf – at **St Francis Bay** and **Jeffrey's Bay** in particular.

↗ SIDE TRACKS
FROM HUMANSDORP

CAPE ST FRANCIS

Cape St Francis is 22 km south of Humansdorp on the R330.

Tourist Office: *Village Centre, St Francis Bay; tel: 0423-940 076* (open Mon–Fri 0900–1700, Sat 0900–1230).

There is no hotel at St Francis Bay, but enquire at the Tourist Office for information on the many self-catering homes and flats. Good guesthouses include **Jyllynga**

Exploring East

Bartolomeu Dias, sailing around the southern coast of Africa in 1488, was the first European to set foot on the shore of what the Portuguese mariners who followed him called the *Bahia de Lagoa*, on which Port Elizabeth now stands. He ventured as far as a headland now known as Kwaaihoek (14.5 km west of Cape Padrone, the eastern extremity of Algoa Bay), where there is now a Dias cross memorial. Here, far from home and not realising that he had already rounded the Cape and completed the most difficult section of the journey, he lost his nerve and hightailed it back to Europe. Ten years later, carefully following his charts, Vasco da Gama sailed south and eventually completed the task.

The first European explorer to come this far east overland was August Friedrich Beutler, an ensign with the Dutch East India Company, stationed at the Cape. At the time, French traders were sniffing their way along the coast, looking for a site to use as a base. On arrival, Beutler raised a beacon on the beach to claim the territory (and everything west) for Holland, thwarting the French plans. His beacon is commemorated in the name of the Bakens (Beacon) river, which flows into the bay. Beutler then returned to Table Bay, with volumes of crucial information, used by the Boer trekkers as they headed east in search of fresh land. It wasn't until the arrival of the British Settlers in 1820, in an attempt to buttress the eastern edge of the colony against the fiersome Xhosa, that the first towns were founded.

Lodge, *Mary Crescent; tel: 0423-940 270, fax: 0423-940 230*; **Seascape**, *Lovemore Crescent; tel/fax: 0423-940 358*, and **Oasis Lodge**, *Grand Comore; tel/fax: 0423-940 456* (all cheap).

For bed and breakfast, try **Fairview Lodge**, *St Francis Village; tel: 0423-940 974* (cheap) or **The Gables**, *Reservoir Rd, St Francis Bay; tel: 0423-941 128* (cheap).

Apart from one or two coffee shops in the village, most places to eat out are in Humansdorp. The exception is **Legends Seafood Grill and Steakhouse**, *St Francis Rd, St Francis Bay; tel: 0423-941 123* (moderate; open daily for lunch and dinner).

Cape St Francis is a little seaside village at the western extremity of the sweeping St Francis Bay, which stretches for 100 km all the way to Cape Recife in the east. Here, at the western end of the bay, winter brings waves celebrated in surfers' lore as 'Bruce's Beauties', which sweep the surfer a good kilometre. It is South Africa's major surfing centre.

JEFFREY'S BAY

Tourist Office: *corner da Gama and Deverland Sts; tel: 0423-932 588* (open Mon–Fri 0800–1700, Sat 0900–1200).

Seaview Holiday Resort, *Drommedaris St; tel: 0423-931 330, fax: 0423-932 365* (moderate) is a luxury holiday resort, with accommodation in chalets. Lower down the price scale, **Eastview B&B**, *24 Spekboom St; tel 0423-961 484*, and **Mount Joy Guesthouse**, *31 Mimosa St; tel/fax: 0423-961 932* (both cheap) are situated on the beachfront. For self-catering accommodation, enquire at the Tourist Office.

For food, try the **Dutch Coffee Shop De Molen**, *Seaview Centre, St Francis St; tel: 0423-932 028* (cheap).

Jeffrey's Bay, *18 km east of Humansdorp*, is a fishing village and holiday resort, with endless stretches of superb beach within walking distance. The surfing here is internationally renowned. At the best spot, known as 'Supertubes', the waves are up to 5 m high and close to a kilometre long. After all, this is home to some of the longest, most perfect waves the world will ever see. Not for nothing has 'J Bay' been voted one of the world's top ten surfing spots. There are opportunities for game-fishing, angling and sailing. 🛥

PORT ELIZABETH

See pp. 290–293.

OUDTSHOORN

Diamonds may have been the treasure of Kimberley, but ostrich feathers were the wealth of Oudtshoorn, a pretty town and capital of the Klein Karoo (Little Karoo). It lies in an area separated from the sea by the Langeberg and Outeniqua Mountains, and from the vast expanse of the Great Karoo by the Swartberg Mountains to the north. Ostriches are still the area's chief industry and tourist attraction; but this is also an area of immense natural beauty.

TOURIST INFORMATION

Tourist Office: *corner Baron van Rheede and Voortrekker Sts; tel: 0443-226 643/222 221* (open Mon–Fri 0830–1700, Sat 0900–1300).

ARRIVING AND DEPARTING

By Car
There is good access to the town from all directions. From the coast, the fastest route is up the N12 from George; the more picturesque route is on the old R328 from Mossel Bay, over the Outeniqua Pass. There is plenty of street parking available in town, with large car parks at all the attractions.

By Bus
Translux links Cape Town with Port Elizabeth via Oudtshoorn and the Garden Route. **Transtate** and **Transcity** both have routes between Plettenberg Bay and Kimberley via Knysna, George and Oudtshoorn.

By Train
A weekly service links Johannesburg with Mossel Bay via Oudtshoorn. There is a fairly regular service between Oudtshoorn and George.

GETTING AROUND

Central Oudtshoorn is small and compact and it is easy to get around on foot. However, the bulk of the town's key attractions are away from the centre. Either hire a car or go on a tour. **TTT Tours**; *tel: 0443-226 643*, offers day tours of all the main sights.

STAYING IN OUDTSHOORN

Accommodation
Hotels: On the edge of town, **Rosenhof Country Lodge**, *264 Baron van Rheede St; tel: 0443-222 232, fax: 0443-223 021* (moderate) is luxurious, comfortable and stylish, with a restaurant serving home-cooked country cuisine. In the same category is the **Altes Landhuis**, *from Oudtshoorn on the R328, 12 km left to Schoemanshoek; tel: 0443-226 112, fax: 0443-292 652* (moderate), situated close to the Cango Caves. It too has its own restaurant. **The Queens's Hotel**, *Baron van Rheede St; tel: 0443-222 101, fax: 0443-222 104* (cheap) is an old-fashioned, comfortable 2-star hotel. Chains include **Hd, Pa**.

There are also a number of excellent guesthouses and bed and breakfasts. Located in a lovely 'feather palace' (see p.284), **Adley House**, *209 Jan van Riebeeck Rd; tel/fax: 0443-224 533* (cheap) is an appropriate place to stay. **De Opstal**, 12 km out of town, on the R328; *tel/fax: 0443-292 954* (cheap) is situated in an early 19th-century farmhouse. In town, try **Bisibee**, *171 Kerk St; tel: 0443-224 784, fax: 0443-292 625* (cheap).

Backpackers should head for **Bedstop Accommodation**, *69 Van der Riet St; tel: 0443-224 746* (very cheap).

Campsites: NA Smit Caravan Park, *Park Rd; tel: 0443-222 220*, has six-bed chalets as well caravan sites; **Cango Mountain Resort**, *2 km from the R328 to the Cango Caves, 27 km from Oudtshoorn; tel: 0443-224 506*, has two-bed chalets and a caravan park.

281

Ostriches

Before the settlers arrived, ostriches were just one wild creature amongst many in the area, but while the population of other wild animals was steadily reduced by hunters, the ostrich remained and flourished. The local desert climate suits them ideally; there are few parasites and diseases; they can find sufficient nourishment in the arid local plant life and, oddly, also like swallowing the sandstone rocks, presumably as an aid to digestion, and possibly for the mineral traces found in sandstone. The ostrich is the largest bird on earth. Without the power of flight, it is now completely terrestrial, has long, strong legs at the end of which are two toes, one of them with a powerful nail used for attack and defence, and can run at a maximum speed of 48 km per hr. The female will lay up to 15 eggs per clutch, each weighing over 1 kg; they take 6 weeks to hatch. The young are a pale, fluffy fawn, which darkens as they grow to maturity (which takes about 2 years). Adults weigh around 100 kg, the male is black and white, the female chocolate-brown. The birds run in herds of 100–150 birds and are plucked every 9 months, losing about 1 kg of feathers each time.

282

Eating and Drinking

Most restaurants in Oudtshoorn serve dishes with ostrich in them. Look out for ostrich steaks, omlettes and biltong (see p.24). Major tourist attractions have their own dining facilities. In town, however, the range of places to eat is rather limited. **The Godfather**, *61 Voortrekker Rd; tel: 0443-225 404* (cheap) is good for steaks. **Headlines**, *Baron van Rheede St; tel: 0443-223 434* (moderate) has a varied menu, with anything from pizza to ostrich steak.

SIGHTSEEING

From the 1880s until World War I, ostrich feathers were at the height of fashion – Europe couldn't get enough of them. The arid Karoo,

named 'the land of thirst' by the Khoikhoi, proved the perfect breeding territory for ostriches and, by the turn of the century, Oudtshoorn was a boom town, filled with millionaires. In 1905, the feathers plucked from just six birds fetched R12,000. Today, the spectacular mansions of the feather barons, the so-called 'feather palaces', are a key feature of a visit. Ostriches, inevitably, are the other.

With World War I, the market collapsed. Oudtshoorn remained desperately poor until the late 1930s, when ostriches again came to the rescue with the opening of the first show farm for tourists. Today, there is once again a steadily growing demand for ostrich meat, which is low fat and almost cholestrol-free. Health-conscious carnivores are flocking to trade in their beef. Ostrich leather has always been popular amongst manufacturers of shoes, bags, belts and other accessories, and is beginning to fall out of the luxury market into everyday use, while the eggs (equivalent to 24 hens' eggs) are eaten or blown, painted or carved as souvenirs. There are now about 300,000 ostriches in the Oudtshoorn area (at the height of the boom there were nearly 750 000), on around 350 farms.

Tourism in Oudtshoorn is basically all about ostriches, but there are also a couple of excellent museums. The **CP Nel Museum**, *Baron van Rheede St; tel: 0443-227 306* (open Mon–Sat 0830–1300 and 1400–1700; free), designed by leading 'feather' architect, Charles Bullock in 1907, inhabits the old Boys' High School. The fascinating exhibits include displays on ostriches and the feather trade, the history of Oudtshoorn, a reconstructed grocery shop and a synagogue. The **Dorpshuis**, *146 High St; tel: 0443-223 676* (open Mon–Sat 0830–1300 and 1400–1700; free), also the work of Charles Bullock (1909), is one of the finest of the 'feather mansions' in Oudtshoorn, carefully restored and luxuriously decorated with stained-glass and wrought-iron. It still contains most of its original furnishings.

Three of the many ostrich farms in Oudtshoorn offer tours and entertainment. **Highgate**, *off the Mossel Bay Rd, R328, 10 km from the town centre; tel: 0443-227 115* (open daily 0730–1700; tours last 2 hrs; R20) was one

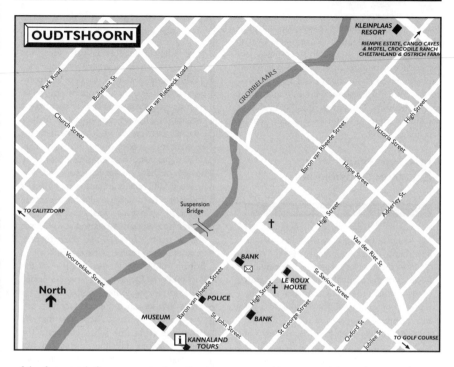

of the first ostrich farms set up in the valley in 1887, and the first to bring in the tourists 50 years later, in 1937. The highlights for most tourists are the ostrich races, with the handlers doubling as jockeys. The **Safari Ostrich Farm**, *off the Mossel Bay Rd, R328, 5 km from the town centre; tel: 0443-227 311* (open daily 0730–1700; R20) also offers a tour of a restored feather baron's mansion, **Welgeluk** (1910), and an explanation of how ostrich products, from feather dusters to handbags, are made. The **Cango Ostrich Farm**, *about 15 km north of Oudtshoorn on the Cango Caves Rd, R328; tel: 0443-224 623* (open daily, 0800–1700; R18), has the same ostrich-based tours, but is a smaller and simpler operation. Added attractions include a wine cellar and butterfly farm.

Nearby, at **Cango Crocodile Ranch and Cheetahland**, *10 km north of Oudtshoorn on the Cango Caves Rd, R328; tel: 0443-225 593* (open daily 0800–1800; R22; restaurant open until late) are a crocodile farm, snake and deer parks, big cats, including lions, cheetahs and jaguars, and small animals, from meerkats, wallabies and pygmy hippos to miniature horses and goats. Almost next door is the **Cango Angora Rabbit Farm**; *tel: 0443-291 259* (open daily 0800–1700; tours every 40 mins; R11).

Continuing north, you come to the **Cango Caves**, *29 km north of Oudtshoorn, R328; tel: 0443-227 410* (open daily 0900–1600; 0800–1700 Dec and Apr school holidays; access to the caves on guided tours only; on the hour, every hour; admission R10, R20 or R25, depending on the type of tour). A local farmer, Jacobus Van Zyl, was the first to 'discover' these massive limestone caves under the Swartberg, in 1780. Although San hunters had lived in the entrance caves for generations, they had not explored the inner reaches. The three sets of caves, diving deep into the heart of the mountain, are a magnificent fantasyland of stalactites and stalagmites, decorating narrow tunnels and huge chambers, the largest of which is a staggering 107m across and 16m high.

There are three possible tours: easy half-hour strolls through 2 caverns; more comprehensive 1 hr tours into 8 chambers; and the full-blown underground experience, lasting about 2½ hrs, with belly-crawls along narrow tunnels and muddy climbs up steep pipes. No experience is required, but for the last option you should be reasonably fit and not claustrophobic. Wear stout shoes with a good grip for any of the tours. The underground temperature remains a constant 18°C, so you may want a sweater or jacket.

SIDE TRACK
FROM OUDTSHOORN

THE SWARTBERGS

Known to the San as the Cango (Water) Mountains, the high, twisted line of the Swartberge (Black Mountains) cuts the coast off from the interior for nearly 200 km, also forming a sharp divide between the lush coastal forests and barren, semi-desert of the Karoo. For centuries, they proved to be almost impassable, but in the 1880s, the great Victorian road builders arrived, of whom the greatest was Thomas Bain. There are seven superbly dramatic passes in the area, of which the finest is the magnificent 24 km **Swartberg Pass** (1881–88), linking Oudtshoorn and the Little Karoo with the charming village of **Prince Albert** in the Great Karoo.

To reach the Swartberg Pass (allow a full day, with plenty of time for a picnic or swim), take the R328 north from Oudtshoorn. The pass itself follows the route used by the Voortrekkers in the 19th century, on their way to the interior. At the top is a remote valley, **Gamkaskloof** (also known graphically as 'Die Hell'), settled for nearly 200 years by a totally isolated group of farmers before the road arrived in 1962 (on the R328 from Oudtshoorn, branch left at the Voortrekker Gedenkteken, then continue on the gravel road for about 40 km; allow at least half a day to explore this section – take a picnic). Beyond the turn off, the northern face of the pass plunges ever deeper into a spectacular ravine, ending in a cauldron of rock at Eerstewater, near Prince Albert.

Founded in 1762, Prince Albert is a

Feather Palaces

The Little Karoo was ideal for ostriches. Nowhere else did they flourish as well, or produce comparable feathers, and the money poured in. Rags-to-riches millionaires built themselves ostentatious homes, the so-called 'feather palaces'. Displays of wealth were manifest in elaborate woodcarving, wrought-iron, stained-glass and rich interior decoration. Several of these homes have survived. The predominant style is art nouveau. In fact, it flourished here, perhaps in part, because the local sandstone was easy to carve. Manor houses, farmsteads and townhouses are all richly ornate – see their turrets, verandas and gables. Charles Bullock, a British immigrant in the employ of the Public Works Department, was the 'prince of the sandstone architects'. Exchanging his Public Works job for more lucrative private practice, he soon discovered that the richer the client, the more elaborate the home required. His buildings seem like ornamental follies, odd in a hot, little town in the midst of an arid, semi-desert.

charming country village, with a range of buildings in different styles – Cape Dutch, Victorian and Karoo vernacular. The **Fransie Pienaar Museum**, *42 Church St; tel: 04436-366* (open Mon–Fri 0900–1230, 1400–1700, Sat 0900–1230, Sun 0930–1200; R2), outlines the location's history.

The **Swartberg Hotel & Lodge**, *77 Church St; tel: 04436 332; fax: 04436-383* (cheap) is the best in town, an atmospheric, old colonial building, laden with photos and memorabilia; and there is also the **Hotel North and South**, *Prince Albert Rd; tel: 02082-4311* (cheap).

Also worth driving are the shorter **Meiringspoort Pass** (take the N12 north from Oudtshoorn towards Beaufort West. The pass, following a river that cuts through the mountains, lies between De Rust and Klaarstroom) and the **7 Passes** (p. 340). ◩

284

PIETERMARITZBURG

In 1838, Voortrekkers colonised the lush Msunduze valley, naming the capital of their tiny new province of Natalia after their leader, Pieter Mauritz Retief, who was killed by Dingane shortly afterwards (see p.64). Over time, the middle 'u' was dropped and the town became Pietermaritzburg. During the centenary celebrations of 1938, it was decided that the town's convenient name should also honour Gerrit Maritz, leader of the second Boer trek into Natal. In spite of these Afrikaaner origins, the republic was annexed by Britain in 1842 and is almost entirely English in construction and personality, priding itself on being one of the last outposts of the empire. Queen Victoria still stands resplendent and scowling in front of the Old Parliament Buildings. This delightful little city has the largest concentration of Victorian and Edwardian architecture in the southern hemisphere, with no fewer than 31 national monuments. It has been the capital of Natal since 1845, although it now shares the honour with Ulundi.

TOURIST INFORMATION

Tourist Office: *177 Commercial Rd; tel: 0331-451 348/9; fax: 0331-943 535.* Open Mon–Fri 0830–1630, Sat 0830–1230.

Most reserves in Kwazulu-Natal come under the jurisdiction of the **Natal Parks Board**, *Queen Elizabeth Park, Duncan McKenzie Dr., PO Box 1750, Pietermaritzburg 3200.*

General enquiries; *tel: 0331-471 891; fax: 0331-471 037;* reservations; *tel: 0331-471 981; fax: 0331-471 980* (all parks open 0500–1900 Oct–Mar; 0600–1800 Apr–Sept).

ARIVING AND DEPARTING

By Air
Pietermaritzburg does have its own small airport, 6 km south of town, on *Oribi Rd; tel: 0331-69286/7,* but the only scheduled flights are an SA Airlink service to Johannesburg. The city is close enough to use the much larger international airport in Durban (see p.149).

By Car
Situated on the main north–south M3, the city has excellent road connections to Durban, all other areas of Kwazulu-Natal and north to Johannesburg. In town, there are numerous free or cheap **car parks**, *behind the City Hall,* on *Longmarket St, Loop St* and *Pietermaritz Rd,* as well as metered on-road parking.

By Rail
Station: *Church St; tel: 0331-958 2525.* Pietermaritzburg has a magnificent colonial station and reasonable train services, being on the main Durban–Johannesburg line.

By Bus
The **City Hopper** is a useful shuttle service to and from Durban and Durban International Airport, departing from the Ulundi car park, *Loop St,* run by **Cheetah Coaches**, *Main City Building, 206 Longmarket St; tel: 0331-422 673.* Other intercity and local buses leave from the car park behind the Tourist Office; **Greyhound**, *tel: 0331-423 026;* **Translux**, *tel: 0331-451 348.*

GETTING AROUND
The historic centre is small and easily explored on foot; much of the immediate *Church St* area is pedestrianised. Walking tour maps are

285

available from the Tourist Office. However, there are a few further-flung sights for which transport is required. There is a **taxi** rank in the car park beside the Tourist Office and City Hall. For radio taxis, contact: **Springbok Taxis**, *tel: 0331-424 444*; **Junior Taxis**, *tel: 0331-945 454*; or **Unique Taxis**, *tel: 0331-911 238*.

For local **guided tours**, including historic walking tours of the city centre, driving tours of the whole city and excursions to the Midland Meander and the Valley of a Thousand Hills (see p.263), contact **Landmarks and Lanes**; *tel: 0331-453 922* (prices from R35 to R240). For Battlefield Tours, contact **PMB Heritage Tours**; *tel/fax: 0331-443 260* (see also p.268 for further details).

(see p.263)
(see also p.268 for further details).

STAYING IN PIETERMARITZBURG

Accommodation

The central, 3-star **Imperial Hotel**, *224 Loop St; tel: 0331-426 551; fax: 0331-429 796* (moderate) is the oldest in town, open since 1878, and named after one of its first guests, the Prince Imperial. It is rather faded these days, but still has a faint recollection of past glories. Much more modern and efficient, catering largely to the business trade, are the **City Royal Hotel**, *301 Burger St; tel: 0331-947 072; fax: 0331-947 080* (cheap–moderate) and the **Karos Capital Tower** *(Ka), 121 Commercial Rd; tel: 0331-942 761; fax: 0331-455 476* (cheap–moderate).

About 5 km north of the city centre, the new **Redlands Lodge**, *1 George McFarlane Lane, Wembley; tel: 0331-943 333; fax: 0331-943 338* (moderate) is a small, elegant neo-Georgian hotel set in a private estate. Its 3-star rating belies the level of comfort and sophistication here. There are also 4-bed self-catering apartments on offer.

The city has a huge number of excellent bed and breakfasts; ask the Tourist Office for a full listing. Next to Redlands, **Briar Ghyll**, *George McFarlane Lane, Wembley; tel: 0331-422 664* (cheap) is a Victorian red brick mansion, recently converted into a charming antique-filled guesthouse, set in 20 hectare gardens. **Le Jardine** *(Pf), 2 Troon Terrace, Muswell Hill; tel/fax: 0331-472 420* (cheap) is a comfortable

family home in the hills with fine views over the town, while the **M'Sunduzi Lodge**, *82 Henderson Rd, Athlone; tel: 0331-944 388* (cheap) prides itself on upmarket accommodation and service. **Reheboth**, *276 Murray Rd, Lincoln Meade; tel: 0331-962 312; fax: 0331-964 008* (cheap) offers self-catering Victorian-style apartments in landscaped gardens, 6 km from the city centre. At the cheapest end of the market, **Debbie's**, *17 Mills Circle, Hayfields; tel: 0331-61719* (cheap) is a friendly, relaxed bed and breakfast that also caters for backpackers, while **Sunduzi Backpackers**, *140 Berg St; tel: 0331-940 072* (cheap) provides self-catering accommodation, meals on request and organises affordable tours of Kwazulu-Natal.

Campsite: **Msunduzi Caravan Park**, *Cleland Rd; tel: 0331-65342*, 5 km south of the city centre.

Eating and Drinking

In the grounds of the Voortrekker Museum, **Christopher's Restaurant and Bar**, *Longmarket St; tel: 0331-428 986* (moderate; open Mon–Fri, lunch and dinner, Sat dinner only; booking essential) is a charming, light and flowery restaurant serving a delicious, imaginative modern menu. The **Café du Midi**, *262 Boom St; tel: 0331-945 444* (moderate; open lunch and dinner) serves good traditional French food in a friendly café atmosphere with a nice courtyard. For seafood, try the **Turtle Bay**, *Wembley Terrace, off the Howick Rd, 5 km north of the city centre; tel: 0331-945 390* (moderate). The best of the local steakhouses is **RJ's Steakhouse**, *66 Durban Rd; tel: 0331-66630* (moderate). For Italian, try the homely and relaxing **Ristorante da Vinci**, *117 Commercial Rd; tel: 0331-456 632* (moderate). The **Keg and Elephant**, *80 Commercial Rd, corner Berg St; tel: 0331-941 357* (cheap) is an English-style pub serving traditional pub grub.

One of the most pleasant places for a light meal (lunch and tea only) is surrounded by trees at the **Botanic Gardens Restaurant**, *Mayor's Walk; tel: 0331-442 207* (cheap). Another is in the **Tatham Art Gallery Café**, *60 Commercial Rd; tel: 0331-428 327*, where all the chairs are painted by local artists – worth a stop on their own.

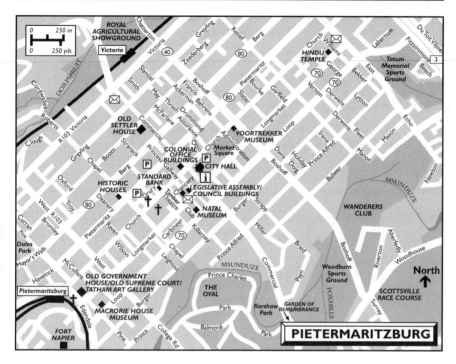

PIETERMARITZBURG

287

Communications

Main Post Office: *Longmarket St; tel: 0331-455 880.*

Money

There are several banks with exchange facilities on *Church St,* of which the finest architecturally is the **Standard Bank Centenary Branch**, *211 Church St; tel: 0331-452 421.* **Thomas Cook/Rennies Travel Foreign Exchange**, *207 Pietermaritz St; tel: 0331-941 571.*

ENTERTAINMENT

There is relatively little going on here from day to day, but the city is easily close enough to take advantage of the Durban nightlife. On Fridays, *What's On* magazine comes free with the *Natal Witness*, or look in the Durban listings *What's On in KZN*, or the Tourist Office's more general monthly *What's On*. **Computicket**, *Furniture OK, Pietermaritz St; tel: 0331-946 203*, handles ticket sales for all local events.

There are two cinema complexes – the **Nu-Metro**, *Cascades Centre; tel: 0331-471 785*, and

Ster Kinekor, *50 Durban Rd; tel: 0331-423 550*, showing first-release movies. Performances at the two theatres, the **Winston Churchill Theatre**, *Leinster Rd, tel: 0331-423 439*, and the **Hexagon Theatre**, *Golf Rd; tel: 0331-260 5537*, are intermittent and often amateur.

One of the town's most popular clubs is the **Buzz Bar**, *204 Longmarket St; tel: 0331-452 638*, a young hang-out where live rock music alternates with kwela – township jazz. *Commercial Rd* has several busy restaurants, clubs and bars.

The local year is punctuated by a number of huge and often horribly energetic events – the massive **Royal Agricultural Show** (May–June, 2 weeks) is followed by the **Midmar Mile**, a mass swimming race, involving some 10,000 people. The **Comrades Marathon** (June) has around 13,000 entrants (see p. 289) and the **Duzi Canoe Marathon** (Jan) is a 3-day canoe race between Pietermaritzburg and Durban. Alexandra Park is home to **Cars in the Park** (Apr) and **Art in the Park** (May/June) open-air exhibitions.

Mahatma Gandhi

Mohandas Karamchand Gandhi began his working life as a lawyer in South Africa. On 7th June 1893, he caught a train at Pietermaritzburg station, naturally choosing a first-class carriage as befit his station. The ticket collector ejected him, sending him to sit in the luggage wagon. When he protested, he was thrown off the train. It was a moment that changed history – and is now marked with a plaque on the station platform.

Gandhi was so disgusted that he put his considerable energy and intellect into fighting for Indian rights. Over the next 20 years, as he won several major concessions from the South African government, including the end of the indentured Indian labour in the cane fields, he also honed his theories of passive resistance *(satyagraha)*. By the time he returned to India in 1914, he was already a national hero, awarded the honorific title 'Mahatma' (Great Soul).

SHOPPING

There are a number of interesting small shops in the narrow lanes behind *Church St*. Amongst them, **The Craft Market**, *Chancery Chambers, Chancery Lane; tel: 0331-948 140*, sells a wide range of excellent souvenirs from across Africa. The **Eco-Shop**, *Chancery Chambers, Chancery Lane; tel: 0331-944 862*, concentrates on all things eco-friendly, from recycled paper and glass to natural cosmetics and herbal teas. **Red Berry**, *11 Caryle Arcade, Chancery Lane; tel: 0331-456 510*, has everything of leather from boots to earrings. The finest arts and crafts in town are sold at the **Tatham Art Gallery shop**, *Commercial Rd*, while on Saturday mornings, the gallery grounds are taken over by the local flea market.

SIGHTSEEING

The best way to experience Pietermaritzburg is slowly and on foot – take care to look both up and down for the extraordinarily detailed decoration in everything from rooflines to lamp posts, many depicting the city's symbols of an elephant or rampant wildebeest. Start next to the massive red brick **City Hall**, *34 Church St, corner Commercial Rd; tel: 0331-951 111*, built in 1902 on the site of the original *Raadsaal* (Afrikaner meeting hall) and said to be the largest brick building in the southern hemisphere, topped by a flamboyant clock tower. Peer inside for a glimpse at the elaborate décor, fine stained-glass, and vast pipe organ with 3806 pipes. Directly opposite is the excellent **Tatham Art Gallery**, *60 Commercial Rd, corner*

Church St; tel: 0331-421 804 (open Tues–Sun 1000–1800; free). The building, completed in 1865, served as the **Supreme Court** (1906–1983). It is now home to a fine collection of late 19th- and 20th-century paintings, with works by Degas, Renoir, Matisse, Hockney, and Henry Moore, together with porcelain and glass, and, increasingly, a powerful collection of traditional and contemporary South African art. Several local artists and craftspeople have small studios in the annexe. Next door, the **Natal Parliament Building**, *47–48 Longmarket St; tel: 0331-355 7720* (open Mon–Fri 0800–1600 by prior arrangement only; free) was designed by three architects, Dudgeon, Snell and Tibbet. It is a magnificent colonial symbol, surrounded by English iron railings. It now shares duty with Ulundi as seat of the state legislature, all 91 MPs switching cities every month. Business is conducted in English, Afrikaans and Zulu. Visitors can sign in to the public gallery when parliament is in session, or request a guided tour at other times. On the other side of the Art Gallery, the magnificent winged **Anglo-Boer War Memorial**, *Carbineers' Garden*, marks the start of the pedestrianised section of **Church Street**, and the lanes which surround it. This is the heart of old Pietermaritzburg and every shop-front is a mass of decorative detail. Particularly beautiful buildings include the **Old Government House** (home of the governors until 1910), whose illustrious guestlist includes Winston Churchill, Rider Haggard and the Empress Eugénie; Philip Dudgeon's fine **Standard Bank building** (1882); **Edgar's Store** (1866), generally acknowledged to be the finest Victorian shop-front in South Africa; and old **Colonial Buildings**. In front of them stands a **statue of Mahatma Gandhi** by Phil Kolbe, unveiled in 1993, on the centenary of the day he was thrown off a local train (see feature box opposite).

On the far side of the City Hall, the small, gabled **Church of the Vow**, built in 1841 in repayment of the Covenant of Blood River (see p.64) is now the **Voortrekker Museum**, *340 Church St; tel: 0331-946 834* (open Mon–Fri 0800–1300, 1400–1600, Sat 0800–1200; free), with a collection of traditional Afrikaner tools, furniture and costumes, and a one-sided account of the Piet Retief storey. Also part of the complex are **Welverdient House**, the original home of Andries Pretorius, and a modern Church of the Vow. The city's only surviving double-storey Voortrekker House, *333 Boom St* (built in 1846) is also administered by the museum. A couple of blocks east, the **Natal Museum**, *237 Loop St; tel: 0331-451 404* (open Mon–Sat 0900–1630, Sun 1400–1700; R2) has an excellent collection of local Victoriana, with a whole gallery of reconstructed shops and homes, authentically furnished in period style. Its Africana section covers the continent with art from San rock paintings to Asante wooden pillows, and there is also section on Portuguese shipwrecks and natural history, with fossilised dinosaurs and stuffed mammals, birds and marine life.

Still on *Loop St,* but away from the centre, the Victorian **Macrorie House Museum,** *11 Loop St, corner Pine St; tel: 0331-942 161* (open Tues–Thur 0900–1300, Sun 1100–1600; R2) was built in 1862. From 1869–1891, it was the home of Bishop Macrorie. It has now been lovingly restored and is furnished with a superb collection of Victorian antiques and costumes. Still further on, **Fort Napier** was built in 1843, as the home of the 45th Regiment (Sherwood Foresters), garrisoned here to protect the town from Zulu invasions. Inside **St George's Garrison Church** (1898) is worth a quick look. Other interesting places of worship include the Anglican **Catheral of St Peters,** *Longmarket St* (1872) and the Hindu temple, the **Sri Siva Soobramoniar and Marriamen Temple**, *Lower Longmarket St* (open Mon–Sat 0700–1800, Sun 0800–1800). Up in the suburbs is one of the city's most unusual museums, the **Comrades Marathon Museum**, *Connaught Rd, Scottsville; tel: 0331-943 510* (open Mon–Fri 0830–1630, Sat–Sun by arrangement; free). This excruciating annual race covers the entire 82 km between Durban and Pietermaritzburg on foot, swapping direction each year. A staggeringly large number of masochists choose to enter; many more camp out in the sun with a cooler of beers to cheer them on their way.

Parks and Gardens

In true 'little England' style, Pietermaritzburg prides itself on its magnificent parks.

The **Natal National Botanic Gardens**, *Mayor's Walk, Prestbury, 4 km north of the city centre; tel: 0331-443 585* (open Mon, Wed–Fri 0730–1800, Sat–Sun 0800–1800 Oct–Mar; Apr–Sept closes 1730; closed Tues; R2) is one of eight in South Africa maintained by the National Botanical Institute, with 12 hectares of landscaped park and a charming central lake. Mature trees provide a canopy of shade over emerald lawns and lush undergrowth bright with flowers, which attract many different species of dragonflies and butterflies, over 100 species of bird and various small game animals such as bushbuck, monkeys and mongooses.

The **Garden of Remembrance**, *corner Durban and Leinster Rds,* is a memorial to the 13,000 South African soldiers who died at the horrific World War I Battle of Dellville Wood. A famous Weeping Cross in the gardens oozes sap on the anniversary of the battle each year.

The 93 hectare **Queen Elizabeth Park Nature Reserve**, *Duncan McKenzie Dr., 8 km north of the city centre, off the Howick road; tel: 0331-472 180* (open daily sunrise–sunset; R2) is filled with indigenous species such as strelitzias, erythrinas and hundreds of spectacular aloes. Impala, zebra, blesbok and duikers roam freely, while white rhinos are kept in a special enclosure. Here too are walking trails, picnic and *braai* sites and the headquarters of the Natal Parks Board (see p.408).

Nature lovers should ask for the *Green Belt Trails* brochure, which has details of various hiking trails around the fringes of the city.

289

PORT ELIZABETH

Port Elizabeth is an historic city, major seaport and popular family resort, whose sandy beaches are washed by the warm Indian Ocean. The city is well located for trips along the Garden Route, to the Settler Hinterland and the Sunshine Coast.

TOURIST INFORMATION

Tourist Office: *Donkin Lighthouse Building, Donkin Reserve, Belmont Terrace, Port Elizabeth; tel: 041-558 884* (open Mon–Fri 0800–1630, Sat and Sun 0930–1530). Information, accommodation advice and reservations. **Branch:** *Brooke Hill, Beach Rd, Humewood, Port Elizabeth; tel: 041-551 977* (open daily 0900–1700).

ARRIVING AND DEPARTING

By Air
Port Elizabeth Airport: *Allister Miller Dr.,* 4 km from the city centre. Taxis and hotel transport are available. Flight information and airport enquiries: *tel: 041-507 7301;* flight reservations and cancellations: *tel: 041-344 444.*

By Car
Port Elizabeth is reached from Cape Town and East London on the N2, and from Johannesburg on the N1, the N9 and the N10. There is plenty of on-street parking and there are multi-storey car parks at *Grey St, Central* and *OK Building, Chapel St, Central.*

By Bus
The following companies operate intercity services linking with Port Elizabeth: **Greyhound Intercity Coach,** *tel: 041-344 550;* **J-Bay Sunshine Express,** *tel: 0423-932;* **Intercape Mainliner,** *tel: 041-560 055;* **Translux Express,** *tel: 041-507 3333* and **The Garden Route Hop-on-Hop-off Hopper Bus,** *tel: 041-554 000.*

By Rail
Railway Station: *Station St,* in the town centre. For enquiries and train timetables, *tel: 041-507 2662* or *041-507 3176* (open Mon–Fri 0730–1600, Sat and Sun 0730–1500). The **Spoornet Information Office,** *The Bridge, Greenacres; tel: 041-507 2222* or *041-507 2111* (after hours), may be contacted for train schedules, fares information and general enquiries.

GETTING AROUND
The central area of the city is compact and most of the historic attractions are within walking distance of one another. There is adequate public transport for those who don't want to walk.

All local **buses** leave from the **Market Square Bus Station,** *beneath the Norwich Union Centre Building, Strand St.* Free timetables from the entrance kiosk. The **Algoa Bus Company,** *tel: 041-414 241,* operates a regular service between the city centre, beachfront, St George's Park, *Rink St,* Greenacres and The Bridge Shopping Centre (Route O).

Taxis: Hurters Taxi Cabs, *tel: 041-557 334,* operates a 24-hour service; **City Taxis,** *tel: 041-342212.* Those who prefer two wheels, contact **Bob's Bicycle Hire,** *111 Russell Rd; tel: 041-554 303* (mountain bikes from R40 per day). **Fat Tracks Mountain Bicycle Club;** *tel: 041-331 921* or *041-554 050.*

STAYING IN PORT ELIZABETH

Accommodation
The city is jam-packed with large resort hotels, bed and breakfasts, time-share and self-catering apartments; full list from the Tourist Office. Chains hotels include *CL, F1, HI, Pa.*

The **Beach Hotel,** *Marine Dr., Humewood, Port Elizabeth; tel/fax: 041-532 161* (moderate) is well placed for the beaches. Nearby, the **Humewood Hotel,** *33 Beach Rd, Humewood; tel/fax: 041-558 961* (cheap) is a recently renovated beachfront hotel, whose low prices bely its comfort and location. In the suburbs,

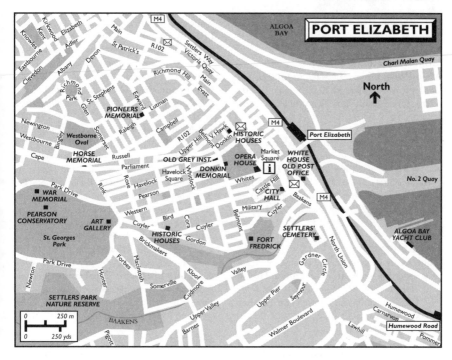

and highly recommended, are **Hacklewood Hill Country House**, *152 Prospect Rd, Walmer, Port Elizabeth; tel: 041-511 300, fax: 041-514 155* (moderate), a stately 19th-century country house, and **Walmer Gardens Hotel**, *10th Ave, Walmer, Port Elizabeth; tel/fax: 041-514 322* (moderate), an old-fashioned hotel with a good restaurant.

Top of the range amongst the guesthouses is **Club 39 Walmer**, *39 Church Rd, Walmer, Port Elizabeth; tel: 041-515 099, fax: 041-514 458* (moderate), while the **Brighton Lodge**, *21 Brighton Dr., Summerstrand, Port Elizabeth; tel: 041-534 576, fax: 041-534 104* (cheap) is an alternative near the the beach.

Bed & Breakfast: One of the most luxurious is **Cuyler Crescent Guest House**, *19 Cuyler Crescent, Port Elizabeth; tel: 041-553 672, fax: 041-556 946* (cheap). Others are **Driftsands**, *2 Marshall Rd, Humewood, Port Elizabeth; tel: 041-560 459, fax: 041-556 513* (cheap), close to all major attractions, and **11 King George's Guest House**, *Millpark, Port Elizabeth; tel/fax: 041-341 825* (cheap).

Hostels: **Port Penguin Backpackers**, *67b Russell Rd, Central; tel: 041-554 499; fax: 041-562 714* (cheap); **Kings Beach Backpackers Hostel**, *41 Windermere Rd, Humewood; tel: 041-558 113* (cheap).

Eating and Drinking

The **Nelson's Arms**, *3 Trinder St; tel: 041-560 072* (cheap; open lunch Mon–Fri, dinner Mon–Sat) offers a variety of fresh seafood with daily specials, while **Aviemore Restaurant**, *67 Parliament St; tel: 041-551 125* (expensive; Mon–Sat dinner, Wed and Fri lunch; booking essential), offers provincial South African cuisine. Probably the most historic restaurant in the city is the **Sir Rufane Donkin Rooms**, *George St, Central; tel: 041-555 534* (expensive; reservation essential), which specialises in French cuisine.

Brooke's Pavilion Entertainment Complex, *corner Beach Rd and Brooke's Hill Dr., Summerstrand; tel: 041-55 5312* (cheap; open early morning until late), has a variety of places to eat and drink, including a tapas bar, a tavern and a popular cocktail bar called **Tequila Sunrise**.

Communications
Main Post Office: *259 Main St; tel: 041-564 666* (open Mon–Fri 0800–1630, Sat 0830–1200). Post Restante service available.

Money
All the major banks are represented, including **Nedbank**, *Nedbank Centre, 88 Main St; tel: 041-523 760*, and **First National Bank**, *68 Main St; tel: 041-506 6111*. Thomas Cook foreign exchange facilities are available at **Rennies Travel**, *Murray & Roberts Building, 48/52 Ring St, Greenacres; tel: 041-343 536*.

Concerts, musicals, opera and theatre are staged at a variety of locations. The **Opera House and Barn**, *White's Rd, Port Elizabeth; tel: 041-561 122*, is the principal theatre. **The Feather Market Centre**, *corner Baaken's St and Military Rd; tel: 041-561 122*, once a centre of the ostrich feather industry (see p.282), is now a concert hall. The **Manville Open Air Theatre**, *St George's Park, Park Dr.*, is the venue for summer's Shakespearean Festival, while the **Ford Little Theatre**, *corner Castle Hill and Belmont Terrace; tel: 041-558 354*, is home to the Music and Drama Society. There are also three multi-screen cinemas – **The Bridge Complex**, *Cape Rd; tel: 041-344 340*; **Kine Montage**, *Kine Park, Rink St, Central; tel: 041-523 311*; and **Walmer Nu-Metro**, *Stanford Rd, Cleary Park Shopping Centre, Walmer; tel: 041-515 380*.

Port Elizabeth has a full calendar of outdoor events; contact the Tourist Office for details.

SHOPPING

The **Bridge Shopping and Entertainment Centre**, *CJ Langehoven Dr., Greenacres; tel: 041-338 914*, adjoining the **Greenacres Shopping Centre**, *tel: 041-343 220*, sells a wide range of goods from fashion accessories to curios. **Walmer Park Shopping Centre**, *Main Rd, Walmer Park; tel: 041-382 690*, is a comprehensive local favourite. **Pier 14 Shopping Centre**, *444 Main St, North End; tel: 041-541 228*, is

innovative and fun to be in, while **Pick 'n Pay Friendly Hyper**, *Old Cape Rd, Hunters Retreat; tel: 041-307 861*, is good for one-stop shopping.

There are several good African art galleries and curio centres, including **Wezandla Gallery and Craft Centre**, *22 Baakens St, Port Elizabeth; tel: 041-551 185*; **African Curios**, *18 Main St, Port Elizabeth; tel: 041-554 679*; and **Momentos of Africa Gift Shop**, *Port Elizabeth Airport; tel: 041-507 7241*.

For antiques, visit *Rink St, Parliament St, Lawrence St, Clyde St, Pearson St* and *Westbourne Rd*. **Tetbury Antiques**, *Parliament St, Port Elizabeth; tel: 041-552 373*, sells high-quality porcelain, furniture and pictures.

Port Elizabeth also has a number of flea markets worth visiting. At **St George's Park** there is a large open-air art exhibition, with arts and crafts for sale (first Sat of every month), while the **Port Elizabeth Beachfront Traders Association** is a collection of stalls scattered along the Humewood beachfronts, every weekend (0800–late afternoon).

SIGHTSEEING

The first settlement here began in 1799, with the construction of Fort Frederick. The city of Port Elizabeth formally began life in 1820, when some 4000 British settlers landed at what is now *Jetty St*, ready to colonise the area. A **campanile**, built in 1923, marks the site. Today, the city, which straddles the shores of Algoa Bay, is the fifth largest in South Africa, as well as one of its busiest ports. It is also a popular resort, with some delightful historic buildings, amongst them the finest collection of art nouveau in Southern Africa, hidden by the modern overgrowth, and some fine swimming beaches beyond the hustle of the port.

At the centre, the **Donkin Reserve**, *abutting Belmont Terrace*, was proclaimed an open space in perpetuity by the Acting Governor of the Cape, Sir Rufane Donkin, after whose wife, Elizabeth, the city was named. She tragically died in India aged 28 and her memorial pyramid stands in the garden today, beside the old 15,000 candlepower lighthouse (1861).

Museums
On the beachfront, the **Port Elizabeth**

Museum, *Beach Rd, opposite Humewood Beach; tel: 041-561 051* (open daily 0900–1700; R2) comprises an Oceanarium (with daily dolphin and seal shows 0900–1300, 1400–1700; R13), the world-famous Snake Park and Tropical House (with a profusion of exotic plants, reptiles and free-flying birds; both open 0900–1300, 1400–1700; R8), and the Museum itself, which focuses on Settler history, early transport vehicles and sailing ships. **No 7 Castle Hill Museum**, *7 Castle Hill; tel: 041-522 515* (open Tues–Sat 1000–1300, 1400–1700, Sun and Mon 1400–1700; donation), is one of the oldest surviving settler cottages in the city. Built in 1827, it was a rectory; restored and lovingly furnished, it now reflects the lifestyle of its original occupants.

The **Port Elizabeth Airforce Museum**, *Forest Hill Dr., Southdene; tel: 041-505 1295* (open Mon–Fri 0800–1530, second Sun of every month 0900–1530; free), houses aviation memorabilia, while the **St Croix Motor Museum**, *Mowbray St, Newton Park; tel: 041-392 5111* (open by appointment), displays a private collection of vintage and classic vehicles, dating from 1901. The **Jewish Heritage Museum**, *Raleigh St; tel: 041-533 671* (open Sun 1000–1200; free), housed in a deconsecrated synagogue, displays an interesting collection of Judaica used by the city's Jewish community. The **King George V1 Art Gallery**, *St George's Park, 1 Park Dr.; tel: 041-561 030* (open Mon–Fri 0830–1700, Sat 0830–1630, Sun 1400–1630; free), houses a permanent collection of 19th- and 20th-century British art, as well as a large South African collection. Stone-built **Fort Frederick**, *Belmont Terrace* (open daily 0900–1700; free), was constructed (1799) in an effort to defend the mouth of the Baakens River, which flows into the port. It has never fired a shot in anger, although it is defended by eight 12-powder guns.

Beaches

Port Elizabeth is also a resort. The beaches of Algoa Bay reach right into the city: **Humewood** and **King's Beach** have excellent, safe swimming, and there are tidal and paddling pools, changing rooms, places for refreshments and a miniature railway (the 'Sea

Breeze Express'). **King's Beach Promenade** overlooks an extensive playground for children. There is go-karting and the chance to go on the **Apple Express**, *tel: 041-507 2333* (departs Humewood Road Station at 0930, returns 1600; R40), a narrow-gauge steam train which operates from Port Elizabeth to Thornhill Village via the world's highest narrow-gauge bridge, over the Van Staden's River.

Wildlife

The city has many natural resources. There is an abundance of bird life, and favourite bird-watching sites include **Settlers Park**, the **Cape Recife Nature Reserve** (with its penguin sanctuary) and the **Zwartkops River Estuary** (which has flamingos in its salt pans). The **Eastern Cape Wild Bird Society** organises bird-watching outings to Settlers Park, *tel: 041-557 715* (first Sat of each month at 0830). **Settlers' Park Nature Reserve**, *St George's Park; tel: 041-559 711* (open daily 0900–1700; admission free), is a 54 hectare wild flower reserve on the Baakens River. Explore the local environment with the **Wildlife and Environment Society of South Africa**, *2B Lawrence St, Port Elizabeth; tel: 041-559 606.*

Tours

There are plenty of tours to be had in and around Port Elizabeth. For the do-it-yourself version, ask the Tourist Office for a map and brochure of the **Donkin Heritage Trail** (5 km), which explores the city's old hill area. **Friendly City Tours**, *tel: 041-551 801*, offer the best city tour (and arrange others to Addo Elephant National Park, see p.184), while **Historical Perspective Tours**, *tel: 041-558 133*, is for history enthusiasts. **John Huddlestone Helicopter Tours & Flips**, *tel: 041-522 597*, arrange aerial trips for views of the bay. Tailor-made tours within the city and further afield (including Addo Elephant National Park), can be arranged by **Gaylards Safaris**, *tel: 041-680 055*, while stimulating package tours are provided by **Springbok Atlas**, *tel: 041-451 2555*, and **Algoa Tours**, *tel: 041-512 403* (excursions to the Settler Country, along the Garden Route, to the eastern cape and the Sunshine Coast).

293

PRETORIA

Pretoria was not designed in a rush but graciously, with gardens, green open spaces and 70,000 jacaranda trees lining the roads, which cloak the city in a beautiful mauve haze each October. Established in 1856 by one of the leaders of the Great Trek, Marthinus Pretorius, and named after his father, Andries Pretorius, leader of the Afrikaans forces at the Battle of Blood River (see p.270), Pretoria became the capital of the Boer Republic in 1860, and is still the administrative capital of South Africa. The impressive Union Buildings, completed in 1913, were the scene of Nelson Mandela's historic inauguration as President of the Republic in May 1994.

294

Although it has long been overshadowed by its noisy, boisterous neighbour, Johannesburg, this is a city of substance, with a great deal to offer. More than 1.5 million people live here. There are four universities, including Unisa, South Africa's correspondence university – the largest in the world.

The city also has nearly three dozen museums and galleries, mzany parks, including Botanical Gardens, a bird sanctuary and zoo, modern shopping malls and entertainment ranging from opera and township jazz to go-karting and gaming. It is within easy reach of the airport and altogether, this is probably a far safer and more pleasant place to stay than

Johannesburg for anyone wanting to spend time in Gauteng.

TOURIST INFORMATION

Pretoria Visitors' Bureau: *Tourist Rendezvous Travel Centre, corner Vermeulen and Prinsloo Sts, Sammy Marks Centre; tel: 012-308 8909/8937; fax: 012-308 8891* (open Mon–Fri 0730–1545). This is one of the best organised tourist offices in the country, providing a good city map, together with a broad range of brochures and leaflets on many of the city's attractions, accommodation, restaurants, transport facilities, entertainments, cultural centres, crafts outlets and places to visit in the surrounding region, including wildlife parks. Staff are willing to deal with any queries and organise accommodation and day trips.

Off-Limits Travel Agency; *tel: 012-323 7993,* and the **Reservations Office;** *tel: 012-323 1222* (open daily 0900–1700), also have desks in the centre. Accommodation at National Parks Board camps and lodges can be booked here or at the **National Parks Board Headquarters:** *643 Leyds St, Muckleneuk (PO Box 787), Pretoria 001; tel: 012-343 1991; fax: 012-343 0905* (open Mon–Fri 0800–1545).

ARRIVING AND DEPARTING

By Air
Johannesburg International Airport (see Johannesburg, p.194) is 45 km south of Pretoria, off the R21. A **bus** service between the airport and the *Sammy Marks Centre* operates daily 0500–2000; *tel: 012-323 1429.* There is also a pick-up **shuttle** service (daily; every hour on the hour between 0700–1900) between the Tourist Rendezvous, Pretoria's main hotels and the airport. Tickets for **Pretoria Airport Shuttle;** *tel: 012-323 0904,* are available from Tourist Rendezvous Reservations. The fare (subject to change) is R38.

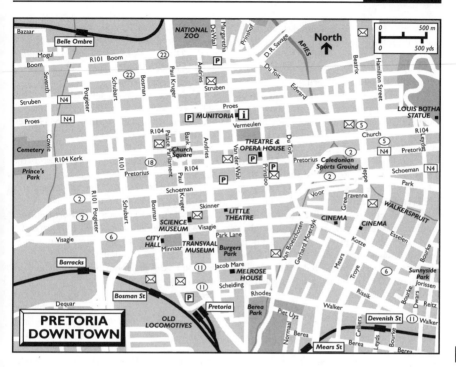

PRETORIA DOWNTOWN

By Car

Pretoria has superb road connections, with easy access to many of South Africa's major freeways. All the main car hire companies have offices in town, including: **Avis**; *tel: 012-325 1490;* **Budget**; *tel: 012-341 4650;* **Europcar Inter-rent**; *tel: 012341 6161;* and **Imperial**; *tel: 012-323 3259.*

Unusually for a capital city, Pretoria has wide roads, traffic problems are rare and **parking** is easy, with plenty of metered on-street parking. There are about a dozen public car parks and parking areas in central Pretoria. The nearest car park to the Tourist Rendezvous and travel centre is on *Vermulen St,* between *Van de Walt* and *Prinsloo Sts.* Others nearby are at the corner of *Prinsloo* and *Pretorius Sts,* and on *Schoeman St,* between *Andries* and *Van der Walt Sts.*

By Train

Railway Station: *Railway St; tel: 012-315 2007* (general information); *012-315 2401* (reservations). Pretoria has one of the most

active rail networks in South Africa, with regular connections to Johannesburg as well as many long-distance services to other major South African cities and neighbouring countries. The magnificent station, designed by Sir Herbert Baker in the style of a renaissance palace, is also the home base of Rovos Rail (see p.55).

By Bus

Coach Station: *1928 Building, Scheiding St, next to the railway station.* A number of intercity bus and coach companies serve the city, including **Greyhound Citiliner**; *tel: 012-323 1154,* **Intercape**; *tel: 012-654 4114* (reservations), *012-386 4400* (information), and **Translux**; *tel: 012-315 2333.*

GETTING AROUND

Central Pretoria is remarkably compact, with many of the major sights in or around *Church St,* within easy walking distance. You will need transport to get to the Union Buildings and the out of town sights.

Church Square is the terminal for **municipal**

buses; *tel: 012-308 0839*. Timetables are available at the information office here, on the buses and also at some chemists' shops. As ever, these are designed primarily for commuters and are not terribly useful for sightseeing.

Metered **taxis** may be flagged down or booked by telephone. There are convenient ranks at the *Tourist Rendezvous, Railway Station, Strijdom Sq.* and *Pretorius St.* Radio taxi companies in Pretoria include **City Taxis**, *tel: 012-215 749;* **City Bug**, *tel: 012-663 6316;* **Rixi Taxis**, *tel: 012-325 8072;* **Transcab**, *tel: 012-324 5051;* **Flash Taxis**, *tel: 012-323 6376/8;* and **Five Star Taxis**; *tel: 012-320 7513*.

Guided city tours, either privately or in groups, are available from the Tourist Rendezvous and several private tour operators. **Expeditionary Force**; *tel: 012-320 7513,* run historical city tours, while **Sakabula Tours**; *tel: 012-981 585,* do tours of the city and the surrounding townships.

STAYING IN PRETORIA

Accommodation

Very much a white collar city with much conference and convention business, Pretoria has a good stock of high-standard accommodation in hotels, guesthouses and bed and breakfast homes. Hotel chains include *BW, Hd* (Crowne Plaza and Garden Court), *Ka, Pa*.

Very few of the good hotels are atmospheric. The exception is the little **Victoria Hotel**, *corner Scheiding and Paul Kruger Sts; tel: 012-323 6052; fax: 012-323 0843* (moderate–expensive), originally the station hotel and the oldest purpose-built hotel in Pretoria (1896). With only 11 rooms, a ladies' bar and a good dining room, this has been lovingly restored to former glories by Rovos Rail (see p. 55).

The other upmarket hotels include the 4-star **Holiday Inn Crowne Plaza** (Hd), *corner Church and Beatrix Sts, Pretoria; tel: 012-341 1571; fax: 012-447 534* (expensive), with 107 double rooms, 129 singles and six suites and a pool; the 3-star **Karos Manhattan** *(Ka), 247 Scheiding St, Arcadia; tel: 012-322 7635; fax: 012-320 0721* (moderate–expensive), well placed for shopping and sports venues, with a pool; and the 3-star **Best Western Pretoria**

(BW), 230 Hamilton St, corner Church St, Arcadia; tel: 012-341 3473; fax: 012-442 258, with 123 air-conditioned rooms, the Hamilton Restaurant and a coffee shop and cocktail bar (moderate–expensive).

Slightly lower down the price ladder, but still very comfortable are the centrally situated, well-equipped 3-star **Holiday Inn Garden Court** *(Hd), corner Van der Walt and Minnaar Sts; tel: 012-322 7500; fax: 012-322 9429* (cheap–moderate), with a pool; and the **Arcadia**, *515 Proes St, Arcadia; tel: 012-326 9311; fax: 012-326 1067* (cheap–moderate), a 3-star property close to the Union Buildings with more than 100 rooms. The **Formula Inn**, *81–85 Pretorius St; tel: 012-324 1304; fax: 012-324 1303* (cheap) is a new no-frills inn with 55 rooms, each with a double bed and full-size bunk for R94 per room per night. There are colour TVs and handbasins in the rooms, adjacent automatically cleaned toilets and shower units, and round-the-clock access, although reception is only open 0630–0930, 1600–2200.

Many guesthouses and bed and breakfasts can be booked direct or through agencies like **Pretoria Guest House**; reservations: *tel: 012-465 327; fax: 012-807 4411;* **Jacana Country Homes** *tel: 012-465 365; fax: 012-346 2499;* **Rikita Guest Houses**; *tel: 012-803 8833;* and the **Bed and Breakfast Association of Pretoria**; *tel/fax: 083-212 1989*. There are plenty to choose from.

Paula's Place, *333 Charles St, Brooklyn; tel/fax: 012-465 934* (cheap) offers bed and breakfast in an elegant old house, with a hostess well informed on Pretoria and its history. **The Waterhouse** *(Pf), 439 Stonewall St, Faerie Glen; tel: 012-991 1808* (moderate) has five double rooms in cool, green surroundings of hill and valley, beyond a pool terrace and mature gardens. The award-winning **La Maison** *(Pf), 235 Hilda St, Hatfield; tel: 012-434 341; fax: 012-342 1531* (moderate) provides luxury accommodation and cordon bleu food in a house more like a small European palazzo, with a pool and fine gardens.

The **Villa Monica**, *308 Hill St, Arcadia; tel/fax: 012-46 1506* (cheap) offers bed and breakfast and secure parking near university, restaurants and rugby stadium. **Brooks**

Cottage, *283 Brooks St, Brooklyn; tel: 012-362 3150; fax: 012-323 0052* (cheap) provides a choice of self-catering unit or double room in an old home recently restored to its original attractive style. **Mellow Place**, *1 Thomas Edison St, Menlo Park; tel/fax: 012-462 887* (moderate–expensive) is a 10-room guesthouse based on English country house style, which offers 24-hour service, meals and many other facilities (no children under 15).

There are also self-catering apartments and clean budget accommodation in dormitories or private rooms in lively areas of the city. The **Courtyard Suite Hotel**, *corner Park and Hill Sts, Arcadia; tel: 012-342 4940; fax: 012-342 4941* (expensive) provides luxury studios and one- or two-bedroom suites with kitchenettes (microwave), bathroom and secure parking. A shopping service operates to stock your kitchen – you can let the management have your list before arrival – and in-suite dining can be arranged with local restaurants.

At rock-bottom price range, **Pretoria Backpackers**, *34 Bourke St, Sunnyside; tel: 012-343 9754;* (cheap) is handy for nightlife, pubs, theatres and cafés, with dormitory or private room accommodation in a well-equipped house. **Word of Mouth Backpackers**, *145 Berea St; tel: 012-341 9661; fax: 012-341 1232,* is centrally situated and open 24 hours a day. Transport from arrival points can be provided and pub crawls are organised for guests. **Campsites**: Amongst several in the area, try the **Joos Becker Caravan Park**, *Mansfield Dr., Pretoria N.; tel/fax: 012-335 2887,* with self-catering chalets, caravan and tent pitches, and a restaurant; and **Polkadraai Caravan Park**, *Hennops River, 12 km south-west of Pretoria city centre; tel: 012-668 8710.*

Eating and Drinking

With so many visiting diplomats and regiments of civil servants around, Pretoria has an excellent selection of upmarket dining establishments. There is also a broad range of middle-of-the-road places offering consistently good value, and efficient but unhurried service. *Esselen St* has a particularly high proportion of good eateries.

Top of the range are **La Madeleine**, *258 Esselen St, Sunnyside; tel: 012-446 076* (expensive; booking advisable), an elegant Belgian-run restaurant serving classic haute cuisine; **Gerard Moerdyk**, *752 Park St, Arcadia; tel: 012-344 4856* (expensive; booking advisable), which offers traditional Cape Dutch food, in a luxuriously appointed neo-Cape Dutch mansion (built in the 1920s); and **Chagall's**, *Fountain Valley; tel: 012-341 7511* (expensive; booking advisable), which serves magnificent French food. Bring the price down a notch or two and there are numerous excellent steak houses and ethnic establishments serving Chinese, Italian, German, Greek, Mongolian, French, Russian, Mexican, Mediterranean, Portuguese, Dutch, Swiss, Austrian, Japanese, and, of course, traditional South African cuisine.

Right in the city centre, **Böhmerwald**, *85 Paul Kruger St; tel: 012-326 7658* (moderate) has a regular following for its satisfying German meat dishes. **Pavarotti's**, *Sammy Marks Sq., Church St; tel: 012-323 4221* (moderate–expensive; open daily till late) is an enjoyable, cosmopolitan restaurant in a first floor position opposite the State Theatre. Italian **Roberto's**, *The Tramshed, Schoeman St; tel: 012-467 258* (moderate) is one of the best of several restaurants, cafés and fast-food joints in the Tramshed shopping arcade.

Further out, at the heart of the city's nightlife area, **The Pavilion**, *corner Jeppe and Esselen Sts, Sunnyside; tel: 012-326 8811* (moderate–expensive) offers a wide choice of continental dishes. **Sirocco**, *109 Gerard Moerdyk St, Sunnyside; tel: 012-341 3785* (moderate–expensive; open Tues–Sun lunch and dinner) serves first-class Mediterranean cuisine in a cheerful setting. The **Mongolian Barbecue**, *Provisus Building, 521 Church St East, Arcadia; tel: 012-44 3423* (moderate; open daily except Sat lunchtime), confusingly, serves Western pub lunches and à la carte meals.

For good Chinese food, try **Hong Kong**, *29-30 Brooklyn Mall, Brooklyn; tel: 012-469 221* (cheap–moderate). For steaks, the **Hillside Tavern**, *Rynlal Building, The Hillside, Lynwood; tel: 012-475 119* (moderate; open daily except Sat lunchtime) is a friendly, trendy steakhouse with a good atmosphere, a string of awards and a menu including Portuguese, British and

297

South African dishes. **A Taste of Texas**, *Crown Ave, at Waterkloof Shopping Centre; tel: 012-466 540* (cheap–moderate) has a long menu and some filling dishes.

It's all fish and no meat at **Uncle's Fishmonger**, *279 Dey St, New Muckleneuk; tel: 012-466 935* (moderate–expensive), a high-profile seafood restaurant decorated with authentic fishing nets, lifebelts, portholes and other fishermen's accoutrements. It is fully licensed, but Uncle does not charge corkage if you bring your own wine.

Coffee bars provide the opportunity for a quick snack or a leisurely light lunch, while most taverns and pubs can be relied on to produce a hearty meal. The **Café Riche**, *Church Sq.; tel: 012-328 3173* (cheap–moderate) is a popular lunch spot for locals in a small art deco building with an owl on the roof sculpted by Anton von Wouw.

In Arcadia, good cafés include the **Café Rose**, *Wenning Park, Eastwood St, Arcadia; tel: 012-342 2064* (cheap); and the **Café Pallette**, *Pretoria Art Museum, Arcadia; tel: 012-343 7564* (cheap).

Pretoria is one of the few places in the country where you can go into a *shebeen* (black beer hall) without a minder. Try **Fana Maseko**, *Motsepe St; tel: 012-373 6402*, or **Justice 'Jaja' Seema**, *12 Ramkatsane St; tel: 012-373 8295*, both in Attridgeville.

Communications

Main Post Office: *corner Pretorius and Van der Walt Sts; tel: 012-409 9111* (open Mon–Fri 0830–1630, Sat 0800–1200). Most other local post offices shut at 1100 on Sat.

Embassies and Consulates

See p. 38.

Money

There are several banks with exchange facilities in the area of *Sammy Marks Sq., Church Sq.* and in the *Tramshed Centre*.

There is a **Thomas Cook/Rennies Travel Bureau de Change** located at *Shop 57, Menlyn Park Shopping Centre, corner Atterbury Rd and Menlyn Dr., Menlo Park; tel: 012-348 3014/6*.

ENTERTAINMENT

Altogether more sober than its neighbour 50 km to the south, Pretoria nevertheless has some decent nightlife, much of it in the form of live music and performances in pubs, township jazz and discos. Classical drama, opera, ballet and music are struggling under hard-hitting subsidy cuts, but they are still performed at the State Theatre and in several smaller venues.

Details of concerts, shows and other events and performances appear in local newspapers and a free publication called *Be My Guest*, available at the Tourist Rendezvous, carry entertainment listings. Bookings can be made through **Computicket**, with offices in the Sanlam and Tramshed Centres, and at the State Theatre; *tel: 012-328 4040*.

The big modern **State Theatre**, *corner Prinsloo and Church Sts; tel: 012-322 1665*, is one of the leading **theatre** complexes in South Africa, with six auditoriums, allowing for the staging of drama, opera, ballet, choral works, recitals and major orchestral performances. Tours, which include a backstage visit, must be booked a week in advance.

The **Pretoria University Amphitheatre**, *Lynnwood St, Hatfield; tel: 012-420 2315*, is a cultural centre regularly presenting music, ballet and opera.

Other venues for live stage performances are **Piet Van der Walt Theatre**, *Showgrounds, Soutter St; tel: 012-237 1487*; **Breytenbach Theatre**, *Gerard Moerdyk St, Sunnyside; tel: 012-444 834*; **Café Richard Basement Theatre**, *Church Sq.; tel: 012-328 3173*, and **Little Theatre**, *Skinner St; tel: 012-322 8484*.

There are scores of **cinemas** in Pretoria. Most of the major shopping centres have excellent multiplexes attached, screening the latest releases. Amongst the most convenient are the **Ster Kinekor**, *Tramshed, cornerVan Der Walt and Schoeman Sts; tel: 012-346 3435*; the **Sterland**, *corner Pretoria and Beatrix Sts, Arcadia; tel: 012-341 7568*; and the **Ster Kinekor**, *Sunnypark Centre, Esselen St; tel: 012-341 9226*.

Jazz and other music festivals are held from time to time at **Moritele Park**, *Mamelodi; tel: 012-805 4669*.

Ed's Easy Diner, *Burnett St, Hatfield; tel: 012-342 2499*, often has live music on the menu. Live music and dancing are a feature at **Oscar's American Diner**, *501 Beatrix St, Arcadia; tel: 012-341 2812*. **Shunter's Tavern**, *202 Esselen St, Sunnyside; tel: 012-341 0751*, and **Paradise Alley**, *cornerSchoeman and Prinsloo Sts; tel: 012-322 6041*, are popular music bars. Several cultural groups are based in the city. For details of **The Gospel Pilots'** engagements, *tel: 012-375 6865;* and for information on **Pretoria Serenaders**, *tel: 012-373 8917*.

Games of all sorts, such as dancing, ten-pin bowling, ice skating, and the latest exciting craze, indoor karting, are popular here. **Kingsley Bowl**, *Kingsley Shopping Centre, corner Church and Beatrix Sts, Arcadia; tel: 012-44 5314*, provides 18 ten-pin bowling lanes. Laser games can be played at **Zone 4**, *Arcadia Shopping Centre; tel: 012-323 1848*, and at **Laserquest**, *286 Esselen St, Sunnyside; tel: 012-341 7314*. Tight cornering and harmless prangs thrill aspiring Schumachers at **Indoor Go-Karting**, *395 Struben St; tel: 083-653 1779*. It costs from R30 for 10 mins or from R175 per hour for an endurance race.

EVENTS

The **Pretoria International Show** takes place in Aug–Sept. The **German Beer Festival** is in Oct, which also sees both the **Lanseria Air Show** and the **Jacaranda Festival**, with the trees in full blossom.

SHOPPING

With a number of major complexes offering a wide range of goods in different parts of the city, shopping is made easy in Pretoria and its environs. There are also some good flea markets and specialist stores, as well as a suggested motor ramble along which arts and crafts maybe bought direct from their creators.

The **Centurion Centre**, *Boulevard, Lenchen Ave, Centurion;* **Sammy Marks Centre**, *Church St, between Van Der Walt and Prinsloo Sts;* **Tramshed**, *corner Van Der Walt and Schoeman Sts;* **Menlyn Park**, *corner Atterbury Rd and Menlyn Dr., Menlo Park;* and **Brooklyn Plaza**, *Bronkhorst St, New Muckleneuk,* are just a few of the enclosed areas of massed shops with safe parking. **Oeverzicht Art Village**, *between Gerard Moerdyk St, Kotze St* and *Boeschoten Lane,*

is a group of 25 restored houses dating from 1895–1920. They are now antique shops, galleries, restaurants and other enterprises, which provide pleasurable browsing. Gift seekers could strike lucky at clothing and curio outlets.

Maps of the **Crocodile Arts and Crafts Ramble**, around the Crocodile River Valley, are available from the Tourist Rendezvous information bureau. Unfortunately, the artists' studios are officially open to the public only on the first Sat–Sun of each month, 0900–1700.

Flea and **art markets** are held at the **Centurion Centre** (see above), *tel: 012-654 2560* (open Sun 0830–1700), and there are others in town on a Sat or Sun. Out of town, there is one on the second and last Sat of each month at **Smuts House/Irene Village Market**, *Nelmapius Rd, Irene; tel: 012-667 1659*.

SIGHTSEEING

By far the largest sight in Pretoria is the massive **Union Buildings**, *on Meintjieskop, a few kilometres from the centre, off the Arcadia end of Church St.* These are still the government administrative headquarters and are not open to tourists, but the surrounding gardens are permanently open and provide good views of Pretoria. A garden tour is available by appointment Mon–Fri; *tel: 012-325 2000*.

This vast complex, generally considered to be one of the great highlights of British Imperial architecture, was designed by illustrious English-born architect Sir Herbert Baker (1862–1946), who also designed the Bank of England in London, the massive Secretariat Buildings in Delhi, and a great many rather dour neo-Gothic churches. The site was chosen not only for its height, but because it had once belonged to President Pretorius. The sweeping symmetrical curves of the great red sandstone building loom powerfully over the city and country. On either side, the office buildings, representing the British and Afrikaans people, are joined in harmony by an elaborately decorative colonnade. The tiny open Council Place, designed to represent the black peoples of South Africa, was never built, but on 10 May 1994, President Mandela was officially sworn in here, taking back the whole country.

The other huge building on the fringes of

299

the city is the dusty, four-square **Voortrekker Monument**, *Monument Hill, off Eeufees Rd (M7); tel: 012-326 6770* (open daily 0900–1645; R8). The granite monolith (40m x 40m x 40m), completed in 1949, commemorates the Great Trek with serious, almost religious fervour. Whatever your political thoughts, this is a fascinating place offering real insight into how the Afrikaners have traditionally viewed themselves and their role in southern Africa. At the entrance, a mother and child represent civilisation, surrounded by the great Boer leaders. Inside is a series of 27 beautiful marble friezes, 92m long, telling the history of the trek from the Afrikaner viewpoint. At the centre is a large slab of stone carved with the worlds *'Ons vir jou, Suid Afrika'* (We for thee, South Africa). At noon, on 16 Dec, the anniversary of Blood River (see p.270), they are highlighted by a shaft of sunlight. The surrounding celebrations are rather more muted these days. Those who climb 260 steps to the top get great views, and there is an interesting little **museum**; *tel: 012-323 0682* (opening times as monument; R5), of Afrikaner life next door, together with a beautifull crafted tapestry version of the frieze.

Church St is the centre of old Pretoria, and many of the city's most interesting sights are either on the street or within a stone's throw of it. In pedestrianised *Church Sq.*, a vast **statue of Paul Kruger**, by the revered South African sculptor Anton van Wouw, gazes down amid four bronze sentries representing burghers of the old Republic, of which he was president. The Transvaal flag was raised here for the first time in 1857 and lowered for the last in 1902. The square is surrounded by magnificent buildings.

President Kruger and his wife lived in the remarkably humble **Kruger House**, *60 Church St; tel: 012-326 9172* (open Mon–Sat 0830–1600, Sun 0900–1600; R5) from 1884–1901. The house is now filled with memorabilia, including items presented to him by friendly governments during the Anglo-Boer War, the president's stage-coach and private railway carriage.

Pretoria is a city of museums and art galleries, and a **Museum Mall** is currently being developed on the lines of Washington's

Smithsonian Institute, incorporating some existing museums together with some new ones still under wraps, in *Visagie St*, from *Van de Walt* to *Schubert Sts*. The Museum Mall will not only become an important focus for tourism, but will be the scene of co-ordinated cultural activities, with such attractions as flea markets around the more formal exhibits.

The Kruger House is one of the museums in Phase I. Amongst the others are: the **Pierneef Museum**, *218 Vermeulen St; tel: 012-323 1419* (open Mon–Fri 0800–1600; free), which displays a collection of paintings by one of South Africa's best-known artists, Jacob Hendrik Pierneef (1904–1957); and the charming, frothily-pink-and-white **Melrose House**, *275 Jacob Mare St; tel: 012-322 2805* (open Tues–Sun 1000–1700; R2), one of the finest examples of Victorian domestic architecture in South Africa. This house, built in 1886, was where the Treaty of Vereeniging was signed, ending the Anglo-Boer War. Allow plenty of time at the **Museum of Natural History**, *Paul Kruger St; tel: 012-322 7632* (open Mon–Sat 0900–1700, Sun 1100–1700; R5), where displays include the whole of Life's Genesis! Geological and archaeological materials and fossils relating to prehistoric man are exhibited. The Bird Hall contains almost every South African bird species. The **National Cultural History Museum**, *corner Bosman and Visagie Sts; tel: 012-324 6082* (open daily 0900–1700; R5) has always been a high-profile, not-to-be-missed attraction. It has recently reopened after complete revamping to reflect the new South Africa, as well as the old – from the Stone Age to President Mandela. Items on show are numbered in millions and cover hundreds of subjects. At the **Museum of Science and Technology**, *Didacta Building, 211 Skinner St; tel: 012-322 6404* (open Mon–Fri 0800–1600, Sun 1400–1700; R5), the wonders of science are brought to life by button-pressing and lever-pulling, with educational entertainment for everyone from toddlers upwards.

There are also a great many other museums, covering the most extraordinary range of subjects, from art to prisons. The **Pretoria Art Museum**, *corner Schoeman and Johann Sts, Arcadia; tel: 012-344 1807* (open Tues and

President Kruger

Born in 1825 and named Stephanus Johannes Paulus, Kruger was the son of Voortrekker parents. He left home at 16 to farm and had little formal schooling, but he was endowed with natural common sense which made his a natural leader. During the first Anglo-Boer War, he became a military and political figurehead, leading the Boers to victory. He was sworn in as the first president of the independent Republic of South Africa (ZAR) in 1881. He served as president until 1900, and was known as the Father of the Afrikaner Nation.

A deeply god-fearing man, who regularly preached at the church opposite his house, he was greatly and justifiably concerned by the discovery of the Witwatersrand gold fields. Not only could he see the terrible influence of the lawless miners who flocked into his country, but also the waiting, greedy hands of the British. Both fears were justified, and try as he might, Kruger's forces lost the Second Anglo-Boer War. He spent his last years in exile in Clarens, Switzerland, where he died in 1904.

Thur–Sat 1000–1700, Wed 1000–2000, Sun 1400–1800; R2) is one of South Africa's most prestigious art collections, with some major works, including 17th-century Flemish paintings by artists as eminent as Hals and Van Dyck, international graphic art, and some of South Africa's best home-grown artists, such as Irma Stern and Pierneef.

In addition to the Pierneef Museum (see above), there are also two other museums dedicated to individual artists: the **Coert Steynberg Museum**, *465 Berg Ave, Pretoria North; tel: 012-546 0404* (open Tues–Fri 1000–1300, Sun 1100–1700; guided tours Tues–Fri 1015, 1115, Sun 1115, 1430, 1530) and the **Anton von Wouw Museum**, *299 Clark St, Brooklyn; tel: 012-346 7422* (open Mon–Sat 1000–1700).

The **South African Association of Arts**, *Mackie St, Brooklyn; tel: 012-346 3100* (open Tues–Fri 1000–1630, Sat 1000–1300; free) is an exciting venue for the work of young, talented up-and-coming and established artists, shown in rotating exhibitions. The **University of Pretoria**; *tel: 012-420 3031,* also has changing exhibitions in various locations, while the guided tours are available at the popular **University of South Africa Art Gallery**, *Theo van Wyck Building, Preller Rd, Muckleneuk; tel: 012-492 6255* (open Mon–Fri 1000–1530, Sat 1430–1630; free), where stimulating temporary exhibitions of different styles are presented.

Two of the most chilling sights in town

were set up under the old regime, but continue to fascinate. Visitors are not spared the gore at the **Police Museum**, *Compol Building, Pretorius St; tel: 012-353 6771* (open Mon–Fri 0830–1530, Sat 0830–1230; Sun 1330–1630; free), which has historic and cultural sections and a vivid crime section with murder weapons displayed. The **Correctional Services Museum**, *Central Prison, Potgieter St; tel: 012-314 1766* (open Tues–Fri 0900–1500; free) is the only museum of its kind in South Africa, outlining the development of the penal system, prisoners' hobbies and some of the illegal items manufactured by inmates.

Other specialist subjects include the **Air Force Museum**, *101 Valhalla (Swartkops Air Force Base); tel: 012-351 2111* (open Mon–Fri 0800–1530, Sat–Sun 1000–1600; free), where some old aircraft are exhibited with uniforms, paintings, medals and other memorabilia; **Coin World**, *R101 (Old Johannesburg Rd), southern outskirts of Pretoria; tel: 012-677 2342* (open daily 0900–1600; free), which displays medallions and jewellery produced by the South Africa Mint; and the **Transport Technology Museum**, *Forum Building, Bosman St; tel: 012-309 3631* (open Mon–Fri 0800–1600; free), which has a fascinating range of displays on meteorology, Antarctic expeditions, civil aviation, road and water transport and road safety.

Open Air Attractions

Finally, there are three fine outdoor attractions. The **National Zoological Gardens**, *corner*

PRETORIA

Paul Kruger and Boom Sts; tel: 012-328 3265 (open daily summer 0800–1730, winter 0830–1700; R16) is rated as world-class, with nearly 140 mammal species and more than 300 types of bird species on display in the park-like gardens. A cable car takes visitors to different lookout points. There is also an aquarium and reptile house. Some 20,000 indigenous plants grow contentedly in the 77 hectare **National Botanical Gardens**, Cussonia Dr., Brummeria; tel: 012-804 3200 (open daily 0600–1800; R5), while a 2-km circular trail leads through about 500 of South Africa's 1000 tree species. An observation hide is provided at the **Austin Roberts Bird Sanctuary**, Boshoff St, New Muckleneuk; tel: 012-348 1265 (open Sat–Sun and public holidays only 0700–1700; free), where more than 100 indigenous species of bird include the spectacular crowned crane, blue crane and sacred ibis.

Out of Town

Sixteen kilometres south of Pretoria is the **Smuts House Museum**, Nelmapius Rd (M31), Irene; tel: 012-667 1176 (open Mon–Fri 0930–1300, 1330–1630, Sat–Sun 0930–1300, 1330–1700; R3). The wood and iron farm-house of Doornkloof was formerly the home of the many-faceted statesman – lawyer, botanist, philosopher and farmer –who became a British Field Marshal during World War I and Prime Minister of South Africa, dying, aged 80, in 1950.

On the way out to Witbank, the **Pioneer Museum**, Pretoria Rd, Silverton; tel: 012-803 6086 (open daily 0830–1600, R7) is an imaginative open-air museum, based around a mid 19th-century Voortrekker cottage and farm. Several other buildings have been reconstructed and furnished in style and the whole complex is alive with demonstrations of butter-making, candle making, bread baking and other rural crafts.

There are similar attractions at the **Willem Prinsloo Agricultural Museum**, 13 km from the city centre, off the R104; tel: 01213-44171 (open daily 0800–1600), which presents an 1880 farmstead with a working watermill,

The Cullinan Diamond

The biggest diamond in the world was excavated at the Premier Diamond Mine in Cullinan in 1905. Named after Sir Thomas Cullinan, it weighed a staggering 3106 carats, or 1 lb 6oz, before it was cut into nine large stones and several smaller ones.

It was given to King Eward VIII, and the largest segment, the 530-carat Star of Africa, (still the largest cut diamond in the world) is set into the Royal Sceptre, while the 317-carat Lesser Stat of Africa is in the Imperial State Crown, both on display with the other British Crown Jewels in the Tower of London. The other stones are all the private property of the royal family.

blacksmith's shop, dairy and peach brandy still, together with demonstrations of traditional farming activities. The annual **Prickly Pear Festival** is held at the museum in Feb.

Nearby, the **Sammy Marks Museum**, Old Bronkhorstspruit Rd, 18 km from the city centre, off the R104; tel: 012-803 6158 (open Tues–Fri 0900–1600, Sat–Sun 1000–1600, Sept–Mar 1000–1700) is the rather eccentric, self-designed home of Randlord Sammy Marks, a Lithuanian Jew who arrived in South Africa in 1868 without a penny and went on to make millions. This lavishly decorated mansion, built to house him, his wife and a flock of daughters, also has fine rose gardens and an excellent café.

The little town of **Cullinan**, 38 km east of Pretoria, dates from the early days of the 20th century, when its corrugated iron and sandstone houses were built during the development in 1902 of the **Premier Diamond Mine**, N4, Witbank Hwy, Rayton tel: 01213-40081. It is possible to do surface tours of the mine (Mon–Fri 1030, 1400, Sat 1400), where the world's largest diamond – 3016 carats – was discovered in 1905 (see feature box above). **Tourist Office**: tel: 01491-313 7694.

302

SIGHTSEEING

PRETORIA–BEIT BRIDGE

This route heads into the far north of South Africa and the gateway to Zimbabwe, across the Limpopo River. It is an area relatively unknown to tourists, but for many this is the real Africa. This can be an exciting trip, whether you stick to the N1 – the Great North Road – or wander into the tea- and coffee-growing highlands and the Venda heartlands to the east. There are historic com-

munities and sites, forests, mountains and sacred places, plus the bonuses of crossing the Tropic of Capricorn and encountering strange-looking baobab trees and cycads.

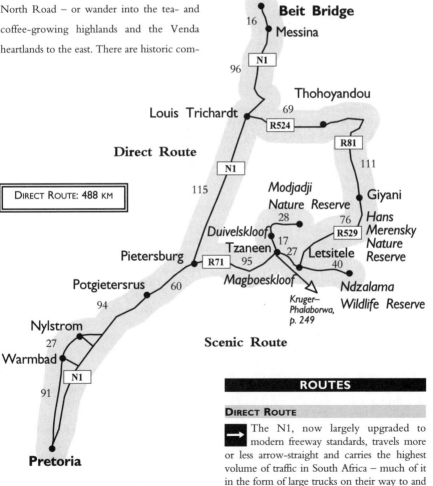

303

DIRECT ROUTE: 488 KM

ROUTES

DIRECT ROUTE

The N1, now largely upgraded to modern freeway standards, travels more or less arrow-straight and carries the highest volume of traffic in South Africa – much of it in the form of large trucks on their way to and from Zimbabwe and Zambia. However, accidents apart, traffic jams are unlikely to occur until you draw close to the Beit Bridge border post, where there can be delays. The early section is now the Kranskop toll road, but the slower old road still runs parallel if you wish to avoid payment. Distance: 488 km; allow 1 day.

If you are planning to continue north into Zimbabwe, consider breaking your journey at Louis Trichardt, which is significantly cooler and has a better choice of hotels than either Messina or Beit Bridge.

Good roads continue north through southern Zimbabwe to join the Zimbabwe route (see p. 388) at Masvingo (290 km) or Bulawayo (320 km). It is worth heading straight for one of them after crossing the border – there is precious little worth stopping for, or in the way of accommodation, in the deep south.

SCENIC ROUTE

▐▶ Leave Pretoria on the old north road up through **Warmbad** (91 km) and **Nylstrom** (27 km), before joining the N1 (toll road) to **Potgietersrus** (94 km) and **Pietersburg**. Leave the main highway here and head east on the R71, which climbs through the delightful Agatha Mountains to **Magboeskloof** and on to **Tzaneen** (95 km). Remain on the R71 for a further 27 km to Letsitele. The R71 continues east for another 84 km through to Phalaborwa (see p. 254) and the central gateway to the Kruger National Park (see p. 239).

To follow this route, turn north at Letsitele on to the R529. It passes **Hans Merensky Nature Reserve** (40 km) to reach Giyani after 76 km. From Giyani, the R81 continues north for 75 km to intersect with the R524. Turn left and head west to **Thohoyandou** (36 km) and **Louis Trichardt** (69 km). Turn back on to the N1 and continue north over Wyllie's Poort and the Soutpan Mountains to **Messina** (96 km). **Beit Bridge** and the borderpost are 16 km further north. Distance: 762 km; allow three to four days.

TRAINS

The Limpopo and the Bulawayo both cover this route. The Limpopo leaves on Fri (journey time 13 hrs), and the Bulawayo leaves on Tues (journey time 15 hrs). See OTT Table 3502.

BUSES

Translux run two services on Tues, Thur, Fri and Sun as far as Messina. Journey time: 8 hrs. OTT Table 3549.

WARMBAD

Tourist Office: *corner Voortrekker and Pretoria Sts; tel: 014-736 3694; fax: 014-736 3288.*

ACCOMMODATION

Most of the accommodation on offer here is self-catering. Said to be fashioned after Germany's Baden-Baden hydro, the **Aventura Spa** *(Av), Voortrekker St; tel: 014-736 2200; fax: 014-736 4712* (moderate–expensive) is the area's main resort, built around the hot springs which give the town its name. It has 104 self-catering units and a full range of facilities, including a restaurant and ladies' bar, hydrotherapy, water-skiing and game drives. Camping and caravan sites are also available. Alternatively, the **Dula Monate Holiday Flats**, *17 Moffat St; tel: 014-736 3168* (cheap–moderate) offer 2–7-bed flats, fully equipped with cutlery, cooking utensils and bedding, but guests must provide their own towels and toiletries. Each flat has its own *braai* and carport. The **Sondéla Nature Reserve**, *Settlers Rd (R516), tel: 014-736 4304; fax: 014-736 4310* (cheap) has 37 two-bedroom self-catering chalets, a small grocer's shop, restaurant and bar. **Thaba Monaté**, *44 Voortrekker St; tel: 014-736 2291* (cheap–moderate) is a time-share complex with luxury thatched chalets available for self-catering rentals. Facilities include a grocery store, fully licensed club house, sporting activities, game-watching and hiking trails.

If you want someone else to do the cooking, the **Mabula Game Lodge**, *off the R516, 35 km west of Warmbad; tel: 014-734 717; fax: 014-734 733* (expensive) is a full-board hotel with 42 rooms and 3 suites, set in 12,000 hectares of private game reserve. Activities include game drives, horse-riding and walking trails. The **Chateau Annique**, *Roodepoort, 1 km from town centre; tel/fax: 014-*

736 2847 (moderate) offers bed and breakfast in a tranquil setting.

SIGHTSEEING

A popular resort town 100 km north of Pretoria on the N1, tourism in Warmbad is based on one attraction, a highly mineralised hot spring (62°C) known to the Tswana locals as *Biela bela* (he who boils on his own), whose supposedly therapeutic powers have drawn visitors since the 1860s. It has been a government-run spa, complete with hospital and leisure facilities since 1873.

NYLSTROOM

Tourist Office: *Public Library; tel: 01470-2211.*

ACCOMMODATION

The 3-star **Shangri-La Country Lodge**, *Eersbewoond Rd; tel: 014-717 5381/1153; fax: 014-717 3188* (moderate; no children under 12) offers dinner, bed and breakfast in 24 rooms and 10 suites.

The **Wees Gerus Holiday Resort**, *off the R517; tel/fax: 01470-512 037*, offers bed and breakfast, self-catering and camping and caravanning facilities (cheap–moderate); and the **Stokkiesdraai Holiday Resort**, *Old Naboomspruit Rd; tel/fax 01470-4005* (cheap) has self-catering chalets and pitches for tents and caravans.

SIGHTSEEING

Nylstroom is the main town of the Waterberg District, a region of mountains, fountains, swamps and streams, which extends from Thabazimbi in the west to the Palala River in the north-east. Its name stems from the Little Nyl River, which flows through the town. Legend has it that a group of fanatically religious Voortrekkers, who were travelling north in search of the Holy Land in the 1860s, came to the river in flood and, in the distance, saw the pyramid-shaped Kranskop, which led them to believe that they were in Egypt and had found the source of the Nile.

There are graves of Anglo-Boer War concentration camp victims in **Old Nylstroom Cemetery**. **J.G. Strijdom House**, *Kerk St;*

(open Mon–Fri 0900–1300, 1400–1700, Sun 1400–1700; free), once the home of a former prime minister of South Africa, is now a museum, largely devoted to his memorabilia.

POTGIETERSRUS

Tourist Office: **Bosveld Publicity Association**, *Voortrekker St; tel/fax: 0154-2244.*

ACCOMMODATION

Located in a parkland setting, the **Protea Park Hotel** *(Pa), 1 Beitel St; tel: 0154-3101; fax: 0154-6842* (moderate), is a three-star hotel with 96 double rooms and two suites, within walking distance of the town centre shops. Children under 16 sharing with adults stay free. The **Lonely Oak**, *Hooge St; tel: 0154-4560* (cheap) and **Jaagbaan Bed and Breakfast**, *N1, 8 km south of town; tel: 0154-7833* (cheap) offer more homely accommodation in comfortable bed and breakfasts.

Campsites: **Kiepersol Holiday Resort**, *Percy Fyfe Rd; tel: 0154-5609* (budget) has caravan and camping sites and rondavels. Pitches are also available at **Potgeitersrus Caravan Park**, *Voortrekker St; tel: 0154-3101.*

There are several restaurants and fast food outlets on *Voortrekker St* in the town centre.

SIGHTSEEING

Although there is little in town, there are several places of interest in the immediate surroundings. **Arend Dieperink Museum**, *Voortrekker St; tel: 0154-2244* (open Mon–Fri 0830–1700, Sat 0900–1500, Sun 1400–1700; free) has a fine cultural-historical collection, including of furniture, ox wagons, horse carts and agricultural machinery, which trace the story of settlement by Voortrekkers and the opposition they met from indigenous people.

The **Makapan Caves**, *off N1, 23 km north-east of Potgietersrus* (tours can be arranged at the museum) have been a national monument since the fossilised remains of early humans (3-million-year-old *Australopithecus africanus*) were uncovered here in 1936. They were also the site of a horrendous tragedy in 1854, when the Boers began snatching local Tlou children for 'indentured labour' (slaves). In September, a party of Voortrekkers was brutally massacred by

305

Tlou warriors in retaliation. The chief, Makapan, feared reprisals, so led 2000 of his people into the caves for safety. A Boer commando followed and, after failing to storm the caves, laid siege for 30 days. When eventually they went in, they found 1500 people dead of hunger and thirst; the rest had managed to escape, or surrendered and were put to work.

The **Potgietersrus Nature Reserve**, *Voortrekker St; tel: 0154-4314* (open Mon–Fri 0800–1600, Sat–Sun 0800–1800; R5) is maintained by the National Zoological Gardens in Pretoria as a breeding centre for a wide range of indigenous and exotic game. Visitors may drive through the reserve. The 3000-hectare **Percy Fyfe Nature Reserve**, *Percy Fyfe Rd, 27 km north of town; tel: 0154-5678* (open daily 0800–1700; admission charge), is also a breeding centre, specialising in rare species of antelope, such as tsessebe and sable.

PIETERSBURG

Tourist Office: *Civic Centre, corner Landros Maré and Bodenstein Sts; tel: 0152-295 2011; fax: 0152-295 4714* (open Mon–Fri 0800–1700). Centrally located, opposite the main post office, this spacious, modern office has a wealth of information about the area, accommodation, restaurants and attractions. Tourist information is also available at **Pietersburg Museum**, *Irish House, Market St; tel: 0152-295 2011, ext 1000; fax: 0152-291 5101*.

The **Dept of Trade, Industry and Tourism**, *Private Bag x9484, Gateway International Airport, Pietersburg 0700; tel: 0152-293 1929; fax: 0152-293 2240*, manages tourism for the whole Northern Province.

ARRIVING AND DEPARTING

Gateway International Airport, *N1, 5 km north of the city; tel: 0152-291 1822*, has been developed with an eye on freight traffic – there is an extensive export park nearby – but SA Airlink operates daily services to Johannesburg and other parts of the country.

The N1 passes through Pietersburg, just skirting the city centre, and there are good **road links** in all directions. **Greyhound** and **Translux coach services** between Johannesburg and Harare, Zimbabwe, stop at **Shell**

Ultra City, *N1, 10 km south of Pietersburg; tel: 0152-293 7278/9*. Passenger **trains** operate to Pretoria and Johannesburg and north to Messina and on into Zimbabwe.

The city has no public transport system.

ACCOMMODATION

There is a broad range of accommodation here, with hotels, guesthouses, bed and breakfast homes, self-catering and country lodges – the exception is anything really luxurious.

Conveniently located near the city centre, the **Holiday Inn Garden Court** *(Hd), Corner Vorster and Bok Sts; tel: 0152-291 2030; fax: 0152-291 3150* (cheap–moderate) has all the amenities to be expected from the chain.

A more attractive option is the **Ranch Hotel**, *N1, 11 km south of Pietersburg; tel: 0152-293 7180; fax: 0152-293 7188* (cheap–moderate), whose bungalows, restaurant and bar are situated in attractive garden, surrounded by 1000 hectares of farmland. Designed as a holiday resort, activities on offer here include a pool, riding, golf, tennis and squash.

Smaller properties include a bed and breakfast, the **Country Lodge**, *128 Third St, Dalmada; tel: 0152-293 6200; fax: 0152-293 6200* (cheap–moderate; dinner available on request); the **Rusoord Overnight Accommodation**, *Kareebosch Farm, signposted off N1, 10 km north of Pietersburg; tel: 0152-289 9284* (cheap), which has spacious farmhouse accommodation and breakfast in rural surroundings; and the **Pietersburg Lodge**, *4 Pringle St, Ivypark; tel: 0152-292 1214* (cheap), which offers excellent self-catering accommodation. **Campsite: Union Park Chalets and Caravan Park**, *Dorp St extension; tel: 0152-295 2011, ext 1003* (cheap) offers self-catering accommodation in four- and six-bed chalets, as well as pitches for tents and caravans.

EATING AND DRINKING

There is nothing too adventurous around here, but there is a sprinkling of cafés, restaurants and pubs in the area around *Civic Sq.*, the attractively landscaped park with a lake and statuary, in the very centre of the city.

O' Hagan's, *77 Biccard St; tel: 0152-297 3281* (cheap–moderate) is another of South

Africa's ubiquitous but dependable chain of pseudo-Irish pubs-cum-restaurants, where the service is friendly and quick. **Pizza & Pasta Magic**, *Palm Centre, Grobler St; tel: 0152-291 1770* (cheap) offers dishes with an Italian flavour, while **Publo's Pub & Dinner**, *Hans van Rensburg St; tel: 0152-295 5329,*(cheap) is a lively place to eat and drink.

Fast-food outlets include **Kentucky Fried Chicken**, *24 Grobler St; tel: 0152-295 4597,* and **Nando's Chickenland**, *59 Schoeman St; tel: 0152-295 6124.* **Sarmi's**, *Nedbank Arcade, Schoeman St; tel: 0152-291 4693,* and **Tassels**, *50 Dorp St; tel: 0152-291 1918,* are coffee shops serving light snacks.

SIGHTSEEING

Capital of the Northern Province, Pietersburg has rather more museums than its size would normally warrant. Most of them are within walking distance of *Civic Sq.,* but a car will be needed to visit other attractions. The prime attraction in town is the **Hugh Exton Photographic Museum**, *Civic Sq.; tel: 0152-295 2011, ext 1004* (open Mon–Fri 0900–1530, Sun 1500–1700; free). This collection of 23,000 glass negatives, taken by a renowned national and local photographer, is housed in the city's first Dutch Reformed church. Hugh Exton, a professional photographer, captured the first 50 years of the city's development from its establishment in 1886, and prints from his negatives form a fascinating exhibition.

Said to be South Africa's most extensive municipal collection outside major centres, the **Pietersburg Art Museum**, *Library Gardens, Jorissen St; tel: 0152-295 2011, ext 1178* (open Mon–Fri 0900–1600, Sat 0900–1200; free) houses some 800 works, including many of South Africa's leading artists. Temporary exhibitions by well known and not so well known South African artists are also staged from time to time. The story of Pietersburg and the surrounding area is displayed in a former department store, now a national monument, housing the **Pietersburg Museum**, *Irish House, Corner Mark and Vorster Sts; tel: 0152-205 2011, ext 1600* (open Mon–Fri 0800–1600, Sat 0900–1200, Sun 1500–1700; free). Exhibits cover the region's history from the

Stone Age to the obtaining of municipal status for Pietersburg in 1903.

Adjoining Union Park, the **Pietersburg Bird Sanctuary and Game Reserve**, *Dorp St Extension; tel: 0152-295 2011* (open daily 0700–1800; free) covers 3200 hectares to form one of the country's largest municipal game reserves. To date, some 280 species of bird have been identified, and the reserve is home to more than 20 species of game. The **Rhino Hiking Trail** is a one-day, 20-km route, covering the most beautiful areas of the reserve.

Out of Town

At the **Bakoni Malapa Northern Sotho Open-air Museum**, *9 km south on the Chuniespoort Rd (R37); tel: 0152-295 2865* (open daily 0830–1230, 1330–1530, closed Mon afternoon; R3), traditional lifestyles are maintained by Sotho people who live on site. There are demonstrations of such skills as basket-making, leatherwork, pottery and fire-making and one section of the museum demonstrates the impact of Western civilisation on the Bakoni tribe.

The monument marking the **Tropic of Capricorn**, *on the N1, about 60 km north of Pietersburg,* consists of a globe set on top of a flat pillar about 15m tall. Travellers may park and picnic here, and many have, as the multi-coloured graffiti – names, initials and religious slogans – on the monument and surrounding rocks testifies.

At **Boyne**, *about 30 km east of Pietersburg, on the R71 towards Tzaneen,* is the massive mission, **Zion City Moria**, headquarters of the Zion Christian Church. There are almost always some robed figures wandering the local roads; at Easter, up to 2 million people descend for religious celebrations.

MAGOEBASKLOOF

Tourist Office: **Letaba Tourism**, *PO Box 129, Haenertsburg 0730; tel: 015276-4307; fax: 015276-4386.* Also contact Tzaneen Tourist Officce (see p.308).

ACCOMMODATION

The 5-star, silver-rated **Coach House**, *Old Coach Rd, Agatha, 15 km south of Tzaneen; tel:*

307

0152-307 3641 or *0800-115 300 (toll-free); fax: 0152-307 1466* (expensive) is one of South Africa's finest hotels. Built on the site of a wayside inn used as a staging post during gold-rush times, it also has a magnificent setting on forested slopes commanding panoramic views across a valley to distant mountain peaks. The service is impeccable and very friendly; the food to die for.

The same management also operates two cheaper properties in the Magoebaskloof area: the 3-star **Magoebaskloof Hotel**; *tel: 015-276 4276* (moderate) and the 2-star **Troutwater Inn and Lakeside Chalets**; *tel: 015-276 4245* (cheap), which also has campsites. Both have pretty mountain settings and are very comfortable. People staying at the cheaper properties are welcome to eat at the Coach House.

SIGHTSEEING

The Magoebaskloof are the last mountainous flourish at the rim of the plateau, marking a dramatic 600 m plunge off the edge of the escarpment to the lowveld. This is an extraordinary area, where soft fruit, tea, bananas and maize flourish within sight of each other, laid out by contour and altitude. Tropical storms can be raging on the lower plain at the same time as cool, almost European mist hangs over the forests of the upper slopes. The Magoebaskloof is a green, pleasant, lazy hideaway of an area, with good fishing, riding, hiking and swimming in mountain streams and waterfalls, such as the **Debengeni Falls** on the Ramadipa River, and magnificent views on clear days. The renowned author John Buchan (1875–1940) once lived here; a monument to him stands in the Georges Valley road (R538), overlooking the **Ebenezer Dam**.

Sapekoe is a contraction of the Chinese word for tea and the initial letters of 'South Africa'; the company is one of the largest producers of tea on the continent. There are huge **Sapekoe Tea Estates**, *Middelkop Tea Estate, Magoebaskloof Rd (R71), 15 km north-west of Tzaneen; tel: 0152-305 3241* (open daily 1000–1700; free) carpeting the uplands. Visitors may enjoy a cup of quality tea at the Pekoe View Tea Garden; tours of the plantation and factory start from the tea garden daily at 1100, or by arrangement.

TZANEEN

Tourist Office: *Municipal Building, adjacent to public library, Agatha St; tel: 0152-307 1411; fax: 0152-307 1507* (open Mon–Fri 0900–1700, Sat 0900–1300). The *Letaba Tourist Guide* (R5) lists hiking and driving trails in the region and provides extensive information on accommodation, dining and shopping opportunities.

ACCOMMODATION

Apart from one hotel, the only accommodation in central Tzaneen is in bed and breakfasts, but standards are high. The centrally located 3-star **Karos Tzaneen Hotel** *(Ka), 1 Danie Joubert St; tel/fax: 0152-307 3140* (moderate) has 44 rooms and four suites, a bar and à la carte restaurant.

Of the various bed and breakfasts, some of the best are the spacious and luxurious **La Borie Guest House**, *23B Circle Rd; tel: 0152-307 5282; fax: 0152-307 1352* (moderate) in a beautifully appointed house on the southern outskirts of Tzaneen; **Steffi's Sun Lodge**, *48 Lushof; tel/fax: 0152-307 1475* (moderate), with six tastefully oak-furnished rooms; the **Tamboti Lodge**, *18 Tambotie St; tel/fax: 0152-307 4526* (cheap–moderate), a luxurious house surrounded by a tranquil, tropical garden with rare orchids and palms; and the **Pension St Georges**, *George's Valley Rd (Rte 528, 4 km south-west of town); tel/fax: 0152-307 1802* (cheap), whose five rooms, each with its own private entrance, are set in lush gardens with an abundance of birdlife.

Campsite: the **Fairview Lodge and Caravan Park**, *1 km from town on the banks of the Letaba River; tel: 0152-307 2679; fax: 0152-307 4809* (cheap–moderate) has 35 caravan stands with electricity points and a range of self-catering chalets. Amenities include a restaurant, shop, pool and bar, bird-watching, boating and 9-hole golf.

EATING AND DRINKING

Tzaneen offers a better choice of eating places than many small South African towns, including the à la carte **Addison's Restaurant**, *Arbor Park Business Centre, Corner Soetdoring and Gelhout Sts; tel: 0152-307 1831* (moderate; open for breakfast, lunch and dinner Mon–Sat);

the roomy and comfortable, **Porterhouse Family Restaurant**, *Oasis Mall, Aqua Park; tel: 0152-307 5730* (cheap–moderate; open daily 1100–midnight), which has a good choice of dishes and speedy, friendly service; the **Villa Italia**, *Danie Joubert St; tel: 0152-307 2792* (moderate), which serves good Italian food in excellent surroundings, marred only by the common South African lack of a non-smoking area; and the inevitable, but convenient **Emerald Creek Spur**, *16 Morgan St; tel: 0152-307 5856* (cheap–moderate), part of the national chain of steakhouses.

The **Bosveld Lapa and Lodge**, *3 km from Tzaneen on Gravelotte Rd (R71); tel: 0152-307 4530* (moderate) is a bush pub, popular with locals, serving superb campfire cooking and a seafood platter. Overnight accommodation is also available.

SIGHTSEEING

Tzaneen, an attractive but busy commercial centre on the Letaba River, is an excellent centre for exploring the beautiful surrounding countryside, whether the tea and coffee plantations, forests of pine and eucalyptus in the mountains, or the cotton fields and citrus orchards of the lowveld. It is also within easy day-trip distance of the Phalaborwa gate of the Kruger National Park (see p.239). At the foot of the escarpment, it is pleasantly warm in winter, bakingly hot in high summer.

At the **Tzaneen Museum**, *adjoining public library, Agatha St; tel: 0152-307 2425* (open Mon–Fri 0900–1700, Sat 0900–1300; free), there is a permanent exhibition of ethnological artefacts, including weapons, pottery, beadwork, the largest collection of pole carvings in South Africa and royal drums from the Rain Queen, Modjadji.

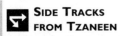 **SIDE TRACKS FROM TZANEEN**

DUIVELSKLOOF

From Tzaneen, the R36 heads north, crossing a finger of the **Fanie Botha Dam** and traversing lovely, hilly countryside clothed with tea and coffee plantations and

magnificent eucalyptus forests, to the small country town of **Duivelskloof** (17 km).

ACCOMMODATION

The 1-star **Imp Inn**, *Botha St; tel: 0152-309 9253; fax: 0152-309 9892* (cheap–moderate) is a typical country town hotel, with a main street frontage, spacious grounds at the back, 22 rooms, restaurant and ladies' bar.

The **Duivelskloof Holiday Resort and Caravan Park**, *within walking distance of the main shopping centre; tel: 0152-309 9561* (cheap) has two- and four-bed self-catering rondavels and caravan pitches with electricity points.

SIGHTSEEING

Set among wooded hills, this is a workaday town of pick-ups and 4x4 vehicles. Two explanations are given for its name, which means 'Devil's Gorge' in Afrikaans. The first is said to refer to the hellish time early settlers had negotiating their wagons up and down the area's muddy hillsides. The second is that the name was an objection to a suggestion that the town should be named Modjadji after the Rain Queen, whom the pioneers regarded as the leader of a devilish sect (see feature box, p.310). The only real reason to come here is to visit the Modjadji Nature Reserve.

MODJADJI NATURE RESERVE

Tourist Office: *Information centre at the reserve; tel: 0156-24147* (open daily 0900–1700; R9). To get there, take the R36 for 6 km north of Duivelskloof, then turn off and follow the signs for 22 km over an increasingly rugged but spectacular route.

This is Jurassic Park without the dinosaurs – a 305 hectare reserve containing the world's largest concentration of a single species of cycads, the Modjadji Palm *(encephalartos transvenosus)*, which has thrived for some 60 million years. There are *braai* facilities and picnic tables set amongst the ancient trees and superb views over the surrounding countryside. A small museum outlines the history of Modjadji, the Rain

She Who Brings the Rain

Modjadji, the Rain Queen, who lives in protected isolation near Duivelskloof, is a rarity in Africa – a monarch whose ascendancy to the throne is passed through the female line. Legend has it that the first Modjadji fled south from Zimbabwe in the 16th century, bringing with her the ability to make rain, a secret which has been handed down through the generations. Until recently, the old queen committed suicide to be succeeded by her eldest daughter, a practice which helped perpetuate the myth of the Rain Queen's immortality and inspire the immortal queen in H. Rider Haggard's adventure story *She*.

Queen, whose home is in the area. Cold drinks and snacks are available at a refreshment kiosk, and craft items and souvenirs are sold in the gift shop.

NDZALAMA

The privately run, luxurious **Ndzalama Wildlife Reserve**, *about 60 km east of Tzaneen, on the R71 to Phalaborwa; tel: 0152-307 3065; fax: 0152-307 3066* (expensive; full board, transfers and game drives included) covers 8000 hectares of indigenous bush, with over 240 species of bird and a wide variety of game, including a large herd of sable antelope – one of the only places in South Africa where you are likely to see them. The emphasis is on eco-tourism and a total bush experience.

Accommodation is in stone and thatch chalets around a restaurant, bar and rock pool, and two remote bush camps with rondavels. ▄

TZANEEN TO LOUIS TRICHARDT

Tourist Office: Venda Tourism, *Private Bag X5045, Thohoyandou 0950; tel: 0159-41577; fax: 0159-41048.* Provides information about accommodations and attractions in the area, and

operates full and half day tours in air-conditioned mini-buses or 4x4 vehicles.

ACCOMMODATION

The leading hotel in the area is the **Venda Sun Thohoyandou** *(SI), PO Box 766, Sibasa 0970; signposted from the town; tel: 0159-21011/2; fax: 0159-21367,* a typically luxurious 82-room hotel with restaurant, bar and casino (moderate–expensive). **Aventura Eiland Resort** *(Av), Hans Merensky Reserve: tel: 015-386 8759/386 8667; fax: 015-386 8692* (cheap–moderate) has nearly 100 one- and two-bedroom self-catering rondavels and chalets, and offers a wide range of facilities, including a restaurant and bar. **Campsites**: Venda Tourism can arrange reservations at **Acacia Park**, *Thohoyandou; tel: 0159-22505*, where there are fully equipped self-catering chalets and caravan and camping sites.

SIGHTSEEING

From the small crossroads community of Letsitele, the R529 leads towards the tropical north and the entrance of the **Hans Merensky Nature Reserve**; *tel: 015-386 8633*, named after the distinguished South African geologist whose finds included diamonds, platinum, gold and chrome in various parts of the country. Covering over 5000 hectares, fronting on the Letaba River, the reserve has an abundance of game and a number of good hiking and nature trails. Bilharzia and crocodiles are very real hazards in the Letaba and other rivers in this northern region, so wading is not recommended.

A major feature of the reserve is the **Tsonga Kraal**; *tel: 015 386 8727* (guided tours Mon–Fri 1000–1500, Sat 1000; admission charged), an open-air museum where villagers wearing traditional dress play out their everyday lives among a village of huts, grain stores and animal enclosures.

Continuing north and crossing the **Tropic of Capricorn**, *about 20 km south of Giyani*, the route leads into the **Venda** region, rightly dubbed the 'Land of Legend'. **Thohoyandou** is the major centre, capital of the former homeland. The VhaVenda were latecomers to South Africa, arriving from the north sometime in the late 18th century. No one knows their exact origins, but they seem to have cultural connections both with the Karanga-Rozwi of Great Zimbabwe and the BaVenda of the Kariba area, both in Zimbabwe (see p.394). This is one of the most remote areas of South Africa, where many people still live according to centuries-old traditions – which makes it particularly fascinating to tourists. The major sightseeing attractions are tightly bound to the culture of the VhaVenda people, and great care must be taken not to offend.

Lake Fundudzi, *north-west of Thohoyandou*, is the sacred home of a great white python and of the *zwidutwane*, strange creatures with one eye, one arm and one leg. No one may visit the lake without permission from the Chief and Priestess of the Lake, but it can be clearly seen from the road winding through the surrounding hills. Nearby, the Thathe Vondo Forest of giant hardwoods and pine plantations contains the Sacred Forest, in which the burial place of the chiefs of the Thathe clan is hidden. Setting foot in the forest is forbidden, for fear of angering ancestral spirits, but visitors are permitted to drive through. The Dzata Ruins, *off R523, about 25 km east of N1* (indicated by a rough signpost) was a stone fortification in the style of Great Zimbabwe (see p.394).

LOUIS TRICHARDT

Tourist Office: Soutpansberg Info, *on the N1 at the northern entrance to the town, next to Ezriel Lodge; tel: 015-516 1037; fax: 015-516 0040* (open Mon–Fri 0800–1700, Sat 0800–1500). This attractive office covers the whole area fanning out to the Zimbabwe border, including Alldays and Pontdrif to the west and Punda Maria and Pafuri to the east. It also serves as a curio shop and an arts and crafts market with locally made products.

ACCOMMODATION

Louis Trichardt has a good selection of hotels, motels and camping and caravan parks. Three-star options include the Bergwater Hotel, *5 Rissik St; tel/fax: 015-516 0623* (moderate), with 23 rooms, one suite, an à la carte restaurant, bar and pool; the cheap–moderate Clouds End Hotel, *N1, 3 km north of Soutpansberg Info office; tel: 015-517 7021; fax: 015-517 7187,* offering dinner, bed and breakfast in 37 rooms and one suite, with table d'hôte restaurant, bar, tennis courts, hiking trails and a pool; and the Ingwe Ranch Motel, *on the N1,15 km north of Louis Trichardt; tel: 015-517 7087; fax: 015-7122* (cheap–moderate), with rondavels and chalets in a beautiful mountain setting, a comfortable bar, à la carte restaurant, scenic hiking trails and a pool. The Ezriel Lodge, *N1, next to Soutpansberg Info office; tel: 015-516 2222* (cheap) claims to offer the area's cheapest overnight facilities, in self-catering rooms equipped with television and telephones. The well-named, 2-star Mountain View Hotel, *N1, 9 km north of Louis Trichardt; tel/fax: 015-517 7031* (moderate–expensive) is situated on the side of the Soutpansberg Mountains with a wonderful view of the town and its surroundings. It has 35 rooms, one suite, an à la carte restaurant, bar, curio shop and pool.

Campsite: Louis Trichardt Municipal Caravan Park, *corner Trichardt and Grobler Sts; tel: 015-516 0212,* has caravan and tent pitches on level grass sites among shady indigenous trees and flowering shrubs.

Camping and caravan facilities are also available at Ben Lavin Nature Reserve (see below), along with cheap self-catering thatched huts, lodges equipped with bedding, towels and soap, and tents with electrical points, refrigerators, gas stoves and picnic baskets. Groceries, venison, braai wood, books and curios are available at the camp shop.

SIGHTSEEING

Located at the foot of the forested Soutpansberg range, Louis Trichardt was founded in 1848 by Andries Potgieter and named after another of the Voortrekker heroes, who died of fever searching for a route through to the Mozambique coast. The town has a more agreeable climate than some parts of the Far North and has long been a favourite holiday area for hikers, bird-watchers and nature lovers. The 'Salt Pan Mountains' stretch 150 km east–west, their lower slopes regimented into commercial forests of pine and eucalyptus, the upper a glorious tangle of primaeval hardwood forest, including splashily coloured aloes, citrus-scented lemonwood and not-quite-so-pleasant

311

The Upside-down Tree, Umbrellas and Worms

The elephantine baobab tree *(Adansonia digitata)*, one of the largest trees in the world – though more for its girth than its height – favours a hot, dry environment, and is found from northern South Africa right up through Central Africa at altitudes of below 1000 m. It is believed to have a life-span well in excess of 1000 years. In some cases, the spongy wood has been eaten away from the inside to cause hollow rooms or tunnels. It blooms with large white flowers in Oct–Nov and bears furry fruit, shaped like maracas, Apr–May. The edible pulp around the seeds is similar to cream of tartar. According to legend, the baobab became so vain over its beauty that God uprooted it and stuck it back in the earth upside-down.

W hile the giant baobab is undoubtedly the star, this mid-level bushveld is dominated by less noticeable trees. The **mopane** has several narrow, grey trunks fanning out from the base and butterfly-shaped leaves. The mopane worm, which feeds on the trees, is a popular local delicacy when deep fried, and is said to be making inroads into the more adventurous end of the gourmet market. There are numerous evergreen **acacias**, which provide crucial shade and even food for some hardy creatures whose mouths can safely negotiate the powerful thorns. The tall (10–15m) **camel thorn** prefers the arid, sandy areas; the distinctive, flat-topped **umbrella thorn** lives in mid-level bushveld, while further south, the most common species is the bushy, yellow-flowering **sweet thorn**. The most dramatic of all is, undoubtedly, the yellow-barked, powdery **fever tree**, which thrives only on hot, low-lying river banks.

stinkwood. The whole area is criss-crossed by hiking trails.

Covering 25 sq. km of typical bushveldt terrain, the **Ben Lavin Nature Reserve**, *Fort Edward Rd, off N1 (signposted), 8 km south of Louis Trichardt; tel/fax: 015-516 4534* (open daily 0630–2130; R15 per person plus R5 per vehicle) is traversed by a network of game-viewing roads, which may be used at any time of day or night. There are 18 km of walking trails, and mountain bikes may be rented. Ben Lavin has more than 230 bird species, and mammals include bushbuck, duiker, giraffe, impala, kudu, tsessebe, warthog and wildebeest.

MESSINA

Tourist Office: see Louis Trichardt, p.311.

ACCOMMODATION

Kate's Hope River Lodge, *Kate's Hope Nature Reserve; reservations tel: 011-476 6217; fax: 011-886 0711* (expensive; inclusive of escorted game-drives and walks; no children under 5) is an exclusive, private 3-star lodge, providing full-board accommodation in four elegant suites. The 1-star **Limpopo River Lodge**, *N1, northern end of town; tel/fax: 01553-40204* (cheap) has 19 rooms and a restaurant.

SIGHTSEEING

Even though it's an international gateway, South Africa's most northerly town, Messina, is not well equipped for travellers. It is best known for copper mining, which has been carried out here for centuries. Iron ore, coal, asbestos, diamonds and semi-precious stones are also mined in the area. The dreadful droughts of recent years caused many farmers to abandon their lands; those that are starting up again are looking to indigenous species and hunting licences instead of cattle. Messina's most notable features are the heat and the baobab trees, which line every approach to the town. A forest of giant baobabs, including one specimen 25m high with a circumference of 16m, lies in the **Messina Nature Reserve**, *on the N1 just south of the town; tel: 01553-3235* (open daily 0800–1600; free). The reserve is home to many species of antelope and to cheetah, giraffe, leopard and more than 200 bird species.

BEIT BRIDGE

Beit Bridge, on the Limpopo River, is the frontier post on the Zimbabwe border. Look closely as you cross the bridge, and you will see both crocodiles and fever trees. See also p.18.

STELLENBOSCH

Sprawling at the foot of the Helderberg, the university town of Stellenbosch has retained much of its early character. Today, it is a charming place of museums, galleries, antique shops and places to eat and drink, and is best explored on a walk around its oak-lined streets. It is the focus of the country's oldest wine route, with over 400 wines to be tasted along the way.

TOURIST INFORMATION

Tourist Office: *36 Market St; tel: 021-883 3584* (open Mon–Fri 0800–1730, Sat 0900–1700, Sun 0930–1630). Information, walking tour routes, accommodation advice and reservations. **Stellenbosch Wine Route Office**: *address as above; tel: 021-886 4310* (open Mon–Fri 0830–1300, 1400–1700).

ARRIVING AND DEPARTING

By Air
Cape Town International Airport is 24 km from Stellenbosch, on the N2. **Airport Shuttle Service**, *tel: 021-794 2772*, can arrange collection to and from the airport (with advance booking).

By Car
Stellenbosch is only 40 mins by car (48 km) from Cape Town. Take the N2, continue until Exit 33 (Eersterivier/Stellenbosch), then follow the R310 and the signs to the town centre. Slightly longer, take the N1 to Exit 39, then follow the R304 into town. There is metered parking throughout the town, and a big municipal car park off *Andringa St*.

By Train
Trains to Stellenbosch depart regularly from Cape Town Station (platforms 9 and 10), and

return from Stellenbosch Station (platform 1). The journey takes 1 hr. For further information, *tel: 021-940 3311.*

GETTING AROUND
Stellenbosch is best seen on foot (see also p.315). The Tourist Office provides maps for an excellent, detailed 'do-it-yourself' walk around town. Guided walking tours are also available: **Sarah-Jane Wessels**, for daily guided walks, cultural walks and Victorian walks; *tel: 021-887 1584* (daytime tours daily 1000, 1200, 1500; 1½ hrs; R15; ghost tours after dusk first and third Thur monthly, 2000; R20). For **coach tours** in and around Stellenbosch: **Country 'Scapes Tours** (wine tasting and cellar tours of the winelands, visits to Cape Town, Cape Point, Hermanus and the West Coast), *tel: 021-881 3707*. **Redwood Tours & Adventures**, *tel: 021-591 7237*.

Taxis: Stellenbosch Taxis, *tel: 021-886 5808;* **Roland's Taxis**, *tel: 021-881 3184;* **Rikki's**, *tel: 021-887 2203.*

Bicycle Hire: **Village Cycles**, *tel: 021-883 8593*, **Stumble Inn**, *tel: 021-887 4049.*

STAYING IN STELLENBOSCH

Accommodation
There is a huge proliferation of high quality accommodation in and around Stellenbosch, most with prices to match. Top of the range **Lanzerac Hotel**, *Lanzerac Rd, Stellenbosch; tel: 021-887 1132, fax: 021-887 2310* (expensive), in the shadow of the Jonkershoek Mountains, is based on a 17th-century Cape Dutch manor. Both the hotel and gardens (with pool) are charming, and the **Vinkel en Koljander Restaurant** is excellent. Also in the de luxe category, the **Auberge Rozendal**, *Omega Rd, Jonkershoek; tel: 021-883 8747, fax: 021-883 8738* (expensive) is situated on a farm 5 mins from town. Small and secluded, meals taken in the homestead are washed down with award-winning Bordeaux-style red wines, produced

on Rozendal Wine Farm. Also just out of town is the wine estate and guesthouse of **L'Avenir**, *take the R44 Stellenbosch-Klapmuts; tel: 021-889 5001, fax: 021-889 7313* (moderate).

Options in the heart of historic Stellenbosch include the **Dorpshuis**, *22 Dorp St; tel: 021-883 9881, fax 021-883 9884* (moderate); the stylish Victorian mansion, **Bonne Esperance**, *17 Van Riebeeck St; tel: 021-887 0225, fax 021-887 8328* (moderate) and the Georgian-style **D'Ouwe Werf**, *30 Church St; tel: 021-887 4608, fax: 021-887 4626* (moderate), South Africa's oldest extant country inn.

Campsite: Mountain Breeze, *take the R44 Stellenbosch-Somerset West, after 7 km turn left; tel: 021-880 0200.*

Eating and Drinking

Most of the hotels listed above have excellent restaurants. Alternatively, try the **Lord Neethling Restaurant**, *Neethlingshof Estate, Polkadraai Rd; tel: 021-883 8966* (expensive; open Tues–Sun 1200–1430, Tues–Sat 1900–2230; closed Mon) is located in the 18th-century Cape Dutch Neethlingshof manor house. Many of the estates on the Wine Route offer light, informal lunches. A trip to the historic wine estate of **Spier**, *on the R310 approach to Stellenbosch, tel: 021-881 3096* (open daily: **Café Spier**, informal lunches; **Jonkershuis**, lunch daily and dinner Tues–Sat; **Taphuys**, informal riverside picnics) makes a good outing, with delicious food. **L'Auberge du Paysan**, *off the R44 between Somerset West and Stellenbosch; tel: 021-842 2008* (open Mon–Sat dinner, Tues–Sat lunch; closed Sun) specialises in venison, game, seafood and fresh farm produce.

Annual events include a **Food and Wine Festival**, *tel: 021-886 4867* (last week of Oct, Wed–Sat), in which to sample traditional food and award-winning local wines. The **Stellenbosch Festival**, *tel: 021-883 3891* (Sept) is predominantly a music event, featuring national and international artists. The **Simon van der Stel Festival**, *tel: 021-883 3584* (Sat nearest Oct 14) is a pageant commemorating Stellenbosch's founder.

On the edge of town, the **Spier Wine Estate**, *tel: 021-434 5423*, has an open-air amphitheatre hosting numerous events, including an annual music festival and jazz season.

Communications

Main Post Office: *corner Plein and Bird Sts; tel: 021-883 2263* (open Mon–Fri 0800–1630, Sat 0800–1200). Post restante service available.

Money

Rennies Travel Bureau de change: *Ground Floor, Meulplein Building, corner Bird and Church Sts; tel: 021-887 0006; fax: 021-886 5259.* Most credit cards are accepted, as are travellers cheques. Banking services are available Mon–Fri 0900–1530, Sat 0830–1230. ATM machines are located throughout the town centre.

Stellenbosch town centre is a busy shopping area. It's a place to buy bric-a-brac, antiques, arts and crafts, and home and fresh produce. **Rarities**, *13 Drosdty St; tel: 021-887 0869*, sells antique furniture, porcelain, silver and paintings. **Oom Samie se Winkel** (Uncle Sam's Shop), *82–84 Dorp St; tel: 021-887 0797*, is a famous historic curiosity selling everything from traditional food to baskets and antiques, and will also export wine. **The Dorp Street Gallery**, *176 Dorp St; tel: 021-887 2256*, sells local art, fine crafts and studio ceramics. **Milieu**, *9 Ryneveld St; tel: 021-883 3441*, sells an array of locally-made shoes, wallets, pewter items and kitchen equipment. **Curios for Africa**, *145 Dorp St; tel: 021-883 9542*, sells curios and gifts. A number of farm stalls sell fresh produce, jams, chutneys, and so on, while the **Simonsberg factory shop**, *9 Stoffel Smit St; tel: 021-883 8640*, sells world-class Simonsberg cheeses and other dairy products. Wine purchases are key: visit **Stellenbosch Wines Direct**, *Doornbosch Wine House, Strand St; tel: 021-883 9315*, a Stellenbosch-based wine exporter. See also wine exporters in Cape Town, p. 108.

Stellenbosch is South Africa's second oldest town, and one of its best preserved. Founded in 1679 as a settlement for European colonists originating from France, Germany and

314

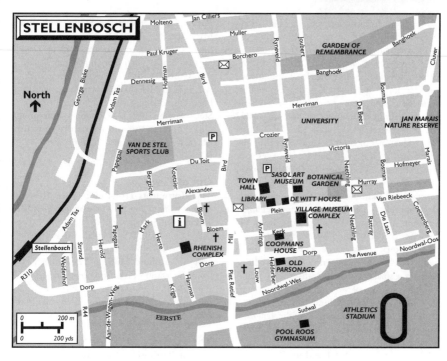

STELLENBOSCH

North ↑

VAN DE STEL SPORTS CLUB

Stellenbosch

GARDEN OF REMEMBRANCE

UNIVERSITY

JAN MARAIS NATURE RESERVE

SASOL ART MUSEUM **BOTANICAL GARDEN**

TOWN HALL

LIBRARY **DE WITT HOUSE**

VILLAGE MUSEUM COMPLEX

RHENISH COMPLEX

COOPMANS HOUSE

OLD PARSONAGE

The Avenue

ATHLETICS STADIUM

POOL ROOS GYMNASIUM

0   200 m
0   200 yds

Holland, land grants were handed out by Governor Simon van der Stel. The presence of water (the Eerste River flows past Stellenbosch to the sea at Macassar Beach) meant that the area quickly became an agricultural centre. It's a town of oaks, planted by Governor van der Stel – hence the colloquial name *Eikestad* (Oak Town).

The Stellenbosch Walk

Start at the Tourist Office in *Market St,* turn right to *Bloem St* and approach **The Braak**, the old village green and former military parade ground. Facing you, at the junction of *Bloem* and *Market Sts,* is the whitewashed, barrel-vaulted **VOC Kruithuis**, the Dutch East India Company's arsenal (1777), now a military museum (open Mon–Fri 0830–1330; closed June–July). Turn right, away from the Kruithuis to the **Rhenish Church**, built in 1852 to train former slaves and coloured people. Retrace your steps past the Kruithuis: on the right-hand side is the charming Anglican church of **St Mary's on the Braak** (also

1852). Turn right into *Alexander St,* then left into *Bird St.* Continue until *Crozier St* at the junction of which, on the left, is an 18th-century smallholding, dominated by a small, restored gabled house called **Bergzicht**. Proceed down *Crozier St,* left into *Andringa St,* then right into *Victoria St.* Here, at nos 11 and 13 are two imposing 19th-century townhouses, **Crozier House** and **Bergville**. Beyond them, turn right into *Ryneveld St.* At no. 52 is the **Sasol Art Museum**; *tel: 021-808 3695* (open Mon–Fri 0900–1600, Sat 0900–1700, Sun 1400–1700; free), which contains the University of Stellenbosch's permanent art collection. Next to it is the 1920s **Synagogue**. Just across the road, **Erfurt House** (no. 37) is an elegant Victorian mansion. Proceed on to *Plein St,* turn right and continue for a block before going oblique left into *Dorp Lane,* a tiny alley which follows the original mill stream. Emerge into *Bird St* and go sharp right into *Church St (Kerk Straat).* **D'Ouwe Werf**, no. 30, is one of the oldest established taverns in the country, in use for paying guests in 1802, it is still going strong (see Accommodation, p.314). **Hofmeyer Hall** (1900), at no. 39, is a centre for student activities, and **Devonshire House**, *corner Ryneveld and Church Sts*, is a fine, mid 19th-century townhouse, showing English influence on the local architectural style. Go left at *Ryneveld St* and enter the wonderful **Stellenbosch Village Museum**; *tel: 021-887 2902* (open Mon–Sat 0930–1700, Sun 1400–1700; R5). This encompasses a large chunk of the oldest part of the town and incorporates four period houses (**Schreuder**, 1709; **Bletterman**, 1789; **Grosvenor**, 1782; and **Bergh**, 1850), restored and furnished to illustrate architectural development and interior style changes between 1709 and 1929. Emerge from the museum complex into *Drosdty St* opposite the **Moederkerk** (1863), the Dutch Reformed mother church. This neo-Gothic edifice replaces a smaller, simpler 18th-century building, the ring wall of which, incorporating family tombs, survives. Continue towards *Dorp St,* to the right of the church. On the left-hand corner of the junction is H-shaped **Church House** (1800), and on the right-hand corner, at *118 Dorp St*, is the **Old Reading Room**. Go right, down *Dorp St,* which displays some of the best historic buildings in Stellenbosch. See in particular **Saxenhof** (Cape Georgian), no. 159, **Loubser House**, no. 157, **Bakker House**, no. 155, where, in 1798, Jans Bakker started a school for slaves, **Hauptfleisch House** (1812), no. 153, and **no. 149**, a typical early Stellenbosch house, far older than the date on its gable (this probably refers to the gable's erection). The **Old Lutheran Church** (1851), *corner Dorp and Bird Sts*, houses the **Art Gallery of the University of Stellenbosch**; *tel: 021-808 3489* (open Mon–Fri 0900–1700, Sat 0900–1300; free), which houses works by South African artists. Further along, **La Gratitude**, no. 95, is a former private house (1798), while opposite, **Voorgelegen**, no. 116, along with its neighbours on either side, represents Georgian Stellenbosch. Continue to the junction with *Herold St*, opposite which is **Libertas Parva**, *31 Dorp St*. This is the **Rembrandt van Rijn Art Museum**; *tel: 021-886 4340* (open Mon–Fri 0900–1245, 1400–1700, Sat 1000–1300, 1400–1700, Sun 1430–1730; free). The **Libertas**

Parva Cellar houses the **Stellenryck Wine Museum**; *tel: 021-881 3875* (same opening times; free). Retrace your steps back up *Dorp St* for two blocks, then branch left into *Market St* and return to the Tourism Bureau, behind which is the **Rhenish Complex**, a group of buildings reflecting the architectural history of Stellenbosch. The old **Rhenish Parsonage** (1815) houses a **toy and miniature museum**, *tel: 021-887 2902* (open Sun–Fri 0930–1700; R2).

Out of Town

The **Hottentots-Holland Nature Reserve**, *enter from the N2 at the Grabouw turnoff (R321)*, 11 km from Stellenbosch; *tel: 0225-4301* (open daily 0800–1630; R9) is a place for longer hikes (1–3 days; R18 for 1 night, R21 for 2 nights), using the **Boland Hiking Trail** (information from the tourist office, or reservations, *tel: 021-886 5858*). Contact the Tourist Office for information about numerous other walks in the area.

The Stellenbosch Wine Route

The **Stellenbosch Wine Route** was established in 1971. Twenty-three local estates and five co-operative wineries are open for tastings, sales and cellar tours.

Exploring the wine route not only gives you a chance to taste the wine, have lunch and relax, but many estates are dominated by 18th-century Cape Dutch homesteads, elegant historic buildings filled with magnificent antiques. Those most worth visiting include the recently restored **Spier, Hazendal, Meerlust, Neethlingshof** (excellent reds), **Rust-en-Vrede** (excellent reds), **Uiterwyk, Vredenheim** and **Zevenwacht**. In addition to these, not to be missed are **Blaauklippen, Clos Malverne, Delaire, Kanonkop** (excellent pinotage), **L'Avenir, Morgenhof, Muratie, Overgaauw** (excellent reds) **Saxenburg** and **Simonsig**. Obtain a map and information on opening hours, tours and wines from the Stellenbosch Wine Route Office (see p. 313). For conducted visits to the winelands, **Vineyard Ventures**, *tel: 021-434 8888*, offers private, tailor-made tours for serious wine tasters (individuals or groups).

SUN CITY–BEIT BRIDGE

This is 'real Africa', remote bushveld of acacia woodland and scrubby grass savannah, punctuated by small rocky mountain ranges. This route takes you through the strange, lonely beauty of some of South Africa's most isolated communities, into the hot, arid region along the Botswana border, a land of baobabs and fever trees, and the great Limpopo River.

Beit Bridge

Scenic Route

R521 R572 N1 25

163 Messina

R572

201 **Alldays**

R510 N1

Ellisras R518

427

126 *Lapalala Wilderness Park*

Thabazimbi 447

Pilanesburg National Park 105 R510 N1

R565

Sun City **Direct Route**

R565 105

50 N4

Rustenberg **Pretoria**

317

DIRECT ROUTE: 633 KM

ROUTES

DIRECT ROUTE

The fastest, if not most direct route, would be to backtrack from Sun City to Rustenberg and join the N4 to Pretoria (see Johannesburg–Gaborone, pp. 209–212), then head north along the N1 (for details of this and the Zimbabwe border, see pp. 303–312). Distance: 633 km; allow one long day.

SCENIC ROUTE

From Sun City, backtrack along the R565 for 4 km, then travel through the **Pilanesburg National Park** from Bakubung

Gate to Manyane Gate, where you join the R510 heading north (remember that the speed restrictions within the park will make this a significantly slower option – but you will be able to do a game drive). For a speedier alternative, leave Sun City in the opposite direction and head north-east on the R565, which also joins the R510 at Manyane Gate. Keep going north on the R510 for the next 231 km, passing through **Thabazimbi** to **Ellisras**. From here, you can either turn right on to the R518, past the **Lapalala Wilderness Reserve** to

Pietersburg to join the Pretoria–Beit Bridge route (see pp.303–312), or continue north on the R510 to the tiny hamlet of Monte Cristo. Here, turn right on to the R572, which roughly follows the line of the Limpopo River along the Botswana border to **Alldays** (201 km). From here, branch left and continue north on the R521 for 58 km, until the road splits. The left fork continues north as the R521 toward the Pontdrif border post and the Mashatu Game Reserve (in Botswana). Take the right fork, now again called the R572, for **Messina** (105 km). At Messina, turn left (north) onto the N1, which continues to Beit Bridge (25 km) and the Zimbabwe border. Distance: 620 km; allow a minimum of 2 days (plus time at Sun City).

SUN CITY

When you first see Sun City, it blows the mind. Everything is bigger, brighter, brasher and busier than you probably expected. It is completely over the top, but not tacky, and once you have glimpsed a little, you have to rub your eyes and stride forward to find out how far an unfettered imagination and reality can go hand in hand.

TOURIST INFORMATION

Sun City Welcome Centre; *tel: 01465-71544*, **Sun International Central Reservations**; *tel: 011-780 7800*. Buses provide free rides to different parts of Sun City and an elevated rail service transports you between hotels and attractions.

Hotel reservations must be made in advance. The Sun City complex provides more than 2000 beds in four hotels, and more than two dozen restaurants, cafés, lounges and bars. Prices do vary, but start high and rise. Guests at any of the hotels are entitled to use all the facilities at any of the other hotels as part of their room charge. Day visitors can pay at the main gate (R20), pick up a map and park inside. Separate charges are made for entrance to some of the attractions and activities. Entertainments, cinemas, shows, sports and recreations, shops and swimming pools, nightclubs and video games, slot machines and gaming tables, exotic gardens and wildlife – you just choose what to do and keep going until the money or the energy, or both, run out.

ACCOMMODATION

The **Sun City Hotel**, *Sun City; tel: 01465-21000, fax: 01465-21470* (expensive) was the first of the four hotels built in Sun City. The architecture is fairly bland, but very comfortable, with 332 rooms and 8 suites built around a central casino. Its restaurants include the popular **Calabash**, the sophisticated **Silver Forest** and a supper club, **Raffles**, within its casino. Next door, the **Sun City Cabanas**; *tel: 01465-21000, fax: 01465-21590* (expensive) is less formal, less expensive, and a favourite with families. Facilities include 284 rooms, a pool with sun deck and bar, a steakhouse, the **Palm Terrace Buffet** (open for breakfast, lunch and dinner), the **Adventureland** playground and mini-golf.

The elegant **Cascades**; *tel: 01465-21000, fax: 01465-7545* (expensive) is built of polished black marble, with internal and external cascading water features, 233 rooms and 10 suites. This is the second grandest hotel in the complex, with an air of city slick and fine dining in the **Peninsula Restaurant**, accompanied by a lagoon view, with swans and pink flamingos. But the last word in grandeur and magnificence, one of the most compelling attractions in the complex, even if you can't afford its lavish prices, is the **Palace of the Lost City**; *tel: 01465-73000; fax: 01465-73111* (expensive), which opened in 1992. Somewhere between Las Vegas and a Maharajah's palace, this is the ultimate fantasy building guarded by life-sized statues of elephants. The interior is sumptuous in the extreme, with a vast painted dome and a 300,000-piece mosaic of amethysts and other semi-precious stones. There are 322 rooms and 16 suites looking over the complex. All its restaurants and bars have elegant decor, but only the **Villa del Palazzo** has ceiling frescoes of jungle scenes.

SIGHTSEEING

Sun City grew out of a chunk of the Pilanesberg region less than a couple of decades ago. At the time, it was in the former homeland

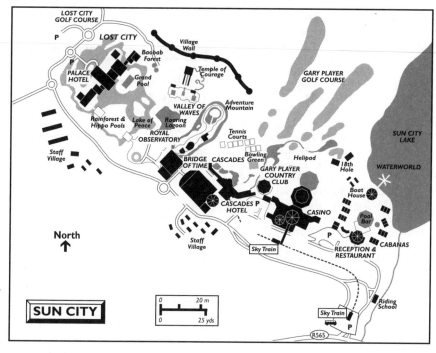

LOST CITY
GOLF COURSE

P   LOST CITY

Village
Wall

Baobab
Forest

P

PALACE
HOTEL

Grand
Pool

Temple of
Courage

GARY PLAYER
GOLF COURSE

VALLEY OF
WAVES

Adventure
Mountain

Rainforest &
Hippo Pools

Lake of
Peace

Roaring
Lagoon

ROYAL
OBSERVATORY

Tennis
Courts

SUN CITY
LAKE

Staff
Village

BRIDGE
OF TIME

CASCADES

Bowling
Green

Helipad

18th
Hole

WATERWORLD

GARY PLAYER
COUNTRY
CLUB

Boat
House

CASCADES P
HOTEL

CASINO

Pool
Bar

North

Staff
Village

Sky Train

P

RECEPTION &
RESTAURANT

CABANAS

SUN CITY

0   20 m

0   25 yds

Sky Train

Riding
School

P

R565

of Bophuthatswana, 'independent' of South Africa, and therefore not subject to the Republic's prohibition of organised gambling. As soon as it opened, people sped there eagerly from Johannesburg and Pretoria, 175 km and 135 km away respectively, and elsewhere, to off-load their rands and indulge their appetite for gaming tables and girlie shows.

Today, South Africa has casinos. The homelands have gone and Sun City is part of South Africa. There is some speculation about how long Sun City will continue to attract huge crowds of glamour-seekers, with fat wallets and massed plastic. But nowhere in the Republic yet competes with the Las Vegas-style and shameless opulence of this oasis of hedonism in a desert of want. It is even attracting gamblers from as far away as Taiwan. These days, however, there is plenty for even the non-gambler to do for a couple of days, and Sun International are actively encouraging the family market. The first step towards this was the creation of the 26 hectares of greenery and water courses known as **The Lost City**, supposedly a

miraculous discovery of an ancient civilisation (who were very fond of swimming pools). Palms, baobab trees, rich vegetation and flowering plants make the extensive **Palace Gardens** a fascinating place for strolling.

The centrepiece of the complex is the **Valley of the Waves** – the resort's answer to holidaymakers' demands for sun, sea, sand and swaying palms. They can ride the surf (thanks to wave machines), enjoy thrilling flumes and sunbathe on a real, if imported, beach. Lakes and waterfalls can be seen in the lush 'African Jungle'. **The Bridge of Time** is another man-made wonder, connecting the Lost City to the Entertainment Centre. Every hour there's an earthquake, with an explosion, smoke and a juddering of the ground. Anyone wanting to experience such heart-stopping situations as hurtling down a steep, bendy bobsled course, or being in a runaway train can spend 10 mins in a simulated ride.

For children, there's **Animal World**, with birds and farm animals (feeding time daily 1100), an aviary with more than 300 bird species, and a crocodile sanctuary, with a supporting cast of other creatures (feeding time 1630), all open daily. A daily programme is organised for resident children aged 4–12.

The **Entertainment Centre** houses a casino with American roulette, blackjack and other games. The **Dream Machine** is said to offer a chance to become a multi-millionaire (in rands), while hundreds of slot machines and a bingo hall offer other chances to win astronomical sums. The **Showcase Theatre**, cinemas, restaurants, bars with live entertainment and banqueting for more than 1000 people are also in the Centre. The **Superbowl**, with state-of-the-art technology, seats more than 6000 and has hosted such events as the Miss World Pageant and international performers like Elton John, Rod Stewart, Queen and Sting.

At nightfall in summer, nature often puts on a pre-dinner spectacular with a display of lightning, bringing the surrounding Pilanesberg Mountains into sharp silhouette, to the accompaniment of reverberating thunder. Indoors, the **Sun City Extravanza** parades high-kicking showgirls half-clad in feathers and fine headdresses.

Sporting Activities

The **Gary Player Country Club** has an 18-hole championship golf course created in a volcanic crater. Some of the world's greatest golfers play in the annual Million Dollar Golf Tournament in December. Gary Player also designed a newer championship course, the desert-style **Lost City Golf Course**, where sleepy crocodiles cool off in the water by the 13th hole. It is compulsory to employ a caddy at the original course, and to hire a golf cart at the Lost City course. Lessons are available at the Lost City driving range.

The Gary Player Country Club also has a dozen tennis courts – some illuminated – and glass-sided squash courts. Other sports facilities include a gymnasium, health club and sauna.

Trail rides on horseback and riding lessons, are available here. Game drives and hot-air balloon rides in nearby **Pilanesberg National Park** are arranged for guests. Ask at the information centre, or your hotel customer services desk.

A large lagoon, home to **Waterworld**, provides waterskiing, jetskiing and pedal boats.

PILANESBERG NATIONAL PARK

PARK INFORMATION AND FACILITIES

Tourist Office: *Manyane Gate; tel: 01465-55351* (open Mon–Fri 0900–1645). There are four gates in and out of the park. **Manyane Gate** is the main entrance; **Bakubung Gate** is the nearest to Sun City (go 4 km west on the R565, then turn right for another 4 km). The park is open daily 0600–1830 Apr–Aug, 0530–1900 Sept–Mar; R13 per person. Pick up the *Welcome to Pilanesberg* official map and guide produced by North West Conservation at the entrance. It is an excellent illustrated publication full of useful information on the different aspects of the park, and lists 'discovery points' to help you locate particular items of interest.

The **Pilanesberg Centre**, built in 1936 as a magistrates' court, is now a charming crafts and curios shop, with refreshments served on the terrace and a small grocery store, which sells cool drinks and ice-creams. The best accommodation options within the park include the main camp, **Manyane**; *tel: 011-465 5423, fax: 011-465 1228* (cheap–moderate), which has campsites, a particularly fine caravan park and self-catering chalets, shop, restaurant, swimming pool, mini-golf and walk-in aviary. **Tshukudu**; *tel: 01465-21861, fax: 01465-21621* (moderate–expensive), has luxurious self-catering thatched chalets on the slopes of a steep hill, linked to a main lodge at the top, overlooking a water hole with fine game-viewing. Game drives and walks with a ranger are offered. **Kwa Maritane** (Place of the Rock); *tel: 01465-21820, fax: 01465-23217* (expensive) is a luxurious hotel and time-share game lodge, whose cabins and chalets all have private patios, while the bar and restaurant overlook an illuminated water hole, viewing hide, two swimming pools, tennis and volleyball courts.

SIGHTSEEING

This 58,000 hectare park was created at the same time, and as a complement to Sun City, out of what was, at the time, Tswana farm land. It is set around a 1200 million-year-old volcanic crater, 27 km in diameter, encircled by three rings of hills. Vegetation includes open grassland, steeply sloping hills, dams, rocky outcrops and thickly wooded gorges. The land, which is in a non-malaria zone, has nearly 200 km of good roads. Because it had been farmed, there were few animals left in the region, and before the park could be opened it became the centre of 'Operation Genesis'. This involved restocking the area with more than 7000 animals of many species, including healthy breeding populations of the Big Five – lion, leopard, rhino (black and white), elephant and buffalo. As the guide puts it, it was 'one of the biggest ever game relocations since Noah's Ark'. More than 300 bird species have also been recorded. **Pilanesburg Safaris**; *tel: 01465-56135,* operate morning and evening game drives, guided walks (daily at 0600) and hot-air balloon rides, with pick-ups at Sun City and Manyane Camp.

THABAZIMBI

Tourist Office: *Main Rd*; *tel: 014773-22590.* Open Mon–Fri 0800–1600.

This small town is home to a massive underground iron mine, but also services the needs of several small game reserves in the area. It is at the heart of a fast-growing concentration of eco-tourism sites, with game drives, night safaris and good accommodation in beautiful surroundings.

Marakele National Park, *near Thabazimbi; 643 Leyda St, Muckleneuk, Pretoria;* reservations: *tel: 012-343 1991, fax: 012-343 1905* (cheap) is one of South Africa's newest parks. It is set in the Waterberg range, with craggy mountains, deep valleys and grassy hills. Rare plants include 13 species of ground orchid and 30 types of fern. An estimated 400 bird species and well over two dozen game animals and many smaller species are also found here. Lions will be brought in when the park is extended to 80,000 hectares. A riverside camp with six furnished tents and private bathrooms can only be reached by 4WD vehicles. The **Nader Guesthouse**, *642 Thabazimbi, adjacent to Marakele National Park; tel: 014-773 22590, fax: 014-773 71575* (cheap) offers self-catering or accommodation with meals.

To experience the solitude of being at least 10 km from the nearest neighbour, spend a night or two at **Rhino Bushveld Eco-Park**; *tel: 014-773 71483, fax: 014-773 71893* (cheap–moderate), in the foothills of the Kransberg range. There's a choice of camps, with bed and breakfast, with or without dinner, or self-catering. For self-caterers there's a butcher on site to supply succulent meat with a dash of spices and herbs. One of the camps is accessible only by 4x4 vehicles. You may see ostriches running ahead of you and any of up to a couple of dozen mammal species. The price at each camp includes a 2-hr afternoon game drive and morning walk.

ELLISRAS

Tourist Office: *Civic Centre, Bedage Wellery-laan*; *tel: 014-763 2193.* Open Mon–Fri 0830–1630, Sat 0900–1100.

Hotel, motel, guesthouse and camping accommodation is available, and there are game lodges and holiday farms. **Machauka Lodge**, *Kotie St; tel/fax: 01536-35360* (cheap) has comfortable rooms by the Mogol River, a swimming pool, squash court, pool tables, bars and restaurant. The family-run **Palm Park Hotel**, *Kotie St; tel: 01476-34385, fax: 01476-36485* (budget–moderate) is the town's main hotel.

The town was only founded in 1960, because of a major open-cast colliery and power station. However, hiking, game-viewing, sailing and golf are major recreational pursuits in the area. It has also become a world-renowned big game hunting centre – the annual **Ellisras Agricultural Show** in May features game slaughter competitions. A big attraction in July is the annual **Bushveld Festival**. The town is prosperous, bright and cheerful – music and singing groups enhance the Saturday shopping experience, with facilities including an 18-hole golf course and swimming pools. The nearby **Mokolo Dam** has a nature reserve, boating, fishing, hiking trails and caravan site.

LAPALALA WILDERNESS

Take the R518 from Ellisras for about 130 km, then turn right and follow the signs for another 30 km on gravel roads; *tel: 011-453 7645.*

Accommodation in the park is in huts in six small, simple bush camps (cheap; self-catering), or at the larger **Lapalala Lodge** (moderate), which has en suite rondavels, a pool, pub and tennis court, while meals are served in the *boma*. This privately run wildlife sanctuary covers some 25,600 hectares of the Waterberg Mountains. The land is being developed in four blocks – one entirely untouched, one used for scientific study and the other two open to the public for game-viewing, hiking and canoeing, while children attend nature study lessons in the Lapalala Wilderness School's outdoor classroom. The game-viewing is rich, although there are no lion or elephant, and sightings can take time and patience. However, there are also 275 species of bird and a stunning array of 150 species of trees and many more plants. Also on offer are 4-night weekend guided hikes, staying in remote bush camps (R800).

ALLDAYS

Tourist Office: *tel: 01554-535.*

Between Ellisras and Messina there is such a dearth of features, apart from the open road, that reaching Alldays is like coming across a mirage in the desert and joyfully discovering that it is real. Traffic is sparse enough for local youngsters to organise a cricket match in the road. You can walk through the shady garden of the **Alldays Inn** and watch a more elevated version of the game in the TV lounge, over a pint and a snack. The story goes that a surveyor on a professional assignment in the area had nothing to do after his day's work in the searing northern heat except to slake his thirst and, in time, pass out. He gave the place its name, remembering 'all days', but no nights. Of course, once you have had a beer and calmed down, there isn't actually anything to see. . .

MESSINA

See Pretoria–Beit Bridge, p.312.

BEIT BRIDGE

See Border Crossings, p.18. Also p.312

UPINGTON–SPRINGBOK

There are areas of the north-west Cape in which game is plentiful and the natural sights are sufficiently stunning to warrant a detour of hundreds of kilometres. However, the region is semi-desert, harsh and dry, with an economy based almost entirely on a few scattered copper and diamond mines. The area is nearly devoid of people and, in many places, un-inhabitable. Large sections of this route are on untarred roads; some even require use of a 4x4 vehicle. Do not choose these options without proper preparations and supplies. Those willing to make the effort will find rich rewards in some of southern Africa's most remote and magnificent wilderness. Some sections of this route are through malarial areas, so take precautions (see p. 22).

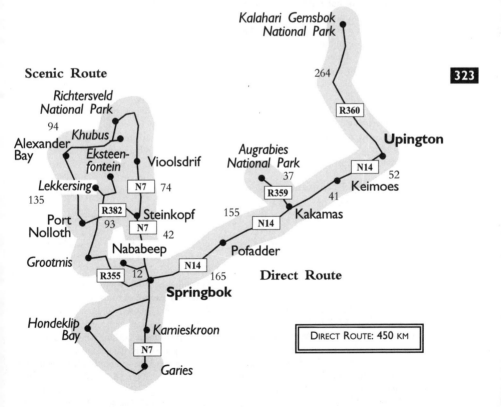

Scenic Route

323

Direct Route

DIRECT ROUTE: 450 KM

ROUTES

DIRECT ROUTE

➡ Leave Upington on the N14, heading south-west for **Keimoes** (52 km). Continue on to **Kakamas** (41 km). Eight km beyond Kakamas, turn right on to the R359 to the **Augrabies Falls National Park** (29 km). Return to the N14 and continue to **Pofadder** (126 km) and, finally, Springbok (165 km). Most of this route is on tarred roads, and it is all easily accessible in a normal car. Distance: 450 km; allow two days.

SCENIC ROUTE

⇢ Follow the instructions on the Direct Route as far as Pofadder. The next section can only be covered using a 4x4 vehicle. Beginning at Pofadder, it ends at the **Richtersveld National Park**. Those wishing to use the Direct Route to Springbok, but who still want to visit the Richtersveld, should head north out of Springbok on the N7. At Steinkopf (42 km), branch left on to the R382 and continue through Port Nolloth to Alexander Bay (total distance Steinkopf to Alexander Bay: 228 km). At Alexander Bay, you pick up the untarred access road to the park (94 km). Return to Springbok via the same route. The road north to Alexander Bay is accessible to normal traffic, but a 4x4 vehicle is required within the park.

4X4 ROUTE FROM POFADDER

Head out of Pofadder on the N14 towards Springbok. After about 20 km, turn right to **Pella** (about 40 km from Pofadder). Here, you pick up the 614 km **Namaqualand** (or Namakwa) **4x4 Trail**, which crosses a complex mix of private and communal land, and state-owned reserves to end at Alexander Bay. A permit is required before you set out. Contact the **Namaqualand District Council**, *PO Box 5, Springbok; tel: 0251-22011*, or *021-222 810* (Cape Town), or *012-343 1991* (Pretoria) to obtain the permit, book your timing and for further information, including detailed, descriptive maps and driving advice (see also Driving in Southern Africa, pp.45–52, and Driving in the Richtersveld, p. 328).

The trail is designed in two sections, which can be covered separately or together. The **Pella to Vioolsdrif**, 'Package 1' (328 km) is easy and perfect for families. Take two hasty days or a leisurely four days. The **Vioolsdrif to Alexander Bay**, 'Package 2' (284 km) is fairly difficult. Allow three days minimum. A fee of R80 per vehicle is charged for each section. If you enter the Helskloof Nature Reserve, a further fee of R10 is required. 'Designated' campsites' are included in the price of each, otherwise, if you prefer, you may stay at pre-booked private campsites.

Pella to Vioolsdrif

Pella is the first stop, followed by **Pelladrif** (about 12 km). Beyond Pelladrif, the route branches inland, around the base of the Pella se Berge, and returns to Pella (24 km). The route heads on to Witbank, Kabis and Abbassas, a few kilometres west of which **Grootmelkboom** marks the first 'designated' campsite. Twenty kilometres further on, a detour heads down to the **Ramansdrif** campsite ('designated'), should you need it. Otherwise head on, past the Henkries date farm. Twenty-five km from the farm, at Witkop, turn north and head for the 'designated' campsite, **Kamgab**, on the banks of the Gariep River (about 18 km from the turnoff). Return to the trail and, continuing west, go through a series of broad plains for 40 km, until it links with the N7 highway to Vioolsdrif. Continue to Vioolsdrif (20 km); on arrival, the first part of the journey is complete.

Vioolsdrif to Alexander Bay

From Vioolsdrif, the second part of the route picks up a gravel trail on the southern bank of the Gariep River and heads for a private camp site, **Peace of Paradise** (25 km). About 9 km beyond this is the entrance to the **Helskloof Nature Reserve**. A round trip of the reserve is 48 km long (allow 5–6 hours). After a visit, return to the trail once again and head for **Wildeperderant** (50 km) using what is considered a particularly dangerous section of road, with a bad surface and blind corners. Accommodation is at either **Sun Valley** or **Rooiberg** (both private) and, further on, at **Spitskloof**, **Bakkranse** and **Black Hill** (all 'designated'

324

campsites). Alternatively, if you have the time and can make it, simply continue on to the private resort-farm of **Brandkaros**, only 30 km from **Alexander Bay**, and the end of the Namaqualand 4x4 Trail. From here, simply follow the signs going east to the **Richtersveld National Park** (64 km).

Return to Alexander Bay using the same route and from there continue south on the coast road to **Port Nolloth** (85 km), then take the R382 going east to **Steinkopf** (143 km) at the junction with the N7. Go south on the N7 to Okiep (42 km), then branch right and head for **Nababeep** (8 km). An untarred route heads south from Nababeep to **Springbok** (about 12km). Distance: 1032 km; allow one week– ten days.

UPINGTON

See Kimberley to Upington, p. 238.

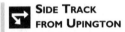

SIDE TRACK
FROM UPINGTON

KALAHARI GEMSBOK NATIONAL PARK

To reach the Kalahari Gemsbok National Park, leave Upington on the R360, staying on it for 147 km. You only leave it when you can go no further, and you must branch left onto an untarred road that heads for Inkbospan (about 40 km). A final 33 km stretch of the R360 is under construction. At Inkbospan, follow the signs to Andriesvale (19 km) and, ultimately, Twee Rivieren and the National Park (58 km).

PARKS INFORMATION AND FACILITIES

Information from the park; *tel: 054-561 0021*, or from **National Parks Board**; *tel: 012-419 5365* (Pretoria), or *021-222 810* (Cape Town). Open daily, 0600–1930 summer, 0730–1800 winter; R20 per vehicle, R12 per person. **Access**: enter at the **Twee Rivieren gate** on the South African side. There is no other gate to the South African section of the park. **Roads:** there are only three roads in the whole vast area, two of them following the river beds

in which the animals cluster near the small amounts of available water. **Walking and hiking:** both are forbidden. Here you are confined to your vehicle.

Accommodation and **facilities:** there are three rest camps – **Twee Rivieren** (the largest, near the Botswana border; moderate), **Mata Mata** (near the Namibian border; moderate) and **Nossob** (cheap). Each has comfortable, if simple, self-catering accommodation and a campsite with ablution facilities. Twee Rivieren has a restaurant, pool, fuel, a landing strip, a shop (groceries, liquor and curios) and car hire facilities (book well in advance). Both Mata Mata and Nossob have fuel facilities and a shop, and Nossob has a landing strip.

SIGHTSEEING

Far up to the north-west, on South Africa's borders with Namibia and Botswana, the Kalahari Gemsbok National Park is truly vast. The 959,103 hectares in South Africa, together with the even more enormous Botswana section, covers over 3.6 million hectares, making it one of the largest conservation areas in southern Africa, and one of the largest unspoilt eco-systems in the world. Set up originally in the 1930s to protect the magnificent gemsbok from poachers, it is now home to a wealth of game of almost every species. Here you can see the 'big five' and literally thousands of wildebeest, hartebeest and springbok, together with leopard, wild dog, jackal, brown and spotted hyena. There are over 215 species of birds, including kori bustards, marabou storks and a variety of raptors, and there is a spectacular range of flora, from the creeping desert melons on the red-gold Kalahari dunes to fertile woodland and savannah wherever there is enough water to sustain life.

KEIMOES

Tourist Office: *Main Rd; tel: 054-461 1016* (open week days 0730–1300, 1400–1630).

Keimoes Hotel, *Main Rd; tel: 054-461 1084* (cheap). **Campsite**: **Caravan Park**; *tel: 054-461 1016*.

325

On the banks of the Gariep River, Keimoes is part of the extraordinarily green and fertile strip which slashes across the desert, home to a growing number of vineyards. The **Orange River Wine Cellars Co-operative** is located just outside the town; *tel: 054-25651* (open for tastings and sales Mon–Fri 0800–1245, 1400–1700, Sat sales only 0800–1200; tours Jan–Mar). This is the largest co-op in South Africa, with five branches (other cellars at Upington, Kakamas, Grootdrink and Groblershoop – all have same hours) stretching along the banks of the Gariep River for several hundred kilometres. Sultanas are a speciality, as are fortified and fruity white wines. The area is also unusual in that the mixed-race Koranna people (Tswana and Griqua; see p.235) managed to remain landowners throughout the apartheid years, and form a significant percentage of the farming population. Four km west of Keimoes is the small **Tierberg Nature Reserve**, *tel: 054-461 1016* (open daily, dawn–dusk; free), where it is possible to see springbok and go walking.

KAKAMAS

Tourist Office: Municipality offices, *Voortrekker St; tel: 054-431 0855* (open office hours).

The 3-star **Waterwiel Protea Hotel** *(Pa), Voortrekker St; tel: 054-431 0838; fax: 054-431 0836* (moderate) is a pleasant, 1960s-style country hotel, with a pool and restaurant. It provides the most comfortable accommodation in the area outside Upington. **Campsite**: **Kakamas Caravan Park**; *tel: 054-431 0857*.

Like Upington and Keimos, Kakamas has developed into a fruit- and wine-growing oasis on the Gariep River, a centre for sultanas, dates, seedless raisins and dried fruit. The **Orange River Wine Cellars Co-operative** has a branch here (see above). However, the most fascinating attraction is its extraordinary network of **waterwheels**, **canals** and **irrigation tunnels**, built 1898–1901 by a self-trained engineer, Japie Lütz. There are two main tunnels, 3–4m wide, 2.5m high, and 97m and 172m long. Fed from the river by a weir a short distance from the town, these tunnels, in turn, supply a smaller open-air irrigation channel, which uses a series of nine giant Egyptian-style paddle-wheels to lift the water to the fields.

AUGRABIES FALLS NATIONAL PARK

INFORMATION AND FACILITIES

Information: *in the Parks Centre, near the Falls; tel: 054-451 0050* (open daily 0700–1900). **Access**: there is one access gate through the main camp (park open 0630–2200 Apr–Sept; 0600–2200 Oct–Mar; R20 per vehicle). **Facilities**: there is a large rest camp (booking through **National Parks Board**; Pretoria, *tel: 012-419 5365; fax: 012-343 1991*, or Cape Town, *tel: 021-222 810*. Accommodation is in a variety of well-spaced 2, 3 and 4 bed self-catering **cottages** (moderate–expensive), and a shady **campsite**, with facilities for tents and caravans. The central block has a small grocery/souvenir shop, petrol station, cafeteria (cheap), bar and the more formal Shibula Restaurant (moderate; open daily lunch and dinner). It also has a good information centre and exhibition on the park geology, flora and fauna.

Away from the park, the **Augrabies Hotel**, *5 km from the Falls; tel/fax: 054-451 0044* (cheap) is a small country hotel, or it is possible to stay in Kakamas (see left).

SIGHTSEEING

The little-known Augrabies Falls, named *'aukoerebis'* ('the place of great noise') by the Khoikhoi, are the fifth largest in the world. In full spate, 400 million litres of water gush over the horse-shoe shaped Falls every minute, plunging around 156m down five flights of solid granite levels into a magnificent canyon. The noise is remarkable. The sight is superb, the cascade of water made all the more stunning by the great boulders and sheets of bare rock surrounding the falls and the barren desert wastelands stretching to the horizon beyond. Below the falls, the pounding force of the Gariep River has carved out a canyon 18 km long. Within the rest camp area, paths leads along the rim of the gorge to a whole series of superb viewpoints, yet the Falls are only one aspect of a huge park.

The National Park actually covers 70,000 hectares, of which 10,000 are accessible to the public via a series of driving and hiking trails.

The 3-day, 40-km **Klipspringer Hiking Trail** runs along the canyon through the park. The actual walking is relatively straightforward, but the intense heat and dryness in the area make any walking a serious business, not to be undertaken lightly. Along with a range of extraordinary desert vegetation and starkly beautiful moonscapes, the park offers a variety of animals, including jackal, bat-eared fox, springbok and steenbok.

The majority of the park is out of bounds; it is currently a breeding ground for the rare black rhino. The **Black Rhino Adventure Tour**, run by the Parks Board, offers an almost guaranteed chance of seeing the animals, as part of a package involving a drive through the park, a river-rafting trip through the canyon and a bush braai. It also includes some steep climbs to and from the river.

POFADDER

Tourist Office: see Pofadder Hotel, below.

The butt of bad jokes about remote 'hick' towns, Pofadder somehow rises above its reputation. Founded in 1875 as a mission station, and named after a cattle rustler, Klaas Pofadder, killed here in the 1860s, it is now a centre for karakul and other sheep. Not much happens here, though the spring flowers adorning the surrounding veld enliven its depressing aspect. The **Pofadder Hotel**, *Voortrekker St; tel: 02532 ask for 43, fax: 02532 ask for 41* (cheap) has a restaurant and bar, and acts as the local Tourist Office. The 4–5 day, 72-km **Pofadder Hiking Trail** heads through Pella to Onseepkans, following the Gariep River for much of the way. For permits, bookings and detailed information, contact the **Pofadder Municipality**; *tel: 02532, ask for 46* (trail open May–Sept only, due to climate).

PELLA TO VIOOLSDRIF

Pella lies at the heart of a goat and sheep farming area, and is also considered a treasure house of gemstones, much frequented by geologists. The settlement was founded in 1814 by the London Missionary Society, as a refuge for people driven out of Namibia during the Nama uprisings, and named after a town east of the Jordan River in the Middle East, where early

Christians found sanctuary from persecution. The elegant mission church, surrounded by date palms, was built by enthusiastic amateurs, Father L. M. Simon and Father Leo Wolf. They had only an encyclopedia to assist them but, astonishingly, the church, now officially a cathedral, is still standing. **Pelladrif**; *tel: 0254-2101*, is a private campsite, not one of the 'designated campsites' on the trail. Very well tended, with lawns and braai areas, it's something of an oasis on this route.

Grootmelkboom is named for an enormous tree, an ancient Namaqua fig *(Ficus cordata)*, thought to be centuries old. At **Henkries**, there are important date orchards, whose fruit ends up in Cape Town. The palms are believed to originate from the rations of German soldiers based in the area at the turn of the century. In season, they can be bought from the farmer. **Vioolsdrif** is the key link with Namibia; the border post is here, on a bridge spanning the Gariep River. Throughout this route, look out for interesting succulents such as the thorny *halfmense* trees and the various quiver trees (see Richtersveld National Park, p.329).

VIOOLSDRIF TO BRANDKAROS

There are canoe river-camps at Vioolsdrif (information from the trail office). The first campsite beyond here is the private **Peace of Paradise**; *tel: 02521-8168*. Nearby are examples of a particular form of rock art – petroglyphs – presumed to be ancient and the work of the San. The 9000 hectare **Helskloof Nature Reserve** preserves extraordinary, dramatic landscape, where you can drive along the beds of dried up rivers, admire breathtaking views and wonder about the naming of some of its features, such as Ice Cream Valley. Outside the reserve, there are private campsites at **Sun Valley** and **Rooiberg**, near Eksteenfontein; *tel: 0255-8064*, where you sleep in traditional dome-shaped reed huts.

Accommodation is basic and there is no water. En route, other campsites are the 'designated' **Black Hill**, a 25 km detour through the foothills of the Rosyntjieberge, and **Bakkranse**, famous for its huge cave. Overnight fees for both are included in the trail package. Beyond this, in the Wildeperderant

327

4x4 driving in the Richtersveld

Four-wheel driving is great fun. However, inconsiderate driving is an easy way to damage the environment irreversibly. Much of the territory covered in this section is suitable for 4x4 driving; most of it is extremely fragile and sensitive to ecological damage. These are the rules:

1. Stick to the marked routes. Never leave them. It may take years for your tracks to be eradicated.
2. Always leave gates as you found them.
3. Established campsites are the only places at which you may camp.
4. All litter should be taken with you; jackals dig up buried litter.
5. Ablutions: go to the loo 'cat style' (that is, bury all the evidence). If you wash in the Gariep River, make sure you use biodegradable soap.
5. Boil drinking water taken from the Gariep River.
6. Never remove plants from the area – there are huge fines if you do.
7. Drive slowly. If you rev, you scar the surface and erosion can result.
8. Ensure that you are self-sufficient; have enough food, water (at least 80 litres) and petrol (at least 200 litres); take spare parts (also tyre repair kit and a set of tools for general repairs), a first-aid kit, insect repellent and camping equipment.
9. Ensure that there are at least two vehicles in your party.

Discuss your plans carefully with the organisers of the route. Be sure you know what you're doing. Off-road driving is exciting, but can be hugely problematic.

328

section towards the coast, the place to stay is at the private resort-farm of **Brandkaros**; *tel: 0256-831 1856* (cheap), which has self-catering chalets, immaculate campsites and a swimming pool.

RICHTERSVELD NATIONAL PARK

INFORMATION AND FACILITIES

For **information**; *tel: 0256-831 1506*, or **National Parks Board** (Cape Town office); *tel: 021-222 810*. The entrance to the Richtersveld National Park is 94 km from Alexander Bay on the gravel road to Sendelingsdrif/Reuning. Drive slowly. Look out for the signboards to Sendelingsdrif and Reuning. Do not turn off to Bloeddrif, but continue on to Reuning Mining Village and look out for the National Parks Board flag on the Park Warden's office. Admission R25 per person; fishing permits R10. Entrance and overnight permits must be obtained at the warden's office at Sendelingsdrif before entering the park. You must arrive by 1600 to enable you to reach your campsite before dark.

Fuel: fill your tanks at Alexander Bay and ensure that you have enough to see you through your stay. Only emergencies can be dealt with at Sendelingsdrif, where fuel may be obtained Mon–Fri 0730–1800, Sat 0800–1600, Sun 0830–1300. **Roads:** sedan cars are not permitted into the park. The roads are classed as 'farm tracks' and are mainly suited to 4x4 vehicles. A **map** of the park and its various campsites is given out at the entrance. Navigation is by numbered signboards at all major turnoffs. Driving is not permitted at night. **Walking and hiking:** walking about the park, and overnight hiking, other than on organised trails, are not permitted (there are three trails of between one and three nights duration). However, visitors are allowed to walk about the campsites.

Accommodation: at Sendelingsdrif there are two 'guesthouses'; otherwise there are five campsites (De Hoop, Kokerboomkloof, Potjiespram, Richterberg and Ou Koei), for which there is a daily charge of R9 per person. To camp anywhere other than in these is a serious offence. Other than at the 'guesthouses', the park has no facilities at all. Visitors at the campsites must be completely self-sufficient (take your own tents and bedding, food, drinking water, toiletries, medicine and refuse bags; remember to stock up at Alexander Bay as there are only limited supplies available at the Sendelingsdrif store). **Extras:** take lots of film; a gas cooker (kindling and firewood cannot be collected in the park); scarves to provide protection from the dust; a spare wheel; extra water containers; and insect repellent. Beware of scorpions when considering how you might like to sleep. Perhaps bring stretchers to sleep on. The best months to come are Apr–Oct. This is a true desert climate. Summer can be almost unbearably hot, so the best part of the day to be active is at dawn and in the early morning. In the winter, it gets chilly and the nights can be cold.

Swimming is permitted in the Gariep River alongside campsites, and you can buy permits for fishing at the park's Sendelingsdrif office.

There are a number of adventure specialists, whose help you may want to enlist. For guided 4x4 tours, contact **Richtersveld Challenge**, *tel: 0251-21905.* **Felix Unite**, a Cape Town-based company, offers 2–3 day canoeing trips on the Gariep River; *tel: 021-762 6935.*

SIGHTSEEING

In the far north, on the Namibian border, the 162,445 hectare Richtersveld National Park is one of the last true wildernesses in South Africa, a magnificent area of mountain desert. Here you will see a forbidding, almost lunar landscape. Slashed by deep gorges and flattened by wide, sandy plains, it is in fact only one section of the huge Richtersveld area, having been enclosed and declared a National Park as recently as 1991. The entire Richtersveld, which fills the area between the Gariep River and the R382 Port Nolloth–Steinkopf, is home to the Nama people, semi-nomadic herders, whose language gave many of the places in this area their names.

The Richtersveld may look barren. In fact, it is a botanist's paradise; 50% of the plants found here are rarities. Of these, the Bastard Quiver tree, *Aloe pillansii;* the Maiden's Quiver tree, *Aloe ramosissima;* and the halfmense ('half-men'), *Pachypodium namaquanum,* are the most interesting. The quiver trees got their name because their light, soft-centred branches were hollowed out by the San for use as quivers. The halfmense are strange extra-terrestial-looking things. Tall and slender, their top halves resemble a human head and nearly all of them grow facing north. According to legend, war-like tribes drove the Khoikhoi southwards over the Gariep River. As they fled, some looked back over their shoulders, and were turned into *'halfmense'*, their faces gazing northwards towards their homeland. Many are thought to be ancient; every stem ring is supposed to represent a year's growth. In addition to these rare plants, some 30 per cent of all South African succulents grow here, representing one of the most diverse collections of succulents in the world.

The area is also well-known for its great variety of lizards, and you can also see klipspringer, Hartmann's zebra, baboon, steenbok, duiker, vervet monkeys and caracals. Leopards live here, but are rarely seen.

ALEXANDER BAY

Tourist Office: *Oranje Rd; tel: 0256-831 1330* (open Mon–Fri 0700–1700).

Campsite: Brandkaros Chalets and Caravan Park, *25 km from Alexander Bay; tel: 0256-856 464.*

Although founded in 1836 by a man called Sir James Edward Alexander, it was only in 1926, when diamonds were found here in any quantity, that the town began to buzz. In 1927, a total of 6890 diamonds (12,549 carats) were recovered here, and alluvial diamonds are still found in the area, at the start of the great coastal beds which stretch up along Namibia's Skeleton Coast. **Alexander Bay Museum**, *Oranje Rd; tel: 0256-831 1330 ext. 2132* (open week days 0700–1600; free) is all about the diamond mines, with underground mine tours starting at the museum (Thur only 0800; R15; no children under 18 or pregnant women). Buying diamonds, rough or polished, from outside the De Beers cartel is strictly illegal and penalties are severe if you are caught. Most of those offered on the black market are fakes – so are some of the street traders, who may well be company security police.

PORT NOLLOTH

Tourist Office: Municipal Offices, *Main Rd; tel: 0255-8229* (open office hours).

The 1-star **Scotia Inn Hotel**, *Kusweg; tel: 0255-8353, fax 0255-8847* (cheap) is basic, but clean and pleasant, with a swimming pool. For greater atmosphere, try the **Bedrock Lodge Guesthouse**, *Kusweg; tel/fax: 0255-8865* (cheap) in a wooden cottage near the sea, with good evening meals on request and a friendly, all-knowing landlady.

✓ Campsite: **McDougall's Bay Caravan Park and Chalets**, *4 km south of Port Nolloth on the R382; tel: 0255-8657*.

Although it was founded in 1854 as a port for shipping copper from Namaqualand, Port Nolloth is now a centre for both alluvial diamond mining and the crayfish industry. It has always been a rough-and-ready place; where prospectors filled the bars in the 1860s following a brief diamond rush, it is now seasonal prospectors who come to see what they can find on the ocean floor. There's not an awful lot to do here, but the beaches are clean and beautiful, and there is good fishing and, of course, crayfish in abundance to eat.

NABABEEP

Tourist Office: see Springbok, opposite.

Options include the 2-star **Okiep Country Hotel**, *Main Rd; tel: 0251-41000, fax 0251-41170* (cheap) and the 1-star **Nababeep Hotel**, *Main Rd; tel: 0251-38461, fax 0251-22257* (cheap).

In the Nama language, Nababeep means 'the water behind the hill', or 'the place where the giraffe drinks', taking its name from the spring near to which it was established. Another town with a copper mining base, it is the headquarters for the Okiep Copper Company. The **Mining Museum**, *Main Rd; tel: 0251-38121* (open Tues, Thur and Sat 1000–1300 and daily Aug–Sept during the flower season; free) chronicles the fortunes of the industry.

Eight km west of Nababeep is **Okiep**, another old copper mining centre, once ranked as the world richest source of this mineral. The boom years are over, but scattered about Okiep are plenty of reminders. The steam-driven **Cornish Beam Pump** (1882) pumped water

from the mine (viewing is from the road only). Near to it, the **Smoke Stack** was erected for the boilers that supplied steam for the Cornish Beam Pump (1880).

SPRINGBOK

Tourist Office: Municipal Offices, *Namaqua St; tel: 0251-22071* (open Mon–Fri 0730–1615, and during the flower season same hours 7 days a week).

ACCOMMODATION

Accommodation throughout Namaqualand is generally simple and inexpensive, and quality places to eat are rare. Rely on country cooking at hotels or in guesthouses and bed and breakfasts. Always book ahead in flower season. Within Springbok, the hotel choices are the newly renovated 3-star **Masonic Hotel**, *2 Van Riebeeck St; tel: 0251-21505, fax 0251-21932* (cheap), or the 2-star **Springbok Hotel**, *87 van Riebeeck St; tel: 0251-21161, fax: 0251-21932* (cheap).

More entertaining is the wide variety of rooms in local houses and cottages, which together make up the **Springbok Lodge**, *Voortrekker St; tel: 0251-21321; fax: 0251-22718* (cheap). Reception is in a popular café/restaurant, with attached newsagent, food, video and curio shops. If you prefer bed and breakfast, try the **Old Mill Lodge**, *69 Van Riebeeck St; tel: 0251-22084, fax 0251-32711* (cheap). Enquire at the tourist information office about self-catering accommodation.

Campsites: Kokerboom Motel and Caravan Park, *off the Cape Town road, 8 km south of Springbok; tel: 0251-22685, fax 0251-22017*; **Springbok Caravan Park**, *off Goegap Rd; tel: 0251-81584*.

SIGHTSEEING

Springbok is the single reasonably-sized town in this region. It's the capital of Namaqualand, and its history is closely linked to that of the copper industry. The first copper mine here came into operation in 1852; Springbokfontein Mine was opened in 1862. The town has always had a tough, frontier character, which it retains even today.

There is not much to see in the town itself.

The chief reason to visit is for the superb display of wild flowers in spring (mid Aug–mid Sept). About 4000 species grow here, and the entire region is transformed by many millions of brightly coloured daisies, mesembryanthemums, perennial herbs, aloes and lilies. Interestingly, Namaqualand's flora belongs to a category dealing with the tropical flora of the ancient world, and is known as the 'Palaeotropical Kingdom' (not to be confused with Cape Flora, which is one of the six Floral Kingdoms found world-wide). A visit to the semi-desert conditions of Namaqualand offers something unique.

The **Hester Malan Nature Reserve**, *15 km south-east of Springbok; tel: 0251-21880* (open daily 0800–1800; R15 per car, R5 per person) is one of the most accessible places to see the flowers, with 581 species of plant, including many rare succulents, a rock garden, 45 species of mammal and 94 species of bird on show. There are 3 hiking trails, horse trails (riders must provide their own horses), mountain bike routes (particularly beautiful during the flower season) and 4x4 routes. There are picnic facilities, but no overnight accommodation.

Remember to contact the **Wildflower Hotline**; *tel: 021-418 3705,* for information about where to find the best displays (see also p.143).

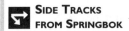

SIDE TRACKS
FROM SPRINGBOK

NAMAQUALAND

Namaqualand takes its name from the Nama people, a Khoi tribe that once occupied the area before migrating to southern Namibia. Although explored in the 17th century, it wasn't until the 1850s that the pioneers began to settle, driving out the nomadic San and destroying the traditional way of life of the Nama Khoi.

It is a vast, wild and rugged area, famous for its sheep farms, its mineral wealth (particularly diamonds – mined at Alexander Bay (see p. 329) and Port Nolloth (see p.330) – and its spectacular displays of wild flowers. The N7 cuts right through the heart of the territory, from the borders of the Western Cape heading for Namibia. To the left, the terrain leads to a sandy, mostly privately owned desert coast on the cold Atlantic, to the right, towards the Gariep River and the hot, red sands of the Kalahari. Ahead, in the far north, is the rough Richtersveld (see pp. 328–329).

Out of flower season, most people speed through the area, but by the middle of August, and certainly by the first week of September, formerly dry, barren regions are transformed into carpets of brightly-coloured flowers.

One way to discover its beauty for yourself is to drive around the untarred back roads on a series of circular trips suggested by the Springbok tourist office (obtain route suggestions and maps from them – see p.330). Take a picnic lunch and a spare can of petrol, start at dawn, and the whole day will be ahead of you.

Route 1: Springbok–Hondeklip Bay–Garies–Springbok (200 km) takes in the seaside resort of Hondeklip Bay, where the farmers go to relax. There is good fishing.

Route 2: Kamieskroon–Leliefontein–Garies (104 km) includes the spectacular Kamiesberg Pass, as well as the oldest village in Namaqualand, Leliefontein. This is a particularly good route for flower-watching.

Route 3: Kamieskroon–Springbok (75 km) runs parallel to the N7 through lovely scenery.

Route 4: Springbok–Grootmis–Port Nolloth–Springbok (286 km), takes you through the coastal desert, bypassing McDougall's Bay, and is good for fishing, windsurfing and swimming.

Route 5: Alexander Bay–Khubus–Eksteenfontein–Lekkersing–Port Nolloth (360 km) penetrates the Richtersveld area (see pp.328–329) Take advice before heading off on this route. You may need a 4x4 vehicle. ◤

331

WORCESTER–GEORGE

Linked to the heartland of the Cape wine industry (see Cape Town–Worcester, pp. 144–1484), the first half of this route remains in important wine-producing country – at Worcester itself, and at Robertson. While the estates themselves are not as interesting or as historic as those in Stellenbosch, Franschhoek and Paarl, they are nonetheless situated in the magnificently lush countryside of the Breede River Valley. The little towns have charm and history, and the wine – and in some cases the port – is excellent. Beyond Montagu, the route heads into the stark beauty of the Little Karoo, through an ever-drier landscape of

flowering aloes, sheep farms and stony mountains. Ostrich farms become increasingly frequent as the road winds through the mountain passes from Ladismith to Oudtshoorn and on to George, which lies near the start of the Garden Route (see pp. 272–280). With such a broad range of scenery and attractions, this is a valuable, but little-known, alternative to the rather boring main road between Swellendam and Mossel Bay. Those who wish to do the stunning coast road from Cape Town–Swellendam (see p. 132–137) can easily pick this route up in Swellendam and Montagu.

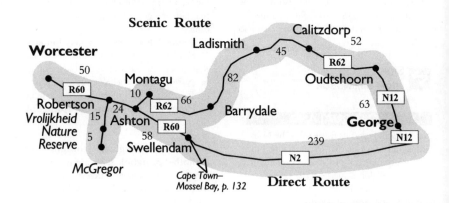

DIRECT ROUTE: 361 KM

ROUTES

DIRECT ROUTE

The most direct route from Worcester to George follows the R60 from Worcester via Robertson and Ashton to Swellendam (122

km). This first half is slower because the road is narrow (although in the process of being widened). At Swellendam, join the national highway, the N2, and remain on it for 229 km, until the junction with the N12. George lies on the N12, about 10 km north of the junction. Distance: 361 km; allow about 5 hours.

SCENIC ROUTE

▶ From Worcester, take the R60 through Robertson (50 km) and Ashton in the lovely Breede River Valley. At Ashton, bear left for 4 km over Cogmanskloof and the dramatic **Thomas Bain's Pass** (built in 1877) to **Montagu**. The R60 continues on from Ashton to **Swellendam** (48 km; see pp.136–137). At Montagu, turn right on to the R62 and continue through the Little Karoo village of **Barrydale** (66 km), **Ladismith** (82 km), in the shadow of the massive Klein Swartberg mountains, and **Calitzdorp** (45 km) to **Oudtshoorn**. At Oudtshoorn, join the N12, which runs directly to George (63 km). There are plenty of lovely stopping places on this route, so take a picnic or plan a lunch stop, and do it in a leisurely fashion. Distance: 392 km; allow one day.

BUSES

Several bus companies run from Cape Town to Port Elizabeth, stopping at Worcester and George. Journey time: 4 hrs. OTT Table 3550.

ROBERTSON

Tourist Office: *corner Robertson and Piet Retief Sts, Robertson; tel: 02351-4437* (open Mon–Sat 0900–1300, 1400–1700). Details about the Robertson Wine Route and its estates and products are available from the **Robertson Wine Trust**, *Kromhout St; tel: 02351-3167* (open Mon–Fri 0830–1700).

ACCOMMODATION AND FOOD

Accommodation in Robertson is fairly run-of-the-mill. Best of the bed and breakfasts is the **Breede Valley Lodge**, *29 Loop St; tel/fax: 02351-2296* (self-catering accommodation also available; moderate). Other good options include the **Rose Room**, *10 Leerdam St; tel: 02351-4729, fax: 02351-5054* (cheap) and **Marina's B&B**, *4 Nassau Crescent; tel/fax: 02351-61403* (cheap). **Campsite: Silverstrand Holiday Resort**, *on the banks of the*

Breede River; tel: 02351-3321 (cheap) has chalets, a caravan park and facilities for golf, swimming and boating.

The best restaurant in town is **Branewynsdraai**, *Voortrekker Rd; tel: 02351-3202* (moderate; open Mon–Sat lunch and dinner; reservations essential), which is attached to the huge KWV Brandy Distillery and has an award-winning wine list drawn from local estates and attractive gardens. **Oudefontein Restaurant**, *Reitz St; tel: 02351-61417* (moderate; open week days 1200–1400 and 1900–late, Sat 1900–late, Sun 1200–late) offers a less formal blend of pizza, steaks and pub lunches. In the neighbouring village of Ashton, the **Normandy**; *tel: 0234-51590*, serves moderately priced French dishes.

SIGHTSEEING

Robertson is a pretty, rural township known for its fruit, wine and race horses, and for the wide stretches of the Breede River that pass it by. A good time to visit is during the October Food and Wine Festival. The **Robertson Museum**, *50 Paul Kruger St, Robertson; tel: 02351-3681* (open Mon–Sat 0900–1200; free) is a cultural history museum, containing an exhibition of lace and the history of its manufacture. As well as wine, the area is important for horse-breeding, with 14 stud farms nearby, so horse-lovers should keep an eye open. **Sheilam Farm**, *off the Ashton Rd (R60); tel: 02351-4133* (open Mon–Sat 0800–1700; R1) has an extraordinary stock of over 3000 species of cacti and succulents.

The Robertson Wine Route

The **Robertson Wine Route**, a key feature of this section of the journey, is confined to the area between Robertson, McGregor, Montagu and Bonnievale. From here come bold chardonnays, chenin blancs, colombards and muscadels. In fact this area was South Africa's champion white wine region in 1989 and 1990. Estates are well-signposted – there are 11 co-operatives and 7 private producers. Visit Rooiberg Co-operative and Roodezandt, in particular.

Rooiberg, *at Umkrivier, about 12 km from Robertson on the Worcester road (R360); tel:*

333

02351-61663 (open for sales Mon–Fri 0800–1730, Sat 0800–1300), has, on several occasions, been named South Africa's champion wine cellar. Look out for the ruby port, often rated the Cape's best (1992–1995). **Roodezandt**, *Voortrekker St, Robertson; tel: 02351-2912* (open Mon–Fri 0800–1300, 1400–1730, Sat 0900–1230; cellar tours by appointment during harvest), produces a wide range of very high quality red and white wines.

⤲ SIDE TRACKS
FROM ROBERTSON

VROLIJKHEID NATURE RESERVE

Fifteen km from Robertson, the **Vrolijkheid Nature Reserve**, *5 km north of McGregor; tel: 02353-621* (open daily dawn to dusk; R3), offers day walks (the Heron Trail – 3 km; the Rooikat Trail – 19 km) in a rocky part of the Little Karoo. The best trail of all is the **Boesmanskloof Trail**, a 16 km hike through the Riviersonderend Mountains, with picturesque fynbos valleys and clear mountain pools. It links McGregor with Greyton (see p. 134). Hikers must have a valid permit from the **Vrolijkheid Nature Conservation Station** (open 0800–1230, 1330–1600; R9), which they must carry with them at all times. There are over 175 species of bird here (the route is well known for its bird-watching potential), and klipspringer, grysbok, grey rhebok and springbok are common.

MCGREGOR

Tourist Office: *Municipality, Voortrekker St; tel: 02353-945* (open Mon–Fri 0800–1300, 1400–1630). Some tourist information is available, but it's better to visit the Robertson Tourist Office (see p.333).

The **Old Mill Lodge**; *tel: 02353-841* (moderate; take the main road through the village until it ends, then follow the signs) offers idyllic accommodation in comfortable thatched cottages, with lovely views of the countryside. It also has an excellent country restaurant (table d'hôte dinner only, daily

from 2000; booking advisable). **McGregor Haus**, *corner Voortrekker and Hof Sts; tel: 02353-925* (moderate) specialises in good Cape food, including the favourite local Karoo mutton. **Villagers Coffee Shop**, *Voortrekker St; tel: 02353-787* (cheap; open Mon–Sat 0900–1700) serves light meals.

The charming village of McGregor (about 22 km south of Robertson) is a quaint settlement of whitewashed cottages, popular with weekending city-dwellers. It has a well-preserved 19th-century townscape – increasingly rare in the Cape – is neither over-prettified nor rundown, and is well worth a visit. It's a good place to head to for an overnight stop, and a good base from which to explore the nearby Riviersonderend Mountains.

BREEDE RIVER

As the Breede River runs from its source high in the mountains above Ceres to the sea, it passes through the Robertson Valley between orchards, towards wine-growing Worcester – where the valley is at its broadest – and between impressive mountains. Viewing this landscape from the water is a novel experience. **Felix Unite Adventure**, *tel: 021-683 6433*, run organised trips in canoes, with experienced and informative guides (food is provided; accommodation is in wagons and dormitories. Optimum period is Oct/Nov–Apr). ⤲

MONTAGU

Tourist Office: *24 Bath St; tel: 0234-42471* (open Mon–Fri 0845–1300, 1400–1645, Sat 0900–1700).

ACCOMMODATION

Avalon Springs, *Uitvlucht St; tel: 0234-41150, fax: 0234-41906* (moderate) is a hotel, timeshare, hot spa and holiday resort, with a variety of accommodation, from luxury hotel rooms to self-catering holiday flats. It also offers a wide range of recreational facilities, including five mineral-water pools at varying temperatures, rock climbing, hiking, gym and sauna.

Of Montagu's many guesthouses, the best are the award-winning Edwardian **Mimosa**

Lodge, *Church St; tel: 0234-42351; fax: 0234-42418* (moderate), or the Victorian **Kingna Lodge**, *11 Bath St; tel: 0234-41066; fax: 0234-42405* (moderate). The **Montagu Rose Guest House**, *19 Kohler St; tel: 0234-42681, fax: 0234-42780* (cheap) has delightful views.

For farmhouse bed and breakfast, try **Lochies Farm**, head for Montagu Springs (see directions below), then continue for another 200 m and follow the signs; *tel/fax: 0234-41474* (cheap–moderate). This also has an excellent restaurant (open daily breakfast, lunch and dinner for guests and non-guests; advance booking essential) serving a traditional farm menu. **De Bos Guest Farm** (head down *Long St* towards Oudtshoorn, turn left at *Barry St*, then first left into *Bath St* and, crossing the low bridge, continue until you see the signs) *tel: 0234-42532* (cheap) specialises in self-catering accommodation for backpackers and rock-climbers, and also has a camp and motor home site. There is also plenty of excellent self-catering accommodation; enquire at the Tourist Office.

Campsite: Montagu Caravan Park, *at the western end of Bath St; tel: 0234-42675* (cheap).

If you don't want to eat at the hotels, **Ye Olde Cape Cart**, *tel: 0234-41644* (moderate; open Tues–Sun 0900–2230) provides continental food – breakfast, snacks and an à la carte menu.

Montagu is well known for its hot mineral springs, muscadel wines, a rugged but scenic location and a dry, healthy climate. It lies at the western end of the Little Karoo and is filled with well-preserved early Cape buildings – 22 of them declared National Monuments. Founded in 1851, and named after a Colonial Secretary called John Montagu, it is today an important fruit-growing region. **Long Street** boasts 14 of the town's national monuments (Cape Dutch houses, barns and cottages). One of them, the oldest, **Joubert House** (open Mon–Fri 0930–1300, 1400–1700, Sat and Sun 1000–1200; free), is now part of the **Montagu Museum** located opposite – *Long St; tel: 0234-41950* (open Mon–Fri 0900–1300, 1400–1700, Sat–Sun 1030–1230; admission free). While

Joubert House is furnished as a country town home of the 19th century, the Montagu Museum houses displays chronicling the history of the town and collections of antique yellowwood and stinkwood furniture. The **Centenary Nature Garden**, *off Van Riebeeck St, on the south bank of the Kinga River* (open daily dawn–dusk, best in Aug–Sept; free) has a particularly fine collection of mesembryanthemums for anyone interested in the local flora.

Montagu is a centre from which to explore the surrounding mountains, with plenty of hiking trails, particularly in the **Montagu Mountain Nature Reserve**, just 2 km to the west of the town; *tel: 0234-41113* and ask for the reserve (open daily dawn–dusk; free for non-hikers; R2 permit for hikers – pick this up at the entrance). Of the various trails, the **Cogmanskloof Hiking Trail**, a 12.1 km circular route, and **Bloupunt Hiking Trail**, a 15.6 circular route through magnificent scenery, are the most worthwhile. Hikers should see klipspringers, baboons, sunbirds, sugarbirds and black eagles.

A rather eccentric attraction is provided by **tractor-trailer rides** (3 hrs) to the summit of the Langeberg (Wed 1000, Sat 0930 and 1400; R25). A delicious *potjiekos* lunch is an optional extra (R28). At the **Montagu Wine Cellar**, *Bath St; tel: 0234-41125* (open Mon–Fri 0800–1230, 1300–1700, Sat 0900–1230) there are excellent sweet muscadels to be tasted (and bought), as well as semi-sweet whites and chardonnays. There are several other local wineries that welcome visitors for tastings and sales.

Ask the Tourist Office for full details of the hiking trails, tractor-rides and local wine route.

Above all, Montagu is famous for its hot springs, a steady source of supposedly therapeutic, radioactive water, which bubbles from the ground at 43°C. The **Montagu Hot Springs Spa**, *4 km north of town (follow the signs from the corner of Long and Cross Sts); tel: 0234-41050, fax: 0234-42235* (open to day visitors daily 0800–1800; R10), is worth a visit. Busy during the day, they are more peaceful at night. There is accommodation to rent – chalets (cheap–moderate) and villas (moderate). The non-commercial alternative, the thermal pools

335

on the farm **Baden**, lie 4 km further on (turn right off the R318 and follow the gravel road). Only open on Sundays, this spot is quiet and worth making the effort to find. For **Avalon Springs**, see Accommodation.

SWELLENDAM

See pp. 136–137.

BARRYDALE

Tourist Office: *Main Rd; tel: 028-572 1572* (open Mon–Fri 0830–1300, 1400–1630, Sat 0930–1030).

The **Tradouw Guest House**, *Van Riebeeck St; tel/fax: 028-572 1434* (cheap) also provides very cheap rooms for backpackers, and runs the **Barrydale Caravan Park**.

Barrydale takes its name from the Barry family, merchants from Swellendam, who laid out the town in 1882. Located in the midst of aloe-covered scenery on the way to the Little Karoo, it is best-known as the base from which to explore the magnificent **Tradouw Pass** (the R324), which heads south for 18 km to join the R322 to Heidelberg. Originally used by the San and the Khoi, the first road over the pass suitable for traffic was constructed in 1873 by Thomas Bain, and has been much modernised since.

LADISMITH

Tourist Office: *Queen St; tel: 028-551 1023* (open Mon–Fri 0900–1200).

Albert Manor *(Pf), 26 Albert St; tel/fax: 028-551 1127* (cheap) provides bed and breakfast and dinner by request, in a delightfully eccentric Victorian homestead.

Like its more famous counterpart (see p. 265–266), Ladismith was named after the Spanish wife of Governor Sir Harry Smith (see p. 99), using an 'i' to differentiate between the two towns. This Ladismith is a pretty village, dominated by the twin peaks of Towerkop (2203 m), which was said to have been split in two by a local witch. There are several good hiking trails nearby in the **Towerkop Nature Reserve**, *3 km north of town*, and **Ladismith Klein Karoo Nature Reserve**, just out of town on the R62 to Barrydale; ask the tourist office for details.

About 19 km beyond the town, on the R62 as you head for Calitzdorp, stop at **Zoar**, just a few kilometres south of the highway (follow the signs). This rural village is an interesting, mostly 19th-century relic, founded as a mission station for the Khoikhoi in 1817. Back on the R62, and just after Zoar on the left, a detour can be made to the awesome **Seweweekspoort Pass**, which climbs up in the shadow of the 2325 m Seweweekspoort Peak. This route links the Central Karoo to the Little Karoo, and provides lots of opportunity for picnicking. There is safe swimming in the river. Just beyond Zoar, the road climbs through the magnificent **Huisrivier Pass**.

CALITZDORP

Tourist Office: Municipality Offices, *Voortrekker Rd; tel: 04437-33312* (open office hours).

Accommodation options in town are simple – the **Queens Hotel**, *Queen St; tel: 04437-33332, fax: 04437-33551* (cheap), or the **Welgevonden Guest House**, *St Helena St; tel/fax: 04437-33642* (cheap; dinner by prior arrangement), in the midst of an excellent wine district.

The **Calitzdorp Spa**, *22 km from Calitzdorp on the Oudtshoorn road – follow the signs from Calitzdorp Main St; tel; 04437-33371, fax: 0443-292667* (Oudtshoorn head office) is located at the site of a natural hot spring, with private baths and saunas. There is a caravan park and several chalets and huts in which to stay (cheap). The restaurant is open daily for breakfast, lunch and dinner.

Calitzdorp, founded in about 1845, sits in the middle of a landscape once heavily populated with game. Buffalo were particularly prolific. Nowadays, it is known for its dried fruit production and for the **Calitzdorp Winery**, *Andries Pretorius St; tel: 04437-33301* (open weekdays 0800–1300, 1400–1700 for tastings and sales). Port is a particular speciality of the area, which holds a Port Festival every July.

OUDTSHOORN

See pp. 281–284.

GEORGE

See Mossel Bay–Port Elizabeth, p. 273–274.

WORCESTER– MALMESBURY

This route begins in the Breede River Valley, an area of exceptional diversity, wedged in between the Karoo and the Swartland. There are fruit estates, vineyards, wine-tasting routes, stud farms, country towns with interesting museums, and an abundance of potential for outdoor activity, from canoeing to riding.

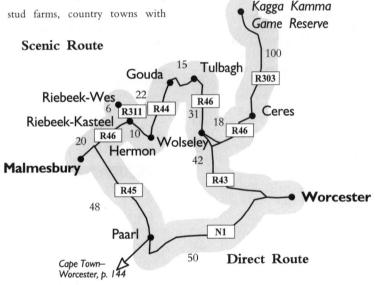

337

DIRECT ROUTE: 98 KM

ROUTES

DIRECT ROUTE

Leave Worcester on the N1, signposted to Paarl or Cape Town, and proceed to Paarl (50 km), using the Huguenot Toll Tunnel through the Du Toit's Kloof Mountains. This section of the N1 is relatively new, and is wide, safe and fast. From Paarl town centre, take the R45 signposted to Malmesbury. After 44 km, turn left and take the R46 into town (4 km). Distance: 98 km; allow 1 hr.

SCENIC ROUTE

Take the R43 out of **Worcester** and follow the signs to Wolseley and Ceres. Ignore the Wolseley sign and continue on to **Ceres** over Michell's Pass (9 km). From Ceres, double back on the R46 down Michell's Pass and continue for 7 km, until you hit the Wolseley turn off. From there it is just 2 km to **Wolseley**. Retrace your steps to the R46 and continue left in the direction of **Tulbagh** (31 km). After Tulbagh, the R46 continues past Gouda and at the village of Hermon does a loop up to **Riebeek-Kasteel**, from where it is

6 km to **Riebeek-Wes** along the R311. From Riebeek-Kasteel, take the R46 to Malmesbury (20 km). This is a comfortable one day trip.

TRAINS AND BUSES

Local train and bus services operate the Worcester to Malmesbury route. Journey time: 2 hrs. OTT Table 3526.

WORCESTER

Tourist Office: *75 Church St, Worcester; tel: 0231-71408* (open Mon–Fri 0800–1630, Sat 0830–1230). Information on Worcester town. **Breede River Valley Tourism:** *Kleinplasie, 23 Traub St, Worcester; tel: 0231-76411* (open Mon–Fri 0745–1630, Sat 0900–1330). Information about the whole Breede River Valley.

Church Street Lodge, *36 Church St, Worcester; tel: 0231-25194, fax: 0231 28859* (cheap) is one of the best guesthouses in the area. There are also many self-catering flats and cottages; ask the Tourist Office for information.

One of the best restaurants around is **Burchell's Restaurant**, *De Breede Estate (4 km from Worcester on the R43 Ceres Rd); tel: 0231-25388* (expensive; open Tues–Sat lunch and dinner, Sun lunch; reservations essential), which serves modern Cape cuisine with excellent Breede River wines.

If the Breede River Valley has a capital, then Worcester is it. Encircled by the peaks of the Hex River, Witsenberg and Skurweberg Mountains, it is a busy commercial town at the heart of fertile farmland. Dominating the main square is the **Dutch Reformed Church**, near which is **Beck House**, *21 Baring St; tel: 0231-22225* (open Mon–Fri 0900–1630; R0.50), a Cape Dutch homestead, furnished in the style of a 19th-century country townhouse. This also houses the **Afrikaner Museum**. The way of life of early pioneer farmers can be studied at the excellent **Kleinplasie Open Air Living Museum**, *23 Traub St; tel: 0231-22225* (open Mon–Sat 0900–1630, Sun 1030–1630; R8), where a series of period farm buildings – a water mill, tobacco shed, farmhouse, smithy – has been re-erected. At weekends, characters in costume give demonstrations of traditional crafts, from candle-making to distilling *witblitz* (literally 'white lightning' – the local firewater).

The Worcester winelands account for roughly 25% of the country's wine production, and Worcester is the central point on the **Worcester Wine Route**, which takes in a variety of local private estates and co-operative cellars. Maps are available from the tourist office. The **KWV Brandy Cellar**, *corner Church and Smith Sts; tel: 0231-20255* (open weekdays for tours 0930, 1100, 1330 Afrikaans; 1530, Sat 0930, 1100 Afrikaans; shop open Mon–Fri 0930–1630, Sat 0930–1200), is the largest of its kind anywhere in the world, organises a daily series of guided tours around its brandy production plant. On the outskirts of Worcester is the **Karoo National Botanical Garden,** *Roux Rd, Panorama; tel: 0231-70785* (open Mon–Fri 0700–1300 and 1400–1700, weekends 0800–1100; free), whose 144 hectares feature an astonishing range of plants from the drier parts of the countryside. Come in winter for the flowering of the aloes, in spring (Sept) for the daisies and mesems, and after October for flowering plants, which attract the brilliant malachite-green birds.

CERES

Tourist Office: *Owen St; tel: 0233-61287* (open Mon–Fri 0830–1700, Sat 0830–1400).

Ceres was established in 1854 as a fruit-growing centre and, because of the fertility of the soil and abundant produce, was dedicated to the Roman goddess of agriculture. Nothing changes. Today, Ceres is the most important deciduous fruit growing and fruit juice producing district of South Africa – illustrated in a tour around the country's largest fruit co-op, **Ceres Fruit Growers**, *3 Bonchretien St, Ceres; tel: 0233-23121* (Tues, Thur 0930 – groups book the day before; free). The district of Ceres is divided into the Warm and Koue (Cold) Bokkeveld, probably named for the millions of springbok that once migrated through this area.

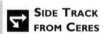 SIDE TRACK FROM CERES

This wonderful, scenic drive reaches far into the Koue Bokkeveld. From Ceres, take the R303, signed to Citrusdal, via **Prince Alfred Hamlet** and the Gydo Pass to Op die Berg (40 km), then branch right and follow the road through Sign Post (18 km), over the Riet River and the Katbakkies Pass to Peerbooms Kloof (19 km). You're now deep in the rough, craggy Koue Bokkeveld region. At Peerbooms Kloof, branch left and follow the signs to the **Kagga Kamma Game Reserve** (18 km), where there is luxury accommodation and the opportunity to go on game drives; *tel: 02211-70888, fax: 02211-70870.* There are also San living on the property (see Background, p.70) and there may be an opportunity to meet them, talk about their traditional life and take some photos. Kagga Kamma is at least 1½ hours from Ceres (100 km; half of the route is on gravel). 🅿

TULBAGH

Tourist Office: *4 Church St, Tulbagh; tel: 0236-301 348* (open Mon–Fri 0900–1700, Sat 1000–1600).

ACCOMMODATION AND FOOD

The best accommodation is out of town at the **Waterval Bush Camp**, *turn off the R46 at the Waterval sign; tel: 0236-300 807, fax: 0236-300 757* (expensive), a luxury ensuite safari-style tented camp. In Tulbagh, **De Oude Herberg**, *6 Church St; tel/fax 0236-300 260* (cheap) is charming, while **Groote Vallei Guest Farm**, *Groote Vallei, Tulbagh; tel: 0236-300 660* (cheap) is very comfortable and quiet. For further accommodation, contact the Tourist Office.

One of the most wonderful restaurants in the Western Cape is in Tulbagh. **Paddagang Restaurant and Winehouse**, *23 Church St, Tulbagh; tel: 0236-300 242* (moderate; open daily 0830–1700, Sat from 1900, reservations essential) serves old-fashioned, traditional Cape cuisine. **De Oude Herberg**, *6 Church St, Tulbagh; tel: 0236-300 260* (moderate; open Mon–Sat lunch and dinner, Sun lunch; reservations essential), is also a charming restaurant, set in a Cape Dutch monument, offering authentic country dishes and light lunches.

SIGHTSEEING

Tulbagh was first settled in 1699. It takes its name from an early 19th-century Dutch governor of the Cape, Ryk Tulbagh. Today, it is chiefly famous for a rich heritage of Cape Dutch and Victorian buildings, concentrated in *Church St.* On Sept 29 1969, an earthquake – 6.5 on the Richter scale – reduced most of them, and much of the rest of Tulbagh to ruins. In *Church St* alone, 32 buildings, many of them whitewashed, gabled homesteads, were shattered. But phoenix-like, Tulbagh was resurrected in one of the biggest restoration programmes ever undertaken in South Africa. Buildings were allowed to revert to their original appearances, stripped of the changes they had accrued over the years. The results are remarkable. Today, Tulbagh – and **Church Street** in particular – forms an almost perfect image of a rural 18th-century South African town. The **Oude Kerk Volksmuseum**, *4 Church St, Tulbagh; tel: 0236-301 041* (open Mon–Fri 0900–1700, Sat and Sun 0900–1600; R4), and its three annexes at *4, 14 and 22 Church St,* house a collection of Cape furniture, porcelain and glass. The old church, the **Oude Kerk** (1743), is the country's earliest surviving example of a cross plan church. *4 Church Street* also houses a photographic exhibition of the earthquake. On the outskirts of town, **De Oude Drostdy**, *4 km outside Tulbagh* (maps from tourist office); *tel: 0236-300 203* (open Mon–Sat 1000–1300, 1400–1700, Sun 1430–1700; free) houses a fine collection of early Cape furniture and household articles and a collection of old gramophones.

RIEBEEK-KASTEEL AND RIEBEEK WES

Tourist Office: see Malmesbury, p.340.

ACCOMMODATION AND FOOD

Riebeek-Kasteel offers two options, the **Royal Hotel**, *33 Main Rd, Riebeek-Kasteel; tel: 02244-378* (cheap), a laid-back, arty hostelry with 7 rooms, 2 bathrooms, a good bar and verandah, and the **Village Tavern**, *Town Sq., Riebeek-Kasteel; tel: 02244-794* (cheap). The accommodation in Riebeek Wes is more luxurious, with both the **Bishop's Lodge**, *4 Dennehof St, Riebeek Wes; tel: 02246-672* (moderate) and **Carolann's Guest House**, *10 Long St; tel: 02246-245* (cheap) highly recommended.

339

The Roadbuilders

In 1830, a systematic programme of road building began in the Cape Colony. The most famous of southern Africa's 19th-century builders were Andrew Geddes Bain and his son Thomas. Between them, using convict labour, they constructed some of the most picturesque, often dramatic, roads in the country. In travelling these routes, never underestimate their engineering skill and aesthetic genius. Best-known is Bain senior's 16 km **Bain's Kloof Pass** (1853) section of the R301 in the Elandskloof and Slanghoek Mountains, following the course of the Witte River and linking Wellington with the R43 Worcester–Ceres. His other great roads in the vicinity are **Michell's Pass, Gydo Pass** and **Karoo Poort**. Thomas continued his father's work with a series of passes no less spectacular. **Prince Alfred Pass** (R339 Knysna–Avontuur), is view-laden, as are **Seven Passes, Garcia's Pass** (R323 Riversdale–Ladismith), gateway to the Karoo, **Cogman's Kloof** (Montagu to the N15 Worcester–Swellendam), **Pakhuis Pass** and the **Swartberg Pass**, one of Africa's most magnificent mountain routes. Those staying in Cape Town should travel the Cape Peninsula's **Victoria Road**, Sea Point–Hout Bay (M6).

SIGHTSEEING

Riding through this region in the 17th century, Dutch corporal Pieter Cruythoff described a landscape filled with lion, rhino, zebra, hartebeest and ostrich. Today, there are only vineyards surrounding these two villages straddling the slopes of the rugged Kasteelberg. This is the Swartland ('black country') settled by Europeans in the 17th century. In quaint Riebeek-Kasteel, the church (1855) is now the **Oude Kerk Museum**, *Main Road, Riebeek-Kasteel* (open by appointment – apply to the tourist office in Malmesbury), which houses a variety of implements used in the 19th century for the cultivation of wheat and wine. Also visit the **Riebeek Wine Cellar,** *follow the signs from the town centre; tel: 02244-213* (open Mon–Fri 0800–1700, Sat 0830–1200).

Riebeek Wes is the birthplace of two of South Africa's most famous Prime Ministers – General Jan Smuts, who became a member of the British Imperial War Cabinet during World War I, and Dr D.F. Malan, one of the principal architects of apartheid. The **General Jan Smuts' Birth House**, *on the road Riebeek Wes-Mooreesberg, follow the signs; tel: 02246-251* (open Tues–Sun 1000–1700; free) details Smuts' history. **Allesverloren**, *at the foot of the Kasteelberg, between Riebeek-Kasteel and Riebeek Wes; tel: 02246-320* (open Mon–Fri 0900–1700, Sat 0900–1200) is the Malan family home

and wine estate, producing sought-after ports and red wines. The first vines were planted in 1780, originally to make brandy and house wine. Open for tasting and sales.

MALMESBURY

Tourist Office: *95a`Voortrekker Rd, Malmesbury; tel: 0224-22996* (open Mon–Fri 0800–1700). Information on the entire Swartland and Sandveld areas, including Riebeek-Kasteel and Riebeek Wes.

Campsite: Malmesbury Caravan Park, *Piketberg Rd, Malmesbury; tel: 0224-23266.*

Malmesbury is the most important of the Swartland towns. A commercial centre founded in 1743, it is surrounded by wheatfields and vineyards. Not a place to stay, due to a lack of good accommodation options, nonetheless it is a pretty country town, with a wide main street and a skyline dominated by the neo-Gothic **Dutch Reformed Church**, built, enlarged and rebuilt between 1751 and 1899. **The Cultural History Museum**, *1 Prospect St, Malmesbury; tel: 0224-22332* (open daily 0800–1300; R1) is housed in a former synagogue. Its collections document Malmesbury's early history and development.

Three km from Malmesbury, the **Swartland Wine Cellar**; *tel: 0224-21134* (open Mon–Thur 0800–1700, Fri 0800–1630, Sat 0900–1200) is famous for its hanepoot and pinotage wines.

BOTSWANA

If any country encapsulates the popular image of Africa it must be Botswana. Here are the rivers and swamps teeming with colourful birdlife and home to vast numbers of crocodiles and hippos. Here is the vast expanse of the Kalahari Desert – harsh, arid, yet redeemed by a rugged beauty. Here are the massive wilderness game reserves – some seventeen per cent of the country's total land area is protected by conservation laws – with a wealth of wild flora and fauna.

Here are the ruins and relics of lost cultures of the kind that set aflame the imagination of the writers John Buchan and H. Rider Haggard. Here is a land of rough roads – sand traps when dry, muddy rivers in the rain – where the most convenient and frequently only practicable forms of transport are boat and light aircraft.

This chapter is roughly laid out as a route from Gaborone north to the Zimbabwe border at Chobe. Roads are few, long and straight and it is virtually impossible to get lost, so any route directions required are inserted in the relevant place. Refer to the colour map of Botswana facing the back cover.

GABORONE

The former British Protectorate of Bechuanaland, now Botswana, was administered from Mafikeng, in South Africa's North-West Province. In 1962, with independence in

prospect, Gaborone, on the railway and the Ngotwane River, seemed a convenient place to put a capital city. Building began in 1964, two years before the country became an independent state. It was to be a small and business-like city.

Three decades later, it has become a seemingly unplanned urban sprawl, with a mixture of industrial, commercial, administrative and residential buildings plonked about haphazardly like weeds colonising a waste site. How such a young town can appear so soulless is difficult to understand.

However, people evidently like living and working there. The population is soaring – 150,000 at the last count and rising – which is around seven times the number that was first thought of. Also the seat of the University of Botswana, Gaborone claims to be Southern Africa's fastest-developing city.

341

TOURIST INFORMATION
Dept of Tourism: *The Mall, Gaborone; tel: 353 024* (open daily 0730–1630). The publication *Consumer Info Gaborone,* usually available at hotels and newsagents, gives details of local events.

ARRIVING AND DEPARTING

By Air
Sir Seretse Khama Airport is 14 km north of the city centre, off the Francistown Road; *tel: 373 307.* The major hotels operate their own airport transfers, but others will need to take a taxi.

Air Botswana, *IGI Building, The Mall; tel: 351 921,* is the national airline, operating daily scheduled flights between Gaborone and South Africa (Johannesburg), Zimbabwe (Harare and Victoria Falls) and Namibia (Windhoek). There are also domestic flights to and from Gaborone, Maun and Kasane.

Charter flights are operated by **Executive Charter**; *tel: 375 257,* **Ngami Air**; *tel: 372*

309, **Okavango Air**; *tel: 313 308* and **Air Charter Botswana**; *tel: 351 804.*

By Rail
Botswana Railways: *Station Rd, Gaborone; tel: 351 401/2.* Tickets are on sale at the station office (open Mon–Fri 0730–1300, 1400–1900, Sat–Sun 1400–1930). See also p. 54.

By Road
Major towns and villages are linked by privately-operated buses. Major operators in Gaborone include: **Seabelo's**; *tel: 357 078,* and **Mahube Express**; *tel: 352 660.* Car hire is available from several companies, including **Avis Rent-A-Car**; *tel: 375 469,* **Holiday Car Rental**; *tel: 353 970,* and **Imperial Car Rental**; *tel: 302 280.*

GETTING AROUND
There is no real city centre – life revolves around a series of spread-out shopping malls. Parking is easy, so the best possible option is to have your own car. Alternatively, taxis are available at Gaborone Airport and in town near major hotels and government buildings. They cannot be flagged down in the street. There are several good town plans on sale in local bookshops, such as the **Botswana Book Centre**, *The Mall.*

STAYING IN GABORONE

Accommodation
Gaborone has some hotels of good standard and a few of more modest character. The bed and breakfast option is beginning to appear. Hotel rooms tend to be snapped up by business visitors, so early booking is advised. Good budget accommodation is the most difficult to find in the city.

The 200-room **Gaborone Sun and Casino** *(SI), Nyerere Dr.; tel: 351 111, fax: 302 555* (expensive) is the glitziest accommodation in town, with a grill, three bars, 24-hr room service, a casino, squash, tennis, swimming and golf facilities. Also attracting business trade, the **President Hotel**, *The Mall; tel: 353 631, fax: 351 840* (moderate–expensive) is a comfortable hotel in a good location, with nearly 100

rooms, a restaurant, grill, coffee shop and bars. The **Grand Palm Hotel**, *PO Box 2025; tel: 312 999, fax: 312 989,* (expensive) provides good value for the money, and is a popular hotel with many facilities on the city's western outskirts.

Lower down the price scale, the **Oasis Motel**, *Tlokweng Rd, about 8km east of the city; tel: 328 396, fax: 312 989* (moderate) has singles, doubles and some chalets, which are a little more expensive.

There are also several good bed and breakfasts. **Pabelelo Way Lodge**, *Pabelelo Way, off Independence Ave; tel: 351 682* (moderate) has single and double rooms; the **Brackenridge Lodge**, *off Independence Ave; tel/fax: 312 886* (cheap–moderate) offers a choice of shared or en suite bathrooms, or family rooms at higher rates; and **Lolwapa Lodge**, *Maakakgang Close, off Mabutu Dr., tel: 359 061* (cheap–moderate) has single and double rooms, either a shared bathroom or en suite.

Mokolodi Nature Reserve, *on Gaborone's southern outskirts, about 12 km from the city centre; tel: 353 959* (cheap–moderate) has clean dormitory accommodation at low cost and self-catering chalets at varying prices, according to size. Several animal species have been introduced to the reserve, which also has scenic hills, valleys and a dam. The dormitory is in the Environmental Education Centre and may be booked by groups. Individuals seeking accommodation should enquire as early as possible.

Campsite: **St Clair Lion Park** (see p. 345).

Eating and Drinking
One can find cheap lunchtime and evening snacks along *The Mall* and in the *Africa Mall*, but to avoid waiting among crowds of office workers, try to eat before or after the midday rush. Ethnic cuisines in town include Indian, Italian, Chinese, French, Portuguese, Mauritian, American and English.

Some of the best restaurants are in the hotels. **Giovanni's**, *Gaborone Sun, Nyerere Dr.; tel: 351 111* (moderate–expensive) specialises in Italian and international dishes, with accompanying live entertainment.

The Pergola, *President Hotel, The Mall; tel:*

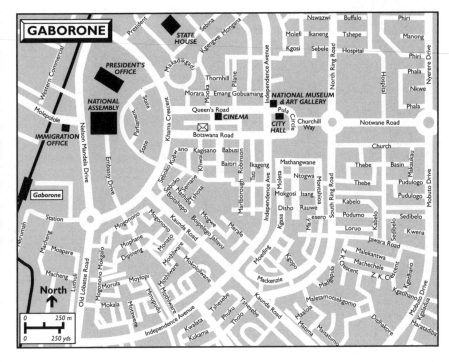

353 631 (moderate–expensive) also serves excellent food, with an eclectic and modern menu.

Elsewhere, the **Bull and Bush Pub**, *off Nelson Mandela Dr.; tel: 375 070* (moderate) has British fare. Go north on *Nelson Mandela Dr.*, and take the left fork when the road divides. **The Kgotla**, *Broadhurst North Mall; tel: 356 091* (moderate) offers a wide choice, which includes vegetarian dishes and salads. The **Mandarin**, *Africa Mall; tel: 375 038* (cheap–moderate) serves good Chinese, Indian and Mauritian dishes.

The **Mokolodi Nature Reserve**, *12 km south of Gaborone; tel: 353 959* (moderate) provides a taste of Africa, with eland or buffalo sometimes on the menu at the outdoor restaurant.

Communications
Gaborone Post Office, *The Mall, Gaborone* (open Mon–Fri 0815–1300, 1400–1600, Sat 0830–1130). **Telephones**: there are public call boxes, but to make international calls, go to **Botswana Telecom**, *Khama Crescent* (open Mon–Fri 0915–1300, 1415–1630, Sat 0815–1130). International dialling from overseas: area code + 267. There are no area dialling codes within Botswana.

Money
There are several large banks with exchange facilities, including Barclays and Standard Chartered, in *The Mall*.

Consulates
See Country by Country, p. 28.

ENTERTAINMENT
A glance at the *Botswana Advertiser* will tell you what's on. The nation's only casino is in the **Gaborone Sun Hotel** (open Mon–Fri 1900–late, weekends and public holidays – except religious holidays – 1600–0300.) There are blackjack and roulette tables. Slot machines can be played from 1000–late daily.

Gaborone has only one cinema, **The Capitol**, *The Mall*.

Botswana

L and-locked Botswana covers an area of 581,730 sq. km – about the size of France – and its people, numbering around 1.4 million, represent one of the lowest population densities in Africa. The northern two-thirds of the country lie within the Tropics.

Effectively, Botswana has only two seasons: rainy and dry. The rainy season comes some-time between October and April, but usually starts in late December and finishes at the end of February. Rainfall during those two months or so can be torrential, and it is at this time that many game camps prudently choose to close.

Between October and March, temperatures can climb as high as 44°C, with night-time temperatures rarely falling below 26°C. In winter, the daytime average is 27°C, dropping to around 6°C at night. Early morning frost sometimes occurs in the south-west between June and August.

The country's largest tribal group are the **Batswana** people, accounting for about 50% of the population. They are the descendants of a splinter group that began a westward movement from the Western Transvaal in the 14th century. About 75% of modern Batswana are to be found in South Africa. The second largest group are the **Bakalanga**, concentrated in the area around Francistown and across the border in Zimbabwe. Many African tribes have been split as a result of the development of international boundaries.

The country's oldest established groups are the **San** (Bushmen) and **Khoi** (Hottentot) (see Background, p.70), also found in neighbouring Namibia, and to a tiny extent in South Africa. Many **Herero**, whose forebears fled from German colonists in Namibia at the beginning of the 20th century, have settled around Maun on the edge of the Okavango Delta. Herero women are distinguished by their colourful long dresses (see Namibia, p.371).

Botswana was one of the poorest countries in the world when it became independent in 1966, but its fortunes took a dramatic turn for the better a year later with the discovery of diamonds, and today the country is the world's largest diamond producer in terms of value, with an annual output of 15 million carats. The country's beef industry is another major source of revenue, much of it earned from exports to the European Union.

The development of tourism, an important growth industry, is being carefully controlled. Already established as one of Africa's prime destinations, Botswana is anxious to make the most of its attractions without ruining them or the environment by over-exposure. Its policy, therefore, is to maintain a tourism industry based on high cost and low volume. For adventure-seeking holidaymakers, this policy is reflected, for example, in game drives and waterborne safaris, with a maximum of four people per vehicle or boat. Many guides feel they have failed in their duty if their party is confronted by another.

'Your vision of the wilderness can be destroyed if you suddenly find other people are around', one guide told us.

Details of what's on and what's coming soon appear on the notice board at the Maitisong **Cultural Centre**, *Mara-a-Pula Secondary School, Metsemasweu Rd; tel: 371 809.* Many entertainment centres world-wide would give their eye teeth for the enthusiastic support the locals give theatre and other cultural programmes at this 450-seat theatre, so if you cannot get tickets in advance don't set your hopes of getting in too

high. Energetic black groups give especially exciting performances.

A sprinkling of discos enlivens the night scene in and around the city. Some are within hotels. In the Gaborone Sun Hotel, **The Platform**, *tel: 351 111,* is a popular spot for African music and dancing.

Soul music is the main attraction at the **Diamond Club** in the Oasis Motel; *tel: 328*

396. **The Night Shift**, *Broadhurst North Mall,* is a lively disco spot.

A calendar of events is available from the **Dept of Culture and Social Welfare**, *Private Bag 00185, Gaborone; tel: 309 222.* Top of the list is the **Maitisong Performing Arts Festival**, which has become a regular celebration at the Maitisong Cultural Centre every March. Nine days of excitement and artistic stimulation with many styles of entertainment, and African enthusiasm and stamina provide a tonic for the town.

SIGHTSEEING

The **National Assembly Building**, *in the Government Enclave,* is probably the city's most beautiful building, its multi-archways reflected in a strip of water.

Across the road from the Tourist Office, near The Mall, the **National Museum and Art Gallery**, *Independence Ave; tel: 374 616* (open Tues–Fri 0900–1800, Sat–Sun 0900–1700; free) has an interesting mix of displays, from San crafts, including decorated ostrich eggs and eggshell necklaces, to the declaration of Gaborone as a city in 1986. The art gallery has a wide selection of African art, including works of the San people alongside paintings by some European artists. A shop sells prints, books, baskets and other handicrafts (open Tues–Fri 0900–1630).

Visitors to Botswana are most likely to be there for its wildlife and nature. The lions do not roam freely in the **St Clair Lion Park**, *18 km south of Gaborone; tel: 306 736.* People who pitch their tents for the night (advance booking essential) may hear them, but need not fear them. This is a good place to cheat and get good close-up pics, but the experience is nothing like seeing real bush lions. The park, by the Ngotwane River, also has entertainments for children.

Gaborone Game Reserve, about 5 km east of central Gaborone, via *Limpopo Dr.; tel: 371 405* (open daily 0630–1830) covers 500 sq. km along the Ngotwane River. It is an educational reserve, opened in 1988 to provide the people of Gaborone with a sense of more typical Botswana terrain than city streets; a number of antelope varieties have been introduced.

GABORONE TO FRANCISTOWN

Leave Gaborone on the Francistown road, the northern extension of *Nelson Mandela Dr.* About 40 km on, stop in the village of **Mochudi** to visit the **Phuthadikobo Museum**, at the top of the sacred Phuthadikobo Hill (open Mon–Fri 0800–1700, Sat, Sun 1400–1700; free, donations welcome). Opened in the 1970s in the first secondary school in the country – built in the 1920s with the aid of voluntary labour and local donations of money – the museum depicts the history of Mochudi and the Kgatla people, who have lived there for 130 years. The original occupants were the Kwena, who moved in during the mid 16th century. On weekdays, visitors can visit a modern silkscreen printing workshop next to the museum.

The drive north, never far from the railway line, is rather featureless until you reach the town of **Mahalapye**, where you can get refreshments and find some of the trappings of civilisation. This is the first town encountered by people entering Botswana from South Africa at the Stockpoort/Parr's Halt border post, about 65 km to the east.

Another 73 km takes you to **Palapye**, and from here you may like to take a side trip westward to the big, busy conurbation of **Serowe**, where Sir Seretse Khama was born, lived and is buried (see feature box p.346). A statue of him stands proudly in the graveyard.

The terrain westward between Serowe and Mahalapye was strictly for 4x4 vehicles only, but a tarred road is being built which, with the tarred road already existing, will form a circle around the Mokgware Hills and the Shoshong Hills.

Less than 1 km from Serowe along the tarred road to Orapa is the **Khama III Museum**; *tel: 430 519* (open Mon–Fri 0830–1630, Sat 0900–1600; free). Also on the Orapa road, near Paje village just north of Serowe, is the **Khama Rhino Sanctuary** (donations welcome; for information, *tel: 430 232)* opened in 1993 for the breeding and preservation of the dwindling species, as a community initiative by the people of Serowe and neighbouring villages.

The Serowe area is also interesting for its

Sir Seretse Khama

An extraordinary man and politician, Seretse Khama (1921–1980) was instrumental in leading the move towards independence. In 1948, he married an English woman, Ruth Williams, whom he met while a law student in London. He and his wife were banished from Botswana for five years from 1951, living in exile in England.

The people of Botswana always held him in high esteem, and on his return he became leader of the Botswana Democratic Party and, subsequently, prime minister and president of the independent country.

He was one of few nationalist leaders to lead his country into independence without blood-shed. He also managed to massively improve the country's economy (thanks largely to the discovery of diamonds), curb corruption and produce a model of what Africa can achieve. He was knighted by the Queen in recognition of his achievements.

In marrying a white woman, however, he displeased his uncle, the regent, and was forced to renounce his claim to the Ngwato chieftainship. His son, Ian, became chief and Lady Ruth Khama was recognised as mother of the chief. Sir Seretse died in 1980, aged 59, and is buried in his family graveyard near Serowe.

ancient sites. Ruins of an 11th-century settlement have been discovered right in Serowe, on **Thathaganyana Hill**, and there have been other finds in the hills south of the town.

Roughly midway between Palapye and Francistown at **Serule**, a tarred road goes 208 km east, almost to the **Tuli Game Reserve**. Only the last few kilometres are gravel, suitable for conventional vehicles. There are other access roads to Tuli farther south, but for most of these you will need a 4x4.

The 90,000 hectare Tuli Game Reserve, bounded by the Limpopo River which forms Botswana's border with South Africa here, is the easternmost part of a region known as the Tuli Block. It is scenically impressive, with areas of rocks, rivers and dry river beds. Trees by the Limpopo grow to an enormous size. It is unlike any other part of Botswana.

People drive or fly 500 km from Johannesburg to spend a night or two at one of the lodges and private reserves. The different habitats attract many bird species, and the little klipspringers which leap about the rocks are more abundant than in other parts of Southern Africa. There is also a big population of elephants.

Two lodges provide accommodation and guided game drives. The **Tuli Safari Lodge**, *by the Limpopo River; tel/fax: 845 303,*

reservations: PO Box 781329, Sandton, RSA; tel: 011-883 434, fax: 011-883 2556, has a tented camp, chalets, a self-catering guesthouse sleeping up to six people, a restaurant and bar. Rates include meals and game drives. (Moderate–expensive.)

The **Mashatu Game Reserve**, *tel: 845 321; reservations: PO Box 2575, Randburg RSA; tel: 011-789 2677, fax: 011-8864382* (expensive) is an extensive private reserve (45,000 hectares), with a luxurious lodge and even more exclusive tented camp. There is a waterhole, floodlit at night, next to the guests' bar, and meals and game drives are included in the price.

FRANCISTOWN

Back in Palapye, continue north for 160 km through open country offering little memorable until you reach Botswana's oldest and second largest town, **Francistown** (population 60,000). It is named after a Briton, Daniel Francis, who started a successful gold mining operation in the area. After adding to his fortune by dabbling in diamonds in Kimberley, he played a part in designing Francistown in the late 1870s.

Archaeological evidence of human habitation of the area many thousands of years ago has been uncovered. Today, apart from shops and

346

one museum, there is little to capture the imagination of the visitor in this workaday industrial town. It is, however, a useful place to stock up on supplies or deal with business.

STAYING IN FRANCISTOWN

Accommodation
In town, **Cresta Thapama Lodge**, *corner Doc Morgan Ave and Blue Jacket St; tel: 213 872, fax: 213 766* (moderate) is reliable and comfortable. About 5 km south of Francistown, the popular **Marang Motel**, *Old Gaborone Rd; tel: 213 991, fax: 212 130* (cheap–moderate) has air-conditioned rooms and a low-cost campsite beside the Tati River. Campers can use hot showers and the motel's swimming pool.

The **YWCA**, *Doc Morgan Ave (southern end); tel: 213 046* (cheap) provides dormitory accommodation for men as well as women.

Eating and Drinking
Several outlets on *Haskins St, Blue Jacket St* and the Mall shopping centre offer budget-priced take-aways. Hotel restaurants are probably the best bet for more formal dining, notably the **Ivory Grill**, at the Cresta Thapama Lodge (see Accommodation, above).

Money
There are several banks with exchange facilities on *Haskins St* and *Blue Jacket St*.

SIGHTSEEING
The **Supa-Ngwao Museum**, *off New Maun Rd, Francistown* (open Tues–Sat 0900–1300, 1400–1700; free) is housed in the Old Court House. It presents the history and culture of Botswana's north-east region.

From Francistown, a good road leads to the Zimbabwe border at Plumtree and on to Bulawayo (see pp. 395–398).

FRANCISTOWN TO KASANE
Much of the long drive up to the eastern limit of the Caprivi Strip and Victoria Falls is fairly dull, but it is a good road. At Nata, 190 km north-east of Francistown, a good road leads left through Gweta to Maun (305 km) on the edge of the Okavango Delta (see p. 350).

Otherwise, the **Sibuyu** and **Kazuma Forest Reserves** provide welcome relief until the environs of **Kasane** compensate for your patience and fortitude.

KASANE
Tourist Office: *between the Immigration regional office and Barclay's Bank Botswana; tel: 650 357.* Information on packages offered by tour operators is available. The Tourism Office also has an information counter at Kasane Airport.

STAYING IN KASANE

Accommodation
On the doorstep of the national park, the area around Kasane has more than its fair share of good hotels. For details, see Chobe Accommodation, p. 348.

Money
The Barclays branch on the main street offers one of the first opportunities to change money for anyone arriving from neighbouring countries (open Mon, Tues, Wed, Fri 0815–1245, Thur, Sat 0815–1045).

Car Hire
Avis, *Kubu Lodge; tel: 650 144;* **Holiday Car Hire**, *Chobe Safari Lodge; tel: 650 226.*

SIGHTSEEING
Kasane is on the doorstep of three neighbouring countries – Zimbabwe, Zambia and Namibia – and at the confluence of the Chobe and Zambezi Rivers. Apart from its importance as a major gateway into Chobe National Park and to other countries of Southern Africa, Kasane has one unusual claim to fame. Behind the police station is a baobab tree, which was apparently used as a prison cell in days gone by. Two or three Kasane hotels run river trips which non-residents may join – enquiries should be made through the hotels. Cruises are held in the late afternoon, with a guide on board to point out birds, mammals and crocodiles. A family of up to two dozen elephants, from toddler to great-grandad, usually puts in an appearance for a drink before sundown, and hippos ease themselves out of the water in the cool of the evening.

347

CHOBE NATIONAL PARK

Parks Information: there is a National Parks Office near the main gate, *about 6 km west of Kasane; tel: 661 265;* open daily 0730–1630. The park is open 0600–1830 Mar–Sept, 0630–1930 Oct–Feb. Admission charge.

ARRIVING

To penetrate the Chobe National Park, you need a 4x4 vehicle and a good sense of direction. Better still, you will find travel easier if you have accumulated the money for flights with bush pilots. Many of the excellent game camps within the park have their own airstrip. This is one of the finest (and most expensive) ways in which to see wildlife at close quarters, with few, if any, fellow travellers. The Kasane entrance to the park is 3 km west of Chobe Game Lodge along the main road, which runs parallel to the Chobe River.

ACCOMMODATION

Centrally situated in Kasane, overlooking the Chobe River, the **Chobe Safari Lodge**; *tel: 650 336, fax: 650 385* (cheap–moderate) has rooms and chalets, a swimming pool, restaurant and bars, together with a popular camping and caravan site – booking advised. **Kubu Lodge**, *at Kazungula, 15 km from Kasane; tel: 650 312, fax: 650 412* (moderate) offers accommodation in log cabins on stilts.

There are also several luxury lodges in the area. The **Mowana Safari Lodge**, *overlooking the Chobe River, near the old airfield, north of town; tel: 650 300, fax 650 301* (expensive) is a rustic-style timber and thatch lodge with top-floor bars and public areas decorated with fine African murals. The lodge's name means 'baobab', a fine example of which is a dominating feature in the grounds. At the opposite end of town, the **Chobe Chilwero Lodge**, *River Rd; tel: 650 505, fax: 650 352* (expensive) stands on top of a hill near the Chobe entrance, with a river view and accommodation in luxury chalets.

Set in beautiful riverside grounds inside the park, the **Chobe Game Lodge**; *tel: 650 340, fax: 650 280* (expensive) provides a busy programme of activities for guests viewing wildlife from water and land. Richard Burton

and Elizabeth Taylor, marrying each other for the second time, held the ceremony here.

Campsites: there are fairly basic parks board campsites at Linyanti, Chobe, Savuti, Nogatsaa/Tchinga, Serondela and Ngome. The Nogatsaa/Tchinga sites are without bathroom facilities.

Luxury Camps

Forget the term 'camping' if you are fortunate enough to stay at one of the luxury tented accommodations in the park, such as **Lloyd's Camp**, *Lloyd Wilmot Safaris, Savuti; PO Box 37, Maun; tel: 660 351, fax: 650 571* (expensive), a comfortable tented camp with its own waterhole and viewing platform, or **Savuti South**, *Savuti; tel: 260 302* (expensive), reservations made through the safari operator **Gametrackers**, *PO Box 2608, Cape Town, RSA; tel: 021-231 054, fax: 021-231 061*. This is an Orient Express property, used by prestigious companies like **Afro Ventures**, *PO Box 323, Kasane; tel: 650 340, fax: 650 280*, who also take bookings for Camp Moremi and Camp Okavango in the Delta, Chobe Game Lodge, Mowana Safari Lodge and other luxury lodges and tented camps in Southern Africa.

Your tent is larger than many hotel rooms. You have a private shower and toilet in separate rooms, two wash-basins, wardrobe and shelf space, electric light, mosquito net drapes over the big white bed, a picture window and a spacious balcony with alluring loungers and somewhere to put your cool drink. All this, and a view into which impala and giraffe may wander. Attentive staff, a big *boma* with bar and restaurant, excellent cuisine, a craft and gift shop and guides who perform miracles complete the heaven-on-earth concept.

SIGHTSEEING

Chobe is the third largest of Botswana's national parks and game reserves, covering nearly 11,000 sq. km. The Chobe River forms the northern boundary. The park's big appeal is the diversity of the terrain – grassland, veldt, marshes, savannah, woodland, rocky outcrops – each attracting different varieties of wildlife.

The **Savuti** region of the park, in the far west (bordering the Moremi Game Reserve), is

Rough Camping in Chobe

Chobe's campsites are not fenced. Even at sites where water and ablutions are provided, hardy souls should not be tempted to sleep under the stars. Keep the tent secure because of marauding animals, particularly lions, which wander freely around the guy ropes. Hyenas are opportunists and likely to grab any food if the chance arises. Keep all food-encrusted tins and other refuse well out of their way. Some places are vulnerable to other hazards. Rough camping in the Savuti can involve the ablution building being vandalised by elephants in search of a drink.

It is vital for self-catering campers to bring enough food and drink to last throughout their trip because the Chobe park has no shops. Also bear in mind that there are long distances between filling stations – not one exists, for instance, in the 400 km between Maun and Kasane – so it is wise to top up the tank wherever possible. Game drives can be tremendously exciting and lead you all over the place, but do not forget to keep an eye on the fuel gauge.

particularly exciting in the rainy season, when vegetation suddenly sprouts green and lush, and antelope, huge numbers of zebra and other plains animals move south with their young. This season (Oct-Apr) is a good time to visit most of Chobe National Park, as long as you are well defended against mosquitoes and the heat of the summer sun. It should be borne in mind that sometimes the rains arrive later – perhaps late Nov or Dec.

Those travelling independently should check with local people which parts of the park are better avoided in the rainy season – the marshy area of the Savuti region in the Mababe Depression may be one – where clay soil can quickly ensnare even robust 4x4 vehicles. Likewise, some of the park's sandy areas become treacherous in the dry season (May–Sept).

Game tends to abandon the Chobe river-front and the Linyanti area in the west of the park in the rains because surface water is available elsewhere. These areas come into their own in the dry season. Chobe is particularly famous for its elephants, with one of the highest concentrations in the world – including visitors from Namibia and Zimbabwe.

OKAVANGO DELTA

A unique eco-system, the Okavango Delta is also a paradox. It is a vast area of wetland surrounded by the world's largest stretch of sand – the Kalahari Desert. Its wildlife, among the finest in Africa, is supported by lush but

fragile vegetation. It is the best-known and, from the tourist's point of view, the least accessible part of Botswana.

Located in the north-west corner of the country, the delta marks the end of the Okavango River, the third longest in Southern Africa, which spreads into a labyrinth of channels and lagoons after flowing 1300 km from its source in central Angola. About the size of Switzerland, the delta covers some 15,000 sq. km, stretching to as much as 18,000 at the peak of the rainy season.

The most popular part of the delta is the **Moremi Game Reserve**, where most of the safari lodges and camps are located. This reserve alone covers nearly 5000 sq. km and offers superb game-viewing and bird-watching as well as boat trips and fishing – all among breathtaking scenery.

Moremi Lodges

In view of Botswana's policy of keeping tourism on a tight rein and promoting quality above quantity, staying at a safari lodge in the Moremi Game Reserve is no cheap option. All the places listed here are expensive, but standards are extremely high, and exciting wilderness experiences are guaranteed.

Camp Moremi, *on the Xakanaxa Lagoon, on the eastern edge of the Okavango Delta;* bookings: **Afro Ventures**, *PO Box 323, Kasane; tel: 650 340; fax: 650 280,* accommodates a maximum of 22 guests. The **Moremi Tree Lodge**, an elevated thatch and timber building,

349

houses a main lounge and cocktail bar, dining room and wildlife reference library. There is a pool, covered boma and an elevated observation platform. Guests who have booked a two-centre stay are transferred to **Camp Okavango**, *on Nxaragha Island in the permanent Okavango Delta;* bookings: **Afro Ventures** (details above), on an exciting 2½ hr boat trip with a picnic stop halfway. 'Camp O', as the island site is affectionately known, can be reached only by water or by light aircraft, and like Moremi accommodates up to 22 guests in East African-style safari tents with private showers. An extensive open-air patio is the setting for alfresco silver service dinners lit by candelabra. Game-viewing is by powerboat, canoe and on foot.

The **Tsaro Elephant Lodge**, *at the reserve's North Gate, near the Khwai River;* bookings: **Hartley's Safaris**, *Private Bag 48, Maun; tel/fax: 660 528,* overlooks the Moremi flood plains. Unlike many safari lodges, this one has 24-hour electricity, in addition to a bar and swimming pool.

MAUN

Tourist Office: *opposite Best Western Riley's Hotel, Sir Seretse Khama Rd; tel: 661 677* (open Mon–Fri 0730–1230, 1345–1630). The office has a good stock of posters, maps, postcards, brochures and souvenirs, and provides information on sightseeing in the area and throughout Botswana.

ARRIVING AND DEPARTING

Maun Airport, *less than a kilometre from the town centre,* has a small, rather old-fashioned terminal building, with a restaurant, post office and a small, inadequately stocked tourist information counter; *tel: 660 492* (open Mon–Fri 0730–1230, 1345–1630).

There are daily scheduled flights between Maun and Johannesburg and Gaborone, and regular flights to and from Kasane, Harare, Victoria Falls and Windhoek.

By Road

Maun is not a difficult place to find and is connected to other major centres by tarred roads, but travelling there involves long journeys. For example, from Gaborone, via Francistown and Nata, the distance is 937 km, a journey, sensibly, of at least two days.

ACCOMMODATION AND FOOD

There is not much choice in town. **Riley's Hotel** *(BW), Sir Seretse Khama Rd; tel: 660 320; fax: 660 580* (moderate) is the only downtown option. The **Sedie Motel**, *4 km north of the airport; tel/fax: 660 177* (cheap) has air-conditioned rooms, a pool, bar and campsites in the grounds, and can arrange transport from town.

Campsite: **Audi Camp**, *Matlapaneng, by the river, 8 km north-east of Maun; tel: 660 599, fax: 660 581* (cheap) is a popular site with some permanent tents, a bar, restaurant, pool and a very cheap sandy golf course. There are several other campsites nearby.

Maun's most popular restaurant is **Le Bistro**, *BGI Shopping Centre; tel: 660 718* (cheap–moderate), which offers an eclectic menu, including pasta, seafood, steaks and Asian dishes. There are a few other restaurants, cafés and fast food outlets.

Money

Both Barclays and Standard Chartered have branches with exchange facilities on *the Mall.*

SIGHTSEEING

Located at the southern end of the delta, the dusty, sprawling town of Maun is the region's major gateway. Few visitors stay long – often less than an hour as they switch from a scheduled jet from Gaborone or Johannesburg to a five- or six-seater light aircraft on their way to a remote lodge or camp.

Sightseeing in the area is restricted to the **Maun Environmental Education Centre** *opposite Riley's Hotel, on the eastern bank of the Thamalakane River;* (open daily 0800–1700), a small nature reserve with four walking trails and a number of animals, including giraffe, impala, lechwe, wildebeest and zebra.

At the **Okavango Swamps Crocodile Farm**, *Sitatunga Camp, Shakawe road, 15 km south of Maun; tel: 660 750* (open daily 0800–1700; free), visitors may take a self-guided tour to learn about the fearsome beasts.

LESOTHO

Aptly dubbed 'The Kingdom in the Sky', Lesotho is encompassed by the Drakensberg Mountains, and is the only country in the world with all its land lying at altitudes of more than 1000m. It is Southern Africa's watershed, the source of most of the region's major rivers, and its highest point, Thabana-Ntlenyana mountain, is the loftiest in Southern Africa at 3841m.

TOURING LESOTHO

'The Land Without Fences', Lesotho is a spectacularly beautiful and exciting country of mountains, waterfalls and streams, and landscapes peopled with colourful Basotho horsemen and young herd boys sporting flamboyant capes and gold or silver rubber boots.

Even with the road improvements brought about by the Lesotho Highlands Development Project (see feature box, p.353), travel is still largely restricted to the northern and southwestern parts of the country. Elsewhere, roads are sparse, rugged and often treacherous, even for 4x4 vehicles. In this chapter are two practical routes, from Maseru to Mokhotlong and Maseru to Moyeni, which will enable you to savour the flavour of Lesotho. All routes from Maseru start at The Circle, a large traffic roundabout at the eastern end of Kingsway, but for extended journeys the self-explanatory roads are *Main Road North* and *Main Road South*. Also refer to the map at the back of the book.

MASERU

Lesotho's capital is a good starting point for excursions to all parts of the country. Animated rather than lively, it is essentially a one-street town, with no specific sights. **Kingsway**, paved for a visit by the British royal family in 1947, carries most of the city's shops and offices and is crowded with street traders, job-seekers,

beggars and car cleaners, who are worth employing if only to keep an eye on the car.

TOURIST INFORMATION

Lesotho Tourist Board: *Kingsway, next to Hotel Victoria, PO Box 1378, Maseru 100; tel: 312 896; fax: 323 638* (open Mon–Fri 0800–1245, 1400–1630, Sat 0800–1200). The office has a very friendly and helpful staff, but is short on printed information. Ask for copies of the colour brochure, *Lesotho – Africa for All Seasons,* which contains a reasonably good map of Lesotho, and the quarterly magazine, *Motsamai,* both published by the tourist board. A small but adequate street map of Maseru goes with the motoring map of the country published by the South African Automobile Association (R5.95, free to members). Listings of hotels and lodges throughout the country and leaflets on ponytrekking, hiking, trout-fishing and camping outfits are also available, as is information on sightseeing tours, historical and cultural sites and handicraft centres. Reservations for full- and half-day conducted tours may be made at the office. Full-day tours start at 0930, return at 1600 and lunch is included in the price.

ACCOMMODATION

The capital's top two hotels are both casinos. The **Lesotho Sun** *(SI), signposted off Nightingale Rd; tel: 313 111; fax: 310 104* (moderate–expensive), is a modern resort hotel in 50 hectares of parkland on a hillside overlooking the city. It is visible from several locations and therefore easy to find. It has six suites, 226 airconditioned rooms, a choice of restaurants and bars and offers evening entertainment and a range of sporting activities. The **Maseru Sun** *(SI), at the end of Orpen Rd, opposite the Victoria Hotel; tel: 312 434; fax: 310 158* (moderate–expensive), has 109 air-conditioned rooms and three suites. The hotel overlooks the Caledon River, and its restaurant is noted for its buffet and à la carte menu; sports facilities include horse-riding, tennis, swimming and volley ball.

351

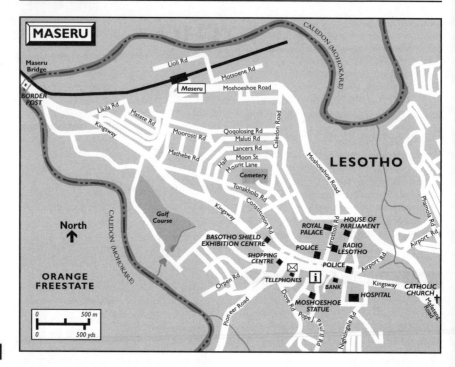

Prominently situated in the centre of town, Maseru's major rendezvous and entertainment spot is the **Victoria Hotel**, *Kingsway, opposite the Basotho Hat; tel: 322 002; fax 310 318* (moderate), with 102 air-conditioned rooms, three restaurants, swimming pool, cinema, patio bar and nightclub. For a more leisurely ambience, try the **Lancer's Inn**, *Kingsway, near corner Pioneer Rd; tel: 312 114; fax: 310 223* (moderate). This is Maseru's oldest hotel, built in colonial times, with self-catering chalets, flats and rondavels, as well as comfortable hotel rooms. Amenities include a restaurant, discotheque and swimming pool.

EATING AND DRINKING

Hotel restaurants and bars are open to the public, with those at the **Victoria Hotel** and **Lancer's Inn** (both cheap–moderate) the most popular. The Lancer's also has a bakery and delicatessen. Other options include the **Auberge**, *Kingsway, on the corner of Airport Rd; tel: 312 775* (moderate) a restaurant and bar popular with local residents, serving classic French-style food in the main dining room and fast food elsewhere; and **Boccaccio Restaurant**, *Bowker Rd, behind the Basotho Hat; tel: 325 583* (cheap–moderate), a relaxed place serving Italian dishes. There are also two popular Chinese restaurants, **China Garden**, *Orpen St; tel: 313 915;* and **China Palace**, *1st floor, Lesotho National Development Corporation Centre, Kingsway; tel: 315 488.*

Money

There are several banks with exchange facilities on *Kingsway.*

Colour section (i): Sun City, Valley of the Waves (pp.318–320); Nama children, Khubus (p.331).
(ii): Kalahari Gemsbok National Park; inset, Northern Kalahari bushpeople (p.325).
(iii): Dunes at Sossusvlei, Namibia (p.375); Basotho people, Lesotho (p.353).
(iv): Cultural Village at Victoria Falls, Zimbabwe (p.400); Reed Dance, Swaziland (p.383).

Lesotho

The stunning mountainous terrain, lying entirely outside the tropics, keeps Lesotho free from tropical diseases. Bilharzia, the scourge of many African waterways and lakes, cannot get a foothold in Lesotho's cool, clear, swift-running streams and rivers, and malaria cannot take hold in the crisp mountain air. For the motorist, however, Lesotho's topography seldom permits driving on the level, and it can be frustrating to be at the tail end of a convoy of crowded buses and pick-ups straining up a mountain pass. Tourism here is all about outdoor activities. Trekking through spectacular scenery on a sure-footed, docile Basotho pony is a memorable experience whether it lasts an hour or several days. Anglers will find mountain streams and lakes brimming with brown and rainbow trout, carp and bass. Bird-watchers and photographers will be in their element, and those with a yen for exploration can go in search of dinosaur footprints, fossils and ancient San rock paintings. Hiking and backpacking will also appeal to those who enjoy fresh air and exercise. The ambitious **Lesotho Highlands Development Project**, centred on the Katse Dam near Bokong in central Lesotho, is opening up new tourism opportunities. The project will create a lake 45 km long, provide water and electricity for a large tract of Southern Africa, introduce a range of water-based recreational activities and improve the wildlife environment.

SHOPPING

The hat-shaped **Basotho Hat**, *Kingsway*, is the best of several good craft shops in Maseru, along Kingsway and in the top-end hotels.

THABA-BOSIU

Tourist Office: *Information centre at base of Thaba-Bosiu, 23 km east of Maseru; tel: 357 212* (open daily 0830–1630; M4 – price includes map, pamphlet and official guide).

   Mmelesi Lodge; *adjacent to Thaba-Bosiu; tel: 357 215* (cheap) offers accommodation in small but comfortable thatched rondavels and has an attractive restaurant. **Thaba–Bosiu** is Lesotho's most important historical site, a mountain fortress that helped preserve the Basotho nation. In 1831, King Moshoeshoe I repulsed the Matabele forces of Mzilikazi and later defeated a Boer attack led by Commandant Louw Wepener, who lost his life in the attempt. Thaba-Bosiu means 'Mountain at Night', and legend has it that what was a hill in daylight became a formidable mountain after dark. Moshoeshoe's grave, his restored house and remains of defensive walls are at the summit.

MOLIMO-NTHUSE

Basotho Pony Trekking Centre, *60 km east of Maseru and signposted from the Mafeteng road, Molimo-Nthuse; tel: 314 165*. Molimo-Nthuse is SeSotho for 'God Help Me Pass', and the centre stands at the top of an awesomely steep and winding pass. Day treks last 1–4 hrs, with longer treks taking up to 6 days. Overnight stops are in Basotho villages.

   Set alongside an impressive waterfall, **Molimo–Nthuse Lodge** lies at the foot of the pass; *tel: 370 211* (cheap). Accommodation is in chalets, while a circular restaurant-bar presents a panoramic view of the surrounding mountains.

MASERU TO MOKHOTLONG

This 270 km route, on a tarred surface the whole way, heads north-east from Maseru on the A1, hugging the border with South Africa until just north of Butha-Buthe, where it curves to the south. The first part of the journey covers reasonably well-populated areas, but from Butha to Buthe communities are tiny and few.

   Teyateyaneng, *42 km from Maseru,* is Lesotho's handicrafts centre (see feature box, p.354). The **Blue Mountain Inn**, *in the centre of town; tel: 500 362* (cheap) is a pleasant hotel, with restaurant and bar, in a tropical garden setting. **Maputsoe**, *86 km from Maseru,* is the border crossing to Ficksburg, 2 km away in the Free State (see pp. 96–97). This is an industrial town and gateway to the Lesotho Highlands Development Project, with one hotel, the **Sekekete**, *Main St; tel: 430 621* (cheap).

353

Craft Tours

The go-ahead Lesotho Tourist Board makes it easy for tourists to visit craft workshops, caves, dinosaur footprints, gorges, waterfalls and some of Southern Africa's most stupendous scenery. It is generally easier to take a conducted half-day or full-day tour from Maseru than to drive your own vehicle along rough highland roads. Some tours make a special feature of crafts, introducing you to local weavers and potters and their work.

The weaving centres have introduced a whole new earning opportunity for Lesotho women living in remote areas. Their work is exquisite – wall hangings, rugs and small tapestries.

Helang Basali Crafts of Lesotho, at the *St Agnes Mission at Teyateyaneng; tel: (27) 5191-40253 (Ladybrand, RSA)*, is a stop on a 52 km conducted tour from Maseru. Visitors can see a courtyard gallery of designs, and select one if they wish, and watch the processes that transform mohair from mountain goats into woven landscapes, scenes of thatched huts or blanket-wrapped Basotho horsemen, or geometric-patterned mats, in the warm, earthy colours of Africa. The high-quality work is sent all over the world. Helang Basali – the name means 'Wonderful Women' – is run by a New Zealander, Christabel Jackson, who co-founded the project in the mid 1980s. It now provides employment for more than 100 women in a peaceful machineless factory. Teyateyaneng, mercifully known as TY, has a number of other weaving and craft workshops open to visitors. Nearby Kolonyama has a pottery centre, where clay and minerals are used to produce fine stoneware products and porcelain jewellery.

Further on, the **Leribe Craft Centre** is a sheltered workshop and philanthropic employment project of the Anglican Church. Some of the women craftworkers are disabled. The mohair yarns are spun at their homes, then brought to the centre where they are washed, moth-proofed, dyed, and woven on looms, knitted or crocheted. The shop on site is stocked with superb stoles, shawls, jackets, ponchos, blankets, cushion covers, shoulder bags, purses, table mats, even saddle girths for horses.

354

Leribe, *15 km beyond Maputsoe*, was developed as a British colonial outpost in 1876. About 10 km north of town are three sets of **dinosaur footprints** embedded in rocks beside the Subeng River. The old-established **Leribe Hotel** is in the town centre; *tel: 400 362* (cheap). **Butha-Buthe**, *30 km further along the A1*, has a road linking with the South African border post at Caledonspoort. The name means 'the Place of Lying Down' – the attractive town, on the banks of the Hlotse River, is dominated by a mountain resembling three crouching lions. In the town centre is the **Crocodile Inn**; *tel: 460 233* (cheap).

Mokhotlong, known as the coldest, driest, most remote place in Lesotho, is near the Thabana-Ntlenyana mountain. From here you can drive on to Kwazulu-Natal by way of the Sani Pass, but the road can be very treacherous (4x4 only), especially in winter. Accommodation is available at the **Senqu Hotel**; *tel: 920 330* (cheap).

MASERU TO MOYENI

This 180 km route takes us out of Maseru on *Main Road South,* then along the A2. Although there are more communities, the scenery is still stunning.

Morija, *45 km south of Maseru*, is the site of Lesotho's oldest church, dedicated 1858, and the country's only **museum**, *tel: 360 308* (open Mon–Sat 0800–1700; Sun 1400–1700; M4), which houses a collection of Stone Age and Iron Age artefacts, dinosaur bones and other fossils, petrified wood and geological samples, as well as shields and spears. A tea shop serves snacks, sandwiches and hot and cold drinks, and there is a crafts centre. Self-catering accommodation is available at **Ha Matela Lodge**; *tel: 316 555 or 360 303*. Visitors can enjoy pony trekking, mounting biking and canoeing. Ten km south of Morija is the start of the worthwhile side track to Malealea Lodge in the aptly-named Paradise Valley. At the Golden

The Land for all Seasons

The mokorotlo is a distinctive conical hat made ornately of woven grass. Its shape represents Mt Qiloane, the last sight seen by King Moshoeshoe's son as he left the kingdom after a quarrel with the British. It became a symbol of nationalism and has since become the symbol of Lesotho, as well as an immensely practical sun hat, useful year-round with an average 300 days of sunshine a year. In winter, both men and women wrap themselves cosily in soft woven blankets of rich colours, necessary when snow blankets the ground and the mountain streams freeze.

The four seasons are well defined in Lesotho. Pale pink peach blossom decorates the towns and villages in spring (Aug–Oct). Eighty per cent of Lesotho is mountainous. Melting snow fills the rivers and waterfalls gather momentum. The backpackers' season starts in earnest. Adventurous young people from every continent explore the formidable but astonishingly beautiful rocks, peaks and plateaux on foot or sure-footed amiable ponies, which give the novice an easy ride. Because of the altitude, Lesotho's summers (Nov–Jan) are rarely overbearingly hot. Brief periods of heavy daytime rain are often followed by clear evenings. Swollen rivers and headstrong waterfalls are at their most spectacular. The tall blooms of the aloes reach for the sky. In the valleys, organically-grown vegetables flourish.

Farming is mainly unmechanised. Young herd boys keep a lonely vigil over a few head of ranging cattle. In autumn (Feb–Apr) the harvested cereals and crops are piled on to ox-drawn carts and there is much dancing and merrymaking at thanksgiving celebrations. Expanses of cosmos bloom red, pink and white. Winter (Mar–July) can be bitterly cold, especially at night, temperatures dropping to -10°C, freezing lakes and streams and petrifying waterfalls. The northern Maluti Mountains provide great conditions for short-range skiing. Daytimes are usually sunny if a bit nippy, and nights are bright with stars.

355

Rose Restaurant and Taxi Stop, turn left on to a gravel road and after a further 10 km fork right. Drive for 15 km, turn left, stop after one kilometre to admire the superb view from the top of the **Gates of Paradise Pass** and continue for 6 km to the lodge.

Located at an altitude of around 2000m, **Malealea Lodge**; *tel: 785 727; fax: 785 326; e-mail: malealea@pixie.co.za* (cheap) offers accommodation in chalets, rondavels and backpackers' rooms. Campsites are also available. There is a simple restaurant, an honesty bar and shop. Originally a trading store built in 1905, the lodge is probably the best place in Lesotho for pony trekking and hiking. The scenery is magnificent, with waterfalls, gorges and rock pools and there are San paintings.

Some 80 km south of Maseru and 18 km east of Van Rooyenshek border post, **Mafeteng** is a large commercial centre. The **Mafeteng Hotel**, in the centre of town; *tel: 700 236* (cheap–moderate) has 27 en suite

bedrooms, a restaurant, 2 bars and a swimming pool. The **Golden Hotel**, *on the northern outskirts; tel: 700 566* (cheap–moderate) has 16 en suite rooms, restaurant, two bars and a pool.

Mohale's Hoek, *42 km south of Mafeteng*, is a pleasant town built by the British as an administrative centre in 1884. **Hotel Mount Maluti**; *tel: 785 224* (cheap–moderate) has 35 en suite rooms, restaurant, bars, a swimming pool and tennis court. **Moyeni** was established in 1877, abandoned three years later during the Gun War, then rebuilt. Today, it is the headquarters of the southern Quthing district, and is the centre for visiting some of Lesotho's best fossils, prehistoric sites and San art. The Tele Bridge border post, leading to the Free State and Eastern Cape Province, is 15 km to the west. **Mountain Side Hotel**, *Lower Moyeni; tel: 750 257* (cheap), has 12 en suite rooms, two bars, restaurant and a night club. The **Orange River Hotel**, *Upper Moyeni; tel: 750 252,* has 16 en suite rooms, restaurant and two bars.

MOZAMBIQUE

Take a long thin tropical country, with 2500 kilometres of pristine Indian Ocean seafront. Into it, pour the rowdy bonhomie of Africa, a small touch of Arabic sophistication and a large dollop of the Latin love of the good life, and you should have – perfection? Mozambique has the potential to be one of the world's great tourist destinations, and is trying desperately to climb aboard the bandwagon. The tourist dollar is seen as the way of saving what is currently one of the three poorest countries in the world.

TOURISM IN MOZAMBIQUE

For tourists, parts of Mozambique are wonderful, if you have the money. Everything other than basic essentials is imported from South Africa, and prices are definitely two-tier, with a gaping void between them. At one end is a shanty town world of subsistence and survival; at the other, a glamorous international playground, with prices in US dollars that would make New Yorkers blink. In between are South African tourists, who arrive with their own accommodation, food and even water, and contribute absolutely nothing to the local economy.

Basically, regeneration has started in the far south, around Maputo, and is gradually working north. The country is safe and easily accessible as far north as Vilanculos and its islands, and there is a semblance of order being re-created around the second city of Beira. During the life of this book, the missing segments of the long coast road from Vilanculos to Beira should be rebuilt; at the time of writing, there were still several hundred kilometres effectively only passable with a 4x4. The inland game parks, such as the once magnificent Gorongosa, suffered dreadfully during the war. They still

have some game, and attempts are being made to recreate their former glories, but it will be a while before they can compare with those in neighbouring countries.

There are potentially beautiful holiday spots in the area north of Beira, such as the coastal town of Pemba, but they are only really accessible by small plane, and there is little development once there. On the ground, the north is still largely impassable, except for those truly dedicated to hard-core adventure. Travellers should expect expedition conditions. Drive a 4x4 in convoy with at least one other vehicle, take your own spares and all supplies.

Never drive off the roads, or walk on unmarked beaches. Mine-clearing operations have been going on for years; known mine-fields are marked, but there are still many lurking underground.

Geographically, the magnificent coast apart, the country is largely low-lying, hot, humid and, in many areas, swampy. Until the determined arrival of modern medicine, the few colonists who came were trapped into small enclaves by disease and, even today, malaria is only one of several tropical diseases that cause serious problems. Take advice, have inoculations and guard against malaria (see Travel Essentials, pp. 20–22).

MAPUTO

In 1498, Vasco da Gama sailed into Delagoa Bay. The European's first port of call was the spot which eventually became the capital, Lourenço Marques. After independence, the city's name changed to Maputo.

Maputo currently has a population of about two million, down dramatically from an over-crowded five million at the height of the war, when refugees flooded into camps and shanty towns. This was the only part of Mozambique that was never under direct attack. The city has also been the centre of all relief and reconstruction efforts, and therefore has a large expat population.

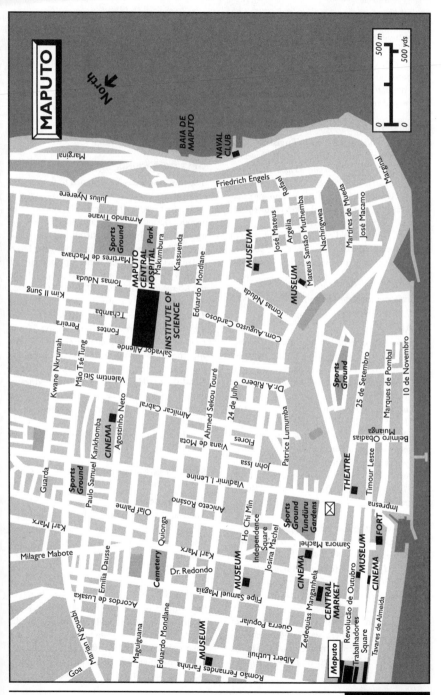

MAPUTO

North

BAIA DE
MAPUTO

NAVAL
CLUB

Marginal

500 m
500 yds

Friedrich Engels

Julius Nyerere

Armando Tivane

Sports
Ground

Mártires de Machava

Makumbura

Kassuenda

Park

Tomas Nduda

MAPUTO
CENTRAL
HOSPITAL

Kim II Sung

Tchamba

Fontes

Pereira

Salvador Allende

INSTITUTE OF
SCIENCE

Kwane Nkrumah

Mão Tsé Tung

Valentim Siti

Eduardo Mondlane

Com. Augusto Cardoso

Tomas Nduda

MUSEUM

José Mateus

Argélia

Rafael

Mateus Sansão Muthemba

Nachingwea

Mártires de Mueda

José Macamo

Marginal

MUSEUM

Dr. A. Ribeiro

Sports
Ground

25 de Setembro

Marques de Pombal

10 de Novembro

Agostinho Neto

Amílcar Cabral

Ahmed Sekou Touré

24 de Julho

Flores

Patrice Lumumba

Belmiro Obadias
Muianga

Paulo Samuel Kankhomba

CINEMA

Viana de Mota

John Issa

Timour Leste

THEATRE

Guarda

Sports
Ground

Olaf Palme

Aniceto Rosado

Vladimir I. Lenine

Imprensa

Karl Marx

Milagre Mabote

Emília Dausse

Quionga

Dr. Redondo

Karl Marx

Ho Chi Min

Independence
Square

Josina Machel

Sports
Ground

Tundúru
Gardens

Samora Machel

MUSEUM

CINEMA

FORT

Acordos de Lusaka

Cemetery

Flipe Samuel Magaia

MUSEUM

Guerra Popular

CINEMA

CENTRAL
MARKET

MUSEUM

Goa

Marian N'goabi

Maguiguana

Eduardo Mondlane

Romão Fernandes Farinha

MUSEUM

Albert Luthuli

Zedequias Manganhela

Revolução de Outubro

Tavares de Almeida

Maputo

Trabalhadores
Square

Nevertheless, the city has a pleasant, welcoming atmosphere. There are street vendors, but few beggars; there is some street crime, but, on the whole, it is safe enough to walk around during daylight. Try not to leave cars unguarded or they will be dismantled before you return.

TOURIST INFORMATION

Empresa Nacional de Turismo (the Mozambique Tourist Office), *Av. 25 Septembre 1203, corner Av. Vlademir Lenine (CP614), Maputo; tel: 01-421 795, fax: 01-421 796.* This office is worth the effort as there is no information available. Instead, use the local tour operators (see Getting Around, opposite).

Above all, get hold of an up-to-date copy of the invaluable *Mozambique Time Out*, published twice yearly, which is available free from most hotels.

ARRIVING AND DEPARTING

By Air

358

Maputo Airport is 8 km from the city centre; *tel: 01-465 074.* There is no public transport except for taxis. Negotiate a price before getting in; it should cost around M100,000 (at the time of writing).

The Mozambiquan national airline, **LAM**, *tel: 01-465 026,* flies to Paris and Lisbon, as well as Johannesburg, Harare and Durban, and domestic services. There are also regular scheduled services to Lisbon and on throughout Europe on the main Portuguese carrier, **TAP**, *tel: 01-465 065/3.* **SAA**, *tel: 01-420 740,* has frequent flights to Johannesburg, with onward connections.

Metavia Airlines runs regular scheduled services between **Maputo**, *tel: 01-465 487,* **Durban**, *tel: 031-469 3400;* **Nelspruit**, *tel: 01311-43141/2* and **Johannesburg**, *tel: 011-394 3780/1.* Other airlines serving Maputo include Air Zimbabwe, Royal Swazi Airlines and Air France.

For scheduled small planned services or charter flights anywhere within Mozambique, contact local charter companies: **NAT Air**, *tel: 01-741 902;* **Sabin Air**, *tel: 01-465 108;* or **STA**, *tel: 01-491 765.*

By Rail

Station: *Praça Dos Trabahadores; tel: 01-431 269.* The only passenger services are to Johannesburg, with occasional visits by the cruise trains (see pp. 54–56).

By Coach

Panthera Azul, *tel: 01-494 238,* run luxury coach services to Johannesburg, Durban and Swaziland.

GETTING AROUND

The few local buses are designed to ferry workers to and from the suburbs and are not terribly useful to tourists. It is generally safe to walk around during the day, although it can get excruciatingly hot; at night always use transport. There are **taxi** ranks beside the Hotel Polana, *tel: 01-493 255;* Banco de Socorros, *tel: 01-428 493,* Maternidade, *tel: 01-494 562;* and the Mercado Central, *tel: 01-429 593.*

Local tour operators, such as **Polana Tours**, *Hotel Polana; tel: 01-493 533; fax: 01-493 538,* or **Nkomati Safaris**; *tel/fax: 01-492 612,* operate regular guided tours of the city and the surrounding area, and are happy to organise private tours. **Arlando Langa Pendula**; *tel: 01-417 507,* is a friendly Mozambiquan, with a good car, who speaks excellent English and will be your driver/guide at an affordable daily rate.

The most convenient option is to hire a car (see p. 52).

STAYING IN MAPUTO

Accommodation

There are now several good hotels up and running in Maputo, but if you have the money and want the style, there is really only one. The **Polana** *(Ka), Av. Julius Nyerere, 1380 Maputo; tel: 01-491 001/7; fax: 01-491 480* (expensive) was designed by Sir Herbert Baker, built in 1920, and is one of the great colonial hotels of the world. After suffering during the war, it was taken over and thoroughly overhauled by the South African Karos group in 1990. Today, it is once again cool, elegant, efficient, beautiful and oozes atmosphere. Even if you can't afford to stay here, have drinks or a meal on the terrace

Bloody Footprints in the Sand

Everything in the country's history has conspired against it. Originally made up of a whole series of small kingdoms, Mozambique's first contact with the outside world came with the Arab traders of the Omani Sultanate, from the 7th century AD onwards. They swept south, setting up their southern capital in Sofala, just south of Beira, and trading inland from there for gold, ivory and slaves. In the late 15th century, the first Portuguese arrived, ousting the Arabs, but looking for the same commodities. Many of the southern Tsonga people are in Mozambique because their ancestors were chased off their own land by Shaka and the Zulu Mfecane (see pp.63–64). When the British moved north in the late 19th century, they got together with the Portuguese to settle the national boundaries on modern lines.

The Portuguese were laid-back colonial masters. They were far less bothered than the British about the development of infra-structure. Roads, schools, health services and all the other practical aspects of the country remained rather shaky. The big plantation owners openly asset-stripped what they could and sent the proceeds back to Portugal. On the other hand, they were far less colour-conscious than their neighbours – many openly and happily married black women, and, despite the later horrors, their liberal attitude has left behind a memory of brotherhood.

In Mozambique, as in the rest of the colonised world, the mid 20th century saw the growth of a powerful and vocal nationalist movement. In 1974, a socialist government gained power in Portugal for the first time. By the following year, they had withdrawn abruptly from all their colonies, taking with them everything they could carry, and leaving a poor, under-developed and under-educated country to fend for itself. Power went overwhelmingly to the hardline Marxist Frelimo, who set about creating a true socialist state, nationalising all land and industry and destroying the few remaining wealth-spinners in the process.

At the same time, the South African and Zimbabwean governments, wary of the effect of having Marxists on their doorstep, helped fund an anarchic violent opposition, Renamo, with the sole purpose of destablising the country. They succeeded all too well and Mozambique spiralled into a devastating civil war that lasted almost 20 years.

Today, things are changing again. In 1986, with the Iron Curtain splintering, hardline President Samora Machel was killed in a plane crash. Joaquim Chissano, Mozambique's current president, was more pragmatic and began to allow the rebirth of private enterprise. In 1990, with harmony breaking out in South Africa, Renamo lost its funding and finally the war ended. A UN-supervised ceasefire was declared in Oct 1992. Progress is slow and often painful, but the country is now peaceful. The people are coming out of shell-shock, billions of dollars of foreign aid are being poured in to help rebuild the shattered community.

359

and dream of the great and inglorious, from Somerset Maugham to Graham Greene, who have been there before you. This is the social centre of upmarket Maputo, with bars, restaurants, laundry, bakery, travel agency and a host of other spin-offs provided to keep expat life ticking over. As an alternative, try the **Hotel Cardoso**, *Av. Martires de Mueda 707; tel: 01-491 071/5; fax: 01-491 804* (expensive), whose clifftop location offers the best views in the city.

A little lower down the price scale, the **Hotel Terminus**, *Av. Francisco Orlando Magumbwé (corner of Av. Ahmed Sekou Touré); tel: 01-491 333; fax: 01-491 284* (moderate) offers less atmosphere, but plenty of efficient comfort. A little way out, along the beachfront, the **Kaya Kwanga**, *Av. D Joao de Castro 321; tel: 01-492 707/492 806; fax: 01-492 704* (moderate–expensive) was first built as an Italian workers' enclave, then used during the ceasefire as housing for Renamo and now operates as a friendly, family-oriented hotel, with accommodation in cabins throughout extensive grounds. Further still along the beach road, the **Costa do Sol**, *The Marginal; tel: 01-455 115; fax: 01-455 162* (cheap) is a cheerfully delapidated Portuguese house, which has a few simple but comfortable rooms above an excellent seafood restaurant. There are no backpackers' lodges, youth hostels or campsites.

Eating and Drinking

All the hotels listed above have good dining rooms. The **Polana** is the smartest (and priciest) in town, while the **Costa do Sol** probably does the best seafood at an affordable price, accompanied by live jazz at the weekends. For elegant drinking, you can't beat the magnificent terraces of the Polana or **Cardoso**; for something less formal, try the noisy, popular Club at **Kaya Kwango**, with live entertainment at weekends.

Outside the hotels, the local yacht club, **Clube Marítimo**, *Marginal; tel: 01-741 345* (moderate) does light lunches, wonderful seafood and an excellent buffet for Sunday lunch on an open terrace beside the sea. **Piri-Piri**, *3842 Av. 24 de Julho; tel: 01-492 379* (cheap–moderate) is one of the city's oldest established restaurants, serving those great Mozambiquan stalwarts, spicy piri-piri chicken and prawns. **Mundo's**, *657 Av. Julius Nyerere; tel: 01-428 872* (moderate; closed Tues) is a lively pub-restaurant serving a typically South African steakhouse mix of steaks, burgers, pizza, and so on. For something cheap and cheerful, the **Feira Popular**, *off R. Marques de Pombal,* beside the docks, has up to 20 small, local restaurants. There is parking inside, but don't go dressed up.

Communication

Main Post Office: *30 Av. 25 de Setembre.* There are public fax and telex facilities here and at the post office at *239 Av. 24 de Julho.*

Embassies and Consulates

See pp. 31–32.

Medical Care

Clínica da Sommerschield, *52 Rua Pereira do*

Largo; tel: 01-493 924/494 278; fax: 01-493 927; **Clinica Cruz Azul**, *414 Av. Karl Marx; tel: 01-430 214; 420 213;* **Red Cross**; *tel: 01-425 297.*

Money

The **Banco Internacional de Moçambique** has two branches at *773* and *2096 Av. 24 de Julho.* These both handle foreign exchange, open longer hours than normal (Mon–Fri 0745–1200, 1400–1500) and have ATMs. There is also an efficient bureau de change in the **Hotel Polana** (see p.358).

SHOPPING

The **Interfranca Shopping Centre**, *Av. 24 de Julho,* and the **Mundo Complex**, *657 Av. Julius Nyerere,* both have a wide range of useful shops. For souvenirs, have a look first at **Artedif**, *20a Marginal; tel: 01-498 239* (open daily 0900–1530), on the beachfront. There are some lovely things on sale, made by disabled people, so your money goes to a worthy cause. A group of disabled women make sturdy leather bags in a small workshop next door. There are two artists' studios/co-ops: the **Núcleo de Arte**, *194 R. da Argélia, off Av. Julius Nyerere; tel: 01-493 211* (open Mon–Fri 0900–1200, 1400–1800, Sat 0900–1200) and the **Cooperativa de Arte Maconde**, *798 Av. Marianne N'guabi; tel: 01-416 331,* both selling a mix of really creative fine art and derivative tat at generally over-inflated prices. There is a good permanent **craft market** camped outside the Hotel Polana, while on Saturday mornings, the **Mercado Artesanato**, *Praça 25 de Junho,* is a hive of activity with everything from wire helicopters and maconde carvings to beautiful handmade furniture on sale.

In this city, much of the best shopping is done at street level. The markets are also buzzing with atmosphere and well worth a stop, just for fun. People are usually OK with cameras, as long as you ask permission first, and give them time to get used to you. Many will ask for copies of prints; if you agree, make sure you send them, for the sake of future travellers. Security is pretty lax, so don't carry valuables. The **Mercado Central**, *between Av. 25 de Setembro and Av. Zedequias Manganhela* (open

Maconde Carvings

The Maconde people of the far north have always had an affinity with wood; their creation myth tells of a wild man who lived alone in the forest and carved himself a wife from a log. Their traditional carvings were ritual – a female form carried to represent the matrilineal origins of the family and bullet-headed *mapico* dance masks. From the 1960s onwards, *Shetanis* (gargoyle-like devils) began to appear in their work, and soon afterwards came the first *Ujamaa* carvings – elaborate, multi-figured, totem-like sculptures, with an entire saga or family history bound into a single piece of wood. Today, a further progression has led to more flowing work, with mystical figures emerging from the natural line of the branch, while the influence of these extraordinary, dream-like, sometimes nightmarish styles has also spread to painting and pottery.

daily, Sun morning only) is the main city centre general market, selling fruit and vegetables, meat and fish, plastic pots and jewellery. The **Mercado Janeth**, *opposite the church on Av. Mao Tse Tung,* is basically a fruit and vegetable market, but does have some other goods. The **Mercado Estrela**, *Bairro Alto Maé, off Av. Emila Daússe,* is also known as the 'Red Cross Market', because it is near the Red Cross Hospital, or the 'thieves' market', for obvious reasons. This is one of the largest markets in the city, selling everything from rip-off designer clothes to fridges, or even the component parts of the car you left parked without security.

Each evening, as the little fishing boats head in, the **Bazar do Peixe** (Fish Market), *opposite Clube Marítimo, on the Marginal,* gears up for a frenzy of selling, amongst others, still wriggling octopus, carpet-flat rays, vivid blue lobsters and, best of all, huge, luscious 'LM' prawns, the local speciality and ranked amongst the finest in the world. To find something to drink with them, head over to the **Barracas do Museu**, *R. dos Lusiadas, off Av. 24 de Julho,* better known as the

'bottle market'. Here, amidst a maze of tiny shanty bars, are stalls selling any sort of alcohol you could possibly desire, most of it at ridiculously low prices.

ENTERTAINMENT

Possibilities are relatively limited but improving all the time. The only decent cinema is the newly reopened **Cinema Scala**, *tel: 01-422 901.* A mix of art movies, theatre, dance and other cultural entertainments is laid on by the **Centro Cultural Franco-Moçambicano**, *Av. Samora Machel; tel: 01-420 786.* The city's better clubs include the loud, bright, upmarket **Clube 7**, *Av. Vladimir Lenine; tel: 01-417 101* (open Thur–Sat, with a bar Tues–Sat), and **Clube Matchedje**, *3785 Av. 24 de Julho; tel: 01-402 153* (open Wed–Sun), a large restaurant/disco with live music on Wed and Thur. There is also live music at **Tchova Xita Duma**, *287 R. Sansão Mutemba; tel: 01-492 271* (jazz; Wed–Sat), known as the local bohemian hangout, and at **Clube Desportivo**, *behind Eagles Bar, Av. Zedequias Manganhela* (local rock, weekends only).

One of the most popular young venues is the **Mini-Golf Complex**, *on the Marginal; tel: 01-490 381,* which has mini-golf, putt-putt, a gym, pool, restaurant, bar and, on Fri and Sat, an open-air disco.

SIGHTSEEING

Maputo sprawls along the river estuary and seafront, and across the inland hills, with no discernible centre. One of the best ways to start is by spending a couple of hours driving round the city's grid layout to get your bearings. Basically, the two waterfronts are roughly at right angles, with the Hotel Cardoso on the high ground near the point where they connect. From here, the **Marginal** stretches north along the **Baia de Maputo** to the marina and beaches, while on the cliff above are the Hotel Polana and the 'posh' district of large, well-groomed houses around *Av. Friedrich Engels* (many now housing embassies). To the southeast, along the estuary waterfront, are the port and, just inland, the so-called business centre around *Av. 25 de Septembre.* Inland are huge apartment blocks of crumbling concrete draped

361

in laundry, shanty towns of reed, cardboard and sun-dried brick, while in the midst of it all still crouch a few beautiful old colonial buildings. Superficially, the city has survived intact. Look more closely and many of its buildings are rotting, with holes in their roofs and glassless windows. Many of those that have been maintained belong to the military or government and should not be photographed; some have been carefully restored as churches or offices, the majority are peeling and neglected and in desperate need of money and attention. The poverty is obvious all around you, but Maputo still has immense charm, as do its laid-back and welcoming inhabitants. Parts of the city centre are currently one large building site as the race to regenerate hots up.

Independence Square

The centre of 'official' Maputo is the *Praça da Independência*, totally dominated by two buildings. The gleaming white art deco **Catedral da Nossa Senhora da Conceição** (Our Lady of Conception), built in 1936–44, has a soaring west front and some fine stained glass. Next door is the **Conselho Executivo**, the imposing, neo-classical City Hall, built in 1945. A short way down the hill, *off Av. Samora Machel,* the entrance to the Jardim Tunduru is presided over by a bronze **statue** of liberator and first President, Samora Machel. Next to it is the extraordinary **Casa de Ferro** (Iron House), a prefab, all-metal, neo-Gothic house designed by the French engineer, Eiffel (of the Tower fame), constructed by a Belgian company and assembled in 1892 to be the governor's mansion. When complete, it proved, inevitably, to be a sweat box and totally unsuitable. Now air-conditioned, it houses the Department of Museums. **Jardim Tunduru** was designed in 1885 by English gardener, Thomas Honney. Today, it is a cool, green wonderland of exotic trees, flowering plants and pretty statuary. For permission to enter the greenhouses, ask at the office opposite.

Museums

There are two must-see museums in Maputo, and several others of more limited interest. The **Museu da Revolução**, *3003 Av. 24 de Julho;*

tel: 01-400 348 (open Mon, Tues, Thur, Fri 0900–1200, 1400–1800, Sat 1400–1800, Sun 0900–1200, 1500–1800; M500) is as frozen in time as any of its exhibits. This is a rivetting, earnest, revolutionary account of the nationalist struggle and its aftermath, filled with photos. Unfortunately none of the many display boards are in English, so try and take a Portuguese speaker with you; it's worth it. The **Museu Nacional de Arte**, *1233 Av. Ho Chi Min; tel: 01-420 264* (open Tues–Sun 1500–1900; free) is a beautifully displayed collection of the best of Mozambiquan art, with a small permanent collection alongside regularly changing exhibitions. Artists represented include Naguib, Reinata Sadimba, Naftal Langa and Chissano. Alberto Chissano also warrants his own gallery, the **Museu Chissano**, *R. Torre de Vale, Bairro Sal, Matola; tel: 01-752 703* (open Tues–Sun 0900–1200, 1500–1700; free), with a number of the great man's works, a small collection of other art, children's toys and a restaurant serving traditional Mozambiquan food.

The much-photographed and elaborately palacial **Museum de História Natural** (Natural History Museum), *Praça de Travessia do Zambeze; tel: 01-491 145,* is currently officially closed to the public, due to the large holes in the roof and permanent inch of water all over the floor. However, the curator, who has been reduced to making film sets in the back yard in an effort to mend the roof, will happily let you in. It is free, but a donation would be greatly appreciated. Inside, a central animal hall (look for the elephant foetuses) is surrounded by collections of fish, insects and other beasties. Also take a stroll in the shady gardens, keeping a wary eye open for concrete dinosaurs. The **Museu de Geologia**, *355 Av. 24 de Julho; tel: 01-743 053* (open Tues–Fri 1500–1800, Sat 0900–1200, 1500–1800; free) is the national geology collection, perhaps of greater interest to those who understand rocks, but with enormous visual appeal for all. The **Museu da Moeda**, *Praça 25 de Junho; tel: 01-420 290* (open Tues, Wed, Thur, Sat 0900–1200, 1400–1630, Fri 0900–1200, Sun 1400–1700; M1000) is the Museum of Money, a fascinating study of local and international currency dating back to the days of cowrie shells, and including all the colonial coppers. The building itself is also worth a visit, as the oldest and one of the most beautiful houses in Maputo, designed in true Latin style, with wide doors and a central courtyard to catch every breath of cool air. Just across the square is the original low clay-built Portuguese fort, the **Fortaleza** (officially open Sat–Sun 0700–1700 only, but a small donation to the watchman can work wonders). Inside are some bits of colonial military history, a few old cannons, and a collection of neglected Portuguese statuary.

Nearby, take a quick look the **CFM Railway Station**, *Praça Dos Trabahadores*, which has to be about the most over-the-top ever built, and now gaudily painted to add impact. In front of it is a World War I memorial by Portuguese sculptor, Rui Cameiro. According to locals, it honours a woman who killed a dangerous cobra, when it dropped out of a tree into the cauldron of boiling porridge on her head.

The Marginal leads along the seafront to Maputo's own **beaches**, a narrow rim of sand backed by casuarina trees. It is pretty, the little beach bars are entertaining and it is worth coming down to watch the fishing boats come home in the late afternoon, but think twice about swimming here.

Out of Town

Many of the most pleasant activities in the area surrounding Maputo involve messing about in boats. To do it in real style, hire the *Free Spirit,* a 56 ft, 4-cabin, 8-berth catamaran, which is fully geared up for water skiiing, snorkelling, diving, and deep-sea fishing, as well as sailing. Booking through **Polana Tours** (see p.358); prices US$125 per person or US$550 per day for the whole boat, all inclusive with drinks.

Letoni Ferries; *tel: 01-743 139* (depart daily on demand at 0900, returning 1500; US$50/R200 per person) can ferry you across to **Inhaca Island**, *34 km offshore*. Much of the little island is a nature reserve, which offers lovely bush rambling. More importantly though, it has wonderful beaches, snorkelling and diving on virtually untouched coral reefs. Accommodation is available at the 3-star **Hotel Inhaca**; *tel: 01-427 372; fax: 01-420 424* (moderate), whose rather basic buildings are set

in pleasant gardens, while along the track, in the village, the local restaurant and bar serves freshly-caught prawns and other seafood on rough wooden tables with the sand beneath your toes, the stars above your head and a sea breeze rattling the palm fronds.

About 110 km south of Maputo, on fairly dire roads (passable slowly in an ordinary car; allow 2–3 hrs), **Ponto do Ouro** is the country's most southerly resort, right on the border with Kwazulu-Natal in South Africa. The recently renovated and reopened **Motel do Mar**; reservations (South Africa), *tel: 012-432 846; fax: 012-436 659* (cheap–moderate) has accommodation in beachfront cabanas, with a restaurant, bar, beach patio and camping and caravan sites. Activities on offer include diving, snorkelling, fishing, boat trips, surfing and nature walks. Nearby, the **Msala Elephant Park** (moderate; bookings through Nkomati Safaris) is gradually being redeveloped, with a luxury tented bush camp. This has the best of all worlds, as it is a game reserve with its own sea frontage. Wildlife in the area includes elephants, a variety of small game, over 450 species of bird, coral reefs for snorkelling and turtles, in season.

Head north from Maputo on the Beira road for 34 km, then turn right, catch the ferry (wait on shore till it is ready to leave; there is a snack bar to entertain you) across the muddy Nkomati River. Continue for about 10 km to **Macaneta** and the little town of **Marracuene**. This was a popular resort in colonial times, and much of the architecture remains, although barely standing in some cases. There is an excellent local market on Saturdays, brilliant fresh fish at any time, the locals are friendly and the beaches great. The only problem is that everyone thinks so, and it gets very crowded at weekends.

If you have the money, head up through grassy wetlands stuffed with birdlife and abandoned cashew plantations to **Jays Camp** (no tel; advance booking through Polana Tours, p.358; cheap), a delightful small, friendly lodge offering self-catering accommodation in comfortably furnished dune-top rondavels, a campsite, bar, safe parking, picnic sites for day visitors (US$5 per car) and a superb beach. A restaurant

363

serving simple meals (salad, bread and the catch of the day) operates at weekends and at other times on request.

VILANCULOS

Vilanculos is about 600 km up the coast from Maputo, on good roads all the way, through various small historic towns, such as Inhambane and Xai-Xai, many of which now have camp-sites, small hotels and rudimentary restaurants. At Inhambane, the **Barra Lodge Beach Resort**; reservations (South Africa); *tel/fax: 011-314 3355* (cheap–moderate) has self-catering cottages, camping and caravan sites, a restaurant, bar, shop, diving and deep-sea fish-ing, and watersports.

The low-lying seafront in the Vilanculos area is generally reckoned to be some of the most beautiful in the country, with coconut palms, cashew trees and baobabs towering over the scrubby sand, while offshore coral reefs calm the waves and add spectacle to the water. Land for miles around is being snapped up by hungry developers and this looks set to become the real centre of mass market tourism in Mozambique. Meantime, for a truly off-beat getaway, **Pontamingo** *(Bv), 32 km south of Vilanculos*, is a small upmarket guest lodge, right on the waterfront.

Vilanculos is also the nearest town to the **Bazaruto Archipelago**, *35 km offshore*, a small group of idyllic islands, which kept Mozam-bique's tourism alive through the worst days of the civil war by flying tourists and supplies straight from Johannesburg. There are now also transfers from Maputo and Vilanculos, but be prepared for the cost of these to mount (Maputo–Bazaruto is US$250 return).

There are four islands, of which the largest is **Bazaruto Island** (35 km by 7 km), with a population of around 2300. Accommodation is provided at the **Bazaruto Island Lodge**; reservations (South Africa) *tel: 011-447 3528; fax: 011-880 5364* (expensive), with A-frame thatched chalets surrounding a pool area, lodge dining room and open-air bar. To the south, on **Benguerra Island**, is the **Benguela Lodge**; reservations (South Africa) *tel: 011-483 2734; fax: 011-729 3767* (expensive), with stilted thatched bungalows, while on **Magaruque**

Island is the **Magaruque Island Lodge** *(La)*, reservations (Zimbabwe) *tel: 14-734 043/6; fax: 14-708 119* (expensive). Activities in all the island lodges include walks, bird-watching, swimming, snorkelling, diving and fishing (beach and deep-sea), while their dining rooms specialise in spectacular seafood. Tiny **Santa Carolina** (3 km by 500 m), nicknamed Paradise Island, was a 19th-century fort and penal colony.

BEIRA

ACCOMMODATION

There are two good hotels in town: the 4-star **Hotel Moçambique**, *R. de Bagamoyo; tel: 03-325 011; fax: 03-325 060* (expensive) and the 3-star **Hotel Embaixador**, *R. Major Serpa; tel: 03-323 121; fax: 03-323 788* (expensive), both of which have satellite TV, modern telephones, coffee shops, restaurants and conference facili-ties. As a reasonable, cheaper alternative, try the **Hotel Infante**, *R. Jaime Ferreira 218; tel: 03-323 042*.

SIGHTSEEING

Mozambique's second city and largest port, Beira was founded as a military post in 1887. It has always been important politically and eco-nomically as the closest port to Zimbabwe, and the only viable alternative to South Africa. It gained in stature in 1902, with the opening of railway inland and again in the 1950s, with the laying of a parallel oil pipeline. It suffered badly from the UN economic sanctions against Rhodesia in the 1960s and 1970s, with a naval blockade cruising off the coast. After indepen-dence, Zimbabwe poured money, arms and troops into Mozambique in an effort to keep the 'Beira Corridor' of road, rail and pipeline open.

Beira was also traditionally the playground of white Rhodesians, who came here for sun, sand, wine, women and song – there were plenty of all on offer. Like Maputo, Beira is making strenuous efforts to recreate a holiday environment and regain some of that valuable custom. So far there is little to do, but there are a number of fine old houses and the beaches and markets are good.

NAMIBIA

Namibia, roughly four times the size of Germany, only has a population of a little over 1 million. Founded as a German colony in 1890, it was handed over to South Africa at the end of World War I under a League of Nations Mandate. It remained part of that country, in spite of protests by the locals and the United Nations, until it eventually received independence in 1990. There is still a distinctly Germanic air about the place, most obvious in the architecture of coastal Luderitz and Swakopmund, and the hilly capital, Windhoek. There is even a local tribe, the Herero, whose married women still wear the full heavy skirts and cloth headdresses of 19th-century German missionaries.

DIRECT ROUTE: 2370 KM

365

ROUTES

DIRECT ROUTE

→ There is a vast amount of driving involved in these routes, but most of it is on good roads. Cape Town to Vioolsdrif on the South Africa/Namibia border is 670 km, straight up the N7 (for a slower journey, see Cape Town–Springbok, pp. 138–143; the border is 118 km north of Springbok).

It is 799 km from the Noordoewer border post (Namibian side; open 24 hrs) to Windhoek up the B1. From Windhoek, continue on up the B1 to Otavi (364 km), then bear right on to the B8 and continue through **Grootfontein** (96 km) and on up to Rundu (258 km). At Rundu, the B8 bears sharp right and hugs the Angola border then the edge of the **Caprivi Game Reserve** as it continues south-east to the Mohembo borderpost (183 km; open

0600–1800) with Botswana. Alternatively, continue right along the B8 through Katima Mulilo to Ngoma and the borderpost with Zimbabwe (open 0600–1800), a short distance from the Victoria Falls (see p. 400). Distance: 2370 km; allow 3–4 days minimum.

SCENIC ROUTE

▶ Cross the South African/Namibian border at the Noordoewer border post, near Vioolsdrif (open 24 hrs). From here, take the main highway, B1, for 37 km, then branch left to the **Ai-Ais Hot Springs** and the **Fish River Canyon** (82 km). From Ai-Ais, take the C10, which leads back to the B1 (74 km). Turn left and head for **Keetmanshoop** (191 km).

From here, head west on the B4, along the first side track to the coast. It is 271 km to **Luderitz**. Retrace your steps to Keetmanshoop and continue north on the B1 through **Mariental** (226 km) to **Windhoek** (267 km) and **Okahandja** (71 km).

At Okahandja, turn left and head west on the B2 to **Swakopmund** (296 km). From here, there are two side tracks, heading south on the B2 to **Walvis Bay** and the **Namib-Naukluft Park**, or north to the **National West Coast Tourist Recreational Area** and the **Skeleton Coast Park** (see relevant sections for detailed directions).

Return to Swakopmund and head back inland along the B2. At Karabib (175 km), turn left and head north on the C33 through Omaruru to **Otiwarongo** (191 km). Here, branch left on to the C38 and continue via Outjo (70 km) to the Andersson Gate of the **Etosha National Park** and **Okaukuejo Camp** (113 km). The C38 passes through the park via Halali camp to **Namutoni Camp**. Exit from Etosha National Park via Namutoni and the Von Lindquist Gate and continue along the C38 to the junction with the B1 (23 km). Turn right and head for Tsumeb (76 km), then take the C42 to **Grootfontein** (57 km). Here, bear left on to the B8 and head up to Rundu (258 km), after which branch right at Katere (113 km) and head for the **Kaudom Game Park** (55 km). Return to the B8 and continue to Bagani (70 km), the entrance to the **Caprivi Game Reserve**. From here, turn right for

Mahango and the **Mohembo** borderpost with Botswana (32 km; open 0600–1800). Alternatively, continue along the B8, which becomes a gravel road through the game reserve, reverting to tar at the far end (191 km), then keep going through Katima Mulilo to Ngoma and the Zimbabwe border (see above). Distance: over 3500 km (excluding the side tracks from Swakopmund to the Skeleton Coast Park, or the Namib-Naukluft Park); allow at least a week, preferably two or three.

FISH RIVER CANYON PARK

Enter the park via Ai-Ais Hot Springs. Open: day visitors are admitted from dawn to dusk but must leave before 2300; overnight visitors with reserved accommodation may enter at any time of the night, but may not leave between 2300 and 0600. For reservations and fees, see box.

Ai-Ais (meaning 'hot spring'), a low-lying resort at the southern end of the canyon (80 km from the main viewpoint), is the best base from which to explore the region. Temperatures here have been known to soar to 48°C at noon and they seldom drop below 35°C. There is a hot spring here, known to the early San and Khoi people. The resort (open daily sunrise–sunset; N$10 per person and N$10 per car, plus N$2 per person for the thermal baths) has accommodation (cheap) in bungalows and huts, a caravan and camping site, a restaurant (open daily 0700–0900, 1200–1400, 1800–2200), shop, swimming pool, thermal spa, petrol station and landing strip. It is closed to the public between early Nov–mid Mar, when it's simply too hot to be here.

At **Hobas**, 10 km from the canyon, near the northern end, has campsites (cheap) and a pool.

SIGHTSEEING

Located in a harsh, forbidding area, between the Fish and Gariep (Orange) Rivers, this awesome canyon, the second largest in the world after America's Grand Canyon, is 161 km long, up to 27 km wide and nearly 550m deep. The geological processes which led to its formation began about 1800 million years ago. A 25 km road running along the eastern edge leads to a number of viewing platforms. The sights are magnificent and should not be missed. Paths

National Parks

Game parks, most of which are state owned, are a special feature of this country. In the north, the Etosha National Park ('the place of dry water') supports one of the largest concentrations of wildlife in Africa. Still more excellent game-viewing can be found in the Caprivi Strip, the oddly shaped neck of land that stretches out into the Zambezi Valley, between Angola and Botswana

Reservation procedures and entry fees are standardised for all state-owned Namibian reserves. Admission is N$10 per person and N$10 per vehicle. Reservations for all accommodation must be made via: **Director of Tourism**, *Kaiserliche Landesvermessung Building, corner John Meinert and Molte Sts (P. Bag 13267), Windhoek; tel: 061-236 975, fax: 061-224 900* (open Mon–Fri 0800–1500). All applications for reservations must be accompanied by an ID or passport number, full address, home and work phone and fax numbers; type of accommodation required; dates of arrival and departure; and number of adults and number/age of children.

wind down to the floor of the canyon, where the Fish River flows through a succession of pools that dry up when there is a drought.

There is excellent hiking in the area, including a famous 85 km-long, 5-day hiking trail running along the canyon's bottom. Only open from early May–end Sept, it has somewhat draconian rules. You must apply well in advance to the Windhoek parks office for a permit, pay a fee of N$50 per person and submit a medical certificate of physical fitness at Hobas before you begin.

KEETMANSHOOP

Tourist Office: *5th Ave; tel: 0631-2095.* Open Mon–Fri 0800–1300, 1400–1700. Information on all southern Namibia available.

The **Canyon Hotel**, *11 Wheeler St; tel: 0631-23361, fax: 0631-23714* (cheap) is well situated and has a restaurant. **Campsite: Lafenis Rest Camp**, *8th Ave; tel: 0631-24316*, has camping and caravan sites, self-catering bungalows and a pool.

Keetmanshoop, originally a mission station – 'the hope of Keetman' – straddles the banks of the Swartmodder River (the Black Mud River), which rarely has water in it. Its bare course is somewhat depressing, except during the odd, violent flash flood. This is the first major Namibian town on the route north. It has a distinctly German air, with many colonial buildings in good repair, including the **old Post Office** (1910), now home to the Tourist Office. The **Keetmanshoop Museum**, *in the*

Rhenish Mission Church (1895); tel: 0631-23316 extension 134 (open Mon–Fri 0700–1230, 1330–1630; free) outlines local history. Near the town, the **Quiver Tree Forest**, *Gariganus Farm, 14 km north-east of Keetmashoop on route 29 (follow the signs)* is a dense stand of about 250 of these extraordinary desert aloes, whose branches were hollowed out by the San for use as quivers for their arrows. Five kilometres further on (signposted) is the so-called **Giant's Playground**, a magnificent landscape strewn with black basalt boulders formed some 180 million years ago.

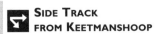 **367**

▼ **SIDE TRACK**
FROM KEETMANSHOOP

LÜDERITZ

Tourist Office: Lüderitz Foundation, *Upper Bismarck St; tel: 06331-2532* (open Mon–Fri 0830–1200 1400–1600, Sat 0830–1200).

ACCOMMODATION AND FOOD

The modern **Hotel Zum Sperrgebiet**, *corner Woermann and Stettinger Streets; tel: 06331-3411, fax: 06331-3414* (moderate–expensive) has rooms overlooking the city, harbour and bay, indoor heated pool and restaurant open to all. Both the **Bay View Hotel**, *Bismarck St; tel: 06331-2288, fax: 06331-2402* (cheap) and the **Kapps Hotel**, *Bay Rd; tel: 06331-2701, fax: 06331-2402* (cheap) have good restaurants, which are open only to hotel guests. The **Lüderitz Rest Camp**; *tel: 06331-3351; fax: 06331-2869* (cheap) has basic bungalows and a good restaurant.

Alternatively, the **Casanova Inn Restaurant**, *Diaz St; tel: 06331-2855* (open lunch and dinner) is good for steaks and seafood, while **Franzels Restaurant**, *Tal St; tel: 06331-2292* (open lunch and dinner) is the place to go for German home cooking and seafood.

SIGHTSEEING

Where the icy South Atlantic meets the flaming Namib desert, the coast is a bleak place. When he first discovered the almost land-locked natural harbour that was to become Lüderitz in 1487, the great Portuguese explorer Bartholomew Dias named it the *Arejas do Inferno* – the 'sands of Hell'. For the next 400 years only whalers, a few traders and guano miners stopped here. Only in 1883 was it developed to any great extent, when a merchant from Bremen in Germany, Adolf Lüderitz, asked Bismarck to place the area under German protection. It was the first step towards the German colonisation of Namibia. The town really began to flourish after the first diamonds were discovered along the coast in 1908. Diamonds are still an important fact of life in Lüderitz – the town is wedged between two restricted diamond areas. Nowadays, it is also an important fishing centre and the point of export for karakul sheep pelts.

The town itself is still definitely Germanic, with some fine colonial and art nouveau architecture, such as the **Railway Station**, *corner Bahnhof and Bismarck Sts*, the **Goerke House**, *Diamond Hill*, and the Evangelical Lutheran **Felsenkirche**, *Kirche St, Diamond Hill*, (open Mon–Sat summer 1800–1900, winter 1700–1800; free, donations welcomed), designed in 1906 by Albert Bause, with a magnificent stained-glass window above the altar donated by Kaiser Wilhelm II. **Lüderitz Museum**, *Dias St; tel: 06331-2061* (open Mon–Fri 1530–1700; free) chronicles the saga of the

diamond prospecting, along with other local history and ethnography.

Kolmanskop Ghost Town, *10 km east of Lüderitz on the B4; tel: 06331-2582* (permit from the Tourist Office required, N\$10; 1 hr guided tours mornings only) was once a centre for the thriving diamond industry. In the early 1900s, it housed over 700 families, but the diggings yielded less and less and the inhabitants gradually departed, finally deserting it altogether after the discovery of Orange River diamonds.

In Lüderitz, **Kolmanskop Tour Company**; *tel: 06331-2445; fax: 06331-2526*, and **Luderitz Safaris and Tours**; *tel: 06331-2719, fax: 06331-2863*, conduct tours of the area; telephone well in advance as some sights require security clearance. ⬛

MARIENTAL

Tourist Office: *Municipality Offices, Stumfe St; tel: 0661-346*. Open Mon–Fri 0800–1230 1400–1700.

The **Sandberg Hotel**, *Marie Brandt St; tel/fax: 0661-2291* (cheap) provides light meals (lunch and dinner). **Anib Lodge**, *34 km east of Mariental on the C20 to Stampriet; tel: 0661-529, fax: 0661-516* (cheap–moderate) is an elegant oasis-like guest farm on the edge of the desert, with its own landing strip, restaurant, bird- and game-watching.

Mariental is a centre for Karakul sheep farming. Marooned in a wide grassy plain, the **Hardap Dam and Recreation Resort** *(head north from Mariental on the B1 for 15 km, branch left and follow the signs for 8.5 km); tel: 0661-381* to make arrangements prior to a visit, is open throughout the year. Overnight visitors with reserved accommodation may enter unrestricted, provided entrance and accommodation fees are paid during office hours; day visitors are admitted from dawn–1800. Accommodation (cheap) is in bungalows or at the camping and caravan sites, and there is a restaurant (open 0700–0900, 1200–1400, 1800–2200). For reservations and fees, see feature box, p.367.

The **Hardap Dam** is Namibia's biggest dam, a vast expanse of water popular with freshwater anglers and other water sports enthusiasts. It is surrounded by a game reserve,

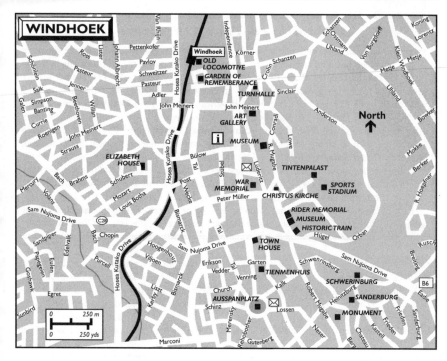

WINDHOEK

North ↑

0	250 m
0	250 yds

in which can be seen black rhino, oryx, spring-bok, Hartmann's mountain zebra and ostrich. Visitors can drive through the reserve or follow a circular walking trail of either 9 or 15 km.

WINDHOEK

Tourist Offices: Windhoek Tourism: *corner Pieter Muller and Independence Aves; tel: 061-290 2056* (open Mon–Fri 0800–1300, 1400–1700) for city information. **Namibia Tourism**: *Independence Ave; tel: 061-284 2366* (open Mon–Fri 0800–1300, 1400–1700) for country-wide information. For city tours, contact **Windhoek City Tours and Hiking**; *tel: 061-221 549; fax: 061-230 960.*

ACCOMMODATION AND FOOD

There are plenty of hotels to choose from in Windhoek. The **Kalahari Sands Hotel**, *Independence Ave; tel: 061-222 300; fax: 061-222 260* (expensive) is a large business hotel with all the trimmings, including a casino and good restaurant. For something with a little more style, try the **Hotel Heinitzburg**, *22*

Heinitzburg St; tel: 061-249 597; fax: 061-249 598 (moderate), a pseudo-castle, complete with battlements, custom-fitted with four-poster beds and handmade wooden furniture. Normally, bed and breakfast and gourmet dinners are available with advance notice. The **Kleines Heim Hotel Garni**, *Voland St; tel: 061-248 200; fax: 061-248 203* (moderate) was the Victorian colonial VIPs guesthouse, with large, airy rooms and a palm garden.

Cheaper hotels include the **Continental Hotel**, *Independence Ave; tel: 061-237 293, fax: 061-231 539*, and the **Hotel Furstenhof**, *Bulow St; tel: 061-237 380, fax: 061-228 751*, noted for its excellent food. Cheap guesthouses include the **Hotel-Pension Christophe**, *33 Heinitzburg St; tel: 061-240 777, fax: 061-248 560*, and the **Hotel-Pension Moni**, *7 Rieks St; tel: 061-228 350, fax: 061-227 124*. The **Cardboard Box**, *15 Johann Albrecht St; tel: 061-228 994; fax: 061-52128* (cheap) is a friendly backpackers' hostel.

Out of town, the **Airport Lodge**, *18 km east of Windhoek on the B6; tel/fax: 061-231 491*

Namibian Tour Operators

The range of tours and safaris on offer here is phenomenal, and with some of the most startlingly beautiful scenery in very remote locations, they often represent the best way to see the country. **Bush Pilots**; tel: 061-248 316; fax: 0651-304 431, charter private small planes for luxury go-as-you-please or specialist tours. **Springbok Atlas**; tel: 061-215 943, fax: 061-215 932 , part of the giant South African operator, and **Trans-Namibia Tours**; tel: 061-221 549; fax: 061-230 960, both run a whole range of scheduled, tailor-made tours using minibuses and self-drive options. **Kaokohimba Safaris**, tel/fax: 061-222 378, operate fly-in tours with a strong emphasis on ecology and community tourism in Kaokoland. **Skeleton Coast Safaris**; tel: 061-224 248; fax: 061-225 713, use small planes and landrovers to roam the desolation of the extraordinary Skeleton Coast. **Karibu Safaris**; reservations (South Africa) tel: 031-839 774; fax: 031-831 957, operate hiking and game-viewing camping safaris in the Namib Desert, Damaraland, the Namib Naukluft and Etosha.

Each of the major towns also has a number of local operators offering specialist tours from half-day city tours to desert camel treks or deep-sea fishing; ask at the Tourist Office for details.

or *236 709* (cheap) has to be one of the world's more unusual airport hotels, a pretty stone and thatch lodge, with six bungalows and a boma dining room. Transfers are available to the city and airport. In the Otjihavera Mountains, the **Midgard Guest Farm** (Namibia Resorts), *on the D2102, 85 km from Windhoek*. Turn on to the D2102 at Kapps Farm, on the Windhoek International Airport road; *tel: 0621-503 888, fax: 0621-503 818* (moderate) caters for quite large conferences, provides a variety of sports, including riding and swimming, and serves excellent alfresco meals.

Gert Klause, *Sanlam Centre; tel: 061-235 706* (moderate; open lunch and dinner) specialises in German dishes. Steaks are popular. Try **Copper Kettle Restaurant**, *corner Joule and Walter Sts, Southern Industrial Ave; tel: 061-225 964* (cheap–moderate), which does excellent spare ribs; or **Okambihi Restaurant**, *A Wessels St, Northern Industrial Area; tel: 061-263 204* (moderate; open lunch and dinner), where they also serve vegetarian options. **Café Restaurant Schneider**, *Jack Levinson Arcade, Independence Ave; tel: 061-226 304* (cheap; daytime only) and **In's Wiener**, *Ground Floor, Wernhill Park; tel: 061-231 082* (cheap; daytime only) are good for cakes and light meals.

SIGHTSEEING

Windhoek has had many names. To the KhoiKhoi it was *Aigrams* ('hot water'), named

after the hot spring rising at its site. In 1836, the location became known as *Queen Adelaide's Bath*, after a British queen who would never visit, then was named as *Winterhoek* by the KhoiKhoi chief, Jonker Afrikaner, to commemorate the Cape farm on which he grew up. When the Germans came, they rather gracelessly called it 'windy corner', *Windhuk*, which South Africans later altered to **Windhoek**.

Built across several low hills, surrounded by the Auas and Eros Mountains, it's a handsome city, whose streets are filled with the evidence of a recent colonial past. The people are a peculiar mix of pinky-brown Europeans of German extraction, some dressed in lederhosen, dark brown Herero women in traditional costume and yellowish-skinned people of San or Khoi extraction. There are several imposing Germanic buildings, such as the Lutheran **Christuskirche**, *Peter Müller St*; to view it, contact the neighbouring church office, *12 Peter Müller St; tel: 061-224 294*, designed by Gottlieb Redecker and consecrated in 1910, which has a graceful spire and striking mix of neo-Gothic and art nouveau styles. The stained glass was donated by Kaiser Wilhelm II. The **Parliament Building**, *off Robert Mugabe Ave; tel: 061-308 9111* (open Mon–Fri by appointment) was built in 1912–13 as the old German administrative headquarters. Known as the **Tintenpalast** (Ink Palace) because of the large amount of writing that took place here, it is now attached to the modern Legislative Assembly. Then there are the three odd 'Beau Geste-style' castle residences in the hills, all battlements and fortifications, built between 1914 and 1917 by Willi Sander; two, Sanderburg and Schwerinsburg, are now private residences, the third the **Hotel Heinitzburg** (see p.369).

Also standing on a hill overlooking the city, the **Old Fort** *(Alte Feste), 74 Robert Mugabe Ave; tel: 061-229 3363* (open Mon–Fri 0800–1800, Sat 1000-1245, 1500–1800, Sun 1100–1230, 1500–1800; free) was the early focus for the developing town. Now a museum, it was built in 1892 by the Germans, becoming the South African army headquarters in 1915. It is Windhoek's oldest surviving building, and today it houses cultural history displays relating to independence, the flag, national musical instruments, and so on. Opposite is the **Rider Memorial** (unveiled 1912), an equestrian statue commemorating the heroism of the German colonial force during the Nama and Herero wars (1904–1908).

The **State Museum**, *103 Robert Mugabe Ave; tel: 061-2934362* (open weekdays 0900–1800, weekends 1000–1230, 1500–1800; free) has interesting displays relating to the Namibian environment and local anthropology. The **National Art Gallery**, *corner Robert Mugabe Ave and John Meinert St; tel: 061-231 160* (open Mon–Fri 0800–1700) has a small permanent collection of historic and contemporary Namibian arts and crafts, together with regular temporary exhibitions and a sales gallery.

Out of Town

Take the C28 west for about 28 km, then bear right to the **Daan Viljoen Game Reserve**, *tel: 061-226 806; fax: 061-232 393*, which offers game-viewing, walks and fishing. Accommodation is in bungalows and there is a camping and caravan site (cheap). Apply to the Windhoek office for reservations. Day and overnight visitors are permitted (the former must leave by 1800, and the latter with reserved accommodation may enter until 2400; N$10).

OKAHANDJA

Tourist Office: *Municipality; tel: 0621-501 051.* Open Mon–Fri 0800–1230, 1400–1700.

The Herero

The Herero, amongst Namibia's most eccentric indigenous people, are best known for the dress of the women. Towards the end of the 19th century, full, ankle-length, Victorian-style dresses were introduced, which are still worn today, although mainly by the older generations. Based on the costume of missionary women, the dresses have high waists and consist of numerous layers of cloth – consuming as much as 25m of material. Modern Herero women have brought their own sense of style to this traditional outfit, with shawls, even in the heat, and jewellery (bead necklaces and metal bangles). Their headdresses are unique, made of cloth folded to resemble the horns of a bull.

ACCOMMODATION

The best accommodation in this area is on private game farms. The **Oropoko Lodge**, *on the B2, 41 km from Okahandja; turn on to the D2156 for a further 18 km to the lodge; tel: 061-262 395, fax: 061-217 026* (moderate–expensive) is a modern complex offering first-class accommodation in private bungalows on an 11,000 hectare game reserve. The old colonial **Okomitundu Guest Farm**, *on the D1967 between Wilhelmstal and Otjimbingwe (go west from Okahandja on the B2); tel: 0621-503 901, fax: 0621-241 186* (moderate–expensive) on a 10,000 hectare estate, and the **Otjisazu Guest Farm**, *approach Okahandja, turn right at route 2102, and continue on a gravel road for 26 km; tel: 0621-501 259, fax: 0621-501 323* (expensive), in an historic mission station, are both smaller and more mellow. All three have pools, and offers game drives and bird-watching.

SIGHTSEEING

Situated on the banks of a tributary of the Swakop River, this site has long been an important site for the Herero people, as their tribal centre and the burial ground for many of their early chiefs, whose graves now lie beneath the trees in the municipal gardens. In 1849,

Rhenish Mission was founded here with the blessing of local leader, Jan Jonker Afrikaner, but the town of Okahandja was actually founded in 1894, when the Germans built a fort and stationed a garrison here. The Herero were finally driven away in 1904, but each year, on the final Sun in Aug, they stage a spectacular memorial service to their long-dead heroes. It's a time to see the women decked in all their traditional finery and the men in full warrior's uniform (see p.371).

Today, Okahandja is a ranching centre and a good place to buy the locally made *biltong*. Stop in at the **Friedenskirche**, *Church St*, the old Rhenish mission church built in 1876. Opposite are the graves of Jan Jonker Afrikaner (d. 1861), Clemens Kapuuo, a notable nationalist politician assassinated in 1978, and Hosea Kutako, considered to be the Father of Namibian Nationalism.

The **Gross-Barmen Hot Springs Resort**, *24 km west of Okahandja; tel: 0621-501 091* (open 0800–1800; N$10 per person and N$10 per car, plus N$2 per person for mineral baths; all visitors, including day visitors must book ahead) is a large, popular and well-run spa, based on a 65°C mineral spring. There are indoor and outdoor pools (a more comfortable 39–45°C), a restaurant, picnic sites, and walks and bird hides around the dam. Accommodation is in self-catering bungalows (cheap) and there are caravan and camping sites.

For tours in the local area, contact **Nazimbo Camping Safaris**; *tel: 06228-4803*, or **Quest Africa**; *tel: 06228-6403; fax: 061-241 186*.

Tourist Office: *5 Bismarck St; tel: 064-402 224* (open Mon–Fri 0800–1300 1400–1700) for local information. **Namibi:** *corner Roon and Kaiser Wilhelm Sts; tel: 064-402 224* (open Mon–Fri 0800–1530) handles the promotion of the whole Namib region.

ACCOMMODATION

Swakopmund has a great many hotels and guesthouses to choose from. For true elegance and luxury, pay a visit to the **Swakopmund Hotel and Entertainment Centre**, *Bahnhof St; tel: 064-400 800; fax: 064-400 801* (expensive), the flamboyant colonial railway station given a new lease of life as a top quality hotel, with a pool, tennis courts, two cinemas, video arcade, crèche and casino. Guests also have access to camel and horse rides in the desert, and one of five desert golf courses in the world. The **Strand Hotel**, *on the seafront; tel: 064-400 315; fax: 064-404 942* (moderate) is far less inspiring, but is the only hotel in town right on the beach. It has a good seafood restaurant. The **Hotel-Pension Prinzessin-Rupprecht-Heim**, *Lazarett St, near the seafront; tel: 064-402 231; fax: 064-402 019* (cheap–moderate) is a charming bed and breakfast, with a lovely garden in the old colonial hospital. It was built in 1902 and is one of the town's oldest buildings. The **Hotel-Pension Deutsches Haus**, *13 Luderitz St; tel: 064-404 896, fax: 064-404 861*, is quietly situated 2 minutes from the town centre (cheap). Ask at the tourist information about self-catering holiday flats.

Campsite: Swakopmund-Mile 4 Caravan Park; *tel: 064-461 781*, also has self-catering bungalows.

EATING AND DRINKING

The best restaurant in town is probably **Platform One**, in the Swakopmund Hotel (see above), which serves heaped seafood buffets. Seafood is obviously a speciality of the town. Other places to try include the **Western Saloon**, *Moltke St; tel: 064-405 395* (moderate; open lunch and dinner), and **Erich's Restaurant**, *21 Post St; tel: 064-405 141* (open lunch and dinner; expensive). For traditional South African dishes, try **Jay Jay's restaurant**, *8 Brucken St; tel: 064-402 909* (moderate; open lunch and dinner) and **Ol' Steamer**, *9 Moltke St; tel: 064-404 806* (moderate; open lunch and dinner). German home cooking can be had at **Bayernstubchen**, *13 Garnison St; tel: 064-404 793* (moderate; open lunch and dinner).

SIGHTSEEING

Swakopmund is where Namibians go to holiday. A resort and port at the mouth of the Swakop River, it was founded in 1892, when the German colonisers attempted to develop an alternative entry port for their colony to Walvis

Bay, which was held by the British. Many of the town's buildings date from this time, with heavy Germanic versions of Victorian architecture, such as the **railway station** (1901) and **courthouse** (1905), both in *Garnisen St*, and colonial variations on their own Baroque and Rococo styles, such as the **Lutheran Church**, *Otavi St*. Plenty of private homes survive from this period and it is not unusual to see castellated or half-timbered mansions dotted about the town and its outskirts, while the seafront is ornamented by several bright-ideas-gone-bad. The **Jetty**, designed in 1911 to extend 500m out to sea, was never completed, and remained a white elephant until restoration began in 1985. Nearby, the 'Mole', intended to be a sheltered harbour, promptly filled with sand and is now the sheltered **Palm Beach**, where the freezing sea provides respite from the hot sun. The local beaches offer sunbathing and windsurfing, but this is a coast which relies on fog for its moisture, and it is not an ideal seaside resort.

At the foot of the lighthouse, the **Swakopmund Museum**, *Strand St; tel: 064-402 046* (open daily 1000–1230, 1500–1730; R4), housed in an old German customs warehouse, is a must-see sight, with displays on all aspects of the Namib region, local history and the ocean.

For safaris into the desert regions, contact **Charly's Desert Tours**; *tel: 064-404 341;* or **Desert Adventure Safaris**; *tel: 064-404 459*. To go shark fishing, contact **West Coast Angling**; *tel: 064-402 377*.

SIDE TRACKS SOUTH OF SWAKOPMUND

WALVIS BAY

Tourist Office: *Municipality, corner 12th Rd and 10th St; tel: 064-205 981* (open Mon–Thur 0800–1300 1400–1700, Fri 0800–1300 1400–1630).

ACCOMMODATION

The **Casa Mia**, *7th St; tel: 064-205 975, fax: 064-206 596* (cheap) is a pleasant hotel, with a good à la carte restaurant; the **Nautilus Bar** attracts a young crowd. The **Esplanade Park Bungalows**, *Esplanade; tel: 064-206 145; fax: 064-204 528* (cheap) offers good self-catering accommodation.

Campsites: Walvis Bay Caravan Park, *1st St, by the Esplanade; tel: 064-205 981*, and the **Langstrand Holiday Resort**, *15 km north of town; tel: 064-203 134*.

SIGHTSEEING

From Swakopmund, take the southbound B2 for 35 km to reach Walvis Bay. This little town is something of an anomaly. Standing on one of the finest natural harbours on the west coast, it was annexed to the Cape Colony as early as 1884, and remained a South African enclave even after Namibian independence. It was only handed over when Mandela took power in 1994. It is now the main port and fishing centre of Namibia, but lacks a certain something as a tourist destination.

The first European to pass this way, Bartholomew Dias (1497), thought the sands inland looked so barren and lifeless that he named them 'the sands of hell'. The Portuguese also noted the abundant life in the surrounding seas, including prodigious quantities of whales, and the bay was charted as 'the bay of whales' – *Bahia das Baleias* in Portuguese; *Walvis Baai* in Afrikaans.

The **Walvis Bay Museum**, *Ground Floor, Public Library, 10th St; tel: 064-205 981* (open Mon–Fri 0900–1230, 1500–1630; N$2.50) has displays relating to local history, costumes, archaeology, natural history and minerals. There are a few historic buildings, such as the prefabricated **Rhenish Church**, *5th Rd*, built in 1880. Ask at the Tourist Office about the possibility of visiting the docks (take your passport to get a permit from the **Railway Police**, *13th Rd*).

Other than that, all the town's attractions are outdoors. The town has good beaches, a lovely bay and a lagoon that is perfect for all types of water sports, such as boardsailing, waterskiing, angling and yachting. The various coastal habitats, including the shallow, 45,000 hectare lagoon, huge commercial salt

373

pans and even the reed-fringed artificial pools of the sewage works, together make up one of the most important wetlands for birds in southern Africa, with up to 150,000 migrants passing through each year, including huge flocks of flamingos and pelicans.

For tours of the area, contact **Gloriosa Safaris**; *tel: 064-206 300, fax: 064-202 455*, or **Inshore Safaris**; *tel: 064-202 609, fax: 064-202 198*.

NAMIB-NAUKLUFT PARK

ACCOMMODATION

There is only basic self-catering accommodation available within the park; see under each section. On the fringes, mainly near Sossusvlei, are several extremely comfortable lodges. The largest, least lovely but closest to the dunes, is the **Karos Sossusvlei Lodge** *(Ka); tel/fax: 06638-4322* (expensive).

The **Naukluft–Namib Lodge**, *on route 36, 19 km from Solitaire and 62 km from Sesriem, the entrance to Sossusvlei; tel: 061-263 086, fax: 061-215 356* (moderate) is located in the midst of real Namib landscape – within walking distance of absolute solitude.

Thatched *'kulalas'* (chalets) are scattered across the baked sand at the **Kulala Desert Lodge**, *on the 826 road, 17 km south of Sesriem; follow the signs to the lodge; tel: 061-221 994, fax: 061-222 574* (moderate–expensive), their terraces all overlooking the the Sossusvlei dunes. Each has a roof platform for those who wish to sleep under the stars. There are walking trails, horse rides, or visits to San rock painting sites available.

At the small, tented **Camp Mwisho**, *50 km south of Sesriem on the D826*, **Namib Sky Adventure Safaris**; *tel: 0663-3233; fax: 0663-3235* (expensive) run hot-air balloon trips over the dunes.

SIGHTSEEING

Swakopmund and Walvis Bay are both convenient bases for exploring the Namib Desert, part of which, the **Namib-Naukluft Park**, is the largest game park in Africa and the fourth largest conservation area in the world. Consisting of a large chunk of the desert (huge tracts of which have been given conservation status, mainly because no other use could be found for them), it covers nearly 5 million hectares of sand dunes, gravel plains, granite inselbergs and dolomite mountain, and is divided into four sections: the Namib; Naukluft; Sesriem/Sossusvlei; and Sandwich Harbour. Permits and all reservations for accommodation must be obtained at the Windhoek parks office (see box, p.367); permits for the Namib Section can also be obtained from the tourist information offices at Lüderitz and Swakopmund (see p.367 and p.372).

The **Namib section** is about 20 km from Swakopmund on the C28; or 20 km from Walvis Bay on the C14. In it, the **Welwitschia Nature Drive** traverses vast plains roamed by herds of oryx, springbok and zebra. Look out too for the hardy *Welwitschia mirabilis*, of which one very large specimen is thought to be over 1500 years old. There are no large rest camps in this section, just campsites at Kuiseb Bridge, Mirabib, Homeb, Kriess-se-rus, Vogelfederberg, Bloedkoppie, Groot Tinkas and Ganab (cheap). Permits are not required if you are simply passing through on the main roads. However, they are required when travelling on signposted tourist roads, such as the Welwitschia Nature Drive.

The **Naukluft section** includes the mountainous escarpment and the edge of the Namib Desert. From Walvis Bay, take the C14 signposted to Bullsport (277 km). After Solitaire, either join route 36 to Maltahohe, which gives access to Sesriem and Sossusvlei (see below), or continue along the C14 to Bullsport and Maltahohe. The entrance gate is on the D854, about 10 km south-west of Bullsport; the park office is about 12 km beyond the entrance gate; in total, it is 249 km from Walvis Bay.

This is a sanctuary for mountain zebra, although other mammals can also be seen here, amongst them springbok, kudu, gemsbok and leopard. There are day hikes in the area (the **Waterkloof** and **Olive Day**

Trails), as well as the arduous 8-day, 120-km **Naukluft Hiking Trail** (N$50 per person to include accommodation; book through the Windhoek office; Mar–Oct only), a hugely exciting option ranging through extremely remote areas, with accommodation in overnight huts. There is also the 73 km **Naukluft 4x4 Trail**, a self-guided, overnight trail (N$150 per vehicle, plus normal entrance fee to include accommodation; book through the Windhoek office).

The **Sesriem section** lies west of the Naukluft Mountains. From Solitaire, continue south towards Maltahohe on route 36 for about 69 km. The entrance gate to Sesriem is reached 12 km beyond the turn off. About 4 km from Sesriem, the River Tsauchab vanishes down a steep kilometre-long gorge in an arid sand and gravel plain broken by occasional pools of water, which attract birds and animals. There is a lovely campsite here (cheap).

The river flows on (during the winter only) deep into a vast sea of sand 300 km long and 150 km wide, its towering red-gold dunes burning flame-like in the evening sun. **Sossusvlei**, *about 65 km from Sesriem and 318 km from Walvis Bay*, is the most accessible part of this monumental landscape. It is actually a huge pan, one of a number which fill occasionally when desert storms break, but the real reason to come here is for the surrounding dunes, some, up to 300m high, the largest in the world.

The **Sandwich Bay** section, only about 40 km south of Walvis Bay, can only be reached using a 4x4 vehicle. You must have a permit (obtainable from the Swakopmund Tourist Office; gates open throughout the year 0600–2000, with overnight camping strictly forbidden). The route is signposted from Walvis Bay; 4 km from town, take the right fork via Paaltjies (8 km) and then continue along the beach to Sandwich. This section is an important wetlands area frequented by migratory birds – to date over 113 have been recorded here (seabirds, waders, waterbirds and landbirds).

SIDE TRACKS NORTH OF SWAKOPMUND

HENTIES BAY

Take the C34 north for 76 km to the little resort of Henties Bay. This is a place to fish, swim and play golf. The long, low, seafront **Hotel de Duine**, *34 Duine St, next to the golf course; tel: 064-500 001, fax: 064-500 724* (cheap) will help arrange surf angling, boat trips, golf and 4x4 excursions into the Namib Desert. There are self-catering apartments at **Die Oord**; *on the main street; tel: 064-500 239* (cheap). See also campsites listed below (National West Coast Recreation Area).

NATIONAL WEST COAST

Further north from here, the coastal C34 gives access to the National West Coast Recreation Area, a protected stretch of coastline for which no entry permits are required. Along its length are popular fishing spots at what are known as **Miles 14** (camping and caravanning; cheap), **72** (camping and caravanning; cheap), **92, 98, 105, 108** (camping and caravanning; cheap) and **110**. At **Cape Cross**, 139 km from Swakopmund (open Sat–Thur 1000–1700; N$10 per person and N$10 per car; no overnight facilities; reservations from the Windhoek office) is a 6000 hectare haven for 60,000 Cape fur seals.

SKELETON COAST PARK

Park Information and Accommodation: Even further north, on the coastal C34, 199 km from Swakopmund, the **Skeleton Coast Park** is only partially open to the public. Enter at the Ugab Mouth gate (open dawn–1500). Entry is with a permit (from the Windhoek parks office, the Swakopmund tourist information office, or the Ugab Mouth gate); admission N$20 per person, N$20 per vehicle; day visitors are allowed, though they are not permitted to visit Torra Bay or Terrace Bay. Day visitors must leave the park no later than 1500.

There are resorts at **Torra Bay** (camping and caravanning, with a shop and a petrol station) and, at the extreme north, **Terrace Bay** (369 km from Swakopmund), a popular angling spot and the administrative centre for the park. Facilities include bungalows (cheap–moderate), a shop and a restaurant. You cannot visit either of these unless you have accommodation booking advices. Bookings from the Windhoek office only. Halfway between Torra Bay and Khorixas, on the Haub River, the **Damaraland Camp** *(Wd;* expensive; ·bookings via Wilderness Safaris, South Africa) is a small, exclusive tented camp offering nature walks, 4x4 expeditions and some of Africa's best rock etchings.

SIGHTSEEING

Covering more than a million and a half hectares, from the Ugab River in the south to the Kunene River on the Angolan border, this is a strange, fog-bound landscape of gravel plains and mirages. A desolate, remote area, it is famous for its lions, which in the past eked out a precarious living surviving on seals and the odd whale. Expect to see the occasional desert elephant, or jackals and hyenas foraging amongst the rocks on the beach. The desert takes its name from the various tragedies that have occurred along its endless empty shoreline – from shipwrecks to plane crashes caused, mostly, by the coastal fog which occurs throughout the year.

SKELETON COAST PARK WILDERNESS AREA

The extreme north, from the Hoanib River to the Kunene River is known as the **Skeleton Coast Park Wilderness Area**. The only way to visit it is by fly-in safaris; **Skeleton Coast Fly-in-Safaris**; *tel: 061-224 248, fax: 061-225 713.*

OTJIWARONGO

Tourist Office: *Municipality Offices, Kreft St; tel: 0651-392 231* (open Mon–Fri 0800–1230, 1400–1700).

ACCOMMODATION

In town, the best of the hotels is the simple

Hamburger Hof; *Bahnhof St; tel: 0651-302 520; fax: 0651-303 607* (cheap). Just south of town, the colonial-style **Otjibamba Lodge**, *tel: 0651-303 133, fax: 0651-303 206* (expensive) is set in its own private game reserve. Even better, the magnificently situated **Okonjima Guest Farm**, *turn off the B1, 48 km south of Otjiwarongo; tel: 0651-4563, fax: 0651-4565* (expensive; no children under 12) is home to the Africat Foundation. Guests can watch leopards and cheetahs at feeding times, take bush walks and watch up to 300 species of bird from purpose-built hides. The **Otjiwa Game Ranch** (Namibia Resorts), *on the B1, 30 km south of Otjiwarongo; tel: 0651-302 665, fax: 0651-302 668* (cheap–moderate) offers safari tours guided by wildlife specialists; animals here include white rhino. **Campsite: Municipal Caravan Park**, *signposted from the main road; tel: 0651-302 231.*

SIGHTSEEING

Not much happens in Otjiwarongo. There is a **Crocodile Ranch**, *beside the caravan park; tel: 0651-302 121* (open daily 0900–1800; about N$5), but the town is really a stopover on the way to the Etosha National Park.

To the east is the **Waterberg Plateau Park**. Go south from Otjiwarongo on the B1 for 29 km, bear left on the C22 and, following the signs, continue for about 65 km until the access road branches left. Head for **Bernabe de la Bat Rest Camp**; *tel: 0651-303 191* (open year-round; admission and reservations, see box, p.367). You must reach the camp before sunset; day visitors must make prior arrangements for their visit and must leave before 1800. The camp has bungalow accommodation (cheap), a camping and caravanning site, restaurant (open 0700–0830, 1200–1330, 1900–2100), shop, petrol station and pool. There are daily guided tours to the plateau – enquire at the office.

This is a vast mountain wilderness with distinctive red sandstone cliffs in an area rich with different types of flora and fauna, as well as interesting rock formations, rock paintings and engravings. This is home to the country's only breeding colony of the rare Cape vulture, as well as black and white rhino, kudu, oryx, sable, roan, buffalo, giraffe, klipspringer and leopard. There is organised game-viewing, as well as walks and trails from the rest camp at Bernabe de la Bat. The guided Waterberg Wilderness Trail takes place every 2nd, 3rd and 4th weekend (Apr–Nov; N$120; reservations from the Windhoek office well in advance).

South-west of Otjiwarongo, on the *Otjihaenamaparero Farm*, a cluster of **dinosaur footprints** is embedded in the rock. They are thought to be between 150 and 185 million years old. To get there, take the C33 to Kalkfield (68 km); just beyond the town bear left on the Okahandja road and continue for 29 km. The site is marked.

ETOSHA NATIONAL PARK

PARK INFORMATION AND ACCOMMODATION

There are information offices in all three camps (open daily 0800–1700). No open vehicles or motorcycles allowed; admission fees must be paid at the Namutoni or Okaukuejo rest camps before proceeding through the park (N$20 per person, N$20 per vehicle). There are three rest camps in Etosha: **Okaukuejo**, the park's administrative headquarters and the most spacious of the camps, *tel: 0671-29800;* **Namutoni**, *tel: 0671-29305,* with accommodation in the old German colonial Fort Namutoni; and **Halali** (no tel; phone either Okaukuejo or Namutoni; only open second Fri in March until 31 Oct). Each has a variety of accommodation (cheap–moderate), ranging from fully equipped luxury bungalows to caravan and campsites. Each has a pool, restaurant, shop, petrol station and landing strip. You must arrive at the camps before sunset (bearing in mind the 60 kph speed limit in the park). Bookings should be made at the Windhoek parks office. Restaurant hours are: 0700–0900; 1200–1400; 1800–2200.

This is one of Africa's premier game parks, and, inevitably, a whole raft of private lodges have grown up around the edges. Namibia Resorts' award-winning **Mokuti Lodge**, *on the B4, 500m from the Namutoni gate; tel: 067-229 084; fax: 067-229 091* (moderate) has luxury rooms and family-sized chalets, a pool, chil-

dren's playground, bushwalks and safaris into the park. The **Ongava Lodge**, *on the C38 between Outjo and Okaukuejo, 5 km from the entrance to Etosha; tel: 061-225 178, fax: 061-239 455* (expensive) is one of the country's most luxurious lodges, with accommodation in thatched chalets, with private terraces overlooking the plains and waterhole. It offers night drives and nature walks on the private 30,000 hectare reserve and game drives on its own land and within the park proper.

SIGHTSEEING

This is the best known of Namibia's game parks. Mainly flat, its most distinctive feature is the large saline **Etosha Pan** (about 120 km long and 55 km at its widest), which takes up nearly a quarter of the total area and gives the park its name, 'the place of great white spaces'. Up to 10 million years ago, Etosha Pan was part of a vast inland sea. It was proclaimed a game reserve in 1907 by German Governor von Lindquist. It's a unique place: this great, white expanse, a place of shimmering mirages, is home to huge herds of game, with over 144 species of mammal. At 22,270 sq. km, the park is vast, but it is nowhere as large as was intended in the original plan. Von Lindquist originally proclaimed a 93,240 sq. km area between the Kunene River and the Atlantic, but, during the 1960s, large tracts were reclaimed to accommodate tribal homelands. In 1970, the reserve was reduced to its present size and declared a national park.

When it rains (Nov–Apr), the animals disperse because water is to be found elsewhere. Plant growth obscures them and many visitors are disappointed to see just a few animals. The best time to visit is during the dry season (May–Oct), when large numbers of animals congregate at the waterholes along the edge of the pan. This is a 'Big Five' park. You will also find zebra, wildebeest, springbok and oryx in their thousands, while at the woodland waterholes, there are eland, giraffe, red hartebeest, black-faced impala, warthog, Damara dik dik and steenbok. Predators present are lion, cheetah, spotted and brown hyena, black-faced jackal, Cape fox, African lynx and African wild cat. Expect to see ostriches, kori bustards, vultures, flamingos and a whole range of other exotic birds.

The rest camp of Okaukuejo has a floodlit waterhole next to it, where you can see important species, such as elephant and black rhino, as well as a myriad of others without ever leaving camp. The other two camps also have waterholes, but they are not as good.

Etosha is well-suited to do-it-yourself safaris. The facilities are not well developed, but there is a network of well-maintained gravel roads linking visitors to 52 watering holes. Identify one, park your vehicle, then sit and wait; the game will come to you. The best are Chudob, Gemsbokvlakte, Goas, Kalheuwel, Klein Namutoni, Rietfontein and Salvadora, where the car parks are literally within a stone's throw of the water.

GROOTFONTEIN

Tourist Office: *Municipality Offices, 499 West St; tel: 067-243 101* (open Mon–Fri 0800–1300, 1400–1700).

ACCOMMODATION

The **Meteor Hotel**, *9 Okavango Rd; tel: 067-242 078, fax: 064-243 072* (cheap) is a typical country town hotel, with a good restaurant specialising in seafood. **Campsite**: the **Municipal Caravan Park**, *next to the swimming pool; tel: 067-243 101*, also has a few self-catering bungalows, a pool and restaurant.

SIGHTSEEING

Grootfontein is a market centre for the local cattle industry, founded around a valuable spring. In 1893, it was made the headquarters of the German South West Africa Company, and, with the building of the **Das Alte Fort** in 1896, it became a garrison town. Das Alte Fort now houses the **Grootfontein Museum**, *Erikson St; tel: 067-202 456* (open Tues–Fri 1600–1800, Wed 0900–1100; N$2), which features local history. There is a mineral collection and restored carpenter's and blacksmith's shops.

However, the town is known chiefly for the meteorite which fell on **Hoba Farm**, *19 km from town*. Leave Grootfontein heading west on the B8; just outside town, there is a signed turn

off on to route D2860. Rich in nickel and iron, this is the largest known meteorite in the world, with an approximate mass of 54,000 kg. It was only discovered in the 1920s, but is thought to have fallen to earth some 80,000 years ago. The **Dragon's Breath Cave**, *46 km from Grootfontein*, contains the world's largest known underground lake (covering 2 hectares). It is closed to casual visitors, but serious cavers should ask the tourist office for details.

KAUDOM GAME PARK

Approach from the B8. This 384,000 hectare park on the Botswana border was opened to the public in 1986. Relatively undervisited, it is located in an area of old Kalahari sand dunes dotted with woodlands of Zambezi teak, wild teak and false mopani, and is home to elephant, lion, leopard, cheetah, giraffe, kudu, reedbuck and a variety of other animals. Only 4x4 vehicles are allowed, with a minimum of two vehicles and sufficient food and water for 3 days, no trailers or caravans (open sunrise–sunset; simple accommodation in huts; apply to the Windhoek office; admission as before). This is a malaria area and prophylactics must be taken (see p. 22).

CAPRIVI GAME PARK

The entrances to this reserve are at Bagani in the west and Kongola in the east. This was once a military zone and the status of the area is still under review; you may not leave the untarred main road (B8). Accommodation is limited to a rather basic campsite at Nambwa. For information and reservations, *tel: 067352-27* (Chief Conservation Officer at Katima Mulilo). This is elephant country – several thousand congregate close to the Okavango and Kwando Rivers, and there are also large herds of buffalo, lion, leopard, cheetah, wild dog and hyena. Note: this is a malaria area and prophylactics must be taken (see p. 22).

The **Lianshalu Lodge**, *in the eastern Caprivi, 150 km west of Katima Mulilo, south of the Kongolo Bridge; tel: 061-225 178, fax: 061-239 455*, is magnificently situated in the still undeveloped **Mudumu National Park**, in a lush wilderness of riverine forest and marsh, were crocodile, hippo and birdlife can be seen.

SWAZILAND

The smallest country in the southern hemisphere, with an area of only 17,360 sq. km and a population of less than a million, Swaziland is a picturesque kingdom whose people cling proudly to their traditions. Headed by King Mswati III, who rules with a Council of Ministers, the Swazi people adhere to a calendar punctuated by sacred ceremonies in which the monarch is the principal player. These are colourful occasions with much traditional dancing and singing.

Road travel within this very compact country is relatively easy. Major highways have tarred surfaces in reasonably good condition and are well-signposted – hazards are cattle, pedestrians and grossly overloaded pick-up trucks – and everywhere is within a three-hour drive of Mbabane. The best way to see Swaziland, therefore, is to select a centre and make day trips. For this reason, we have suggested below a number of places with good accommodation and sightseeing possibilities, rather than particular routes. See also the colour map of Swaziland at the back of the book.

TOURING SWAZILAND

If you would prefer to take a rest from driving, **Swazi Trails**, *Royal Swazi Sun Hotel, Ezulwini; tel/fax: 62180,* is a local tour company offering a wide range of Land Rover or minibus tours covering culture, crafts, wildlife, scenery and adventure sports. Tours range from

half a day to a week – some cross the borders to the Kruger National Park and Mozambique. A sundowner safari with game-watching by spotlight, followed by Swazi dancing, costs about E130.

MBABANE

Surrounded by mountains, Swaziland's capital city was established in 1902 by the British, who liked its relatively cool, healthy highveld climate. Today, it is a modern commercial centre with a pleasantly relaxed atmosphere. Most of the area's sights and best places to stay are in the Ezulwini Valley (p.382), which extends from the city's southern outskirts to Lobamba, the country's spiritual capital, where the royal palace and Houses of Parliament are located.

TOURIST INFORMATION

Tourist Office: *Swazi Plaza, opposite the Caltex filling station on Commercial Rd; tel: 42531.* Open Mon–Fri 0800–1300, 1400–1700, Sat 0830–1300. The office is run by friendly, informative staff, who are ready to help with information on accommodation, dining and sightseeing. *Swaziland Complete* is a useful 40-page booklet.

Dept of Tourism, Ministry of Commerce, Industry and Tourism: *PO Box 338, Mbabane; tel: 44556; fax: 42774.* **Big Game Parks**: central reservations office and display centre, *The Mall, Commercial Rd* (open Mon–Fri 0800–1300, 1400–1700, Sat 0830–1300), for enquiries, bookings, itineraries, transfers and custom-made packages. **Head Office**: *PO Box 23, Mbabane; tel: 44541; fax: 40957,* manages and markets Hlane, Mlilwane and Mkhaya Game Reserves.

ARRIVING AND DEPARTING

By Air
Matsapha Airport, *34 km from Mbabane, 8 km from Manzini.* There are international flights to Johannesburg, Durban, Harare, Maputo and

Swaziland

Completely land-locked and almost surrounded by South Africa – Mozambique runs along its eastern border – the country ranges from mountainous terrain and rain forests in the west to lowveld savannah in the east. Summer is the wettest season when the western region suffers severe, torrential thunder storms. In the east at this time, temperatures often reach more than 40°C. The coolest period is May–Aug and frosts can occur in June–July at higher altitudes. Swaziland has five major national parks and reserves. Other activities for visitors to the country are hiking, white water rafting, rock climbing and abseiling, horse-riding and bird-watching, with over 280 species of birds recorded at Malolotja, which is also noted for wild flowers and rare plants. Traditional handicrafts thrive in Swaziland. Woven grassware, wood carvings, jewellery, pottery and traditional implements and weapons make attractive souvenirs. Craft shops and stalls are abundant. The Swazi Market in Mbabane offers a wide range of goods (see p.382).

Legend has it that the ancestors of the Swazi people came from a site near what is now the Mozambique capital, Maputo, and in the late 1700s, were led across the mountains into south-eastern Swaziland by cheif Ngwane II. Over the years that followed, other African peoples who had settled in the area became united with them. White settlers, mainly British traders and Boer farmers, began arriving in Swaziland in the 1830s, and the discovery of gold brought a rush of prospectors in the 1880s. Illiterate Swazi leaders signed over mineral rights and grazing and farming grants without realising they were losing control of their land. At the end of the Anglo-Boer War, Britain took control of Swaziland, which had been governed by the South African Boer Republic since 1894. Repeated calls for Swaziland to be placed under South African jurisdiction were resisted by Britain and the Swazi people, and the country achieved internal self-government in 1967. A year later it received full independence with King Sobhuza II as head of state. King Sobhuza died in 1982 after a reign of 82 years. One of his sons, 15-year-old Prince Makhosetive, was named heir to the throne and was installed as King Mswati III in 1986.

Maseru. There are taxis at the airport, regular bus services to Manzini, Mbabane and the Ezulwini Valley, and Swazi Trails (see p.379) run a door-to-door shuttle to the hotels. **Car Hire: Avis**, *tel: 84928;* **Hertz**, *tel: 84393.*

GETTING AROUND

Pleasant though Mbabane is, the only reasons for going there are (a) so you can say you have been; and (b) shopping. The best shops are located in *The Mall* and *Swazi Plaza*, on opposite sides of *Commercial Rd.* Although the city centre is reasonably compact, some streets are fairly steep and walking is uncomfortable in hot weather. There are ample car parks, especially around the two shopping malls.

STAYING IN MBABANE

Accommodation

The area's three top hotels, and many of the

other local establishments, are all in the Ezulwini Valley (p.382), on the Manzini road, about 20 mins from the city centre. A shuttle bus service links all three hotels.

Close to the central business district in town, the popular colonial-style **City Inn**, *Allister Miller St; tel: 42406; fax: 45393* (cheap) has undergone a major refurbishment, with additional en suite bedrooms and improved bar and dining areas. Its 28 rooms are available on a bed and breakfast basis. Also close to the city centre, within walking distance of the Mbabane Club golf course, the **Tavern Hotel**, *off Griffin St; tel: 42361; fax: 45229* (cheap) has 40 rooms, an à la carte restaurant and a bar, which is popular with local residents as well as guests.

The **Mountain Inn**, *off the Manzini road, 2 km south of the city centre; tel: 42781; fax: 45393* (moderate) stands above the Ezulwini Valley with magnificent views of the Lubombo Mountains to the east. Designed in Spanish

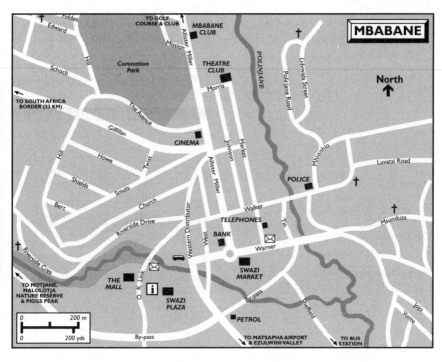

MBABANE

style, it has 60 en suite rooms built around a swimming pool, a bar and à la carte restaurant. Nearby, the **Swazi Inn**, *Malagwane Hill, Manzini road, 3 km from the city centre; tel: 42235; fax: 46465* (cheap) is a country-style thatched-roof hotel overlooking the Ezulwini Valley, with 42 en suite rooms, a pool, restaurant and bar.

Campsite: Timbali Caravan Park, *Manzini road, 10 km from Mbabane; tel/fax: 61156* (cheap) has caravan and camping pitches on a shady 2 hectare site, and offers self-catering accommodation in cottages, rondavels and caravans. Cooking and eating utensils are available. The park has a swimming pool, and a general store and post office are nearby.

Eating and Drinking

Mbabane has no shortage of restaurants and bars, many of them concentrated on *Allister Miller St*. One of the most popular city centre restaurants is **Pablo's** at the City Inn (see left), where food is served all day long. The bar here is also a favourite meeting place. The other hotel restaurants and bars listed above also welcome non-residents. The **Phoenix Spur**, *The Mall; tel: 49103* (open Sun–Thur 0900–2300, Fri–Sat 0900–2400; moderate), in an attractive location next to the Mbabane River, offers steaks, above-average 'Tex-Mex' dishes and an excellent salad bar. All dishes available for take-away. The **Longhorn Restaurant**, *Swazi Plaza; tel: 44302* (moderate) is another steak-house popular with shoppers and office workers. **La Casserole**, *Omnicentre, Allister Miller St; tel: 46426* (moderate) is a city centre restaurant serving German and continental dishes, while aficionados of Portuguese food make their way to **LM**, *corner Allister Miller and Gilfallan Sts; tel: 43097* (moderate). Those in search of Italian food head to **Marco Trattoria**, *Allister Miller St; tel: 45029* (budget–moderate), a first-floor restaurant with some alfresco dining on a small patio.

The Mediterranean, *Allister Miller St; tel: 43212* (moderate) offers some seafood, but is actually an Indian restaurant serving curries and vegetarian dishes, and for a change of cuisine and location, there is the Chinese **Hwa Li**, *Dhlanu'beka House, Walker St; tel: 45986* (cheap–moderate).

Communications

Main Post Office: *Warner St* (open Mon–Fri 0830–1700, Sat 0830–1300).

There are no telephone area codes in Swaziland. Mbabane has an automatic exchange, but calls to some parts of the country must be made through an operator (dial *90*).

Money

There are banks with exchange facilities on *Alistair Miller St* and in *Swazi Plaza*.

Consulates

See Country by Country, p. 40.

ENTERTAINMENT

Bars apart, there is little in the way of nightlife in the city itself, but most hotels in the Ezulwini Valley have discos, and the Royal Swazi Sun has a casino. The **Cinelux Theatre**, *Allister Miller St*, shows general release films. Traditional ceremonies are an essential part of Swazi life (see feature box, opposite).

SHOPPING

Mbabane's two major shopping centres – *The Mall* and *Swazi Plaza* – cater for most everyday needs and include shops selling more exotic arts and crafts items. There is a big **OK Bazaar** supermarket in Swazi Plaza. **African Fantasy**, *The Mall; tel: 40205*, sells T-shirts, ceramics, ethnic jewellery, craft pieces, postcards, posters and stationery.

Indingilizi Art and Craft Gallery, *Johnstone St; tel: 46213*, specialises in contemporary African art and collectables, including batiks, mohair, ethnic jewellery and studio pottery. Exhibitions featuring the work of local and other artists are regularly staged. A restaurant adjoining the gallery serves African dishes from the Cape to Cairo at lunchtime Mon–Sat. The **Mantenga Craft Centre**, *Swazi Plaza; tel: 61136*, also sells work by many of Swaziland's leading crafts workshops, including T-shirts, batiks, candles, silverware and Ngwenya glass.

Stalls in the **Swazi Market**, at the *Warner St* end of *Allister Miller St* (open Mon–Sat 0800–1700) offer a range of craft items in wood, metal, basketry and other materials, but similar items can be found, usually cheaper, at roadside stalls out of town.

EZULWINI VALLEY

Home of the Swazi royal family and focal point of the country's political activity, the 22 km Ezulwini Valley, reached by the Manzini road south of the capital, is the area's main accommodation and sightseeing centre, and the heart of Royal Swaziland.

TOURIST INFORMATION

See Mbabane.

ACCOMMODATION

The **Royal Swazi Sun Hotel and Casino** *(SI); tel: 61001; fax: 61859* (expensive) is Sun International's flagship property in Swaziland, with 140 rooms, seven suites, three restaurants and, of course, a casino. Sports facilities include golf, lawn bowls, tennis, squash, swimming and horse-riding. There are banking facilities, an automatic teller machine, children's video arcade and a cinema. The chain also has two other hotels here. The **Lugogo Sun** *(SI); tel: 61550; fax: 61111* (moderate–expensive) is Swaziland's largest hotel, a family resort with 202 rooms, a full range of sports facilities and live entertainment. The 120-room **Ezulwini Sun** *(SI); tel: 61201; fax: 61782* (moderate) is pitched more at the business traveller, but does have a swimming pool, tennis courts and riding stables. The **Valley Blues Restaurant** is open daily 0700–2230.

There are also several options for the less affluent. The multi-faceted **Happy Valley Motel**, *Manzini road; tel: 61061; fax: 61050* (cheap), has 57 en suite rooms around a swimming pool, a pizzeria, roadhouse, take-away cafeteria and steakhouse. Food is available until 0400. The **Why Not? Night Club and Disco** features international cabaret performers, disco music and current video shows. The **If Not, Why Not? Go Go Bar** appeals to locals as well as visitors and **Sir-Loin Cocktail Bar** serves drinks until after midnight.

Ceremonial Swaziland

It is unusual for overseas visitors to attend the main Swazi festivals, but it is well worth making an effort to do so. There is no regular annual date, some proceedings being dictated by the phases of the moon.

The two main ceremonies in the calendar are the **Ncwala**, or Festival of the First Fruits (Dec/Jan), in which youths and men take part, and the **Umhlanga**, or Reed Dance, involving maidens of marriageable age (Aug/Sept). Each ceremony, in which Royalty plays a major part, lasts for several days, although not all are spectator occasions.

Anyone hoping to take pictures or recordings must apply in writing, enclosing two passport-style photographs of the applicant, to the **Government Information Service**, *PO Box 451, Mbabane, Kingdom of Swaziland.* You may receive a form to be completed, so allow time for this to be returned and accepted. It is strictly forbidden to record during sacred parts of the event.

The **Ncwala** is the Swazis' most important ceremony, involving many hundreds of men and boys. Its purpose is to renew the strength of the King and the nation for the coming year. At the time of the new moon preceding the Ncwala, water-gatherers visit Swaziland's main rivers and collect water from the Indian Ocean at Maputo in Mozambique, the Swazis' ancestral home. When the moon is full, many of the nation's youth march 40 km to fetch branches or the *lusekwane* (acacia) tree, with which elders construct a sacred bower for the King next to the Royal Cattle byre. Everyone gathers round as a bull is driven into the bower for the mystic and sacred parts of the ceremony, and then released. The most spectacular scenes are played out on the fourth day of Ncwala. The King joins 1000 or more of his warriors, all in costumes of ox hide and leopard skins, carrying shields and tall sticks. The King joins in a long session of dancing and singing as the warriors whistle piercingly in unison and the hard earth trembles with the ritual stamping of feet. Once the King has eaten a piece of pumpkin, the Swazi people can sample the fresh fruit and crops. On the final day, articles are burnt on a huge bonfire, symbolising the year just ended. Then ancestral spirits are entreated to send rain to quench the fire, signifying the start of a new year, with singing, dancing and feasting.

Swazi maidens have their **Umhlanga** to honour the Queen Mother at the Somhlolo Stadium in Lobamba. They gather reeds to repair the windbreak around her house, and prepare elaborate costumes for rhythmic dancing and singing on the sixth and seventh days.

There are rigid rules for visitors privileged to attend the ceremonies: no recording of the sacred songs, no hats or umbrellas, and women must wear long skirts (not trousers).

In early April, **Tinkhomo Temadloti** honours the nation's ancestors. Visitors are permitted without their cameras or cars.

383

Accommodation at the **Mantenga Lodge**, *Manzini road, Ezulwini; tel: 61049; fax: 62168* (budget–moderate) is in 26 cottages with views of the surrounding mountains. The à la carte restaurant is open daily 0700–2200 and there is a bar, sauna and swimming pool. Some of the 30 en suite rooms at the **Mgenule Motel**, *foot of Malagwane Hill, near Royal Swazi Hotel, Manzini road; tel: 61041; fax: 46465* (cheap) are self-catering. The **Tandoori Restaurant** in the grounds serves halaal curry dishes as well as the more traditional steaks and seafoods.

The **Smokey Mountain Village**, *Matenga*

Falls road, off Manzini road, Ezulwini; tel: 61291; fax: 46465 (cheap–moderate) is surrounded by forest. This small resort has 18 self-catering 'A' frame chalets, each with its own verandah and braai area. A restaurant serves simple lunch and dinner and bar snacks are available all day long in the 'village' pub. Finally, the unique **Yen Saan Hotel**, *Manzini road; tel/fax: 61051* (cheap–moderate) is designed in Chinese style, a theme which is carried through to the interior, which contains 34 air-conditioned guest rooms. The restaurant, naturally, serves Chinese dishes.

EATING AND DRINKING

Restaurants in the hotels and motels listed above are open to non-residents. There are also a fair few non-hotel options. The **Calabash Continental Restaurant**, *signposted off Manzini road near Royal Swazi Sun Hotel; tel: 61187* (open daily for lunch and dinner; expensive) features dishes from Austria, France, Germany, Italy and Portugal, along with traditional haute cuisine. The **First Horse Restaurant**, *near Yen Saan Hotel, Manzini road; tel: 61137* (moderate) serves international and curry dishes.

The **Great Taipei Restaurant**, *next to Mantenga Craft Centre, Mantenga Falls road; tel: 62300* (cheap–moderate) serves Chinese food to eat in or take away. **Hippo Haunt**, *Mlilwane Wildlife Sanctuary; tel: 61591* (cheap–moderate) serves traditional Swazi fare.

SIGHTSEEING

The **Mlilwane Wildlife Sanctuary** *signposted off Manzini road, Ezulwini; tel: 44541* (open daily 0600–1800; weekdays E7, off-season weekends E10, peak season and long weekends E13) provides a glimpse of wild Africa just a 20-min drive from either Mbabane or Manzini. The 4450 hectare reserve is home to a wide range of game, including eland, kudu, impala, caracal and serval cats, giraffe, zebra, crocodile, hippo, buffalo and warthog. Rest camp accommodation (cheap) is available in thatched huts, dormitories and a thatched cottage. There are camping and caravanning sites, and accommodation in **Sondzela House**, Swaziland International Travellers Hostel, costs from E27.50 to E38.50 per night plus tax.

Lobamba is the royal village and real political capital of Swaziland. The **Embo State Palace**, home of King Mswati III, is closed to the public, but stop to look at the **King Sobhuza II Monument** and the **Somhlolo National Stadium**.

Visitors may listen to debates in **Houses of Parliament**, *next to the Somhlolo Stadium, off Manzini road, Lobamba*, from the public gallery, but must be properly attired – jacket and tie for men. The imposing building may be photographed from outside, but photography inside is strictly forbidden.

Aspects of the history and culture of Swaziland from the early Stone Age are shown at the **Swaziland National Museum**, *next to the Houses of Parliament, Lobamba tel: 61151* (open Mon–Fri 0900–1545, Sat–Sun 1000–1545; E10). Costumes, weapons, household pots and other items, together with an original homestead and cattle byre, help build a picture of Traditional Swazi life. The flesh is put on the bones at the **Swazi Cultural Village**, *Mantenga Nature Reserve, Mantenga Falls road, Ezulwini; tel: 61516* (open daily 0600–1800; free; charges for traditional dancing other activities and events). This is a new development in which traditional cultures and heritage are demonstrated – household chores, hairstyles, folklore, dance and song. In a collection of traditional beehive huts, authentically built of local materials – poles, saplings, thatching grass – without the use of modern tools, visitors can study how a polygamous Swazi family lives. The healer's hut, cattle byre, grain store and various huts reflect the traditional lifestyle. Local artists exhibit their sculpture, pottery, ceramics, basketry and weaving. In the nature reserve are highveld and middleveld habitats, hiking trails, picnic sites and, a short (1 km) but rough walk from the Cultural Village, the **Mantenga Falls**, a spectacular sight in the summer rains. In the reserve, accommodation is available in 20 traditionally-built rondavels and a campsite with an attached restaurant and kitchen.

The workshops of **Swazi Candles**, *Malkerns, signposted from Mbanane-Manzini road, 5 km south of Lobomba; tel: 83219* (open daily 0900–1700; free) are one of the country's more unusual attractions. Craftsmen and women make each candle individually – owls, tortoises, ducks, more intricate elephants and rhinos, or simple globular or egg shapes as colourful as stained glass. Each animal candle turns out with whatever expression its creator chooses, so the sea of faces on show provides an amusing scene and there are no two alike. Each candle is formed and then coated with an outer shell. These make lovely presents.

MANZINI

Almost at the centre of Swaziland, 42 km south

Swazi Royalty

Swaziland, which was ruled by Britain as a Protectorate for 66 years, achieved indepen-dence without undue birth pangs in 1968. King Sobhuza II, who was born in 1899, succeeded to the Swazi throne when he was 21, reigning until his death in 1982 and mak-ing the record books as the world's longest-reigning monarch of the 20th century.

The British had drawn up the Constitution. He altered it to maintain traditional tribal values in a changing world, and is still revered for this by the people. A memorial statue of King Sobhuza II is displayed in a park at Lobamba, together with photographs of him and words of wisdom he uttered over the years.

Also held in high esteem is the present king, Mswati III, who returned from his English public school (Sherborne in Dorset) to ascend the throne in April 1986.

The King has to be a member of the Dlamini family and must be unmarried at the time of his accession – though he may take a number of wives afterwards. It is not usual for the King's eldest son to succeed him, or any son of the King's first marriage, because by the time the King dies these older sons are likely to be already married.

Nobody knows for certain who the heir to the throne is. Only when the King dies do the Royal Council, who are members of the Royal Dlamini Family, decide who is to succeed. The Royal Council will already have decided who the new Queen Mother will be. She will be one of the late King's senior wives, chosen for her status in the family rather than for the duration of her marriage.

The Queen Mother, as First Lady of the Royal Household, is the most influential woman in the Kingdom. As soon as the King dies, however, she loses her status.

of Mbabane, Manzini is a large commercial and industrial city with nothing to interest the tourist except a daily handicrafts market.

The refurbished colonial **New George Hotel**, *Ngwane St; tel/fax: 52061* (moderate) has 56 air-conditioned en suite rooms, coffee shop and grill room. The **City Pub** in the hotel, is a popular watering hole for local residents and visitors alike, serving basic pub food. For a little more variety, try the Portuguese **Mocambique Restaurant**, *Mahleko St; tel: 52489.*

MHLAMBANYATSI

This pleasant small town is 27 km south-west of Mbabane on a newly tarred road. It stands in mountainous country at the heart of the Usutu Forest, with tumbling streams teeming with trout and bass. The **Luphole Dam** is ideal for canoeing, sailing, water skiing and windsurfing. The **Foresters Arms Hotel**, *PO Box 14, Mhlambanyatsi (signposted from road); tel: 74177; fax: 74051* (moderate) is one of Swaziland's most popular getaways, especially at weekends, when people are drawn from all parts of

Swaziland and neighbouring South Africa by the prospect of Sunday lunch. Standing in 585 hectares of highland country estate, it has 24 en suite rooms, each with a magnificent view and most overlooking the swimming pool. There is fishing in six stocked dams, and there are a number of self-guided walks. Horse-riding, tennis, squash, bowls and table tennis are avail-able and the **Usutu Golf Club** course adjoins the estate.

NGWENYA

Five kilometres from the Oshoek border post, the town is an important crafts centre, close to the Malolotja Nature Reserve. The Phuma-langa tapestries woven at the **Endlotane Studios**; *tel: 24149* (open daily 0800–1700; free) have achieved recognition in southern Africa, Europe and North America. Only re-cycled glass is used to make ornamental and functional glassware at **Ngwenya Glass**; *tel: 24053* (factory open Mon–Fri, showroom and coffee shop daily 0900–1530; free). Animals and birds of Africa, and vases and tableware, can

Highland Adventures

Swaziland has some sporting activities for the adventurous. Tourists on a tight budget are offered a 'No Frills' white-water rafting experience on the Great Usutu River – two nights' hostel accommodation in Mlilwane Wildlife Sanctuary, with a full day's rafting for about E300. A day's rafting can also be part of a 'Rhinos and Rafting' 2-night self-catering stay at Hlane Royal National Park. White-water rafting takes place all year. Capsizing is almost inevitable in some of the rapids. Participants are taught techniques in still water before they set out. Rafters who lose their nerve mid stream are allowed ashore to walk around the bigger rapids. Those eager for yet more thrills can combine rafting with abseiling – lowering themselves down a 48 m cliff face alongside the Bulunga Waterfall into the raft.

Advance booking is necessary for these adventures, available through **Big Game Parks**, *PO Box 234, Mbabane; tel: 44541*. The same organisation runs mountain bike rides in Mlilwane Wildlife Sanctuary, Swaziland's most visited park. Hardy cyclists can take a gruelling three-hour ride among wildlife and great scenery – and tracks strewn with obstacles.

be bought or ordered. Look for the ingenious glasses reshaped from old bottles. From a balcony, visitors can watch glassblowers at work.

The **Malolotja Nature Reserve**; *tel: 43060; reservations, tel: 61178* (open daily 0600–1800; E10 for foreigners, E6 for locals; camping E15, cabins Sun–Thur E130, Fri, Sat E180) covers more than 18,000 hectares from mountains, including two of the kingdom's highest peaks – Ngwenya (1829 m) and Silotfwane (1680 m) – to the Nkomata River gorge, and has many species of animals, reptiles, plants and over 280 species of bird, including secretary birds and the rare sacred ibis. There are 25 km of game-viewing roads and 200 km of hiking trails, from easy to strenuous. Of special interest is an ironstone mine said to date back 41,000 years. Visitors may see it in the company of a ranger. You will need to arrange this at least 24 hrs in advance. Accommodation is in self-catering log cabins, in the camping and caravan site or, for hikers, 17 basic trail camps. Water is available here, but as open fires are prohibited, walkers must take portable cookers. Day visitors may use a picnic site and braai.

Outside the park, the **Hawana Park Resort**, *Piggs Peak road; tel: 24335; fax: 43420*, offers self-catering chalets with en suite bathrooms and traditional Swazi huts, with nearby showers and toilets and an outside cooking area with electrical power points. There are campsites and a fully licensed restaurant.

Appropriately, the town's name means 'meeting place'. Here, in 1947, King Sobhuza II met the British monarch George VI, and in 1961, Swaziland was set on the road to independence when Prime Minister Harold Macmillan had talks with Swazi leaders. Close to the Mahamba border post, today it is a destination for travellers on their way to and from Piet Retief in South Africa.

The **Nhlangano Sun and Casino** *(SI); tel: 78211; fax: 78402* (moderate–expensive), set in 20 hectares overlooking the stupendous Makhosini Valley, has 47 air-conditioned chalet-type rooms, each with en suite bathroom and private terrace. There are bars, a restaurant, lounge and sports facilities.

In north-west Swaziland, about halfway between the Mbabane and Matsamo border post and 19 km east of Bulembu border post, this highland timber town owes its name to a prospector who found gold here in 1884. The seam ran out nearly 40 years ago.

Originally a farmhouse, the **Highlands Inn**, *1 km south of the town centre; tel: 71144* (moderate) stands in 2 hectares of gardens and has 18 rooms with private bath or shower. The **Phophonyane Lodge**, *14 km north of Piggs Peak; tel: 71429; fax: 71319* (budget–moderate) has self-catering thatched cottages, a guest suite and tents. Guests who prefer to have meals prepared may be served in their own accommodation or dine in the small à la carte restaurant overlooking the Phophonyane River.

Each of the 106 luxury rooms at the **Protea Piggs Peak Hotel and Casino** *(Pa), 10 km north of Piggs Peak; tel: 71104/5; fax: 71382* (moderate–expensive) faces the mountains and forests of the Phophonyane Valley. There is a renowned restaurant, and the coffee shop is open throughout the day serving light snacks and full à la carte menu. Activities include squash, tennis, swimming, horse-riding and walking. A disco and live entertainment are available at night.

BIG BEND

A small town among the sugar cane fields of Swaziland's Eastern Lowveld, where the Great Usutu River plunges through the Lubombo Mountains down to the lowveld and into Mozambique, Big Bend is well placed for visits to Mkhaya and Mlawula nature reserves and Hlane Royal National Park.

The **New Bend Inn**, *overlooking the river just south of the town; tel: 36111/2; fax: 36384* (cheap) has 24 rooms, a restaurant and a relaxing patio bar. The **Riverside Motel**, *10 km south of Big Bend, on the Lavumisa road; tel: 36012; fax: 36032* (cheap) is an attractive stopover built in Portuguese style. Each of its eight en suite rooms has a private car port. The restaurant, overlooking the Great Usutu River, specialises in Portuguese cuisine.

GAME RESERVES

The **Hlane Royal National Park** is 60 km north of Big Bend on the Lamahasha road; reservations with Big Game Parks essential; *tel: 44541, fax: 40957, weekdays; tel: 61591, fax: 61594 after hours.* (Open daily sunrise to sunset; peak season E13, out of season weekdays E7, weekends E10.) The park offers self-catering accommodation at **Ndlova Camp**, in rondavels without electricity (E77 per person based on two sharing to E88 in peak season), or two-bedroom modern cottages at **Bhubesi Camp** (E99–E115 according to season). Bhubesi Camp overlooks the Umbuluzana River, a popular drinking spot for local wildlife.

Walks with a Swazi guide are available for E10 per person. Among lowveld animals which may be seen are rhino (black and white), buffalo, elephant, hippo, giraffe, crocodile and many species of antelope. The park has the most southerly known nesting colony of Marabou storks and many birds of prey.

It is claimed that the upmarket private reserve of **Mkhaya Game Reserve**, *32 km west of Big Bend on the Manzini road; tel: 44541* (see Big Game Parks information, p.386) provides the best opportunity in Africa to photograph the endangered black rhino. There is certainly abundant wildlife. Day visits in open Land Rovers or on foot with highly skilled Swazi rangers cost E120; overnight stays E240, in luxury safari tents. Overnight guests have dinner cooked over a central log fire under the stars, and may be entertained by an impromptu performance of traditional dancing.

The **Mlawula Nature Reserve**, *83 km north of Big Bend, off the Lamahasha road; tel: 61178* (open 0600–1800, charges as for Malolotja; see Ngwenya, p. 385) covers 16,500 hectares near the border with Mozambique. Tools more than 100,000 years old have been found in river beds here. Rare cycads and succulents are amongst the 1000 species of plant growing in the reserve, and there are over 350 species of bird. Among animal occupants are a wide variety of antelope and the rare samango monkey.

> ### Bride Price
>
> As in many Southern African countries, marriage in Swaziland involves *lobola*, a custom in which a bridegroom has to pay a dowry – usually in the form of cattle – to the bride's parents.
>
> A Swazi man may point to his cows in a kraal by his home and tell foreign visitors, 'That is my bank.' The number of cattle a man pays for a bride measures his social status. Formal divorce is not recognised in Swaziland, but if a wife behaves disgracefully – by committing adultery, for instance – she is returned to her family and the husband has his lobola returned.

ZIMBABWE

Directly north of South Africa, bounded to the south by the Limpopo River and to the north by the legendary Zambezi, modern Zimbabwe is a relatively new country, only achieving independence and its present name in 1980. Its borders were drawn in 1890–92 by Cecil Rhodes, who colonised the lands of the Mashona, Manyika and Ndebele during his perpetual quest for more gold, land, wealth and power. The settlers rewarded his ambitions by naming their new country Rhodesia after him.

Today, after a bloody civil war in the 1970s, the country is calm, stable and relatively sound economically. It is also friendly, welcoming and extraordinarily beautiful, with a wealth of opportunities for tourists, including some of the best game-viewing in Africa, the magnificent Victoria Falls and the ruins of Great Zimbabwe, former capital of the Mwene Mutapas, powerful Karanga emperors who ruled much of central Africa in the 13th–15th centuries (p. 62).

TOURING ZIMBABWE

The route in this chapter is in the form of a rough circle around Zimbabwe, starting in Harare. It would be equally easy to pick it up in Masvingo or Bulawayo, if arriving from South Africa; or in Bulawayo or Victoria Falls if arriving from Botswana. Any route directons required are inserted in the relevant place in the text, and you can also refer to the colour map of Zimbabwe at the back of the book. To do it all by road, allow a minimum of two weeks.

HARARE

Tourist Information: **Harare Publicity Association**: *corner Jason Moyo Ave and 2nd St (African Unity Sq.); tel: 14-705 085/6.* City information and accommodation advice; pick up a free copy of the monthly *What's On* listings. **Zimbabwe Tourism Development Authority**, *Three Anchor House, 54 Jason Moyo Ave; tel: 14-758 712/4 or 752 570; fax: 04-758 828,* for information on the whole country.

ARRIVING AND DEPARTING

By Air
Harare Airport: *15 km south-east of the city centre.* The terminal on the left is for domestic flights; the larger one on the right for international services. Banks are open for all flight arrivals, and there are hotel and car hire desks. There is a rudimentary café, but shopping facilities are limited. Air Zimbabwe runs **airport buses** every hour (on the half-hour) from the **City Air Terminal**, *corner of 3rd St and Speke Ave, opposite Meikles Hotel (just behind African Unity Sq.); tel: 14-794 481; fax: 14-796 039.* Taxis are cheap as a speedier alternative (see Getting Around, see p.389).

By Rail
Station: *Kenneth Kaunda Ave; tel: 14-700 011 (14-700 033 after hours).* See also p. 54.

By Road
There are good road connections with all other major towns in Zimbabwe, and, through them, with neighbouring countries. **Car Hire**: p. 52.

By Bus

Express Motorways; *tel: 14-720 392*; **Ajay Motorways**, *tel: 14-703 421;* and **Blue Arrow**, *tel: 14-729 514*, are the main intercity coach operator. Most **local buses** are run by **Zupco**, *109 Belvedere Rd; tel: 14-750 570*. Times and destinations are posted at the **main bus terminal**: *2nd St*. Buses to outlying districts and rural areas run from the **Mbare Bus Terminal**, *Chaminuke and Ardbennie Rds*. There are no timetables here, so just turn up and wait for the next one.

GETTING AROUND

The city centre is small enough for walking. Small city centre **maps** are available from the Tourist Office. More detailed maps and full street guides are on sale in most bookshops and stationers. Metered on-street **parking** is usually easy to find and there are a couple of multi-storey car parks, on *Julius Nyerere Way*, and between *Union Ave and Samora Machel Ave*, for longer stays. Most hotels have secure parking areas. Elsewhere, someone will usually offer to guard your car for a few dollars. Take up the offer; it's a bargain. There is a fair amount of car crime, so always lock your car and never leave anything valuable in view.

Alternatively, the elderly **taxis** are cheap, metered and only break down occasionally. The main rank is on *African Unity Sq*. For reliable phone taxis, call **Rixi**; *tel: 14-753 080/1/2* or **Creamline**; *tel: 14-703 333*.

For **guided tours** of Harare and the surrounding area, contact **UTC** (see feature box, p.393) or **African Explorations**, *tel:14-721 586.*

To hire **bicycles**, contact **Bushtrackers**, *Bronte Hotel, corner 4th St and Baines Ave; tel: 14-303 025* or *796 631.*

STAYING IN HARARE

Accommodation

None of the city centre hotels are particularly atmospheric; all are in modern buildings. There are three large, 5-star hotels in central Harare (all expensive). The most famous, **Meikles**, *African Unity Sq.; tel: 14-795 655; fax: 14-707 754,* has a modern case built around the core of

the city's first hotel. Near the art gallery, the highrise **Holiday Inn Crown Plaza Monomotapa**, *(Hd/ZS), Julius Nyerere Ave; tel: 14-704 501; fax: 14-791 920*, is efficient, comfortable and has great views. Slightly further out, opposite the museum, is the **Sheraton**, *Pennefather Ave; tel: 14-729 771; fax: 14-728 450 .*

Slightly cheaper are the **Jameson Hotel** *(BW), corner Samora Machel Ave and Park St; tel: 14-794 641; fax: 14-794 655*, and the **Holiday Inn** *(Hd), corner Samora Machel Ave and 5th St; tel: 14-795 611; fax: 14-735 695* (both moderate). Good cheap options include the **Ambassador** *(Rb), 88 Union Ave; tel: 14-708 121; fax: 14-708 126*, which is right in the centre; while the **Courteney**, *corner Selous Ave and 8th St; tel: 14-704 400;* the **Selous**, *corner Selous Ave and 6th St; tel: 14-727 940/8/9; fax: 14-727 885;* and the **Bronte**, *152 Baines Ave; tel: 14-796 631* (all 2-star) are about 1.5 km from the centre.

Backpackers lodges in the suburbs include: **Kopje 221**, *221 Enterprise Rd, Chisipite; tel/fax: 14-499 097;* the **Backpackers' Lodge**, *72 King George Rd, Avondale; tel/fax: 14-335 341/335 176;* and the **Hillside Backpackers Lodge**, *71 Hillside Rd, Hillside; tel: 14-747 961.* A full list is available from the Tourist Office.

Campsite: Coronation Park, *6 km from the centre, off the Mutare Rd; tel: 14-46282*, is a large, comfortable shady site with full facilities.

Some of the best accommodation in the Harare area is a short distance out of town, still within commuting distance, but able to take advantage of the beautiful bush. **Imba Matombo**, *3 Albert Close, Glen Lorne; tel: 14-499 013/4; fax: 14-499 071* (expensive) is a small, luxurious thatched hotel – the only Relais & Chateaux property in Zimbabwe, with a French chef (see p.390). **Landela Lodge** *(La), Ruwa, 29.5 km from Harare on the Mutare road; tel: 14-702 634; fax: 14-702 546* (expensive) is a small, relaxed colonial country house hotel. Transport into Harare is available on request.

Eating and Drinking

As food prices are not tiered, the exchange rate works in favour of overseas visitors and it is

389

almost impossible to have an expensive meal in Zimbabwe – so splash out.

Some of the best food in town is inevitably to be found in the best hotels – **Meikles**, the **Monomotapa** and the **Sheraton** all have a range of eateries, while **L'Escargot**, *at the Courteney Hotel; tel: 14-706 411*, is one of the best restaurants in the city. The **Imba Matombo** (see above) offers superb French haute cuisine, given a local twist by available ingredients. Also excellent is **Victoria Twenty-Two**, *22 Victoria Dr., Newlands; tel: 14-776 429*, run by a German/Italian couple.

For local food, try the very touristy **Ramambo Lodge**, *corner Samora Machel Ave and Leopold Takawira St; tel: 14-792 029*, which serves game (such as crocodile, ostrich and zebra); the **Pan-African Restaurant**, *National Handicraft Centre, corner Grant and Chinhoyi Sts; tel: 14-721 816*, which serves traditional African food from various areas of the continent; or the jolly but very haphazard **Roots of Africa**, *corner 7th and Livingstone Aves; tel: 14-721 494*, where the fascinating menu seems to boil down to rabbit or goat stew – but you are well-entertained.

Communications

Main Post Office: *Inez Terrace; tel: 14-794 491*.

Money

Most large commercial banks have exchange facilities. Two conveniently central branches are: **Barclays**, *corner Jason Moyo Ave and 1st St; tel: 14-758 280*; **Standard Chartered**, *John Boyne House, corner Speke Ave and Inez Terrace; tel: 14-796 930*.

SHOPPING

The city centre is small and has plenty of useful shops interspersed with curios and souvenirs. Amidst the usual run of T-shirts and copper ashtrays are several galleries selling magnificent Shona sculpture, which are worth a visit even if you can't pay the rapidly climbing prices. Amongst the finest are the **Matombo Gallery**, *6 Zimre Centre, 114 L. Takawira St; tel: 14-792 472*; the **Vukutu Gallery**, *9 Harvey Brown Ave, corner Blakiston St; tel: 14-720 767*; and the

Dendera Gallery, *65 Speke Ave, between 1st and 2nd Sts; tel: 14-725 666*.

Mbare is the largest of the high density suburbs (former townships), and at its centre is a huge, throbbing **market**, *about 8 km from the city centre, just behind the main Mbare bus station*, (open daily until around 1730). To get there, leave central Harare on *Cameron St*, head past the huge football stadium, turn left and head down behind the bus station. Park near the large pie shop sign and the Musicaa supermarket. Beside the supermarket is the undercover tourist market, a huge hall crammed with souvenirs of good quality at reasonable prices; the main local market is in the concrete enclosure across the road. It is a feast of experience, with everything on sale from deep-fried grubs in a twist of paper and shoes made of old car tyres to pumpkin and sunflower seeds and strange-looking medicinal roots. People are friendly, happy to chat, and won't pressure you too hard to buy. It is a wonderful introduction to black Africa.

SIGHTSEEING

Originally known as Fort Salisbury, this town was founded by the white pioneers on 13 Sept 1890, and has been capital of Rhodesia, and then Zimbabwe, ever since. Today, Harare, named after a local chief with a reputation for alert vigilance (the name means 'the one who does not sleep') is a bustling city, with a population of about 1.5 million. It is reasonably attractive, a useful business centre and the main international gateway, but there are relatively few real attractions for tourists. As with all southern African cities, it still has a split personality, with a pristine, high-rise city centre and rich garden suburbs on one side, and a sprawl of tightly packed low-income housing on the other.

A very few nice colonial buildings are dotted between the 1950s and 1960s concrete blocks and 1980s mirrored skyscrapers, amongst them **Cecil House** (1901); the neo-renaissance **Town House** (1932), *Julius Nyerere Way*; the **Old Market Hall** (1894), *Market Sq., corner Mbuya Nehanda and Bank Sts*; **Jameson House** (1896), *Samora Machel Ave;* and the **Anglican Cathedral** (1913–61), *corner Baker*

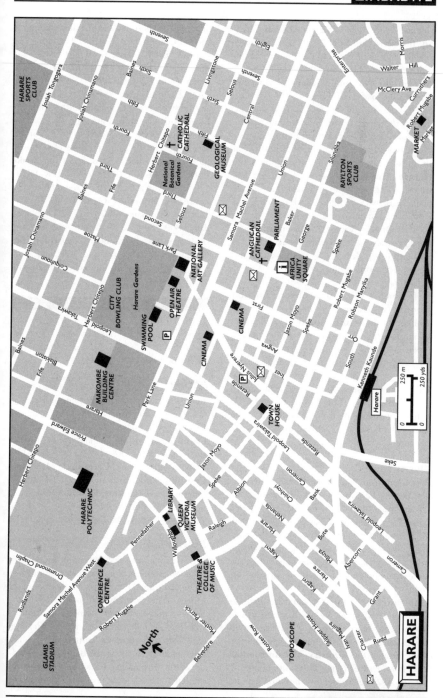

HARARE

North

0   250 m
0   250 yds

HARARE SPORTS CLUB

Josiah Tongogara

Baines

Sixth

Seventh

Fifth

Josiah Chinamano

Fourth

Third

Fife

Baines

Herbert Chitepo

National Botanical Gardens

CATHOLIC CATHEDRAL

Fourth

Third

Second

Selous

Park Lane

Mazoe

Coiynoun

Josiah Chinamano

Eighth

Livingstone

Selous

Sixth

Central

Seventh

GEOLOGICAL MUSEUM

Samora Machel Avenue

Union

Morris

Walter Hill

McClery Ave

Robert Mugabe

Curruthers

MARKET

Market

Silundika

RAYLTON SPORTS CLUB

Baker

George

Speke

PARLIAMENT

ANGLICAN CATHEDRAL

AFRICA UNITY SQUARE

First

Robert Mugabe

Robson Manyika

Union

Jason Moyo

Speke

Speke

South

Kenneth Kaunde

Harare

Harare

Takawira

Herbert Chitepo

Leopold

CITY BOWLING CLUB

Harare Gardens

NATIONAL ART GALLERY

SWIMMING POOL

OPEN AIR THEATRE

P

Baines

Blakiston

Fife

Harare

Prince Edward

Herbert Chitepo

MAKOMBE BUILDING CENTRE

Park Lane

CINEMA

Union

CINEMA

Julius Nyerere

Rezende

Angwa

Inez

TOWN HOUSE

Jason Moyo

Speke

Albion

Leopold Takawira

Rezende

Cameron

Chinhoyi

Bank

Bute

Abercorn

Leopold Takawira

Cameron

Seke

Drummond Chaplin

Samora Machel Avenue West

Rudlands

GLAMIS STADIUM

CONFERENCE CENTRE

Robert Mugabe

Pennefather

Willowvale

LIBRARY

QUEEN VICTORIA MUSEUM

Raleigh

Mother Patrick

THEATRE & COLLEGE OF MUSIC

Nehanda

Harare

Kaguvi

Mbuya

Harare

Kaguvi

Rotten Row

Belvedere

TOPOSCOPE

Skipper Hoste

Ivan Maguire

Charter

Rudd

Grant

HARARE POLYTECHNIC

Ave and 2nd St. This stands on **African Unity Sq.** (formerly *Cecil Sq.*), a pretty park originally established as a memorial to the pioneers on the spot where they first raised their flag.

The little **National Gallery,** *corner Julius Nyerere Ave and Park Lane; tel: 14-704 666* (open Tues–Sun 0900–1700; Z$1) is the one sight of real interest, with a second-rate permanent collection of lesser known European artists and a wonderful exhibitions of Zimbabwean art, in particular Shona sculpture. Behind it, the **Harare Gardens,** *between Park Lane and Leopold Takawira St,* are a lovely, lush, shady public park with a children's playground, and art displays and concerts at weekends.

The **Queen Victoria Museum,** *Pennefather Ave, opposite the Harare Sheraton; tel: 14-790 044* (open daily 0900–1700) is small and ragged, but worth a quick visit for the displays of local fauna.

In season, a visit to the **Tobacco Auction Rooms** is fascinating; details from the **Tobacco Marketing Board,** *TSF Building, Gleneagles Rd, Willowvale; tel: 14-666 311/5* (open Mon–Fri 0745–1200, late Apr–Sept; free). Zimbabwe is one of the world's largest tobacco growers and this massive complex has three simultaneous auction floors, selling up to 20,000 bales a day. **The Kopje,** reached from either *Rotten Row* or *Robert Mugabe Rd,* is the only hill in the area, with a toposcope and panoramic views over the city.

Out of Town

The **Chapungu Sculpture Garden,** *1 Harrow Rd, Beverley East, Msasa, 8 km from Harare off the Mutare road; tel: 14-486 648/487 113* (open Mon–Fri 0800–1800, Sat–Sun 0900–1800; Z$5) has a permanent display of over 350 magnificent pieces of Shona sculpture, together with a sales gallery, traditional Shona village and a *n'ganga,* who you can consult about your fortune.

Many of the best sights around are along the Bulawayo road. Built by the Koreans, in best Soviet style, **Heroes Acre,** *7 km from the city centre* (open Mon–Fri; visits by appointment only through the **Ministry of Information,** *5th Floor, Liquenda House, Baker Ave, Harare; tel: 14-706 891;* free) is the awe-inspiring national

memorial to those who led or died during the Second Chimurenga (War of Liberation). The **Larvon Bird Gardens,** *13a Oatlands Rd, Merwede, 17 km from Harare; tel: 14-229 816* (open Mon–Fri 0930–1700, Sat–Sun 0900–1700; Z$20) has over 400 species of birds from around world, while a little further out, the **Lion and Cheetah Park,** *Le Rhone Game Farm, about 24 km from Harare; tel: 172-27567/9* (open daily 0830–1700), provides close-ups of the big cats, while next door, at the **Snake Park;** *tel: 14-226 0056* (open daily 0830–1700), you can actually handle the reptiles. The **Ewanrigg Botanical Gardens,** *41 km from Harare on the Shamva road; tel: 174-23720* (open daily 0800–1800; Z$10) include 40 hectares of landscaped gardens, famous for their indigenous flora, water gardens, cacti and herbs, and a further 200 hectares of untouched bush with walking trails.

MASVINGO

Tourist Office: *Robert Mugabe St (opposite the Chevron Hotel), at the southern entrance to the town; tel: 139-62643. Open Mon–Fri 0800–1300, 1400–1600, Sat 0830–1300).*

ACCOMMODATION

There are two reasonable but boring hotels in town: the **Chevron,** *Robert Mugabe St; tel: 139-62054/5; fax: 139-65961;* and the **Flamboyant Motel,** *1.5 km from town on the Beit Bridge Road; tel: 139-53085; fax: 139-52899* (both cheap). **Campsite: Municipal Camping and Caravan Site:** *1 km from the centre on the Mutare Road; tel: 139-62431.*

Most people choose to stay at Great Zimbabwe or Lake Mutirikwe (see opposite).

SIGHTSEEING

This was the very first settlement founded by Rhodes' pioneer column as it headed north in 1890, and named Fort Victoria in honour of the Queen. The town moved in July 1892 to a better-watered site, and changed its name to Masvingo on independence, in 1980. The original **Fort** and **pioneer cemetery** lie a few kilometres south, along the Beit Bridge Road.

In the surroundings are a trio of noteworthy churches. Five kilometres from Masvingo, off

Main Zimbabwean Tour Operators

Most major tour operators in the country are based in Harare, although some also have branch offices elsewhere, and it is worth spending time here at the start of your trip to iron out all your requirements.

UTC, 4 Park St (PO Box 2914), Harare; tel: 04-793 7011 fax: 04-756 060, is the country's largest operator, running 'meet and greet' services, transfers, and local and countrywide tours from all the major tourist centres. They are also linked to Hertz Car Hire, Block Hotels and Frontiers Adventures. **Touch the Wild Safaris**, P. Bag 6, Hillside, Bulawayo; tel: 19-74589; fax: 19-44696, specialise in very exclusive, upmarket lodges and safaris, at a price to match.

Adventure tour specialists, offering a whole range of activities, from canoeing and white-water rafting to bush hiking, mainly in the Zambezi Valley, include: **Frontiers Adventures**, 1st Floor, Throgmorton House, corner Julius Nyerere Way and Samora Machel Ave; tel: 14-732 911/2/3; fax: 14-732 914; **Safari Par Excellence**, 3rd Floor, Travel Centre, Jason Moyo Ave, Harare; tel: 14-700 911; fax: 14-722 872; and **Shearwater Safaris**, Edward Building, corner 1st St and Baker Ave, Harare; tel: 14-757 831; fax: 14-757 836. All three have offices in Victoria Falls.

For walking safaris, contact **Backpackers' Africa**, Victoria Falls; tel/fax: 113-4510; for bird-watching, try **Birds of a Feather**, Harare; tel: 14-882 478; fax: 14-728 744; for canoeing on the Zambezi, there are several options, including **Kandahar Safaris**, Victoria Falls; tel: 113-4502; fax: 113-4556 and **Buffalo Safaris**, Kariba; tel:161-2645; fax: 161-2827.

the Mutare Road, the **Italian Church of St Francis**, *turn right on to Thorn Rd by Masvingo town sign,* was built by Italian prisoners of war held here between 1942–46; many chose to stay on afterwards, and one of them, a civil engineer, covered the apse with paintings and mosaics. The aisle decorations, wings and the tombs of 71 men who died in the camps were added by the Italian authorities in 1956–57. Work on the **Serima Mission Church**, *20 km from Masvingo on the Mvuma Rd,* began in 1948 under the auspices of a Swiss priest, Father John Gröber, who used it as an exercise to teach art to his students. The result is an extraordinary fusion of Catholic and Zimbabwean iconography, with every space covered in frescos, carvings and sculptures.

Mushandike Sanctuary, *27 km west of Masvingo along the Mashava Road, tel: 135-497,* is a 13,360 hectare wildlife sanctuary surrounding a beautiful lake. The mopane woodland supports a wide variety of antelope, including sable, as well as white rhino, wildebeest, zebra, warthog and other plains animals. Fishing permits and bookings for the small **camping and caravan site** are both available from the Park Warden.

From Masvingo, it is 290 km due south on

the A4 to Beit Bridge and the South African border (see p.312). The basic **Lion and Elephant Motel**, *on the Bubi River, 80 km north of Beit Bridge; tel: 114-336; fax: 114-358* (cheap) provides the best accommodation in the region. It is better, if possible, to continue on to Louis Trichardt (see pp.311–312).

GREAT ZIMBABWE AND LAKE MUTIRIKWE

ARRIVING AND DEPARTING

Leave Masvingo heading south on the A4 Beit Bridge road for about 3 km, then turn left on to the road signed to Great Zimbabwe and follow it for a further 25 km. Continue along this same road for a further 15 km to the Mutirikwe dam wall. It is possible to drive right round the lake, but the road is poor in places. For faster access to the Mutirikwe Recreational Park (Game Reserve) on the north bank, leave Masvingo on the Mutare road, head east for 20 km, turn right and follow the dirt road for a further 2.5 km to the gate.

A **local bus** service to Morgenster Mission, which goes within 1 km of the ruins, operates twice daily from the **Mucheke Bus Terminal**, *beside Musica, Charumbira St.* Ask the Publicity Association for details of times, and ask the driver when to let you off. There are also private taxis and organised tours from town.

ACCOMMODATION

The 2-star **Great Zimbabwe Hotel** *(ZS), Post Bag 9082, Masvingo; tel: 139-62449* (moderate–expensive) is a pretty, thatched hotel with good facilities (including a pool) and food, within easy walking distance of the ruins. There are also two new bush lodges on private game farms in the area: **Pa-Nyanda Lodge**, *between Masvingo and the ruins; tel: 139-63412; fax: 139-62000* (moderate), and **Karanga Lodge**, *overlooking the lake; tel: 139-62718; fax: 139-65791* (moderate). **Norma Jeane's Lake View Chalets**; *tel: 139-64879; fax: 139-65083* (cheap) and the **Mtirikwe Lake Shore Lodges**; *tel: 139-7151* (cheap) both offer pleasant self-catering chalets on the water's edge; activities on offer include fishing and game-viewing by boat.

Campsites: there are two wonderful campsites in the area. The **National Museums and Monuments Camp**; *tel: 139-7055*, provides camping and caravan sites and basic rondavels in the grounds of Great Zimbabwe itself; this is your chance to see the ruins at night or dawn, a breathtakingly beautiful experience. On the far side of the lake, the campsite in the **Mutirikwe Recreational Park**; *tel: 139-62913*, again has rondavels and space for campers on a rocky spur right on the shore, with the animals roaming freely around you.

SIGHTSEEING

Great Zimbabwe (open daily sunrise–sunset; US$5 for non-residents; Z$5 for Zimbabwean residents) is an enigma, even though people have finally given up the idea that it was King Solomon's mines, built by Phoenicians, or various other bizarre theories concocted to explain away the 'lost city'. In fact, although much of the architecture still has to be explained fully, it is only one of around 200 known 'zimbabwes' – stone-built towns, mainly scattered through southern Zimbabwe and the Northern Province of South Africa. But it is, of course, gloriously different from the others, in that it is

many times the size – the largest stone structure in Africa, after the Pyramids – and a sophisticated complex, where trade and industry flourished alongside the government of a great empire and the centre of a powerful religion.

The word 'zimbabwe' could derive from either *dzimba dza mabwe* ('houses of stone') or *dzimba woye* ('venerated houses') in Shona. It is a name given to all royal residences, chiefs' houses and graves; during the Chimurengas (freedom struggles), this remnant of an older, black empire, became the symbol of freedom, which eventually gave its name to the new country.

The earliest people to settle here appear to have been the Gokomere, in about 300 AD, but it only became a significant settlement from the 11th century onwards, when the Nguni Karanga-Rozwi people began to consolidate their empire. The first stone buildings date to the early 13th century and, within the next hundred years, it boomed as a powerful city-state, with a population of up to 20,000, who traded, via the Arabs, as far as China. From the 14th century onwards came the first written accounts by merchants of visits to the court of the all powerful *mambo* (priest-king), the *Mwene Mutapa* (Great Plunderer), whose empire covered all of modern Zimbabwe and spread across parts of Botswana, Zambia, Mozambique and South Africa. Within another hundred years, the glory days were over, as the empire fragmented amidst family squabbles, and the real seat of remaining power moved to Fura Mountain, north of modern Harare. Zimbabwe remained a royal city until 1834, when it was destroyed and all its inhabitants, including the last of the mambos, were massacred by the newly arrived Zulus.

Understanding the ruins can be difficult, so allow yourself time, buy the detailed site guide and plan, and start in the little **museum**, where you can also see the extraordinary stone Zimbabwe birds, which have become the national emblem of the country. Seven and a half of these greeny-grey soapstone birds, each about 40cm high, have been found; most stood on 1m pillars around the walls of the Hill Enclosure, and are thought to have been a family totem or memorials to dead ancestors.

The **Hill Enclosure** was the earliest inhabited site and had great significance as the spiritual temple/home of the priest-kings. There are two paths up: the steep, uneven Old Route and the gentler modern New Path. The old, which squeezes between giant rocks and defensive walls, is the more dramatic; try it coming down. At the top, the outer walls surrounds two enclosures, thought to have been an outer public court and private living area.

The **valley settlement** was where the mass of the people lived, while one enclosure is thought to have been the royal treasury as it contained large numbers of precious iron hoes, gongs and spearheads, copper and bronze wire, Indian glass beads and Chinese dishes. There is also now a reconstruction village, with dancers and souvenir sellers.

On the far side of the valley is the **Great Enclosure**, the largest and most important of all the buildings, with a 255 m outer wall, built with a million granite blocks weighing some 15,000 tonnes. The quality of the work improved dramatically as it was built, in an anti-clockwise direction, with the latest sections sporting chevron designs around the top. Inside are numerous old hut floors, animal enclosures and ceremonial platforms, all leading to the famous **conical tower**, which stands 10 m high, is 5 m in diameter at the base and is solid right through. With no other sensible explanation forthcoming, it appears to be the world's largest phallic symbol. It is known that the health of the nation was dependent on the health of the king, so it makes sense that the fertility of its land would also be connected. This enclosure is generally thought to have been the home of the Royal family from the mid 13th century, with five or six households living here.

A granite ridge covered by small enclosures and terraces, possibly the work of 18th-century invaders, leads back to the museum.

Nearby **Lake Mutirikwe** is, when full, the third largest lake in Zimbabwe, still commonly referred to as Lake Kyle. Unfortunately, it has suffered badly during recent droughts, at one stage emptying completely, and is still nowhere near full. It is a particularly beautiful lake, its shores bounded by great slabs of granite gleaming in the sun from tiny flecks of mica. Along

the southern shore and near the dramatic 305 m wide dam wall are several small holiday resorts (see Accommodation), viewpoints and picnic sites. Look out for huge monitor lizards basking on the rocks.

Most of the north shore is taken up by the 7600 hectare **Mutirikwe Recreational Park** (open sunrise–sunset), an oddly-named, but well-stocked game park that was at the forefront of the drive to preserve the rhino. It still has a particularly good rhino population, and large quantities of antelope and small game, while the lake has hippo and crocodiles. There are no large predators. Guided horse rides are available from the parks office near the main gate (advance booking essential).

To reach Bulawayo, return to Masvingo and take the A9 road to Bulawayo via Zvishavane. Distance: 293 km; allow about 3 hrs. There are no worthwhile stops en route.

BULAWAYO

Tourist Office: *City Hall Car Park, off Robert Mugabe Way, between Leopold Takawira and 8th Aves; tel: 09-60867.* Open Mon–Fri 0830–1645.

ARRIVING AND DEPARTING

By Air

Bulawayo Airport, *Queens Rd, 22 km north of the city centre; tel: 19-26491/2,* has regular flights from Harare, Hwange and Victoria Falls. An airport bus connects all inward and outbound flights with the Bulawayo Sun Hotel (see Accommodation).

By Road

Good tarred roads lead to Bulawayo from all other major centres in Zimbabwe, as well as from the Botswana border at Plumtree (100 km) and the South African border at Beit Bridge (321 km). **Parking** in town is free and easy, with plentiful on-street parking and a large car park behind the City Hall.

There are regular **coach** services to Bulawayo from Johannesburg, Harare, Victoria Falls and Masvingo. Companies serving Bulawayo include: **Ajay's Motorways,** *c/o Manica Travel, 10th Ave between Main and Fort*

Sts; tel: 19-540 535; **Express Motor ways**, *c/o UTC corner 14th Ave and George Silundika St; tel: 19-61402;* **Blue Arrow**, *Unifreight House, 73a Fife St; tel: 19-65548,* and the **Zimbabwe Omnibus Company**, *Lobengula St; tel: 19-67291.*

By Rail

Station: *Lobengula St; tel: 19-363 111,* or *322 284* after hours. There are regular services to Harare, Victoria Falls, Botswana and South Africa, and all the cruise trains to Victoria Falls call here (see p.54).

GETTING AROUND

There are several **taxi** ranks within the city, with the largest beside the City Hall. The most reliable service is **Rixi**, based at the Bulawayo Sun; to book a taxi: *tel: 60666, 61933, 72454, 60154* or *60704.* **Car hire**: see p. 52.

Frequent **local bus** services only travel as far as the high density suburbs. Services for the northern, eastern and southern suburbs leave from *City Hall, 8th Ave, between Fife St and Robert Mugabe Way; tel: 09-67172;* those for the western suburbs go from the corner of *Lobengula St* and *6th Ave.* Most are geriatric, deeply uncomfortable and belch black smoke. Timetables are, theoretically, available from the terminals.

Local **tours** are available from **UTC**, *tel: 19-61402,* and **Black Rhino Safaris**, *tel: 19-41662.*

ACCOMMODATION

The **Bulawayo Sun** *(Hd/ZS), corner 10th Ave and Josiah Tongogara St; tel: 19-60101; fax: 19-61739* (moderate) is the largest and most central of the local hotels, mainly used by businessmen. There is also a more basic **Holiday Inn** *(Hd/ZS), Ascot Centre, PO Box AC88, Bulawayo; tel: 19-72464; fax: 19-76227* (cheap–moderate) near the racetrack. The mock-Tudor **Churchill** *(BW), about 6 km from the centre, corner Matopos Rd and Moffat Ave; tel: 19-41016; fax: 19-44247* (moderate), belongs more properly near a motorway exit in England's Home Counties, but is nevertheless one of the city's better hotels. Right in the centre, Eland Hotels have two old colonial hotels,

the **Selborne**, *Leopold Takawira Ave, corner George Silundika St; tel: 19-65741,* and **Grey's Inn**, *73 Robert Mugabe Way, corner Leopold Takawira Ave; tel: 19-540 318* (both 2-star; cheap). There are several good bed and breakfasts and guesthouses in the suburbs, including the **Induna Lodge**, *16 Fortunes Gate Rd, Matsheumhlope; tel: 19-45684; fax: 19-45627,* and **McAllister's Lodge**, *57 Southway Dr., Burnside; tel: 19-44462/78525* (both expensive for overseas visitors thanks to three-tier pricing).

There is an official **HI Youth Hostel**, *corner Townsend Rd and 3rd St; tel: 19-76488,* with strictly enforced lock-up times (all out 1000–1700, all in by 2230). There are also several more lenient backpackers' hostels, including **Africa Sun Backpackers' Lodge**, *398 Thurso Rd, Killarney; tel: 19-31528/76523;* and **20 Devon Road Backpackers**, *Hillside, 6 km from the centre; tel: 19-41501* (both cheap).

Campsite: Bulawayo boasts the country's finest **Municipal Caravan Park**, *Centenary Park; tel: 19-75011.* It is lush, cool, shady and centrally located, with a few basic chalets as well as camping and caravan pitches.

Out of town, the **Coach House**, *27 km from Bulawayo, on Robert Mugabe/Turk Mine Rd; tel: 19-226 009* (cheap) does bed and breakfast, full board by prior arrangement, and has caravan and camp sites on a working cattle ranch. The owners have a fine collection of carriages and other horse-drawn vehicles. Many people also choose to stay in the Matobo (see p.398).

EATING AND DRINKING

Outside the hotels, **Cape to Cairo**, *77 Robert Mugabe Way; tel: 19-72387* (moderate) is an attractive restaurant and cocktail bar in a restored colonial building. Of the towns various steakhouses, the best is probably **The Cattleman**, *corner 12th Ave and Josiah Tongogara St; tel: 19-76086* (moderate). **Morgans Restaurant**, *Ramji's Complex, corner Robert Mugabe Way and 11th Ave; tel: 19-79404* (cheap–moderate) is a popular local pub-restaurant.

SIGHTSEEING

When Mzilikazi fled north from the wrath of Shaka (see p. 64), he eventually stopped

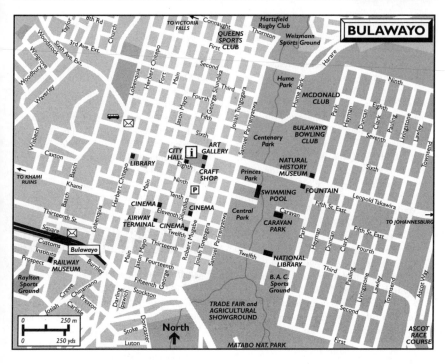

running once he had crossed the Limpopo and settled down in what is now Matabeleland, in south-western Zimbabwe. In 1868, when Lobengula inherited the throne, he moved the capital to KwaBulawayo (the place of killing), 6 km from the present city. It was to this spot that Cecil Rhodes sent negotiators, in 1888, to gain the concessions leading to the colonisation of Rhodesia. During the Matabele Wars of 1893–96, Lobengula fled and died in the hills, his city was demolished, a new colonial State House was built on the ruins, and Bulawayo became the Matabeleland headquarters of the British South Africa Company. It is still Zimbabwe's second city.

At the centre are the imposing **City Hall**, *in the square formed by Leopold Takawira Ave, Fife St, Robert Mugabe Way and 8th Ave*, and Tourist Office. Just north of it, the **Art Gallery**, *75 Main St, corner Leopold Takawira St; tel: 09-70721 (open Tues–Sun 0900–1700; Z$1)* is housed in a magnificently restored colonial building, **Douslin House**. The gallery is small, focussing on some excellent contemporary local

art, and also has a number of artists's studios in the courtyard behind, a good shop and café.

To the south, green and leafy **Centenary Park** and **Central Park**, together cover 45 hectares between *Samuel Parirenyatwa St* and *Park Rd*. In Centenary Park, visit the **Natural History Museum**, *corner Park Rd and Leopold Takawira Ave; tel: 19-60045* (open daily 0900–1700; non-residents US$2, Zimbabwe residents Z$3), undoubtedly the best museum in Zimbabwe, with a mammal collection alone that includes 75,000 specimens. Relatively few are on permanent display, but the presentation is excellent, with galleries devoted to animals, birds, insects, archaeology, anthropology and geology. Highlights include a reproduction gold mine and a fascinating collection of Rhodes memorabilia.

Bulawayo has been the headquarters of the national railways since 1897. Behind the station, the **Railways Museum**, *corner Prospect Ave and 1st St, Raylton* (open Tues, Wed, Fri 0930–1200, 1400–1600, Sat–Sun 1400–1700; Z$5) is interesting to everyone, not just enthusiasts, with numerous old steam locomotives and carriages, including Rhodes' private train, together with memorabilia and photos covering a hundred years of railway history.

Township Square, *corner Old Falls Rd and Basch St, next to Makokoba Township; tel: 19-76673/79379*, is an open-air cultural centre, where art and craft sales, fashion and fairs combine with the best of Zimbabwean music, dance, theatre and any other artistic endeavour going. Nearby, **Makokoba Market** is a lively African market selling everything from spare tyres to traditional medicine.

To combine shopping and sightseeing, visit the **Mzilikaze Art and Crafts Centre**, *Taylor Ave, 4 km from the centre of town, off the Old Falls Rd near Mpilo Hospital, Western Suburbs; tel: 19-67245* (open Mon–Fri 1000–1230, 1400–1700), a thriving local pottery, sculpture and arts centre and school. Opposite, at **Bulawayo Home Industries**; *tel: 19-65376*, workers create a wide variety of carpets, woven or batik textiles, ilala palm basketware and other crafts. Both were originally set up as community projects.

Out of Town

The **Chipingali Wildlife Orphanage**, *26 km from Bulawayo along the Gwanda Rd; tel: 19-70764* (open Tues–Sun 1000–1730; Z$15) cares for orphaned, sick or abandoned wildlife and operates a captive breeding programme for endangered species. Those that cannot be returned to the wild are given a permanent home, with a 100 hectare park and large aviaries alongside the main orphanage. This is a chance to take close-up photos.

On the opposite side of town, the **Tshabalala Sanctuary**, *8 km from Bulawayo along the Matopos Rd* (open 0600–1800), is a small National Parks game reserve, with plenty of smaller animals, but no large predators; walking and cycling are permitted.

The **Cyrene Mission**, *32 km from Bulawayo along the Plumtree Rd,* was founded in 1939 by Canon Edward Paterson, who was also responsible for creating an artists' studio in Harare (see p. 392). This time, he used the simple stone chapel as a training ground for his art students, who have turned it into a joyous festival of

colour, with the biblical message presented in purely African style.

The **Khami (or Kame) Ruins**, *22 km west of Bulawayo; take 11th Ave and follow it as it turns into Khami Road* (open daily 0800–1700), are a magnificent ruined stone city, second only to Great Zimbabwe. Although humans have lived in the area for about 100,000 years, building began in about 1400 AD. The city was destroyed in 1830 by Ndebele invaders. Massive granite walls support a series of terraces used for building, farming and defence. As at Great Zimbabwe, the high ground is thought to have been the royal enclosure. There is a small site museum and guide.

MATOBO (MATOPOS) NATIONAL PARK

PARK INFORMATION AND ACCOMMODATION

The main gate is about 30 km from Bulawayo along the Matopos Road (a continuation of *Robert Mugabe Way*). Open daily sunrise–sunset; Z$50 (non-resident), Z$10 (resident) per person, plus Z$10 per car. There is an information office at the Maleme Rest Camp (open 0600–1200, 1400–1800). Walking and cycling are permitted everywhere but in the fenced game park.

Pretty **Maleme Dam**, *overlooking a small lake; follow the signs,* is the main camp, with chalets and rondavels, camping and caravan sites. The approach is steep, so be careful if towing. There are smaller camping and caravan sites at **Mtshelele Dam**, *in the south-east of the park,* and at the **Arboretum**, *near the north entrance.* Take all supplies, including food and fuel, as there are no stores or garages. Accommodation bookings via **National Parks Central Reservations Office** *(ZN),* or their office at *140a Fife St, Bulawayo; tel: 19-63646/7.*

Outside the park, several small safari lodges have recently been opened. **Camp Amalinda**, *45 km south-west of Bulawayo on the Matopos road (7 km from the park gate); tel: 183-8268;* reservations: *19-439 5410 fax: 19-78319* (expensive) has thatched rooms built into the granite outcrop, with the main living area a traditional San cave. The price includes full board and two activities a day (game-drives or walks, riding, local village visits, San paintings), and there are 3 small elephants. Guests can interact as they are groomed and washed, and go for rides (extra cost). The **Matobo Hills Lodge**, *near the northern boundary; tel: 19-74589; fax: 19-44696* (expensive) is also magnificent, set in a wild natural rock garden which has been drawn into the architecture with a true artist's eye. Less expensive is the motel-style **Matobo Ingwe Lodge**, *Gladstone Farm, off the Figtree Rd; tel: 183-8233; fax: 183-8217* (cheap), where accommodation is in simple thatched rondavels. Ask the Bulawayo Tourist Office for many other options. It is possible to see the Matopos in a single day, but if possible allow yourself longer.

SIGHTSEEING

This superb area, covering almost 2000 sq. km, is a giants' playground of vast granite boulders, some 3000 million years old. Over the endless millenia, wind and water have stripped the rock bare, and twisted and carved it into a thousand impossible formations of balancing rocks, sweeping vistas of stone and sculpted outcrops stained red, gold and green by lichens. To the Rozwi, this was a sacred place; Mzilikazi named the hills Matobo ('bald-headed ones'); Rhodes created a 43,200 hectare National Park.

The main road loops through the park. Look out for small game, and for snakes if climbing the rocks. There are numerous caves which have well-preserved San rock paintings, of which the best known are at the **Mjelele Cave**, **White Rhino Shelter**, **Pomongwe Cave** and **Nswatugi Cave** – the best preserved of all the Matobo paintings are reached via steep rocky steps. A tiny **museum** offers a little background and a detailed map of the area.

The **View of the World** is a massive granite dome, considered sacred by locals, who call it **Malindidzimu** ('the place of spirits'). Cecil Rhodes, who was always aware of the potent symbolism of sacred ground and found good views wherever he went, chose to be buried here in 1902. It took two weeks to bring his body up from Cape Town by train to Bulawayo then out to the Matopos by ox-cart. His seemingly simple grave had to be blasted

out of solid granite. Also buried up here are Rhodes' right-hand man, Dr Leander Starr Jameson, famous as the leader of the failed Jameson Raid (see p. 66) and Sir Charles Coghlan, who became first prime minister of Rhodesia in 1923. There is also a **Memorial to the Shangaan Patrol**, a group of 34 Rhodesian soldiers, headed by Allan Wilson, who faced down a Zulu impi of 30,000 men on 3 Dec 1893, during the Matabele Wars. They died bravely, killing 400 Zulus, and were honoured for their courage by both sides.

The western sector of the park is fenced off as the **Whovi Game Park**, which has a broad range of small game, together with a relatively large concentration of both white and black rhino.

HWANGE NATIONAL PARK

For drivers, all three main camps are accessed off the main Bulawayo–Victoria Falls road, and both **Express** and **Ajay's coaches** make stops here. The small **Hwange National Park Airport**, *about 18 km from Main Camp*, has regular scheduled flights to Bulawayo, Victoria Falls, Kariba and Harare (the same plane doing a milk-run). The **railway** station in Dete, *26 km from Main Camp*, is a regular stop on the Bulawayo–Victoria Falls line. Most local hotels or safari operators will organise transfers if informed of your arrival in advance.

For those doing self-drive tours, detailed road maps of the park, advice on where game has been spotted recently and the condition of the roads are available from information desks in the camps. Inform them of the direction you are taking, so they can send out search parties in case of trouble. No trailers, open vehicles or motorbikes are allowed into the park, and there is a speed limit of 40 kph. You must leave the park or report into a camp by 1800, so you will need to leave by 1200 if travelling between Main and Robins Camps, by 1400 between Main Camp and Sinamatella, and by 1500 between Sinamatella and Robins.

For those who prefer guided game-viewing drives with a knowledgeable ranger, **UTC** operates from Main Camp and the Hwange Safari Lodge; **Touch the Wild Safaris** operate from Hwange Safari Lodge, or

399

contact **Shamwari Safaris**; *tel/fax: 118-248,* who also run longer camping trips inside the park. All the private game lodges run their own vehicles. **Guided walks** are run by rangers from all three main camps.

PARK INFORMATION AND ACCOMMODATION

Advance information and bookings for all accommodation within the park should be made through the **National Parks Central Reservations Office**, *Harare (ZN).* There are information desks at all three main camps within the park (see Accommodation below). **Main Camp**, *15 km from turning off the Bulawayo–Victoria Falls Road, by the 264.5 km peg; tel: 118-371,* is the largest, with facilities including self-catering cottages and lodges, a camping and caravan site, restaurant, bar, store and fuel pumps. **Sinamatella**, *about 50 km from Hwange town; tel: 118-44522,* is much smaller, with self-catering cottages and lodges, a camp site and store. Both are open all year. **Robins Camp**, *in the far northern Matetsi area, about 118 km from Victoria Falls; tel: 118-70220,* has only basic chalets with communal facilities and is closed Nov–Apr. The road is being upgraded to allow year-round access.

There are also several small 'exclusive' camps, available for private hire, including the **Nantwich Lodges**, *11 km from Robins Camp;* **Bumbusi and Lukosi Camps**, *in the Sinamatella area;* and **Deka Camp**, *25 km west of Robins Camp.* Bambusi and Deka are only accessible in a 4x4.

Recent years have seen a positive explosion in the number of small upmarket lodges springing up along the eastern boundaries of Hwange, mainly around the **Dete** area (all expensive). The largest and oldest-established is the **Hwange Safari Lodge** *(ZS), about 11 km from Main Camp; tel: 118-331/2,* set in its own extensive game reserve, overlooking a waterhole for evening viewing from the terrace. They also operate a **bush camp**, with grass huts and tree houses. **Touch the Wild Safaris** operate several luxury camps: the **Sikumi Tree Lodge**; *tel: 118-2105,* with accommodation in thatched, stilted huts, and the pink-brick **Sable Valley Lodge**. Others include **Chokamella**

Camp *(La),* with thatched cottages on a sandstone cliff above the Chokamella River; the **Detema Safari Lodge** *(Bk), tel: 118-256; fax: 118-269,* with thatched Ndebele-style painted chalets overlooking a waterhole for the animals and pool for the humans, and **Makololo Plains** *(Wd),* a tented camp in a remote section of the park proper.

In the Matetsi area, **Sizinda Lodge** *(Bv),* turn right about 1 km beyond the Robin's Camp turn off, about 45 mins drive north of Hwange town; tel: 181-3498, is a small, friendly lodge on a hill, with wonderful views over the surrounding plains. The rangers here are particularly keen on bush-walks, but will take you driving on their own land for full days inside the park, or on sightseeing tours of Victoria Falls.

SIGHTSEEING

Founded in 1929, Hwange is the biggest of Zimbabwe's game reserves, covering a massive 14,650 sq. km in the north-west corner of the country. It is also the third largest in Africa and home to 107 species of mammal and 410 species of bird, including an estimated 22,000 elephants. The best time to visit is May–Sept, when the vegetation has been eaten down and water shortages force animals to concentrate round the pans and boreholes.

Within the park, there are 482 km of road, most of them dirt and some impassable in the rainy season. Most people stay in the dryish teak woodland area around Main Camp, specifically on the circular **Ten Mile Drive**, which connects three large waterholes, **Dom Pan, Balla Balla Pan** and **Nyamandhlovu Pan**, where there is a high level observation platform overlooking the water to give you a break from the car. It is here, if anywhere, that you will see the magnificent sable antelope. Sinamatella is situated on a small hill that gives excellent views of the surrounding area. The vegetation is mixed here, with open grassland, rocky kopjes and mopane woodland, offering a variety of meals to a range of animals. The more remote Robin's Camp is particularly noted for large concentrations of lion, buffalo and roan antelope.

VICTORIA FALLS

Tourist Office: *Parkway; tel: 113-4202.* Open

Mon–Fri 0800–1300, 1400–1700, Sat 0800–1300.

Parkway is the main street of Victoria Falls village, also known as Wimpy Corner. Almost all the travel agents, car hire companies and tour operators have offices crammed into this short stretch, with billboards outside to advertise their products. They all open daily 0700–2000, seem happy to make bookings for each other, and prices are fairly uniform (and high). The only decision left to you is what you can afford of the many activities on offer, and which whitewater or canoe company to start with. The three main contenders are **Frontiers, Shearwater** and **Safari Par Excellence** (see box, p.393).

ARRIVING AND DEPARTING

There are good road and rail connections to Bulawayo, good roads across the borders to Zambia, Namibia and Botswana, and frequent flights from Harare, Bulawayo and Johannesburg. Air Zimbabwe runs a bus to meet all flights into the **airport**, about 40 km from town, and most hotels have courtesy coaches to the airport, the town centre and the falls. Once in the village you can get around fairly easily on foot. The main **car hire** companies are represented (see p. 52), but book ahead to ensure that there will be a car available; the local fleets are small. Several local tour operators run general sightseeing tours. **Bicycles** can be hired from **Bushtrackers**, *behind the Post Office; tel: 113-2024* (about Z$25 per hour, or Z$150 per day).

ACCOMMODATION

Victoria Falls is exploding with tourists and hotels to cater for them all. The bad news is that the owners are cashing in, and prices are routinely double those in the rest of the country.

In the town centre, the **Victoria Falls Hotel** *(ZS); tel: 113-4751/4203; fax: 113-4586* (expensive) is not only the oldest hotel in town, but undoubtedly the best. This is one of the great classic hotels of Africa, a calm, almost monastic colonial building, with lovely gardens and superb views over the gorges and bridge. Visit for a drink if you can't afford to stay.

Lower down the price scale, the 3-star

Rainbow Hotel *(Rb); tel: 013-4583; fax: 013-4654* (moderate) is a recently refurbished hotel with Moorish architecture, while the 2-star **Sprayview Motel**, *near the old aerodrome; tel: 113-4344; fax: 13-4713* (moderate) provides some of the cheapest accommodation in the area.

A short distance upstream of the falls, the vast **Elephant Hills Hotel** *(ZS); tel: 113-4793; fax: 113-4655* (expensive) is an eyesore, but from the inside, it is a huge, 5-star family resort, with a games room, golf course and casino among its many entertainments. A little further on, the **A'Zambezi River Lodge** *(Rb); tel: 113-4561-4; fax: 113-4536* (moderate) is an attractive sprawling, thatched complex.

Campsites: There is a municipal **Rest Camp**, *next to the Tourist Office, in the centre of the village*, with a selection of dormitory accommodation, one-and two-bedroomed chalets and a camping site, and a 60-berth **caravan site** *on the river, 3 km from the village; tel for both: 113-4210/4311.*

The **National Parks Authority** *(ZN)* has some self-catering lodges inside the game park at **Zambezi Camp**, *6 km upstream from the falls*, and three remote fishing camps, at **Kandahar** (open all year), **Sansima** and **Mpala Jena** (open May–Oct).

Out of town, there is a rapidly growing number of delightful small safari lodges scattered along the river and through various areas of bush around Victoria Falls, including the tented **Masuwe Lodge** *(La), 7 km on the Bulawayo road; tel: 113-4699*, and **Sekutis Drift** *(La), about 15 km from town, on the Chamabonda National Park road (7 km from the Airport Road); tel: 113-426 524*, a turn-of-the-century-style colonial lodge (both expensive). One of the most beautiful is **The Gorges** *(Bk; expensive; no children under 12), about 12 km from town, off the Airport Rd*, where wood and thatch chalets teeter right on the clifftop overlooking the gorges and the rafting.

SIGHTSEEING

When David Livingstone first canoed cautiously along the Zambezi to the rim of the falls and peered over in Nov 1855, he was

401

completely entranced. Ignoring the fact that all the locals and quite a few Afrikaner hunters already knew all about them, he discovered them officially, discarded their musical traditional name, *Mosi-Oa-Tunya* (the smoke that thunders), and named and claimed them for his queen, Victoria. They are truly superb, the largest waterfalls in the world, standing 61–105m high, 1688m wide, with some 545 million litres of water cascading over the rim every minute in flood season, shooting a fog of spray 500m into the air.

The **Victoria Falls** (open daily; US$5) is a protected national park. Vendors rent out umbrellas and raincoats in the car park by the entrance; be careful to have some way of keeping cameras dry; the falls spray creates a permanent light rain along the path. The best time to visit is in mid winter (July–Aug), when the rainfall and flow of water are low, the falls are not obscured by too much spray and rainbows play in the mist.

Just inside the gate, a display board details the unique geology, flora and fauna of the falls and the cloud forest along the rim. From here, a 2–3 km loop walking path heads first to Devil's Cataract and a memorial statue to Livingstone, then leads along the rim of the gorge to a series of lookout viewing points before returning to the gates via the woods behind.

The **bridge**, a road and rail link and the border between Zimbabwe and Zambia, was built, on the orders of Cecil Rhodes, so close to the Falls that passengers could feel the spray as they crossed. He died before it was completed in 1905, but it is a monumentally beautiful work. Take your passport to be allowed on for a look, or across to Zambia on a day-trip. The bridge's most spectacular function these days, however, is as the home of the world's tallest and most beautiful **bungee jump** (US$90), operated by African Extreme.

You need to plan your time and finances carefully here. There are so many activities on offer that it is almost impossible to slot them all in. First priority must be to see the falls from the air – a totally magical experience. However, the range of options is wide, starting with the original **Flight of Angels**, in a 6-seater Piper Aztec

plane (US$45). Other possibilities include a **helicopter** (US$65), **sea plane** (US$60), or **microlight** (US$92). For safety reasons, the **hot-air balloons** (US$130) keep clear of the Falls themselves.

Next comes the watery experience. **White-water rafting** here (US$85 for a half-day; US$95 for the full day) is some of the wildest, commercially-run water in the world. There is a choice between paddling yourself, or riding with professional paddlers, all on large inflatables. There is a strong chance that you will go in at some point along the way, but the safety record of the operators here is impeccable, and for most of the 60,000 people a year who do the rafting expeditions, it is the highlight of their holiday. Be warned: there is a 250m climb down to the river – and back up at the other end. Upstream of the falls, the boat trips are less frenzied, with gently alcoholic **river cruises** (US$25) and peaceful **canoe** trips (US$65 for a half-day). Back on land, try an old-fashioned Safari Train into Zambia (see p. 57), or just cross into Livingstone for a morning's sightseeing. You can go **horse riding** (US$50), on full day **game-drives** (US$100) in the Zambezi National Park, **walking safaris** (US$52), or **game-viewing by elephant** (US$345, including accommodation and full-board; or US$110 for a half-day; no children under 16). In between, more normal pastimes, such as swimming, tennis and golf are available. Do not swim in the river upstream of the falls, where hippos, crocodiles and bilharzia are all waiting to get you.

To give your pocket a rest, spend a more gentle half-day exploring the village and surrounding area. The **African Craft Village**, *behind the Post Office; tel: 113-4309* (open Mon–Sat 0830–1630, Sun 0900–1230; Z$28) has a variety of authentically decorated and furnished huts belonging to all main tribal groups in Zimbabwe, such as a Venda chief's hut, San shelter, Shona funerary hut and Batonka children's hut. Go round on your own, with their excellent guidebook, or take a guided tour. The resident *n'ganga* promises good fortune to all, and there is a traditional dance programme each evening (1830–2000; Z$75), displaying the masked dances of the Makishi, war dances of the Shangaan, and other highly dramatic, often funny, dance dramas. The other regular dance programme is the very commercial **African Spectacular**, *in the grounds of the Elephant Hills Hotel* (daily, 1900).

Beyond the Village, the road bowls into a huge **craft market**, surrounded by more elegant souvenir shops, selling everything from jewellery to stuffed lions. The **Snake Park**, *Adam Stander Dr., behind the Post Office; tel: 113-4236* (open Mon–Sat 0800–1700, Sun 0900–1600; Z$30), offers a chance to see some of Africa's most deadly reptiles under controlled conditions. The **Zambezi Nature Sanctuary**, *opposite the A'Zambezi River Lodge, about 4 km from the village centre, tel: 113-4604* (open daily 0800–1700), includes a crocodile farm, small natural history museum, aviaries and a few other animals, including leopard. The **Big Tree**, *on the road to the Falls car park,* is a particularly resplendent baobab (see p. 312), which measures about 20 m around the trunk and 25 m high, and was used as the local landmark and meeting point by pioneers a century ago.

The **Game Park** (open May–Oct only) along the river does have a wide range of animals, including elephant, but pales next to Hwange.

KARIBA

Tourist Office: *by the Observation Post, Kariba Heights, Kariba; tel: 161-2328.* Open daily 0800–1700.

Visitors should remain alert to the local wildlife. Elephants and hippos frequently visit the centre of town and the grounds of the hotels and campsites. If you do meet one unexpectedly, keep calm, quiet and back off slowly. The lake has a great many crocodiles, so swimming is not recommended.

ARRIVING AND DEPARTING

There is no connecting road between Victoria Falls and Kariba, and the only driving route is back via Bulawayo and Harare. **Kariba Ferries**, *8 km Peg, Simon Mazorodze Rd, Harare; tel: 14-614 162/7; fax: 14-614 161*, operate a **car ferry** along the length of Lake Kariba between Mbilizi, near Binga, and Kariba town (depart Kariba Mon, Tues, Thur, Fri; depart

Mblilizi Tues, Wed, Fri, Sat; sailing time 22 hrs; Z$560 per adult and Z$385 per saloon car). The fare covers full board and there is a cash bar. Otherwise, there are regular **flights** to Kariba from Harare, Hwange, Victoria Falls and Bulawayo (the same plane hops round the country). There are no **rail** services.

On arrival, **taxis** are thin on the ground, while many of the game lodges on the lake are reached only by boat or small plane. Organise your transfers before arriving, and be prepared for them to add significantly to the bill. There are only two roads of any significance in town – the very long road that snakes around the edge of the lake, connecting all the hotels, boat yards, and so on, and the road which winds up the hill near the dam wall through the town to the observation point. Navigating is easy; there are no street addresses.

You can also hire **boats**, either motor cruisers or yachts, for sailing and fishing. For details, contact the **Boating Association of Zimbabwe**, *PO Box AY20, Amby, Harare; tel: 14-487 587/487 881-3; fax: 14-497 021*, or **Kariba Cruises**, *PO Box 186, Kariba; tel: 161-2839; fax: 161-2885*. For day or sunset cruises, contact **UTC** (see feature box, p.393) or **Bonaventure Tour Operators**, *Caribbea Bay Hotel; tel: 161-2453/4*. To charter a houseboat, arrange canoe trips and transfers, contact **Zimbabwe Reservation**; *tel: 161-2423*, or **Kariba Boating and Safaris**; *tel: 161-2553; fax: 161-2227*. **United Air Safaris**; *tel: 161-2305/2498*, offer sightseeing flights over the dam wall and Matusadona.

ACCOMMODATION

There are several pleasant hotels in town, strung out along the water's edge, but the best accommodation is undoubtedly in the remote houseboats (see above) or game lodges. The large, Mediterranean meringue-style **Caribbea Bay** *(ZS), Kariba; tel: 161-2453/4; fax: 161-2765* (moderate) is the town's main resort, with several pools, a casino, camping and caravan site, water sports (in spite of the crocodiles!) and lots of enthusiastic noise; day entry is Z$2. By contrast, the **Lake View Inn** *(ZS); tel: 161-2411/2* (moderate) is quiet and peaceful, with lovely lake views and gardens. The 2-star

Cutty Sark; *tel: 161-2321;* reservations: *tel: 14-751 908/9, fax: 14-753 038* (moderate) is a pleasant family hotel with full amenities but no beach; the day-trip boats leave from here. For attractive self-catering cottages, try the **Tamarind Lodges**; *tel: 161-2697/2948* (cheap). **Campsites: Mopani Bay Camping and Caravan Park**, *2.5 km east of Kariba town on the Makuti Road; tel: 161-22313;* **Caribbea Bay** (see above); and the **MOTH Holiday Resort**, *near the Lake View Inn; tel: 161-2809,* with pleasant self-catering cottages as well as camping and caravan pitches.

Out of town, the accommodation, mainly clustered around the fringes of the Matusadona National Park, is more varied, more sophisticated and almost always more expensive. Game-viewing is offered by boat, open vehicle, on foot, at night, and, in some cases, by canoe, and the quality of wildlife to be seen is excellent. Access to them all is by boat or small plane. **Bumi Hills Safari Lodge** *(ZS;* expensive) is a large, comfortable lodge in a private game park next to Matusadona National Park; access is by small plane only. Each room has a private verandah, with hilltop views of the lakeshore and floodplain. Nearby **Water Wilderness** *(ZS;* expensive) provides comfortable accommodation on houseboats on the Chura River, mainly for fishermen. **Fothergill Island** *(ZS;* expensive) is a wonderful island/spur, just off Matusadona National Park, with luxury thatched cottage accommodation and an enormous range of wildlife, including swimming elephants. **Spurwing Island**; *tel: 161-2466; fax: 161-2301* (expensive) really is an island, with an exclusive tented camp and knowledgeable staff. Probably the most luxurious of the lot is **Gache Gache** *(La;* very expensive), a lodge with brick-built bungalows and all the trimmings on a river estuary. Those who are looking for luxury houseboat accommodation should try the **Matusadona Water Lodge** *(Wd),* where four 'floating chalets' surround the 'mother ship', guests commuting by canoe or motorboat.

Tiger Bay; *tel: 161-2569;* reservations *tel: 14-792 211; fax: 14-792 617* (moderate–expensive), with thatched chalets on the Ume River, is primarily a game-fishing camp.

SIGHTSEEING

In 1912, someone first suggested damming the high, narrow Kariba Gorge on the Zambezi River for irrigation. When work eventually began in 1951, it was a much more complex project, designed to supply both Zambia and Zimbabwe (still Northern and Southern Rhodesia) with cheap hydro-electric power. It was a massive project, completed in June 1959. On 17 May 1960, the power station was officially opened by the Queen Mother.

The toll was staggering. It cost Z$180 million and took 10,000 men' four years to build. The dam wall is 134m high (including the foundations), 24m wide at the base, 12m wide and 633m long at the top. It holds back a lake 290 km long, up to 32 km wide and up to 120m deep. It is still the fifth largest reservoir in the world. Take your passport to be allowed on to the dam wall without going through full border formalities. There is an excellent view over the wall from the Observation Point at the top of **Kariba Heights**, next to the Tourist Office.

The town, a popular holiday resort for middle-class Zimbabwe, has no real centre. There are one or two sights, however. Near Kariba Heights is a monument to **Operation Noah**, an astounding programme of animal rescue as the lake waters rose behind the wall. In all, some 4700 animals, large and small, were captured on isolated islands and ferried to safety. Nearby, **St Barbara's Chapel**, dedicated to St Barbara (the patron saint of engineers), St Joseph (the patron saint of carpenters) and Mary, was built by the Italian construction workers in memory of the 87 men who died on the project. Its circular shape and six surrounding pillars represents the coffer dams built before the main wall. There is also a **Crocodile Farm**, *near the airport; tel: 2822* (open daily 0800–1700).

On the south side of the lake, the **Matusadona National Park** *(ZN)* covers 1407 sq. km between the Umi and Sanyati rivers. It can be reached by road with great difficulty, but is mainly accessed by air or water from the various luxury lodges around the edge (see above). There is a self-catering camp at Tashinga, in the park.

GREAT BUSINESS LOCATIONS

WORLD CLASS ELEGANCE

UNIQUE HABITATS

ZIMBABWE AT ITS BEST

Zimbabwe Sun has a prestigious portfolio of exclusive safari lodges, city hotels and resorts located throughout the country. Each property, while being a part of the largest hotel group inZimbabwe, has its own distinctive style and character. Discover a country blessed with spectacular scenery, a rich culture and exceptional wildlife, and experience the comfort and the warmth of Zimbabwe Sun.

ZIMBABWE SUN
HOTELS, RESORTS & LODGES

99 JASON MOYO AVENUE, HARARE, ZIMBABWE. TEL :(263-4) 737944 / 735681, FAX : (263-4) 734739. E MAIL: zimsuncro@zimsun.gaia.co.zw

DRIVING DISTANCES AND TIMES

Approximate distances from major cities to main attractions and centres are given following the most direct routes. Driving times are meant as an average indication only, allowing for the nature of the roads but not for traffic conditions, which can be very variable (see the route descriptions throughout the book). They do not include allowance for stops or breaks en route.

Bloemfontein to . . .	Kilometres	Hours
East London	570	7¼
Johannesburg	398	5
Kimberley	177	2¼
Ladysmith	410	5¼
Pretoria	456	5¾

Johannesburg to . . .	Kilometres	Hours
Durban	578	7¼
Maseru	438	5½
Port Elizabeth	1075	13½
Pretoria	58	¾
Sun City	193	2½

Cape Town to . . .	Kilometres	Hours
Johannesburg	1402	17½
Kruger National Park	1756	22
Springbok	539	6¾
Sun City	1595	20
Windhoek	1500	18¾

Kimberley to . . .	Kilometres	Hours
East London	780	9¾
Hluhluwe	1027	12¾
Kruger National Park	826	10⅓
Ladysmith	587	7⅓
Port Elizabeth	743	9¼

Durban to . . .	Kilometres	Hours
Bloemfontein	634	8
Johannesburg	578	7¼
Kruger National Park	932	11⅔
Ladysmith	236	3
Sun City	771	9⅔

Port Elizabeth to . . .	Kilometres	Hours
Bloemfontein	780	8½
Cape Town	769	9½
Maseru	822	10¼
Sun City	1268	15¾
Worcester	705	8¾

East London to . . .	Kilometres	Hours
Cape Town	1099	13¾
Durban	632	8
Gaborone	979	12¼
Hluhluwe	994	12½
Johannesburg	578	7¼

Sun City to . . .	Kilometres	Hours
Harrismith	467	5¾
Kimberley	665	8⅓
Kruger National Park	489	6¼
Ladysmith	549	6¾
Mbabane	554	7

HOTEL CODES
AND CENTRAL BOOKING NUMBERS

The following abbreviations have been used throughout the book to show which hotel and motel chains are represented in a particular town. Central booking numbers of these, or the numbers to call for information, are shown in bold – use these numbers whilst in Southern Africa to make reservations at any hotel in the chain. Where available, numbers that can be called in your own country are also noted. (Aus=Australia, Can=Canada, Ire=Ireland, NZ=New Zealand, UK=United Kingdom, US = United States of America). Some telephone calls are free, usually incorporating *800*.

Av **Aventura Resorts**
(012) 428 7600
fax: (012) 346 2293
Large self-catering and camping resorts, usually based on spas.

Bb **Bed 'n' Breakfast (South Africa)**
(011) 482 2206/7
fax: (011) 726 6915
UK (01787) 228 494
Small guesthouses, bed and breakfasts and self-catering resorts in South Africa.

Ce **Cresta Hospitality**
(012) 341 3473
fax: (012) 442 258
Established chain in South Africa, Zimbabwe and Namibia. Brands include 5-star Safari Lodge, 3–4-star Best Western, Cresta Lodge business hotels and budget Travel Inn.

Ck **Caraville Resorts**
(031) 701 4156
fax: (031) 701 4159
e-mail: *caravill@iafrica.com*
National network of lodges, self-catering resorts and caravan parks.

CL **City Lodge**
(011) 884 5327
fax: (011) 883 3640
Broad range of properties, including self-catering Courtyard, moderate City and Town Lodges and budget Road Lodges.

Cv **The Conservation Corporation**
(011) 784 6832
fax: (011) 784 7667
Exclusive game parks, with luxury bush lodges.

Hd **Holiday Inn**
(011) 482 3500
(0800) 117 711
fax: (011) 726 3019
Aus 02-262 2663/2111
UK 0800 897 121
US 800 421 8905
Chain of 2–5-star hotels, many belonging to **Southern Sun Hotels** (South Africa) and **Zimbabwe Sun Hotels** (Zimbabwe). Brands include 3-star Crowne Plazas and 4-star Garden Courts.

Hl **Hostelling International (South Africa)**
(021) 419 1853
fax: (021) 216 937
Local youth hostel affiliate.

Hn **Hilton**
(011) 880 3108
fax: (011) 788 4802
Aus (800) 222 255
NZ (800) 448 002
UK (0800) 856 8000
US (800) 445 8667

Hy **Hyatt**
(0800) 991 029
fax: 44 181 335 1250
Ire (800) 535 500
NZ (800) 441 234
UK (0345) 581666
US 800 233 1234

Ic **InterContinental**
(0800) 999 136
fax: 44 181 568 9555
Aus (800) 221 335
Can/USA (800) 327 0200
NZ (0800) 654 343
UK (0345) 581 444

Jc **Jacana Country Homes and Trails**
(012) 346 3550/1/2
fax: (012) 346 2499
Farm stays and country cottages.

Ka **Karos Hotels**
(011) 484 1641
fax: (011) 484 6206

407

UK (0181) 544 0151
Large 3–5-star, mainly
business, hotels.

**LH Leading Hotels of
South Africa**
(011) 884 3583
fax: (011) 884 0676
Lavish hospitality and
luxury at high prices.

**NP National Parks Board
(South Africa)**
(012) 343 1991
fax: (012) 343 0905
SA (021) 343 2007
fax: (021) 343 2006
All accommodation with-
in the national parks,
from campsites to lodges.

Nt Natal Parks Board
0331 471 981
fax: 0331 471 980
Lodges and self-catering;
camping and caravan
reservations must be
made directly with the
individual reserve.

Pa Protea Hotels
(021) 419 5320
fax: (021) 254 362
UK (01789) 204 269
Business-like moderate
South African chain,
with over 90 properties
in 11 countries.

**Pf Portfolio Town and
Country Retreats**
(011) 880 3414
fax: (011) 788 4802
South Africa's best
listings of b&bs, guest-
houses and luxury hotels.

Rx Relais & Châteaux
33 1 45 72 96 50
fax: 33 1 45 72 96 69

Aus (02) 957 4511
UK (0800) 960 239
USA (212) 856 0115

**Sb Stocks Hotels and
Resorts**
(011) 302 3800
fax: (011) 784 6759
Upmarket city hotels
and game lodges.

SI Sun International
(011) 780 7444
fax: (011) 780 7701
UK (01491) 411 222
US (00-1-954) 713 2501
Large, comfortable to
luxurious hotels in
southern Africa.

SS Southern Sun
See Holiday Inn.

**SX Small Exclusive
Hotels of
Southern Africa**
UK (0171) 930 1717
fax: (0171) 930 1515
Luxurious country
house hotels in mag-
nificent surroundings.

TR Three Cities Group
(011) 331 8911
fax: (011) 331 8467
Luxury city hotels,
business hotels and
leisure lodges.

Wd Wilderness Safaris
(011) 884 1458
fax: (011) 883 6255
e-mail: wildrsa@iafrica.com
Upmarket safaris, game
camps and lodges in
South Africa, Botswana,
Namibia and Zimbabwe.

The following refer to accommodation in Zimbabwe:

Bk Block Hotels
04 700 6615/792 792
fax: 04 735 080
e-mail: utczim@
Luxury game lodges.

Bv Bushveld Safaris
04 307 945/921
fax: 04 796 432
e-mail: bushveld@mail.
pci.co.zw
Charming bush lodges.

La Landela Safaris
147 340 4326
fax: 147 08119
e-mail: landela@samara.
co.zw
Exclusive bush camps.

Rb Rainbow Hotels
04 733 781
fax: 04 790 585
Friendly mid-range hotels.

**ZN Zimbabwe National
Parks Service**
04 706 077/8
fax: 04 726 089

ZS Zimbabwe Sun
04 737 944
fax: 04 734 739
Aus 02-956 6620
SA (011) 886 2130
UK (0181) 908 3348
USA (213) 256 1991
Zimbabwe's premier
chain of large 3–5-star
hotels; linked with
Holiday Inn.

The following refers to
accommodation in Namibia:

Nb Namibia Resorts
(061) 233 145
fax: (061) 234 512
Broad-based range of
international hotels.

CONVERSION TABLES

DISTANCES (approx. conversions)
1 kilometre (km) = 1000 metres (m) 1 metre = 100 centimetres (cm)

Metric	Imperial/US	Metric	Imperial/US	Metric	Imperial/US
1 cm	3/8ths in.	10 m	33 ft (11 yd)	3 km	2 miles
50 cm	20 in.	20 m	66 ft (22 yd)	4 km	2½ miles
1 m	3 ft 3 in.	50 m	164 ft (54 yd)	5 km	3 miles
2 m	6 ft 6 in.	100 m	330 ft (110 yd)	10 km	6 miles
3 m	10 ft	200 m	660 ft (220 yd)	20 km	12½ miles
4 m	13 ft	250 m	820 ft (275 yd)	25 km	15½ miles
5 m	16 ft 6 in.	300 m	984 ft (330 yd)	30 km	18½ miles
6 m	19 ft 6 in.	500 m	1640 ft (550 yd)	40 km	25 miles
7 m	23 ft	750 m	½ mile	50 km	31 miles
8 m	26 ft	1 km	5/8ths mile	75 km	46 miles
9 m	29 ft (10 yd)	2 km	1½ miles	100 km	62 miles

24-HOUR CLOCK
(examples)

0000 = Midnight	1200 = Noon	1800 = 6 p.m.
0600 = 6 a.m.	1300 = 1 p.m.	2000 = 8 p.m.
0715 = 7.15 a.m.	1415 = 2.15 p.m.	2110 = 9.10 p.m.
0930 = 9.30 a.m.	1645 = 4.45 p.m.	2345 = 11.45 p.m.

TEMPERATURE
Conversion Formula: $°C × 9 ÷ 5 + 32 = °F$

°C	°F	°C	°F	°C	°F	°C	°F
-20	-4	-5	23	10	50	25	77
-15	5	0	32	15	59	30	86
-10	14	5	41	20	68	35	95

409

WEIGHT
1kg = 1000g 100 g = 3½ oz

Kg	Pounds	Kg	Pounds	Kg	Pounds
1	2¼	5	11	25	55
2	4½	10	22	50	110
3	6½	15	33	75	165
4	9	20	45	100	220

FLUID MEASURES
1 litre(l) = 0.88 Imperial quarts = 1.06 US quarts

Litres	Imp.gal.	US gal.	Litres	Imp.gal.	US gal.
5	1.1	1.3	30	6.6	7.8
10	2.2	2.6	35	7.7	9.1
15	3.3	3.9	40	8.8	10.4
20	4.4	5.2	45	9.9	11.7
25	5.5	6.5	50	11.0	13.0

MEN'S CLOTHES

SA/UK	Europe	US
36	46	36
38	48	38
40	50	40
42	52	42
44	54	44
46	56	46

MENS' SHOES

SA/UK	Europe	US
6	40	7
7	41	8
8	42	9
9	43	10
10	44	11
11	45	12

LADIES' CLOTHES

SA/UK	France	Italy	Rest of Europe	US
10	36	38	34	8
12	38	40	36	10
14	40	42	38	12
16	42	44	40	14
18	44	46	42	16
20	46	48	44	18

MEN'S SHIRTS

SA/UK	Europe	US
14	36	14
15	38	15
15½	39	15½
16	41	16
16½	42	16½
17	43	17

LADIES' SHOES

SA/UK	Europe	US
3	36	4½
4	37	5½
5	38	6½
6	39	7½
7	40	8½
8	41	9½

AREAS
1 hectare = 2.471 acres

1 hectare = 10,000 sq meters

1 acre = 0.4 hectares

411

412

413

SOUTH AFRICA...

'A world in one country'. Experience it and more with Thomas Cook Holidays.

There are many ways to see South Africa - but not many with the experience of Thomas Cook. We offer innumerable combinations to make each holiday unique - whether you want to "go as you please" or join one of our fully escorted Cook's Tours.

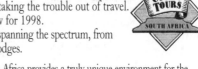

- ◆ Competitively priced.
- ◆ Fly drives and car hire.
- ◆ The best in rail journeys - including Rovos Rail and the Blue Train.
- ◆ Independent and Scheduled tours.
- ◆ Fully escorted Cook's Tours - accompanied by a highly experienced Tour Manager, taking the trouble out of travel.
- ◆ Star value Cook's Tour - new for 1998.
- ◆ A range of accommodation - spanning the spectrum, from economy comforts to luxury lodges.

South Africa provides a truly unique environment for the traveller - explore it with Thomas Cook Holidays. Preview your South Africa holiday before you go. The "Thomas Cook in South Africa" video is available for just £10.

Call the experts now on 01733 267171 or simply drop into your local Thomas Cook shop.

Thomas Cook Holidays, P.O. Box 5, 12 Coningsby Road, Peterborough. PE3 8XP. ABTA: V6434 ATOL: 265

414

READER SURVEY

If you enjoyed using this book, or even if you didn't, please help us improve future editions by taking part in our reader survey. Every returned form will be acknowledged, and to show our appreciation we will give you £1 off your next purchase of a Thomas Cook guidebook. Just take a few minutes to complete and return this form to us.

When did you buy this book?

Where did you buy it? (Please give town/city and if possible name of retailer)

When did you/do you intend to travel around Southern Africa?

For how long (approx.)?
How many people in your party?

Which countries, cities, parks and other locations did you/do you intend mainly to visit?

Did you/will you:
☐ Make all your travel arrangements independently?
☐ Travel on a fly-drive package?
Please give brief details:

Did you/do you intend to use this book:
☐ For planning your trip?
☐ During the trip itself?
☐ Both?

Did you/do you intend also to purchase any of the following travel publications for your trip?
Thomas Cook Travellers: *South Africa*
A road map/atlas (please specify)
Other guidebooks (please specify)

Have you used any other Thomas Cook guidebooks in the past? If so, which?

Please rate the following features of Touring Southern Africa for their value to you (Circle VU for 'very useful', U for 'useful', NU for 'little or no use'):

The 'Travel Essentials' section on pages 15–27	VU	U	NU
The 'Driving in Southern Africa' section on pages 45–52	VU	U	NU
The 'Touring Itineraries' on pages 74–77	VU	U	NU
The recommended driving routes throughout the book	VU	U	NU
Information on towns and cities, National Parks, etc	VU	U	NU
The maps of towns and cities, parks, etc	VU	U	NU
The colour planning map	VU	U	NU

Please use this space to tell us about any features that in your opinion could be changed, improved, or added in future editions of the book, or any other comments you would like to make concerning the book:

Your age category: ☐ 21-30 ☐ 31-40 ☐ 41–50 ☐ over 50

Your name: Mr/Mrs/Miss/Ms
(First name or initials)
(Last name)

Your full address: (Please include postal or zip code)

Your daytime telephone number:

Please detach this page and send it to: The Project Editor, Touring Southern Africa, Thomas Cook Publishing, PO Box 227, Peterborough PE3 6PU, United Kingdom.

We will be pleased to send you details of how to claim your discount upon receipt of this questionnaire.

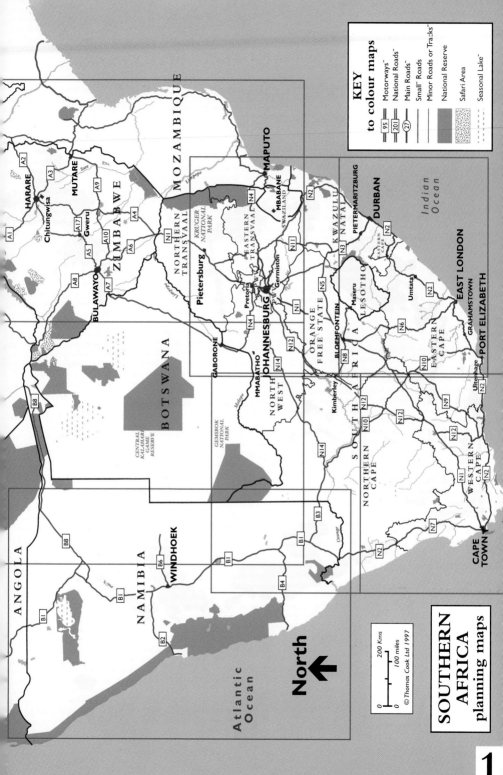

KEY
to colour maps

Motorways⁻
Motorways⁻ 95
National Roads⁻ 201
Main Roads⁻ 27
Small⁻ Roads⁻
Minor Roads or Tracks⁻
National Reserve
Safari Area
Seasonal Lake⁻

North

200 Kms
100 miles
© Thomas Cook Ltd 1997

SOUTHERN
AFRICA
planning maps

1

Indian Ocean

Atlantic Ocean

ANGOLA

NAMIBIA

WINDHOEK

BOTSWANA

CENTRAL KALAHARI GAME RESERVE

GEMSBOK NATIONAL PARK

GABORONE

ZIMBABWE

HARARE

MUTARE

Chitungwisa

Gweru

BULAWAYO

MOZAMBIQUE

MAPUTO

MBABANE

SWAZILAND

KRUGER NATIONAL PARK

NORTHERN TRANSVAAL

Pietersburg

EASTERN TRANSVAAL

Pretoria

Germiston

JOHANNESBURG

MMABATHO

NORTH WEST

ORANGE FREE STATE

BLOEMFONTEIN

LESOTHO

Maseru

KWAZULU NATAL

PIETERMARITZBURG

DURBAN

SOUTH AFRICA

Kimberley

NORTHERN CAPE

EASTERN CAPE

Umtata

GRAHAMSTOWN

EAST LONDON

PORT ELIZABETH

Uitenhage

WESTERN CAPE

CAPE TOWN

A1 A2 A3 A9 A17 A5 A10 A4 A6 A7 A8

B8 B1 B6 B1 B2 B4 B1 B3

N1 N4 N4 N2 N2 N3 N11 N5 N1 N12 N14 N8 N6 N10 N2 N2 N9 N12 N10 N12 N12 N1 N2 N7

Limpopo

Sare

Manduri

Molopo

Orange

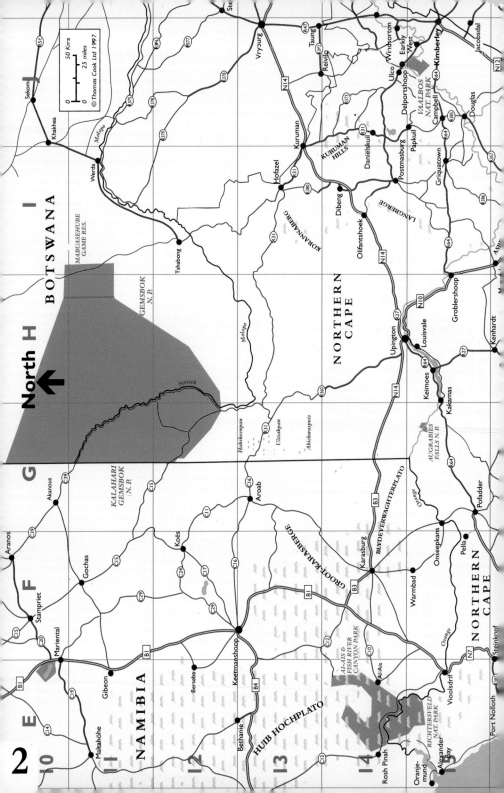

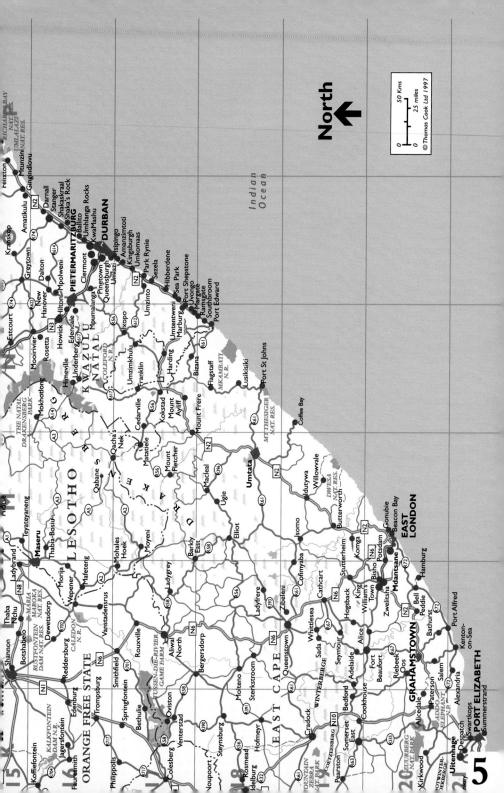

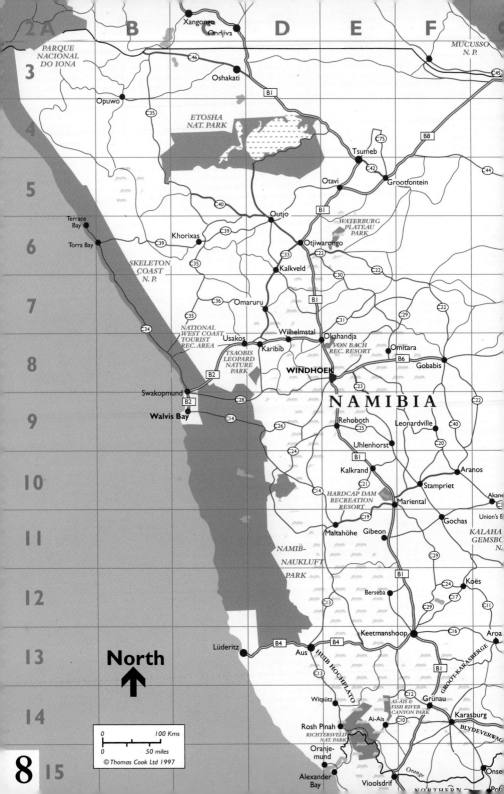